HANDBOOKS

D0650990

OAXACA

BRUCE WHIPPERMAN

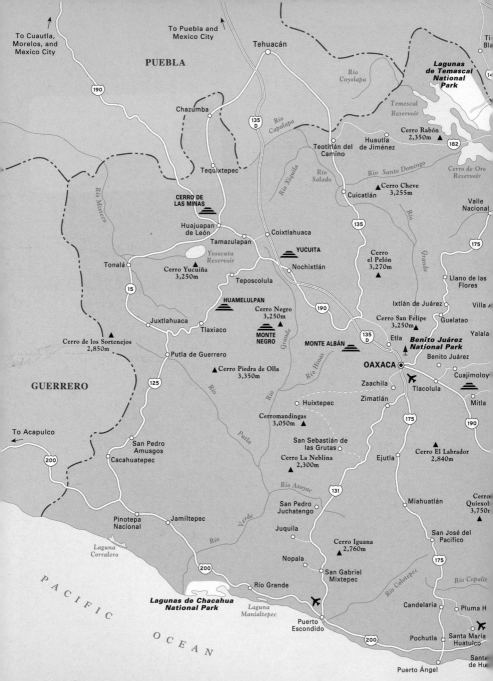

Contents

Discover Oaxaca

Experience the best of Mexico, both old and new, in Oaxaca. Once isolated and little visited, this Mexican state is now fulfilling its promise. Superhighways and airline routes have increased access to its capital city, the gateway to an abundance of arts and handicrafts, renowned native cuisine, fascinating history, and rich cultural heritage, which includes 16 separate living languages, spoken in dozens of distinct dialects and spread among hundreds of ethnically separate indigenous groups.

A generation ago, the United Nations recognized Oaxaca City's unique gifts by naming it a UNESCO World Heritage Site. The city acknowledged the compliment, rebuilding and refurbishing its graceful colonial-era buildings, churches, and monuments, including the stunning 16th century Iglesia de Santo Domingo. But the city is as much about the present as the past. By day, people linger at plaza-front sidewalk cafés. By night, the same central plaza comes alive with entertainment, from arts and crafts stalls to folkloric dance.

The cultural wealth is also abundant outside the city. The surrounding Valley of Oaxaca is ringed by the ruins of ancient civilizations, including magnificent Mitla, celebrated for the unique *Greca* stone fretwork decorating its walls. The vibrant market of Zaachila coexists with the mysterious and revered ruins of its pre-conquest old town. And on a high

western hill overlooking everything, regal Monte Albán, Mesoamerica's first metropolis, still reigns from its mountaintop throne.

These ghosts of the ancients exist side by side with vibrant native markets, one for practically each day of the week, decorated with stalls offering everything from colorful carpets and pottery to embroidered dresses and *alebrijes*, Oaxaca's celebrated wooden animals. The less-traveled Mixteca region offers its share of magnificent Dominican churches, barely explored ancient kingdoms, and natural wonders such as emerald waterfalls, limestone caves, and crystal springs. More contemporary pleasures can be found on the golden strands of Pacific coastal resorts like Puerto Ángel, the Bahías de Huatulco, and Puerto Escondido. And southeast on the Isthmus, where the continent shrinks to a narrow land bridge, you can join the celebration at near-continuous festivals.

Wherever you wander in this rich land, you'll find excitement, lots of friendly folks, relatively low prices, and a host of traditional Mexican delights.

Planning Your Trip

▶ WHERE TO GO

native markets with colorful arts and crafts at villages such as Teotitlán del Valle and Tlacolula on the east side; San Bartolo Coyotepec and San Antonino Castillo Velasco on the south side; and Zaachila, Arrazola, and Atzompa in the southwest. Or seek out lost cultures at noble, timeless Mitla, regal Monte Albán, monumental San José El Mogote, and ancient Suchilquitongo.

Pacific Resorts and Southern Sierra

This long, lazy land of eternal summer is embellished by its resort trio: Puerto Ángel and Huatulco, on the east side, and Puerto Escondido on the west. Enjoy beachcombing, sportfishing, swimming, snorkeling, and scuba diving. On the Puerto Ángel–Huatulco side, add plenty of golf and tennis, river rafting, and jungle coffee farms. On the Puerto Escondido side, add abundant wildlife-viewing at Laguna Manialtepec and Parque Nacional Lagunas de Chacahua.

Oaxaca City

At the crossroads of the mountain-rimmed Valley of Oaxaca, the capital city offers virtually everything within its strollable downtown. Start from its charming central plaza to explore baroque churches, fetching handicrafts markets, distinguished galleries and museums, and inviting restaurants serving both authentic Oaxacan and international cuisine.

The Valley of Oaxaca

The banquet of old-Mexico experiences continues in the valley outside the city. Visit

The Mixteca

This homeland of the Mixtecs, Oaxaca's "People of the Clouds," is a virtually untouristed domain, ripe for adventuring. Visit monumental 16th century Dominican ex-convents at Coixtlahuaca and Yanhuitlán, and the elegant open chapel at Teposcolula. Farther south, the cool, pine-tufted plateau of the High Mixteca offers groves of ancient *sabino* trees, plunging waterfalls, and Tlaxiaco, the "Paris of Oaxaca" with its splendid Saturday market. Even more is tucked in the Mixteca's hidden corners: the

Tlaxiaco's Saturday market

hammocks for sale in Tuxtepec

idyllic Valley of Apoala, the ruins of Monte Negro, and emerald springs at Laguna Encantada. Farther south, the indigenous heartland around Pinotepa Nacional offers a trove of handicrafts.

Northern Oaxaca

An exploration of northern Oaxaca begins in the villages of the Sierra Juárez, scarcely an hour north from Oaxaca City. Farther north, past the picturesque towns of Tuxtepec and Ixcatlán, the highway climbs past the gigantic whale-back massif of the Cerro Rabón, the holy mountain of the Mazatec people, to the summit, at Huautla de Jiménez, their spiritual home. Stroll the *tianguis* and shop

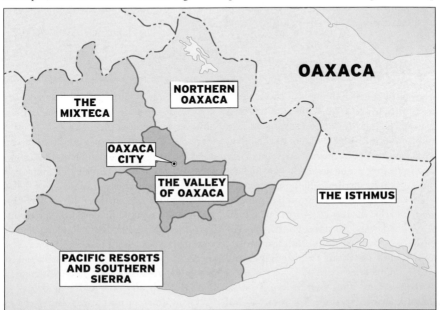

OAXACA

NORTHERN OAXACA

THE MIXTECA

OAXACA CITY

THE VALLEY OF OAXACA

THE ISTHMUS

PACIFIC RESORTS AND SOUTHERN SIERRA

the Mar Muerto

for prized *huipiles.* Or continue another half an hour to enjoy the twin waterfalls of Las Regaderas, or explore the limestone cave near Eloxochitlán.

The Isthmus

Nothing embodies the independent Isthmus spirit more than its near-continuous menu of fiestas, especially in Tehuántepec and Juchitán, where *istmeño* hearts beat fastest. Women dress in their spectacular floral *huipiles* and sway to the lovely, lilting melody of "La Sandunga," the song of the Isthmus. Exciting excursions include crystal-blue springs at Tlacotepec, the fishing hamlet of Rincón Juárez, on the shore of the Mar Muerto, and the grand canyon of the Río Zanatepec.

▶ WHEN TO GO

The most popular times to visit Oaxaca City are Christmas–New Year's, the Guelaguetza (gay-lah-GET-zah) dance festival in July, and Día de los Muertos (Day of the Dead) week, around November 1. Although the crowds are biggest and hotel prices are highest, the city is at its merriest and most colorful.

By contrast, beaches are most popular twice yearly: during the Christmas–New Year's holiday and Semana Santa, pre-Easter week. Droves of folks, both foreign and local, crowd restaurants and lodgings and push up hotel rates.

Oaxaca (and most of Mexico) has two sharply defined seasons: wet summer–fall and dry winter–spring. People sometimes say Oaxaca is too hot in the summer. This, however, isn't necessarily the case. In fact, increased summer cloud cover and showers can actually create average daily temperatures in July, August, and September that are cooler than clear and very warm late April, May, and early June temperatures. If you like lush, green landscapes, summer–fall may be your season. This is true especially in the highlands around Oaxaca City, northern Oaxaca, and the Mixteca, where multicolored wildflowers decorate the roadsides and the clouds seem to billow into a 1,000-mile-high blue sky.

If you don't mind crowds and want to

experience lots of local color, go during one of Oaxaca's festivals. If, however, you shun crowds but like the sunny, temperate winter, January, a low-occupancy season, is a good bet, especially on the beach.

October, November, and the first half of December are also good times to go (except possibly for the crowded, expensive high-holiday Día de los Muertos week). Hotel prices are cheapest, the landscape is lush and green, beaches are beautifully uncrowded, and it's cooler and not as rainy as July, August, and September.

Passports, Tourist Cards, and Visas

Your passport (or birth or naturalization certificate) is your positive proof of national identity. Mexican authorities won't let U.S. and Canadian citizens, including children, enter

DÍA DE LOS MUERTOS

Instead of mourning the dead, Mexicans celebrate the memory of their deceased relatives with a festive holiday, the Día de los Muertos (Day of the Dead). The roots of this festival go back for countless generations, long before the Spanish Conquest, to the ancient holiday of Mictecacihuatl, the guardian-goddess of the dead, whom many of the original Mexicans celebrated around the month of August.

The Spanish shifted the date to November 1 and 2, to coincide with the Catholic double holiday of All Saints Day and All Souls day. Now, Mexicans celebrate November 1 as the Día de los Angelitos ("Little Angels") and November 2 as the Día de los Muertos, in remembrance of their deceased children and their deceased adult relatives, respectively. Although universal throughout Mexico, the holiday is most intensely celebrated in the indigenous southern regions, of Michoacán, Guerrero, Chiapas, and the entire state of Oaxaca.

The Día de los Muertos, named after the second day of the two-day holiday, amounts to a joyous reunion of all family members – both living and dead. At the end of October, people gather in their hometowns and villages to reunite with their loved ones. Around noon, on November 1, they arrive at the cemeteries and begin sweeping up the gravesites, polishing the tombstones, scattering flower petals, and lighting candles to mark the path. By early evening, all is ready. The graves are festooned with fruit, flowers, and glowing candles, and decorated with toys and candy for the *angelitos* and

dishes loaded with the favorite foods and drinks of the deceased adults. Most importantly, most everyone has arrived; people drink, eat, and tell favorite family stories. As the evening wears on, people begin to drowse and curl up beneath blankets and spend the night in a happy vigil to welcome their departed loved ones back into the family fold once again.

Mexico without one, and U.S. Immigration rules require that all U.S. citizens must have a valid passport in order to re-enter the United States.

For U.S. and Canadian citizens, entry by air into Mexico for a few weeks could hardly be easier. Desk clerks check your passport, airplane attendants hand out tourist cards *(tarjetas turísticas)*, and officers make them official by stamping them at the immigration gate. Business travel permits for 30 days or fewer are handled by the same simple procedures.

Immunizations and Precautions

A good physician can recommend the proper preventatives for your Oaxaca trip. If you are going to stay pretty much in town, your doctor will probably suggest little more than updating your basic typhoid, diphtheria-tetanus, hepatitis, and polio shots.

For remote tropical areas—below 1,200 meters (4,000 ft)—doctors often recommend a gamma-globulin shot against hepatitis A and a schedule of chloroquine pills against malaria. Use other measures to discourage mosquitoes and other tropical pests. Common precautions include mosquito netting and rubbing on plenty of pure DEET (N,N dimethyl-meta-toluamide) "jungle juice," mixed in equal parts with rubbing alcohol (70 percent isopropyl).

Getting There and Around

The majority of visitors reach Oaxaca by air, and a large fraction of those through Mexico City. There, travelers transfer to flights bound for either Oaxaca City, Puerto Escondido, or Bahías de Huatulco–Puerto Ángel.

But bus travel rules in Mexico. Hundreds of sleek luxury- and first-class bus lines roar out daily from the border, headed south. The route to Oaxaca along the Pacific shore, although the longest, requiring one or two transfers and at least three full 24-hour days,

Bus travel rules in Mexico.

is the most scenic. Within Oaxaca, a host of lines connect virtually every town and most villages. Three distinct levels of service—luxury or super-first class, first class, and second class—are generally available.

If you're adventurous, but still want to have all the comforts of home, you may enjoy driving your car or RV to Oaxaca. On the other hand, the cost, risk, wear on both you and your vehicle, and the congestion hassles in towns may change your mind. Oaxaca car rentals are not cheap. With a 15 percent or more "value added" tax tacked on and mandatory Mexican car insurance, they run more than in the United States.

What to Take

Everyone should bring a hat for sun protection and a light jacket or sweater for the occasional cool evening. Loose-fitting, hand-washable, easy-to-dry clothes make for trouble-free tropical vacationing. Leave showy, expensive clothes and jewelry at home. Stow valuables in your hotel safe or carry them with you in a sturdy zipped purse or a waist pouch on your front side.

Explore Oaxaca

▶ THE BEST OF OAXACA

This two-week adventure explores Oaxaca's most fascinating, charming, and beautiful places. First-time visitors will want to spend their time in and around Oaxaca City and Valley and enjoy a few days relaxing on the coast. Returning visitors might choose to wander off the beaten path into other regions, such as the Mixteca or the Isthmus.

Although you could successfully begin this itinerary any day of the week, the ideal would be to plan your Thursday, Friday, and Sunday for visiting the Valley of Oaxaca towns of Zaachila, Ocotlán, and Tlacolula, when their *tianguis* (native markets) are at their biggest and best. The itinerary below consequently starts in Oaxaca City on Monday, Tuesday, and Wednesday, and then switches to the valley towns, beginning with Zaachila, on Thursday.

Day 1

Monday: Arrive in Oaxaca City. Stroll the *zócalo* (central plaza), visiting the cathedral and mysterious Santa Cruz de Huatulco. Take a table and enjoy the scene and dinner at a plaza-front café, or at Casa de la Abuela upstairs.

Days 2-3

Tuesday: After breakfast, stroll through the Mercado Juárez and continue to the adjacent San Juan de Dios church and market. Return uphill along Andador de Macedonio Alcalá, sampling the handicrafts shops and the sights (Museo de Arte Contemporaneo, Ex-Convento de Santa Catalina). Enjoy lunch at the Hostería Alcalá restaurant.

Spend the full afternoon at the Iglesia y

after-church procession in Oaxaca City

Iglesia y Ex-Convento de Santo Domingo

Ex-Convento de Santo Domingo and the Museo de las Culturas de Oaxaca. Eat dinner at either Restaurant los Pacos or La Manantial Vegetariana. In the evening, take in a Guelaguetza folkloric dance performance.

Wednesday: Follow your individual interests. For arts and handicrafts, check out the shops and galleries you missed on Day 2, or visit the Museo Arte Prehispánico de Rufino Tamayo or the ethno-botanical garden by the Iglesia de Santo Domingo. Visit the beloved San Agustín church and the Basilica de Nuestra Señora de la Soledad and its museum. During the evening, enjoy a music concert (Oaxaca State Band, Marimba Ensemble, or Oaxaca Orchestra) in the *zócalo*.

Alternatively, you might travel northwest of town, first to San José El Mogote archaeological zone and its community museum, continuing to the market at Etla, and then northwest to Suchilquitongo Community Museum and the Cerro de la Campana archaeological zone.

Days 4-5

Thursday: By 8 A.M. head southwest to Zaachila to explore the archaeological site and the market. Have lunch at a Zaachila market food stall or Restaurant La Capilla. Return via the Cuilapan de Guerrero church and Arrazola woodcarver's village.

Friday: Head out early to the Ocotlán market. In town, visit the Casa de Cultura Rudolfo Morales and the Templo de Santo Domingo and do lunch either at a plaza-front restaurant or La Cabaña restaurant, on the highway at the south edge of town.

On your return, visit handicrafts villages San Antonino Castillo Velasco, Santo Tomás Jalieza, San Martín Tilcajete, and San Bartolo Coyotepec.

Days 6-7

Saturday: Enjoy a midmorning visit to

Monte Albán. Allow around three hours, including the bookstore and museum. Eat lunch in the cafeteria or bring a picnic. Return downhill via Santa María Atzompa pottery village and handicrafts market.

Sunday: Head east early, first to the great El Tule tree. Continue to the wool textile store-workshops and community museum at Teotitlán del Valle. Have a noon lunch at either Restaurant El Descanso in town, or Restaurant El Patio on the highway.

Continue to Tlacolula for 1.5 hours at the market and the Capilla del Señor de Tlacolula. By 2:30 P.M. head east for at least an hour's visit to the Mitla archaeological zone.

Day 8

Monday: Since the Oaxaca coast stretches about 320 kilometers (200 mi) from east to west, it's best to divide your overnights between Puerto Ángel, on the east side, and Puerto Escondido, on the west side. Arrive in Puerto Ángel. Stroll the beachfront and follow the *andador* (walkway) to Playa Panteón for sunning, swimming, or snorkeling. Have dinner at Casa de Huéspedes Gundi y Tomás in Puerto Ángel or Restaurant El Alquimista in Playa Zipolite.

Days 9-10

Tuesday: Spend Day 9 enjoying the nearby beaches. Drive or bus west to Playa Zipolite and its diminutive Roca Blanca district. Have breakfast at Posada Mexico hotel restaurant; swim, surf, and sun for an hour or two, and then continue via Playa San Agustinillo village for a visit to the Centro Mexicano de la Tortuga turtle museum at Playa Mazunte. Stroll Mazunte village and beach; visit the Fábrica Ecología de Cosméticos Naturales de Mazunte, a cosmetics and soap factory. Have lunch or an early dinner at either Tania's or Armadillo restaurant.

Wednesday: Drive, tour, or ride a *colectivo*

the archaeological ruins of Mitla

to Crucecita for a day in Huatulco; transfer to a taxi to Santa Cruz de Huatulco early enough to catch one of the excursion boats to tour Bahías de Huatulco. Return mid-afternoon and go to Crucecita for a walk around the plaza-front handicrafts shops and market. Dine at Restaurant La Crucecita, or Cafe Oasis on the plaza.

Days 11-12

Thursday: Travel west an hour to Puerto Escondido. Stroll the *adoquín* (pedestrian walkway) and soak in the scene from a shady beachfront restaurant. Catch a boat ride (or a taxi) for either or both Bahía Puerto Ángelito and Bahía Carrizalillo for more beach fun, and lunch at a beachfront *palapa* restaurant. Head back east over to Playa Zicatela for a sunset dinner at the Hotel Santa Fe restaurant. Cap the evening with a balmy stroll, shopping, and nightclubbing along the *adoquín.*

Friday: Head out for a wildlife-viewing excursion at Laguna Manialtepec by private tour, car, or bus (independent travelers get off and hire a boat at lagoon-front Isla El Gallo).

Days 13-14

Saturday: Day 13 might be a good time for simple poolside or beachfront relaxing, watching the daredevil surfers at Playa Zicatela, or perusing the *adoquín* shops. If you're up for adventure, enjoy a day (or overnight) excursion west to Lagunas de Chacahua or an upland overnight in either Nopala or Juquila, to visit Oaxaca's adored Virgen de Juquila.

Sunday: Wind down by taking a morning walk along Playa Zicatela or the seafront *andador* from the main Puerto Escondido beach. Alternatively, go on a fishing excursion, do some snorkeling at Bahía Carrizalillo, get a scuba lesson, or ride horseback along Playa Zicatela.

Palms and bougainvillea decorate Puerto Escondido's *playa principal.*

TIANGUIS: NATIVE MARKETS

Most important Oaxaca towns have a public outdoor market every day, but a *tianguis* (tee-AHN-gees) only once a week. The word *tianguis* is an ancient native expression, synonymous with "awning," the colorful tarpaulins that shade the mini-mountains of fruits, vegetables, crafts, and merchandise. Native people flock to *tianguis* everywhere in Oaxaca to buy and sell.

Although trade appears to be the prime mover, people really come to *tianguis* for human contact, not only in the buying and selling itself, but for gossip, entertainment, flirtation – all of the other diversions that make life worth living.

Oaxaca City
- Abastos: Saturday
- Juárez: every day

The Valley of Oaxaca
- Sola de Vega: Sunday
- Tlacolula: Sunday
- Miahuatlán: Monday
- Etla: Wednesday
- Zimatlán: Wednesday
- Ejutla: Thursday
- Zaachila: Thursday
- Ocotlán: Friday

Pacific Resorts and Southern Sierra
- Juquila: Friday, Saturday, and Sunday
- Nopala: Saturday and Sunday
- Santa María Huatulco: Saturday and Sunday
- Cacahuatepec: Sunday
- Pinotepa Nacional: Monday
- Pochutla: Monday
- Astata: Tuesday
- Huamelula: Thursday
- Jamiltepec: Thursday

Mixteca
- Nochixtlán: Sunday
- Yosundua: Sunday
- Putla: Sunday

- Huajuapan: Wednesday, Saturday
- Tamazulapan: Wednesday
- Chalcatongo: Thursday
- Juxtlahuaca: Thursday, biggest on Friday
- Tonalá: Friday
- Tlaxiaco: Saturday

Northern Oaxaca
- Cuicatlán: Saturday and Sunday
- Huautla: Sunday
- Ixtlán de Juárez: Sunday
- Tuxtepec: Sunday
- Valle Nacional: Sunday
- Yalalag: Sunday
- Villa Alta: Monday
- Ojitlán: Wednesday
- Teotitlán del Camino: Wednesday and Sunday
- Jalapa de Díaz: Thursday and Sunday

The Isthmus
- Juchitán: every day
- Salina Cruz: every day
- Tehuántepec: Wednesday and Sunday

The Juchitán *tianguis* is every day.

► TREASURES OF OLD MEXICO

Oaxaca preserves a wealth of tradition in its museums, galleries, festivals, historic churches, pilgrimage shrines, and archaeological sites. You can also find Oaxacan culture alive today in its shops and native markets.

Oaxaca City

Along your city route, be sure to include the Museo de las Culturas de Oaxaca and its neighboring Iglesia de Santo Domingo. Of the churches, don't miss the Basilica de Nuestra Señora de la Soledad and the Catedral de Oaxaca, with its legendary Santa Cruz de Huatulco (Holy Cross of Huatulco).

Oaxaca City overflows with handicrafts. Stroll along the Andador de Macedonio Alcalá to visit the finest source shops, such as La Mano Mágico (masks and textiles), Oro de Monte Albán (gold jewelry), and the first-rate, female-operated MARO (Mujeres Artesanías de las Regiones de Oaxaca) on Calle Cinco de Mayo, a block south of Macedonio Alcalá.

The Valley of Oaxaca

Three very worthwhile community museums welcome visitors in Teotitlán del Valle, Santa Ana del Valle, and San José El Mogote. Along the way, don't miss the beautifully restored, lovely 16th-century churches in Tlacolula and Ocotlán.

Make certain to visit the monumental ruins, unmissable at Mitla and Monte Albán. The sites at Yagul and Lambityeco on the east side, and San José El Mogote and Suchilquitongo on the west side are also worthwhile if you have the time.

Go to the source in the celebrated handicrafts villages of Teotitlán del Valle (for

the Catedral de Oaxaca at Christmas

the *danzantes* sculptures at the ancient ruins of Monte Albán

wool weavings), San Bartolo Coyotepec (for black pottery), San Martín Tilcajete and Arrazola (for carved wooden animals), San Antonino Castillo Velasco (for embroidered blouses and dresses), and Santa María Atzompa (for pottery).

Pacific Resorts and Southern Sierra

The Oaxaca Pacific's must-see museum is the Centro Mexicano de la Tortuga (Turtle Museum) in Playa Mazunte. The most interesting churches to visit are (moving east to west) the shoreline chapel at Santa Cruz de Huatulco and the pair of beloved pilgrimage shrines, the Santuario de Nuestra Señora de Juquila and La Capilla del Pedimento, at Santa Catarina Juquila.

Most of Pacific Oaxaca's handicrafts are made on the west-side Mixtec coast. Primary are masks, in Huazolotitlán and Pinotepa

Don Luis; *pozahuancos* (indigenous Mixtec wraparound skirts), in Pinotepa Nacional and vicinity; and the embroidered *huipiles* sold at San Pedro Amusgos.

The Mixteca

Some professionally prepared community museums in the Mixteca welcome visitors: Memorias de Yucundaayee at San Pedro y San Pablo Tequixtepec, Museo Regional de Huajuapan at Huajuapan, and Museo Comunitario Ihitalulu at San Martín Huamelulpan are all well worth a visit. Furthermore, the Mixteca boasts some of Mexico's most celebrated Dominican church gems, notably at Teposcolula, Yanhuitlán, and Coixtlahuaca.

You can also visit a number of archaeological sites, the most accessible being the Cerro de las Minas, at Huajuapan, and the site at Huamelulpan. For pure wonder, visit the

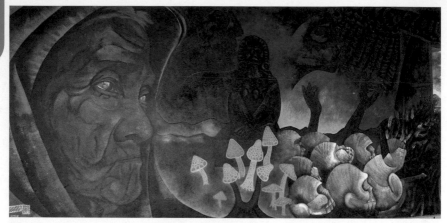

the María Sabina mural, by Mario Enrique Fernández Medina

haunting and fascinating mountaintop ruined city at Monte Negro (near Tilantongo). For the rarest of archaeological treats, hike to the Puente Colosal, near Tepelmeme, to view the big red glyph of the yet-undeciphered Mesoamerican Ñuiñe language.

The entire Mixteca Baja is a source of soft, pliable palm sombreros, baskets, and mats. One shop, Artesanías de Palma in Huajuapan, sells all these and more. At the Juxtlahuaca market, indigenous Trique women offer embroidery and their richly decorated *huipiles,* while master artisan Alejandro Jesús Vera Guzmán offers expertly carved masks. At the big Tlaxiaco Saturday market, there are also carved *calabazas* (gourds), embroidered *huipiles,* and leather belts, purses, and billfolds.

Northern Oaxaca

Head north to visit petite Guelatao and its shrine and museum in honor of Benito Juárez. Farther north in Tuxtepec, find the remarkable, unreconstructed El Castillo de Moctezuma pyramid. Up the mountain, at the Huautla de Jiménez market, shop for bright, ribbon-decorated Mazatec *huipiles,* and don't miss the mysterious María Sabina mural.

The Isthmus

Circle southeast to the Isthmus for a visit to Tehuántepec and its early-16th-century Templo y Ex-Convento de Santo Domingo. While in both Tehuántepec and neighboring Juchitán, shop for the famous flower-embroidered *huipiles.*

► ECOTOURISM LODGES

Cabañas ecoturísticas offer a unique opportunity for visitors weary of the tourist rush who desire more contact with local people and cultures. Many of the participating communities produce fine handicrafts and enjoy scenic, wildlife-rich locations. For modest fees, these local communities furnish guides who lead visitors along scenic trails, past springs, caves, meadows, and mountain vistas, identifying useful plants and birds and animals along the way. Some communities rent mountain bikes and offer instruction in rappelling and rock climbing and other outdoor diversions.

The Oaxaca Federal-State Department

of Tourism (SEDETUR) first built these tourist cabin complexes on the east side of the Valley of Oaxaca during the 1990s. Although five of the original nine are not being used, several more *cabañas ecoturísticas* have been built, mostly in Northern Oaxaca and the Mixteca, raising the total to about 14 operating complexes. About two dozen Oaxaca communities now invite visitors to stay in their community tourist lodging.

The *cabañas* are government constructed but locally managed, modern but usually rustic. Each bungalow typically sleeps four, with private hot-water shower-baths and toilet, and perhaps a kitchenette. The following are the locales for the best *cabañas ecoturísticas*.

The Valley of Oaxaca

Santa Ana del Valle: Master weavers' shops, museum, lake, scenic views, hikes.
San Sebastián de las Grutas: Limestone caves, hikes, riverside picnicking, groves of grand old *sabino* trees.
Hierve El Agua: Hikes, scenic vistas, mineral springs, frozen stone cascades.

The Mixteca

Apoala: Idyllic village, wild canyon, cave, cascade, springs, camping.
Yosocuta: Reservoir, boating, fishing, RV and tent camping.
San Martín Huamelulpan: Ruined city, museum, hikes to other archaeological sites.
San Miguel Tequixtepec: Museum, hike to hieroglyphic rock paintings, palm weaving, restored 17th-century church.
Tepelmeme de Morelos: Museum, canyon hike to Puente Colosal natural bridge and rare Ñuiñe glyph.

Northern Oaxaca

Ixtlán de Juárez: Cloud forest, wildlife-viewing, Benito Juárez's birthplace and museum, limestone cave.

Santa Catarina Ixtepeji: Hiking trails, campground, colonial-era church.
Benito Juárez: Cool pine-scented air, camping, panoramic views.
Cuajimoloyas: Mountain-top village, hiking, rock climbing.
Llano Grande: Woodland hikes, wildflowers.
Valle Nacional: Two separate locations. San Mateo Yetla: Riverside park, pool, kayaking, hiking, wildlife viewing. Balneario Monte Flor: Forest picnicking, kayaking, swimming in natural spring.

Reservations

Two agencies handle reservations for most of the *cabañas*. The Oaxaca state ecotourism (703 Av. Juárez, tel./fax 951/516-0123, info@ aoaxaca.com, www.aoaxaca.com) reserves Santa Ana del Valle, Hierve El Agua, Ixtlán de Juárez, Santa Catarina Ixtepeji, Apoala, and Yosundua. They've also published an informative *Guía Ecoturística* (Ecotourism Guidebook), written in Spanish.

cabaña ecoturística in Valle Nacional

The other reservations agency, Expediciones Sierra Norte (M. Bravo 210, tel./fax 951/514-8271, sierranorte@oaxaca.com, www.sierra norte.org.mx), handles *cabaña* reservations for the several communities collectively organized as the Pueblos Mancomunados: Benito Juárez, Cuajimoloyas, and Llano Grande, and three neighboring communities, Santa Catarina Lachatao, La Guacamaya, and San Miguel Amatlan.

You can also make the reservations yourself, by phone (in Spanish), or email. Even without a prior reservation, you can nearly always rent a *cabaña* if you arrive by 5 or 6 P.M.(especially on non-holiday weekdays).

▶ NATURAL WONDERS

Oaxaca abounds with natural wonders and outdoor adventures: hiking, climbing, kayaking, rafting, caving, bird-watching, and much more. It's also home to myriad species, from white herons to iguanas and crocodiles, dolphins and whales.

Hiking, Biking, and Horseback Riding

In Oaxaca City, walk uphill to the top of breezy Cerro del Fortín, or, at Hierve El Agua (best by tour), follow the *sendero peatonal* (footpath) that circuits the entire fascinating site.

In Huatulco, follow the forest paths to Bahía El Organo and Bahía Cacaluta, hike or ride horseback along the Río Copalita, or hike to the coffee farm downhill from Pluma Hidalgo.

The Mixteca abounds with unforgettable walks. For example, in Apoala, follow the spectacular trail into the gorge of Las Dos Peñas Colosales to the hidden valley of the La Peña Donde Murió El Aguila con Dos Cabezas. In Tepelmeme, hike to the spectacular natural bridge, Puente Colosal.

Oaxaca's northern mountains offer plenty

The fierce-looking iguana is actually very shy.

catch of the day in Puerto Ángel

near Puerto Escondido. For deep-sea fishing, either launch your own boat or rent a launch in Huatulco, Puerto Ángel, or Puerto Escondido. You can also rent a fully equipped fishing boat at either Huatulco or Puerto Escondido.

If you prefer to go after freshwater fish, such as *mojarra* (bass) or tilapia, launch at either Yosocuta reservoir in the Mixteca or Temascal reservoir in northern Oaxaca.

Caverns, Waterfalls, and Natural Springs

In the Valley of Oaxaca, start your exploring at the limestone cavern complex near San Sebastián de las Grutas down Highway 131, south of Zimatlán.

Moving counterclockwise around the Mixteca, start at Apoala to explore the limestone cavern, natural spring, and waterfall. Farther northwest, continue to Juxtlahuaca to Laguna Encantada, a crystal-clear, spring-fed lake. Nearby, explore the triple wonder of limestone cavern, natural spring river, and lake at San Miguel de la Cueva.

In northern Oaxaca and on the Isthmus, most spectacular are the crystalline springs Monte Flor and El Zuzul and the limestone cavern at Eloxochitlán, near Huautla de Jiménez.

Kayaking

At Huatulco, for easy bay boating or kayaking, start out from the sheltered Bahía Chahue marina with your own boat or by kayak from Playa Entrega in the Bahía Santa Cruz or the beach at Bahía El Maguey. More challenging kayaking opportunities abound in the less-sheltered Huatulco bays of El Organo, Cacaluta, and San Agustín. Near Puerto Escondido, easy boating or kayaking is possible from the landings at Las Hamacas, La Alejandria, or Isla El Gallo in Laguna Manialtepec.

of hiking and mountain biking, beginning not far from Oaxaca City, around the pine-scented Benito Juárez, Cuajimoloyas, and Ixtlán de Juárez villages.

River Rafting and Kayaking

When the water conditions are right (usually in the fall), outfitters take parties for rafting on the Río Copalita near Huatulco. A number of other coastal rivers, notably (moving from east to west) the Ríos Zimatán, Colotepec, Verde, and Arena, appear negotiable during the fall and early winter seasons for skilled rafters and kayakers with their own equipment.

Fishing

Fish thrive all along Pacific Oaxaca. From the beach or shoreline rocks, pluck them out of the surf with a net or rod and tackle at Huatulco's Bahía Chahue, at the Bahía Puerto Ángel, and at Bahía Carrizalillo

BEST BEACHES

BEST OVERALL
- **Playa San Agustinillo** (Puerto Ángel and vicinity, page 126)
- **Playa Entrega** (Huatulco, page 152)
- **Playa Manzanillo** (Puerto Escondido, page 177)

BEST SURF-FISHING
- **Bahía Chahue** (Huatulco, page 149)
- **Playa Bachoco** (Puerto Escondido, page 177)

BEST SNORKELING
- **Playa Estacahuite** (Puerto Ángel and vicinity, page 126)
- **Playa Manzanillo** (Puerto Escondido, page 177)

BEST SURFING
- **Playa Zipolite** (Puerto Ángel and vicinity, page 126)
- **Playa Zicatela** (Puerto Escondido, page 176)

BEST SUNSETS
- **Playa Zipolite** (Puerto Ángel and vicinity, page 126)
- **Playa La Ventanilla** (Puerto Ángel and vicinity, page 130)

- **Bahía Tangolunda** (Huatulco, page 149)
- **Playa Zicatela** (Escondido, page 176)

BEST FOR KIDS
- **Playa Panteón** (Puerto Ángel and vicinity, page 126)
- **Bahía El Maguey** (Huatulco, page 152)
- **Playa Principal** (Puerto Escondido, page 176)

BEST FOR CAMPING
- **Playa Zipolite** (Puerto Ángel and vicinity, page 126)
- **El Playon at Bahía San Agustín** (Huatulco, page 153)

MOST PRISTINE
- **Playa La Ventanilla** (Puerto Ángel and vicinity, page 130)
- **Bahía Chachacual** (Huatulco, page 153)
- **Bahía Carrizalillo** (Puerto Escondido, page 177)

MOST INTIMATE
- **Bahía El Organo** (Huatulco, page 152)
- **Bahía Carrizalillo** (Puerto Escondido, page 177)

MOST SPECTACULAR
- **Bahía Cacaluta** (Huatulco, page 152)

Playa Manzanillo

OAXACA CITY

The fortunate city of Oaxaca (pop. 400,000, elev. 1,778 meters/5,110 feet) is both the governmental capital of Mexico's fifth-largest state by area (about tenth largest by population) and the de facto capital of Mexico's southern indigenous heartland. And Oaxaca is southern indeed. It lies farther south than all of Mexico's state capitals save one, Tuxtla Gutiérrez, the capital of the state of Chiapas. Oaxaca nestles in a temperate highland valley, blessed with a year-round balmy, springlike climate, prized by both residents and visitors alike.

Every year, for two weeks starting in mid-July, Oaxaca (wah-HAH-kah) City becomes the focus of the extraordinary diversity of its entire state. In the celebrated Guelaguetza (The Giving) festival, indigenous Oaxaca people, speaking 16 unique languages and representing hundreds of Oaxaca's separate ethnic groups, converge in the city for a grand two-week party of food, dancing, music, and general merrymaking.

The Guelaguetza (gay-lah-GAY-tzah), like virtually all of Oaxaca's civic revelries, starts at the *zócalo* (central plaza), sprinkled all around by relaxing sidewalk cafés and bordered by the porticoed Palacio de Gobierno on its south side and the distinguished baroque bulk of the Catedral de Oaxaca on its north side.

From there, the city's street grid, originally laid out by city founders in 1529, spreads south past the town's vibrant pair of central markets, the Mercado Juárez and the Mercado San Juan de Dios, and north, uphill, along the very strollable pedestrian walkway, the Andador Macedonio Alacalá. The walkway connects the

© BRUCE WHIPPERMAN

HIGHLIGHTS

◖ Mercado Juárez: A regiment of stalls offers the best traditional Oaxaca merchandise, from *huipiles* to mountain-gathered remedies and spit-roasted chickens (page 36).

◖ Catedral de Oaxaca: The recently restored facade and the inner chapel, which enshrines one of the four replicas of the Holy Cross of Huatulco, highlight a visit to this plaza-front gem (page 37).

◖ Basilica de Nuestra Señora de la Soledad: Five pounds of gold and 600 diamonds crown Oaxaca's adored patron, and a fascinating adjacent museum preserves her beloved legacy (page 38).

◖ Ex-Convento de Santa Catalina: Wander the tranquil inner courtyards of this richly restored ex-convent, now a distinguished hotel (page 39).

◖ Centro Cultural de Santo Domingo: Explore the celebrated duo: the art-swathed Iglesia y Ex-Convento de Santo Domingo and the adjacent Museo de las Culturas de Oaxaca, with its golden treasure of Monte Albán's Tomb 7 (page 39).

◖ Los Arquitos: The original 18th-century aqueduct still stands in Oaxaca City's uptown northwest corner, in a quaint string of arches called Los Arquitos. The surrounding neighborhood is ripe for strolling winding village lanes and lingering at a sprinkling of shops, small cafés, and an all-natural Saturday food market (page 41).

◖ MARO: Do a major part of your Oaxaca handicrafts shopping at this store, run by a remarkable group of native Oaxacan women artisans (page 64).

LOOK FOR ◖ TO FIND RECOMMENDED SIGHTS, ACTIVITIES, DINING, AND LODGING.

zócalo with Oaxaca's uptown monuments, most notably Oaxaca's jewel, the Centro Cultural de Santo Domingo, made up of the Iglesia y Ex-Convento de Santo Domingo and the adjacent magnificent Museo de las Culturas de Oaxaca.

Finally, the city streets climb even more steeply, and as the Guelaguetza throng does in July, the westbound streets reach the grand outdoor dance stage and amphitheater atop Oaxaca's storied hillside of Cerro del Fortín.

This hill, originally known as the hill of Huaxyacac, was named for the forest of podbearing trees that still cover its slope. In fact, Huaxyacac was the city's original name, which the Spanish transliterated as Oaxaca.

HISTORY
Before Columbus

As early as perhaps 20,000 years ago, small bands of people, whose ancestors had migrated from Asia, were gathering wild grains, vegetables, and fruits and hunting wild game in the present Valley of Oaxaca. They foraged from the bounty of forest and meadow while following the great herds—bison, camels, deer, horses, and mammoths—that roamed Ice Age America.

Later, around 8000 B.C., the climate had warmed and the animal herds were gone. The people, no longer following the vast game migrations, settled into a more sedentary life. They began to sow and cultivate the fruits, vegetables, and grains they had originally gathered. A few thousand years later, many of those original humble fields and gardens had become productive fields supporting permanent settlements of thatched houses, not unlike many remote Oaxacan hamlets today.

Finally, around 600 B.C., people speaking a Zapotec mother tongue founded Monte Albán, on a mountaintop above the present city of Oaxaca. Monte Albán ruled the Valley of Oaxaca for more than a millennium, climaxing as a sophisticated metropolis of as many as 40,000, controlling a large and populous area of southern Mexico, and enjoying diplomatic and trade relations with distant kingdoms. But for reasons unknown, Monte Albán declined to a shadow of its former glory by around A.D. 800.

Zapotec-speaking city-states such as Zaachila, Dainzu, Mitla, and Lambityeco in the surrounding valleys filled the power vacuum left by the decline of Monte Albán. They ruled small valley-floor kingdoms, each controlling a small flock of satellite towns. Later, Mixtec-speaking people from the northwest invaded the Valley of Oaxaca and took over Monte Albán, using it mostly as a burial ground. Their chiefs subjugated many of the Zapotec city-states and ruled as upper-crust nobility over much of the Valley of Oaxaca, until the Aztecs invaded during the 1440s.

In 1488, after a generation of struggle against combined Mixtec and Zapotec forces, the victorious Aztecs established a garrison on the hill of Huaxyacac (oo-ash-yah-KAHK), now called Cerro del Fortín, overlooking the present city of Oaxaca. Although Aztec settlers had established a model colony by 1500 (including

districts with well-known Valley of Mexico names that still exist, such as Xochimilco), their rule was brief. On December 25, 1521, after a token skirmish, conquistador Francisco de Orozco and his soldiers replaced the Aztecs on the hill of Huaxyacac scarcely five months after the Spanish tide had flooded the Aztecs' Valley of Mexico homeland.

Conquest and Colonization

Spanish settlers began arriving soon after the conquistadors. Hernán Cortés, hearing of the beauty and bounty of the Valley of Oaxaca from both his lieutenants and emissaries from the Zapotec king, decided early on to stake out the Valley of Oaxaca as his personal domain. Time and again during the 1520s he ordered the settlers evacuated from Huaxyacac, only to find a year or two later that they had returned. During Cortés's absence on an expedition to Honduras, the settlers petitioned for and received a charter from King Carlos V for their town, which they christened Antequera after the old Roman city in Spain. Determined not to be outmaneuvered, Cortés personally went to Spain to plead his case and returned triumphant with the royal title of Marqués del Valle de Oaxaca. This included a grant of hundreds of thousands of acres and rights to the labor of thousands of indigenous subjects in a grand checkerboard domain stretching from the Valley of Mexico to the Isthmus of Tehuántepec. Cortés's lands surrounded the settlers' entire town of Antequera. In desperation, the townspeople petitioned the queen of Spain for land on which to grow vegetables: They were granted a one-league square in 1532, now the core of the modern city of Oaxaca.

For hundreds of years, Cortés's descendants reigned; the townspeople prospered; the church grew fat; and the natives toiled—in corn, cattle, cane, and cochineal.

Independence, Reform, and Revolution

In contrast to its neighbors in the state of Guerrero, conservative Oaxaca was a grudging player in the 1810–1821 War of Independence.

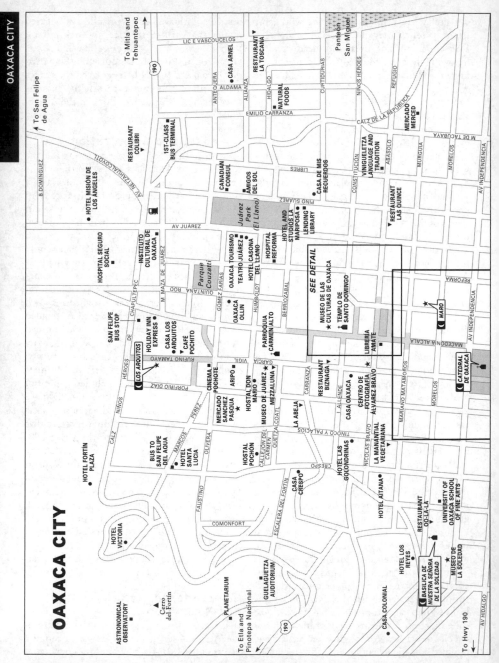

OAXACA CITY

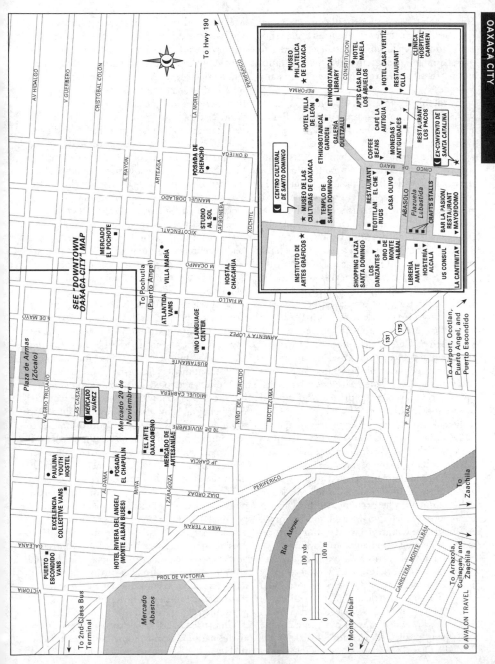

But as the subsequent republican tide swept the country, local fervor produced a new state constitution, including a state legislature and governmental departments, such as public instruction and the Institute of Arts and Sciences.

By the 1850s, times had changed. Oaxacans were leading a new national struggle. Benito Juárez, a pure Zapotec native Mexican, was rallying liberal forces in the War of the Reforms against the oligarchy that had replaced colonial rule. Born in Guelatao, a mountain village north of the Valley of Oaxaca, Juárez at age 12 was an orphan sheepherder. A Catholic priest, struck by the boy's intelligence, brought him to the city as a servant and taught him Spanish in preparation for the priesthood.

Instead, Benito became a lawyer. He hung out his shingle in Oaxaca as a defender of the poor. He then became state legislator, governor, chief justice, and finally the president of Mexico. In his honor, the city's official name was again changed—to Oaxaca de Juárez—in 1872.

In 1861, after winning the three-year civil war, Juárez's Reformista forces had their victory snatched away. France, taking advantage of the preoccupation of the United States with its own civil war, invaded Mexico and installed an Austrian Hapsburg prince as Emperor Maximilian of Mexico.

It took Juárez five years to prevail against Maximilian and his conservative Mexican backers. Although Maximilian and Juárez paradoxically shared many of the same liberal ideas, Juárez had Maximilian executed after his defeat and capture in 1867. Juárez bathed Mexico in enlightenment as he promulgated his Laws of the Reform (which remain essentially in force). Although the country rewarded him with re-election, he died of exhaustion in 1872.

Another Oaxacan of native Mexican descent, General Porfirio Díaz, vowed to carry Juárez's banner. Díaz, the hero who defeated the French in the battle of Puebla on Cinco de Mayo (May 5) of 1862, was elected president in 1876. *"No Reelección"* was his campaign cry. He subsequently ruled Mexico for 34 years.

Under Díaz's "Order and Progress" programs,

Mexico, and to a lesser degree Oaxaca, was modernized at great human cost. As railroads, factories, and mines mushroomed, property ownership increasingly became concentrated among rich Mexicans and their foreign friends. Smashed protest marches, murdered opposition leaders, and rigged elections returned Díaz to office time and again.

But not forever. The revolt that ousted Díaz in 1910 has, in theory, never ceased. For the last three generations of the 20th century, the PRI (Partido Revolucionario Institucional, or the Institutional Revolutionary Party) presided over a uniquely imperfect Mexican form of democracy. During that time, the lives of native Oaxacans improved gradually. Although indigenous families now go to government health centers and more of their children attend government rural schools, the price for doing so is to become less indigenous and more Mexican.

In the late 1980s, UNESCO recognized Oaxaca as one of several world sites belonging to the "cultural patrimony of mankind." The government took notice and began preparing Oaxaca for an influx of visitors. Museums were built, monuments refurbished, and the venerable buildings restored. Burgeoning tourism during the 1990s visibly improved the economic well-being of many Oaxaca families. In 1995, moderate PRI governor Diodoro Carrasco Altamirano pushed through an unprecedented law that legalized Oaxacan native rights to their indigenous language and their traditional, town-meeting form of government.

Nevertheless, by developed-world standards, most Oaxaca City families remain poor. The political system, moreover, remains far from perfect. In 2000, the victory of opposition presidential candidate Vicente Fox promised a new day for democracy in Oaxaca. Although Fox couldn't work miracles during his six-year term, one of his major achievements was to add transparency to the workings of the Mexican government.

Unfortunately, despite President Fox's efforts at the national level, serious political trouble surfaced in Oaxaca in mid-2006. It started mildly enough. In May 2006, Oaxaca's statewide teachers union went on their perennial strike for much-needed higher wages. They accused PRI governor Ulises Ruiz of diverting millions of dollars in education funds to his controversial pet public works projects.

By mid-June, when teachers began barricading streets around the *zócalo,* Ruiz sent in his police, who brutally roughed up the nonviolent middle-class demonstrators. The protest escalated quickly. The teachers allied themselves with their left-leaning supporters, forming an umbrella protest organization, the APPO (Popular Assembly of the People of Oaxaca), and added the demand for Governor Ruiz to step down.

During the summer months of 2006, the protests turned violent. Highways were blocked, buses were burned, a radio station was occupied, and a handful of people were shot to death. By the end of September, tourism had evaporated and, consequently, most businesses, including hotels and restaurants, had shut their doors.

In late October, President Vicente Fox, spurred by the killing of an American news reporter, acted. He sent a brigade of federal troops and police to Oaxaca, where they removed the street barricades and dispersed the protestors while inflicting only minimal injuries.

The local townspeople, relieved and encouraged, turned out, and in two days they swept up the mess, painted over the accumulated graffiti, and opened their businesses. Townspeople filled the streets, buying flowers to celebrate their subsequently peaceful November 1–2 Day of the Dead holiday, and equally tranquil and joyful Christmas celebrations.

During 2007, aside from a few minor APPO ("AH-poh") demonstrations, relegated to the city outskirts, Oaxaca continued returning to normal. Local and national visitors responded, frequenting downtown hotels, restaurants, and shops in increasing numbers. By November 2007, a growing trickle of foreign visitors was joining the influx, fueling predictions by some experts that in 2008 international visitors would come back, big-time.

Oaxaca was certainly ready for them. By 2009, virtually all of the favorite restaurants and shops were open for business; the same was true of hotels, several of which remodeled and welcomed visitors with bargain rates, making the prospect of a long Oaxaca stay more tempting than ever. The city and state welcomed the returned visitors with big Guelaguetza celebrations in both 2009 and 2010. And best of all, despite past political tensions, the people of Oaxaca remained appreciative of visitors and looked forward with renewed enthusiasm to sharing their lovely city's celebrated handicrafts, delicious cuisine, and beloved fiestas with them.

Moreover, the 2010 Oaxaca election results seemed to improve prospects for a peaceful Oaxaca. On July 4, 2010, Oaxaca voters statewide, contrary to the national trend, rejected 90 percent of the PRI (Governor Ruiz's party) candidates, from city council hopefuls all the way up to governor, in favor of a battalion of PRD and PAN candidates. Finally, after 81 years of statewide rule, the Oaxaca PRI had suffered near-total defeat. At the top of the list, Governor Ruiz's hand-picked PRI candidate for governor was steamrolled by Convergence (United PRD and PAN) Party candidate Gabino Cué Monteagudo, allowing Oaxacans a much-needed sigh of relief with the departure of the Ruiz administration in late 2010.

PLANNING YOUR TIME

You could spend a month exploring the city of Oaxaca and still have plenty to see. However, in about four fairly relaxed days, you can take in most of the downtown highlights. Start out with a leisurely day of people-watching and café-lounging around the invitingly tranquil old *zócalo.* For activity, explore the nearby Palacio de Gobierno, the colorful **Mercado Juárez**, the exquisitely baroque **Iglesia y Ex-Convento de San Agustín**, and the **Catedral de Oaxaca** with its mysteriously intriguing Santa Cruz de Huatulco.

Spend your second day relaxing along the **Andador de Macedonio Alacalá pedestrian mall,** checking out the many fine handicrafts

OAXACA CITY

© BRUCE WHIPPERMAN

Ex-convento de Santo Domingo

shops, the **Museo de Arte Contemporaneo,** and the **Ex-Convento de Santa Catalina,** now restored as the Hotel Camino Real. Be sure to enjoy lunch on the relaxingly cool patios of the Danzantes or Hostería Alcalá restaurants.

Highlight your downtown exploration with at least a day around the **Centro Cultural de Santo Domingo,** which includes a pair of not-to-miss stops: the world-class **Museo de las Culturas de Oaxaca** and Oaxaca's pride, the radiantly lovely **Iglesia y Ex-Convento de Santo Domingo.**

Spend your fourth day following your own interests, such as investigating more handicrafts stores, especially **MARO** (Mujeres Artesanís de los Regiones de Oaxaca); visiting small museums, notably, the **Casa de Juárez** and the **Museo Arte Prehispánico de Rufino Tamayo;** or taking in sights, such as the intimate Arquitos and San Felipe del Agua village neighborhoods or the gemlike **Basilica de Nuestra Señora de la Soledad** and adjacent museum, **Museo de la Soledad.**

Sights

GETTING ORIENTED

The streets of Oaxaca still run along the same simple north–south grid the city founders laid out in 1529. If you stand at the center of the old *zócalo* and look out toward the *catedral* across Avenida Hidalgo, you will be looking north. Diagonally left, to the northwest, you'll see the smaller plaza, **Alameda de León,** and directly beyond that, in the distance, the historic hill of Huaxyacac, now called **Cerro del Fortín.**

Along the base of that hill, the Pan American Highway (National Highway 190) runs generally east–west through the northern suburbs. Turn around and you'll see the porticoed facade of the former **Palacio de Gobierno,** now a museum, where Oaxaca's governor used to tend to the state's business. In 0.8 kilometers (0.5 mi) behind that (although you can't see

it from the *zócalo*), the **periférico** (peripheral boulevard) loops around the town's south end. There it passes the yawning but often dry wash of the **Río Atoyac** and the sprawling **Mercado Abastos,** a market and second-class bus terminal on the southwest. Finally, if you find a clear vantage point, you'll see the hill of **Monte Albán** looming 300 meters (1,000 ft) above the southwest horizon.

AROUND THE ZÓCALO

The venerable restored downtown buildings and streets, some converted to traffic-free malls, make a delightful strolling ground for discovering traditional Mexico at its best. The shady old *zócalo* basks at the heart of it all, a perfect place for taking a seat at one of many sidewalk cafés and watching the world glide by. Officially called Jardín Juárez, the *zócalo* was laid out in 1529. Its portals,

OAXACA CITY

DOWNTOWN OAXACA CITY

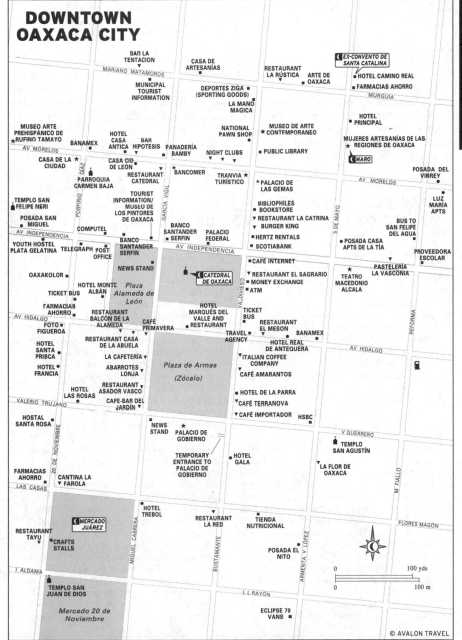

BAR LA TENTACION

CASA DE ARTESANÍAS

RESTAURANT LA RÚSTICA

ARTE DE OAXACA

EX-CONVENTO DE SANTA CATALINA

HOTEL CAMINO REAL

FARMACIAS AHORRO

MARIANO MATAMOROS

MUNICIPAL TOURIST INFORMATION

DEPORTES ZIGA (SPORTING GOODS)

LA MANO MAGICA

MURGUIA

MUSEO ARTE PREHISPÁNICO DE RUFINO TAMAYO

HOTEL CASA ANTICA

BAR HIPOTESIS

NATIONAL PAWN SHOP

MUSEO DE ARTE CONTEMPORANEO

HOTEL PRINCIPAL

BANAMEX

PANADERÍA BAMBY

NIGHT CLUBS

PUBLIC LIBRARY

MUJERES ARTESANÍAS DE LAS REGIONES DE OAXACA

AV MORELOS

CASA DE LA CIUDAD

CASA CID DE LEÓN

MARO

POSADA DEL VIRREY

PARROQUIA CARMEN BAJA

RESTAURANT CATEDRAL

BANCOMER

TRANVIA TURÍSTICO

PALACIO DE LAS GEMAS

AV MORELOS

LUZ MARÍA APTS

TEMPLO SAN FELIPE NERI

TOURIST INFORMATION/ MUSEO DE LOS PINTORES DE OAXACA

BIBLIOPHILES BOOKSTORE

RESTAURANT LA CATRINA

POSADA SAN MIGUEL

COMPUTEL

BURGER KING

BUS TO SAN FELIPE DEL AGUA

AV INDEPENDENCIA

BANCO SANTANDER SERFIN

PALACIO FEDERAL

HERTZ RENTALS

POSADA CASA APTS DE LA TÍA

YOUTH HOSTEL PLATA GELATINA

TELEGRAPH POST OFFICE

BANCO SANTANDER SERFIN

AV INDEPENDENCIA

SCOTIABANK

PROVEEDORA ESCOLAR

NEWS STAND

CAFÉ INTERNET

PASTELERÍA LA VASCONIA

OAXAKOLOR

HOTEL MONTE ALBÁN

Plaza Alameda de León

CATEDRAL DE OAXACA

RESTAURANT EL SAGRARIO

MONEY EXCHANGE

TEATRO MACEDONIO ALCALA

TICKET BUS

ATM

FARMACIAS AHORRO

RESTAURANT BALCÓN DE LA ALAMEDA

CAFÉ PRIMAVERA

HOTEL MARQUÉS DEL VALLE AND RESTAURANT

TICKET BUS

RESTAURANT EL MESON

AV HIDALGO

FOTO FIGUEROA

TRAVEL AGENCY

BANAMEX

HOTEL SANTA PRISCA

RESTAURANT CASA DE LA ABUELA

HOTEL REAL DE ANTEQUERA

AV HIDALGO

LA CAFETERÍA

ITALIAN COFFEE COMPANY

HOTEL FRANCIA

ABARROTES LONJA

Plaza de Armas

(Zócalo)

CAFÉ AMARANTOS

HOTEL LAS ROSAS

RESTAURANT ASADOR VASCO

HOTEL DE LA PARRA

REFORMA

VALERIO TRUJANO

CAFÉ-BAR DEL JARDIN

CAFÉ TERRANOVA

CAFÉ IMPORTADOR

HSBC

HOSTAL SANTA ROSA

NEWS STAND

PALACIO DE GOBIERNO

V. GUERRERO

TEMPLO SAN AGUSTÍN

FARMACIAS AHORRO

CANTINA LA FAROLA

TEMPORARY ENTRANCE TO PALACIO DE GOBIERNO

HOTEL GALA

LA FLOR DE OAXACA

LAS CASAS

HOTEL TREBOL

RESTAURANT LA RED

TIENDA NUTRICIONAL

FLORES MAGON

RESTAURANT TAYU

MERCADO JUÁREZ

CRAFTS STALLS

POSADA EL NITO

I ALDAMA

TEMPLO SAN JUAN DE DIOS

Mercado 20 de Noviembre

L L RAYÓN

ECLIPSE 70 VANS

MIGUEL CABRERA

BUSTAMANTE

ARMENTA Y LÓPEZ

M. FIALLO

20 DE NOVIEMBRE

PORFIRIO

DIAZ

GARCÍA VIGIL

V.L DIVISO

5 DE MAYO

| 0 | 100 yds |
| 0 | 100 m |

© AVALON TRAVEL

clockwise from the west side, are named Flores, Clavería, Juárez, and Mercaderes.

Palacio de Gobierno

Give the guards at the temporary entrance (near southeast *zócalo* corner, on Bustamante) of the former statehouse—now museum (south side of the *zócalo*, 951/501-1662, 10 A.M.–7 P.M. Mon.–Sat., 10 A.M.–5 P.M. Sun., $3) a cheery *"buenos días"* or *"buenas tardes"* and step inside. City fathers first built a city hall on the same site in 1576. Repeated earthquakes led to reconstructions, until 1948, when the present building, a modernized and strengthened version of the previous 1884 structure, was finished.

Inside, you'll find a beautifully renovated museum, highlighted by dramatic historic murals, and an excellent 2nd-floor science and natural history sub-museum. After entering, continue straight ahead, to the middle of the central patio, where, along the stairs on the left, spreads the main mural, by Arturo Bustos, completed during the 1980s. It depicts the

MARGARITA MAZA: A LIFE OF COURAGE AND CONVICTION

Calle Margarita Maza, a modest two-block lane on Oaxaca City's northern downtown edge, memorializes Margarita Maza, wife of Mexico's revered president Benito Juárez and heroine who gave her all for love and country. Her greatness and that of her husband were inextricably intertwined by their own strong liberal ideals and their collective fate. Years before Margarita was born, Benito, of pure Zapotec blood, came to Oaxaca City seeking both his sister and his fortune. He found his sister working as a cook in the household of Italian immigrant and merchant Antonio Maza and his wife, Petra Parada.

Benito also found refuge and warmth in the Maza household; through the Mazas, Benito found work and social connections that led to an education and introduction into Oaxacan society. Benito was 20 years old when Margarita, the Mazas' youngest child, was born. He bounced the baby on his knee and played with her like an older brother as she matured and while Benito's career as a lawyer, then Oaxaca state legislator, blossomed.

By the time Margarita was 17, their mutual affection had bloomed into love, and Benito, a successful attorney at 37, proposed marriage. They were married in the church of San Felipe de Neri, in Oaxaca City, on July 31, 1843. Even today such a match would be unusual; in the Oaxaca of 1843 it was unheard of. That he, a poor, dark brown Zapotec, and she, a lily-white daughter of a prominent merchant, were even able to associate, much less to marry, is testament to the Mazas' liberal views.

The same liberal views and their iron determination to do something about them scarred the last half of Benito and Margarita's 26 years of married life. From around 1854, when Benito was driven into exile in New Orleans, civil war, foreign invasion, and assassination attempts forced the family to be nearly always on the move, living in unfamiliar and trying circumstances, hounded and threatened by enemies, and continually lacking money.

One of the most dangerous episodes came in 1858, when Margarita, at the age of 32, had to move her brood of five children and entire household from Oaxaca to Veracruz, where Benito was running the liberal Mexican government-in-exile. Fearing spies and assassins, Margarita took the tortuous, roundabout route over the heart of the Sierra Madre, traveling at night, on foot beside their burro-train, disguising herself in native *huipil*, and sleeping by day in farmhouses of friendly Zapotec campesinos.

Later, Benito and Margarita enjoyed two years of peace together, beginning in 1861, after the liberal triumph in the War of the Reform. Their marriage, although severely tried by hardship and separation, was a supremely happy one. Twelve children resulted; seven — six girls and a boy — outlived their parents.

struggles of Oaxaca's independence, reform, and revolutionary heroes. On the upper right, in his trademark bandanna, is *insurgente* José María Morelos y Pavón, who published the famous *El Correo del Sur* newspaper in Oaxaca during Mexico's War of Independence. In the center is Oaxaca's favorite son and Mexico's revered *presidente*, Benito Juárez, and his wife, Margarita Maza. Below them is Juárez's *reformista* cabinet (notice the young, restive General Porfirio Díaz third to the right of Juárez, with the sword on the right), which

struggled through two bloody wars, finally emerging, with Juárez, triumphant in 1867. On the mural's far left is Oaxaca's 1910 revolutionary hero—Ricardo Flores Magón—in turn-of-the-20th-century Marxian-style spectacles. Also take a look at Bustos's other mural, above the east (entry) side staircase, upstairs. It dramatically depicts Mexico's pre-Hispanic and conquest eras.

Before you leave, you might spend an extra few minutes on the museum's airy, renovated upstairs floor, enjoying the intriguing hands-on

Two boys and three girls died when still young. Their love, although profoundly deep, had few pretensions. Benito called her his "old lady." She called him "Juárez" and, when asked, replied that "he is very homely but good."

Their peace together was short-lived. The French invasion forced Benito to travel the country, managing the government in a black carriage, one jump ahead of the French army. Margarita took the family on a hopscotch path into northern Mexico and finally to New York and Washington, D.C. There, she reached the depths of despair when two of her three sons died. She wrote to Benito: "The loss of my sons is killing me...I prefer death a thousand times more than life...I do not blame persons who kill themselves...If I had been braver I should have done it a year ago."

Eventually Margarita recovered her equilibrium, buoyed by the birth of her first grandchild, a baby girl, and the admiring attention of American society, including General Ulysses S. Grant and President Andrew Johnson.

On June 19, 1867, Juárez had the French-installed Emperor Maximilian executed. This was Margarita's signal to return home. A month later, with her party of 14, she arrived in Veracruz, showered by bouquets as she walked down the gangplank.

Reunited for three happy years with Margarita in Mexico City, Benito worked like a demon to turn his dreams for Mexico into reality. But overwork took its toll, and Benito suffered a stroke in October 1870. He recovered partially to discover that Margarita was fatally ill. She died on January 2, 1871, of cancer. Although weak, Benito strained with all of his strength and with tears in his eyes to lift her body into the coffin. All of Mexico, both friends and former enemies, joined in grief with their president for their beloved Margarita Maza, who had given as much as any heroine could for both love and country.

© BRUCE WHIPPERMAN

portrait of Margarita Maza and Benito Juárez

Kids enjoy the new hands-on interactive displays at the museum in the Palacio de Gobierno.

© BRUCE WHIPPERMAN

science and natural history exhibits that run from the creation of the universe, all the way through dinosaurs, early humans, and Darwin.

Mercado Juárez

The traditional Juárez market (most shops open by 8 A.M. and close by 6 P.M. daily) occupies the one-block square that begins just one block south and one block west of the *zócalo*. Stroll around for fun and perhaps a bargain in the honeycomb of traditional leather, textile, and clothing stalls.

While at the market, be sure to step to the southwest corner of 20 de Noviembre and Rayón for a history lesson in art inside the **Templo y Ex-Convento de San Juan de Dios,** which stands on the site of Oaxaca's oldest church. The present structure, completed in 1703, replaced the former earthquake-damaged 1535 town cathedral, which itself replaced the original 1521 adobe structure. Big paintings lining the nave walls depict landmarks in Oaxaca's religious history. Inside the front door, to the left, see Bishop las Casas protecting his native charges against soldiers

and settlers. Farther inside is an oil painting of the Santa Cruz de Huatulco (Holy Cross of Huatulco); next comes Oaxaca's first mass, on the banks of the Río Atoyac, on November 25, 1521, and after that, the baptism of Cosijoeza, the last Zapotec king. Also, you'll find a series of oil paintings showing the discovery, persecution, revolt, and reacceptance of the so-called "Idolators of Los Cajonos," whom Spaniards discovered worshipping their native gods on September 14, 1700.

Templo y Ex-Convento de San Agustín

Off-*zócalo* side streets are studded with Oaxaca's old church gems. One of the most precious and most accessible is the San Agustín church and ex-convent (on Calle Guerrero), one block due east from the Palacio de Gobierno. One of the few Oaxacan works of the Augustinian order, the original adobe church on this site was finished in 1596, but it was seriously damaged by subsequent earthquakes. The present church, finished in 1722, replaced the original. A generation after the Augustinians were expelled in the 1860s, Bishop Gillow of Oaxaca acquired and reactivated the church in 1893 and started the Casa de Cuna, a children's home and school, which still exists next door.

San Agustín's baroque facade blooms with a pious pastoral sculpture of a bearded San Agustín, 5th-century Bishop of Hipona, North Africa, above the entrance arch. Below, flanking the entrance portal, stand sculptures of Augustinian Saints Alipio, on the left, and Thomas of Valencia, on the right.

Inside, the same saints grace the grand, gilded main altarpiece, with the addition of Augustinian founding fathers San Juan Sahagún and San Fulgencio. The gilded south (right) transept altarpiece displays a heavenly image of Santa Monica, mother of San Agustín. Finally, look below the pulpit for the glass capsule that contains a bone-fragment relic of San Agustín, gift from the Roman Augustinians.

◖ Catedral de Oaxaca

Return to the *zócalo*'s north side for a look at the present cathedral. It replaced the 1550 original, demolished by an earthquake in 1696. Finished in 1733, with appropriately burly twin bell towers, the present cathedral is distinguished by its Greek-marble main altar, where a polished Italian bronze Virgin of the Ascension is being drawn upward to the cloud-tipped heavenly domain of the Holy Spirit (the dove) and God (the sunburst). Notice the glass images of noble, bearded St. Peter and St. Paul flanking opposite sides of the altar.

Of considerable historical interest is the **Santa Cruz de Huatulco** (Holy Cross of Huatulco), enshrined in a chapel at the middle, south (right) side of the nave. The cross, about two feet high, in the glass case atop the chapel altar, is one of four made in 1612 by Oaxaca bishop Juan Cervantes from the original mysterious cross worshiped by the natives on the southern Oaxaca coast long before the conquest. An explanation, in Spanish, gives three versions of the story of the cross, which, as the natives reported to the conqueror Pedro Alvarado in 1522, was erected long before by a strange, white-robed holy man who soon

© BRUCE WHIPPERMAN

Oaxaca City's sturdy, earthquake-resistant cathedral rises from the broad plaza that marks the city center.

departed and never returned. Bishop Cervantes sent the three other copies of the cross, respectively, to authorities at Santa María Huatulco municipality, Mexico City, and Rome.

NORTHWEST OF THE *ZÓCALO*
Templo de San Felipe Neri

Just two blocks west of Catedral de Oaxaca rises the distinguished facade of the Templo de San Felipe Neri (on Independencia, corner of Tinoco and Palacios, open for worship 8 A.M.–11 P.M. daily). The building is immediately notable, for it faces south, unlike the great majority of Oaxaca's churches, which follow tradition and face west.

Its builders finished the structure, once a convent of the order of San Felipe Neri, and dedicated it to the Virgin of Patrocinio in 1773. The subsequent 1795 earthquake caused extensive damage, which was not completely repaired until the 20th century. Unfortunately, more earthquakes, in 1928 and 1931, inflicted additional destruction. The present restoration was completed in 1985.

The result appears well worth the effort. Original builders crafted the facade in the 17th-century "plateresque" tradition, so named for the designs, similar to those of fine silverware, using muted green volcanic *cantera* stone. The sole exception is the noble statue of San Felipe Neri, carved of contrasting yellow *cantera,* in clerical hat and bishop's cape, that presides above the front door.

Walk inside to admire the temple's glorious golden *retablo* (altarpiece). It towers three stories, inhabited by a host of apostles, saints, angels, and cherubs, all reigned over by the Virgin and finally San Felipe Neri at the very top.

Museo Arte Prehispánico de Rufino Tamayo

Just one block farther north, this museum (503 Morelos, tel. 951/516-4750, 10 A.M.–2 P.M. and 4–7 P.M. Mon. and Wed.–Sat., 10 A.M.–3 P.M. Sun., $3) exhibits the brilliant pre-Columbian artifact collection of celebrated artist Rufino Tamayo (1899–1991). Displays include hosts of animal motifs—Colima dogs, parrots, ducks,

snakes—whimsically crafted into polychrome vases, bowls, and urns.

(Basilica de Nuestra Señora de la Soledad

Continue three blocks west, past the University of Oaxaca School of Fine Arts and the airy Plaza of Dances, to the baroque Basilica de Nuestra Señora de la Soledad. Inside, the Virgen de la Soledad (Virgin of Solitude), the patron of Oaxaca, stands atop the altar with her five-pound solid golden crown, encrusted with 600 diamonds.

Step into the **Museo de la Soledad** (Calle Morelos, at the Plaza de las Danzas, tel. 951/516-5076, 9 A.M.–2 P.M. and 4–6 P.M. daily, free admission) at the downhill side of the church, on the rear end. A multitude of objects of adornment—shells, paintings, jewelry—crowd cabinets, shelves, and aisles of musty rooms. Large stained-glass panels tell of the images of Jesus and the Virgin that arrived miraculously in 1620, eventually becoming Oaxaca's patron symbols.

the basilica of Oaxaca's patron, La Señora de la Soledad

© BRUCE WHIPPERMAN

ANDADOR DE MACEDONIO ALCALÁ

The tranquil Andador de Macedonio Alcalá pedestrian mall, named after the composer of the Oaxacan hymn "Dios Nunca Muere" ("God Never Dies"), leads north from the *zócalo.* Paved with Oaxaca green stone in 1985 and freed of auto traffic, the mall connects the *zócalo* with a number of not-to-be-missed Oaxaca sights.

Teatro Alcalá

Christened by a 1909 opening performance of *Aida,* the Teatro Alcalá (900 Independencia, tel. 951/516-8312 or 951/516-8344, 9 A.M.–5 P.M. Mon.–Fri., admission free, except during events) houses a treasury of Romantic-era art. Above the foyer, a sumptuous marble staircase rises to a bas-relief medallion allegorizing the triumph of art. Inside, soaring above the orchestra, a heavenly choir of muses, representing the arts, decorates the ceiling. Check at the theater box office for a list of performances, which customarily include classical ballet, folkloric dance, opera, and orchestral music.

To get to the theater from the back of the Catedral de Oaxaca head right one block along Independencia to the corner of Independencia and Cinco de Mayo.

Museo de Arte Contemporaneo de Oaxaca

Continuing north along the Macedonio Alcalá pedestrian mall and past the bookstore (which sells some English-language history, art, and travel books), you soon reach the so-called **Casa de Cortés,** now the Museo de Arte Contemporaneo de Oaxaca (Macedonio Alcalá 202, tel. 951/514-1055, www.museomaco .com, 10 A.M.–6 P.M. daily, free admission). Exhibitions feature works of local and nationally known modern artists. Although named popularly for Hernán Cortés, the building is at least a hundred years too new for Cortés to have lived there. The coat of arms on the facade above the door reveals it to have been the 17th-century home of a different Oaxaca family.

For a change of pace, enjoy an airy 45-minute ride around town on the motorized trolley **Tranvia Turístico** (corner of Macedonio Alcalá and Morelos, $3 pp), which takes off hourly, half a block downhill from the Museo de Arte Contemporaneo.

◖ Ex-Convento de Santa Catalina

Continue uphill and, at Murguia, detour right again, to the Ex-Convento de Santa Catalina (Cinco de Mayo 600, tel. 951/516-0611, public tours 5 P.M. Tues.–Fri., free), the second-oldest women's convent in New Spain, founded in 1576. Although the quarters of the first novitiates were spare, the convent grew into a sprawling chapel and cloister complex decorated by fountains and flower-strewn gardens. Juárez's reforms drove the sisters out in 1862; the building has since served as city hall, school, and movie theater. Now it stands beautifully restored as the Hotel Camino Real. Note the native-motif original murals that the renovation revealed on interior walls.

◖ Centro Cultural de Santo Domingo

Return to the Macedonio Alcalá pedestrian mall and continue another block uphill to Oaxaca's pride, the Centro Cultural de Santo Domingo (corner of Macedonio Alcalá and I. Allende, 951/516-2991 or 951/516-3721, free admission), which contains two main parts, side by side: the Museo de las Culturas de Oaxaca and the Iglesia y Ex-Convento de Santo Domingo, both behind the broad Plaza Santo Domingo maguey garden and pedestrian square.

Inside, the **Iglesia y Ex-Convento de Santo Domingo** (tel. 951/516-2991 or 951/516-3721, 7 A.M.–1 P.M. and 5–8 P.M. daily) glows with a wealth of art. Above the antechamber spreads the entire genealogical tree of Santo Domingo de Guzmán, starting with Mother Mary and weaving through a score of noblemen and women to the saint himself over the front door.

Continuing inside, the soaring, Sistine Chapel–like nave glitters with saints, cherubs,

© BRUCE WHIPPERMAN

Museo de las Culturas de Oaxaca is housed in the cloister of the Santo Domingo church.

and Bible-story paintings. The altar is the climax with a host of cherished symbols—the Last Supper, sheaves of grain, loaves and fishes, Jesus and Peter on the Sea of Galilee—in a riot of gold leaf.

Continue next door to the **Museo de las Culturas de Oaxaca** (tel. 951/516-2991 or 951/516-3721, 10 A.M.–6 P.M. Tues.–Sun., admisssion $6, audio tour $5), which occupies the completely restored convent section of the Santo Domingo church. A very informative audio tour with headset and player is available for rent just past the entrance security gate.

Exhibitions begin on the bottom floor in rooms adjacent to the massive convent cloister, restored in 1998 to all of its original austere beauty. A downstairs highlight is the long-neglected but now safely preserved Biblioteca (Library) de Francisco Burgoa, which you can walk right through and examine some of the more important works on display. The collection, 23,000 titles in all, includes its earliest work, a 1484 commentary on the works of Aristotle by Juan Versor.

A Museo sign points you upstairs via a glittering, restored, towering domed chamber, adorned overhead with the Dominican founding fathers, presided over by Santo Domingo de Guzmán himself.

It's hard not to be impressed by the seeming miles of meticulously prepared displays divided into about two dozen long rooms covering various historical periods. One room exhibits priceless Monte Albán–era artifacts, including one of the most important of the original so-called *danzantes,* with the typically mutilated sex organs. The climax comes in the Tesoros de Tumba 7 (Treasures of Tomb 7) room, where the entire gilded treasure discovered at Monte Albán Tomb 7 is on display. Beside a small mountain of gold and turquoise ornaments, notice the small but masterfully executed golden head of Ecéchatl, god of the wind, made eerie by the omission of facial skin over the jaw, which produces a nightmarishly skeletal piece of jewelry.

The museum also includes a **jardín etno-botánico** (ethno-botanical garden; enter at northwest corner of Reforma and Constitución, tel./fax 951/516-5325 or 951/516-7915; tours in Spanish 5 P.M. Fri. and Sat., $5 pp; tours in English 11 A.M. Sat., $10 pp) in its big backyard. The staff conducts tours regularly and there is an announced schedule, but the schedule seems to change often. Inquire (check for the tour schedule on the door) at the ethno-botanical library at the garden entrance, two blocks behind the Santo Domingo churchfront.

Small Museums

Back outside, step across Macedonio Alcalá, a few doors uphill, into the rust-colored old building now tastefully restored as the museum of the **Instituto de Artes Gráficos de Oaxaca** (Macedonio Alcala 507, tel. 951/516-6980, 10 A.M.–8 P.M. Mon.–Sun., free admission). Inside, displays exhibit mostly contemporary etchings, wood-block prints, and paintings by artists of both national and international renown. Exhibits change approximately monthly.

Head west one block (along the Plazuela del Carmen, off Macedonio Alcalá across from the museum) to the **Casa de Juárez** museum (609 Garcia Vigil, tel. 951/516-1860, 10 A.M.–7 P.M. Tues.–Sun., $3). The modest but beautifully restored house was the home of Juárez's benefactor, priest, and bookbinder: Father Antonio Salanueva. Rooms decorated with homey mid-19th-century furnishings realistically illustrate the life and times of a man as revered in Mexico as his contemporary, Abraham Lincoln, was north of the border.

Later, if you have time, return to the Santo Domingo church plaza and continue east past the church along Constitución to the new **Museo Filatelia de Oaxaca** (Reforma 504, just uphill from the corner of Constitución, tel. 951/514-2366 or 951/514-8028, www.mufi.org.mx, 10 A.M.–8 P.M. Tues.–Sun., $2). Inside, showcases display the noted collection of José Cosino y Cosio—a library of international postal paraphernalia. Planners project that the museum's collection, of mostly Mexican and Oaxacan postage stamps, will grow steadily during succeeding decades.

Return a block and a half down Reforma and turn right at Abasolo, which, past Macedonio Alcalá, becomes M. Bravo. Continue a block to the **Centro de Fotografía Manuel Alvarez Bravo** (M. Bravo 116, corner of Garcia Vigil, tel. 951/516-9800, 9 A.M.–8 P.M. Wed.–Mon., free admission). Galleries display the work of both locally prominent and internationally acclaimed photographers, while instructors in classrooms conduct photography classes for children, adult beginners, and professionals.

Back downhill, at the north edge of the *zócalo* stands a regally restored colonial-era house, formerly the Oaxaca state tourism headquarters, now home to the **Museo de los Pintores Oaxaqueños** (Museum of Oaxacan Painters, corner of Independencia and Garcia Vigil, tel. 951/516-5645, 10 A.M.–6 P.M. Tues.–Sun., $2). It houses an eclectic, revolving collection of modern art, sometimes primitive, sometimes erotic, and mostly abstract, on two floors around a central patio. The house itself, built in 1695, has gone through several transformations: first a girl's school, then, in succession, the Manuel Fiallo family home, a regional

museum, city hall, and finally the Oaxaca *Turismo* (Tourism Secretariat) for several years before its 2004–2005 restoration to its austerely noble present incarnation. Presently, state *Turismo* maintains a tourist information desk to the left as you enter the museum.

LOS ARQUITOS

Long ago, Oaxaca's city founders provided for a permanent local water supply. They tapped the bountiful natural springs flowing from the mountains rising directly north of the city, topped by the towering Cerro San Felipe (elev. 3,100 meters/10,200 feet). The aqueduct they built gave rise to the name San Felipe del Agua, the foothill village where the aqueduct begins. Although now replaced by underground steel pipes, the original 18th-century aqueduct still stands, paralleling the downhill road from San Felipe and ending in a quaint string of arches, called Los Arquitos, in the city neighborhood several blocks northwest of Iglesia y Ex-Convento de Santo Domingo.

Walking Tours

The following are two walking tours: first, a one- or two-hour stroll (best in morning or early afternoon to incorporate breakfast or lunch) through the relatively close-in Los Arquitos neighborhood; and next, an out-of-downtown one- or two-hour exploration (best in the afternoon to incorporate a late lunch) of the cooler, leafy heights of picturesque San Felipe del Agua village.

Starting from the Santo Domingo church-front, at the corner of Macedonio Alcalá and Allende, walk north, uphill along Macedonio Alcalá three blocks to Humboldt. Turn left and continue two blocks to busy Porfirio Díaz, where, across the street rises a towering fig tree that marks the **Mercado Sánchez Pasqua.** Cross with care and continue straight past the tree to the entrance of the market. Inside, you'll first find a squadron of tiny dry goods, clothes, and handicrafts shops, and then a rainbow mix of colorful fruit and vegetable stalls. Continue in the same direction and you'll arrive at the *fondas* (food stalls), for which Mercado Sánchez

© BRUCE WHIPPERMAN

strolling in Los Arquitos

Pasqua is famous, were you can enjoy a home-style breakfast or a special lunch treat.

Retrace your steps back outside, across Porfirio Díaz, to Humboldt, one block and turn left at Garcia Vigil. Continue north, uphill, a block, to the corner of Calle Xolotl (show-LOH-tuhl), where Garcia Vigil changes to Calle Rufino Tamayo. Pass (on the left, above the street), the art **Cinema Pochote,** where you can check the film schedule on the door.

Continue uphill along Tamayo, paralleling the arches for three blocks, until you reach busy east–west thoroughfare Calzada Niños Héroes. Along the way, you'll be entertained by the ways the residents have adapted to the aque-duct, ingeniously tucking their individual home and store doorways beneath the arches. Don't miss the little shrine built beneath one arch, at Tamayo 802, and also the tiny café, El Pavito (The Little Peacock), beneath another. Also notice the colorfully picturesque contrast be-tween the arches' red brick and light green vol-canic *cantera* stone construction. Furthermore, be sure to explore some of the side lanes, such as the one opposite Tamayo 818 that heads

beneath an arch and opens into a tiny plaza presided over by Archangel Gabriel.

During your walk, you might also stop by the diminutive **Café Pochotita** (Rufino Tamayo 814, no phone, 9 A.M.–8 P.M. Mon.–Sat., $3–6) for some good coffee and maybe a snack (*tortas,* banana bread, baguettes, light meals). If you'd like to linger overnight in Los Arquitos, ring the doorbell at **Casa Los Arquitos** bed-and-breakfast (818 Rufino Tamayo, tel. 951/132-4975, ventas@casalosar-quitos.com, www.casalosarquitos.com, $60–100) and take a look inside.

For the **San Felipe del Agua** part of these north-end tours, it's easiest to first hire a taxi ($5) to San Felipe del Agua village. Alternatively, you can save money by having a taxi take you to a San Felipe del Agua city bus stop (such as on upper Calle Crespo, corner of Marcos Pérez, or on Calz. Niños Héroes, uphill six blocks from Santo Domingo church). Or, near the *zócalo,* catch a bus labeled San Felipe, heading north, either from the corner of Independencia and Reforma, or uphill along Pino Suárez.

Alternatively, you can drive the five miles

uphill to San Felipe del Agua village. The jumping-off point is Avenida Netzahualcoyotl (nay-tzah-oo-wahl-coh-YOH-tuhl), which heads uphill at its intersection with the Highway 190 thoroughfare (Calz. Niños Héroes) at the big green San Felipe sign.

Continue about one kilometer (0.6 mi) uphill; bear left around the curve onto Calle Naranjos. A block later, pass a hospital on your left. After another block, turn right at the big divided intersection Calzada San Felipe. Notice the old stone aqueduct, on your left, that divides the thoroughfare. In a few miles the road becomes San Felipe's Calle Hidalgo, which leads you to San Felipe Apostol Church behind the pocket-sized village plaza on the right.

At this point you can enjoy a leisurely stroll, taking a turn around the plaza and church and a couple side streets. For a real treat, walk a couple of blocks uphill from the plaza, along the main street, to the lovely, relaxing **Hacienda Los Laureles** (driveway on the right, at Hidalgo 21, tel. 951/501-5300 or 951/520-0890) for a walk around the luscious grounds and perhaps lunch or early dinner ($10–20 pp).

Accommodations

Oaxaca offers a wide range of good lodgings. Air-conditioning is not particularly necessary in temperate Oaxaca, although hot-water showers (furnished by all lodgings listed here) feel especially comfy during cool winter mornings and evenings. Many of the less expensive hotels, which generally do not accept credit cards, are within easy walking distance of the colorful, traffic-free *zócalo*. (Note: In Oaxaca, as in much of Mexico, clean water is an increasingly scarce commodity. A few common-sense actions, such as turning off faucets, refraining from half-hour showers, and making hotels aware of continuously running toilets, will do much toward alleviating the problem. Kindly use no more water than you need.)

With but a few exceptions, Oaxaca's plush, resort-style hostelries dot the northern foothill edge of town. During holidays and festivals (pre-Easter week, July, August, late October–early November, December 15–January 6), most Oaxaca hotels and bed-and-breakfasts raise their prices 10–50 percent above the rates listed here. (Note: Several of the following lodgings and many more not listed here are advertised on websites, such as www.hoteles deoaxaca.com for hotels, www.oaxacabed andbreakfast.org for bed-and-breakfasts, and www.vrbo (Vacation Rentals by owner) for long-term house and apartment rentals.)

All accommodations listed in this section are positive recommendations, grouped by location in relation to the *zócalo,* and listed, within each location group, in ascending order of double-occupancy price.

HOTELS
Near the *Zócalo*
UNDER $50
For economy and value, consider **Hotel El Chapulin** (Aldama 317, 951/516-1646, hotel-chapulin@hotmail.com, $16 s, $20 d, $24 t), one of Oaxaca's good (and increasingly hard-to-find) budget lodgings. The welcoming owners carefully tend to the eight rooms, which are tucked away from street traffic noise. The result: a restful, clean, and comfy retreat of two compact stories climaxed by an airy rooftop patio with a superb view of town, with the towering Monte Albán ridge above the southern horizon as the backdrop. All of this plus private shower-bath, in-house Internet, and inviting lobby–sitting room available for less than $25. There's $4 overnight parking nearby.

Alternatively, try the nine-room **Hotel Santa Prisca** (20 de Noviembre 204, tel. 951/516-4008, $22 s, $27 d, $35 t), just a block west of the *zócalo,* next door to the big Hotel Francia. Here, you can get a plain but clean upstairs room with bath and the bonus of good breakfasts and people-watching on the *zócalo* only a block away. There is no parking and they don't accept credit cards.

Another good, budget option is the modest, gay-friendly **Posada Nito** (Armenta y López 416, tel. 951/514-6668, $25 s, $33 d, $43 t), a block east and two blocks south of the *zócalo*'s southeast corner. Guests at this simple, 10-room hotel enjoy clean, light rooms, thoughtfully decorated with handmade bedspreads, rustically attractive tile floors, reading lamps, and shiny hot-water bathrooms. There is no parking or telephones, and credit cards are not accepted. Downstairs, guests enjoy a tranquil, intimate inner patio, with chairs, table, and a shade umbrella for relaxing and socializing. Reserve one of the upstairs rooms for maximum privacy and light.

Head northeast a few blocks east of the *zócalo*'s northeast corner to the busy, budget traveler–favorite, the 39-room **Posada del Virrey** (1001 Morelos, tel. 951/516-5555, fax 951/516-2193, $35 s or d in one bed, $45 d in two beds, $50 t). Only four blocks (five minutes) east of the *zócalo*, the authentically colonial Posada del Virrey offers two floors of rooms surrounding a spacious inner restaurant patio, which in the mornings and evenings is often half-full with mostly foreign travelers, reading, conversing, and relaxing. The rooms are clean and comfortably furnished, including one, two, or three double beds, with attractive brown and bright-orange bedspreads and handsome rustic handmade wooden furniture. Rooms come with cable TV, phone, fan, parking (9 P.M.–9 A.M.), and MasterCards accepted. Get your reservations in early, especially during holidays.

Even closer in, just half a block west of the *zócalo*'s southwest corner, is the petite and popular **Hotel Las Rosas** (Trujano 112, tel./fax 951/514-2217, $41 s, $47 d, $53 t). Climb a flight of stairs to the small lobby, relatively tranquil by virtue of its 2nd-floor location. Beyond that, a double tier of rooms surrounds a homey inner patio. Adjacent to the lobby is a cheery sitting room with a big, beautiful tropical aquarium and a TV, usually kept at subdued volume. In the rear, guests enjoy an airy terrace

for reading and relaxing. The rooms themselves, although plainly furnished, are clean and tiled (except some bathrooms, which could use an extra scrubbing). Prices are very reasonable for such a well-located hotel. Discounts are negotiable for a one-week stay. No credit cards, parking, or wheelchair access, however.

A block west of the *zócalo*'s southwest corner, find the **Hóstal Santa Rosa** (Trujano 201, tel. 951/514-6714 or 951/514-6715, fax 951/514-6715, hostalsantarosa@hotmail.com, $40 s, $48 d). The streetside lobby leads past an airy restaurant to the rooms, recessed along a meandering inner passageway and courtyard. Inside, the rooms are very clean, comfortably furnished, and decorated in pastels. Rates continue to be reasonable except during festivals and holidays, when they might rise as much as 40 percent. Hóstal Santa Rosa offers TV, phones, parking, limited wheelchair access, and an in-house travel-tour agency, but no credit cards are accepted.

$50-100

Just a block south of the *zócalo*'s southwest corner, the **C Hotel Trebol** (Flores Magón 201, tel./fax 951/516-1256, hoteltrebol@hotmail.com, www.oaxaca-mio.com/trebol.htm, $50 s or d in one bed, $70 d in two beds, $80 t) remains an enduring jewel among Oaxaca's moderately priced hotels. Guests can choose from about 40 rooms, artfully sprinkled in three stories around an airy, plant-decorated inner patio. The recently renovated rooms are comfortably furnished with rustic tile, hand-hewn wooden furniture, table lamps, color-coordinated bedspreads, and shiny, modern-standard shower-baths. Rooms include fans, telephone, cable TV, and in-house Internet; there's also a travel agent and good restaurant in the hotel.

A block west of the *zócalo*, find the long-time **Hotel Francia** (20 de Noviembre 212, tel. 951/516-4811 or 951/516-4120, fax 951/516-4251, info@hotelfrancia.com.mx, www.hotelfrancia.com.mx, $55 s or d, $65 t). Savvy new managers have brightened up the Francia with fresh white paint, a bright chandelier, potted palms, shiny lobby tile, and a new restaurant. They have also added a renovated colonial-era section (once a separate hotel next door) built around an invitingly traditional interior patio. Rooms are clean and spacious, with high ceilings and old-world dark wood furniture. The 62 rooms feature private baths, fans, cable TV, phones, and limited parking; credit cards are accepted.

Ideally situated just east of the *zócalo*'s northeast corner, the best-buy colonial-era **Hotel Real de Antequera** (Hidalgo 807, tel. 951/516-4635, fax 951/516-4020, www.oaxaca-mio .com/real.htm, hra5109@prodigy.net.mx, $45 s, $55 d, $65 t) offers plenty for reasonable rates. The 29 comfortable rooms, in two stories around an inviting old world–style restaurant-patio, include breakfast, bath, fans, cable TV, phones, and parking (8:30 P.M.–8:30 A.M.), and credit cards are accepted.

On the northwest side of the *zócalo,* at the leafy Alameda de León square in front of Catedral de Oaxaca, you'll find **Hotel Monte Albán** (Alameda de León 1, tel. 951/516-2777 or 951/516-2330, fax 951/516-3265, hotelmontealban@prodigy.net.mx, $54 s, $59 d, $68 t). This popular old standby hostelry encloses a big patio/restaurant that hosts folk-dance shows 8:30–10 P.M. nightly. During your first evening this could be understandably exciting, but after a few days you might feel as if you were living in a three-ring circus. The 20 rooms, which surround the patio in two floors, are genuinely colonial, with high-beamed ceilings and big bedsteads. Rates are modest for such a well-located hotel; there's no parking, but credit cards are accepted.

Although somewhat removed (three blocks south, three blocks west, 10 easy minutes) from the *zócalo,* the **Hotel Rivera del Ángel** (Mina 518, tel. 951/516-6666, fax 951/514-5405, reservaciones@hotelriveradelangel.com, www.hotel riveradelangel.com, $55 s, $60 d, $65 t) offers a number of advantages. Downstairs, an airy, shiny, but busy lobby and restaurant area offers nothing special, but through the lobby windows, feast your eyes on the inviting big blue pool and sunny central patio. Upstairs, you'll find the rooms semi-deluxe, clean, spacious, and comfortable, several with private terraces

overlooking the pool patio. The hotel's main drawback, besides the questionable neighborhood (streetwalkers, low-life bars, and drunks at night), is street noise from buses along Mina. Avoid this by reserving a *tranquilo* off-street room, next to or above the inner pool-patio. Amenities include cable TV, fans, phones, passable restaurant, secure parking, a travel agency, and tour buses to Mitla and Monte Albán. Credit cards are accepted, though discounts are customarily available for payment in cash.

Just a few doors south of the *zócalo*'s southeast corner, consider the popular 1980s-mod **Hotel Gala** (Bustamante 103, tel. 951/514-2251 or 951/514-1305, fax 951/516-3660, Mex. toll-free 800/712-7316, galaoax@prodigy.net. mx, www.gala.com.mx, $60 s, $68 d, $76 t, $86 junior suite). Guests enjoy comfortable, modern, deluxe accommodations at relatively moderate prices right in the middle of the *zócalo* action. The 36 rooms, although tastefully decorated and carpeted, are smallish. Get one of the quieter ones away from the street. They include private shower-baths, phones, TV, and fans; conveniently, the downstairs has a restaurant, and there is parking (10 P.M.–8 A.M.); credit cards are accepted.

Return just two blocks west of the *zócalo*'s northwest corner to the class-act **◖ Parador San Miguel** (Independencia 503, tel./fax 951/514-9331, info@paradorsanmiguel.com, www.paradorsanmigueloaxaca.com, $95 s or d, $110 t). Here, little seems to have been spared in transforming a colonial-era mansion into a lovely hotel. Inside, a plethora of old-world details—leafy, tranquil inner patio, sunny upstairs corridors, brilliant stained glass–decorated staircase, scrolled wrought-iron railings, handsome hand-carved wooden doors—are bound to please lovers of traditional refinement. A correspondingly elegant restaurant, the Andariega, completes the gorgeous picture. The 19 rooms and four suites are no less than you'd expect, attractively furnished with custom-woven bedspreads and curtains, handcrafted bamboo and leather furniture, elegantly tiled shower-baths, and a choice of king, single, or double beds. If the Parador San Miguel has a drawback, it's the traffic noise from busy Independencia, just outside the front door; ask for a room away from the street. But never mind, the place is simply exquisite and prices are not unreasonable; add about 50 percent during festivals and holidays. All rooms come with air-conditioning, cable TV, phones, and wireless Internet. Credit cards are accepted.

Alternatively, check out the queen of *zócalo*-front hotels, the long-time **Hotel Marques del Valle** (Portal Clavería, tel. 951/514-0688 or 951/516-3474, fax 951/516-9961, reservaciones@hotelmarquesdelvalle.com.mx, www .hotelmarquesdelvalle.com.mx, $100 s or d, $110 t) on the north flank of the *zócalo*. Guests enter through a restored lobby, bright with a grand, glittering chandelier, gleaming mirrors, and burnished dark-wood paneling. Upstairs, however, massive wrought-iron fixtures cast gloomy nighttime shadows through the soaring, balconied central atrium. The 96 rooms, nevertheless, retain their original 1940s polish, with handcrafted cedar furniture and marble-finished baths. Deluxe rooms have TV, carpets, and some balconies looking out onto the *zócalo*. The hotel has a good restaurant/bar, exercise room, wireless Internet, limited wheelchair access, credit cards accepted, and parking (8:30 P.M.–8:30 A.M.).

North of the *Zócalo*
UNDER $50

Much closer in, halfway between the *zócalo* and Iglesia de Santo Domingo, right in the middle of the tranquil Calle Cinco de Mayo restaurant and shopping district, find the charmingly old-fashioned (**Hotel Principal** (Cinco de Mayo 208, tel./fax 951/516-2535, hotelprincipal@gmail.com, $30 s, $35 d, larger, superior rooms $60), like a slice out of the 1940s. Past the entry, the two stories of 14 rooms surround a quiet, geranium-decorated interior patio. A few sofas line the patio and upstairs corridor. The rooms are clean, with high ceilings, tiled floors, and shaded bed lamps. There are no TVs or phones, but there are hot-water baths all day. All rooms have private shower-baths and fans, but no parking available nor credit cards accepted.

A few blocks farther north stands another well-located, moderately-priced choice, the **Hotel Villa de León** (Reforma 405, tel. 951/516-1958, fax 951/516-1977, www.hotelesdeoaxaca.com/hotelvilladeleon.html, $30 s, $40 d, $45 t), adjoining the back side of the Iglesia de Santa Domingo grounds. Past the reception and inner-courtyard restaurant, about half of the 20 rooms encircle an upstairs balcony; the remainder are tucked in the rear, fortunately removed from street and restaurant noise. All rooms are attractively renovated, with tile floors, handmade wooden furniture, and private shower-baths. Credit cards are accepted and you get a 10 percent discount for reservations made on the Internet. Reserve a room away from the heavily trafficked street.

One of the most popular modestly-priced options, **Casa Arnel** (Aldama 404, Colonia Jalatlaco, tel./fax 951/515-2856, oaxaca@casa-arnel.com, www.casaarnel.com.mx, standard rooms $40 s, $45 d, $50 t) is also farthest north (actually, less than a mile) from the *zócalo*. Casa Arnel stands at the edge of downtown, so removed from the urban bustle that it feels as if it's embedded in another era. As one local resident explained, Jalatlaco, the formerly separate village, is "old, with stone streets…It's *so* Oaxaca." In front of Casa Arnel, the streets are indeed cobbled with stone, and across from it stands the ancient village church, San Matias Jalatlaco, beside its shady neighborhood plaza. Casa Arnel is a family home that grew into a hotel, with about 20 rooms with baths, around a jungly garden blooming with birdcalls, flowers, and big, leafy plants, with a monument of a library in the middle of it all. Additional amenities include a broad roof deck with umbrellas, tables, and chairs for sunning and relaxing. The rooms, all renovated, are attractively furnished with new bedspreads, curtains, and shiny furniture and fixtures. The owners offer a travel agency and decent restaurant, and it's just three blocks from big, shady El Llano Park, with its good restaurants and services. Bargain for a cheaper long-term rate.

$50-100
In the Santo Domingo neighborhood,

discerning travelers should also consider the low-key but inviting **Hotel Maela** (Constitución 206, tel./fax 951/516-6022, maela@prodigy. net.mx, www.mexonline.com/maela.htm, $41 s, $51 d, $58 t, suites for four $70), one block east of the Iglesia de Santo Domingo compound. Inside, just past the petite reception, the hall tiles shine, the ceilings are gracefully high, and the 23 rooms and three suites, in two stories, are spacious, with private shower-baths and attractive handmade wood dressers, beds, and end tables. Ceiling lights are bare-bulb, but nighttime reading lamps are shaded. Rooms come with fans, some air-conditioning, TV, wireless Internet, and parking.

On the northwest side, about three blocks west of the Iglesia de Santo Domingo, is the very inviting and super-popular **Hotel Las Golondrinas** (Tinoco y Palacios 411, tel. 951/514-3298 or tel./fax 951/514-2126, hotel-lasgolondrinas.com.mx, lasgolon@prodigy.net. mx, lasgolonoax@yahoo.com, $50 s, $55 d, and $60 t). Rooms enfold an intimate garden, lovingly decorated with festoons of hothouse verdure. Leafy bananas, bright bougainvillea, and platoons of potted plants line pathways that meander past an intimate fountain patio in one corner and lead to an upstairs panoramic vista sundeck in the other. The care also shows in the rooms, which, although smallish, are immaculate and adorned with spartan chic, pastel earth-toned curtains and bedspreads, and natural wood furniture. Guests additionally enjoy use of laundry facilities, a TV sitting room, on-line computer, shelf of paperback books, and a breakfast café (8–10 A.M.). In addition to the 27 regular rooms, two honeymoon suites rent for about $60 each.

Several blocks north of Iglesia de Santo Domingo stands the **Hotel Casona de Llano** (Av. Juárez A701, tel. 951/514-7719 or 951/514-7703, fax 951/516-2219, www.hotelcasonade llano.com, $55 s, $65 d, and $75 t). This hotel is a favorite of visitors who enjoy the shady, untouristed ambience of Oaxaca's big Sunday park, officially called Parque Paseo Juárez, but popularly referred to as El Llano (YAH-noh, Plain or Flat Place). The memorable time to arrive is in the evening, when the hotel puts on its most impressive face: You enter the lobby, crowned with high ceilings hung with gleaming chandeliers, continue past polished mahogany Doric columns, and enter a graceful Porfirian dining room, where guests often linger after dinner. Your room, by contrast, is modern, comfortably furnished, and very clean. In the morning, you open your door and look out upon a tranquil, grassy, inner tropical garden. The 28 rooms include fans, TV, phones, parking, and credit cards accepted. Reserve ahead.

On the other side and a block south of El Llano, step into **Hotel Casa Vertíz** (Reforma 404, tel. 951/516-1700 or tel./fax 951/516-2525, reservaciones@hotelvertiz.com. mx, www.hotelvertiz.com.mx, $80 s, $85 d, $97 t), one of the most inviting small hotels in Oaxaca. Here you find a masterfully rebuilt former colonial house with air, light, and space that encourages lingering. Inside the entrance, guests enjoy a refined, airy patio restaurant and a petite, exquisitely naturalistic tropical rear garden. All 14 rooms, both upstairs and down, are thoughtfully tucked away from the busy street. Upstairs, rooms open onto a spreading top-floor terrace, shaded on one side by a grand leafy tree. Accommodations are luxuriously appointed with designer-rustic tile floors, earth-toned bedspreads and curtains, deluxe tiled baths (four rooms have tubs), and queen-size beds. Rentals include cable TV, phone, in-room Internet connection, air-conditioning, parking, and credit cards accepted.

OVER $100

If you're exhausted from a long flight or arrive on a crowded holiday without a reservation, or simply hanker for a North American–style lodging, you might try landing at the **Holiday Inn Express** (Díaz Quintas 115, 951/512-9200, fax 951/512-9292, U.S./Can. toll-free tel. 800/315-2621, www.holidayinn.com, $140 d). Tucked away from the downtown bustle, on the very pleasant north-end neighborhood Parque Conzatti, the hotel offers American-style amenities at American-style prices. Although from the outside its faux–colonial box design leaves much to be desired and the inside ambience is strictly Holiday Inn contemporary, its 100 rooms are spacious and beds are super comfortable. Moreover, besides soaking in the hotel's tranquil Parque Conzatti location, you can also relax in its secluded and oft-sunny interior patio with heated pool (a Oaxaca rarity). Try a travel website such as Expedia or Travelocity for the best rates.

For genuine urbane class, try Oaxaca's most distinguished downtown hotel, the C Camino Real (Cinco de Mayo 300, tel. 951/516-0611, toll-free U.S./Can. tel. 800/722-6466, fax 951/516-0732, oaxaca@caminoreal.com, www.caminoreal.com/Oaxaca, $300 d), which occupies the lovingly restored former convent of Santa Catalina, four blocks north and one block east of the *zócalo*. Flowery, secluded courtyards, massive arched portals, soaring beamed ceilings, a big blue pool, and impeccable bar and restaurant service combine to create a refined but relaxed old-world atmosphere. Rooms are large, luxurious, and invitingly decorated with antiques and folk crafts and furnished with a plethora of modern conveniences. If street noise is likely to bother you, request a room away from bustling Calles Abasolo and Cinco de Mayo, or bring earplugs. The hotel entertains guests and the paying public (about $35 pp) with a weekly class-act in-house buffet and folkloric dance performance. Rooms have phones and cable TV, but parking is not included; credit cards are accepted. Sometimes the hotel offers promotional packages that run about $260 for a double, including breakfast.

North-Side Suburban Luxury Hotels

$50-100

Just above north-side Calzada Niños Héroes (Hwy. 190), the **Hotel Fortín Plaza** (Av. Venus 118, Colonia Estrella, tel. 951/515-7777, Mexico toll-free 800/718-9647, fax 951/515-1328, reservaciones@hotelfortinplaza.com.mx, www.hotelfortinplaza.com.mx, $90 s or d) is hard to miss, especially at night. Its yellow-lit six-story profile tops everything else in town.

The hotel offers resort facilities—restaurant/bar, pool, live music Tuesday–Saturday, disco, and parking—in a compact, attractively designed layout. Upstairs, guests enjoy deluxe, clean, and comfortable rooms with private city-view balconies (whose tranquility is reduced, however, on the highway side, by considerable traffic noise—best reserve a more *tranquilo* mountain-view room on the opposite side). The 90-odd rooms come with phones, TV, wireless Internet, wheelchair access, and parking; credit cards are accepted. Ask for a discount or a *paquete* (package), especially during weekdays and the low-occupancy months of January, May, June, and September.

OVER $100

Hotel Misión de Los Angeles (Porfirio Díaz 102, tel. 951/502-0100, fax 951/502-0111, info@misiondelosangeles.com, www.misiondelosangeles.com, $140 d, junior suites $155) rambles like a hacienda through a spreading oak- and acacia-decorated garden-park two blocks uphill from Calzada Niños Héroes (Hwy. 190), about a mile uphill, north, of the city center. After a rough few days on the sightseeing circuit, this is an ideal place to kick back beside the big pool or enjoy a set or two of tennis. The 162 rooms and suites are spacious and comfortable, decorated in earth tones and pastels and have big garden-view windows or balconies. Upper rooms are quieter and more private. Some rooms, however, may not be as favorably located; request a garden-view (*vista del jardín* room). Additional amenities include phones, air-conditioning, parking, and a restaurant; credit cards are accepted.

Several blocks west, a couple of blocks past the Hotel Fortín Plaza, the **Hotel Victoria** (Km 545, Blvd. Adolfo Ruiz Cortínez 1306, Carretera Panamericana, tel. 951/515-2633, fax 951/515-2411, reservaciones@hotelvictoriaoax.com.mx, www.hotelvictoriaoax.com.mx, rooms $125, villas $150, junior suites $240) spreads over a lush hillside garden of panoramic vistas and luxurious resort ambience. The 1960s-modern lobby extends from an upstairs bar, downhill past a terrace restaurant, to a flame tree and jacaranda-decorated pool patio. Rooms come in three grades, all comfortably deluxe, that vary by size and location. The smallest are the rooms in the original hotel building; somewhat larger are the villas downstairs around the pool; and most spacious are the junior suites, in the newer wing detached from the lobby building, with double-size bathrooms and private-view balconies. The 150 rooms come with cable TV, phones, air-conditioning, wireless Internet, tennis courts, live music seasonally, handicrafts shop, parking, and wheelchair access; credit cards are accepted.

Cooler, breezier San Felipe village, in the foothills north of Oaxaca town, has recently become home to a number of restful luxury lodgings. Choicest among them, **(Hacienda Los Laureles** (Hidalgo 21, San Felipe del Agua, tel. 951/501-5300 or 951/520-0890, fax 951/501-5301, bookings@hotelhaciendaloslaureles.com, www.hotelhaciendaloslaureles.com, or agent Mexico Boutique Hotels toll-free U.S./Can. tel. 800/728-9098, www.mexico boutiquehotels.com, deluxe rooms $300 s or d, superior deluxe $330 s or d) is the labor of love of personable German expatriate owner-managers Ligia and Peter Kaiser. After a career of managing hotels in Europe, Africa, and the United States, Peter and Ligia decided to create their version of heaven in Oaxaca. During the late 1990s they rebuilt a venerable hacienda, tenaciously preserving its rustic old-world essence while installing the best of the new. Now, Hacienda Los Laureles's centerpiece is its lush interior garden of grand tropical trees and climbing vines that, at night, is transformed by shadowed lighting and the serenades of crickets and tree frogs into an enchanted forest. The Hacienda's 25 rooms, which all open onto this precious scene, are decorated in elegant simplicity, with high ceilings, handsome tile floors, and hand-hewn mahogany furniture. Bathrooms are likewise luxurious and comfortable. Suites for 3–6 or more people are also available. All come with air-conditioning, cable TV, pool with whirlpool tub, and breakfast at their excellent terrace restaurant. A *temazcal*

ceremonial hot room and a menu of spa services are also available at an extra cost.

BED-AND-BREAKFASTS
The number of Oaxaca bed-and-breakfast–style lodgings has increased in response to the influx of North American visitors. From only a scant few a generation ago, Oaxaca has blossomed with perhaps two dozen attractive bed-and-breakfasts located mostly on the north side, uphill from the town center. As a group, they are not particularly economical, since they are a North American transplant that appeals to foreign visitors who are accustomed to paying somewhat elevated prices.

The recommendations that follow present a sampling of several of the most solid, long-standing Oaxaca bed-and-breakfasts. For even more choices, check out the good website, www.oaxacabedandbreakfast.org.

North and East of the *Zócalo* $50-100
Just south of El Llano park, **(Hotel and Studios Las Mariposas** (Pino Suárez 517, tel. 951/515-5854, from U.S./Can. direct tel. 619/793-5121, ventas@lasmariposas.com.mx, www.lasmariposas.com.mx, $45 s, $50 d, rate includes breakfast) is strongly recommended by previous customers as either a bed-and-breakfast, hotel, or apartment rental. Welcoming and knowledgeable owner Teresa Dávila offers seven rooms (with baths, but without kitchenettes) in her restored 19th-century family house for about $40 s, $45 d without breakfast, $45 and $50 with. She also rents six comfortable studio kitchenette suites with private baths for $45 s, $50 d without breakfast. Ask for a discount for a longer-term stay. Besides the happy customers, pluses include use of fax machine, wireless Internet access, coffee, TV, and use of credit cards; kids under 12 are not welcome.

For another worthy, moderately-priced option, check out the **Casa los Arquitos** (Rufino Tamayo 818, tel. 951/132-4975, ventas@casa-losarquitos.com, www.casalosarquitos.com, $60–100), where a welcoming Mexican couple have converted their modest home into an inviting small bed-and-breakfast tucked into the heart of the charming north-end Los Arquitos neighborhood. Their five immaculate rooms with bath, simply but attractively decorated, offer a choice of either one single bed, two single beds, or one king-size bed with full kitchenette, including refrigerator, stove, microwave oven, dishes, and utensils, and a private patio to boot. Amenities include in-house Internet and a generous continental breakfast with choice of savory organic coffee, hot chocolate, or tea, and breads, yogurt, granola, and fresh seasonal fruit.

Much closer in, just two blocks behind Iglesia de Santo Domingo, you'll find **Casa de las Bugambilias** (Reforma 402, tel./fax 951/516-1165, U.S./Can. toll-free 866/829-6778, bugambilias@lasbugambilias.com, www.lasbugambilias.com, $65–95 s, $75–105 d), with seven rooms and one suite, artfully tucked behind its good street-front restaurant. The rooms, immaculate and thoughtfully appointed with art and handicrafts, are all unique. Some open onto a lovely rear garden. Take a look at as many as possible before choosing. Rules include a minimum three-night stay, $50 cancellation fee, children over 12 only, no pets, and no smoking. Amenities include private bath, breakfast, Internet access, a *temazcal* hot room (at extra cost); credit cards are accepted, but parking is not included.

Another promising bed-and-breakfast in the same north-side neighborhood (but a few blocks west of El Llano park) is 🌙 **Bed-and-Breakfast Oaxaca Ollin** (oh-YEEN; Quintana Roo 213, tel. 951/514-9126, U.S./Can. tel. 619/787-5141, reservations@oaxacaollin.com, www.oaxacaollin.com, $80–90 d, honeymoon suite $120), the life project of guide Judith Reyes López and her husband Jon McKinley. Judith and Jon offer 11 comfortable double rooms in their large house, located on a quiet side street a block north and a block east of the Centro Cultural de Santo Domingo. Rooms are immaculate and comfortably appointed with natural wood furniture, reading lamps, and lovely Talavera-tile bathrooms. Extras abound, such as a lovely blue swimming pool

(not heated, however) and patio, living room, library, reading room, gratis Internet access and local phone calls, and much more. Prices include a hearty breakfast.

Back on the northeast side, from Casa de las Bugambilias, go east two blocks and turn north a block to the bed-and-breakfast gem **Casa de Mis Recuerdos** (House of My Memories, Pino Suárez 508, tel. 951/515-8483, tel./fax 951/515-5645, misrecue@hotmail.com, www.misrecuerdos.net, U.S. toll-free 877/234-4706, $60–80 s, $95–105 d). Enter the front gate and continue through a blooming, bougainvillea-festooned garden to the private home of the Valenciana family, which has been accommodating students and foreign visitors for a generation. The rented rooms occupy rear and front sections. The four front rooms, immaculate, spacious, and lovingly decorated with folk art and furnished with handmade wooden furniture, have two bathrooms between them. They are closer to the busy streetfront than the five similarly furnished rear rooms, which, although they have private baths, are smaller. Guests also have the use of an airy, shaded rooftop gazebo for reading and relaxing. Breakfast, included with rentals, is served in the inviting downstairs family dining room. Rates approximately double during festivals and holidays; all linens and cleaning service are included.

OVER $100

Elegant Hotel **Casa Oaxaca** (Garcia Vigil 407, tel. 951/514-4173, fax 951/516-4412, casaoax@prodigy.net.mx, www.casa-oaxaca.com, $180 s or d for the four smallest, yet spacious units, $320 s or d for a larger suite, and $350 for a two-story apartment above the rear courtyard) is straight uphill four blocks and a world apart from the *zócalo*. Its sky-blue colonial facade reveals nothing of its singularly unique interior. The lobby, which appears more like an art museum foyer than a lodging entrance, provides the first clue. Past that, you enter a spacious, plant-decorated courtyard, with the wall plaster artfully removed here and there to reveal the brick underlay. Continue to a rear courtyard, which centers on a blue designer pool and a *temazcal*. All six rooms, which border the courtyards, are luxuriously austere and uniquely appointed with antiques, crafts, and contemporary wall art. Rates include gourmet continental breakfast in the exclusive Casa Oaxaca restaurant; credit cards are accepted. *Temazcal* treatments, complete with native healer, run about $50 per person.

South and West of the *Zócalo*
$50-100
Only a few bed-and-breakfast lodgings dot the south and west sides of town. Here are two gems.

Start several blocks southeast of the *zócalo* with **Posada de Chencho** (4ta Privada de la Noria 115, tel./fax 951/514-0043, pchencho@ prodigy.net.mx, www.mexonline.com/chencho.htm, $39 s, $58 d). Part of the attraction here is the spark-plug owner, Inocencio "Chencho" Velasco, a friendly Mixtec version of Santa Claus. Such a stream of visitors from all over the world stay at his place that he seems to know someone everywhere. Moreover, very well-informed, English-speaking Chencho is a treasury of information about Oaxaca, both local and statewide. His compound, 22 immaculate rooms in two stories, surrounds an inviting, green garden patio. The rooms themselves are comfortably and thoughtfully decorated, with Western-standard baths. Downstairs, guests enjoy a dining room and a big sitting room/library, as well as patio nooks for reading and relaxing. Some rooms in the sun might get hot during the summer. If heat bothers you, be sure to select one in the shade, with a ceiling fan. If your room has no fan, ask Chencho to supply one. Rates include breakfast. Add $24 per person for all meals. Ask for a cheaper long-term rate. Get to Chencho's by walking east, along Guerrero, from the southeast corner of the *zócalo*. After four blocks, at Xicotencatl (shee-koh-tayn-KAH-tuhl), turn right and continue another four blocks south to Calle La Noria; 4ta Privada de la Noria is one of the one-block streets to your left that run south from La Noria.

On the west edge of downtown, about 10 blocks due west of the *zócalo*, stands **Casa Colonial** (Calle Miguel Negrete 105, tel./fax 951/516-5280, toll-free U.S./Can. tel. 800/758-1697, oaxaca@casa-colonial, reservations@ casa-colonial.com, www.casa-colonial.com, $40–110). Personable owner Jane Robison, who seems to know everyone in town, calls her domain the "posada with no sign," because she doesn't advertise and only accepts guests with reservations. Upon arrival, you immediately see why Casa Colonial is such a favorite among savvy visitors. Low-rise rooms and apartments enfold a spacious, gracefully lovely inner garden. Rooms vary from high-ceilinged, antique-decorated Victorians to smaller, one-person garden-side units. Besides the leisurely tropical ambience, guests enjoy the use of a spacious, refined-but-homey living room with a fine library and Internet connection. Room prices vary according to size and elegance; there's a 10 percent discount if you pay in cash. For information on Casa Colonial Tours, visit the website.

APARTMENTS
Many Oaxacans offer apartment or house rentals and lodging in their homes. If you're interested, be sure to see the classified sections of the English-language newspaper *Oaxaca Times,* either online (www.oaxacatimes.com) or at their editorial office (Macedonio Alcalá 307, tel. 516-3443), or log on to the local site, www.rentapartmentsinoaxaca.wordpress.com. For house rentals, check out the excellent website www.vrbo.com (Vacation Rentals by Owner). If you'd like to experience a homestay with a Mexican family, ask for information at one of the several Oaxaca language schools that arrange homestays.

In the meantime, consider the following worthwhile apartment options.

South and East of the *Zócalo*
UNDER $50
In the southeast quarter, an easy five-block walking distance to the *zócalo,* you'll find the attractive ◖ **Villa María** (Arteaga 410 A, tel. 951/516-5056, fax 951/514-2562, villamaria22@hotmail.com, $45–65 d per night, $400–600/month). Villa María is the labor of

love of trilingual (English, French, Spanish) owner-manager María Garcia and her sister Mari Carmen. Step inside their domain and you'll see the other reason for Villa María's popularity: about 15 apartments surrounding an inviting, plant-adorned inner patio, where stairways rise to rooftop sundecks furnished with comfortable chairs and shady umbrellas. The immaculate, thoughtfully decorated one-bedroom housekeeping apartments, with themes such as "Mixteco," are completely furnished, including dishes, silverware, in-house Internet, optional phones, and maid service. The one- and two-bedroom apartments vary in cost depending on location, size, and amenities.

Just three blocks from the *zócalo*, find the secluded and attractive, **Casa Luz María** (1002 Morelos, tel. 951/514-6280 or 951/516-2378, luzmago30@hotmail.com, $450/month for two). The sprightly, grandmotherly owner, who retired from running her lodging as a bed-and-breakfast, now offers four smallish furnished apartments, around a pair of flowery interior patios. They include kitchenettes, a double bed, a shower-bath (either private or shared), and in-house Internet. The owner prefers monthly rentals.

North of the *Zócalo*
UNDER $50

About five blocks north of the *zócalo*, right in front of Iglesia de Santo Domingo, is **Departmentos del Fraile** (Macedonio Alcalá 501, tel./fax 951/516-4310, humbertobenitezc@ yahoo.com, $550/month). Family owner-managers offer four, compact, modern, and historic (former Santo Domingo priests') apartments, hidden behind a street-front wall and tucked within a quiet, leafy inner courtyard. The renovated units have one bedroom, bathroom, and kitchenette. Rentals are monthly only.

Behind (east of) the Iglesia de Santo Domingo block, find **La Casa de Rosita** (Reforma 410, tel. 951/516-1982 or 951/514-9815, lacasadelosabuelos@hotmail.com, www .lacasa-de-rosita.com, $60/day, $400/week), formerly La Casa de los Abuelos (House of the Grandparents). This charmingly quirky colonial-era complex is the life project of personable owner-builder Luis Arroyo Nuñez, who inherited it from his *abuelos* (grandparents). This former priests' residence for Iglesia de Santo Domingo was confiscated by the government after the *cristero* revolt of the late 1920s. Luis's six completely renovated apartments, built around two quiet inner patios, are replete with unique details, such as exposed original brick walls, old family photos, bric-a-brac, and sturdy wooden staircases leading up to bedroom lofts. Rentals include invitingly furnished living-dining rooms, kitchenettes, queen-size beds, and shower-baths. Asking rates are negotiable by the month; apartments come with fans, TV, purified bottled water, and wireless Internet connections.

HOSTELS

Oaxaca's best hostel by far is the beautifully restored **[Paulina Youth Hostel** (V. Trujano 321, tel. 951/516-2005, reservations@paulina-hostel.com, www.paulinahostel.com, dorms $14 pp, rooms $22 s, $28 d, $42 t, $56 q), just three blocks west of the *zócalo*. The owners created the best of all possible hostelling worlds, with a good cafeteria and inviting, spacious common areas, all within attractive garden grounds. The comfortable, squeaky-clean rooming options include separate male and female dorms and private rooms with shower-baths, all with comfortable orthopedic mattresses, roof terrace, hot water, and hearty breakfast thrown in for free. Get your reservations in early.

Also worthy are two hostels in the picturesque Los Arquitos neighborhood on the far northwest side of downtown. First, consider **Hostal Pochón** (Callejon del Carmen 102, tel. 951/516-1322, hostalpochon@yahoo.com, www.hostalpochon.com, dorms $10 pp, rooms $25–32 d, includes breakfast), two blocks west and nine blocks north (15 min.) from the *zócalo*'s northwest corner. The owners offer lodging for about 30 guests in six separate four-person dorms, three rooms with shared bath, and one suite with private bath. Amenities include in-house Internet, library, use of phone, cable TV, free popcorn, and more.

In the same northwest neighborhood is the very worthy **Posada Don Mario** (Cosijopi 219, tel./fax 951/514-2012, hostaldonmario@hotmail.com, www.posadadonmario.com, dorms $13 pp, rooms with shared bath $23 s, $32 d, $40 t, rooms with private bath $30 s, $40 d) on a quiet side street. Hardworking owner Norma Moran offers 10 rooms and a dormitory, tucked around an intimate downstairs patio and an airy upstairs porch, furnished with comfy chairs and couches for reading and relaxing. Continental breakfast and in-house Internet are included.

TRAILER PARKS AND CAMPING

Oaxaca has two trailer-camping parks. Most accessible, but less inviting, is the long-time **Oaxaca Trailer Park** (900 Av. Violetas, tel. 951/515-0376, hookups $15, tents $10), at the far northeast side of town. Once a very popular facility, the Oaxaca Trailer Park has been partly converted to offices and apartments during the past few years. Nevertheless, it lives on, still with dozens of all-hookup spaces and tent spaces remaining. Amenities include big shade trees, diagonal parking spaces for the largest rigs, clean hot-water showers and toilets, a manager-watchperson, and the original sturdy security fence. Get there by turning left at Violetas, marked by the big green Colonia Reforma sign over the highway, a block or two past the baseball stadium, several blocks east of the first-class bus terminal on Highway 190. Continue uphill six long blocks to the trailer park entrance on the left.

Although much more remote, the second choice trailer park has its advantages. For those who prefer a bit of adventure and wide-open spaces, the **San Felipe del Agua Trailer Park** (Camino de la Chigolera 10, San Felipe del Agua, tel. 951/516-0654, fax 951/516-4239, scorpionmezcalo@yahoo.com, www.oaxacanstuff.com, tents $7, RVs $15; furnished apartment $40/day, $450/month) will probably be the best choice for tenters and for rigs 7.5 meters (25 ft.) or smaller. It perches atop a steep, valley-view knoll above foothill San Felipe del Agua village, about six kilometers (four mi.) north of downtown. The owner— San Francisco, California, expatriate Doug French—offers all hookups for about 10 rigs in a large country lot with scant shade but plenty of mezcal plants and room for tents. A small clubhouse with kitchenette, shower, and toilet is also available for resident use. Prices include water, electricity, and drainage. A furnished apartment with private bath and kitchenette is also available. Reservations are possible but probably not necessary, except on holidays.

Get to San Felipe del Agua village by bus, taxi, or car. By bus: From anywhere in town hire a taxi to take you to the nearest San Felipe bus stop, or, from the town center, catch a San Felipe–marked bus from the corner of Independencia and Reforma, two blocks east of the *zócalo*. Get off the bus at the San Felipe del Agua village plaza (see the old church on the right) and follow the driving directions that follow.

For drivers, the jumping-off point to the trailer park is Avenida Netzahualcoyotl (nay-tzah-oo-wahl-coh-YOH-tuhl), which heads uphill at its intersection with the Highway 190 thoroughfare (Calz. Niños Héroes), at the big green San Felipe sign. Continue about one kilometer (0.6 mi) uphill; bear left around the curve on to Calle Naranjos. After a block, pass the hospital on your left, and, a block later, turn right at the big divided intersection, Calzada San Felipe. Notice the old stone aqueduct, on your left, that divides the thoroughfare. In a few miles the road becomes San Felipe's Calle Hidalgo, which leads you to San Felipe Apostol Church behind the pocket-sized village plaza on the right.

To continue to the trailer park, turn left (west), just before the church and village plaza, on to Calle Iturbide, then right again at the first street, Morelos, then another quick left onto the "Prologation of Iturbide." After another long block or two downhill, at the arroyo bottom, turn right onto Chigolera; continue, climbing steeply uphill 0.6 kilometer (0.4 mi.) to the trailer-park sign and gate steeply uphill on your left.

Food

SNACKS, FOOD STALLS, AND COFFEEHOUSES

Despite the onset of worldwide hard economic times, the cost of meals at many of Oaxaca's popular restaurants has risen sharply during the past few years. Nevertheless, plenty of tasty, reasonably priced food is out there for the discerning diner to enjoy. This is especially true if you go where the local folks go. Read on for a plethora of possibilities.

During fiestas, snack stalls along Hidalgo, at the cathedral-front Alameda de León square, abound in local delicacies. Choices include *tlayudas,* giant pizza-like crisp tortillas loaded with avocado, tomato, onions, and cheese; and *empanadas de amarillo,* huge tacos stuffed with cheese and red salsa. For dessert, have a *buñuelo,* a crunchy, honey-soaked wheat tortilla.

At non-fiesta times, you can still fill up on the sizzling fare of tacos, *tortas,* hamburgers, and hot dogs (eat 'em only when they are served hot) at stands that set up in the same vicinity, especially late afternoon and evenings.

For additional economical sit-down meals, visit the acre of food stalls inside the **Mercado 20 de Noviembre,** two blocks south and one block west of the *zócalo's* southwest corner. Adventurous eaters will be in heaven among a wealth of succulent *chiles rellenos;* piquant *moles* (moh-LAYS); fat, banana leaf–wrapped *tamales Oaxaqueños;* and savory *sopas* (soups) and *guisados* (stews). Insist, however, that your selection be served hot.

Alternatively, on the northwest side of downtown, take a look around the completely untouristed **Mercado Sánchez Pasqua** (8 A.M.–2 P.M. Mon.–Sat.) for some pleasant surprises. (To get there, from the *zócalo* cathedral, walk uphill along Garcia Vigil seven blocks to Humboldt and turn left a block to Porfirio Díaz. It's the market across the street, past the gigantic wild fig tree.) Here, you can enjoy the town's tastiest *comal* (charcoal-fired griddle) cooking. Enjoy a hearty, homestyle breakfast (perhaps *huevos a la mexicana* with hot tortillas, or hotcakes with honey and bacon).For a special lunchtime treat, ask for (**Carmen Hernández Ramírez** and order her *memelas* (big, thick, open-face tortillas smothered in beans, $1.50) or the luscious, plump tamales ($1.50) of **Señora Catalina Minerva Paz.**

Much farther up the economic scale, sample the delicious offerings of (**Hostería Alcalá** (Macedonio Alcalá 307, 8:30 A.M.–11 P.M. daily, $5–15), four blocks north of the *zócalo.* The airy, tranquil patio ambience is ideal for a relaxing refreshment or lunch break from sightseeing along the Macedonio Alcalá pedestrian mall.

For coffee and dessert, you have a number of additional downtown choices, notably **Coffee Beans** (Cinco de Mayo 400, 8 A.M.–11 P.M. daily), five blocks north of the *zócalo;* or nearby **Restaurant La Antigua** (a block east at Reforma 401, tel. 951/516-5761, noon–11 P.M. daily, $3–8), just uphill from Abasolo.

For baked goods, a trio of good carryout bakeries stand within a stone's throw of the *zócalo.* First, try the sweet offerings of **Tartamiel Pastelería Frances** (on Trujano, half a block west from the southwest corner of the *zócalo,* tel. 951/516-7330, 7 A.M.–8 P.M. Mon.–Sat., 8:30 A.M.–7 P.M. Sun.). Continue clockwise, north of the *zócalo* a block, to **Panadería Bamby** (northwest corner of Garcia Vigil and Morelos, 6 A.M.–9 P.M. Mon.–Sat.). A block east of the *zócalo,* stop by (**Pastelería and Café La Vasconia** (Independencia 907, between Cinco de Mayo and Reforma, tel. 951/516-2677, 8 A.M.–9 P.M. daily, $2–6), with an inviting arched interior patio and a luscious selection of pastries, cakes, salads, and sandwiches.

CAFÉS AND RESTAURANTS
Around the *Zócalo*

Oaxaca visitors enjoy a number of good, reasonably priced eateries right on or near the *zócalo.* In fact, you could spend your entire Oaxaca time enjoying the fare of the several *zócalo-*

front sidewalk cafés. Of the eight cafés, seven offer recommendable food and service. Moving counterclockwise from the northwest corner, they are Primavera, La Cafetería, Del Jardín, El Importador, Terranova, Amarantos, and the *zócalo*-front café of the Hotel Marques del Valle.

First place overall goes to the middle-to-upper-class **Terranova** at the southeast corner, and the **Hotel Marques del Valle** on the north side, for their professionally prepared and served lunch and dinner entrées. For good, reasonably priced breakfasts, however, go to **Primavera,** at the northeast (Hidalgo) corner. The adjacent west-side **La Cafetería** and **Del Jardín** (with

---

A OAXACAN MENU

Oaxacan food adds another layer to the already rich Mexican food tradition. Oaxacan meals must start off with appetizers, such as *quesillo a la plancha,* Oaxaca's famous white cheese, served melted with guacamole and black beans. An appetizer list wouldn't be truly Oaxacan without *chapulines*, small grasshoppers grilled with minced onion in oil until crunchy.

Next come the Oaxacan *sopas* (soups), such as *sopa de guias,* a delicious stewed medley of squash flowers, tender baby squash, small corn dumplings, fresh whole corn kernels *(elote),* and tender vine shoots. Other typically served soups include *caldillo de nopales,* a broth of fleshy cactus leaves, often cooked with bits of pork, chicken, or small shrimps, and *sopa de frijoles,* black bean soup with cheese chunks and tortilla chips.

Main courses must include *moles* (MOH-lays), the most Oaxacan of all dishes. Very typical is *mole negro* (black *mole*), a spicy-sweet mixture of chocolate, chilies, garlic, peanuts, and a score of spices and other flavorings, cooked to a sauce, then baked with chicken or turkey. The turkey variation, called *mole de pavo,* is so *típica* that it's widely regarded as the national dish.

The *mole* list goes on, through *mole amarillo* (yellow *mole*) to *mole colorado* (red *mole*), a sauce of chilies, sesame seeds, almonds, raisins, bananas, tomatoes, and spices, served over chicken with rice seasoned with *chepil,* a wild local herb.

Oaxacan main-dish sauces are not necessarily chili based. Some menus feature fruit- and nut-based sauces, such as *almendrado,* an almond sauce spiced with tomatoes, green olives, and herbs and served over chicken.

Oaxacans also enjoy local variations on the usual Mexican *antojitos* (native Mexican snacks), such as *chiles rellenos de picadillo.* Here the cook replaces the usual chiles rellenos cheese stuffing with minced spiced pork, beef, or chicken and serves them with guacamole, grilled onion, and retried black beans.

Menu meat selections often include *cecina* (say-SEE-nah), thin slices of spicy cured pork, frequently served with bean sauce and cheese, or *tasajo,* thinly sliced grilled beef, often dished up with *chilaquiles* (tortillas cooked in chili-tomato sauce).

Finally, top off your meal with a local dessert, such as flan (egg custard), and a drink, such as *té de poleo,* a tea brewed from *poleo,* a local, mint-like herb, or *café de la olla,* a rich regional coffee sweetened with *panela,* the dark brown sugar that market vendors sell by the chunk.

Dried chilies are a basic ingredient for flavoring Mexican dishes.

© BRUCE WHIPPERMAN

loud marimba music most nights) rate generally good for food (notably Del Jardín's tummy-warming apple strudel), but their service can be spotty. While service at **Amarantos** is usually good, its food is only fair. Newcomer **El Importador** is trying harder with entertaining, not-too-loud live music and passably good food, at lower prices than neighboring Terranova. They all are open long hours, about 8 A.M.–midnight daily, and have typical menus: morning breakfasts ($2–5); soups and salads ($3–6); pasta, meat, poultry, and fish ($5–12).

Note: The *zócalo*'s west side is generally shadier, cooler, and more pleasant during the warm March, April, and May dry season. On the other hand, the east side, which gets the afternoon sun, is the warmer and often more pleasant side during the cooler months of November, December, and January. As for *zócalo*-front seating, nonsmokers can escape to the open-air tables, thus avoiding the cigarette and cigar smoke beneath the portal.

The one drawback of *zócalo*-front eating is the persistent flow of vendors, which can be unnerving. If, however, you refuse (or bargain for) their offerings gently and with humor, you might begin to accept and enjoy them as part of the entire colorful scene. (If vendors really get to you, it's best to take an inside table or retreat to the two restaurants, Terranova and Marques del Valle, that shoo them away.)

As for *zócalo* restaurants with a view from upstairs, serious-eating longtimers return to **El Asador Vasco** (Portal Flores 10A on the 2nd-floor balcony above Del Jardín, tel. 951/514-4755, 1 P.M.–midnight daily, $25–35). The menu specializes in hearty Basque-style country cooking: salty, spicy, and served in the decor of a medieval Iberian manor house. Favorites include fondues (bean, sausage, and mushroom), garlic soup, salads, veal tongue, oysters in hot sauce, and the carnes asadas (roast meats) house specialties.

Longtimers also swear by the Oaxacan specialties at **Casa de la Abuela** (Grandmother's House; above the Primavera café, tel. 951/516-3544, 10 A.M.–11 P.M. daily, $7–20) at the *zócalo*'s northwest corner. Here you can enjoy tasty,

professionally prepared regional dishes and airy *zócalo* vistas from the balcony. Call for reservations and a table with a view.

On Hidalgo, just past the *zócalo*'s northeast corner, the spotless little *fonda* **(El Mesón** (Hidalgo 805, tel. 951/516-2729, 8 A.M.–11:30 P.M. daily, $5–7) specializes in buffet food. For less than $10, you can select your fill of fresh fruit, salads, *frijoles charros* (chili beans), and several entrées, including roast beef and pork, chicken, *moles*, tacos, tamales, and enchiladas.

For fine Oaxacan specialties in a graceful, old-world setting, try **Andariega Restaurant** (Independencia 503, tel./fax 951/514-9331, 7:30 A.M.–9 P.M. daily, $8–14) in the Parador San Miguel, two blocks west of Catedral de Oaxaca. Here's one of your best chances to try some of Oaxaca's *moles,* such as *almendrado* (almond), *verde* (greena), *amarillo* (yellow), or *negro* (black), over chicken, beef, or pork. Other favorites are *chiles rellenos,* stuffed with cheese and *picadillo* (spiced meat), and red snapper in orange sauce. An excellent daily four-course *comida* (set lunch) runs about $8.

Moving uphill, the **Restaurant Catedral** (Garcia Vigil 105, tel. 951/516-3285, 9 A.M.–midnight Mon.–Fri., 8 A.M.–2 A.M. Sat.–Sun., $8–16), two blocks north of the *zócalo*, at the corner of Morelos, serves as a tranquil daytime business and middle-to-upper-class refuge from the street hubbub. The refined ambience—music playing softly in the background, tables set around an airy, intimate fountain patio crowned by the blue Oaxaca sky above—is half the show. The finale is the very correct service and quality food for breakfast, lunch, or supper. The Aguilar family owners are especially proud of their *moles* that flavor their house specialties. These include fillets, both meat and fish, and regional dishes, such as banana leaf–wrapped *tamales Oaxaqueños.*

More good eating, in a genteel, relaxed atmosphere, awaits you at the very popular **Restaurant El Sagrario** (120 Valdivieso, tel. 951/514-0303 or 951/514-3319, 8 A.M.–midnight daily, $7–14), behind Oaxaca Cathedral. Mostly local, youngish, upper-class customers enjoy a club/bar atmosphere (lower level), pizza parlor booths (middle level), or restaurant tables (upper level). At the restaurant level, during the evening, you can best take in the whole scene around you—chattering, upbeat crowd; live guitar, flute, jazz, or salsa melodies; and elegantly restored colonial details. Then, finally, comes the food, beginning, perhaps, with an appetizer, continuing with a soup or salad, then an international or regional specialty, which you top off with a light dessert and a savory espresso. Music volume goes up later in the evening.

North of the Zócalo

Devotees of light, vegetarian-style (and economically priced) cuisine get what they're hungering for at 【 **La Manantial Vegetariana** (corner of west-side Calle Tinoco y Palacios 303, tel. 951/514-5602, 9 A.M.–9 P.M. Mon.–Sat., lunch $6, dinner $8), located just north (uphill) of Matamoros, two blocks west and three blocks north of the zócalo. A tranquil patio ambience sets the tone for the house specialty, a set lunch *comida*. Typically they might offer soup (onion or cream of zucchini), salad (mixed greens or tomato cucumber), stew (mushroom or soya steak), bread, fruit drink, dessert, and coffee or tea.

Step into the unpretentiously elegant, vine-hung atrium-courtyard of the 【 **Hostería Alcalá** (307 Macedonio Alcalá, tel. 951/516-2093 or 951/514-0820, 8 A.M.–11 P.M. Mon.–Sat., 7 A.M.–10 P.M. Sun., $12–14), and choose from a long menu of professionally prepared and presented salads, soups, pasta, meats, and fish. In addition to its excellent food, Hostería Alcalá is so relaxing that you, like I, may decide to dine there practically every day. It provides an invitingly cool and soothing refuge on a warm afternoon. Find it one block downhill from the Santo Domingo churchfront.

Right across from the Santo Domingo church, enjoy some relief from high restaurant prices at the **Pizza Nostrana** (Macedonio Alcalá 501A, tel. 951/514-0778, 1–11 P.M. daily, $7–12). In the cozy, five-table, old-country Italian dining room, relax and choose from a long menu of genuine Napolitano (the welcoming owners are recent Italian immigrants)

country cooking. Choices include prosciutto, salads, plenty of pizza, pasta, all washed down by good Chilean red wine.

If you're unfamiliar with (or unconvinced about) Oaxaca's *mole* sauces, erase your doubt by walking two blocks east of the front of Iglesia de Santo Domingo to **Restaurant los Pacos** (Abasolo 121, tel. 951/516-1704, 10 A.M.–10 P.M. daily, $12–14). Your meal automatically comes with a *mole* appetizer sampler, which treats you to six—*coloradito, verde, negro, estofado, Amarillo,* and *chichilo*—of Oaxaca's *moles* right off the bat. It only gets better after that, especially if you continue with one of the good salads, from Caesar to tomato, then follow up with a traditional Oaxaca specialty, such as *enchiladas coloradito con picadillo, espinazo de puerco con mole verde,* or *entomatadas,* either *solas* (alone) or with beef.

Also behind Santo Domingo, half a block north of Abasolo, **Café La Olla** (Reforma 402, in front of Casa de las Bugambilias bed-and-breakfast, tel. 951/516-6668, 8 A.M.–10 P.M. daily, $6–15) enjoys a loyal following of longtime North American residents and visitors. Here, the dark-beamed ceiling, subdued spotlighting of the art-decorated walls, quiet music, and candlelight set a refined, romantic tone. Select from a long but light menu of skillfully prepared and presented soups (Aztec soup is nearly a meal in itself), salads, Oaxacan specialties, and meats. (Café La Olla's main drawback is street noise, which you can minimize by taking an upstairs table.)

Right across the street is **Café La Antigua** (Reforma 401, tel. 951/516-5761, 9 A.M.–11 P.M. Mon.–Sat., $3–10), enjoyed by a long list of loyal patrons for entirely different reasons. Here, the main course is conversation and fine on-site roasted Oaxaca "Pluma" coffee (from the farms around Pluma Hidalgo village, in the sierra above Huatulco). Along with their savory lattes, cold cappuccinos, and mocha frappés, patrons can enjoy fresh baked goods, crepes, sandwiches, eggs, and juices. The prime mover behind all this is friendly coffee grower and owner Diego Woolrich Ramírez.

Finally, if you're hankering for good seafood,

take a table in the relaxing garden of north-east-side **Mariscos Jorge** (on Pino Suárez, across from El Llano park, tel. 951/513-4308, 8 A.M.–6:30 P.M. daily, $8–16), the standout standby of local middle- and upper-class patrons. Choose from a long menu: 14 cocktail selections including shrimp, squid, and clams; salads and soups; and entrées, including fish fillets, from breaded and baked to *a la diabla*, octopus, and much more. It's also a good place to go for breakfast.

South of the *Zócalo*

Only a few good sit-down restaurants sprinkle the neighborhoods south of the *zócalo*. A trio of them, two well known for Oaxacan cuisine, and one for seafoood, stand out.

Local folks strongly recommend the no-nonsense, country-style (but refined) **La Flor de Oaxaca** (Armenta y López 311, tel. 951/516-5522, 7:30 A.M.–10 P.M. Mon.–Sat., 9 A.M.–3 P.M. Sun., $8–10), a block east and half a block south from the *zócalo*'s southeast corner. Along with spotless linen and very professional service, you'll get the customary bottomless plate of warm corn tortillas to go with your entrée. The *mole*-smothered regional specialties come mostly in four styles: *con tasajo* (thin broiled steak), *con pollo* (chicken), *con cecina* (roast pork), or *sola* (without meat). Besides those, you can choose from an extensive menu of equally flavorful items, such as *tamales Oaxaqueños* (wrapped in banana leaves), pork chops, several soups, spaghetti, and much more. Vegetable lovers get started off right with their crisp *ensalada mixta* (sliced tomato, cucumber, onion, avocado, and lettuce with vinegar and oil dressing). Credit cards are accepted.

A block west and two blocks south of the *zócalo*'s southwest corner, **(Restaurant Tayu** (20 de Noviembre 416, tel. 951/516-5363, 8 A.M.–6 P.M. Mon.–Sat., $3–7) allows you to step in to Oaxaca "as it used to be." Take a table and relax in the refined, old-world, TV-free ambience. In the mornings, select from a host of tasty breakfasts; in the afternoons, choose one of their four-course $6 *comidas* that

include a choice between several hearty entrées, such as short ribs, chicken, *chiles rellenos*, with soup, rice, and dessert included. Arrive in the afternoon, 2:30–4:30 P.M., and enjoy their live instrumental music.

Lovers of fresh seafood can join the loyal brigade of local folks who frequent the airy and unpretentious **Restaurant La Red** (The Net; corner of Bustamante and Colón, tel. 951/514-8840, noon–9 P.M. daily, $10–16), one of five Oaxaca branches, located one block south of the *zócalo*'s southeast corner. Customers get their heart's delight of generous seafood cocktails, heaping bowls of shrimp, fish fillets, octopus, and much more.

Splurge Restaurants

The Oaxaca visitor influx during the 1990s nurtured a crop of fine restaurants. If at all possible, visit the uniquely elegant **(Los Danzantes** (Macedonio Alcalá 402, tel. 951/501-1184 or 951/501-1187, 1:30–11:30 P.M. daily), where everything seems designed for perfection. We were lucky to enjoy a surprisingly economical ($10 until 6 P.M.) set lunch, which, when offered, changes every day. In the luxuriously airy dining atrium, beneath blue sky and sunlight filtering through curtains artfully draped overhead, waiters scurried, starting us off with yummy chilled artichoke soup, and continuing with savory spinach lasagna with Oaxaca *requesón* cheese, accompanied by mildly delicious pressed guava-apple juice. They topped it all off with delectable dark-Oaxaca chocolate mousse and espresso coffee. Bravo! After such an introduction, you'll be tempted to return on another day. Normally, expect to pay about $20 for lunch, and about least $35 per person for dinner. Reservations are strongly recommended.

Hotel manager and chef, Alejandro Ruiz, of **Casa Oaxaca** (Garcia Vigil 407, tel. 951/514-4173 or 951/516-8889, 1–9 P.M. Mon.–Sat., $23–28) puts his all into blending the best of old and new cuisine. For example, start off with duck pâté and continue with *flor de calabaza,* stuffed with cheese and accompanied by *tostaditas* (toasted corn) and guacamole. Follow through with broiled shrimp in their juice with lentils, or baked *robalo* (snook) with lemon, all accompanied with a bottle of Concha y Toro Sauvignon Blanc from Chile. Finish off with either baby coconut custard, mango pie, or *guanabana* mousse, or a sampling of all three. Reservations are mandatory.

In the far northeast corner of downtown, showplace **Restaurant La Toscana** (corner of Cinco de Mayo and Alianza, tel. 951/513-8742, 2–10 P.M. daily, $10–20), in the old northeast-side Jalatlaco neigborhood, offers a long, elegant Mediterranean menu, spiced with a dash of traditional Oaxaca. Although it would be hard to go wrong with most anything here, I enjoyed the lettuce and tomato salad with goat cheese, shrimp fettuccine, leg of *jabalí* (wild pig), and, for dessert, croquettes of coconut and banana. Reservations are recommended.

GROCERIES, WINE, AND NATURAL FOOD

For fruits and vegetables, the cheapest and freshest are in the Juárez market, which takes up the square block immediately southwest of the *zócalo.*

For simpler, straightforward grocery shopping, plus a small selection of good wines, go to handily located **Abarrotes Lonja** (8 A.M.– 9:30 P.M. daily), on the *zócalo*'s west side, next to La Cafetería café.

Local devotees go to **Xiguela** café and natural food store (Hidalgo 104C, corner of Cinco de Mayo, in the northeast-side Jalatlaco district, no phone, 9 A.M.–6 P.M. Mon.–Fri., 9 A.M.–3 P.M. Sat.). There they stock up with healthy goodies, teas—arnica, anise, manzanilla—organic grains, granola, yogurt, honey, jams, and a ton more.

Entertainment, Events, and Recreation

AROUND THE *ZÓCALO*

The Oaxaca *zócalo,* years ago relieved of traffic, is ideal ground for spontaneous diversions. Regular concerts serenade from the *zócalo* band kiosk beginning around 6 P.M. virtually every evening: the Oaxaca state band, Tuesday and Thursday; Marimba band, Wednesday (at 6:30 P.M.); and the Oaxaca orchestra, Sunday. Furthermore, the Oaxaca state band also plays Wednesdays and Saturdays, at noon. (Schedules may change; verify with Oaxaca state tourism, 703 Av. Juárez, tel. 951/516-0123.)

At other times, divert yourself by running like a kid over the plaza, bouncing a 10-foot-long *aeroglobo* into the air. (Get them from vendors in front of Oaxaca Cathedral.) If you're in a sitting mood, watch the world go by from a *zócalo* sidewalk café. Later, take in the folk dance performance (about $9) at the Hotel Monte Albán on the adjacent Plaza Alameda de León, 8:30–10 P.M. nightly. After that, return to a *zócalo* café and enjoy the musicians who entertain most evenings until midnight.

© BRUCE WHIPPERMAN

The Oaxaca state marimba band entertains at the *zócalo.*

FESTIVALS

There seems to be a festival somewhere in the Valley of Oaxaca every week of the year. Oaxaca's wide ethnic diversity explains much of the celebrating. Each of the groups celebrates its own traditions. Sixteen languages, in dozens of dialects, are spoken within the state. Authorities recognize around 500 distinct regional costumes.

The Guelaguetza

All of this ethnic ferment focuses in the city during the July **Lunes del Cerro** (Mondays on the Hill) festival, so named because it kicks off on the first Monday following July 16— the **Día de la Virgen de Carmen** (Virgin of Carmen day)—and continues for two weeks, when Oaxaca City is awash with both travelers, and native Oaxacans in costume from all seven traditional regions of the state.

This gathering was known in pre-Hispanic times as the Guelaguetza (gay-lah-GAY-tzah, or "offering"), a time of feasting, when tribes reunited for rituals and dancing in honor of Centeotl, the god of corn. The ceremonies, which climaxed with the sacrifice of a virgin who had been fed hallucinogenic mushrooms, were changed to tamer, mixed Christian–native rites by the Catholic Church. Lilies replaced marigolds—the flower of death—and saints sat in for the indigenous gods.

During recent times, the two-week Guelaguetza festival has grown to include a grand crafts exposition at the *zócalo* and an agricultural fair. Festivities climax on each of the two Mondays at the Guelaguetza dance amphitheater on the Cerro del Fortín hill northwest of the city. Thousands of spectators thrill to the whirling, stomping, and swaying performances of dozens of brightly costumed troupes, which wow the crowd by throwing offerings of fruit, candy, and handicrafts from the stage.

If you're coming, bring sunglasses and a hat for shade, and make hotel reservations several months ahead of time. Hotels customarily offer packages that include tickets (about $40) for each Guelaguetza performance. Alternatively, local Ticketmaster outlets usually sell tickets,

adding a fee of about $15. For more information, contact the Oaxaca state tourist information office (703 Av. Juárez, tel. 951/516-0123, 8 A.M.–8 P.M. daily, info@aoaxaca.com, www .aoaxaca.com) on the west side of El Llano park. Find them three blocks uphill, north, and two blocks east, of the Santo Domingo church.

Note: If the first Monday after July 16 happens to fall on July 18, the anniversary of Benito Juárez's death, the first Lunes del Cerro shifts to the succeeding Monday, July 25.

On the Sunday before the first Lunes del Cerro, Oaxacans celebrate their history and culture at the Plaza de Danzas, adjacent to the Iglesia de la Virgen de la Soledad. Events include a big sound, light, and dance show and depictions in tableaux of the four periods of Oaxaca history.

If you miss the Lunes del Cerro festival, some towns and villages stage smaller Guelaguetza celebrations year-round. So do a number of hotels, most frequently, at the **Hotel Monte Albán** (Alameda de León 1, tel. 951/516-2777, usually 8:30 P.M. daily, $10), adjacent to the *zócalo;* or most elaborately, at hotel **Camino Real** (Cinco de Mayo 300, tel. 951/516-0611, www.caminoreal.com/Oaxaca, 7 P.M. Fri., $35 show with buffet, not including drinks). Also, **Restaurant Casa de Cantera** (on northside Calle Dr. Federico Armengal, at the top of Av. Porfirio Díaz, tel. 951/514-7585 or 951/514-9522, www.casadecantera.com, 9 P.M. several nights a week, $15 pp, including a snack) has staged a popular Guelaguetza show for years.

Day of the Dead

As in many southern-Mexico locales, Oaxaca folks celebrate a robust **Día de los Muertos** (Day of the Dead; Oct. 31–Nov. 2). Families gather at cemeteries, where they decorate their family graves with flowers and the favorite foods of the deceased and festoons of glowing candles to guide the beloved spirits to reunite (albeit temporarily) with the family once again.

Festivities kick off on the afternoon of October 31, with the arrival of the *angelitos* (spirits of deceased infants and children), who it is said, depart the next day, November 1, to make room for the arrival of the adult spirits, who are feted for the next two nights.

Contrary to the somber graveyard traditions of Europe and North America, the Día de los Muertos (which should actually be called the *Days* of the Dead) is a three-night celebration. At the gravesites, folks eat, drink, and make merry, and finally cover themselves with blankets through the wee hours. Being a celebration, they often welcome others, even strangers, to rejoice with them. Be sure to bring your camera (but do ask permission to take photos; you'll seldom be refused).

If, however, you still feel uncertain how to behave, or where to go, either your hotel (make reservations months in advance), tour agencies, or professional guide will gladly set up a tour for you. If you prefer to go on your own, simply hire a taxi or walk to Oaxaca's main cemetery, Panteón San Miguel, around sunset. (From Macedonio Alcalá, on the downhill front corner of the Santo Domingo churchyard, walk east along Constitución for eight blocks, to the Panteón, at thoroughfare Av. Lic. E. Vasconcelos.)

Guadalupe, Soledad, and Navidad

The month of December in Oaxaca nearly amounts to a nonstop fiesta that kicks off with celebrations leading up to Mexico's patron, **Virgen de la Guadalupe** (Dec. 12). Oaxacans continue, feting their own patron, the **Virgen de la Soledad** (Dec. 16–18). Festivities, which center around the Virgin's basilica (on Independencia, six blocks west of the *zócalo*), include fireworks, dancing, food, and street processions of the faithful, bearing the Virgin's gold-crowned image decked out in her fine silks and satins.

Soon comes the **Fiesta de los Rábanos** (Festival of the Radishes; Dec. 23), when celebrants fill the Oaxaca *zócalo*, admiring amazing displays of plants, flowers, and whimsical figures crafted of giant radishes. Ceremonies and prizes honor the most innovative designs. Food stalls nearby serve traditional delicacies, including *buñuelos* (honey-soaked fried tortillas), plates of which are traditionally thrown into the air before the evening is over.

Oaxaca people culminate their *posada* pre-Christmas week on **Nochebuena** (Christmas

© BRUCE WHIPPERMAN

a street procession honoring the Virgen de la Soledad, the patron saint of Oaxaca

Eve) with candlelit processions from their parishes, accompanied by music, fireworks, and floats. They converge on the *zócalo* in time for a midnight cathedral mass.

ARTS EVENTS

Many Oaxaca institutions, such as the **Museo de Arte Contemporaneo de Oaxaca** (Macedonio Alcalá 202, tel. 951/514-1055, www.museomaco.com), the **Teatro Alcalá** (900 Independencia, tel. 951/516-8312 or 951/516-8344), the **Instituto de Artes Gráficos de Oaxaca** (across Macedonio Alcalá, tel. 951/516-6980), and the art-film **Cinema El Pochote** (Garcia Vigil 817, tel. 951/514-1194, films at 6 and 8 P.M. Tues.–Sat.), sponsor first-rate cultural events. Local sources of events information include resident Diane Barclay's top-notch website (www.oaxacacalendar.com), the weekly Spanish *El Grito* events newsletter of the Oaxaca State Secretary of Culture (www.cultura.oaxaca.gob.mx), and Oaxaca state tourist information office (703 Av. Juárez, west side of El Llano Park, www.aoaxaca.com).

Other Festivals

Besides the usual national holidays, a number of other locally important fiestas liven up the Oaxaca calendar. The first day of spring, March 21, kicks off the **Juegos Florales** (Flower Games). Festivities go on for 10 days, including the crowning of a festival queen at the Teatro de Alcalá, poetry contests, and performances by renowned artists and the National Symphony.

On the second Monday in October, residents of Santa María del Tule venerate their ancient tree in the **Lunes del Tule** festival. Locals in costume celebrate with rites, folk dances, and feats of horsemanship beneath the boughs of their beloved great cypress.

NIGHTLIFE

When lacking an official fiesta, you can create your own at a number of nightspots around town.

Some sidewalk cafés around the *zócalo* regularly have live music. Just follow the sound to either café **Terranova** or **El Importador** next door (southeast *zócalo* corner), or the marimba band in front of the café **Del Jardín** (southwest corner), and seasonally at the **Hotel Marques del Valle** restaurant (Portal Clavería, tel. 951/514-0688 or 951/516-3474, www.hotelmarquesdelvalle.com.mx), on the north side of *zócalo*. Music typically continues until about 11 P.M.

Nearby, behind Oaxaca Cathedral, **Restaurant El Sagrario** (120 Valdivieso, tel. 951/514-0303 or 951/514-3319, 8 A.M.–midnight daily, $7–12) has live music nightly, beginning around 9 P.M.

Bar La Farola (20 de Noviembre 314, corner of Las Casas, 951/516-5352, 11 A.M.–2 A.M. daily), a block west and a block south of the *zócalo*, founded 1916, claims to be Oaxaca's longest-running cantina. The Farola's dignified old-style-pub ambience attracts a middle-to-upper-class local clientele, some young, some old, who come to relax over food, drinks, and the rhythms of a live latin-jazz-salsa trio.

Moving uphill, north from the *zócalo*, the action is often livelier and louder (recorded hip-hop, reggae, and salsa) at restaurant-bar **Tentación** (Matamoros 101, 951/514-9521, 8 A.M. until sometimes as late as 2 A.M. Tues.–Sat.).

One of the most intense in-town nightspots is **Candela** (Murguia 413, corner of Pino Suárez, tel. 951/514-2010, from about 10 P.M. Thurs.–Sat.), which jumps with hot salsa and African-Latin rhythms. Arrive at 10 P.M. for dance lessons; call to confirm. (Women, be aware that a well-known cadre of local Romeos regularly frequents this and other such downtown spots.)

Very popular among 20-somethings is the class-act **Bar La Pasion** (tucked beyond the rear of Restaurant Mayordomo, Macedonio Alcalá 302, tel. 951/514-4363 or 951/516-6113, noon–3 A.M. daily) with giant flat TV screens, studio lighting, and loud, live music. On Friday, Saturday, and Sunday, you can recognize it easily after about 8 P.M. by the large crowd out front.

The success of Bar La Pasion has spawned a number of newer nightspots. One of the liveliest is across the street, restaurant-bar **La Cantinita** (Macedonio Alcalá 303, tel. 951/516-8961, 1 P.M.–2 A.M. daily). Above the front door, a sign announces, "entrance prohibited to all persons who like to fight, are in a bad mood, or are angry." The attraction is loud, with live salsa and hip hop and lots of folks in their twenties and thirties dancing, drinking, and eating.

For a more subdued atmosphere, try the luxury hotels, which host live dance music in their lobby bars, especially on weekends and holidays. Call to confirm programs at **Camino Real** (Cinco de Mayo 300, tel. 951/516-0611, www.caminoreal.com/Oaxaca), **Hotel Victoria** (Km 545, Blvd. Adolfo Ruiz Cortínez 1306, Carretera Panamericana, tel. 951/515-2633, www.hotelvictoriaoax.com.mx), and **Hotel Fortín Plaza** (Av. Venus 118, Colonia Estrella, tel. 951/515-7777, Mexico toll-free 800/718-9647, www.hotelfortinplaza.com.mx).

SPORTS AND RECREATION

A modest sporting goods and clothing selection (no tennis rackets at this writing, however) is available at **Deportes Ziga** (southwest corner of Macedonio Alcalá and Matamoros, next to La Mano Mágico handicrafts shop, tel. 951/514-1654, 9 A.M.–3 P.M. and 4–9 P.M. Mon.–Sat., 11 A.M.–2 P.M. Sun.).

Swimming, Tennis, and Golf

Swimmers can do their laps and laze the afternoon away by the big pool (unheated but usually swimmable) at in-town **Hotel Rivera del Ángel** (Mina 518, tel. 951/516-6666, $10 adults, $5 kids ages 5 and under).

For both tennis (about seven courts) and a nine-hole golf course, go to the relaxed country club–style **Club Brenamiel** (intersection of Hwy. 190 and Calle San Jacinto, tel. 951/512-6822, clubbrenamiel@hotmail.com), about three miles north of the town center, on the left just past the Hotel Villas del Sol. Alternatively, on the other side of town, try the well-equipped (half a dozen tennis courts, two pools, gymnasium) YMCA-like **Deportivo Oaxaca** (Km 6.5, Carretera a El Tule, tel. 951/517-5271, 951/517-5974 or 951/517-7312), off Highway 190 on the way to El Tule, about four miles east of town. *Note:* Although both Club Brenamiel and Deportivo Oaxaca are membership organizations, they do accept day guests for a fee.

For both swimming and tennis, you can also stay at either the **Hotel Victoria** (Km 545, Blvd. Adolfo Ruiz Cortínez 1306, Carretera Panamericana, tel. 951/515-2633, www.hotel victoriaoax.com.mx) or the **Hotel Misión de los Angeles** (Porfirio Díaz 102, tel. 951/502-0100, www.misiondelosangeles.com).

Jogging and Walking

For jogging, try the public fields, **Ciudad Deportiva** (Sports City; west side of Hwy. 190), about three kilometers (two mi) north of the town center. Closer in, you might also jog around the big **Parque Paseo Juárez** (El Llano, on Av. Juárez), 3 blocks east and about 10 blocks north of the *zócalo*.

For an invigorating in-town walk, climb the **Cerro del Fortín.** Your reward will be a panoramic city, valley, and mountain view. The key to getting there through the maze of city streets is to head to the **Escalera del Fortín** (staircase), which will lead you conveniently to the instep of the hill. For example, from the northeast *zócalo* corner, walk north along the Macedonio Alcalá mall. After five blocks, in front of the Iglesia de Santo Domingo, turn left onto Allende, continue four blocks to Crespo, and turn right. After three blocks, you'll see the staircase on the left. Continue uphill, past the sprawling Guelaguetza open-air auditorium, to the road (Av. Nicolas Copernicus) heading north to the **Planetarium** (tel. 951/514-5379, 7–9 P.M. Nov.–May, check the events schedule), where you can enjoy the panoramic city and valley view. (Besides daytime movies and star shows, the planetarium is customarily open for evening telescopic viewings of the moon, planets, and stars.)

Past the planetarium, you can keep walking along the hilltop for at least another mile. Take a hat and water. The round-trip from the *zócalo* is a minimum of three kilometers (two mi); the hilltop rises only a few hundred feet. Allow at least a couple of hours.

Shopping

The city of Oaxaca is renowned as a handicraft shopper's paradise. Prices are moderate, quality is high, and sources—in both large traditional markets and many dozens of private stores and galleries—are manifold. In the city, however, vendors do not ordinarily make the merchandise they sell. They buy wholesale from family shops in town, the surrounding valley, and remote localities all over the state of Oaxaca and Mexico in general. If your time is severely limited, it's best to buy from the good in-town sources, many of which are recommended here.

TRADITIONAL MARKETS

The original town market, **Mercado Juárez**, covers the entire square block just one block south and one block west of the *zócalo*. Many dozens of stalls offer everything; cotton and wool items—such as dresses, *huipiles*, woven blankets, and serapes—are among the best buys. Despite the overwhelming festoons of merchandise, bargains are there for those willing to search them out.

Before diving into the Juárez market's cavernous interior, first orient yourself by looking over the lineup of stalls on the market's west side, along the block of 20 de Noviembre, between Las Casas and Trujano. Here, you'll be able to select from a reasonably priced representative assortment—*alebrijes* (fanciful wooden animals), black and green pottery, cutlery, filigree jewelry, *huipiles*, leather goods, pewter, tinware—of much that Oaxaca offers.

If organic food and produce suits your style, visit the modest **Pochote Market** (411 Rayon, corner of Xicotencatl, most shops 9 A.M.–4 P.M. daily), four blocks east and two blocks south of the *zócalo's* southeast corner. A sprinkling of vendors from all over the Valley of Oaxaca offer fruit, vegetables, homemade mescal, honey, delicious hot tecate (tay-KAH-tay) chocolate-flavored drink, and lots of fresh food cooked on the spot.

After your Juárez market tour, walk along Aldama, a block west, to J. P. Garcia, then left,

one and a half blocks south, to between Mina and Zaragoza, for a look inside the **Mercado de Artesanías** (handicrafts market). Here, you'll find a ton of textiles—fetching *huipiles* and *camisas* (shirts), *flowery blusas* (blouses), fine wool *tapetes* (carpets), colorful *alfarería* (pottery), whimsical *alebrijes*, festive handmade masks, and much more.

PRIVATE HANDICRAFTS SHOPS

Although pricier, the private shops generally offer the choicest merchandise. Here you can select from the very best: *huipiles* from San Pedro de Amusgos and Yalalag, richly embroidered "wedding" dresses from San Antonino Castillo Velasco, rugs and hangings from Teotitlán del Valle and Santa Ana del Valle, pottery (black from San Bartolo Coyotepec and green from Atzompa), carved *alebrijes* from Arrazola, whimsical figurines by the Aguilar sisters of Ocotlán, mescal from Tlacolula, and masks from Huazolotitlán.

Most of the best individual shops lie scattered along three streets—Cinco de Mayo, Macedonio Alcalá, and Garcia Vigil, which run uphill, north of the *zócalo*.

◖ MARO

Somewhere along your handicrafts route, you must take a serious look around MARO, **Mujeres Artesanías de las Regiones de Oaxaca** (Craftswomen of the Regions of Oaxaca; 204 Cinco de Mayo, tel./fax 951/516-0670, 9 A.M.–7:30 P.M. daily). From behind Oaxaca Cathedral, walk uphill, along Macedonio Alcalá, first passing Independencia; one block farther, at Morelos, turn right, continue a block and turn left on Cinco de Mayo, and walk half a block uphill to MARO, on the right.

Here, a remarkable all-Oaxaca grassroots movement of women artisans sell their goods and demonstrate their manufacturing techniques. The artisans are virtually pure native

Mexicans from all parts of Oaxaca, and their offerings reflect their unique effort. The shelves of several rooms are filled with hosts of gorgeous handicrafts: wooden masks, toys, carvings; cotton *traje* (native clothing), such as *huipiles, pozahuancos,* and *quechquémitles;* wool serapes, rugs, and hangings; woven palm hats, mats, and baskets; fine steel knives, swords, and machetes; tinplate mirrors, candlesticks, and ornaments; and leather saddles, briefcases, wallets, and belts. Don't miss it. Better still, do a major part of your Oaxaca shopping at this store.

Other Private Shops

South of the *zócalo,* head up J. P. Garcia and visit the unique private store **El Arte Oaxaqueño** (Mina 317, corner of J. P. Garcia, tel. 951/516-1581, 10 A.M.–8 P.M. Mon.–Sat., 10 A.M.–5 P.M. Sun.). Their diverse, carefully selected offerings run from lovely wool weavings and bright one-of-a-kind pottery to fetching wooden toys and precious metal Christmas ornaments. Each piece comes with a detailed explanation of its history and a description of the craftsperson that made it.

From the *zócalo,* head north along the Macedonio Alcalá pedestrian mall; just a block north of Oaxaca Cathedral, you'll arrive at a Oaxaca favorite, the **Palacio de las Gemas** (corner of Morelos and Macedonio Alcalá, tel. 951/514-4603, 10 A.M.–8 P.M. Mon.–Sat.). Although specializing in semiprecious stones and jewelry, it has much more, including a host of charming hand-painted tinware Christmas decorations, Guerrero masks, and pre-Columbian reproductions in onyx and turquoise.

Continue north on Macedonio Alcalá for a block and step into **La Mano Mágico** (Macedonio Alcalá 203, on the west side, just below corner of Murguia, tel./fax 951/516 4275, 10:30 A.M.–3:00 P.M. and 4–8 P.M. Mon.–Sat.). The shop offers both a colorful exposition of crafts from all over Mexico and a patio workshop where artisans work, dyeing wool and weaving examples of the lovely, museum-quality rugs and serapes that adorn the walls.

Take a one-block detour west along Matamoros to **Casa de Artesaniás** (Matamoros 105, corner of Garcia Vigil, tel. 951/516-5062, 9 A.M.–9 P.M. Mon.–Sat., 10 A.M.–6 P.M. Sun.).

© BRUCE WHIPPERMAN

Decorative tinware is a Oaxacan speciality.

Here, a cooperative of about six dozen Oaxaca artisan families offers a wide handicrafts selection, including rainbows of fantastic *alebrijes,* from Tilcajete and Arrazola, a treasury of glistening black pottery from Coyotepec, and preciously embroidered dresses from San Antonio Castillo Velasco.

Return and continue uphill on Macedonio Alcalá, a block farther north, to the Plaza Alcalá complex (southwest corner of M. Bravo), which has both an outstanding courtyard restaurant, Hostería Alcalá, and some good shops. Best among them is an exceptional bookstore, **Librería Amate** (307 Macedonio Alcalá, tel. 951/516-6960 or 951/516-7181, amatebooks@ prodigy.net.mx, 10:30 A.M.–7:30 P.M. Mon.– Sat., 2–7 P.M. Sun.). Personable owner Henry Wangeman stocks an expertly selected library of English-language books about Mexico, including archaeology, cookbooks, ethnography, guides, history, literature, maps, postcards, and much more.

If you're interested in fine weavings, step directly across Macedonio Alcalá at the corner of Gurrion to **Tapetes de Teotitlán** (Macedonio Alcalá, 11 A.M.–7:30 P.M. Mon.–Sat., 1–7 P.M. Sun.), the shop of the Martínez family from the famous Teotitlán del Valle weaving village. Here, you're looking at the real thing: fine, mostly traditional designs, made of all-natural dyes.

Half a block farther uphill, be sure to look inside jewelry store **Oro de Monte Albán** (Macedonio Alcalá 403, tel. 951/514-3813, 10 A.M.–8 P.M. Mon.–Sat., noon–8 P.M. Sun.), across from the Iglesia de Santo Domingo. This extraordinary family-run enterprise carries on Oaxaca's venerable goldsmithing tradition as the sole licensed manufacturer of replicas from the renowned treasure of Monte Albán Tomb 7. Besides the luscious, museum-quality reproductions, Oro de Monte Albán offers a fine assortment of in-house silver and gold earrings, charm bracelets, necklaces, brooches, and much more.

While you're on Macedonio Alcalá, be sure to peruse the colorful outdoor displays of for-sale local paintings and native-style women's *blusas, enredos, vestidos* (blouses, skirts, dresses), and *huipiles* that decorate **Plaza Labastida,** just south, across Abasolo, from the Santo Domingo church.

FINE ARTS GALLERIES

The tourist boom has stimulated a Oaxaca fine-arts revival. Several downtown galleries bloom with the sculpture and paintings of masters, such as Rufino Tamayo, Rudolfo Morales, Francisco Toledo, and a host of up-and-coming local artists. Besides **La Mano Mágico** (Macedonio Alcalá 203, on the west side, just below corner of Murguia, tel./fax 951/516-4275, 10:30 A.M.–3:00 P.M. and 4–8 P.M. Mon.–Sat.), one of the private handicrafts shops, a number of galleries stand out. Foremost among them is **Arte de Oaxaca** (Murguia 105, between Macedonio Alcalá and Cinco de Mayo, tel. 951/514-0910, www.arte deoaxaca.com, 11 A.M.–3 P.M. and 5–8 P.M. Mon.–Fri., 11 A.M.–6 P.M. Sat.), the gallery of the Rudolfo Morales Foundation.

Also outstanding is **Galería Quetzalli** (Constitución 104, between Reforma and Cinco de Mayo, tel. 951/514-2606, fax 951/514-0735, www.galeriaquetzalli.com, 10 A.M.–2 P.M. and 5–8 P.M. Mon.–Sat.), local outlet for celebrated artist Francisco Toledo. It's located opposite the south flank of Iglesia de Santo Domingo.

Across the street and just as fascinating is the longtime coin, antique bric-a-brac, and art store **Monedas y Antiguidades** (Coins and Antiques; Abasolo 107, between the upper end of Cinco de Mayo and Reforma, tel. 951/516-3935, 11 A.M.–3 P.M. and 6–9 P.M. Mon.–Sat.). Browsers enjoy a potpourri of art, from kitsch to fine, plus a for-sale museum of dusty curios, from old silver coins and pioneer clothes irons to revolutionary photos and Porfirian-era tubas.

CUTLERY AND METALWORK SHOPS

Oaxaca is well known for its fine metal crafts. A few families produce nearly everything. A couple of the families sell their wares from their own shops. While in Mercado Juárez, stop by stall number 5 to see the fine swords, knives, and scissors of **Miguel Martínez** and family (tel. 951/514-4868, 9 A.M.–9 P.M. Mon.–Sat., 9 A.M.–6 P.M. Sun.). Walk a few blocks west and south to see an even wider selection, plus artisans at work, at **Guillermo Aragon's** street-front shop (J. P. Garcia 503, tel. 951/516-2658, 10:30 A.M.–3 P.M. and 4–8 P.M. Mon.–Sat.).

Information and Services

TOURIST INFORMATION

The state tourism secretariat maintains an **information office** (703 Av. Juárez, tel./fax 951/516-0123, www.aoaxaca.com, info@ aoaxaca.com, 8 A.M.–8 P.M. daily) on the west side of El Llano Park. They also staff a town center **information desk** (on Independencia, corner of Garcia Vigil, tel. 951/516-5645, 10 A.M.–6 P.M. Tues.–Sun.) at their former headquarters (now the Museum of Oaxacan Painters), at the north edge of the *zócalo*, half a block north of the cathedral-front.

Furthermore, the city (Coordinación de Turismo Municipal) also maintains a town-center **tourist information office** (102 Matamoros, tel. 951/516-9901 or 951/516-8365, 9 A.M.–6 P.M. Mon.–Sat.). Follow Garcia Vigil two blocks north of the *zócalo*, turn left (west) and continue half a block.

Travel and Tour Agencies and Guides

Formerly American Express, now **Lohbi Tours and Travel** (corner of Valdivieso and Independencia, tel. 951/516-6522 or 951/516-2700, fax 951/516-7475, 9 A.M.–2 P.M. Mon.–Sat., lohbitour@yahoo.com.mx), one block northeast of the *zócalo*, behind the cathedral, is a good source for most travel services, especially air tickets.

Other agencies are likewise experienced, especially with tours. Among them is **Viajes Xochitlán** (M. Bravo 210A, tel. 951/514-3271 or 951/514-3628, www.xochitlan-tours .com.mx, oaxaca@xochitlan-tours.com.mx, 9 A.M.–2 P.M. and 4–7 P.M. Mon.–Sat.). Travel in comfort to Oaxaca City and Valley sites and villages, such as Monte Albán, Mitla, Teotitlán del Valle, Tlacolula, and much more. They specialize in individuals and groups, tourist and business services, and travel agent services, such as air and bus tickets and hotel bookings.

Another reliable, long-time travel and tour agent is **Viajes Turísticos Mitla** (at Hóstal Santa Rosa, Trujano 201, tel./fax 951/514-7800 or 951/514-7806, fax 951/514-3152), a block west of the *zócalo*'s southwest corner. They offer many tours, including guide and transportation, for small- or medium-size groups. Their main office (Mina 501, tel./fax 951/514-3152) is three blocks west, three blocks south of the *zócalo*'s southwest corner. They also provide very economical bus-only tourist transportation to a plethora of Valley of Oaxaca sites, with multiple daily departures to Monte Albán. For more information and reservations, contact the bus departure ticket desk (tel. 951/516-5327).

A Oaxaca regiment of **private individual guides** also offers tours. Among the most highly recommended is the fluent-in-English **Juan Montes Lara** (Prol. de Eucaliptos 303, Colonia Reforma, tel./fax 951/513-0126, jmonteslara@yahoo.com, $25/hour), backed up by his wife Karin Schutte. Besides cultural sensitivity and extensive local knowledge, Juan and Karin also provide comfortable transportation in a big Chrysler van.

Moreover, satisfied customers rave about guide **Sebastian Chino Peña** (home tel. 951/562-1761, cell tel. 044-951/508-1220 in Oaxaca City, sebastian_oaxaca@hotmail.com, $20/hour). He offers tours by car of anywhere you would like to go in the city or valley of Oaxaca.

More athletic travelers might enjoy the services of **Zona Bici** (Garcia Vigil 409, tel. 951/516-0953, www.bikeoaxaca.com, boccaletti @prodigy.net.mx), five blocks due north of the *zócalo*, which rents bikes and also conducts bike tours into the countryside.

For even more extensive backcountry adventure bicycling, hiking, and camping in the mountains just north of the Valley of Oaxaca, contact **Expediciones Sierra Norte** (M. Bravo 210, tel./fax 951/514-8271, www.sierranorte .org.mx, sierranorte@oaxaca.com).

You might inquire for a guide recommendation at the state tourist *information office* (703 Av. Juárez, tel./fax 951/516-0123, www.aoaxaca .com, info@aoaxaca.com, 8 A.M.–8 P.M. daily).

HEALTH AND EMERGENCIES

If you get sick, ask your hotel desk to recommend a doctor. Otherwise, go to the 24-hour **Clínica Hospital Carmen** (Abasolo 215, tel./ fax 951/516-0027), staffed by English-speaking IAMAT Doctors Horacio Tenorio S. and Germán Tenorio V. Alternatively, go to highly recommended northside **Hospital Reforma** (Reforma 613, tel. 951/516-6100), a block west of El Llano park.

For routine medicines and drugs, go to one of many pharmacies, such as the **Farmacia Ahorros** (on Cinco de Mayo, near the northeast corner of Murguia, 7 A.M.–11 P.M. daily), one block east, two blocks north of the cathedral. After hours, call Farmacia Ahorros's free 24-hour delivery service (951/515-5000).

For fire or police emergencies, call the emergency number 066, or take a taxi to the municipal **police station** (*policia municipal*; Morelos 108, tel. 951/516-0455), or call the **firefighters** (*bomberos*; tel. 951/506-0248).

BOOKSTORES AND PUBLICATIONS

One of the absolute best sources of English-language books about Mexico is the **Librería Amate** (Macedonio Alcalá 307, ground floor of Plaza Alcalá, tel. 951/516-6960, fax 951/516-7181, www.amatebooks.com, amatebooks@ prodigy.net.mx, 10 A.M.–8:30 P.M. Mon.–Sat., 2–7 P.M. Sun.), four blocks north of the *zócalo*.

The interesting **Librería de Bibliofiles de Oaxaca** (Bibliophiles' Bookstore of Oaxaca; Macedonio Alacalá 104, tel. 951/516-9901,

10 A.M.–9 P.M. daily), downhill from Iglesia de Santo Domingo, offers a big collection of new, mostly Spanish books, but with a good number of art, crafts, archaeology, and cultural books in English.

Oaxaca's largest general book source (nearly completely in Spanish, however) is **Proveedora Escolar** (Scholar's Supplier; Independencia 1001, tel. 951/516-0489, fax 951/514-5655, 9 A.M.–8 P.M. Mon.–Sat.), which, as its name implies, is especially useful for those seeking a wealth of detailed historical, geographical, touristic, cultural, and archaeological information about Oaxaca. It's a cultural experience in itself to visit the place. The materials you'll probably most want to peruse are on the upper floors.

Pick up a copy of the good daily English-language *News,* from Mexico City, available late mornings, except Sunday, at the newsstand near the *zócalo*'s southwest corner, a few steps south on Cabrera.

Also, you can print out copies of the useful tourist newspapers, *Oaxaca Times* (www .oaxacatimes.com) and *Go-Oaxaca* (www.go-oaxaca.com)on the Internet; pick up the *Oaxaca Times* paper edition at hotels, shops, travel agents, the local tourist information offices, or at the publisher (Macedonio Alcalá 307, upstairs, tel./fax 951/516-3443).

MONEY EXCHANGE

Several banks, all with ATMs, sprinkle the downtown area. (*Note:* Remove your ATM card promptly; some local machines are known to "eat" them if left in for more than about 15 seconds after the transaction is finished.) One of the most convenient is the **Banamex ATM** (on Valdivieso, directly behind Oaxaca Cathedral, 9 A.M.–4 P.M. Mon.–Fri.).

The best-bet, full-service bank with long hours is **HSBC** (one block north, one block east of the *zócalo* corner of Guerrero and Armenta y López, tel. 951/514-7040 or 951/516-9754, 8 A.M.–6 P.M. Mon.–Fri., 9 A.M.–6 P.M. Sat.).

A full-service **Banamex** branch (Hidalgo at Cinco de Mayo, tel. 951/516-5900, 9 A.M.–4 P.M. Mon.–Sat.) nearby, receives customers just one block due east of the *zócalo.* If Banamex is too crowded, go to HSBC or **Banco Santander Serfin** (on the Independencia corner, north of the Oaxaca Cathedral, tel. 951/516-1100, 9 A.M.–4 P.M. Mon.–Sat.); they change U.S. and Euro currencies and travelers checks.

If banks are closed, try money-changer **Ce Cambio** (on Valdivieso, corner of Independencia, tel. 951/516-3399, 9 A.M.–6 P.M. Mon.–Fri., 9 A.M. -5 P.M. Sat.), just north of the *zócalo,* behind the Oaxaca Cathedral. Although it may pay about a percent less than the banks, it changes many major currencies and travelers checks.

COMMUNICATIONS

The Oaxaca **post office** (*correo;* corner of Alameda de León plaza and Independencia, tel. 951/516-1291, 8 A.M.–7 P.M. Mon.–Fri., 10 A.M.–5 P.M. Sat.) is across from the cathedral-front. A block west of the post office, the **telecomunicaciones** (corner of Independencia and 20 de Noviembre, tel. 951/516-4902, 8 A.M.–7:30 P.M. Mon.–Fri., 9 A.M.–4 P.M. Sat., 9 A.M.–noon Sun.) offers money orders, telephones, and public fax machines.

For long-distance and local telephone service, buy a Ladatel phone card (widely available in stores; look for the yellow Ladatel sign) and use it in public street telephones.

Answer your email and access the Internet at any one of a number of spots around the *zócalo.* For example, try the small shop behind the cathedral (Valdevieso 120, tel. 951/514-9227, 9 A.M.–11 P.M. daily).

LIBRARIES

Visitors starving for a good read in English will find satisfaction at the **Oaxaca Lending Library** (Pino Suárez 519, tel. 951/518-7077, library@oaxlibrary.org, www.oaxlibrary .org, 10 A.M.–2 P.M. and 4–7 P.M. Mon.–Fri., 10 A.M.–1 P.M. Sat.), about five blocks north of the *zócalo* on the west side of Pino Suárez, a block north of Constitución.

The city **biblioteca** (public library; corner of Morelos and Macedonio Alcalá, tel. 951/516-1853, 9 A.M.–8:30 P.M. Mon.–Fri.,

10 A.M.–2 P.M. Sat.), two blocks north of the *zócalo* in a lovingly restored former convent, is worth a visit, if only for its graceful, cloistered Renaissance interiors and patios. The library holdings are nearly all in Spanish.

CONSULATES AND IMMIGRATION

The **U.S. Consulate** (Macedonio Alcalá 407, tel. 951/514-3054 or 951/518-2853, fax 951/516-2701, 11 A.M.–4 P.M. Mon.–Thurs.) is upstairs at Plaza Santo Domingo, across from the Santo Domingo church. In an emergency, call the U.S. Embassy (tel. 01-55/5080-2000). The **Canadian Consulate** (700 Pino Suárez, local 11B, tel. 951/513-3777, fax 951/515-2147, 11 A.M.–2 P.M. Mon.–Fri.) services Canadian citizens. In an emergency, call the Canadian Embassy in Mexico City (toll-free Mex. tel. 800/706-2900).

Other consulates that may be available in Oaxaca are the **Italian Consulate** (Macedonio Alcalá 400, tel. 951/516-5058) and the **Spanish Consulate** (Porfirio Díaz 340, Colonia Reforma, tel. 951/515-3525 or 951/518-0031). For more information, look for consulate contact numbers in the *Oaxaca Times* or the telephone directory Yellow Pages, under *Embajadas, Legaciones, y Consulados,* or call the U.S. or Canadian consulates for information.

If you lose your tourist permit, make arrangements with **Migración** (at the airport, tel. 951/511-5733, 7 A.M.–9 P.M. daily) at least several hours before your scheduled departure from Mexico. Bring with you proof of your arrival date in Mexico—stamped passport, airline ticket, or copy of the lost permit.

LAUNDRY

Get your laundry done at conveniently located **Super Lavandería** (corner of Hidalgo and J. P. Garcia, tel. 951/514-1181, 8 A.M.–8 P.M. Mon.– Sat.), two blocks west of the *zócalo*'s northwest corner.

PHOTOGRAPHY

At this writing the only good photo store in downtown Oaxaca is **Foto Figueroa** (Hidalgo

516, corner 20 de Noviembre, tel. 951/516-3766, 9 A.M.–8 P.M. Mon.–Sat.). With plenty of Kodak digital accessories, it offers quick digital and develop-and-print services.

VOLUNTEER WORK AND DONATIONS

Local residents and visitors have banded together to provide help for Oaxaca's street children and poor single-parent families. A formerly grassroots organization, **Centro de Esperanza Infantile** (Crespo 308, tel. 951/501-1069, www.oaxacastreetchildrengrassroots.org, streetchildren@spersaoaxaca.com.mx, 9 A.M.–4 P.M. Mon.–Fri., 9 A.M.–2 P.M. Sat.) operates cooperatively out of its center, about four blocks north and three blocks west of the *zócalo*. The all-volunteer organization raises money for food, schoolbooks and uniforms, housing, foster care, and much more for homeless children and destitute single mothers and their children. They welcome donations and volunteers, and visitors are always welcome. Check the website for an address for sending donations within the United States or Canada.

LANGUAGE INSTRUCTION AND COURSES

A long list of satisfied clients attest to the competence of the language instruction of the **Instituto Cultural de Oaxaca** (northside corner of Calz. Niños Héroes/Hwy. 190 and Av. Juárez, tel. 951/515-3404, fax 951/515-3728, www.icomexico.com, info@icomexico.com), in a lovely garden campus.

Also very highly recommended is the **Becari Language School** (M. Bravo 210, tel./fax 951/514-6076, www.becari.com.mx, becarioax @prodigy.net.mx, becari@becari.com.mx). Offerings include small-group Spanish instruction, as well as cooking and dancing classes. If you desire, the school can arrange homestays with local families.

Similarly experienced is the **Vinigulaza Language and Tradition School** (Vinigulaza Idioma y Tradición; Abasolo 503, corner of Los Libres, about six blocks east, four blocks north of the plaza, tel. 951/513-2763, www.vinigulaza

.com, vinigu@prodigy.net.mx), associated with the local English-language Cambridge Academy. Offerings include informative (and even fun) small-group Spanish instruction. Schedules are flexible, and prices are reasonable.

Alternatively, for more lightweight instruction, try **Español Interactivo** (Interactive Spanish; Armenta y López 311B, tel./fax 951/514-6062, www.studyspanishinoaxaca .com), one block east and half a block south of the *zócalo*, by Iglesia de San Agustín. The school offers several levels that provide 15–40 instructional hours per week. Classes have a maximum of five students.

All the language schools also arrange **homestays** with Oaxaca families and often offer classes in folkloric and salsa dancing, weaving, and painting on clay and wood.

Inexpensive Spanish instruction is customarily available from volunteers at the **Oaxaca Lending Library** (Pino Suárez 519, tel. 951/518-7077, www.oaxlibrary.org, library@ oaxlibrary.org), about five blocks north of the *zócalo* and a block north (uphill) from Constitución.

OAXACAN COOKING AND CULTURE

Susana Trilling, Oaxaca resident and author of *My Search for the Seventh Mole* (as in MOH-lay), offers an unusual mix of Oaxacan culture, cooking, and eating, with a lodging option, at her **Seasons of My Heart cooking school** (Rancho Aurora; in Oaxaca, local cell tel. 044-951/508-0469; in Mexico, long-distance 045-951/508-0469; from Canada or U.S. 011-52-1-951/508-0469; www.seasonsofmyheart .com, info@seasonsofmyheart.com) in the Etla Valley, north of the city. Susana's simplest offering is a half-day cooking lesson ($50). She also offers a one-day group cooking adventure ($75), which includes a morning trip to a local native market to buy food, then preparing and eating later at Susana's ranch. Farther-ranging cooking courses (six days, $1,500) regularly include trips to outlying parts of Oaxaca, such as the Isthmus of Tehuántepec or northern Oaxaca, around Tuxtepec.

Getting There and Away

BY AIR

The Oaxaca airport (code-designated OAX) has several daily flights that connect with Mexico City and other Mexican and international destinations. Many of the Mexico City flights allow same-day connections between Oaxaca and many U.S. gateways.

Note: **Mexicana Airlines,** which ran daily Mexico City–Oaxaca flights for years, went bankrupt and closed operations on August 17, 2010. As of this writing, plans are afoot to restart operations on a much-reduced scale. In the meantime, a number of other reliable carriers are filling the gap.

Continental Airlines, (toll-free in Mex. tel. 800/900-5000) fortunately, has eliminated the oft-difficult stop in Mexico City en route to Oaxaca and now flies nonstop to and from Houston daily (flight time only 2.5 hours).

Aeroméxico (reservations toll-free in Mex. tel. 800/021-4000, tel. 951/516-1066, 951/516-7101, or 951/516-3765; flight information tel. 951/511-5055 or 951/511-5044) has flights that connect daily with Mexico City.

Budget carrier **Volaris Airlines** (toll-free in Mex. tel. 800/122-8000 and 800/865-2747) currently offers a direct Tijuana-Oaxaca connection, which is especially handy for southern California travelers.

Alternatively, light charter airlines (in the general aviation terminal, the building to the right as you face the main terminal) connect Oaxaca City with various points within Oaxaca. **Aerotucan** (tel. 951/502-0840, toll-free in Mex., outside Oaxaca tel. 800/640-4148, www.aerotucan.com.mx, infor@aerotucan.com.mx) regularly connects Oaxaca City with Puerto Escondido, Huatulco, and sometimes with Tuxtla Gutiérrez and Puebla.

From the same general aviation terminal, **Aerovega,** the dependable local air-taxi service, routinely connects Oaxaca City with Puerto Escondido and Huatulco. Book through a travel agent, such as **Lohbi Tours and Travel** (corner of Valdivieso and Independencia, one block northeast of the *zócalo,* behind the Oaxaca Cathedral, tel. 951/516-6522 or 951/516-2700, fax 951/516-7475).

The Oaxaca airport provides a modicum of services, such as a good upstairs restaurant with a view; a few shops for last-minute purchases; an international newsstand (seasonally only) with magazines and paperback novels; car rentals; a mailbox *buzón* (downstairs by the staircase to the restaurant); public Ladatel card-operated telephones; and an ATM upstairs.

Travel to and from the Airport

Arrival transportation for the 10-kilometer (six mi) trip into town is easy. Buy tickets at the booth at the far right end of the terminal as you exit. Fixed-fare *colectivo* (shared taxi) tickets run about $4 per person for downtown ($7 to northside Hotels Misión de los Angeles, Fortín Plaza, and Victoria). For the same trip, a *taxi especial* (private taxi) ticket runs about $15 for four people; larger Nissan Vans cost $17 and $28 (depending on destination) for up to eight passengers. No public buses run between the airport and town.

Car rental agents stationed regularly at the Oaxaca airport are: Hertz (cell tel. in Oaxaca 044-951/508-8721 and 044-951/139-8845, oax60@avasa.com); Alamo (951/511-8534, toll-free in Mex. tel. 800/002-5266, tel./fax 951/514-8534, oaxalamo@hotmail.com); and Europcar (tel. 951/516-8258, 951/516-9305 or 951/143-8340, toll-free in Mex. tel. 800/201-1111 or 800/201-2089, www.europcar.com.mx).

For **departure,** save taxi money by getting your *colectivo* airport transportation ticket ahead of time, at **Transportacion Terrestres** (on the west side of Plaza Alameda de León, across from the cathedral, tel. 951/514-4350, 9 A.M.–2 P.M. and 5–8 P.M. Mon.–Sat.).

Furthermore, keep enough dollars or pesos for your $12 international departure tax (which may be collected in Mexico City), if your air ticket doesn't already cover it. If you lose your tourist permit, take proof of your arrival date in Mexico, such as a stamped passport, airline ticket, or copy of lost permit, to airport **Migración** (tel. 951/511-5733, 8 A.M.–9 P.M. daily) a minimum of several hours prior to departure from Mexico.

BY CAR OR RV

Paved (but long, winding, and sometimes potholed) roads connect Oaxaca City with all regions of Oaxaca and neighboring states.

Four routes connect Oaxaca City south to the Pacific coast; two of them, via Highways 175 and 131, connect directly south over the super-scenic but rugged Sierra Madre del Sur. Especially during the June–October rainy season, travelers are subject to landslides and bridge washout delays. The longer but less rugged (and most dependable in bad weather) route connects Oaxaca via Highway 190 southeast to Tehuántepec, and from there to the Pacific coast Highway 200 west. The fourth route, also less direct, but still rugged and winding, travels west from Oaxaca, via Highway 190, and then south to the Pacific coast, via Highway 125.

The most direct route, narrow national **Highway 175,** runs along 238—winding, sometimes potholed—kilometers (148 mi), with its junction with coast Highway 200 at Pochutla (from there, it's 10 km/6 mi to Puerto Ángel). The road climbs to more than 2,700 meters (9,000 ft) through winter-chilly pine forests and indigenous Chatino and Zapotec villages. Fill up with gas at the last-chance Pemex in Mihuatlán heading south and at Pochutla (north edge of town) heading north; carry water and blankets and be prepared for emergencies. Under dry, daylight conditions, count on about seven hours at the wheel if heading south from Oaxaca to Puerto Ángel, or about eight hours in the opposite direction.

About the same is true for the paved **National Highway 131** route south from Oaxaca, which splits off of Highway 175 three kilometers (two mi) south of San Bartolo Coyotepec. On your way out of town, fill up with gasoline at the Oaxaca airport Pemex. Continue, via Zimatlán

and Sola de Vega (fill up with gas again), over the pine-clad Pacific crest, a total of 254 kilometers (158 mi) to Puerto Escondido. Under dry, daylight conditions, allow about seven hours southbound, or about eight hours in the opposite direction. Unleaded gasoline is regularly available mid-route at the Sola de Vega Pemex only.

Highway 190 connects Oaxaca City southeast with Tehuántepec, along 250 kilometers (155 mi) of well-maintained but winding highway. Allow about 4.5 hours to Tehuántepec (downhill), or 5 hours in the opposite direction.

At Tehuántepec, connect west with Highway 200, via Salina Cruz, to the Oaxaca Pacific coast, and Bahías de Huatulco (161 km/100 mi, three hours), Pochutla–Puerto Ángel (200 km/124 mi, four hours), and Puerto Escondido (274 km/170 mi, five hours) via a paved, lightly traveled but secure highway.

The very long but super-scenic 368-kilometer (229 mi) **Highway 190-Highway 125** route connects Oaxaca southwest with coastal Pinotepa Nacional, via the Mixtec country destinations of Yanhuitlán, Teposcolula, and Tlaxiaco. Although winding most of the way, the generally uncongested road is safely drivable (subject to some potholes, however) from Oaxaca in about 10 driving hours if you use the *cuota autopista* northwest of Oaxaca City (exit to old Highway 190 at Nochixtlán). Add an hour for the 2,100-meter (7,000 ft) climb in the opposite direction.

The 564-kilometer (350 mi) winding **Highway 190-Highway 160** from Oaxaca to Cuernavaca, Morelos, and Mexico City via Huajuapan de León requires a very long day, or better two days for safety. Under the best of conditions, the Mexico City–Oaxaca driving time runs 11 hours either way. Take it easy and stop overnight en route. (Make sure you arrive in Mexico City on a day when your car is permitted to enter. There are restrictions in place to reduce smog and traffic congestion in the city.)

Alternatively, you can cut your Mexico City–Oaxaca driving time significantly via the Mexico City–Puebla–Oaxaca *autopista*, combined 150D–131D, which, southbound, takes off from the southeast end of Mexico City's Calzada General Ignacio Zaragoza. Northbound, follow the signs on Highway 190 a few miles north of Oaxaca. Allow about six hours driving time at a steady 100 kph (60 mph). Tolls, which are worth it for the increased speed and safety, run about $30 for a car, much more for a big RV.

Car Rentals

Car rentals offer a convenient means of exploring Oaxaca City and environs. Although town and valley roads present no unusual hazards, drive defensively, anticipate danger, and keep a light foot on the accelerator. Also be aware that road hazards—animals, people, potholes, barricades, rocks—are much more dangerous at night.

To rent a car, all you need is a current driver's license and a credit card. However, car rentals, which by law must include adequate Mexican liability insurance, are expensive, running upwards of $40 per day. Save *mucho dinero* by splitting the tariff with others.

Get your rental through either a travel agent or, before departure, through U.S. and Canadian toll-free car rental numbers, or in Oaxaca locally: **Hertz** (at airport, or Valdivieso 100, tel. 951/139-8845, cell tel. 044-951/508-8721, oax60@avasa.com); **Alamo** (at airport or Cinco de Mayo 203, tel. 951/511-6220, tel./fax 951/514-8534, fax 951/514-8686, oaxalamo@hotmail.com); and **Europcar** (at airport, or at Matamoros 101, tel./fax 951/143-8340, toll-free tel. in Mexico, tel. 800/201-1111 or 800/201-2084).

BY VAN

Eight-to-sixteen-passenger vans, although less comfortable than first-class buses, provide faster service (at a much cheaper price). They are becoming increasingly popular for medium-distance connections, especially for the Pacific coast destinations of Pochutla–Puerto Ángel and Huatulco, northwest destinations in the Mixteca, and Northern Oaxaca destinations in the Sierra Norte, the Cañada, and around Tuxtepec.

At least two operators provide Oaxaca–Pochutla connections, from stations about one block east, three blocks south of the *zócalo's* southeast corner. The first option is **Eclipse 70** (tel. 951/516-1068, Pochutla $12), which departs about every half hour during the day from Armenta y López 540. Alternatively, around the second left downhill corner, you can ride **Atlantida** (Noria 101, tel. 951/514-7077, $12) every two hours for the same price.

For a direct Huatulco connection, try competent carrier **Van 2000** (Hidalgo 208, westside, near Soledad Church, tel. 951/516-3154), which offers about eight daily departures, connecting with Crucecita on the Huatulco coast.

The northwest (Nochixtlan, Teposcolula, Tlaxiaco, Putla) van connection is **Excelencia** (Díaz Ordaz 305, tel. 951/516-3578), three blocks west, one block south, from the *zócalo's* southwest corner.

For northern Cañada (Cuicatlan and Teotitlan del Camino) and Sierra Mazateca (Huautla de Jiménez) destinations, go by **Transportes Turistico Oaxaca-Cañada** vans (600 Trujano, five blocks west of the *zócalo*, tel. 951/378-1080).

BY BUS
Luxury and First Class

In contrast to vans, buses are much more comfortable and remain a popular option, especially for longer trips. Oaxaca's major luxury- and first-class carriers, Autobuses del Oriente and Omnibus Cristóbal Colón and their associated minor carriers, operate out of their shiny new **terminal** (toll-free in Mex. tel. 800/702-8000, Calz. Héroes de Chapultepec 1036, at Carranza, on the north side of town) on Highway 190. Bus lines accept credit cards for luxury- and first-class bookings. Passengers enjoy some amenities, such as Ladatel-card public telephones (on the terminal south end), snack stands, luggage lockers, air-conditioned first- and luxury-class waiting rooms, and cool, refined Restaurant Colibri across the street.

Moreover, all of the carriers that use the Héroes de Chapultepec terminal cooperate through the joint agency **Boletotal** (formerly Ticket Bus, toll-free in Mex. tel. 800/702-8000 or 800/009-9090, www.boletotal.com.mx, 8 A.M.–10 P.M. Mon.–Sat. and 8 A.M.–9 P.M. Sun.), which sells tickets at three town-center offices: on the *zócalo*'s south side, by the Internet store (tel. 951/513-3773); a block west of the *zócalo* (20 de Noviembre 103D, tel. 951/514-6655); and behind the Oaxaca Cathedral (corner of Independencia, tel. 951/502-0560).

Omnibuses Cristóbal Colón (OCC) offers first- and luxury-class connections with many Oaxaca and national destinations. Buses connect northwest with the Mixteca destinations of Nochixtlán, Tamazulapan, and Huajuapan de León, then continuing on to Puebla and Mexico City. Westerly, they connect with the Mixteca Alta, via Teposcolula, Tlaxiaco, Juxtlahuaca, Putla de Guerrero, and Pinotepa Nacional. Southerly, they connect (via the surer, but 11-hour long, Isthmus route) via Salina Cruz, with Huatulco, Pochutla–Puerto Ángel, and Puerto Escondido; and southeasterly, with Tehuántepec, Juchitán, Tapachula, Tuxtla Guitiérrez, and San Cristóbal de las Casas.

Autobuses del Oriente (ADO) also offers both first- and luxury-class Oaxaca connections, mostly along the Highway 190 corridor. First-class buses connect northwest with Mexico City (Tapo Tasqueña and Norte stations), via Nochixtlán and Huajuapan de León, and southeast with Tehuántepec and Salina Cruz. Other departures connect northeast with Coatzacoalcos, Villahermosa, Palenque, and Mérida; others connect north, with Tuxtepec, Veracruz, and Tampico.

ADO luxury-class buses mostly connect with Mexico City: ADO Platino (Platinum-class) connects, nonstop northwest, with Mexico City's Tapo and Norte stations, and southeast, with Tuxtla Gutiérrez in Chiapas. Furthermore, ADO GL luxury-class buses connect northwest, with Mexico City's Tapo and Tasqueño stations; southeast, with Tuxtla

Gutiérrez and San Cristóbal de las Casas; and north, with Veracruz.

Also, first-class **Estrella de Oro** departures connect with Acapulco, via Huajuapan de León in the Mixteca, and Chilapa and Chipancingo in Guerrero.

Regional first-class **Cuenca** buses connect with northern Oaxaca points along Highway 175, including Ixtlán de Juárez, Valle Nacional, Tuxtepec, and Tierra Blanca, continuing all the way to Veracruz.

Note: Although first-class **Sur** and **Autobuses Unidos** (AU) tickets for reserved seats are sold at the Héroes de Chapultepec first-class station, they nevertheless depart from the Oaxaca Second-Class terminal. (Be sure to double-check your departure station when you buy Sur or AU tickets.)

Sur departures connect with Mexico City's Tapo station, along old Highways 190 and 160, via Huajuapan de León, Izucar de Matamoros, Puebla, and Cuatla, Morelos.

Autobuses Unidos departures connect with either Mexico City along the fast *autopista* expressway via Nochixtlán, Coixtlahuaca, and Puebla; or along the old Highway 131 via Cuicatlán, Teotitlán del Camino, Tehuacán, and Puebla.

Second Class

A swarm of long-distance second-class buses runs from the **camionera central segunda clase** (second-class bus terminal), southwest of downtown, just north of the Abastos market. Get there by taxi or by walking due west about eight blocks from the *zócalo* to the west end of Calle Las Casas. Take care crossing the busy *periférico* straight across the railroad tracks. Keep walking the same direction, along the four-lane street for two more blocks, to the terminal gate on the right. Inside, you'll find an orderly array of snack stalls, a cafeteria, luggage lockers, a long-distance telephone and fax, and a lineup of *taquillas* (ticket booths).

With one exception all ticket booths line up along the terminal to your left as you enter. **Fletes y Pasajes** (tel. 951/516-2270) dominates the terminal, with three separate ticket booths. All three Fletes y Pasajes booths sell tickets to most of their destinations. They offer very broad second-class service, connecting with nearly everywhere in Oaxaca except north: westerly, with Mixteca destinations of Nochixtlán, Tamazulapan, Huajuapan, and Tlaxiaco, connecting all the way via Highway 125 to Pinotepa Nacional on the coast; easterly, with Mitla and Mixe destinations of Ayutla, Zacatepec, and Juquila Mixes; and southeasterly, with Isthmus destinations of Tehuántepec, Juchitán, and Salina Cruz. Besides all of the above, Fletes y Pasajes offers luxury-class "super" expressway connections with Mexico City.

In approximate consecutive order, moving left from the entrance, first find **Transportes Oaxaca Istmo** (tel. 951/516-3664). Departures connect with dozens of destinations east and south. These include the east Valley of Oaxaca destinations of Tlacolula and Mitla, continuing to the Isthmus destinations of Tehuántepec, Juchitán, and Salina Cruz. From Tehuántepec and Salina Cruz, they connect west, with the Pacific coast destinations of Huatulco, Pochutla–Puerto Ángel, and Puerto Escondido.

Cooperating **Auto Transportes Oaxaca-Pacífico** (tel. 951/516-2908) and **Autobuses Estrella del Valle** travel the Highway 175 north–south route between Oaxaca and Pochutla–Puerto Ángel. Both lines continue,

connecting along east–west coastal Highway 200 with Bahías de Huatulco, Puerto Escondido, and Pinotepa Nacional.

Estrella Roja del Sureste and **Trans Sol** (tel. 951/516-0694), with some first-class buses, connect directly with Puerto Escondido along Highway 131 north-south via Sola de Vega (with a side-trip to Juquila pilgrimage shrine). From Puerto Escondido, you can make coastal connections with Pochutla–Puerto Ángel, Bahías de Huatulco, Jamiltepec, and Pinotepa Nacional.

Several other semi-local lines connect mostly with Valley of Oaxaca points: **Choferes del Sur,** with the northwest Valley of Oaxaca, ranging from San Felipe del Agua north of the city to Etla northwest; **Autobuses de Oaxaca** connects south with Cuilapan and Zaachila; and **Sociedad Cooperativa Valle del Norte** connects west with Teotitlán del Valle and Tlacolula. Lastly, if you hanker for a long, sometimes rough but scenic back-roads adventure, ride **Flecha de Zempoaltépetl** northeast to the remote Zapotec mountain native market towns of Villa Alta and Yalalag, via Tlacolula and Cuajimoloyas.

Finally, to the right of the entrance as you enter, **Pasajeros Benito Juárez** buses climb the mountains edging the Valley of Oaxaca's north side to the cool, pine-shadowed mountain-top communities of Benito Juárez and Cuajimoloyas (koo-ah-hee-moh-LO-yahs).

THE VALLEY OF OAXACA

The riches, both cultural and economic, of the city of Oaxaca flow largely from its surrounding hinterland, the Valley of Oaxaca, a mountain-rimmed patchwork expanse of fertile summer-green (and winter-dry) fields, pastures, villages, and reed-lined rivers and streams. By far Oaxaca's largest valley, both in size and population, with an aggregate population of about half that of the central city, the Valley of Oaxaca consists of three subvalleys—the Valley of Tlacolula, the Valley of Ocotlán, and the Valley of Etla—that each extend, respectively, about 30 miles east, south, and northeast of Oaxaca City.

The Valley of Oaxaca is unique in a number of ways. Most importantly, the inhabitants are nearly all indigenous Zapotec-speaking people. You will often brush shoulders with them, especially in the big markets in Tlacolula, Ocotlán, Zaachila, and Etla. The women traditionally dress in attractive bright skirts and blouses, with their hair done up in colorful ribbon-decorated braids. Although only a fraction of them speak fluent Spanish, they will nearly always understand and appreciate a smile and friendly *"buenos dias"* or *"buenas tardes."*

The Valley of Oaxaca's vibrant and prosperous native presence flows from a fortunate turn of history. During the mid-1800s, Mexico's Laws of the Reform forced the sale of nearly all church lands throughout the country. In most parts of Mexico, rich Mexicans and foreigners bought up much of these holdings, but in Oaxaca, isolated in Mexico's far southern region, there were few rich buyers, so the land was bought at very low prices by the local people, most of

© STEPHAN SCHERHAG/123RF.COM

HIGHLIGHTS

◖ Santa María del Tule: Townsfolk have literally built their town around their gigantic beloved El Tule tree, a cousin of the giant redwood trees of California (page 82).

◖ Teotitlán del Valle: Fine wool carpets and hangings, known locally as *tapetes*, are the prized product of dozens of local family workshop-stores (page 84).

◖ Mitla: Explore the monumental plazas and columned buildings, handsomely adorned by a treasury of painstakingly placed *greca* (Grecian-like) stone fretwork (page 91).

◖ San Bartolo Coyotepec: A small city of roadside home-workshops and a must-see museum display of the pearly-black pottery pioneered by celebrated potter Doña Rosa a generation ago (page 98).

◖ Zaachila: Its monumental archaeological zone and riotously colorful *tianguis* (native market) make Zaachila a Thursday destination of choice in Oaxaca (page 106).

◖ Monte Albán: Any day is a good day to visit this – Mesoamerica's earliest true metropolis – which to some still rules from its majestic mountain-top throne (page 108).

◖ San José El Mogote: Its regal reconstructed pyramids and plazas and the un-forgettably red *diablo enchilado* sculpture displayed in its community museum, plus the neighboring **Etla market**, make San José El Mogote a worthwhile Wednesday excursion (page 115).

LOOK FOR **◖** TO FIND RECOMMENDED SIGHTS, ACTIVITIES, DINING, AND LODGING.

© AVALON TRAVEL

them indigenous farmers. Moreover, after the Revolution of 1910–1917, progressive federal-government land-reform policies awarded many millions of acres of land to campesino communities, notably to Oaxaca Valley towns Teotitlán del Valle and Santa Ana del Valle, whose residents now conserve many thousand acres of rich valley fields and foothill forests.

Although the grand monuments, fascinating museums, good restaurants, and inviting handicrafts shops of Oaxaca City alone would be sufficient, a visit to Oaxaca is doubly rich because of the manifold wonders of the surrounding Valley of Oaxaca. The must-see highlights of the valley are the timeless Mitla and Monte Albán archaeological sites and the fetching crafts—wool weavings, pearly black pottery, floral-embroidered blouses and dresses, and *alebrijes* (wood-carved animals). You could easily spend a week or more of your time touring the Valley of Oaxaca from a base in Oaxaca City.

You can even let the valley's *tianguis* (literally, "shade awnings" and synonymous with "native

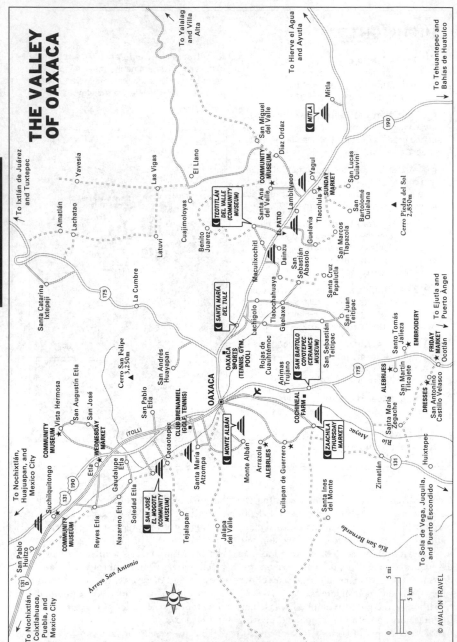

THE VALLEY OF OAXACA

To Ixtlán de Juárez and Tuxtepec

To Yalalag and Villa Alta

To Hierve el Agua and Ayutla

To Tehuantepec and Bahías de Huatulco

MITLA

Mitla

190

San Miguel del Valle

Díaz Ordaz

COMMUNITY MUSEUM

San Ana del Valle

Santa Catarina Ixtepeji

Amatlán

Lachatao

Yavesia

El Llano

Las Vigas

Cuajimoloyas

Benito Juárez

Latuvi

175

La Cumbre

TEOTITLÁN DEL VALLE (COMMUNITY MUSEUM)

Macuilxochitl

Lambityeco

Yagul

SUNDAY MARKET

Tlacolula

San Lucas Quiavini

EL PATIO

Dainzú

San Bartolomé Quialana

San Marcos Tlapazola

Cerro Piedra del Sol 2,850m

Guelavia

SANTA MARÍA DEL TULE

Lachigolo

Tlacochahuaya

Guelaxe

San Sebastián Abasolo

San Cruz Papalutla

San Andrés Huayapan

Cerro San Felipe 3,250m

San Pablo Etla

OAXACA SPORTS (TENNIS, GYM, POOL)

Rojas de Cuauhtémoc

Ánimas Trujano

SAN BARTOLO COYOTEPEC (CERAMICS MUSEUM)

San Sebastián Teitipac

San Juan Teitipac

175

Santo Tomás Jalieza

To Ejutla and Puerto Ángel

Vista Hermosa

San Augustin Etla

San José

COMMUNITY MUSEUM

WEDNESDAY MARKET

(TOLL)

CLUB BRENAMIEL (GOLF, TENNIS)

OAXACA

COCHINEAL FARM

ALEBRIJES

San Martín Tilcajete

San Antonino Castillo Velasco

EMBROIDERY

FRIDAY MARKET

Ocotlán

DRESSES

Santa María Zegache

To Nochixtlán, Huajuapan, and Mexico City

Suchilquitongo

131

190

Etla

Guadalupe Etla

Cacaotepec

Santa María Atzompa

MONTE ALBÁN

Monte Albán

Arrazola

ALEBRIJES

Cuilapan de Guerrero

ZAACHILA (THURSDAY MARKET)

Río Atoyac

Huixtepec

131

Nazareno Etla

Soledad Etla

SAN JOSÉ EL MOGOTE (COMMUNITY MUSEUM)

Tejalapan

Jalapa del Valle

Santa Ines del Monte

Zimatlán

Reyes Etla

COMMUNITY MUSEUM

San Pablo Huitzo

131 D

To Nochixtlán, Coixtlahuaca, Puebla, and Mexico City

Arroyo San Antonio

Río San Bernardo

To Sola de Vega, Juquila, and Puerto Escondido

5 mi

5 km

© AVALON TRAVEL

0

0

markets") guide you along your excursion path. Along the way, beneath the shadowed market canopies and the shops of Oaxaca's welcoming local people, you can look, choose, and bargain for the wonderful handicrafts that travelers from all over the world come to the Valley of Oaxaca to buy.

PLANNING YOUR TIME

If your time is limited, your enviable task is to pick, according to your own interests, the best of the best from the Valley of Oaxaca's treasury of colorful markets, bucolic handicrafts villages, mysterious archaeological sights, and community museums. In a whirlwind four or five days, you can soak in the valley's celebrated highlights, scheduling your time according to the weekly market days.

Given the limited hotel choices in the Valley of Oaxaca and the relatively short distances (16–48 km/10–30 mi) to valley sights from Oaxaca City, you could use your lodging in the city as a home base and take excursions from there to explore the valley.

For transportation, you could hire a guide for about $150–200 per day, which should include a car for 4–5 people; rent a car for around $50 per day ($250 per week); or use private tourist bus transportation for $10–15 per person. Each of these options can get you to most of the valley's highlights over three or four days. A fourth option, touring by local public bus from *camionera central segunda clase* (second-class bus station) is much cheaper, but it requires twice the time.

Some sights you won't want to miss are the archaeological zones of **Mitla,** on the east side, and **Monte Albán,** on the southwest side of the valley. Of the markets, the biggest are the **Tlacolula** Sunday market, the **Ocotlán** Friday market, the **Etla** Wednesday market, and the **Zaachila** Thursday market. Fascinating crafts villages along the way are **Teotitlán del Valle** (on the way to Tlacolula and Mitla); Santo Tomás Jalieza, San Martín Tilcajete, and **San Bartolo Coyotepec** (on the way back to Oaxaca City from Ocotlán); and the **Santa María Atzompa** pottery village (on the way to or from Monte Albán).

If your time is very limited, you could skip the Tlacolula market, but make sure to visit the Thursday market in **Zaachila,** unbeatable for its intensely colorful ambience and exotic fruits and other food. Be sure to include the nearby Zaachila archaeological site in your visit.

On the other hand, if you have an extra day, it would be worthwhile to visit the **San José El Mogote** archaeological site and the adjacent community museum. Continue to the **Etla** market, especially good on Wednesdays.

GETTING AROUND
Taxis, Buses, and Rental Cars

For short runs in downtown Oaxaca, street taxis ($2–3, 25–35 pesos) are quick and secure. Be sure to establish the price before getting into the taxi. If it's too high, hail another taxi.

For Oaxaca Valley touring, the cheapest (but not quickest) option is to ride a bus from the west-side Abastos market *camionera central segunda clase* (second-class bus terminal). The buses run everywhere in the Valley of Oaxaca and beyond. Arrive early any day and you could cover most major valley destinations in about a week: two days east (Teotitlán, Tlacolula, Mitla), two days south (crafts villages, Ocotlán market), two days southwest and west (Zaachila market and archaeological site, Cuilapan, Arrazola, Monte Albán, and Atzompa), and one day northwest (Etla market and San José El Mogote).

Get to the second-class bus terminal by walking one block south from the *zócalo*'s southwest corner, turn right at Las Casas, and keep walking about seven blocks. With caution, cross the *periférico*. The big terminal is two blocks farther, on the right.

More leisurely options include renting a car or riding a private tourist bus, or both. Get your car rental through either a travel agent or U.S. and Canadian toll-free car rental number before you leave home, or in Oaxaca locally: **Hertz** (at airport, or Valdivieso 100, tel. 951/139-8845, cell tel.044-951/508-8721, oax60@avasa.com); **Alamo** (at airport or Cinco de Mayo 203, tel. 951/511-6220, tel./fax 951/514-8534, fax 951/514-8686, oaxalamo@hotmail.com); and **Europcar** (at airport, or at

Matamoros 101, tel./fax 951/143-8340, toll-free tel. in Mexico, tel. 800/201-1111 or 800/201-2084).

For economical private transportation-only tourist buses, a good bet is to go with **Viajes Turísticos Mitla** (at Hóstal Santa Rosa, Trujano 201, tel./fax 951/514-7800 or 951/514-7806, fax 951/514-3152), a block west of the *zócalo*'s southwest corner. They offer many tours, including a guide and transportation, for small- or medium-size groups. You can also contact their main office (Mina 501, tel./fax 951/514-3152), three blocks west, three blocks south of the *zócalo*'s southwest corner.

Guided Tours

Many private individual guides offer tours. One of the the most highly recommended is fluent-in-English **Juan Montes Lara** (Prol. de Eucaliptos 303, Colonia Reforma, tel./fax 951/513-0126, jmonteslara@yahoo.com, $25/hour), backed up by his wife Karin Schutte. Besides cultural sensitivity and extensive local knowledge, they can also provide comfortable transportation in a Chrysler van.

Moreover, satisfied customers rave about guide **Sebastiañn Chino Peña** (local cell tel. 044-951/508-1220, tel. 951/562-1761,

COMMUNITY MUSEUMS

Oaxaca's many community museums *(museos comunitario)* provide visitors with a potentially rewarding alternative for getting to know local people. The museums, which now number about 20, sprinkle the Valley of Oaxaca, the Mixteca, and the Pacific coast. The first community museums began as a result of archaeological digs. Later museums arose from the local need to house historic community documents and the myriad artifacts that folks have been digging up in their own backyards for centuries.

During the 1980s and 1990s, the government funded the construction of museums and installation of exhibits in a number of indigenous communities, in both the Valley of Oaxaca and the Mixteca. Now, excellent small museums in the communities of **Teotitlán del Valle** and **Santa Ana del Valle,** in the east Valley of Oaxaca, and **San José El Mogote** and **Suchilquitongo,** in the northwest valley, welcome visitors during regularly maintained hours.

The same is more or less true for the well-organized Mixteca museums in **Huajuapan de León, San Pedro y San Pablo Tequixtepec, Huamelulpan,** and **Tututepec** on the Mixtec Coast.

A number of other small communities also established museums but do not yet maintain regular hours. Nevertheless, local contact people are available to open their museums for visitors. In the Valley of Oaxaca, such museums exist at San Pablo Huixtepec (on Hwy. 131, south of Zimatlán) and San Pablo Huitzo (northeast, off of Hwy. 190). The same is true in the Mixteca for the communities of Yucuita, San Miguel Tequixtepec, Tepelmeme de Morelos, San José Progeso, San Juan Mixtepec, Santa María Cuquila, and Santa María Yucuhiti.

REACHING OUT

By establishing museums for public viewing, the communities are reaching out as never before. Your interest in visiting them will most likely be seen as a compliment by the local people. If you're interested in seeing more than just the museum, ask the museum attendant to suggest a guide who can show you around. Most of these museums have regular guides who are available to lead visitors to notable local sites, such as ruins, sacred caves, lakes, springs, mountain summits, and artisans' shops.

Always volunteer to pay – *donar al museo* (donate to the museum) – for such services. If necessary, be sure to bring along your own English-speaking guide or a Spanish-speaking friend to interpret.

For details, see museum information in the individual community sections. Also, you might contact Oaxaca state tourism (Av. Juárez 703, west side of El Llano park, Oaxaca City, tel. 951/516-0123, www.aoaxaca.com., info@aoaxaca.com, 8 A.M.-8 P.M. daily).

sebastian_oaxaca@hotmail.com, $20/hour). He offers tours of anywhere you would like to go in the Valley of Oaxaca.

Another promising guide option is **Judith Reyes López** (B&B Oaxaca Ollin, Quintana Roo 213, tel./fax 951/514-9126, judithreyes37@hotmail.com or reservations@ oaxacaollin.com, www.oaxacaollin.com), who operates through her Art and Tradition tours. Judith offers tours ranging from half-day city tours and whole-day Valley of Oaxaca archaeological and crafts-village outings to farther-reaching explorations of the art and architecture of venerable Dominican churches in the Mixteca. Contact her at her bed-and-breakfast, Oaxaca Ollin, a block north and a block east of the Centro Cultural de Santo Domingo.

On the other hand, folks interested in the exceedingly diverse natural world of Oaxaca might appreciate a tour led by biologist Fredy Carrizal Rosales, owner-operator of **Tourism Service in Ecosystems** (tel. 951/515 3305, in-town cell tel. 044-951/164-1897, ecologiaoaxaca@yahoo.com.mx). Fredy offers customized explorations of many Oaxaca locations—pine-oak woodlands, coastal mangrove wetlands, semi-desert highlands, lush coastal foothill forest coffee plantations—viewing and identifying plants and animals and enjoying nature in general

Customized explorations of Oaxaca's indigenous communities, traditions, and natural treasures are the specialty of native Zapotec guide Florencio Moreno, who operates **Academic Tours in Oaxaca** (Nieve 208A, Colonia Reforma, home tel. 951/518-4728, in-town cell tel. 044-951/510-2244, info@ academictoursoaxaca.com, www.academic toursoaxaca.com). Florencio's tours reflect his broad qualifications: fluency in native dialects, historical knowledge, cultural sensitivity, personal connections with indigenous crafts communities, and expertise in wildlife-watching and identification. His excursions can be designed to last a day or a week and include any region of Oaxaca, exploring anything from folk art and hidden archaeological sites to the colorful indigenous markets and festivals of the Mixteca or the Isthmus.

Higher up the economic scale, **commercial guided tours** also provide a hassle-free means of exploring the Valley of Oaxaca. Travel agencies, such as **Viajes Turísticos Mitla** (at Hóstal Santa Rosa, Trujano 201, tel./fax 951/514-7800 or 951/514-7806, fax 951/514-3152), **Viajes Xochitlán** (M. Bravo 210A, tel. 951/514-3271 or 951/514-3628, www.xochitlan-tours .com.mx, oaxaca@xochitlan-tours.com.mx, 9 A.M.–2 P.M. and 4–7 P.M. Mon.–Sat.), and others, offer such tours.

For even more guide recommendations, check at the Oaxaca state **tourist information office** (Av. Juárez 703, west side of El Llano park, tel. 951/516-0123, www.aoxaca.com, info@aoxaca.com, 8 A.M.–8 P.M. daily).

THE VALLEY OF OAXACA

East Side: The Textile Route

The host of colorful enticements along this path could tempt you into many days of delightful exploring. For example, on Saturday you could head out, visiting the great El Tule tree and the weavers' shops in Teotitlán del Valle and continuing east for an overnight at Mitla. Next morning, explore the Mitla ruins, then return, stopping at the hilltop Yagul archaeological site and the Sunday market at Tlacolula. In either direction, going or coming from the city, you could pause for a brief exploration at the Dainzu and Lambityeco roadside archaeological sites.

One more day would allow time to venture past Mitla to the remarkable mountainside springs and limestone mineral deposits at Hierve El Agua. Stay longer and have it all: a two- or three-day stay in a colorful market town, such as Tlacolula, with a side trip to visit the textile market and community museum at Santa Ana

THE VALLEY OF OAXACA

del Valle and also perhaps to a quiet backcountry village, such as San Bartolomé Quialana or San Marcos Tlapazola, south of Tlacolula.

EL TULE AND TLACOCHAHUAYA
◖ Santa María del Tule

El Tule is a gargantuan Mexican *ahuehuete* (cypress), probably the most massive tree in Latin America. Its gnarled, house-size trunk divides into a forest of elephantine limbs that rise to bushy branches reaching 15 stories overhead. The small town of Santa María del Tule, 14 kilometers (nine mi) east of Oaxaca City on Highway 190, seems built around the tree. A crafts market, a church, and the town plaza, where residents celebrate their El Tule with a fiesta on October 7, all surround the beloved 2,000-year-old living giant.

Note: Eastbound Highway 190 to El Tule divides inbound traffic, either to the left along a town bypass, beneath a viaduct, or to the right, passing over the viaduct to the town and the El Tule tree.

Tlacochahuaya

At San Jerónimo Tlacochahuaya (tlah-koh-chah-WYE-yah), about seven kilometers (four mi) east of El Tule, stands the village's pride and joy, the venerable 16th-century **Templo y Ex-Convento de San Jerónimo.** Dominican padres and their native acolytes, under the guidance of Father Jordán de Santa Catalina, began its construction in 1586 and completed it a few decades later.

Tlacochahuaya is usually a quiet little town except during holidays, notably the eight days of processions, dances, fireworks, and food that climax on September 30, the feast day of San Jerónimo.

The church's relatively recent 1991 restoration glows so brilliantly, especially from the white baroque facade, that, standing beneath the spreading wild fig tree in the courtyard (or more precisely, atrium), you can feel the facade reflecting the warmth of the late afternoon sun. The atrium appears big enough to assemble a crowd of about 5,000 folks, probably the number of local *indígenas* the padres

© OTTO DUSBABA/123RF.COM

El Tule may be the largest cypress tree in Latin America.

hoped to convert during the 16th century. At the atrium's corners stand the three open-air but arch-roofed chapels, or *pozas,* where the conversions took place.

Above the entrance portal, see San Jerónimo standing piously, his left hand on a skull, listening for the voice of God. Inside, glance upward at the lovely nave ceiling and appreciate the still-vital spirit of those long-dead artists who created its flowery, multicolored swirls. Look for the group of oil paintings depicting the legend of the **Virgin of Guadalupe,** with the last showing the roses miraculously tumbling from Juan Diego's cape, emblazoned with her image.

Once when I visited, near the entrance was the pledge of the Sacerdote de Cristo (Priest of Christ), which, translated, reads:

The priest of Christ offers
THIS MASS
As if it were your
FIRST MASS
As if it were your
ONLY MASS
As if it were your
LAST MASS

Get there by car, guide, or the Sociedad Cooperativa Valle del Norte or Fletes y Pasajes local bus from the *camionera central segunda clase* in Oaxaca City.

DAINZU AND LAMBITYECO ARCHAEOLOGICAL SITES

Among the several Valley of Oaxaca buried cities, Dainzu and Lambityeco, both beside Highway 190, are the most accessible. Dainzu comes first, on the right, about nine kilometers (six mi) east of El Tule.

Dainzu

Dainzu (in Zapotec, "Hill of the Organ Cactus"; Hwy. 190, no phone, 10 A.M.–5 P.M. daily, $3) spreads over an approximate half-mile square, consisting of a partly restored ceremonial center surrounded by clusters of unexcavated mounds. Beyond that, on the west side, a stream runs through fields, which

at Dainzu's apex (around A.D. 300) supported a town of about 1,000 inhabitants.

The major excavation, at the foot of the hill about a hundred yards south of the parking lot, reveals more than 30 bas-reliefs of ball players draped with leather head, arm, and torso protectors. Downhill, to the west, lies the partly reconstructed complex of courtyards, platforms, and stairways. The northernmost of these was excavated to reveal a tomb, with a carved door supporting a jaguar head on the lintel and arms—note the claws extending down along the stone doorjambs. The jaguar's face, with a pair of curious vampire teeth and curly nostrils, appears so bat-like that some investigators have speculated that it may represent a composite jaguar-bat god.

A couple of hundred yards diagonally southwest you'll find the ball court running east–west in the characteristic I-shaped layout, with a pair of "scoring" niches at each end and flanked by a pair of stone-block grandstand-like seats. Actually, archaeologists know that these were not seats, because the blocks were once stuccoed over, forming a pair of smooth inclined planes (probably used for glancing shots) flanking the central playing area.

Lambityeco

Ten kilometers (six mi) farther, Lambityeco (Hwy. 190, 10 A.M.–5 P.M. daily) is on the right, a few miles past the Teotitlán del Valle side road. The excavated portion, only about 100 yards square, is a small but significant part of Yegui (Small Hill in Zapotec), a large buried town dotted with hundreds of unexcavated mounds covering about half a square mile. Salt-making appears to have been the main occupation of Yegui people during the town's heyday, around A.D. 700. The name "Lambityeco" may derive from the Arabic-Spanish *alambique,* the equivalent of the English "alembic," or distillation or evaporation apparatus. This would explain the intriguing presence of more than 200 local mounds. It's tempting to speculate that they are the remains of *cujetes,* raised leaching beds still used in Mexico for concentrating brine, which workers subsequently evaporate into salt.

In the present small restored zone archaeologists have uncovered, besides the remains of the Valley of Oaxaca's earliest known *temazcal* (a curative hot room), a number of fascinating ceramic sculptures. Next to the parking lot, a platform, mound 195, rises above ground level. If, after entering through the gate, you climb up its partially restored slope and look down into the excavated hollow in the adjacent east courtyard, you'll see stucco friezes of a pair of regal, lifelike faces, one male and one female, presumably of the personages who were found buried in the royal grave (Tomb 6) below. Experts believe this to be the case, because the man was depicted with the symbol of his right to rule—a human femur bone,

probably taken, as was the custom, from the grave of his chieftain father.

Mound 190, sheltered beneath the adjacent large corrugated roof about 50 yards to the south, contains a restored platform decorated by a pair of remarkably lifelike, nearly identical divine stucco masks. These are believed to be of Zapotec rain god Cocijo (see the water flowing from the mouths). Notice also the rays, perhaps lightning, representing power, in one hand, and flowers, for fertility, in the other.

◖ TEOTITLÁN DEL VALLE

Teotitlán del Valle (pop. 5,000), 14 kilometers (nine mi) east of El Tule, at the foot of the northern Sierra, means "Place of the Gods" in Nahuatl; before that, it was known, appropriately, as Xa Quire (shah KEE-ray), or "Foot of the Mountain," by the Zapotecs who settled it at least 2,000 years ago (by archaeologists' estimate). From the age of artifacts uncovered beneath both the present town and at nearby sites, experts estimate that approximately 1,000 people were living in Teotitlán by A.D. 400.

Present-day Teotitlán people are relatively well off, not only from sales of their renowned *tapetes* (wool rugs), but from their rich communal landholdings. Besides a sizable swath of valley-bottom farmland and pasture, which every Teotitlán family is entitled to use, the community owns a dam and reservoir and a small kingdom of approximately 100,000 acres of sylvan mountain forest and meadow, spreading for about 32 kilometers (20 mi) along the Valley of Oaxaca's lush northeastern foothills.

Getting Oriented

Teotitlán del Valle has two principal streets: Juárez, the entrance road, which runs northerly about four kilometers (2.5 mi) from the highway; and Hidalgo, which intersects Juárez at the center of town. Turn right at Hidalgo (where the pavement becomes cobbled) and you'll be looking east, toward the town plaza and the 17th-century town church behind it.

Textile Shops

Nearly every Teotitlán house is a mini-factory

TOWN NAMES

Town names in Oaxaca (and in Mexico) generally come in two pieces: an original native name accompanied by the name of the town's patron saint. Very typical is the case of San Jerónimo Tlacochahuaya, a sleepy but famous little place. Combining both the saint's name (here, San Jerónimo) and the native name (here, Tlacochahuaya) often makes for very unwieldy handles; so, many towns are known only by one name, usually the native name. Thus, in the west side of the Valley of Oaxaca, San Jerónimo Tlacochahuaya, Santa María del Tule, Tlacolula de Matamoros, and San Pablo Villa de Mitla, for example, are commonly called Tlacochahuaya, El Tule, Tlacolula, and Mitla, respectively.

Nevertheless, sometimes a town's full name is customarily used. This is especially true when a single name – such as Etla, northwest of Oaxaca City – identifies an entire district, and thus many towns, such as San Agustín Etla, San Sebastián Etla, and San José Etla, must necessarily be identified with their full names. In this book, although we may mention the formal name once on a map or in the text, we generally conform to local, customary usage for town names.

© BRUCE WHIPPERMAN

THE VALLEY OF OAXACA

The Teotitlán del Valle church is built on the original Zapotec temple's foundation.

where people card, spin, and color wool, often using hand-gathered natural dyes. Each step of wool preparation is laborious; obtaining pure water is even a chore—families typically spend two days a week collecting it from mountain springs. The weaving, on traditional handlooms, is the final, satisfying part of the process. The best weaving is generally the densest, typically packing in about 18 strands per centimeter (45 strands per inch); ordinary weaving incorporates about half that. Please don't bargain too hard. Even the highest prices typically bring the weavers less than a dollar an hour for their labor.

Visiting the workshop-stores should be first on your itinerary. The home workshops, once confined to the town center, now sprinkle nearly the entire mile-long entrance road. Half a kilometer (about 0.25 mi) from Highway 190, be sure to visit the cooperative shop **Mujeres Que Tejan** (Women Who Weave; Juárez, old number 86, new number 162, tel. 951/166-6174), on the right side. The shop is managed by welcoming sparkplug Josefina Jiménez and displays the fine for-sale woven products of 28 women weavers.

In the town center, also be sure not to miss the shop of renowned master **Isaac ("Bug in the Rug") Vasquez** (turn left at main cross-street Hidalgo, number 30, tel. 951/524-4122, 10 A.M.–6 P.M. daily).

A number of Teotitlán workshops are especially welcoming. For example, step into the workshop-restaurant-hotel **El Descanso** (Juárez 51, tel. 951/524-4152, 8 A.M.–7 P.M. Mon.–Sat., 8 A.M.–3 P.M. Sun.), at the town-center corner of Juárez and Hidalgo.

Also well worth a visit is the charming garden shop of friendly **Luis Martínez Jiménez** (Juárez 48, tel. in Oaxaca city, 951/516-1675), on the main street. (Luis also arranges very reasonably priced tours by car, check with him at petite Oaxaca City shop: Macedonio Alacalá 402, at the Santo Domingo church corner.)

For some good Teotitlán del Valle tips, visit Ron Mader's super website (www.planeta.com/ecotravel/mexico/oaxaca/teotitlan.html).

Community Museum

Allow enough time to visit the community museum **Balaa Xtee Guech Gulal** (Hidalgo, tel. 951/524-4463, 10 A.M.–6 P.M. Tues.–Sun., $3), whose name translates from the local Zapotec as "Shadow of the Old Town." It's on the north

THE VALLEY OF OAXACA

© BRUCE WHIPPERMAN

woolen weavings for sale in Teotitlán del Valle

side of Hidalgo, about a block east of Juárez. Step inside and enjoy the excellent exhibits that illustrate local history, industry, and customs. One display shows the wool-weaving tradition (introduced by the Dominican padres, that replaced the indigenous cotton-weaving craft), including sources of some natural dyes—*cochinilla* (red cochineal), *musgo* (yellow moss and lichens), *anil* (dark blue indigo), and *quizache* bean (black). Another exhibit shows the local practice of a prospective groom's service to the bride's parents. A house mock-up shows the prospective bride making tortillas. Be sure to get a copy of the good English-language explanatory pamphlet.

A Walk Around Town

If you ask, a community museum volunteer may be available to lead you on a walking tour of the town and environs. English-speaking Zeferino Mendoza is especially recommended. Walking tour highlights often include visits to weavers' homes, the church, a traditional *temazcal*, the recently reconstructed foundation stones of the ancient town, the dam and

lake, and the hike to Picacho, the peak above the town's west side.

Lacking a guide, simply stroll out on your own self-guided tour. After seeing the community museum, head east on Hidalgo. If you haven't already, take a look around the plaza-front textile stalls, then continue to the **Templo de la Precioso Sangre de Cristo** (Church of the Precious Blood of Christ). This is the central location for both the **patronal festival** (July 1–15) and the **Fiesta del Señor de La Natividad** (Festival of the Lord of the Nativity; first Sun. in Sept.), which include processions, fireworks, and the spectacular Danza de las Plumas (Dance of the Feathers).

The Teotitlán Church

The church itself, built over an earlier Zapotec temple, contains many interesting pre-Columbian stones, which the Dominican friars allowed to be incorporated into its walls. Notice the corn motif carved into the front doorway arch, similar in style to the monolith built into the outside wall at the right of the church entrance steps. Inside, admire the nave's

© BRUCE WHIPPERMAN

THE VALLEY OF OAXACA

the Dance of the Feathers

flowery overhead decorations and the colorful Bible-story paintings. Continue from the nave into the intimate *claustro* (cloister) and see the Zapotec god of the wind, with stone curls curving upward to represent the wind (on the southwest corner column, to the right as you enter from the nave).

Outside, behind the church, continue to the reconstructed foundation corner, on the street, downhill, of the original **Zapotec temple.** Notice the uniquely Zapotec stone fretwork, similar to the famous *Greca* remains at Mitla, 32 kilometers (20 mi) farther east.

Farther Afield

If you have time, you can venture even farther afield. One option is to walk or drive along the bumpy, but passable, uphill gravel continuation of main street Juárez about 1.6 kilometers (one mi) to the **town dam.** After the summer rains, the reservoir fills and forms a scenic lake, good for swimming, picnicking, and even possibly camping, along its pastoral mountain-view shoreline. If you plan to camp at the Teotitlán reservoir, first ask for permission

at the community museum (Hidalgo, tel. 951/524-4463, 10 A.M.–6 P.M. Tues.–Sun.) or the *presidencia municipal* (951/524-4123, www .teotitlandelvalle.gob.mx).

Travelers can extend their Teotitlán adventure all the way into the neighboring mountains. From the Teotitlán reservoir, hike (be prepared with water, good shoes, and a hat), hitchhike, taxi, or drive about 19 more kilometers (12 mi) uphill (with an elevation gain of 1,500 meters/5,000 feet) along the good gravel road to pine-shadowed **Benito Juárez** and **Cuajimoloyas** mountain hamlets in northern Oaxaca.

Back at the Teotitlán reservoir, you can also venture up the slope of **Picacho,** the steep, peaked hill 1.6 kilometers (one mi) west of town. The usual route from town is along Calle 2 de Abril, which heads west, bridging the west-side arroyo. Continue uphill, bearing right at the fork, on to the dirt road at the base of the hill. First you'll pass some houses, then continue, curving left around the hillside. Eventually, before the summit, you'll pass some *cuevitas* (small caves), a holy site where local folks have been gathering for sacred ceremonies each New Year's Day since before anyone can remember.

Accommodations and Food

Sample Teotitlán's best at the traditional **Tlamanalli** restaurant (on Juárez, about a block south of Hidalgo, no phone, 1–4 P.M. daily except possibly Mon. and Thurs., longer hours when more people stop by, $5–10). Their menu of made-to-order Zapotec specialties, such as *sopa de calabaza* (squash soup) and *guisado de pollo* (chicken stew) is limited, but highly recommended by Oaxaca City chefs.

If Tlamanalli is closed, go to the inviting **Restaurant El Descanso** (Juárez 51, tel. 951/524-4152, weaving shop and restaurant 8 A.M.–7 P.M. Mon.–Sat., 8 A.M.–3 P.M. Sun.; lodging $40 d). Your hosts will be the welcoming family of Edmundo and Alicia Montaño, who, besides crafting and selling lovely wool weavings, also serve tasty country fare and offer a number of rooms that open on to their leafy and lovely inner garden-patio. Choices include king-size, regular double, and single beds.

Alternatively, for a lunch or early dinner treat, stop at showplace **⟨ Restaurant El Patio** (Hwy. 190, 1.2 km/0.8 mile east of the Teotitlán entrance road, tel. 951/514-4889, 10 A.M.–6 P.M. Tues.–Sun.). The restaurant centers around an airy patio, decorated by antique country furniture and a fetching gallery of scenes from the 1940s-era films of the Mexican Golden Age of cinema. The finale is the food: tasty traditional Oaxacan dishes, such as *ensalada Oaxaqueña,* Zapotec soup, and the house specialty *botana* Don Pepe.

Getting There

You can go to Teotitlán del Valle by car, tour, taxi, or bus. Drivers: Simply turn left from Highway 190 at the signed Teotitlán del Valle side road, 14 kilometers (nine mi) east of El Tule. By bus: Ride a **Fletes y Pasajes** Tlacolula- or Mitla-bound bus from the *camionera central segunda clase* (in Oaxaca City by the Abastos market at the end of Las Casas, past the *periférico* west of downtown). Alternatively, ride the hourly **Valle del Norte** bus from the *camionera central segunda clase* parking lot. Get off at the signed bus stop and walk, taxi, or hitchhike the four kilometers (2.5 mi) into town.

SANTA ANA DEL VALLE

This is a sleepier version of Teotitlán del Valle, where virtually every family speaks the Zapotec tongue at home and earns at least part of its living through weaving. Many older folks understand Spanish only with difficulty. Santa Ana del Valle, like Teotitlán, has thousands of acres of communal lands in the valley bottom and mountains north of the town. Nearly all households tend plots of corn, beans, and vegetables. Most also graze cattle, sheep, and goats in specified communal areas. These lands have been traditionally held by the town since before the conquest. Families may buy or sell shares of their allotted land, but only within the Santa Ana del Valle community.

Community Museum

Your first stop should be at the excellent community museum **Shan Dany** (tel. 951/562-1705, 11 A.M.–3 P.M. and 4–7 P.M. Mon.–Sat.), on the town plaza opposite the *presidencia municipal.* The exhibits include an archaeological section with pre-conquest remains found during a recent plaza-front construction project. Also notice the ponderous monolith, brought from the mountain above town, carved with the visage of Cocijo, the god of lightning and rain. Another museum section details 1910–1917 revolutionary history, when townsfolk had to flee to the hills and wage a guerrilla war against rampaging forces of "Primer Jefe" General Venustiano Carranza.

Toward the rear of the museum, a pair of excellent displays illustrate more community lore: one shows many of the naturally occurring dyes, including avocado seeds, *guaje* bark, and *copal* bark, that local weavers gather and use; the other explains the Danza de la Pluma (Dance of the Feathers), in which a dozen young men dance and brighten the town plaza with their huge, round feathered hats. This dance takes place during the July 26 and August 14–16 split-date festival in honor of Santa Ana.

A Walk Around Town

Ask and a museum volunteer may be able to find a guide (offer to pay) to lead you on a two- or three-hour *recorrido* (tour) around town, including the *presa* (dam and small reservoir); a creek, where you can cool off during the summer rainy season (bring your bathing suit); a breezy *mirador* (viewpoint) for a spectacular valley vista; and an old gold, silver, and copper mine. During the walk, your guide might identify and explain the uses of the many medicinal plants along the path. Be sure to ask them to point out the poison oak–like *mala mujer* (bad woman) bush to you. Finally, ask them to take you to shops of outstanding local weavers for demonstrations and possible purchases of their work.

If you can't get a guide, you can still do most of the walk on your own. The path to the dam takes off from Calle Plan de Ayala, on the east, uphill side of town. After about 0.8 kilometers (0.5 mi), bear left, around the hill. If you get confused, ask a younger person (they're most likely to understand Spanish), *"¿Donde está la presa"* (PRAY-sah), *"por favor?"* The viewpoint, the big moss-mottled rock about halfway up the steep, left-hand slope, sticks out of the hillside above the path to the dam.

Accommodations

The comfortable Santa Ana del Valle tourist ◖ **cabaña ecoturística** is at Calle Moreles #2, on the entrance road to town. It is well situated for exploring, being just a few blocks from the center of town. The nightly rate is approximately $30 for one to four people, with toilet, hot-water shower-bath, and two double or bunk beds. Reserve at the community museum (on the town plaza, tel. 951/562-1705, 11 A.M.–3 P.M. and 4–7 P.M. Mon.–Sat.), either in person or by telephone.

Shopping

Although Santa Ana del Valle weavers sell much of their work through shops in Teotitlán del Valle and Oaxaca City, they also sell directly in town, from both the **Mercado de Artesanías** on the town plaza and their home workshops. For suggestions of who to visit, ask at the community

museum (on the town plaza, tel. 951/562-1705), or go directly to **Casa Martínez** (Matamoros 3, corner of V. Carranza, tel. 951/562-0366), the house of personable master weaver Ernesto Martínez. His house is around the corner, a few doors downhill from the town plaza. You'll also be welcome at the home shop of the friendly weaving family of **Alberto Sánchez Garcia** (Sor Juanes Inés de la Cruz 1, no phone), a few blocks from the town plaza.

For some good Santa Ana del Valle tips, visit Ron Mader's super website (www.planeta.com/ecotravel/mexico/oaxaca/santana.html).

Getting There

You can go to Santa Ana del Valle by car, tour, taxi, or bus. Drivers: Turn left at the fork across Highway 190 from the Tlacolula Pemex *gasolinera* 38 kilometers (24 mi) east of Oaxaca City. After 0.8 kilometers (0.5 mi), turn left again at the signed Santa Ana del Valle side road. Continue another few minutes; pass the tourist *cabaña ecoturística* on the right, and arrive at the town plaza a few blocks farther. By bus, you can ride a Tlacolula- or Mitla-bound bus from the *camionera central segunda clase* in Oaxaca City by the Abastos market (end of Las Casas, west of downtown). Get off at the Tlacolula stop on Highway 190 by the Pemex station. Cross to the side road on the north side of the highway and take a taxi, ride the Transportes Municipal del Santa Ana del Valle local bus, or hike the 6.4 kilometers (four mi) from the highway—walk the side road 0.8 kilometers (0.5 mi) to a signed Santa Ana del Valle fork; go left and continue for 3.2 more kilometers (two mi), passing the *cabaña ecoturística,* at Calle Moreles #2, on the right, and then on to the town plaza a few blocks farther.

TLACOLULA

The Zapotec people who founded Tlacolula (pop. 15,000, 38 km/24 mi east from Oaxaca City) around A.D. 1250 called it Guichiibaa ("Place Between Heaven and Earth"). Besides its beloved church and chapel and famous Sunday market, Tlacolula is also renowned for mescal, a Tequila-like alcoholic beverage distilled from the fermented hearts of maguey. Get a good free sample at the friendly **Pensamiento shop** (Juárez 9, tel. 951/562-0017, 9 A.M.–7 P.M. daily), about four blocks from the highway gasoline station (along Juárez) toward the market. Besides many hand-embroidered Amusgo *huipiles* and Teotitlán weavings, proprietor Guadalupe Pensamiento offers fruit and spice-flavored mescal, which, at this writing, came in 40 flavors, 16 for men and 24 for women.

Just before the market, take a look inside the main town church, the 1531 **Parroquia de la Virgen de la Asunción.** Although its interior is distinguished enough, the real gem is its attached chapel, **Capilla del Señor de Tlacolula,** which you enter from the nave of the church. Every inch of the chapel's interior gleams with sculptures of angels and saints, paintings, and gold scrollwork. Notice the pair of floating angels, each holding a great pendulous solid silver censer, on opposite sides of the altar; also, admire the solid silver fence in front of the altar. Saints seem to live on in every corner of the chapel. Especially graphic are the martyrs, who reveal the way they died, such as a sorrowful San Sebastián, his body shot full of arrows, and a decapitated San Pablo, above the right transept, his head on the ground.

Ordinarily tranquil, the church grounds seem to nearly burst with the faithful during the five-day **Fiesta del Santa Cristo de Tlacolula,** climaxing on the second Sunday of October, when the plaza is awash with merrymakers. It is then that folks enjoy their favorites, the **Danza de los Jardineros** (Dance of the Gardeners) and the spectacular **Danza de las Plumas** (Dance of the Feathers), along with a *pelota mixteca* (traditional Mixtec ball game) tournament.

The big gate bordering the church grounds leads you to the Tlacolula **market.** One of Oaxaca's biggest and oldest, the Tlacolula market draws tens of thousands from all over the Valley of Oaxaca every Sunday. Wander around and soak it all in—the diverse crowd of buyers and sellers, and the equally manifold galaxy of merchandise. How about a hand-hewn yoke for your oxen, or a new stone *mano* (roller) and *metate* (flat stone) for your kitchen? If not, perhaps some live (or ground) *chapulines* (grasshoppers), maybe a live turkey for dinner tomorrow, or a hunk of sugarcane to chew on while you stroll?

For food and accommodations, try the basic but clean downtown Tlacolula lodging, the **Hotel and Restaurant Calenda** (Juárez 40, tel. 951/562-0660, food $3–8, lodging $20 s or d, $30 t). They offer about 30 rooms with fans and hot-water shower-baths in three floors around an interior restaurant courtyard. Their restaurant serves a wholesome country menu that, although specializing in *barbacoa pollo, chivo,* or *borrego* (barbecue chicken, goat, or lamb), offers many more hearty choices, such as pork chops, spaghetti, eggs, fish, and chiles rellenos.

YAGUL ARCHAEOLOGICAL ZONE

The regal remains of Yagul (Zapotec for "Old Tree"; 45 km/28 mi east of Oaxaca City, just north of Hwy. 190, 10 A.M.–5 P.M. daily, $3) preside atop their volcanic hilltop. Although only 12 kilometers (7.5 mi) from Mitla and sharing architectural details, such as Mitla's famous *Greca* fretwork, the size and complexity of its buildings suggest that Yagul was an independent city-state in its own right. Local folks call the present ruin the Pueblo Viejo (Old Town) and remember it as the forerunner of the present town of Tlacolula. Archaeological evidence, which indicates that Yagul was occupied for about a thousand years, at least until around A.D. 1100 or 1200, bears them out.

One of Yagul's major claims to fame is its **Palace of Six Patios,** actually three nearly identical but separate complexes of two patios each. In each patio, rooms surround a central courtyard. The northerly patio of each complex is more private and probably was the residence, while the other, more open patio served administrative functions.

South of the palace sprawls Yagul's huge **ball court,** the second largest in Mesoamerica, shaped in the characteristic Oaxaca I configuration. Southeast of the ball court is Patio 4, consisting of four mounds surrounding a courtyard. A boulder sculpted in the form of a frog lies at the base of the east mound. At the courtyard's center, a tomb was excavated; descend and explore its three *greca*-style, fretwork-decorated chambers.

If it's not too hot, gather your energy and climb to the hilltop above the parking lot for a fine view of the ruin and the entire Valley of Oaxaca. The name for this prominence—the Citadel—was probably accurately descriptive, for Yagul's defenders long ago added rock walls to enhance the hilltop's security.

◖ MITLA

The ruins at Mitla (Hwy. 176, about 57 km/35 mi east of Oaxaca City, 8 A.M.–5 P.M. daily, $5) are a "must" for Valley of Oaxaca sightseers. Mitla (Liobaa in Zapotec, the "Place of the Dead") flowered late, reaching a population of perhaps 10,000 during its apex around A.D. 1350. It remained occupied and in use for generations after the conquest.

During Mitla's heyday, several feudalistic, fortified city-states vied for power in the Valley of Oaxaca. Concurrently, Mixtec-speaking people arrived from the north, perhaps under pressure from Aztecs and others in central Mexico. Evidence suggests that these Mixtec groups, in interacting with the resident Zapotecs, created the unique architectural styles of late cities such as Yagul and Mitla. Archaeologists believe, for example, that the striking *Greca* (Grecian-style) frets that honeycomb Mitla facades are the result of Mixtec influence.

Exploring the Site

In a real sense, Mitla lives on. The ruins coincide with the present town of San Pablo Villa de Mitla, whose main church actually occupies the northernmost of five main groups of monumental ruins. Virtually anywhere archaeologists dig within the town they hit remains of the myriad ancient dwellings, plazas, and tombs that connected the still-visible landmarks.

Get there by forking left from main Oaxaca Highway 190 onto Highway 176. Continue about two miles to the Mitla town entrance,

THE VALLEY OF OAXACA

© BRUCE WHIPPERMAN

Hundreds of thousands of pieces of *Greca* stone fretwork make up Mitla's magnificent buildings.

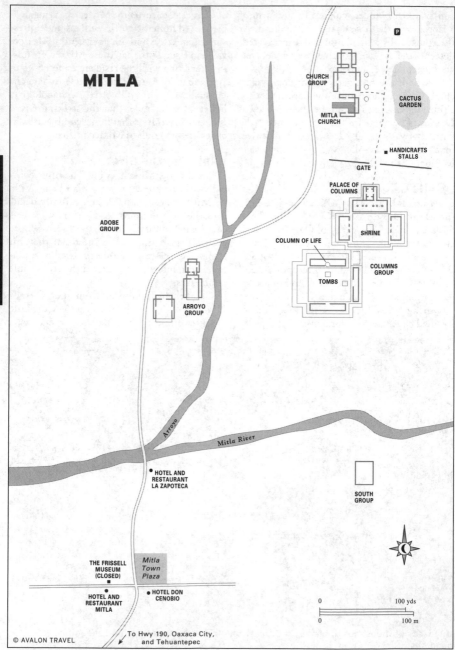

MITLA

CHURCH GROUP

MITLA CHURCH

P

CACTUS GARDEN

HANDICRAFTS STALLS

GATE

PALACE OF COLUMNS

SHRINE

COLUMN OF LIFE

COLUMNS GROUP

TOMBS

ADOBE GROUP

ARROYO GROUP

Arroyo

Mitla River

HOTEL AND RESTAURANT LA ZAPOTECA

SOUTH GROUP

THE FRISSELL MUSEUM (CLOSED)

Mitla Town Plaza

HOTEL AND RESTAURANT MITLA

HOTEL DON CENOBIO

0   100 yds

0   100 m

To Hwy 190, Oaxaca City, and Tehuantepec

© AVALON TRAVEL

on the left. Head straight through town, cross a bridge, and, after about a mile, arrive at the site. Of the five ruins clusters, the best preserved is the fenced-in Columns Group. Its exploration requires about an hour. Three of the others—the Arroyo and Adobe Groups beyond an arroyo, and the South Group across the Mitla River—are rubbly, unreconstructed mounds. Evidence indicates the Adobe and South Groups were ceremonial compounds, while the Arroyo, Church, and Columns Groups were palaces.

The interesting **Church Group** (marked by the monumental columns that you pass first on your right after the parking lot) is on the far north side of the Palace of Columns. Builders used the original temple stones to erect the church here. Although the Church Group has suffered from past use by the local parish, it deserves a few minutes' look around inside. It consists of a pair of regal courtyards, labeled A and B, adjacent to the triple red-domed 16th century church. You first enter courtyard B, enclosed by monumental stone-framed doorways. A passageway leads to smaller courtyard A, where you can see the fascinating remnants of the red hieroglyphic paintings of personages, name-dates, and glyphs that once covered its walls.

Back outside, on the main entrance path, continue past the tourist market and through the gate to the **Columns Group.** Inside, two large patios, joined at one corner, are each surrounded on three sides by elaborate apartments. A shrine occupies the center of the first patio. Just north of this stands the **Palace of Columns,** the most important of Mitla's buildings. It sits atop a staircase, inaccurately reconstructed in 1901.

Inside, a file of six massive monolithic columns supported the roof. A narrow "escape" passage exits out the right rear side to a large patio enclosed by a continuous narrow room. The purely decorative *Greca* facades, which required around 100,000 cut stones for the Columns Group complex, decorate the walls. Remnants of the original red and white stucco that lustrously embellished the entire complex hide in niches and corners.

Walk south to the second patio, which has a

THE MYSTERY OF MITLA'S FRISSELL MUSEUM

The Frissell Museum (a block west of the town entrance road, by the Mitla town plaza) has been closed since 1995, presumably for remodeling. Even worse, sometime between 1995 and 2007, the museum's entire priceless 40,000-80,000 piece collection (such as masterfully carved ceramic figurines, yet-to-be-deciphered Zapotec glyphs, and a Zapotec marriage certificate in stone) disappeared. Local folks shake their heads when they sadly report that none of the stolen artifacts have yet been recovered.

Besides its collection, the museum's venerable hacienda-style home is notable in its own right. From the mid-19th century, as the **Posada La Sorpresa,** it served as a lodging, owned and operated by the longtime local Quero family. In 1950, they sold it to American artifact collector Edwin R. Frissell, who turned the hotel into both his home and a re-pository for his growing collection and that of his friend, Howard Leigh, noted scholar of Mixtec language and culture. Upon their deaths, the entire building and artifact collection passed to the Mexico City University of the Americas.

In 2001, Mitla residents, notably Rufino A. Quero, descendant of the historic owners, suspected foul play and hired attorneys to investigate. By 2007 they had gathered enough evidence to denounce the "sacking" of the collection and hinted that Oaxaca state officials were responsible. In 2008, they filed legal charges, and in 2009 a group of local residents petitioned the National Institute for Archaeology and History (INAH) to return at least 30 percent of the collection. Meanwhile, local folks wait and hope that their cherished, lost legacy will someday be returned home.

similar layout. Here the main palace occupies the east side, where a passage descends to a tomb beneath the front staircase. Both this and another tomb, beneath the building at the north side of the patio, are intact, preserving their original crucifix shapes. (The guard, although he is not supposed to, may try to collect a tip for letting you descend.) No one knows for certain who and what were buried in these tombs, which were open and empty at the time of the conquest.

The second tomb is similar, except that it contains a stone pillar called the **Column of Life;** by embracing it, legend says, you will learn how many years you have left.

Fiesta del Apóstol de San Pablo

Mitla (pop. 15,000), although famous, is a quiet town where tranquility is disturbed only by occasional tourist buses along its dusty, sun-drenched main street. A major exception occurs during Mitla's key fiesta, which centers on the town's venerable 16th-century church, dedicated to San Pablo Apóstol (St. Paul the Apostle). If you plan your visit during the eight days climaxing around January 25 (or also around June 29, the day of St. Pablo and St. Pedro), you can join with the townsfolk as they celebrate their *patrón* with masses, processions, a feast, fireworks, *jaripeo* (bull roping and riding), and dancing.

Accommodations and Food

Stop for a refreshment at the homey **Hotel and Restaurant Mitla** (Benito Juárez 6, tel. 951/568-0112, cell tel. 044-951/115-5676, food 8 A.M.–7 P.M. daily; lodging $15 s, $22 d), domain of the sparkplug mother-daughter team of Teresa and Gloria González de Quero. Here you can enjoy Mexico as old-timers remember it, in a charmingly ramshackle hacienda-style farmhouse, where roosters crow, dogs snooze, and guests can have their seasonal fill of bananas, avocados, mandarins, and zapotes from a shady backyard *huerta* (orchard). Their 16 rooms vary. Most rooms in the upstairs tier—plain but clean (if you don't look too hard), with the essentials, including hot water—are acceptably rustic.

Diagonally across the plaza from the museum is the shiny, four-star neo-colonial-style **Don Cenobio Banquet Salon and Hotel** (Benito Juárez 3, tel. 951/568-0330, fax 951/568-0050, informes@hoteldoncenobio.com, www.hoteldoncenobio.com, $70 d), with about 20 beautifully decorated rooms built around a large, inviting pool and grassy patio. Guests enjoy a wealth of facilities, including a restaurant and banquet hall for 500 people. Rooms come with air-conditioning, cable TV, queen and king-size beds, and much more. The only drawback to all of this is that they rent the place out to hundreds for conferences and parties quite often. Best to check by telephone before reserving an overnight.

Alternatively, about five blocks north, closer to the archaeological zone, try the family-run **(Hotel and Restaurant La Zapoteca** (5 de Febrero 12, tel. 951/568-0026, ivettsita_revelde@hotmail.com, food 8 A.M.–6 P.M. daily; lodging $15 s, $20 d, $27 t), on the right just before the Río Mitla bridge. The spic-and-span restaurant, praised by locals for "the best mole negro and chiles rellenos in Oaxaca," is fine for meals, and the 20 clean, reasonably priced rooms, with hot water, in-house Internet, and parking, are good for an overnight.

Shopping

Instead of making handicrafts, Mitla people concentrate on selling them, mostly at the big **handicrafts market** adjacent to the archaeological zone parking lot. Here you can sample from a concentrated all-Oaxaca assortment, especially textiles: cotton *huipiles,* wool hangings and rugs, onyx animals and chess sets, fanciful *alebrijes* (wooden animals), and leather huaraches, purses, belts, and wallets.

Getting There

Bus travelers can get to Mitla from Oaxaca City by Fletes y Pasajes or Oaxaca-Istmo bus from the *camionera central segunda clase.* Drivers get there by forking left from main Oaxaca Highway 190, at the big Mitla sign, onto Highway 176. Continue about 3.2 kilometers (two mi) to the Mitla town entrance, on the left. Turn left, and head straight past the town plaza. Continue across the bridge over the (usually dry) Río Mitla, and after about 1.6 kilometers (one mi), arrive at the archaeological site.

HIERVE EL AGUA MINERAL SPRINGS

Although the name of this place translates as boiling water, the springs that seep from the side of the limestone mountain less than an hour's drive east of Mitla aren't hot. Instead, they are loaded with minerals. These minerals over time have built up into rock-hard deposits, forming great algae-painted slabs in level spots and, on steep slopes, accumulating into what appear to be grand frozen waterfalls. *Note:* A local community dispute has unfortunately led to periodic closures of the Hierve El Agua park. Before planning a visit, check at the Oaxaca state tourist information office (Av. Juárez 703, west side of El Llano park, tel. 951/516-0123, 8 A.M.–8 P.M. daily, info@aoaxaca.com, www .aoxaca.com, 8 A.M.–8 P.M. daily). You can also consult with a tour agency or guide, such as the excellent **Juan Montes Lara** (tel/fax 951/513-0126, cell 951/170-3239).

The Springs

Although Hierve El Agua (9 A.M.–6 P.M. daily, $2) may be crowded on weekends and holidays, you'll probably have the place nearly to yourself on weekdays. The first thing you'll see after passing the entrance gate is a lineup of snack and curio stalls at the cliff-side parking lot. A trail leads downhill to the main spring, which bubbles from the mountainside and trickles into a huge basin that the operators have dammed as a swimming pool. Bring your bathing suit.

Part of Hierve El Agua's appeal is the panoramic view of mountain and valley. On a clear day, you can see the tremendous massif of Zempoatepetl (saym-poh-ah-TAY-pehtl), the grand holy mountain range of the Mixe people, rising above the eastern horizon.

From the ridge-top park, agile walkers can hike farther down the hill, following deposits curiously accumulated in the shape of miniature limestone dikes that trace the mineral water's downhill path. Soon you'll glimpse a towering limestone formation, like a giant petrified waterfall, appearing to ooze from the cliff downhill straight ahead, on the right.

Back uphill by the parking lot, operators have augmented the natural springs with a resort-style swimming pool, where, along with everyone else, you can frolic to your heart's content.

Hikers can also enjoy following a *sendero peatonal* (footpath) that encircles the entire zone. Start your walk from the trailhead beyond the bungalows past the pool, or at the other end, at the cliff edge between the parking lot and the entrance gate. Your reward will be an approximately one-hour, self-guided tour, looping downhill past the springs and the great frozen rock cascades and featuring grand vistas of the gorgeous mountain and canyon scenery along the way.

The Hierve El Agua zone and surrounding country is habitat for a hardy dry-country palm you'll probably see plenty of while strolling around. Lack of winter–spring moisture usually keeps the palms small, sometimes clustering in great wild gardens, appearing like regiments of desert dwarfs. Local people gather and weave their fronds into *tenates* (baskets), *petates* (mats), *escobas* (brooms), and more, which they sometimes sell in the stalls by the parking lot.

Accommodations and Food

The Hierve El Agua tourist **☾ cabañas ecoturísticas** have in the past provided the key for a restful one- or two-night stay. The several clean and well-maintained housekeeping bungalows, with shower-baths and hot water, rent for about $10 per person, or around $40 for up to six in a bungalow, with refrigerator, stove, and utensils. For information about cabaña reservations, contact the Oaxaca state tourist information office (Av. Juárez 703, west side of El Llano park, tel. 951/516-0123, 8 A.M.–8 P.M. daily, info@aoaxaca.com, www .aoxaca.com, 8 A.M.–8 P.M. daily).

BUILDING CHURCHES

Although European architects designed nearly all of Mexico's colonial-era churches, embellishing them with old-world Gothic, Renaissance, baroque, and Moorish decorations, native artists blended their own geometric, floral, and animal motifs. The result was a hybrid that manifested in intriguing variations all over Mexico. This was especially true in Oaxaca, where faithful droves worship before gilded altars and flowery ceilings built and decorated by their long-gone ancestors. Local materials further distinguish Oaxacan churches from others in Mexico. The spectrum of soft pastels of local *cantera* volcanic stone, from yellow through gray, including green in Oaxaca City, marks Oaxacan walls and facades.

Sometimes the native influence led to poor ("provincial") versions of European designs; other times (notably, the Templo y Ex-Convento de Santo Domingo in Oaxaca City), artists merged brilliant native decorations with the best of European-style vaults, arches, and columns.

THE LAYOUT

Mexican church design followed the Egypto-Greco-Roman tradition of its European models. Basically, architects designed their churches beginning with the main space of the nave, in the shape of a box, lined with high lateral windows. Depending on their origin and function, the churches fit into three basic groups – the monk's **convento** (monastery or convent), the bishop's **catedral** (cathedral), and the priest's **templo** or **parroquia** (parish church). Most Oaxacan monastic churches (nearly all now ex-convents) were begun during the 16th and 17th centuries by the missionary orders – a handful by the Franciscans, Jesuits, and Augustinians, and the overwhelming remainder by the Dominicans.

In Oaxaca, faced with the constant threat of earthquakes, the Dominican padres built massively thick walls supported on the exterior with ponderous buttresses. Key elements were naves, with or without **cruceros** (transepts), cross spaces separating the nave from the altar, making the church layout resemble a Christian cross. They placed the **coro** (choir) above and just inside the entrance arch.

At the opposite, usually east (or sunrise) end of the church, builders sometimes extended the nave beyond the transept to include a **presbiterio** (presbytery), which was often lined with seats where church officials presided. The building ended past that at the **ábside** (apse), the space behind the altar, frequently in semicircular or half-octagonal form. Within the apse rose the gilded **retablo** (retable or altarpiece) adorned with sacred images, attended by choirs of angels and cherubs.

Larger churches usually incorporated side altars presided over by images of locally popular saints, nearly always including the Virgin of Guadalupe.

THE FACADE

Outside, in front, rises the **fachada** (facade), sometimes in a uniform style, but just as often with a mixture of Renaissance, Gothic, and baroque, with some *mujedar* (Moorish) worked into the mix. A proliferation of columns nearly always decorates Oaxacan church facades, from the classic *Toscano, Dórico, Jónico,* and *Corintio* (Etruscan, Doric, Ionic, and Corinthian) pillars to spiraled *Salomónico* (Solomonic) barber's poles and bizarre *estipites.* The *estipite* columns, a baroque feature of Plateresque facades (so-named for their resemblance to elaborate silverware designs), usually begin with a classical capital (base) but rise, curiously, like an inverted obelisk, widening to a pair or trio of elaborately carved prismatic blocks and narrowing quickly again to an identical capital at the top.

CONVENTS

The monastery- (or convent-) style churches included, in addition to all of the above, living and working quarters for the members of the order, typically built around a columned patio called the **claustro** (cloister). A corridor through an arched **portería** (porch) adjacent to the nave usually leads to the cloister, from which monks and nuns could quickly reach the dining hall, or **refectorio** (refectory), and their private rooms, or **celdas** (cells).

The Oaxacan missionary fathers always designed their churches with an eye to handling the masses of natives whom they hoped to convert. For them, padres included an *atrio* (atrium), a large exterior courtyard in front of the facade. For the partly initiated natives, they often built a *capilla abierta* (open chapel) on one side of the atrium. Conversions also occurred at smaller open chapels called *pozas*, built at the corners of the atrium.

OAXACA STANDOUTS
(an asterisk "*" denotes especially recommended churches)
Outstanding examples (nearly all Dominican) of Oaxacan church architecture are scattered throughout the state, notably in the following locations:

Oaxaca City
- Basilica y Ex-Convento de Nuestra Señora de la Soledad*
- Catedral de Oaxaca*
- Iglesia y Ex-Convento de San Agustín
- Iglesia y Ex-Convento de Santo Domingo*
- Templo de San Felipe Neri

Valley of Oaxaca
- Cuilapan*
- Ocotlán
- Tlacochahuaya
- Tlacolula*

Mixteca
- Coixtlahuaca*
- San Juan Teposcolula
- San Miguel Achiutla*
- Santo Domingo Tonalá
- Tamazulapan
- Tejupan
- Teotongo
- Teposcolula*
- Tlaxiaco*
- Yanhuitlán*

Northern Oaxaca
- Capulalpan*
- Ixtlán de Juárez*
- Santa Catarina Ixtepeji

The Isthmus
- Juchitán
- Tehuántepec*

THE VALLEY OF OAXACA

© TOMAS HAJEK/123RF.COM

Catedral de Oaxaca architectural details

For food, you can bring and cook your own in your bungalow or rely upon the strictly local-style beans, carne asada (roast meat), tacos, tamales, and tortillas offered by the parking-lot food stalls. In any case, fruit and vegetable lovers should bring their own from Oaxaca City. Produce selection in local San Lorenzo village stores will most likely be minimal.

Getting There

Get there by riding an Ayutla-bound Fletes y Pasajes bus east out of either Oaxaca City (departing from *camionera central segunda clase*) or from Mitla on Highway 179 just east of town. Get off at the Hierve El Agua side road, about 18 kilometers (11 mi) past Mitla. Continue the additional eight kilometers (five mi) by taxi or the local bus marked San Lorenzo. At this writing, the road is open for cars and buses only to the edge of San Lorenzo village, from which you can walk or continue by taxi the additional mile to the Hierve El Agua entrance.

South Side: The Crafts Route

Travelers who venture into the Valley of Oaxaca's long, south-pointing fingers, sometimes known as the Valleys of Zimatlán and Ocotlán, can discover a wealth of crafts, history, and architectural and scenic wonders. These are all accessible as day trips from Oaxaca City by car or combinations of bus and taxi. Most reachable are the renowned crafts villages of San Bartolo Coyotepec, San Martín Tilcajete, Santo Tomás Jalieza, and others along Highway 175, between the city and the colorful market town of Ocotlán (best to plan a visit to all on Friday, Ocotlán's market day; start at Ocotlán early and work your way north back to Oaxaca City). Another day, you can either continue farther south, off the tourist track, to soak in the feast of sights at the big market in Ejutla, or fork southwest, via Highway 131 through Zimatlán, to the idyllic groves, crystal springs, and limestone caves hidden around San Sebastián de las Grutas.

◖ SAN BARTOLO COYOTEPEC

San Bartolo Coyotepec (Hill of the Coyote), on Highway 175, 23 kilometers (14 mi) south of Oaxaca City, is famous for its pottery and its August 23–28 festival, Fiesta de San Bartolomé. During the fiesta, masked villagers costumed as half-man half-woman figures in tiaras, blond wigs, tin crowns, and velvet cloaks dance in honor of their patron.

The town's black pottery, the renowned *barro negro* sold all over Mexico, is available at the signed **Mercado de los Artesanias** market on the right and at a number of cottage factory shops (watch for signs) off the highway, scattered along the left (east side) of Calle Juárez, marked by a big Doña Rosa sign. Doña Rosa, who passed away in 1980, pioneered the technique of crafting lovely, big, round jars without a potter's wheel. With their local clay, Doña Rosa's descendants and neighbor families regularly turn out acres of glistening black plates, pots, bowls, trees of life, and fetching animals for very reasonable prices (figure on about $20 for a pearly black three-gallon vase, and perhaps $2 for a cute little rabbit).

San Bartolo Museum

Across the highway from the town church, on the town plaza's southern flank, stands the large, new **Museo Estatal de Arte Popular** (Plaza Principal, tel. 951/551-0083, 10 A.M.–6 P.M. Tues.–Sun., $4). Although the main event is a fine exposition of San Bartolo Coyotepec's famed black pottery, the museum also exhibits a surprisingly innovative range of some of the best crafts that the Valley of Oaxaca offers. Besides Doña Rosa's classic pearly-black examples, a host of other pieces—divine angels, scowling bandidos, fierce devils—reveal the remarkable talent of Doña Rosa's generation of students and followers.

Cochineal Farm

On your way either to or from San Bartolo Coyotepec and Ocotlán, you're in for an unusual treat if you stop at the small demonstration cochineal farm and museum **Rancho la Nopalera** (Km 10.5 Carretera Oaxaca–Puerto Ángel, Calle Matamoros 100, tel. 951/551-0030, fax 951/551-0053, info@aztecacolor.com, www.aztecacolor.com, 9 A.M.–1 P.M. and 2–5 P.M., $3), a few blocks off the highway at San Bartolo Coyotepec.

The farm, officially called the **Centro de Difusión del Conocimiento de la Grana Cochinilla y Colorantes Naturales,** is the labor of love of retired chemical engineer Ignacio J. del Río Dueñas and his son-in-law, engineer Manuel Loera Fernández. They graciously welcome all visitors—schoolchildren, visiting scholars, neighbors, tourists—to their ranch for the purpose of breathing life into the ancient Oaxaca tradition of cochineal dye, the source of the bright reds in many of the Oaxaca weavings.

Many others besides Señores Dueñas and Fernández believe in cochineal and support its use as a natural dye. Its color, so intensely scarlet that it is sometimes known as the "blood of the nopal," is produced from the bodies of the scale insect, *Dactylopius coccus,* that thrives on the thick leaves of the nopal (prickly pear) cactus, found all over Mexico and much of the western United States. Precisely *because* cochineal is a natural, non-synthetic product, it's gaining favor as a food and cosmetic (lipstick) coloring. The modest cochineal crop that the farm produces requires the processing of about 600 nopal leaves for each kilogram of cochineal, which sells for about $200.

They (or an assistant) will be happy to show you around their cactus cultivation house and demonstrate how the insects are harvested, and explain their several interesting museum exhibits, which illustrate the history and uses of cochineal.

Get there by bus from the *camionera central segunda clase* in Oaxaca City, via regional buses Estrella del Valle, Oaxaca Pacifico, or Estrella Roja del Sureste, or more local Choferes del Sur or Halcón buses, which will let you off at

THE VALLEY OF OAXACA

© BRUCE WHIPPERMAN

Cochineal, a brilliant red dye, is made from an insect that lives on nopal (prickly pear) cactus.

the highway, where you can taxi or walk according to the following driver's directions: By car, from Highway 175, about 7.5 kilometers (4.7 mi) south of the Oaxaca airport, turn right, southbound, at the small blue roadside sign ("El Museo Centro Reproducióa Grana Cochininilla") at Calle Unión, at the northern, Oaxaca edge of San Bartolo Coyotepec village; after a few hundred yards westbound, on a dirt road, another sign directs you left to the rancho.

CRAFTS VILLAGES ON THE ROAD TO OCOTLÁN

Each of the three crafts villages not far north of Ocotlán has something unique to offer. In order to visit all of them, plus San Bartolo Coyotepec and Ocotlán, on Friday, you'll need to get an early start. If you're inclined to linger, it's best to allow two days for your visit, with an overnight in Ocotlán. Under any circumstances, visit **San Antonino Castillo Velasco** on the same Friday that you visit Ocotlán, because it also has its *tianguis* (native market) on Friday. Two things to look for are the wonderful breads (in the morning, sold out by afternoon), fresh and yummy as you come into town, and the famous *vestidos de San Antonino,* sometimes known as "Oaxaca wedding dresses," marked by their elaborately fancy and colorful animal and floral embroidery.

First stop for the *vestidos de San Antonino* should be the small **Artesanías de Castillo Velasco** (on the San Antonino entrance road, Av. Castillo Velalsco, on the right, two blocks from the highway, tel. 951/571-0623). Your hosts will be friendly Enrique Lucas G. and his wife Maria Luisa Amador H., who manufacture and offer lovely embroidered *vestidos, blusas,* and *servilletas* (dresses, blouses, and napkins), and much more. Their finest *vestidos,* elaborately adorned with fetchingly colorful floral and animal designs, sell for $100 and up. Besides the goods they display up front, they can show you much more, including men's wedding shirts, from their rear storeroom.

For more embroidery options, a few women sell dresses and blouses in the regular market on Friday (turn left at the first block after the bread stalls). If you arrive and no one seems to be selling any dresses, mention *vestidos de San Antonino,* and someone will lead you to a woman who makes them. Alternatively, ask for friendly **Rosa Canseco Godines** (go-DEE-nays; Calle Guerrero 33, no phone), one of the local *maestras* of the craft. If she's home, she'll gladly show you examples of her beautiful work.

Bus passengers, take a taxi or walk 1.6 kilometers (one mi) from Ocotlán. Drivers, turn west at the San Antonino Castillo Velasco sign just at the northern (Oaxaca) edge of Ocotlán.

San Martín Tilcajete and Santo Tomás Jalieza

San Martín Tilcajete (teel-kah-HAY-tay; Hwy. 175, not far north of the Hwy. 131 fork), about 37 kilometers (21 mi) south of Oaxaca City, is a prime source of *alebrijes,* fanciful wooden creatures occupying the shelves of crafts stores the world over. Both it and Santo Tomás Jalieza (Hwy. 175, south of the Hwy. 131 fork), a mile or two farther south, can be visited as a pair on any day.

The label *alebrije,* a word of Arabic origin, implies something of indefinite form, and that certainly characterizes the fanciful animal figurines that a generation of Oaxaca woodcarvers has been crafting from soft copal wood. Dozens of factory-stores sprinkle San Martín Tilcajete. Start on the front main street, but also be sure to wander the back lanes and step into several cottage workshops, whose occupants will be happy to show you what they have and demonstrate how they make them. You'll find lots more than funny animals. Artisans branched out to plants such as purple palm trees and yellow cacti. Some items, such as imaginatively painted jewel boxes and picture frames, are practical, while others, such as miniature sets of tables and chairs, are for kids 3–90. Find some of the most original examples at the back-street shop of **Delfino Gutiérrez** (Calle Reforma, tel. 951/524-9074), who specializes in free-form elephants, frogs, turtles, armadillos, and much more.

Santo Tomás Jalieza, on the other hand, is known as the town of embroidered *cinturones* (belts). Women townsfolk, virtually all of whom practice the craft, concentrate all of their selling in a single many-stalled **market** (Centro de Artesanías, Plaza Principal, no phone,9 A.M.–5 P.M. daily) in the middle of town. Step inside and you'll be tempted not only by hundreds of hand-embroidered leather belts, but also by a wealth of lovely hand-loomed and embroidered purses, shawls, dresses, blouses, small backpacks, and much more. Furthermore, asking prices are very reasonable.

A couple of local restaurants received favorable reviews. Although it caters to the tourist crowd, the food is good and innovative at **Restaurant Azucena** (on the Tilcajete entrance road). On the other hand, for truly rustic, ranch-style ambience, complete with old wagon wheels, wooden picnic-style tables and plenty of savory barbeque, stop by **Restaurant Huamuches** (on the highway, by the Santo Tomás Jalieza entrance road).

OCOTLÁN

Your first stop in district capital Ocotlán (pop. 20,000, 42 km/26 mi south of Oaxaca) should probably be the interesting trio of family workshops (9 A.M.–6 P.M. daily) run by the Aguilar sisters, Irene, Guillermina, and Josefina. Watch for signs reading "Aguilar," on the right, on the outskirts, about 0.4 kilometers (0.25 mi) on the Oaxaca side from the town plaza. Their creations include a host of charming figures in clay: vendors with big ripe strawberries, green and red cactus, goats in skirts, and bikini-clad blondes.

The main Ocotlán attraction (unless you're lucky enough to arrive for the big fiesta on the third Sunday of May) is the huge **Friday market.** Beneath a riot of colored awnings, hordes of merchandise—much modern stuff, but also plenty of old-fashioned goodies—load a host of tables and street-laid mats. How about a saddle for your donkey? If not that, why not four or five turkeys, a goat, or perhaps half a dozen bags of hard-to-get wild medicinal

plants? And be sure to pick up a kilo or two of *cal* (lime or quicklime) for soaking your corn. If you're looking for lots of native costumes, you'll have to head for the mountains, because few women (except for their ribbon-decorated braids) and virtually no men wear *traje* (traditional indigenous dress). You'll hear plenty of Zapotec, however. At least half of the local people are native speakers.

Since markets are best in the morning, you should make Ocotlán your first Friday stop. Drivers could get there by heading straight south out of the city, arriving in Ocotlán by mid-morning. Spend a few hours, then begin your return in the early afternoon, stopping at the sprinkling of crafts villages along the road back to Oaxaca. Gasoline is available at the Pemex *gasolinera,* on the highway, on the north edge of Ocotlán.

Bus travelers could hold to a similar schedule by riding an early Autobuses Estrella del Valle, Autotransportes Oaxaca–Pacífico, or Choferes del Sur from the *camionera central segunda clase,* then returning, in steps, by bus, or more quickly by taxi, stopping at the crafts villages along the way.

Casa de Cultura Rudolfo Morales

During the 1980s and 1990s, Ocotlán came upon good times, largely due to the late Rudolfo Morales, the internationally celebrated but locally born artist who dedicated his fortune to improving his hometown. The Rudolfo Morales Foundation has been restoring churches and other public buildings, reforesting mountainsides, and funding self-help and educational projects all over Ocotlán and its surrounding district. The bright colors of the plaza-front *presidencia municipal* and the big church nearby result from the good works of Rudolfo Morales.

The Morales Foundation's local efforts radiate from the Casa de Cultura Rudolfo Morales (Morelos 108, tel. 951/571-0198, 9 A.M.–2 P.M. and 5–8 P.M. Mon.–Fri., 9 A.M.–3 P.M. Sat.), in the yellow-painted mansion three doors north from the Ocotlán plaza's northwest corner. In the Casa de Cultura's graceful, patrician interior, the Morales family and staff manage the foundation's affairs, teach art and computer classes, and sponsor community events.

The foundation staff welcomes visitors. For advance information, contact the foundation's headquarters in Oaxaca City (Murguia 105, between Macedonio Alcalá and 5 de Mayo, tel. 951/514-2324 or 951/514-0910, galeria@artedeoaxaca.com, www.artedeoaxaca.com, 11 A.M.–3 P.M. and 5–8 P.M. Mon.–Sat.).

Templo de Santo Domingo

Local people celebrate Rudolfo Morales's brilliant restoration of their beloved 16th-century Templo de Santo Domingo. Gold and silver from the infamous Santa Catarina Minas (mines), in the mountains east of Ocotlán, financed the church's initial construction. When overwork and disease tragically decimated the local native population by around 1600, the mines were abandoned, and work on the church stopped. Although eventually completed over the succeeding three centuries, it had slipped into serious disrepair by the 1980s.

Fortunately, the Templo de Santo Domingo is now completely rebuilt, from its bright blue, yellow, and white facade to the baroque gold glitter of its nave ceiling. Inside on the right side, you'll pass a pious Saint John the Baptist, with Mary Magdalene at his feet. Up front, above the main altar, a white-haired, bearded Creator reigns, resembling an indigenous Father Sun, with a halo of golden rays bursting from behind his head. Below him, Jesus hangs limply on the cross, flanked below by Mother Mary with a knife in her breast and St. John the Baptist lamenting at Jesus's feet.

Walk to the nave's south (right) side, to a gilded chapel dedicated to the Señor de la Sacristía (Lord of the Sacristy), the image above the altar. Also notice the adjacent oil painting of the Virgin of the Rosary, singular for her mestizo facial features. The Señor de la Sacristía is the object of community adoration in a festival of food, fireworks, processions, high masses, and dances climaxing on the third Sunday in May.

Practicalities

Free yourself of the Friday downtown crowd at the rustic-chic restaurant **La Cabaña** (Hwy. 175, tel. 951/571-0201, 8 A.M.–7 P.M. daily, $4–10), an open-air palapa by the *gasolinera* on the highway, at the north, Oaxaca, side of town.

If you decide to linger overnight in Ocotlán, the newish, clean, and modern **Hotel Rey David** (16 de Septiembre 248, tel. 951/571-1248, $13 s or d in one bed, $22 d or t in two beds) can accommodate you. The hotel offers about 20 comfortable, attractively decorated rooms. Find it on the south-side Highway 175 ingress-egress avenue, Avenida 16 de Septiembre, where it runs east–west, about three blocks east of the market and central plaza.

Do your money business at the Ocotlán **Banamex** (9 A.M.–4 P.M. Mon.–Fri.), with ATM, on the north side of the town plaza.

EJUTLA

Tour buses usually skip Ejutla de Crespo (pop. 20,000) because of its distance, about 59 kilometers (36 mi, one hour) from Oaxaca City. This is a pity, because Ejutla (ay-HOOT-lah) hides some surprises, not the least of which is its huge, colorful **Thursday market.** Folks troop in from country villages all over the huge Ejutla governmental district and farther to haggle over everything from *hamacas* (hammocks) and huaraches to radios and refrigerators. Moreover, Ejutla also offers accommodations at Hotel 6, the graceful hacienda-turned-hotel at the south edge of town.

Sights

Take a walk around Ejutla's shady plaza to get your bearings. The portico-fronted *presidencia municipal* stands on the plaza's south side, the market is on the north, and the big, proud **Templo de la Natividad** towers above the southeast corner. Sometime around 1750, the present church replaced the 16th-century original (which itself replaced a big preconquest Zapotec pyramid). Over the years, earthquakes took their toll; it was extensively restored around 1900.

Several large hieroglyph-decorated stone blocks built into the church's walls attest to the fact that the entire town remains an unexplored archaeological zone. You can find more evidence of this about two blocks north and two blocks east of the church, near the corner of Calles Altimirano and 16 de Septiembre. A big house compound encloses what appears to be a small hill, which is actually a buried temple-topped pyramid. Look for the several hieroglyph-decorated pre-conquest monoliths that have been incorporated into modern walls.

Since the church is usually open, you might as well step into the cool interior and contemplate the town's patron, the **Virgin of the Nativity,** presiding in front of the altar in what at first glance appears to be a bridal gown. In the lovely transept chapel on the right of the nave, you'll see another image of the same patron. Local people celebrate both, with a big fiesta centering around December 8.

For something else interesting, step over to the *presidencia municipal* and look on the wall for Ejutla's official *escudo* (coat of arms), which incorporates no arms at all. It's a portrait in tile of a bean vine, encircling a view of the sun rising from behind a likeness of Cerro El Labrador, the town's sacred mountain, towering in the east. A poem in praise of the "Sun, which rises here earlier than other lands…the source of life…without which there would be nothing" is included at the base of the *escudo.*

Practicalities

Another of Ejutla's surprises is the ⟨ **Hotel 6** (Km 61.5 Carretera Oaxaca–Puerto Ángel/Hwy. 175, tel. 951/573-0350, $20 s or d in one bed, $30 d or t in two beds), "probably the best in North America," claims the owner-operator, cordial former Olympic wrestler and civil engineer Mario E. Corres. A sign, which strikingly resembles Motel 6 signs all over the United States and Canada, draws you into the parking lot. You know you're in for something unique when you pull up to an old hacienda as big as a baseball field, with a mini-jungle on one side, complete with a tree house and a swinging rope suspension bridge.

© BRUCE WHIPPERMAN

THE VALLEY OF OAXACA

The Hotel 6 in Ejutla is more impressive than its ho-hum name suggests.

Inside, you'll find everything completely in order, from three spreading courtyards and a spacious pool, to two big function rooms and a grand living room, dining room, and spotless, shining, old-fashioned kitchen. The climax to all this is Señor Corres's museum, which includes his family tree and which he gladly explains to visitors (in Spanish, of course).

The 14 rooms, which after everything else seem an afterthought, are plain but clean. Some are more inviting than others. Take a look at two or three, small and large, before choosing. If the weather's warm, you'll need a fan, which some rooms have. This hotel offers all this plus parking, hot-water shower-baths, and an elegantly homey dining room.

You'll encounter most of Ejutla's **services** during your stroll around town—most of the available stores and institutions are right on or near the plaza. Starting at the *presidencia municipal,* on the south and moving clockwise, at the plaza-front eatery **Taquería Mary** (8 A.M.–7 P.M. daily, $2–6), at the southwest plaza corner, a squad of hardworking teenage girls serve hearty country food.

For pizza and hamburgers, go to **Restaurant Rulis** (roo-LEES; 8:30 A.M.–10 P.M. Mon.–Sat., noon–10 P.M. Sun.). To get there, walk a block west (downhill) from Taquería Mary, to Díaz, then turn left and continue, passing the **Banamex bank** (9 A.M.–5 P.M. Mon.–Fri.), for a block and a half.

Alternatively, for fresh and home-cooked food on the plaza's north side, visit the **market** (8 A.M.–6 P.M. daily) where permanent *fondas* (eateries) serve plenty of hearty breakfasts, soups, and stews, and stalls offer mounds of luscious fruit and veggies.

Continuing east, uphill at the street corner past the market, find the *huarachería* **La Principal** (tel. 951/573-0717, 9 A.M.–7 P.M. Mon.–Sat.) with a huge assortment of footwear, some still made onsite by the owner's daughter. One short block behind that (north) is the **Clínica San Gabriel** (tel. 951/573-0244), with a gynecologist and a general practitioner–surgeon on call 24 hours a day. If you need a *farmacia,* you have your choice of either the **Santa Fe** (9 A.M.–9 P.M. daily), on the plaza's northeast corner, or the **Farmacia Liliana** (pharmacy 9 A.M.–9 P.M. daily; doctor 4–8 P.M. Mon.–Fri.) with general practicioner Doctora Concepción Carballido, a block east of the plaza, next to the church. Gasoline is available at the highway **Pemex** *gasolinera* at the north edge of town.

DOWN HIGHWAY 131
Zimatlán

Travelers who head far enough along Highway 131, which branches west about 35 kilometers (22 mi) south of Oaxaca City through the Valley of Oaxaca's southwest side, are in for more than just one treat. They pass some of Oaxaca's most productive farmland: lush fields and pastures that in summer and fall appear like a verdant carpet reaching to the foot of pine- and oak-studded mountains.

Zimatlán (pop. 20,000), the capital of all this, appears simply as a workaday farming town, with a modicum of strictly local-style

services. Zimatlán's pace quickens, however, on Wednesdays, when the town market overflows with a flood of Zapotec buyers and sellers from the surrounding mountains. Excitement peaks during the eight days around January 15, when folks celebrate the unique **Fiesta del Dulce Nombre de Jesús.** Keeping by their traditional ways, townspeople enjoy old-fashioned events including processions, a big everyone-invited barbecue, *jaripeo* (bull roping and riding), and the Danza de las Plumas (Dance of the Feathers) and Danza de los Jardineros (Dance of the Gardeners), plus a *pelota mixteca* (pre-conquest ball game) tournament.

San Sebastián de las Grutas

It's hard not to fall in love with this idyllic hidden corner of the Valley of Oaxaca. Don't be put off by the tourist restaurants that clutter Highway 131 as you follow the right turnoff, 73 kilometers (45 mi) south of Oaxaca City. After 0.4 kilometers (0.25 mi) toward the *grutas* (caves), the road becomes a gently winding, sylvan, creekside drive. The jade-green brook (sometimes muddy in wet season) gurgles downhill over little rocks and giant boulders, pausing here and there in picture-perfect swimming holes. Meanwhile, from overhead, a regal host of towering, gnarled *sabinos* (bald cypress trees; *tules* or *ahuehuetes*) shades the creek, appearing every bit as ancient and grand as their northern cousins, the California redwoods. Now and then, you pass by the rustic wooden homes and cornfields of the local farm families. Or you might glimpse the big cylindrical fermentation vats of a rough-and-ready roadside mescal factory.

About 12 kilometers (seven mi) after the Highway 131 turnoff, and half a mile past San Sebastián de las Grutas village (pop. 900), you reach the caves. The creek emerges clear and pristine, as if by magic, from beneath a big rock at the foot of a mountain.

A hundred yards uphill are the caves, which you can tour for a fee of about $2. A guide, armed with strong flashlights, will lead you on an easy, mostly level walk through the cave's several chambers, which vary from about 6

© BRUCE WHIPPERMAN

Cabañas ecoturísticas invite an overnight stay in San Sebastian de las Grutas.

meters (20 ft) to more than 60 meters (200 ft) in height. The guide is used to receiving a tip of about $2 per person.

The cave you will see is only one of the several partly explored caves honeycombing the mountain, Cerro Cruz del Lado. Its five or six main chambers stretch about 0.5 kilometers (500 yards) into the mountain. Inside, the formations, which include many towering stalagmites and plenty of bulging stalactites, initially appear, in the semi-darkness of the flickering flashlights, to be gargantuan mounds and columns of half-melted vanilla-chocolate-swirl ice cream. However, when your eyes get accustomed to the darkness, many of the formations take on fanciful shapes. Bring your own flashlight and have fun dreaming up your own interpretations instead of merely seeing the guide's camel, turtle, shark, alligator (which looked like a seal to me), or tiger.

PRACTICALITIES

One could spend two or three enjoyable days hiking, bird-watching, swimming in the creek, sitting in the town plaza, and getting to know the local people. They're generally friendly, having seen enough visitors that they're not afraid and don't think you're too strange.

Moreover, the local folks are ready for you, with a pair of cozy, rustic wooden **cabañas ecoturísticas** (tel. 951/488-4640, $25 d, $30 t or q), with hot-water shower-bath, for up to six people in an inviting, forested creekside setting.

The shady streamside park, furthermore, appears ripe for camping ($15), either in your tent or (self-contained) RV. For food and drinking water, bring your own or go to stores in the village (or possibly food stalls near the caves).

Get there by bus via the Trans-Sol or Estrella Rojo del Sureste bus from the *camionera central segunda clase* next to the Abastos market on the southwest side of Oaxaca City. The Trans-Sol buses, some of which may (ask when you buy the ticket) go right to the caves, leave several times a day, beginning around 6 A.M. The Estrella Rojo del Sureste may only drop you at the intersection, 13 kilometers (eight mi) from the caves. Take a taxi or *colectivo* van or truck from there. Drivers, follow Highway 131, a total of 76 kilometers (53 mi) south of Oaxaca City. Allow about two hours' driving time. In the reverse, north direction, the *grutas* (caves) are 190 kilometers (119 mi) north of Puerto Escondido. For safety, under the best of conditions, allow about four hours of daylight driving time.

Sola de Vega

San Miguel Sola de Vega (pop. 5,000), diminutive capital of the remote, sprawling governmental district of the same name, is the main service stop on Oaxaca–Puerto Escondido Highway 131. The town, 95 kilometers (59 mi) south of Oaxaca City (159 km/99 mi north of Puerto Escondido), presides over a lush mountain-valley checkerboard of corn, cane, and cattle. The lovely *sabino*-shaded Río Sola de Vega ripples right past the town, crossed by quaint but practical footbridges. It looks as if the people have plenty of fun, spending about half their Sunday afternoons in the water. Informal camping by tent or RV appears seasonally promising in shady spots by the river. Get permission from authorities at the *presidencia municipal* at the town plaza, about three blocks north from the highway.

If you arrive on Sunday, Sola de Vega's traditional market day, be sure to visit the local *tianguis* (native market) around the town plaza.

PRACTICALITIES

A few stores near the plaza can supply basic groceries. For cooked food, the town's best bet is the 24-hour dining room of the plain but clean **Hotel Aguirre** (Hwy. 131, tel. 951/574-0046 or 951/574-0047, food $3–8; lodging $15 s, $22 s or d one bed, $31 d, t, q in two beds) on the highway. Its 25 rooms come with private hot-water shower-baths. You will not generally need a reservation, unless you're arriving late (perhaps after 9 P.M.).

Drivers: Fill up with gasoline at the **Pemex** station (about a mile north of town), since gasoline is scarce in most of the country along Highway 131. For other essential services,

you have the *correo* (post office), *telégrafo*, and Internet stores by the plaza; a *centro de salud* (health clinic) on Independencia, off the plaza; and a private physician, Dr. Vicente Mendoza Martinez, also on Independencia (neither have phones). For nonprescription medicines and phone calls, go to the *farmacia-caseta larga distancia* San Miguel, right on the highway at the south (Puerto Escondido) end of town. Also on the highway you'll find the Trans Sol and Estrella Roja del Sureste bus stations.

SOUTHWEST SIDE
◖ Zaachila

About 16 kilometers (10 mi) south of Oaxaca City, Zaachila (pop. 30,000), like Mitla, overlies the ruins of its ancient namesake city, which rose to prominence after the decline of Monte Albán. Although excavations have uncovered many Mixtec-style remains, historical records nevertheless list a number of Zapotec kings (including the greatest, Zaachila Yoo, for whom the town is named) who ruled Zaachila as a virtual Zapotec capital during the 14th and 15th centuries. Nevertheless, by the eve of the conquest, in the early 16th century, a noble Mixtec minority dominated the Zapotec-speaking inhabitants, whose leaders the Mixtec warriors had sent fleeing for their lives to Tehuántepec.

The big forested hill that rises north of the market plaza is topped by the large, mostly unexplored **Zaachila pyramid** (8 A.M.–5 P.M. daily, $4). Several unexcavated mounds and courtyards dot the hill's north and south flanks. The site parking lot and entrance gate are adjacent to the colonial church just north of the plaza.

In 1962, archaeologist Roberto Gallegos (guarded from hostile residents by armed soldiers) uncovered a pair of unopened tombs beneath the summit of the pyramid. They yielded a trove of polychrome pottery, gold jewelry (including a ring still on a left hand), and jade fan handles. Tomb 1 descends via a steep staircase to an entrance decorated with a pair of cat-motif heads. On the antechamber walls a few steps farther are depictions of owls and a pair of personages (perhaps former occupants) inscribed respectively with the name-dates 5-Flower and 9-Flower. Do not miss the bas-reliefs on the tomb's back wall that depict a man whose torso is covered with a turtle shell. (Tomb 2, although open for inspection, contains no remaining sculptures or inscriptions.)

Hint: The narrow tomb staircase is negotiable by only a few persons at a time and often requires an hour for a tour-bus crowd to inspect it. Rather than waste your time standing in line, go downhill, stroll around the market, and return when the line is smaller. If driving, arrive early, around 9 A.M. on Thursday, to avoid tour-bus crowds. Return in early afternoon, allowing time to visit Cuilapan and Arrazola.

After visiting the archaeological site, you might take a look inside the smallish but robustly buttressed colonial-era Zaachila church, which appears to have been erected atop one of the town's original pre-conquest ceremonial platforms. Inside, atop the altar, an unusual black Jesus presides above the glass-encased town patron, the Virgin of the Nativity. In her honor, townsfolk stage a big fiesta during the eight days around September 8, which, besides the exhilarating carnival rides, challenging games of chance, tasty food, and flashing fireworks, also features the spectacularly colorful Danza de las Plumas (Dance of the Feathers).

The Thursday **tianguis** (native market) is Zaachila's weekly main event. It spreads for blocks below the archaeological site and church. Thousands of Zapotec-speaking country people stream into town to buy, sell, gossip, flirt, and fill up with their favorite delicacies. A few highlights are the luscious, scarlet-red *pitacaya* (pee-tah-KAHY-yah) fruits, and the foamy-tan *tecate* (tay-KAH-tay) drink, corn-based and deliciously flavored with chocolate, *rosita* flower petals, and ground seeds of *mamey,* all sweetened with brown sugar juice and honey. For a breezy change of pace, hop into one of the buzzing *moto-taxis* (motorized rickshaws) for a 10-minute jaunt (for about $1.50) around town.

If you're in the mood for food, wholesome country fare (make sure you get it served hot) is available at the regiment of *fondas* in the permanent, roofed section of the market. Pork is a Zaachila ("Town of Pork") specialty, and any one of a small acre of pork stalls will be ready to barbeque a pork chop for you on the spot. Alternatively, enjoy lunch at the showplace **《 Restaurant La Capilla** (tel. 951/528-6115, 7 A.M.–7 P.M. daily, $5–10). Get there on foot or by asking your *moto-taxi* driver to let you off at La Capilla (kah-PEE-yah), on the main east–west Oaxaca ingress street, a few blocks west of the market.

By bus, get to Zaachila via **Autobuses de Oaxaca,** from the *camionera central segunda clase* in Oaxaca City, or by private tourist bus.

By car from Oaxaca City, head south from downtown to the *periférico.* Do not continue south via the airport Highway 131–175. Instead, from the *periférico* a block west of the airport-highway intersection (watch for the Monte Albán sign), follow the four-lane boulevard that angles southwest, away from the *periférico,* across the Río Atoyac bridge. Just after crossing the bridge, do not continue straight ahead toward Monte Albán, but take the second left (south) onto the old (scenic route) Zaachila road, which also passes Cuilapan de Guerrero and Arrazola. (*Note:* The first left fork heads along the no-nonsense—but at this writing, potholed—highway, in a straight four-lane bee-line toward Zaachila, bypassing Cuilapan de Guerrero and Arrazola.)

Cuilapan de Guerrero and Arrazola

Southwest of Oaxaca City, on the old road between Zaachila and Arrazola, Cuilapan de Guerrero is famous for its elaborate but unfinished **Ex-Convento de Santiago** (Saint Jame, 9 A.M.–5 P.M. daily). It's visible from the Oaxaca City–Zaachila Highway (via Xoxocotlan). This is where Vicente Guerrero, father of the Mexican republic, was infamously executed in 1831. Although construction began in 1535, the cost of the basilica and associated monastery began to balloon. In 1550, King Philip demanded humility and moderation of the builders, whose work was finally ended by a 1570 court ruling. The extravagances—the soaring, roofless basilica, magnificent baptismal font, splendid Gothic cloister, and elaborate frescoes—remain as national treasures.

Arrazola, a few miles farther north, toward Oaxaca City, is one of the sources (along with San Martín Tilcajete) of the intricately painted *alebrijes* (ah-lay-BREE-hays)—fanciful wooden creatures that decorate the shelves of handicrafts shops all over Mexico and foreign countries. Bus travelers: Get there either by second-class bus or by tourist bus from Oaxaca City. Drivers: Turn west (left) onto signed Highway 145 a few miles north of Cuilapan de Guerrero or, traveling south, turn right 5.1 kilometers (3.2 mi) south of the Río Atoyac bridge in Oaxaca City.

Pass through San Javier village and continue from the turnoff a total of five kilometers (three mi) to the Arrazola town plaza. Turn right immediately before the plaza onto Calle E. Zapata and turn left after one block, at Independencia. After one more block you will be at Calle Obregón, where everyone seems to be making *alebrijes*. Although you should visit a number of family workshops along the street, be sure to visit **Pepe Santiago** (no phone, 10 A.M.–6 P.M. daily) and his Santa's workshop of craftspeople. Inside the Santiago compound (on the right, just below the hilltop), men and boys saw and carve away while a cadre of young women and girls painstakingly add riots of painted brocade to everything from whimsical dragons and gargoyles to armadillos, giraffes, and rabbits.

West Side: The Archaeological Route

Although all of these interesting destinations are readily reachable from Oaxaca City, they are far too rich to be visited in a single day. As a minimum, be sure to visit Monte Albán, which can be conveniently combined with a side trip to Atzompa. On another day, preferably a Wednesday, visit the Etla market, with stops at the community museums and key archaeological sites at El Mogote and Suchilquitongo nearby.

◖ MONTE ALBÁN

Monte Albán ranks among Mesoamerica's most regally spectacular ruined cities. Known in ancient times by its Zapotec name, Danni Dipaa, the site's present "Monte Albán" label was probably coined by a local Spaniard because of its resemblance to a similarly named Italian hilltop town.

Monte Albán's original inhabitants cultivated beans, chilies, corn, fruits, and squash on the hillsides and in adjacent valleys, occasionally feasting on meat from deer, small game, and perhaps (as did other native Mexicans) domesticated dogs. Tribute from surrounding communities directly enriched Monte Albán's

ruling classes and, by extension, its artisans and farmers.

The great city atop the hill reigned for at least 1,200 years, between 500 B.C. and A.D. 750, as the capital of the Zapotecs and the dominant force between Teotihuacán in the Valley of Mexico and the Maya kingdoms of the southeast. Archaeologists have organized the Valley of Oaxaca's history from 500 B.C. to the conquest into five periods, known as Monte Albán I–V. Over those centuries, the hilltop city was repeatedly reconstructed with new walls, plazas, and staircases, which, like layers of an onion, now overlie earlier construction.

Remains from Monte Albán Period I (500 B.C.–A.D. 1) reveal an already advanced culture, with gods, permanent temples, a priesthood, a written language, numerals, and a calendar. Sharply contrasting house styles indicate a differentiated, multilayered society. Monte Albán I ruins abound in graceful polychrome ceramics of uniquely Zapotec style.

Concurrent Olmec influences have also been found, notably in the buildings known as the Danzantes (Dancers), decorated with unique bas-reliefs similar to those unearthed along the Veracruz and Tabasco coasts.

The people who lived during Monte Albán Period II (A.D. 1–300), by contrast, came under heavy influence from Chiapas and Guatemala in the south. They built strange, ship-shaped buildings, such as Monte Albán's mysterious Building J, and left unique remains of their religion, such as the striking jade bat-god now on display in the Anthropology Museum in Mexico City.

Monte Albán reached its apex during the classical Period III (A.D. 300–800), attaining a population of perhaps 40,000 in an urban zone of about eight square kilometers (three sq mi), which spread along hilltops (including the El Gallo and Atzompa archaeological sites) west of the present city of Oaxaca.

Vigorous Period III leaders rebuilt the main hilltop complex as we see it today. Heavily influenced by the grand style of the Teotihuacán structures in the Valley of Mexico, the buildings were finished with handsome sloping staircases,

corniced walls, monumental carvings, ball courts, and hieroglyph-inscribed stelae depicting gods, kings, and heroic scenes of battle.

By A.D. 750, few foreign influences were continuing to enrich Monte Albán's uniquely Zapotec pottery styles. Quality declined until they seemed like mere factory copies. Concurrently, the Zapotec pantheon expanded to a horde of gods, as if mere numbers could protect the increasingly isolated Valley of Oaxaca from the outside world.

In A.D. 800, Monte Albán, mysteriously cut off from the rest of Mesoamerica, was declining in population and power. By A.D. 1000, the city was virtually abandoned. The reasons—whether drought, disease, or revolt—and the consequent loss of the necessarily imported water, wood, salt, and food supplies remain an enigma.

During Periods IV and V, Mixtec peoples from the north invaded the Valley of Oaxaca. They warred with valley Zapotecs and, despite their relatively small numbers, became a

THE VALLEY OF OAXACA

© BRUCE WHIPPERMAN

Monte Albán's enigmatic Building J, foreground

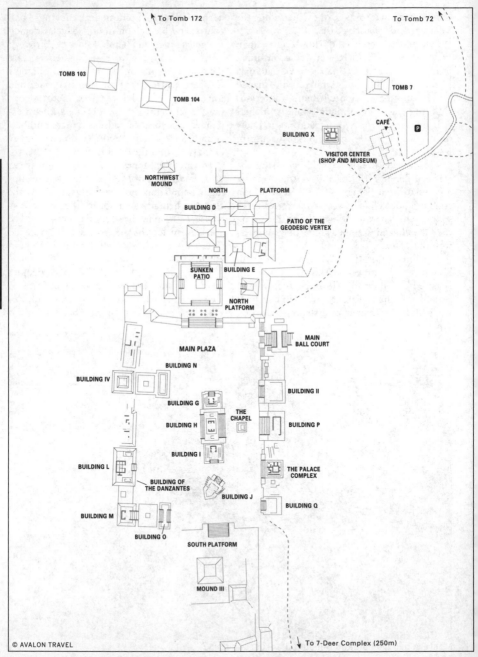

To Tomb 172

To Tomb 72

TOMB 103

TOMB 104

TOMB 7

CAFÉ

BUILDING X

VISITOR CENTER
(SHOP AND MUSEUM)

NORTHWEST
MOUND

NORTH   PLATFORM

BUILDING D

PATIO OF THE
GEODESIC VERTEX

SUNKEN
PATIO

BUILDING E

NORTH
PLATFORM

MAIN
BALL COURT

MAIN PLAZA

BUILDING N

BUILDING IV

BUILDING II

BUILDING G

THE
CHAPEL

BUILDING H

BUILDING P

BUILDING I

BUILDING L

BUILDING OF
THE DANZANTES

THE PALACE
COMPLEX

BUILDING J

BUILDING M

BUILDING Q

BUILDING O

SOUTH PLATFORM

MOUND III

© AVALON TRAVEL

To 7-Deer Complex (250m)

To Oaxaca City

SMALL BALL COURT

TOMB 105

MONTE ALBÁN

0   100 yds
0   100 m

ruling class in a number of valley city-states. The blend of Mixtec and Zapotec art and architecture sometimes led to new forms, especially visible at the west valley sites of Yagul and Mitla.

Monte Albán, meanwhile, although abandoned, was not forgotten. It became both a refuge and a venerated burial place. In times of siege, local people retreated within the walls of a fortress built around Monte Albán's South Platform. At other times, Mixtec nobles opened tombs and reused them as burial vaults right up until the eve of the conquest.

Exploring the Site

Visitors to Monte Albán (tel. 951/516-9770, 8 A.M.–5 P.M. daily, entrance $5) enjoy a panoramic view of green mountains rising above the checkerboard of the Valley of Oaxaca. Monte Albán is fun for a picnic; alternatively, it is an auspicious place to perch atop a pyramid above the grand Main Plaza, etched by lengthening afternoon shadows, and contemplate the ages. Allow at least two hours for your visit.

A good **guide** (about $10 pp for a two-hour tour) can certainly enhance your Monte Albán visit. Many are licensed by the authorities. You can often hire someone on the spot. Or, make an appointment with one of the best: very knowledgable and English-fluent Juan Carlos Peralta (cell tel. 044-951/103-4004, guiasjuan@hotmail.com).

Past the visitor's center, as you enter the Main Plaza, north will be on your right, marked by the great **North Platform,** topped by clusters of temples. The **Ball Court** will soon appear on your left. Twenty-foot-high walkways circumscribe the sunken I-shaped playing field. To ensure true bounces, builders spread smooth stucco over all surfaces, including the slopes on opposite sides (which, contrary to appearances, did not seat spectators). This, like all Oaxacan ball courts, had no stone ring (for supposed goals), but rather four mysterious niches at the court's I-end corners.

The **Main Plaza,** 1,000 feet long and exactly two-thirds that wide, is aligned along a precise north–south axis. Probably serving as a market and civic/ceremonial ground, the monumentally harmonious Main Plaza was the Zapotec "navel" of the world.

Monte Albán's oldest monumental construction, the **Danzantes** building (surmounted by newer Building L, on the west side of the plaza between Buildings M and IV), dates from Period I. Its walls are graced with a host of personages, known commonly as the *danzantes* (dancers) from their oft-contorted postures—probably chiefs vanquished by Monte Albán's armies. Their headdresses, earplugs, bracelets, and necklaces mark them among the nobility, while glyphs around their heads identify each individual.

Building J (circa A.D. 1), one of the most

THE TRAGIC STORY OF PRINCESS DONAJI

The fabled marriage of King Cosijoeza (koh-see-hoh-AY-zah) of the Zapotecs to Coyolli-catzin (koh-yoh-yee-KAH-tseen), daughter of Emperor Moctezuma II of the Aztecs, around 1490, was a happy one. It resulted in five children, the youngest of whom was a charming little girl.

The king asked his soothsayers what their divinations told of his little daughter's future. They replied that her life would be filled with tragic events and that she would finally sacrifice herself for her people. The king, saddened by the news but happy that she would turn out to be so selfless, named her Donaji (Great Soul).

Earlier, Cosijoeza, who ruled the Zapotec Isthmus domains from his capital at present-day Tehuántepec, had been an uneasy ally of his old enemy, King Dzahuindanda (zah-ween-DAHN-dah) of the Mixtecs. In 1520, with the Aztec threat diminished by the Spanish invasion, Cosijoeza recklessly attacked the fierce Mixtecs, losing the initial battle and then nearly his life as the Mixtecs pressed their advantage.

However, the Spanish, in the person of Hernán Cortés's lieutenant, Francisco Orozco, soon imposed a Mixtec-Zapotec treaty in which Dzahuindanda received Princess Donaji as a hostage to guarantee the peace.

Having Donaji as a prisoner at Monte Albán (known as Danni Dipaa in those days) was not exactly an advantage to Dzahuindanda, for he suspected that she was as much a spy as a hostage. His guess was right. Donaji gleaned intelligence vital to the Zapotec counterattack her father Cosijoeza was planning. At the moment Dza-huindanda's forces were most vulnerable, she sent her father a secret message to attack, which he did, with complete success, except for one thing.

With the treaty broken, the outraged Mixtecs decided to do away with Donaji. They decapitated her and buried her body before her father could rescue her. Later, some Zapotecs found Donaji's remains on the bank of the Atoyac river. They were surprised to see a lovely violet wild iris blossoming from her blood. Even more surprising, they found the flower's roots growing around her head, which was without any sign of decomposition.

Three hundred years later, the Oaxaca government decided to honor the heroine who sacrificed herself for her people by adding an image of Donaji's head to the Oaxacan coat of arms, where it remains to the present day.

Princess Donaji sacrificed her life in order to protect the safety of her Zapotec kinfolk.

© BRUCE WHIPPERMAN

remarkable in Mesoamerica, stands nearby in mid-plaza at the foot of the South Platform. Speculation has raged since excavators unearthed its arrow-shaped base generations ago. It is not surprising that Alfonso Caso, Monte Albán's original principal excavator, theorized it was an astronomical observatory (perhaps since it does point in the direction of the setting sun at its winter solstice).

In the mind's eye, however, it seems like some fantastic ocean (or space?) vessel, being navigated to some mysteriously singular southwest destination by a ghostly crew oblivious of its worldly, earthbound brother monuments.

Aficionados can't resist claiming that Building J represents some other-worldly influence. They assert that the figure, visibly inscribed on the building's upper northwest corner, is an extraterrestrial wearing a space helmet. Expert professionals refute this with a more earthly explanation, that the figure simply represents a ball player wearing the customary protective leather helmet.

The **South Platform** affords Monte Albán's best viewing point, especially during the late afternoon. Starting on the right-hand, Palace-complex side, **Building II** has a peculiar tunnel on its near side, perhaps covertly used by priests for privacy or some kind of magical effect. To the south stands Building P, an undistinguished, albeit multi-room palace.

The South Platform itself is only marginally explored. Looters have riddled the mounds on its top side. Its bottom four corners were embellished by fine bas-reliefs, two of which had their engravings intentionally buried from view. You can admire the fine sculpture and yet-undeciphered Zapotec hieroglyphs on one of them, along with others, at the South Platform's plaza-edge west side.

Still atop the South Platform, turn southward, where you can see the Seven-Deer complex, a few hundred yards away, labeled for the name-date inscribed on its great lintel.

Turning northward again, look just beyond Building J to Buildings G, H, and I at the plaza center, erected mostly to cover a rocky mound, impossible to remove without then-unavailable dynamite. Between these buildings and the palace complex on the right stands the small chapel where the remarkable bat-god jade sculpture was found.

On Monte Albán's northern periphery stand a number of tombs that, when excavated, yielded a trove of artifacts, now mostly housed in museums. Walking west from the Northern Platform's northeast base corner, you will pass Mound X on the right. A few hundred yards farther comes the **Tomb 104** mound, presided over by an elaborate ceramic urn representing Cocijo, the Zapotec god of rain. Just north of this is **Tomb 172,** which has its skeletons and offerings left intact when it was first opened.

Heading back along the northernmost of the two paths from Tomb 104, you will arrive at **Tomb 7** a few hundred feet behind the visitors center. Here, around 1450, Mixtec nobles removed the original eighth-century contents and reused the tomb, burying a deceased dignitary and two servants for the netherworld. Along with the bodies, they left a fabulous treasure in gold, silver, jade, alabaster, and turquoise, now visible at the museum at the Centro Cultural de Santo Domingo in Oaxaca City.

A few hundred feet toward town on the opposite side of the road from the parking lot is a trail leading past a small ball court to the Cerro de Plumaje (Hill of Plumage), site of **Tomb 105.** A magnificent entrance door lintel, reminiscent of those at Mitla, welcomes you inside. Past the patio, descend to the mural-decorated tomb antechamber. Inside the cruciform tomb itself, four figures walk in pairs toward a great glyph, flanked by a god and goddess, identified by their name-dates.

Visitors Center

The Monte Albán Visitors Center (tel. 951/516-9770, 8 A.M.–5 P.M.) has an excellent museum, good café with airy terrace, and information counter. Also, a well-stocked store offers many books—guides, histories, art, folklore—on Mesoamerica. First, take a look inside the museum, which displays a number of Monte Albán's famous finds. Most notable are several

THE VALLEY OF OAXACA

of the original *danzantes* monolith reliefs, recognizable by their mutilated genitals.

In the bookstore (tel. 951/516-9180), you might purchase a copy of the very useful *Guide to Monte Albán,* by Monte Albán's director, Neli Robles. You could also pick up a copy of the very authoritative, in-depth *Oaxaca, the Archaeological Record,* by archaeologist Marcus Winter, that covers many Oaxaca archaeological sites, including the valley sites of Dainzu, Lambityeco, Mitla, San José El Mogote, Suchilquitongo, and several other important sites in the Mixteca.

Getting There

Get to Monte Albán economically and very conveniently by one of the several **tourist buses,** run respectively by Hotel Rivera del Ángel (Mina 518, tel. 951/516-6666), and Viajes Turísticos Mitla (Mina 501, tel. 951/516-5327). Find them three blocks south and four blocks west of the *zócalo* in Oaxaca City.

By car, get to Monte Albán via the most scenic route. Start from Oaxaca City's south side, at the *periférico,* about a mile due south from the *zócalo* past the end of southbound Calle M. Cabrera. At the *periférico,* watch for a Monte Albán sign. Cross the *periférico,* then bear right (southwest) and immediately cross over the Río Atoyac bridge. Continue ahead, following other Monte Alban signs, about eight kilometers (five mi), uphill, to Monte Albán.

Alternatively, get to Monte Albán by following Highway 190 northwest from downtown Oaxaca City. After just about three kilometers (two mi) from the city center (look for a Monte Albán sign), curve left, around the big monument and traffic circle, reversing your direction, then immediately turn right (west) and continue across the Río Atoyac bridge. Follow the signs about 10 more kilometers (six mi) uphill to Monte Albán.

SANTA MARÍA ATZOMPA

The present-day town of Santa María Atzompa (pop. 5,000) spreads over the western end of the greater Monte Albán archaeological complex, overlying hundreds of acres of unexplored

pottery selection, Atzompa Mercado de Artesanías

© BRUCE WHIPPERMAN

ancient remains. The majority of modern Atzompans, however, have little time for the past. They are busy producing their distinctive pottery creations—attractive emerald green–glazed cooking pots, bowls, baking dishes, plates, and more—famous all over Mexico and the world.

Now, however, they make much more than these, having developed a host of new styles such as multicolored vases, some with artfully cut holes for placing dried or fresh flowers, as well as lily-adorned crosses, vases, plates, and red pottery, inscribed with fetching floral motifs.

Atzompa's artists, moreover, make it very easy to select from their wares, with an inviting **Mercado de Artesanías** (Handicrafts Market, tel. 951/558-9232, or local cell tel. 044-951 516-5062, 9 A.M.–7 P.M. daily), on the entrance road (right side) after a long initial lineup of private stores. Each of the *mercado* displays contains the name and address of the artist, whom you can contact nearby in town. (*Note:* Recently, some artists have been trying harder, building individual stores on the road before the official Mercado de Artesanías. For the best selection, however, pass these and go straight to the official market.)

For lunch at the handicrafts market, try the adjacent, airy **[** **Restaurant Patio** (11 A.M.–6 P.M. daily, $4). They offer an inviting menu of many Mexican country specialties, including a number of *moles* (with chicken) and the reliable favorite, chiles rellenos.

Atzompa Archaeological Zone

The line of hilltops stretching west from Monte Albán to Atzompa is peppered with buried pyramids, ceremonial plazas, and ball courts. Archaeologists have recently been investigating the hilltop above Atzompa. They have excavated a mound (known locally as *el mogote*) and partly restored a regal platform and pyramid. At this writing, they're not yet welcoming visitors, but a visitor's center and museum are in the works.

Get there by taxi, car, or on foot, climbing main Atzompa street Calle Independencia (the first street past the Mercado de Artesanías). Turn left and continue uphill about a mile to the visitor's center and parking lot.

Get to Atzompa by bus, from the Abastos *camionera central segunda clase* in Oaxaca City, or by car, heading northwest out of town, along the Highway 190 exit boulevard in the direction of Mexico City. After about three kilometers (two mi) from the city center, follow the Monte Albán sign, bearing left around the traffic circle, which heads you momentarily back toward town. Immediately turn right, cross the Río Atoyac bridge, and continue for 0.8 kilometers (0.5 mi), turning right (north) at an Atzompa-signed intersection. Continue another four kilometers (2.5 mi) to the Mercado de Artesanías and the restaurant on the right.

[SAN JOSÉ EL MOGOTE

Finds uncovered at San José El Mogote have shed considerable light on Valley of Oaxaca prehistory, especially during the thousand-year period preceding the founding of Monte Albán, around 500 B.C. Remains reveal that San José El Mogote was founded around 1500 B.C. and developed into a sophisticated center, with factory workshops supervised by elite merchants, which manufactured mica mirrors and jewelry for local and regional trade.

Old San José El Mogote lives on, literally, in the backyards of its present Zapotec residents. The people had forgotten what was buried in the seven or eight *mogotes* (mounds) dotting their village. From the pottery shards littering their fields, however, they suspected something was buried beneath the mounds. Archaeologists came and dug up the treasures now displayed in the community museum.

Museum

San José El Mogote people take justifiable pride in their museum, the **Hacienda del Cacique,** housed in a gorgeously restored old hacienda, the former ranch home of a local founding *cacique* (political boss) family. Its intriguing displays include shell jewelry, ceramic and stone burial offerings, a reconstructed tomb, a pre-Columbian adobe wall, a photo of a *danzante* (dancer) monolith (still situated in the ruins) like those found at Monte Albán, and exquisite ceramic sculptures. Outstanding among these is the amazing *diablo enchilado,* with a half-scowling, devilish grin, exactly like a scary red Halloween demon.

Note: The museum's hours are irregular. If you arrive unannounced, you may find the museum closed. However, someone is usually in charge, and, if available, he or she will open it for you. To inquire, say (or point to) this phrase *"¿Donde está el encargado del museo?"* ("Where is the person in charge of the museum?") The *presidencia municipal* (town hall) is usually the best place to make your inquiry.

Exploring the Site

The archaeological zone consists of eight mounds in all, which extend over a local half-mile square. Only one of them, the biggest, immediately behind the museum, has been extensively explored. Climb its reconstructed stone staircase to a broad courtyard. On the courtyard's north side is an excavated shaft, customarily locked,

THE VALLEY OF OAXACA

© BRUCE WHIPPERMAN

the ancient restored staircase at San José El Mogote

with the *danzante* (dancer) monolith at its bottom. Climb the regal, stair-stepped pyramid adjoining the courtyard. At the summit, you can glimpse the other mounds, scattered near and far. Most notable among these is a partly excavated ball court, a five-minute walk to the northwest, once used for the *pelota mixteca* ball game, which is still played locally.

Farther afield, a 10-minute walk to the southwest side of the zone past a modern but now unused stone *era* (threshing circle), local people can lead you to a corrugated iron roof that shelters the stone foundation of what archaeologists believe to be an elite family house.

While exploring the site, you may see a scattering of tiny yellow daisies. Local folks call this *yerba de conejo* (herb of the rabbit). They take it as a tea, or mixed with beans, especially before siestas. Some say that its aphrodisiac effect is indeed potent.

Festival of San José

Arrive during the third week in March and join in the fun of the patronal festival of San José, which climaxes on the weekend closest to March 19. Festivities include processions, fireworks, dances of giant figures (called *monos* or *marmotas*), and a *pelota mixteca* tournament. While at the museum, ask the volunteers to show you the *hule* (natural rubber) ball and the leather mitts currently used to play the game.

Getting There

You can reach San José El Mogote in a number of ways. The easiest way is to go by tour or taxi from downtown Oaxaca City. You can also go solo by second-class bus from the *camion-era central segunda clase,* just north of Abastos market. Catch the Choferes del Sur bus to Nazareno town. Alternatively, you can catch a *colectivo* on the prolongation of V. Trujano, which runs along the north side of the second-class bus station.

Drivers: Head north along Highway 190 out of Oaxaca City. About 12 kilometers (7.5 mi) from downtown, at the fork to the new *cuota autopista,* stay on the *libre* (free) old route. After about three kilometers (two mi), turn left (west) at the San José El Mogote (also Nazareno) side road (marked by the pyramid archaeological symbol sign). Pass over the railroad tracks, continue 0.8 kilometers (about 0.5 mi), and at the bus stop shelter, turn left. Continue to the museum just past the water towers on the left.

SIDE TRIP TO SAN AGUSTÍN ETLA

Renowned Oaxaca artist Francisco Toledo encourages the public to visit and support hillside art center that he, with others, founded in 1999. His efforts continue to fulfill his goal of inspiration, education, and encouragement of art appreciation in his native state of Oaxaca. Toledo, now over 70, was honored with the Mexico National Prize in 1998 in recognition of his work (which included the Oaxaca Institute of Graphic Arts and the Museum of Oaxaca Contemporary Art in Oaxaca City).

You can view some results of his work in the suburban village of Vista Hermosa, above small San Agustín Etla town. First you arrive at the factory-shop of **Arte Papel Vista Hermosa** (tel./fax 951/521-2394, 9 A.M.–5 P.M. Mon.–Fri., 9 A.M.–2 P.M. Sat.), with an airy showroom in an antique high-ceilinged former power-generating house. Overhead a festoon of colorful paper banners hang like kites in the wind, while in a next-door rear workshop a cadre of young artisans diligently execute Toledo's sometimes whimsical, but sometimes stark, graphic designs-in-paper.

Up the hill two blocks, find the **Centro de Artes San Agustín** (Calle Independcia, tel. 951/521-3042, 951/521-3043, or 951/521-2574, www.casanagustin.org, 9 A.M.–6 P.M. daily), the art exhibition hall and educational center. The main building resembles a Greek temple much more than the cotton-weaving mill that it once was. There's an expansive pond surrounding a massive iron boiler—the only hint of the site's former identity.

San Agustín Etla makes a good side trip from San José Mogote (it's about 20 minutes by car or taxi), and can also be combined with a visit to Etla. On Highway 190, drive shortly past the San José El Mogote exit (archaeological sign on left), to a paved road (watch for a Vista Hermosa sign) on the right. Turn right and continue uphill for about 7.2 kilometers (4.5 mi), to the paper factory *(fábrica de papel)* on the right.

To get there from Oaxaca City, start at the second-class bus station, much like going to San José El Mogote. Ask the Choferes del Sur bus driver to let you off at the branch road to San Agustín Etla, from Highway 190. Ride a taxi or collective taxi from there the 6.4 kilometers (four mi) to Vista Hermosa.

ETLA

The name Etla strictly refers to a county-size district northwest of Oaxaca City that contains a number of small towns (such as Soledad Etla, San Miguel Etla, and San Gabriel Etla) that cluster around the central hub town of San Pedro y San Pablo Etla, site of the famous **Etla Wednesday market.** Consequently, this is the place that most folks refer to simply as Etla (or sometimes Villa de Etla). Although the Etla Wednesday market invariably has stalls overflowing with its celebrated "Oaxaca" (but more correctly "Etla") cheese, vendors offer plenty of other old-fashioned merchandise. How would you like, for example, some fresh sheepskins, burro pack frames, green Atzompa pottery, or banana-leaf-wrapped red Oaxaca tamales? The market's main attraction, however, is the battalion of native country women offering mounds of carrots, forest-gathered herbs, nopal cactus leaves, onions, and much more.

For food, either pick one of the platoon of very clean *fondas* (food stalls) on the upper level of the main market, or head outside, to country-style *comedor* **(La Fonda** (no phone, 8 A.M.–7 P.M. daily, $2–5), adjacent to the market's southeast side. Elderly Señora Julia both cooks and directs a bustling cadre of helpers in serving up a wholesome menu of homemade breakfasts, *sopas* (soups), and *guisados* (stews), all served up with generous portions of rice and beans and steaming stacks of handmade tortillas. Alternatively, try **Restaurant Chefy**

(8 A.M.–8 P.M. daily, $3–8) for a wholesome, home-style breakfast or lunch, on the left side of the main street as you enter town from the highway.

Get to Etla much as you would get to San José El Mogote. Preferably arrive at the market by about 10 A.M. to allow time for visits to San José El Mogote, Suchilquitongo, and/or San Agustín Etla later. By bus from Oaxaca City: Ride a Choferes del Sur Etla–marked bus from the *camionera central segunda clase,* or a *colectivo* from the north side of the bus station.

By car: Head north along old *libre* (toll-free) Highway 190 for about 15 kilometers (nine mi) from the center of Oaxaca City and turn left at the big green Etla sign above the highway. The market is the prominent light-yellow *cantera* stone building, uphill from the rail station, about 0.4 kilometers (0.25 mi) from the highway.

SUCHILQUITONGO AND CERRO DE LA CAMPANA ARCHAEOLOGICAL ZONE
Suchilquitongo

Before heading uphill to investigate the important Cerro de la Campana archaeological zone, look around the nearby Suchilquitongo town plaza. Suchilquitongo ("Place of Flowers" in the Mixtec language; pop. 5,000) is the seat of the surrounding Suchilquitongo *municipio,* a rich domain of hills and mountains enclosing the emerald vale of the upper Río Atoyac. Using irrigation, bottomland farmers routinely bring in three crops per year, achieving some of Mexico's highest yields per acre in corn, beans, alfalfa, and squash. If only the rest of Oaxaca were so productive. Although virtually all of the bottomland is privately owned, much of the surrounding hills and mountains are undeveloped town communal pasturelands.

The Suchilquitongo **Museo Comunitario** (Community Museum; no phone, but check with the *presidencia* tel. 951/528-4616, 10 A.M.–2 P.M. and 4–8 P.M. Tues.–Sun.) is on the town plaza. It's one of best of the network of community museums sprinkled around the state, with artifacts, reproductions, and an

actual-size mock-up model of the famous Tomb 5, discovered in the Cerro de la Campana archaeological zone in 1985. A glance at the archaeological displays reveals why it's considered the most important Zapotec city-state tomb uncovered to date. It was literally a house of the dead, with the remains of about 20 noble personages from at least three generations, with calendrical birth names, such as 5-Earth, 5-Serpent, and 12-Monkey. Before the excavation, they lay at rest in a massive three-room, 15-foot-deep crypt complex among piles of jewelry, supplied with elaborate goods for the afterlife, and surrounded by bright murals of ceremonial scenes, including a grand procession of feathered and helmeted ball players. Before you leave the Tomb 5 mock-up, be sure to see the Sphere of Day and Night, and the richly engraved columns and tomb entrance door, both embossed with as-yet-untranslated Zapotec glyphs.

Another museum room illustrates the Spanish-Mexican custom of *mayordomía,* as acted out by Suchilquitongo people for their major fiesta, the July 22–27 fiesta of Santiago (St. James). Everyone participates—cooking food, making costumes, rehearsing for the dancing, setting up *ramadas* (temporary roofs) for shade, spiffing up the church, donating money—especially the *mayordomo,* the man or woman nominated by the *presidente municipal* and approved by a grand church meeting of the entire community to head all this up. The *mayordomo,* nearly always a person of means, usually ends his or her term of office poorer, but rich with community affection and prestige.

Before you leave Suchilquitongo, you might want to visit one of the town's **basket weavers** at work. For a small fee, maybe the equivalent of a couple of dollars, the person at the museum desk may be able to guide you (or find someone who can) to one of their workshops.

Suchilquitongo's other significant craft is **stonemasonry.** Local quarries mine three types—*morada* (pink), *blanco* (meaning white, but actually a pale green), and *amarillo* (pale yellow)—of the soft *cantera* (volcanic tufa) for which Oaxaca is famous. As you exit at the highway, go left a few hundred yards, and on the right you'll see the covered workshop of master stonemason **Cenobio Ausencio Pinelo Martínez** (tel. 952/528-4569), who is teaching his sons his disappearing craft.

Exploring Cerro de la Campana

From the town plaza, you can see the Cerro de la Campana cluster of hilltops above the northern horizon. The site is about a three-kilometer (two mi), 150-meter (500 ft) climb. If it's hot, hire a taxi. If not, be sure to wear a hat, sturdy shoes, and take water. Atop the hill, you'll find Tomb 5 (hopefully open to the public after years of restoration), a ball court, three courtyards, and three partly restored pyramids.

After you arrive atop the hill, look closely at the knolls in the immediate vicinity and you'll see that they too are topped by pyramids, approximately 20 in all. Also, as you walk next to a road-cut section of hillside, look carefully and you'll be able to spot and examine 1,500-year-old pottery shards.

Climb to the highest—the cross-topped—pyramid, and your reward will be a breezy view of the entire Etla Valley and mountain panorama. Notice the dark Monte Albán ridge, far to the southeast, to the right of distant Oaxaca City (below the Cerro San Felipe massif on the left). You can immediately see Cerro de la Campana's advantages: direct signal-fire communication with its contemporary, Monte Albán; a strong defensive position; and fertile riverbank fields. Why it was abandoned, like Monte Albán, around A.D. 800, remains a puzzle for future generations of archaeologists

to decipher from the bones, stones, and mute, mysterious glyphs Cerro de la Campana's builders left behind.

Getting There

Get to Suchilquitongo by bus via one of the Cooperativo de Autobuses Suchilquitongo buses, which leave from the *camionera central segunda clase* just north of the Abastos market in Oaxaca City, west of the *periférico*. Alternatively, you can go by a Suchilquitongo-bound *colectivo* on the prolongation of V. Trujano, which runs along the bus station's north side.

Drivers: Head out of Oaxaca City along Highway 190 in the direction of Mexico City, northwest. Bear right onto *libre* (toll-free) Highway 190 where the *cuota autopista* (toll expressway) splits off to the left, about 12 kilometers (7.5 mi) from the city center. Continue another several kilometers along *libre* Highway 190, pass an industrial park entrance on the left and, within a few minutes, turn left 27 kilometers (17 mi) from the city center at the big Suchilquitongo entrance arch on the left. Pass over the railroad tracks and continue straight ahead to the Community Museum, another 0.8 kilometers (0.5 mi) to the town plaza. Climb the plaza stairway on the right to the museum.

For the Cerro de la Campana archaeological zone, return to the railroad tracks, where Calle Victoria forks left, uphill north, passing a church, continuing a total of about 2.5 kilometers (1.5 mi) to the hilltop archaeological zone.

THE VALLEY OF OAXACA

PACIFIC RESORTS AND SOUTHERN SIERRA

Historically, Oaxaca's southern coastal residents have both earned their livelihoods and sought their connections with the outside world by the Mar del Sur, the Southern Sea, the traditional Mexican name for the Pacific Ocean. Before roads were built, the Oaxaca coast slumbered, every bit like an isolated South Seas island, dependent upon occasional ships for trade and news from the exterior world.

The major cause of the isolation was the towering, cloud-capped wall of the Sierra Madre del Sur (Mother Range of the South). Oaxaca's high southern Sierra, always remote and mysterious, was finally unveiled in its majesty only in the 1980s, when satellite photo measurements revealed that Cerro Quiexobra (kee-ay-SHOW-brah), at 3,750 meters (12,300 ft), was by far Oaxaca's tallest mountain massif, a scarce 64 kilometers (40 mi) due north of the Bahías de Huatulco.

From such high, cool, pine-crested summits along its entire 320-kilometer (200 mi) rampart, the Sierra Madre del Sur plunges precipitously downward more than three kilometers (two mi) through lush vine-hung canyon and foothill forest to the Pacific shore, an acacia-tufted expanse of endless summer.

There, as if forced southward by the weight of the high mountains, the coastline bulges to Oaxaca's (and nearly the entire country's) most southerly point, near the petite bay and resort of Puerto Ángel. From there, the Oaxaca coastline bends northerly—on its east side toward the Isthmus, and on its west side toward the Mixtec Coast, often called the Costa Chica (Little Coast) in southern Mexico.

© BRUCE WHIPPERMAN

HIGHLIGHTS

◖ Playa Estacahuite: This intimate cove, sheltered by friendly offshore rocks, enfolded by breeze-swept headlands, and teeming with colorful fish, ranks among Oaxaca's loveliest beaches (page 126).

◖ Playa Zipolite: A little bit for everyone – surf, sun, and plenty of clean, golden sand – makes Zipolite a choice spot for a relaxing day, week, or even a season (page 126).

◖ Centro Mexicano de la Tortuga: Far-seeing government action and community cooperation has converted a former turtle processing factory into a center for the recovery of Oaxaca's Pacific sea turtles (page 128).

◖ Cascadas Mágicas: Enjoy a day of strolling, swimming, picnicking, and admiring this lovely collection of bubbling blue waterfalls, in the sylvan tropical foothill forest not far from Huatulco (page 170).

◖ Playa Zicatela: The two types of Zicatela waves, simply mountainous and super-mountainous, make for lots of excitement, for both the intrepid surfers and the spectators on the beachfront (page 176).

◖ West-Side Beaches: Manzanillo, Carrizalillo, and Bachoco: Rewarding off-beach snorkeling, golden sand, and *palapa* restaurants make these three playas the local favorites for Sunday family outings (page 177).

◖ Laguna Manialtepec: Easy access, mirror-smooth oft-fresh water, and dozens of bird species identifiable in an afternoon make this a prime adventure ground for kayakers, boaters, and campers (page 192).

◖ Santuario de Nuestra Señora de Juquila: Several duplicate images of the beloved patron are accessible to accommodate the hundreds of thousands of adoring pilgrims who arrive in Juquila yearly (page 199).

◖ La Capilla del Pedimento: This small hilltop chapel is a necessary second devotional stop for Juquila pilgrims, who adorn a life-size replica image of the Virgin of Juquila daily with dozens of *milagros* (metal wish tokens) (page 200).

◖ Pinotepa Market: Among the picked-from-the-garden vegetables, mountain-gathered herbal remedies, and piñatas, you may see an heirloom *pozahuanco* (Mixtec wraparound skirt) for sale at this market (page 210).

PACIFIC RESORTS

LOOK FOR ◖ TO FIND RECOMMENDED SIGHTS, ACTIVITIES, DINING, AND LODGING.

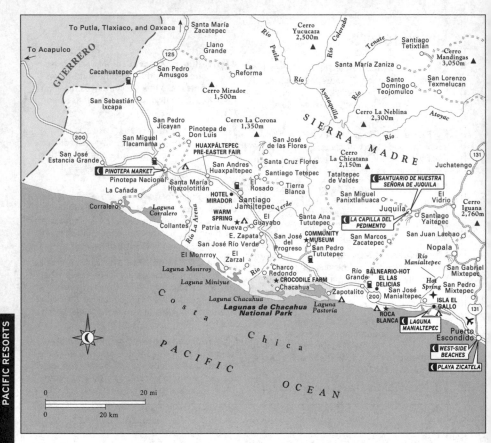

During the 1970s and 1980s, paved highways and airlines ended the Oaxaca coast's isolation and brought a trickle of Mexican and foreign visitors to the region. The government recognized the area's potential and began developing a new, ecologically correct vacationland at the Bahías de Huatulco. Meanwhile, visitors were discovering the South Seas village resorts of Puerto Ángel and Puerto Escondido.

Now the steady stream of vacationers can choose from a growing menu of outdoor diversions, from strolling the sand and snorkeling in hidden coves to rescuing sea turtle eggs, splashing in upland waterfalls, and lodging comfortably overnight at rustic jungle coffee farms.

PLANNING YOUR TIME

Where you go and how much time you spend on Oaxaca's sun-drenched southern coast depends on what you prefer. The prime resorts of Puerto Ángel (and its neighboring villages Zipolite and Mazunte), the Bahías de Huatulco, and Puerto Escondido each have their distinct charms. In all three, you will be able to enjoy beautiful beaches and good restaurants; but there the similarity ends. Puerto Ángel is heaven for those who prefer sleepy Mexico beach-village ambience. On the other hand, Puerto Escondido has the spectacularly awesome breakers of Playa Zicatela, the most famous (and most challenging) surfing beach

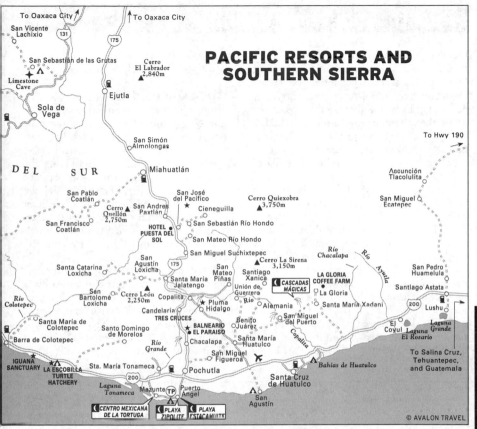

in Mexico; plenty of handicrafts shopping; and a pair of lovely hidden coves. And, the up-to-date Bahías de Huatulco resort has the widest range of hotels, from modest to luxurious; several very good restaurants; and a small kingdom of sylvan forests that enfold its nine, coral-strewn blue bays.

If you have a week, you could spend it all at one place, spending half of your time on the beach, in the water, and by the pool. For more activity, in Puerto Ángel, spend two or three days on excursions, to **Playa Estacahuite,** the **Centro Mexicano de la Tortuga** in Mazunte, La Ventanilla for bird- and crocodile-watching, maybe continuing for a day upcountry in

Chacalapa for a stroll to the waterfall, and continuing to the pine-scented sierra summit at San José del Pacífico. In Huatulco, you can easily spend a day on a catamaran tour exploring the bays, another day rafting or kayaking the Río Copalita, and a third day visiting La Gloria coffee farm and the **Cascadas Mágicas** in the tropical foothill forest. In Puerto Escondido be sure to spend a day wildlife-viewing at sylvan **Laguna Manialtepec,** maybe continuing farther afield to explore Parque Nacional Lagunas de Chacahua, and finally heading uphill into the Chatino indigenous heartland to visit the **Santuario de Nuestra Señora de Juquila** pilgrimage shrine.

Puerto Ángel and Vicinity

During his three presidencies, Oaxaca-born Benito Juárez shaped many dreams into reality. One such dream was to better the lot of his native brethren in the isolated south of Oaxaca by developing a port for shipping the lumber and coffee they could harvest in the lush Pacific-slope jungles of the Sierra Madre del Sur. The small bay of Puerto Ángel, directly south of the state capital, was chosen, and by 1870 it had become Oaxaca's busiest port.

Unfortunately, Benito Juárez died two years later. New priorities and Puerto Ángel's isolation soon wilted Juárez's plan, and Puerto Ángel lapsed into a generations-long slumber.

In the 1960s, Puerto Ángel was still a sleepy little spot connected by a single frail land link—a tortuous cross-Sierra dirt road—to the rest of the country. Adventure travelers saw it at the far south of the map and dreamed of a South Seas paradise. They came and were not disappointed. Although that first tourist trickle has grown steadily, it's still only enough to support the sprinkling of modest lodgings and restaurants that now dot the beaches and hillsides around Puerto Ángel's tranquil little blue bay.

Getting Oriented

Puerto Ángel is at the southern terminus of Highway 175 from Oaxaca City, about nine kilometers (six mi) downhill from its intersection with Highway 200. It's a small place, where nearly everything is within walking distance along the beach, which a rocky bayfront hill divides into two parts: Playa Principal, the main town beach; and sheltered west-side Playa Panteón, the tourist favorite. A scenic boulder-decorated shoreline *andador* (walkway; watch out for gaps and holes in the concrete) connects the two beaches.

A paved road winds west from Puerto Ángel along the coastline a couple of miles to Playa Zipolite, lined by a colony of beachfront *cabañas,* popular with an international cadre of budget-minded seekers of heaven on earth. Continuing west, the road passes the former turtle-processing village beaches of Playa San

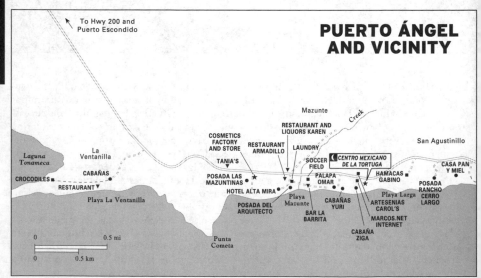

PUERTO ÁNGEL AND VICINITY

Agustinillo and Playa Mazunte. From there it goes on another 6.4 kilometers (four mi), past the joining with Highway 200 (and thence Puerto Escondido) at San Antonio village at Kilometer 198.

The major local service and transportation center is **Pochutla** (pop. 35,000), a mile north along Highway 175 from its Highway 200 junction.

Getting Around

Local *colectivo* taxis ferry passengers frequently between Pochutla and Puerto Ángel (fare around $1) from about 7 A.M. until 8 P.M., stopping at the Highway 200 intersection. Some taxis continue to Zipolite after stopping on Bulevar Virgilio Uribe, Puerto Ángel's main bayfront street. To continue to Playa San Agustinillo and Playa Mazunte, you must transfer to another *colectivo* (arriving from the opposite direction) in Zipolite. Private taxis also routinely make runs between Puerto Ángel and either Zipolite or Pochutla for about $7.

You can also get around (much more expensively) by boat. Captains routinely take parties of up to eight for sightseeing, snorkeling,

Puerto Ángel's village church bell

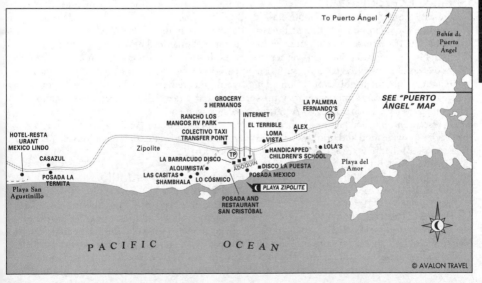

© BRUCE WHIPPERMAN

PACIFIC RESORTS

and picnicking to a number of nearby beaches. Bargain at Playa Panteón: The rate should run about $30/hour for a whole boat rented privately for 6–8 people or about $15 per person per day for a shared boat.

Tours and rental cars are other options for getting around.

SIGHTS AND BEACHES
Playas Principal and Panteón

Playa Principal's 400 yards of wide golden sand decorate most of Puerto Ángel's bayfront. Waves can be strong near the pier, where they often surge vigorously onto the beach and recede with a sometimes-strong undertow. Swimming is always more tranquil at the sheltered west end toward Playa Panteón. The clear waters are good for casual snorkeling around the rocks on both sides of the bay.

Sheltered Playa Panteón (Cemetery Beach) is Puerto Ángel's sunning beach, lined with squadrons of beach chairs and umbrellas in front of beachside restaurants. **Playa Oso** (Bear Beach) is a little dab of sand beside a rugged seastack of rock beyond Playa Panteón. It's fun to swim to Playa Oso from Playa Panteón.

◖ Playa Estacahuite

Decorating the rocky shoreline, about half a mile outside the opposite (east) side of Puerto Ángel bay, Playa Estacahuite (ay-stah-kah-WEE-tay) is actually two beaches in one: a pair of luscious coral-sand nooks teeming with fish grazing the living reef just offshore. (Don't put your hands in crevices; a moray eel may mistake your finger for a fish and bite.) A pair of *palapa* restaurants perched picturesquely above the beaches provide food and drinks. Get there in less than a mile by taxi ($3) or on foot via the dirt road (watch for sign) that forks right off the highway, about 400 yards uphill from beachfront Bulevar Uribe.

◖ Playa Zipolite

Playa Zipolite (see-poh-LEE-tay), a wide, mile-long strand of brilliant golden sand enfolded by headlands and backed by palm groves, is simply stunning. It stretches from the intimate little cove and beach of **Playa del Amor,** tucked on its east side, to towering cactus-festooned sea cliffs rising behind the new-age Shambala retreat on the west end.

Playa Zipolite, although often good for wading and for casual swimming (with care), its surf, usually tranquil in the mornings (but always with significant undertow), can turn thunderous by the afternoon, especially when offshore storms magnify both the swells and the undertow. Experienced surfers love these times, when everyone but experts should stay out.

Playa Zipolite has evolved from a lineup of stick and thatch beachfront *cabañas* to mostly concrete hotels, most with oceanfront *palapa* restaurants. Many of these hotels share a new, paved two-block street-front known locally as the **adoquín** (ah-doh-KEEN), along with a procession of home-grown restaurants and small businesses, from grocery and pharmacy to surf shop, laundry, and Internet stores. All of this, in a neighborhood known as **Colonia Roca Blanca,** is now Playa Zipolite's town center. Get there, heading west from Puerto Ángel, by turning left, past Piñ Palmera, the children's school.

Good surfing notwithstanding, Playa Zipolite's renown stems from its status as one of the very few nude beaches in Mexico. Bathing au naturel, practiced nearly entirely by visitors and a few local young men, is tolerated only grudgingly by local people, many of whose livelihoods depend on the nudists. If you're discreet and take off your clothes at the more isolated west end (behind the big rock), no one will appear to mind (and women will largely avoid voyeuristic attention from Mexican boys and men).

Playas San Agustinillo and Mazunte

About a mile west of Playa Zipolite, a wide, mile-long, yellow-sand beach curves past the village of San Agustinillo. On the open ocean, but partly sheltered by offshore rocks at the west, its surf is much like that of Playa Zipolite, varying from gentle in the morning to rough

PUERTO ÁNGEL

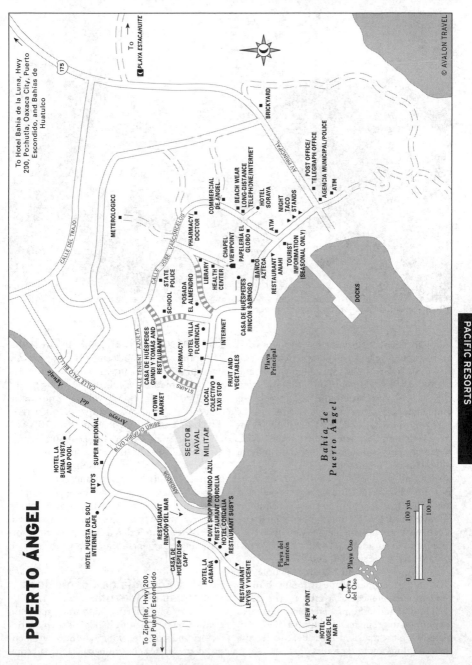

© AVALON TRAVEL

To Hotel Bahia de la Luna, Hwy 200, Pochutla, Oaxaca City, Puerto Escondido, and Bahias de Huatulco

175

To ► PLAYA ESTACAHUITE

METEOROLOGICO

BRICKYARD

CALLE DEL TRAJO

CALLE JOSÉ VASCONCELOS

AV PRINCIPAL

COMMERCIAL DE ÁNGEL

BEACH WEAR
LONG-DISTANCE TELEPHONE/INTERNET

POST OFFICE/
TELEGRAPH OFFICE

AGENCIA MUNICIPAL/POLICE

ATM

HOTEL SORAYA

PHARMACY/
DOCTOR

CHAPEL
VIEWPOINT

PAPELERIA EL GLOBO

NIGHT TACO STANDS

ATM

LIBRARY

HEALTH CENTER

BANCO AZTECA

SCHOOL

STATE POLICE

POSADA EL ALMENDRO

RESTAURANT ANAHI

TOURIST INFORMATION (SEASONAL ONLY)

CASA DE HUÉSPEDES RINCÓN SABROSO

DOCKS

CALLE TENIENT AZUETA

HOTEL VILLA FLORENCIA

INTERNET

CASA DE HUÉSPEDES GUNDI Y TOMAS AND RESTAURANT

PHARMACY

STAIRS

FRUIT AND VEGETABLES

Playa Principal

CALLE PALO BELLO

Arroyo del

TOWN MARKET

LOCAL COLECTIVO TAXI STOP

Bahía de Puerto Ángel

BLVD VIRGILIO URIBE

SECTOR NAVAL MILITAR

Arroyo de Andador

HOTEL LA BUENA VISTA AND POOL

SUPER REGIONAL

BETO'S

HOTEL PUESTA DEL SOL/ INTERNET CAFE

RESTAURANT RINCÓN DEL MAR

DIVE SHOP PROFUNDO AZUL

RESTAURANT CORDELIA

HOTEL CORDELIA

RESTAURANT SUSY'S

CASA DE HUÉSPEDES CAPY

HOTEL LA CABAÑA

RESTAURANT LEYVIS Y VICENTE

Playa del Panteón

Playa Oso

VIEW POINT

Cueva del Oso

HOTEL ÁNGEL DEL MAR

To Zipolite, Hwy 200, and Puerto Escondido

100 yds
100 m

0
0

Playa San Agustinillo, a top Oaxaca beach

© BRUCE WHIPPERMAN

in the afternoon, depending mostly upon wind and offshore swells. Small village groceries and beachside *palapa* restaurants supply food and drinks to the occasional Playa Zipolite overflow as well as to local families on weekends and holidays. Fishing is excellent either in the surf from nearby rocks, by rented *panga,* or from your own boat launched from the beach. Beach camping is customary, especially in front of beachfront restaurants.

The half-mile-long, yellow-sand Mazunte Beach, like San Agustinillo, is semi-sheltered and varies from tranquil to rough. Fishing is likewise good, beach camping is customary (as a courtesy, ask nearby business owners if it's okay), and local stores and seafood *palapa* restaurants sell basic supplies and food.

San Agustinillo and Mazunte people, including a group of European (many Italian) resident-entrepreneurs, have been renovating their houses and building hotels and *cabañas* to accommodate an increasing number of visitors. Signs along the road and at the beach advertise their lodgings and restaurants.

◖ Centro Mexicano de la Tortuga

The former turtle-processing plant at Mazunte lives on as the Mazunte Turtle Museum (on the main road, east end of the village, tel./ fax 958/584-3376, www.centromexicano delatortuga.org, www.tomzap.com/turtle .html, 10 A.M.–4:30 P.M. Wed.–Sat., 10 A.M.– 2:30 P.M. Sun., $4). At the museum, which includes an aquarium, study center, and turtle hatchery, you can peruse displays illustrating the ongoing turtle research and conservation program and see members of most of Mexico's turtle species paddling in tanks overlooking the beach where their ancestors once swarmed. Guided tours are offered in a number of foreign languages, including English, German, and Italian.

Fábrica Ecología de Cosméticos Naturales de Mazunte

About half a mile farther west along the main road through Mazunte village is a cosmetics factory and store (tel. 958/587-4860, www.cos meticosmazunte.com, cosmenat@hotmail.com,

9 A.M.–5 P.M. daily). Initially funded partly by the Body Shop Foundation and spearheaded by the local community, the project has grown into an important local industry, with dozens of workers and a sizable shop filled with thousands of bottles of locally produced all-natural shampoo, skin cream, hair conditioner, and much more. The staff is working hard to assure that the effort continues to grow, so that locally grown products such as coconut, corn,

A TURTLE ARRIVES AT PLAYA LA VENTANILLA

It was raining, and the wind, although not cold, was driving the surf high on Playa La Ventanilla. On the rocky headland above the beach, a small hole, like a round window, appeared to have been carved in the rock. Our guide, Pedro, who had just rowed us through the community wetland ecological preserve, explained.

"That's why we call this La Ventanilla. Because of that hole that the sea and wind have carved out."

"It's like a little window, a *ventanilla*."

"Yes, that's right."

He then went on to tell us something we didn't expect.

"We are waiting for the turtles to arrive. They come this time of year, especially when the wind blows toward shore like this. Yesterday afternoon and night nearly 80 turtles came and laid about 8,000 eggs."

It seemed too many.

"Eight thousand? Are you sure?"

"Yes...and they're buried right here."

He pointed to a fenced-off area in the sand, laid out in a grid of several dozen stakes.

"Each turtle lays about 100 eggs, and we buried each one's eggs separately under each of these stakes."

Before I could answer, a lookout atop the headland yelled something.

"A turtle has come ashore."

We scanned the beach. A black, pointed silhouette showed at the edge of the sand.

"There it is."

Two or three young male villagers raced toward the beach. They stopped several steps short of the turtle, however.

"We don't want to interfere with its egg-laying."

For several minutes, we watched the turtle, not large, perhaps 50 pounds and two feet long, struggle to climb one last small sand ridge before reaching the flat part of the beach. We asked what kind of turtle it was.

"It's a *golfina* turtle," Pedro explained. "Two other kinds arrive here. The *laut*, and the *sacasillo*. The *laut* can be big, maybe as much as a ton. They arrive in February."

After watching the turtle struggle for a few minutes longer, Pedro decided to help. He picked it up by the shell and placed it on level sand a dozen feet farther inland. He sympathized with the turtle's plight.

"The turtle seems very tired. It's small and weak."

The boost seemed to encourage the turtle. It immediately began digging with its flippers. After 10 minutes it began depositing its eggs in a foot-deep hole. Pedro promptly removed the eggs and placed them in a bucket. After a few minutes, the seemingly near-exhausted turtle was finished. Pedro had kept count.

"Seventy-five eggs. Not many."

"But it's better than nothing."

Pedro nodded his head in agreement

He let the turtle cover up the empty hole. After doing so, it packed down the sand over where it had deposited the eggs, rocking its body back and forth with its flippers. Then it turned and headed back toward the waves. Pedro gently lifted it up and placed it near the water. Soon the turtle was gone, beneath the surf.

Pedro took the bucket of 75 eggs and buried them beneath a new marker alongside the other 80 markers.

"You are the turtle papa," we said. He laughed.

"Soon these eggs will hatch into thousands of little turtles, which we will return to the sea."

"And maybe many of them will return here."

"Yes, we hope so."

PACIFIC RESORTS

and avocado oils and natural aromatics will form the basis for a thriving cottage cosmetics industry.

Playa La Ventanilla

Continue about 2.4 kilometers (1.5 mi) west along the main road over the low hill west of Mazunte and turn left at the signed dirt road to pristine wildlife haven **Playa and Laguna La Ventanilla** (cocodrilianos@hotmail.com, 8 A.M.–6 P.M. daily). Now protected by local residents, swarms of birds, including pelicans, cormorants, and herons, and a population of wild *cocodrilos* and *lagartos* is making a comeback in a bushy mangrove wetland.

Boat workers headquartered at the sturdy **visitors center** *palapa,* past the beach village road's end parking lot, guide visitors on a two-hour ecotour (adults $4, kids $2), which includes a stop for refreshment at a little mid-lagoon island. The boat workers are known for their wildlife sensitivity and allow no motor vehicles within 100 yards of their communally owned lagoon-sanctuary.

The Playa La Ventanilla community has taken responsibility for protecting the turtles that arrive on their beach against poachers. During both February and June–October, hundreds of sea turtles come ashore to lay eggs. If necessary, community volunteers help the exhausted turtles up the steep beach, where they lay their eggs. Volunteers then gather the eggs and rebury them in a secure spot. After the hatchlings emerge about a month and a half later, volunteers nurture them for about three months and release them safely back into the ocean. For more information and photos, visit www.tomzap.com/ventanil.html.

Besides lagoon tours and saving turtles, La Ventanilla cooperative maintains the excellent beach-view **Restaurant Maiz Azul** (8 A.M.–7 P.M. daily, $2–6), run by half a dozen dedicated women. They specialize in local recipes, such as savory banana-leafed-wrapped tamales, baked turkey smothered in *mole* sauce, and yummy chiles rellenos. They also sell their own home-ground fresh peanut butter.

Furthermore, the Ventanilla community

invites visitors to stay in their very rustic accommodations. They offer two options: either four clean *cabañas* (on the left as you enter), with choice of one king-size bed, two double beds, or one double bed, all with mosquito nets and private hot-water shower-bath, for $35 s or d; or, a four room dormitory-style *cabaña,* each room with two bunk beds for a total of four people per room, with shared toilets and showers, for $15 per person. Email cocodrilianos@ hotmail.com for more information.

ACCOMMODATIONS

The Puerto Ángel area offers about a dozen accommodations, most of which are modest, homegrown guesthouse-style lodgings. The successful ones have given their legion of savvy repeat customers what they want: clean, basic, tepid-water accommodations in tranquil, television-free settings where Puerto Ángel's natural isolation and tropical charm set the tone for long, restful holidays.

Visitors have their choice of several neighborhoods. In Puerto Ángel itself, hotels and guesthouses dot the hillside above the main town beach, the pier, and the single main business street. The Playa Panteón lodgings, by contrast, are on the sleepier west side of the bay, above the lineup of rustic *palapa* restaurants along petite Playa Panteón.

Outside of Puerto Ángel visitors also have many choices, mostly right on the beach, but some atop breezy hillsides, above the plumy, west-side country beachfront hamlets of Zipolite, San Agustinillo, and Mazunte.

Unless otherwise specified, prices listed here are year-round rates, excepting Christmas–New Year's and Easter holiday seasons, when rates customarily rise 25–50 percent, depending on demand.

Puerto Ángel: Main Town
$25-50
Puerto Ángel's most welcoming lodging is the exceptional ◖ **Casa de Huéspedes Gundi y Tomás** (tel. 958/584-3068, gundtoma@ hotmail.com, www.puertoangel-hotel.com, $25–50 depending on room), the life project

Every day seems like Sunday at guesthouse Casa de Huéspedes Gundi y Tomás.

© BRUCE WHIPPERMAN

PACIFIC RESORTS

of personable German-born Gundi Ley and her sons, Bastian and Fabian López. Their homey, rustic-aesthetic complex rambles up a leafy hillside to a breezy bay-view *palapa,* where patrons relax, socialize, and enjoy food and drink from their kitchen. Below and above that, guests enjoy two rows of several clean, simply, but colorfully furnished rooms, shaded by two hammock-strewn view porches. Besides all this, they change U.S.-dollar travelers checks, volunteer information about local sights, do laundry, and pick up and drop off guests at the Huatulco airport. In addition, Bastián and Fabián, both accomplished surfers, offer surfing lessons in English, German, or Spanish, and take parties out for beach tours in their sturdy boat.

Their accommodations, which also include the **Almendro** tropical-garden *posada* (lodging) near the beach downhill, consist of 14 rooms—some shared shower and toilets, some private—and one bungalow (50 percent discount for a one-week rental), all with fans and a good restaurant. Get there via the lane (see

the sign, uphill side) that stair-steps uphill near the west end of Puerto Ángel's main beachfront street.

Travelers who enjoy being right in the middle of the Puerto Ángel beachfront street scene choose the petite **Hotel Villa Florencia** (Blv. Virgilio Uribe, tel./fax 958/584-3044, villaserenaoax@hotmail.com, $20 s, $30 d, $35 t, add $3 for a/c). Here, in the shady interior lobby-patio, past the porch-front café, tranquility reigns as soft classic songs and instrumental music play in the background and guests read and relax on comfortable chairs and couches. Upstairs, the approximately 15 rooms with bath are immaculate and thoughtfully decorated with local art and handicrafts.

Enjoy the variety and luxury of west-side (two blocks past the bridge) hilltop castle-in-the-palms at solid long-time **Hotel Puesta del Sol** (Barrio del Sol, tel. 958/584-3096, tel./fax 958/584-3315, www.puertoangel.net/puesta_del_sol_s.html, $25–50 d). Luxuriant tropical verdure festoons a sunny inner patio, leading up to the main building, with 14 immaculate,

PACIFIC RESORTS

semi-deluxe rooms, quaintly (but invitingly) appointed with ruffled bedspreads and curtains (with private baths, two with hot water.) A dining room serves breakfast (8–11 A.M., $3–6). An open air, hammock-hung patio overlooks it all. Web-access computers are available for guest use.

Back on the east side of town, find the 1960s-modern style **Hotel Soraya** (Priv. José Vasconcelos 2A, tel./fax 958/584-3009, hotelsorayadepuertoangel@hotmail.com, $45 s or d, $50 t fan only, $55 s or d, $60 with a/c), perched on the bluff above the pier. The well-managed hotel includes a restaurant (closed Sept.–Oct.) with a luminous bay view, fine for morning breakfasts and sunset-glow dinners. Outside, two tiers of semi-deluxe, light and comfortable rooms enclose a parking patio. Although some rooms have air-conditioning, the fan-only ones may be preferable, since they avoid the air-conditioner noise and oft-associated mildew. Rooms vary; some have bay-view balconies, such as #24 and #29. Check more than one before moving in. Rent on the upper story for maximum privacy, air, and light.

Another worthy west-side Puerto Ángel accommodation is **Hotel La Buena Vista** (Calle Palo Bello, tel./fax 958/584-3104, reservations@labuenavista.com, www.labuenavista.com, $50–70), tucked on the hillside that rises just west of the mid-town Arroyo de Aguaje bridge. The hotel's five accommodations levels stair-step artfully (but steeply) up the forested slope. First- and second-level rooms look out onto verdure-framed garden forest views. On the 3rd level are more rooms and a luxuriously airy restaurant *palapa* that opens to an airy bay vista. The hotel climaxes with several large onyx-tile-floored 4th- and 5th-floor rooms that share an entire private view patio with hammocks. There, the owners have provided a luxurious view pool-patio for their guests ($3 entrance for non-guests). All rooms are immaculate, light, and simply but tastefully furnished, with spotless bathrooms. Several of the approximately 20 rooms have private hammock-hung view balconies; all rooms come with fans, mosquito curtains,

and breakfast and supper at the restaurant (in season only, $4–14), but with room-temperature water only.

Playa Panteón
UNDER $25
Heading around the curve of the bay to the Playa Panteón neighborhood, you'll find one of Puerto Ángel's old standby budget lodgings, **Casa de Huéspedes Capy** (Playa Panteón, tel./fax 958/584-3002, $12 s, $18 d in one bed, $22 d, $25 t in two beds), perched on the bay-view hillside by the road fork to Playa Zipolite. Rooms are stacked in two stories, many of which enjoy views toward the beach. The rooms are basic but clean, with fans and cool-water private baths. The upper rooms open to an airy bay-view porch. The restaurant, with TV, is handy for breakfast.

$25-50
Downhill stands Puerto Ángel's only truly beachfront lodging, **Hotel Cordelia** (right on Playa Panteón, tel. 958/584-3109, fax 958/582-3231, azul_profundomx@hotmail.com, $40 s or d, $60 d, t, or q in two beds). The Cordelia's seven rooms, most with expansive bay views, are pleasingly decorated with rustic whitewashed walls, attractive native floor tiles, natural wood furniture, and artful tile touches in the bathrooms (with room-temperature water). No phones, no TV, just the murmur of the gentle Playa Panteón surf to lull you to sleep. With in-house Internet, fans, and handy beachfront restaurant for breakfast downstairs (seafood is a bit pricey for dinner).

Bahía de la Luna
$50-200
Visitors who long for the delights of a hidden south seas hideaway can have it at **Bahía de la Luna** (on the coast about two miles east of Puerto Ángel, tel. 958/584-3460, info@bahiadelaluna.com, www.bahiadelaluna.com, $70 s, $80 d, $130 suite, $200 villa). New owners have revitalized this mini-paradise, set on a petite, palm-shaded half-moon strand, lapped by gentle waves and enfolded by rocky headlands.

They offer about a dozen comfortable rustic-chic thatched, adobe *cabañas,* some with panoramic views, on the forested hillside above the beach, and others, tucked in the leafy shade, right on the beach below. *Cabaña* rentals feature one room with big bed, reading lamps, and private tepid-water shower-bath. Two larger similarly comfortable units—a suite accommodating four, and a villa accommodating eight—are also available. All include a hearty breakfast in the beachfront restaurant. There, guests enjoy shady beach *palapas* with recliners, hammocks for snoozing, and snorkeling equipment.

Get there via the signed but rough side road, east off of Highway 175, about eight kilometers (five mi) downhill from the Highway 200 Pochutla junction, or three kilometers (two mi) uphill from Puerto Ángel. After about two bumpy miles from the turnoff, the road steepens and becomes impassable for all but sturdy four-wheel-drive vehicles. It's best to go by taxi.

Playa Estacahuite
OVER $200
Nestled on the west flank of gorgeous Playa Estacahuite, **Casa Bichu** (Playa Estacahuite, tel. 958/584-3489, -90, -91, from Canada or U.S. toll-free direct 877/223-9590, reservaciones@casabichu.com, www.casabichu.com, $350–500 d) is graced by an abundance of natural, hand-fashioned décor. From regal inlaid mahogany floors and luxuriously thick thatched roofs, to polished liana vine handrails and stunning ocean views, nothing has been spared at Casa Bichu to create heaven on earth. All 14 rooms and suites, are large and superbly furnished with all possible amenities, including comfy king-size beds, soft couches, and garden and vine-framed ocean view windows, all of which blend to create a feeling of luxurious seclusion.

Accommodations, all called "villas" come in three variations, Garden ($350), Deluxe ($460), and Resort ($500), depending upon size and location. All villas come with breakfast, exercise machines, sauna, in-house Internet, and

gourmet restaurant ($10–35). Spa services, such as massage and temazcal ceremonial hot room, are extra. Pets ($50 extra) and young adults 16 and over are welcomed.

Zipolite
UNDER $25
The *cabañas* of **Lo Cósmico** (Playa Zipolite, no phone, admin@locosmico.com, www.locosmico.com, $20–40 d) nestle on a cactus-decorated rocky knoll at Playa Zipolite's sheltered west end. White spheres perched on their thatched-roof peaks lend a mystical Hindu-Buddhist accent to the *cabañas'* already picturesque appearance. In the restaurant atop the knoll, you're likely to find Antonio Nadurille, Lo Cósmico's Mexican owner-manager. He watches after the *cabañas* and the restaurant, specializing in a dozen varieties of tasty crêpes. His hillside and beach-level *cabañas* are clean, candle-lit, and equipped with hammocks and concrete floors, with shared bath and toilets. Recently, Antonio has built a number of sturdy, rock-walled, hurricane-proof designer rooms with bath on his hilltop with a view. *Note:* All of Lo Cósmico's very clean shared toilet and shower facilities are separate from the accommodations, a short walk downhill.

$25-50
Shambhala (Playa Zipolite, tel. 958/584-3152, fax 958/584-3151, shambhala_vision@excite.com, www.advantagemexico.com/shambhala, $25–50), which shares the same forested, west-side headland as Lo Cósmico, is—as it sounds—a tranquil Buddhist-style retreat. Shambhala's driving force is the articulate owner–community leader Gloria Esperanza Johnson, who arrived in Zipolite by accident in 1970 and decided to stay, eventually adopting Mexican citizenship.

Shambhala is a peaceful, alcohol-free haven for lovers of reading, sunbathing, hiking, yoga, and meditation. It perches atop an enviable few acres at the edge of a sylvan hinterland. Adjacent cactus-studded cliffs plummet spectacularly to surf-splashed rocks below, while paths fan out through lush green (in July–Dec.)

wall art at Shambhala retreat

© BRUCE WHIPPERMAN

tropical deciduous forest. An excellent macrobiotic restaurant with panoramic view completes the attractive picture.

Gloria has built Shambhala from the ground up; she now offers five rustic *cabañas* on a no-reservation, first-come-first-served basis only. Choices include one large beachfront *cabaña* with kitchen, accommodating four with shared toilet and shower, and a second beachfront *cabaña* for two with shared toilet and shower. Also in the leafy (green in summer–early winter) uphill forest overlooking lovely Zipolite beach, are a pair of smaller *cabañas*, each with private toilet and shower-bath, and a larger-view *cabaña*, accommodating three, with shared toilet and shower. All *cabañas* come with fans and mosquito nets.

Get to both Shambhala and Lo Cósmico by turning toward the beach from the main Puerto Ángel–Zipolite road onto the signed dirt driveway at Zipolite's west end (where the *colectivos* stop to transfer passengers). Bear right at the first fork, then left at the next for Lo Cósmico or right for Shambhala.

Smack at the center of the Zipolite beachfront scene stands **Posada Mexico** (Playa Zipolite, tel./fax 958/584-3194, info@posadamexico.com, www.posadamexico.com, $20 s, $30 d private bath, $28 d shared bath), with its dozen South-Seas rustic *cabañas* basking in a flowery beachfront garden. The *cabañas* come in two styles. The four most attractive are right on the beach, each with upstairs bamboo and thatch sleeping *palapa,* with a private toilet and room-temperature shower and a hammock-hung porch below at beach level. The six shared bath units line up in a row on one side, and are plain, with only double bed and mosquito net.

The ambience at Posada Mexico invites relaxation, by private hammock or at the hotel's popular Italian-Mexican beachfront restaurant, where the mostly youthful guests enjoy late breakfasts, stroll out for swims, read thick novels, and kick back and enjoy convivial conversation with mostly North American and European fellow vacationers. Rentals include beds with mosquito nets.

$50-100

For a touch of luxury right on the gorgeous Zipolite west-end beach, consider **El Alquimista** (Playa Zipolite, tel. 958/587-8961, www.el-alquimista.com, el-alquimista.com, $65). Although mostly known as a good restaurant, El Alquimista also offers half a dozen comfortably rustic beachfront *cabañas,* each with double bed, fan, private room-temperature bath, and a beachview porch with hammock, perfect for a relaxing week on the beach. Get there by turning toward the beach from the main Puerto Ángel–Zipolite road onto the signed dirt driveway at Zipolite's west end (where the *colectivos* stop to transfer passengers). At the first fork, bear left straight toward the beach.

Bungalows **(Las Casitas** (Playa Zipolite, local cell tel. 044-958/587-8464, info@las-casitas.net, www.las-casitas.net, $28–100), also on Zipolite's far west end, occupy the same leafy hilltop as, but west of, Shambhala. Las Casitas is the labor of love of friendly Italian builders-owners Daniela and Bruno Canibus, who have created their vision of paradise in Zipolite's summer-green tropical forest. They offer five rustically picturesque housekeeping bungalows, meticulously hand-built of all-natural materials, in a lovingly tended naturalistic garden of meandering stone pathways, sea views, refreshing breezes, and a thatched *palapa* restaurant (breakfast $3–6, supper $9–14), fine for enjoying leisurely meals and conversation with fellow guests. A path leads downhill to Zipolite beach.

The five bungalows, each unique, come with kitchenettes equipped with gas stove, utensils, and purified water. Two of the bungalows, El Organo and La Tortuga, the most private options, are spacious studios, furnished with one double bed and private toilet and shower-bath. The other two bungalows, Los Platanos and La Ceiba, accommodate six and nine people respectively in three separate bedrooms with shared kitchen and bathroom facilities. The Los Platanos bungalow has rooms for one, two, and three people each. The rooms in the larger La Ceiba bungalow are for two, three, and four

people each. A fifth large and luxurious bungalow, El Sueño, is the most expensive and comes with kitchen and private bath. The attraction of all the bungalows is lots of outside tropical living. On the other hand, be sure to bring mosquito repellent.

Get to Las Casitas via the dirt road to Lo Cósmico and Shambhala, which you will pass along the way. Continue uphill about two hundred yards more to the Las Casitas gate.

Alternatively, folks who want peace and quiet and don't mind climbing stairs might enjoy **Loma Linda retreat** (no phone, info@lalomalinda.com, www.lalomalinda.com, $40–95). Here, welcoming European-born yoga instructor Brigette Longueville manages a yoga retreat and Feldenkreis center, while also renting out six unique rustic lodging bungalows. Her suite of charming stone, wood, and adobe accommodations decorate a steep, hillside with panoramic ocean views above the middle of Zipolite beach. A stairway winds among the bungalows (three roomy, for four people, and three petite, for two people). All bungalows have private toilets and room-temperature shower-baths. Two of the larger bungalows have lofts; one has a kitchen. Prices vary according to size. Children are welcome. Add $10 per extra person. Yoga and Feldenkreis activities are held in an adjacent, similarly decorated building. The atmosphere is tranquil and austere, with no restaurant, nor any alcohol sold.

San Agustinillo
$25-50

A number of lodgings sprinkle the San Agustinillo beachfront and hillside above the road. Here, you can enjoy it all: charming Mexican beach village ambience; stores and small restaurants nearby; hammock-hung verandas with gorgeous views of the foaming San Agustinillo surf; and hundreds of yards of golden sand to wander upon.

One of the most popular options, where you can walk out your door right onto the sand, is **Mexico Lindo** (Playa San Agustinillo, no phone, faustojasso@gmail.com, $40 d), at the west end of the village. Italian-born owner-manager Fausto offers five spacious individually decorated *cabañas* in two stories, with soft beds and private shower-baths. Amenities include fans and Fausto's good restaurant next door.

$50-100

In the middle of San Agustinillo is **Casazul** (tel. 958/584-6489, casazulplus@hotmail.com, www.casazulposada.com, $35–85), the lovely life-project of friendly owner Yolanda Quintana. It's situated uphill two long blocks, at the end of a driveway signed "Casa Azul." This hillside-perched stucco-and-tile, art-decorated complex offers four guest lodgings, including a rustic whitewashed *cabaña* in-the-round, with queen-size bed, small refrigerator, and private bath, by the swimming pool. Two "casitas" each come with a double bed and kitchenette, sharing a panoramic ocean-view veranda. One two-bedroom deluxe kitchenette apartment has two double beds and one bath, and a patio with a view. Extras include breakfast service at additional cost, mosquito nets, and a lovely blue lap pool.

If you prefer the beach, consider **Posada La Termita** (Playa San Agustinillo, local cell tel. 044-958/589-3046, www.posadalatermita.com, info@posadalatermita.com, $70–80), right on the dazzling San Agustinillo beachfront. Italian-born owner Isabel Bresci offers four comfortable upstairs rooms, with choice of one king-size bed, one queen-size bed, or two queen-size beds, with private hot-water shower-bath, fan, mosquito net, in-house Internet, and a downstairs ocean-view restaurant, with good cappuccino, breakfasts, and pizza.

Innovative **Posada Rancho Cerro Largo** (Playa Cerro Largo, ranchocerrolargomx@yahoo.com.mx, $80 s, $95 d), half a mile west of San Agustinillo village, is the creation of builder Mario Corella, descendant of a longtime Hermosillo, Sonora, hotel family. After knocking around in the hospitality trade for several years, Mario decided to create his own version of utopia. Mario says that he wanted to "be in contact with nature and live among the community with as little impact as possible." He's done it, with six rustically charming tile-floored, wood-and-adobe *cabañas,* furnished with handloomed bedspreads and opening to hammock-hung ocean-view verandas. There's also a reception area and restaurant. The entire complex nestles in a summer-green and lovely hillside deciduous forest, linked by a path that meanders, between panoramic ocean viewpoints, to a gorgeously isolated, wave-washed sandy beach below. Rates include dinner and breakfast. Email for reservations (necessary in winter, and highly recommended anytime). Get to Rancho Cerro Largo via the signed driveway on the Puerto Ángel–Mazunte road, 6.4 kilometers (four mi) from the Puerto Ángel bus stop.

OVER $100

❰ Casa Pan de Miel (about a third of a mile west of San Agustillo village, tel. 958/584-3509, casapandemiel@yahoo.com.mx, www.casapandemiel.com, $110–250), the lifelong dream-come-true of French-born co-owner Anne Gillete, perches on its airy hilltop above the blue Pacific. Only superlatives can describe the architecturally designed amenities: spacious veranda breakfast restaurant; a blue designer pool; soft couches and chairs for sitting inside; lounge chairs and umbrellas by the pool; and panoramic ocean views east, toward San Agustinillo, south, out to sea, and west, toward Mazunte's gracefully curving strand. Guests enjoy eight spacious, comfortable, and artfully decorated deluxe rooms, with private view porches, hot-water bathrooms, fans, air-conditioning, and credit cards accepted, but no children under 12, please.

Mazunte

Mazunte folks offer a number of lodgings, from rough beachfront *cabañas* to semi-deluxe architecturally designed thatched *palapas.*

$25-50

Very popular among the Mazunte beachfront accommodations is **❰ Posada Ziga** (Mazunte, tel. 958/583-9295, www.posadaziga

.com, $25–40), just west of the Mazunte Turtle Museum, with 15 rooms in three floors and a palm-shaded beach-view restaurant, just above the waves. The plainly decorated, spacious, and clean tile-floored rooms come with fans, in-house Internet, a safe, and mosquito nets.

Also invitingly rustic (frequented mostly by youthful international travelers) on the stunning, palm-shadowed Mazunte beachfront is **Posada del Arquitecto** (Calle Rinconcito, Mazunte, no phone, info@posadadelarquitecto.com, www.posadadelarquitecto.com, $25–45 s or d, $6 pp dorm or camping). The owner (who really is an architect), offers about 10 clean, bamboo and thatch *palapa*-sheltered *cabañas*, picturesquely sprinkled atop a palm-shadowed ocean-view knoll. All lodgings include mosquito nets, fans, and private room-temperature shower-baths. Also available are dormitory bunks and a beach-level campground with *palapa* shelters and hammocks. Find it at the beach end of Calle Rinconcito, a block west of the bridge in Mazunte.

Another solid option is **Posada las Mazuntinas** (Calle Bugambilias, Mazunte, tel. 958/589-5845, mazuntinas@aol.com, www.tomzap.com/mazuntinas.html, $30–55 d). Welcoming owners Tiki Scott and David Flynn offer four cozy but spacious (three thatch-roofed, one red-tiled) *cabañas,* with views of the surrounding leafy jungle verdure. All are attractively appointed in 1980s modern style, with furnished kitchenettes, soft beds, hot-water shower-baths, and in-house Internet. It's a five-minute walk to the beach, and there's a good restaurant (Tania's) a block away, as well as parking.

The fanciest accommodation in Mazunte, and sister to the Hotel La Buena Vista in Puerto Ángel, is the lovely hillside **(Alta Mira Bungalows** (reserve via the Hotel La Buena Vista in Puerto Ángel, tel./fax 958/584-3104, reservations@labuenavista.com, www.labuenavista.com/alta_mira, $50–60 d). Guests enjoy a beautiful ocean-view hillside setting with restaurant, the murmur of the waves, and a stepped path (5–10 minutes) down to glorious Mazunte beach. The approximately 10 separate *cabañas* have comfortable rustic-chic decor, including handcrafted furniture, soft beds, and hurricane lamps. Rentals include private shower-baths and mosquito nets. At this writing, Alta Mira's lingering drawback is low-power (solar-panel) electricity, which results in weak fans and dim light bulbs.

Get to Alta Mira Bungalows from the main through-town road. A block west of the bridge, turn toward the beach at the side road, Calle Rinconcito. Continue about a block, where you turn right at a signed uphill fork road. Continue 300 yards to Alta Mira's signed driveway on the left.

Trailer Parks and Camping

The **Trailer Park La Palmera Fernando's** (958/584-0646, trailerparkfernandos@hotmail.com, $5 pp tent, $12–20 RV) has about 20 parking (big rigs possible) and camping spaces beneath a shady, tufted grove by the road at the east end of Playa Zipolite. A spirit of camaraderie often blooms among the tents and assorted RVs of travelers from as far away as Miami, Medicine Hat, and Murmansk. RV rates get you a space for two people, including electricity, water, shared dump station, shower, and toilets.

Alternatively, park or camp at Zipolite's former hacienda and now shady paradise RV and camping park, **(Rancho Los Mangos** (cell tel. 044-958/109-1316, Mex. toll-free 800/546-4693, $20 RV, $50 hotel room, $150 bungalow). Soak in the lush tropical garden ambience, bask in the swimming pool and patio, and feast on all the mangos you can eat in season, April–June. The RV rate includes electricity, water, and drainage. Also available are two deluxe two-bedroom bungalows, sleeping up to five, with living room, kitchen, and air-conditioning, and two comfortable hotel rooms with bath and air-conditioning. Find it on the Puerto Ángel–San Agustinillo main road, at a signed driveway about half a mile past the Zipolite-*Adoquín*-Roca Blanca intersection.

One of Zipolite's best informal beach tenting spots is on the strand below Shambhala, with good food available from neighboring Restaurant El Alquimista or Shambhala's restaurant uphill. The Shambhala owner, Gloria Johnson, will probably allow you to use Shambhala's showers and toilets for a small fee. Ask at the Shambhala office for the privilege.

Camping is also customary on the beach in **Mazunte,** in front of Palapa Omar and Cabañas Yuri, or at Posada del Arquitecto ($6 pp).

FOOD
Puerto Ángel
Cheap eats abound, especially in Puerto Ángel **food stalls** ($2–3), on the beachfront street by the pier, beginning daily around noon and going until midnight. Although tacos are the favorite, fish, *carnitas* (roast pork), chicken, beef, *pozole* (savory pork and hominy soup), *guisados* (chicken, pork, or beef stew), and delicious Oaxaca-style tamales are also common.

Even though its list of sit-down restaurants has dwindled in recent years, Puerto Ángel still offers some good choices. Most welcoming of all Puerto Ángel places to eat is the relaxingly simple restaurant at (**Casa de Huéspedes Gundi y Tomás** (tel. 958/584-3068, 8 A.M.–9 P.M. daily, $4–8). It's uphill on the west end of Puerto Ángel's beachfront street; see the streetside sign. Owner Gundi Ley and her family offer hearty breakfasts, light lunches, and a couple of tasty dinner entrées. Over the winter holidays be sure to attend Gundi's not-to-be-missed gala **Christmas and New Year's Eve dinners** ($14).

Of the *palapa* restaurants right on the beach, the best is **Anahi** (tel. 958/584-3142, 8 A.M.–9 P.M. daily, breakfast $3, seafood $6). Here you'll find a cool palm-shaded beachview spot for breakfast (fresh orange juice, fruit salad, ham and eggs) and super-fresh seafood (conch salad, dorado filet, grilled shrimp, seafood pasta Alfredo).

Most visible along the beachfront main street is the café at the **Hotel Villa Florencia** (Blv. Virgilio Uribe, tel./fax 958/584-3044, 8 A.M.–11 P.M. daily, $5–12). Lulu, the wife of the late Italian-born owner-chef, carries on his

tradition, specializing in antipasti, salads, and meat and seafood pastas.

Playa Estacahuite
Finally, you can top everything off by enjoying a splurge gourmet dinner at **Casa Bichu** (Playa Estacahuite, tel. 958/584-3489,-90,-91, reservations mandatory, about $40 pp including wine). Although the innovative menu often derives from Oaxaca-style cuisine, you can also anticipate seafood, such as super-fresh lobster, shrimp, or fish, or the tenderest filet mignon, or maybe the crispest possible Caesar salad.

Zipolite
Zipolite also has some good eating places. For tasty macrobiotic fare and a breezy beach view, go to the restaurant at **Shambhala** (on the Playa Zipolite west-end headland above the beach, 8 A.M.–8 P.M. daily, $3–6). Personable owner Gloria Johnson runs a very tidy kitchen, which serves good breakfasts, soups, salads, and sandwiches. There is no alcohol at this restaurant.

A regiment of satisfied patrons of (**Restaurant El Alquimista** (on far westside of Zipolite beachfront, tel. 958/587-8961, www.el-alquimista.com, 8–10 P.M. daily, $6–12) choose from a seemingly milelong menu of appetizers (hummus, guacamole), soups (onion, cream of carrot), salads (Greek, romaine), *tortas* (egg, ham, cheese), fish (10 styles of fillet), pastas (*al burro,* cream, Bolognese), hamburgers (fish, beef, chicken), and much, much more.

The restaurant of **Posada Mexico** (on the beach, a few steps from Zipolite's *adoquín* main-street, in Colonia Roca Blanca, tel./fax 958/584-3194, 8 A.M.–9 P.M. daily, $6–9) is among the best. In a beachfront candlelit setting, the food seems especially good. Such as breakfast eggs and pancakes, salads (Mediterranean), seafood (shrimp brochette), pasta (fetuccini arabiata), and steak (T-bone). Bravissimo!

Enjoy an excursion into French cuisine, at restaurant **Terrible** (at the entrance corner of the *adoquín,* cell tel. 044-958/106-4037,

6 P.M.–midnight Tues.–Sat., $10–12) which isn't so bad after all. Instead, it's the candlelit domain of friendly Brittany-born chef Thierry Pati, who invites you to sample his crepes (Provençal cheese, tomato with garlic; and Hawaiian cheese-pineapple-ham), pepper steak filet, butter-grilled fish with capers and wine vinegar, and chocolate nutella pudding for dessert.

San Agustinillo and Mazunte

In San Agustinillo, longtimers like shady beachfront *palapa* **Restaurant Mexico Lindo** (at the east, Mazunte end of the beach, 8 A.M.–10 P.M. daily, closed Sept.–Oct., $5–10). Owner Fausto and his wife serve from a short but tasty menu of salads, sandwiches, tacos and tostadas, and seafood.

In Mazunte, tasty vegetarian-style goodies are the specialty at **Tania's** (on the west end, uphill from the cosmetics factory-store, tel. 958/101-8455, 9 A.M.–11 P.M. daily, $5–12). Besides super-fresh seafood, Tania offers plenty of tasty juices, salads, and burgers, both meat and soy.

A fortunate addition to Mazunte's list of good restaurants is bakery and restaurant **Armadillo** (Calle Rinconcito, tel. 958/101-3834, armadillo.mazunte@yahoo.com.mx, 8 A.M.–11 P.M. daily high season, 3–11 P.M. daily low season, $9). Armadillo is the life project of a personable Mexican-French husband-wife team, Raoul and Beatrix, who, beneath their sculpture-decorated *palapa* (he's the sculptor), offer a delicious, eclectic menu (she's the chef), including breakfasts (omelets), lunch (tuna salad), and, for dinner, the Armadillo specialty, stuffed fish fillet. (They also rent a large, comfortable, *palapa* lodging in the tropical forest behind their restaurant, with a king-size bed and hot-water shower-bath, just a block from the beach, $40 low, $50 high.) Find them a block and a half down Calle Rinconcito, the street that heads toward the beach, a block west of the Mazunte bridge.

Also worthy for a light breakfast or lunch, is breezy beachfront **Café Chez l'Arquitecto,** (at Posada del Arquitecto, Calle Rinconcito, no phone, info@posadadelarqitecto.com, www .posadadelarquitecto.com, 8 A.M.–6 P.M.). For breakfast, you can enjoy espresso coffee, sweet rolls, croissants, eggs your style, and fruit; for lunch and supper salads, sandwiches, tortas, gazpacho, and chocolate brownie.

ENTERTAINMENT AND EVENTS

Puerto Ángel's entertainments are mostly spontaneous. If anything exciting is going to happen, it will most likely be on the beachfront Bulevar Uribe, where people often congregate during the late afternoon and evenings. A small crowd may accumulate by the food stalls and the pier for tacos, talk, and beer.

Sunset-watchers get their best chance from the unobstructed hilltop perch of the Hotel Ángel del Mar (atop Puerto Ángel's west-side headland). The same is true at the beach restaurants in Zipolite, such as mod restaurant **Nude** (North end of the adoquin, tel. 958/584-3062, www.nudezipolite.com, 8:30 am-10 pm daily), which has an airy top floor bar. It also offers something to enliven the occasion even if clouds happen to block the view.

For livelier nightlife, in Zipolite, follow the youthful folks who (especially on Saturdays) crowd into **Disco La Puesta** (on the Zipolite *adoquín,* 9 P.M.–late Tues.–Sat. high season, Fri.–Sat. only in low season).

Similar diversions go on at salsa-rock disco **La Barracuda** (near the west end of the Zipolite *adoquín,* no phone, most nights of the week in season, until midnight).

Alternatively, in Mazunte, join the regulars who relax at hangout **La Barrita** (Calle La Barita #20, no phone, 6 P.M.–midnight nightly) with drinks and dancing (usually to recorded music) in the garden-patio. Find it in mid-village, on Calle Barrita, by the beach.

For additional nighttime diversions, head west to Puerto Escondido or east to Bahías de Huatulco, each about an hour by car or bus.

Festivals

Puerto Ángel's major scheduled event is the big **Fiesta de San Miguel Arcangel** (Oct.

PACIFIC RESORTS

1 and 2). Then the *mascaritas* (masked children) dancers romp, carnival games and rides light up the streetfront, and a regatta of fishing boats parades around the bay.

Mazunte folks enjoy more than their share of fiestas. The year kicks off with the exciting **Fiesta Popular** (around Jan. 15), an old-fashioned carnival, complete with ferris wheel, loop-the-loop, a platoon of coin-tossing, bottle-knocking, balloon-popping games, and loads of popcorn, tacos, and hot dogs, all topped off by a colorful riot of fizzing, whirling, and booming fireworks.

Curanderos (traditional healers) converge from all over to celebrate the beginning of spring with a feast of **traditional healing arts** (Mar. 21). They offer treatments, from temazcal hot room, native herb potions and poultices, to massage and spine straightening by the *curanderos de huesos* bone healers.

Finally, Mazunte celebrates the fall with an all-Oaxaca **Jazz Festival** around the end of November.

RECREATION
Swimming and Surfing

Swimming provides cooler exercise opportunities, especially in the sheltered waters off of Playa Panteón. Off of Playa Zipolite, bodysurfing, boogie boarding, and surfing can be rewarding, depending on wind and swells. For surfing lessons contact expert and friendly surfers Bastián and Fabián López at Casa de Huéspedes Gundi y Tomás (tel. 958/584-3068, localsur_13@hotmail.com or gundtoma@hotmail.com, $20 for two hours).

Be super careful of **undertow**, which is always a threat, even on calm days at Zipolite (where authorities maintain a skilled cadre of lifeguards). If you're inexperienced, don't go out alone. Novice and even experienced swimmers have sometimes drowned at Zipolite. If you get caught in a current pulling you out to sea, don't panic. Experts advise that you simply float and paddle parallel to the beach a hundred yards or so, to a spot where the offshore current is not so severe (or may even push you back toward the beach). Alcohol and surf, moreover, don't

mix. On rough days, unless you're an expert, forget it. Bring your own board, or rent one at one of the sprinkling of shops along the beach and the Zipolite *adoquín*.

Sailing and Windsurfing

If you have your own boat or sailboarding gear, sheltered **Playa Panteón** would be a good place to put it into the water, although the neighboring headland may decrease the available wind. Calm mornings at **Playas Zipolite, San Agustinillo,** or **Mazunte,** might also be fruitful. Afternoons typically have more wind, but also rougher waves.

Snorkeling and Scuba Diving

Rocky shoals at the edges of Puerto Ángel Bay, especially just off **Playa Panteón,** are fine for casual snorkeling. **Playa Estacahuite,** on the open ocean just beyond the bay's east headland, is even better. Snorkel rentals are available on the beach, at both Playa Estacahuite and Playa Panteón.

Puerto Ángel divers enjoy a well-equipped, professional scuba diving shop, **Profundo Azul** (Deep Blue; at Playa Panteón, tel. 958/584-3109, tel. 958/584-3015 at Zipolite, azulprofundomx@hotmail.com, www.tomzap.com/azulprofundo.html), run by very experienced Juan José de Nova Reyes, known locally as Chepe. He offers snorkel trips ($15 pp), scuba dives (two tanks, for certified scuba divers, $100), and scuba instruction, from the basics (beginners, $70) all the way up to a complete open-water advanced certification course (3–5 days, $350).

Fishing

Puerto Ángel's Playa Principal, Playa Panteón, and Playa Zipolite are the best places to bargain for a boat and captain to take you and your friends out on a fishing excursion. Prices depend on season, but you can figure on paying around $60 for a half-day excursion for three or four people with bait and two or three good rods and reels.

During a three-hour outing a few miles offshore, a competently captained boat will typically bring in three or four big, good-eating *dorado* (mahi-mahi), *huachinango* (snapper), *atún* (tuna), or *pez de gallo* (roosterfish). If you're uncertain about what's biting, go down to the Playa Principal in Puerto Ángel around 2 or 3 P.M. and see what the boats are bringing in.

Experienced scuba instructor Chepe at **Profundo Azul** (Deep Blue; at Playa Panteón, tel. 958/584-3109, tel. 958/584-3015 at Zipolite, azulprofundomx@hotmail.com, www.tomzap.com/azulprofundo.html), also offers fishing trips (three hours in motor *lancha* for $100, including tackle and bait, for up to four people). Experienced swimmer and surfer Bastián López, at Casa de Huéspedes Gundi y Tomas (tel. 958/584-3062, gundtoma@hotmail.com) offers about the same.

SHOPPING
Market
The biggest local market is the Monday *tianguis,* which spreads along the Pochutla main street, Highway 175, about seven miles from Puerto Ángel, one mile inland from the Highway 200 junction. It's mostly a place for looking rather than buying, as throngs of vendors from the hills line the sidewalks, even crowding into the streets, to sell their piles of onions, mangoes, forest herbs, carrots, cilantro, and jícama.

On other days, vendors confine their displays to the permanent Mercado 5 de Octubre, east side of the main street, between Calles 1 and 2 Sur.

In Puerto Ángel, the freshest fruit and vegetables are available at the tiny fruit and vegetable store (on the main beachfront street, west end, 8 A.M.–9 P.M. daily) by the pharmacy. Alternately, go to the smallish Puerto Ángel market, near the corner of main beachfront street Bulevar Uribe and the west-side bridge.

Handicrafts
For fine custom-made **hammocks,** visit local craftsman Gabino Silva at his country shop, off a jungly stretch of the road between Zipolite and San Agustinillo. He also rents out two very

rough *cabañas.* (However, he does have a solid sea-view *palapa,* apparently orginally intended to be a restaurant, that would be fine for camping if you have mosquito repellent.) Watch for his sign labeled Hamacas and Cabaña on the beach side of the road, 6.7 kilometers (4.2 mi) from the Puerto Ángel village center.

A handful of handicrafts have arrived in Puerto Ángel at **La Carey** beachware (on Vasconcelos, directly uphill from the pier, tel. 958/584-3251, 9 A.M.–10 P.M. daily).

In Mazunte, stop by **Artesanias Carol's** (no phone, 9 A.M.–6 P.M. daily) across from the turtle museum, for a carefully selected assortment of mostly women's wear, including *huipiles,* resort wear, straw hats, shells, bathing suits, black Oaxaca pottery, interesting bamboo drinking cups, and *palos de lluvia* ("rain sticks") to restore your jangled nerves.

INFORMATION AND SERVICES
Money Exchange, Banks, and Tourist Information
In Puerto Ángel, only a few shopkeepers change money. For example, manager Bastián López, at the **Casa de Huéspedes Gundi y Tomás** (uphill on the west end of Puerto Ángel's beachfront street, tel. 958/584-3068, gundtoma@hotmail.com, www.puertoangel-hotel.com), changes U.S. dollars cash and travelers checks. You can also change U.S. dollars at the local **Banco Azteca** (which is not a real bank, only a high-fee credit and money-wiring agency), but their fee, around 10 percent, is excessive.

The best Puerto Ángel money source is the pair of 24-hour **ATMs,** a Bancomer machine (on Bulevar Uribe at the corner of Vasconcelos), by the taco stands, and HSBC (a block east, behind the agencia municipal).

For more complete banking services, go to the real banks in **Pochutla.** Your best bet is **HSBC** bank (on the Pochutla main street, Lázaro Cárdenas, tel. 958/584-0699, 8 A.M.–5 P.M. Mon.–Fri.). Alternatively, go to **Bancomer** (corner of Lázaro Cárdenas and Av. 3A Norte, tel. 958/584-0053, 8:30 A.M.–4 P.M. Mon.–Fri.), or, a few doors south, **Scotiabank**

Inverlat (Lázaro Cárdenas, tel. 958/584-0145, 9 A.M.–5 P.M. Mon.–Fri.).

Pochutla tourism runs a seasonal **information office** (upstairs at the foot of the Puerto Ángel pier, 9 A.M.–2 P.M. and 4–8 P.M. daily in season).

Health and Emergency

Puerto Ángel's **doctor** is Dr. Constancio Aparicio Juárez, who is available at the **pharmacy** (Calle Vasconcelos, tel. 958/584-3058, 9 A.M.–2 P.M. and 5–9 P.M. Mon.–Sat., 9 A.M.–2 P.M. Sun.) on the left side of Calle Vasconcelos, a block uphill from the pier. For serious illness requiring diagnostic specialists, Dr. Juárez recommends you go to the government **Hospital Regional in Pochutla** (tel. 958/584-0236), or the **Seguro Social in Crucecita** (Bahías de Huatulco, tel. 958/587-1182).

Another option is to go to Puerto Ángel's small government **Centro del Salud** health clinic, which concentrates on preventative rather than diagnostic medicine, on the hill behind the church. Go up Vasconcelos a long curving block, go left at the first corner, and continue past the library to the health center (by the church).

For police emergencies, contact the **state police** (uphill on Vasconcelos, tel. 958/584-3207), or call or go to the **Agencia Municipal** (at the foot of Hwy. 175., tel. 958/584-3101) at the end of the beachfront main street, past the pier in Puerto Ángel.

Communications

The Puerto Ángel **correo** and **telecomunicaciones** stand side by side at the Agencia Municipal (at the foot of Hwy. 175., tel. 958/584-3101, 9 A.M.–3 P.M. Mon.–Fri.).

The Puerto Ángel **larga distancia** telephone, fax office, and **Gela Net** Internet access is on Calle José Vasconcelos (on Vasconcelos, just uphill from the pier, tel. 958/584-3046 or 958/584-3054, fax 958/584-3210, shenalo@hotmail.com, 8 A.M.–10 P.M. daily).

Internet access is also available in Puerto Ángel, at **Cyber Zone Café** (uphill, about a block west of the Blv. Uribe bridge, 9 A.M.–10 P.M. daily, tel. 958/584-2034).

Internet access has also arrived in Zipolite, at **Danydoquin** (at the far end of the *adoquín*, tel. 958/584-3363, 9 A.M.–9 P.M. daily), with fax, copies, and public telephone. In Mazunte, answer your email at **Marcos Internet** (10:30 A.M.–8 P.M. daily) on the main road through town, about a block west of the turtle museum.

Groceries and Photography

The best general grocery store in Puerto Ángel (with a healthy wine selection) is **Comercial del Ángel** (on Vasconcelos, a block straight uphill from the pier, tel. 958/584-3237, 7 A.M.–9:30 P.M. Mon.–Sat., 11 A.M.–1:30 P.M. Sun.).

In Zipolite, go for groceries to **Abarrotes Tres Hermanos** (in the middle of the *adoquín*, no phone, 7 A.M.–11 P.M. daily).

The best local photo store is professional **Foto Garcia** (Lázaro Cárdenas 76, tel. 958/584-0735, 8 A.M.–8 P.M. Mon.–Sat.), on the main street in Pochutla. They offer digital and film development services, and stock several digital point and shoot cameras and other supplies.

GETTING THERE AND AWAY
By Air

Scheduled flights to Mexican and international destinations connect daily with airports at **Huatulco,** 30 kilometers (19 mi) east, or **Puerto Escondido,** 71 kilometers (44 mi) west, by road from Puerto Ángel.

By Car or RV

National highways connect Puerto Ángel to the west with Puerto Escondido and Acapulco, north with Oaxaca, and east with the Bahías de Huatulco and the Isthmus of Tehuántepec.

Highway 200 connects westward with Puerto Escondido in an easy 71 kilometers (44 mi), continuing to Pinotepa Nacional (217 km/135 mi, three hours) and Acapulco in a total of seven hours (469 km/291 mi) of driving. In the opposite direction, Bahías de Huatulco (actually Crucecita town), 45 kilometers (28 mi) is reachable in about 45 minutes. The continuation to Salina Cruz stretches another 148 kilometers (92 mi), or around 2.5 additional hours of driving time.

North to Oaxaca, paved but narrow and winding National Highway 175 connects 238 kilometers (148 mi) over the Sierra Madre del Sur from its junction with Highway 200 at Pochutla. The road climbs to around 9,000 feet through cool (chilly in winter) pine forests and hardscrabble Chatino and Zapotec native villages. Fill up with gas in Pochutla. Unleaded gasoline is available at the Pochutla Pemex stations, both on through-town Highway 175, about 300 yards toward town from Highway 200, and on the north, uphill, edge of town. Carry water and blankets, and be prepared for emergencies. The first gas station after Pochutla is at Miahuatlán, 145 kilometers (90 mi) north. Allow about eight hours behind the wheel from Puerto Ángel to Oaxaca, about seven in the opposite direction.

By Bus and Van

All long-distance bus connections must be made in Pochutla. Operating out of separate stations, several long-distance bus lines and two van shuttle services connect with points west, east, and north. The stations cluster less than a mile north from the Highway 200 junction along Avenida Lázaro Cárdenas, the Highway 175 main street into Pochutla.

As you enter the Pochutla business district, first you'll come to combined first-class **Omnibus Cristóbal Colón** and second-class **Sur** station (Av. Lázaro Cárdenas 84, tel. 958/584-0274) on the left. From there, several departures per day connect east with Huatulco at Crucecita. Some continue east, connecting with Salina Cruz and Tehuántepec, continuing to Chiapas destinations of Tuxtla Gutiérrez San Cristóbal and Tapachula, at the Guatemala border. A few buses connect north with Oaxaca via the relatively level, long (10-hour) Isthmus route, via Salina Cruz and Tehuántepec. During the dry season, buses also connect with Oaxaca, via the shorter (eight-hour) trans-Sierra Highway 175. One bus continues to Puebla

and Mexico City daily. A few buses also connect daily west with Puerto Escondido.

Next, **Estrella Blanca** (94 Lázaro Cárdenas, tel. 958/584-0380) and subsidiary-line buses (such as first-class Elite, luxury-class Turistar and Futura) connect west daily with Puerto Escondido, continuing to Acapulco, where connections are available for the entire Mexican Pacific coast, all the way to the U.S. border. They also connect east (many per day) with the Bahías de Huatulco destination of Crucecita, and Salina Cruz on the Isthmus. A few "plus" (pronounced "ploos") luxury-class buses connect daily, all the way to Mexico City, via Acapulco.

About a block farther, across Lázaro Cárdenas street, **Autobuses Estrella del Valle, Autobuses Oaxaca Pacífico,** and **Fletes y Pasajes** (tel. 958/584-0138) operate out of their joint central bus station *(central de autobus)*. Frequent second-class and some first-class service is offered, connecting west with Puerto Escondido and Pinotepa Nacional; north with Oaxaca, Puebla, and Mexico City; and east with Bahías de Huatulco.

Farther north, **Atlantida** shuttle vans (Av. Lázaro Cárdenas 62, tel. 958/584-0116) connect north, via Highway 175, about every two daylight hours, with Oaxaca. Next door, **Eclipse** vans (Av. Lázaro Cárdenas, tel. 958/584-0840) also offer frequent Oaxaca connections.

UPLAND EXCURSIONS FROM PUERTO ÁNGEL

Highway 175 curves its way from Puerto Ángel north, rising from the coast, continuing past a scattering of villages set in luxuriant forests, and finally climbing to cool, pine-tufted heights, where on a clear day the shining blue Pacific far below seems half a world away.

Travelers who hurry along this route find little; many of those who linger discover pleasant surprises along the way.

Pochutla

The capital of the Pochutla governmental district was founded around 1600. One look along the busy, cluttered main street of Pochutla (officially San Pedro Pochutla, pop. 30,000) reveals that it's a market town. This is most apparent on Mondays, when the side streets off the main street—Highway 175, locally known as Avenida Lázaro Cárdenas—bloom with colorful *tianguis* of vendors offering a collective mountain of merchandise.

On other days, vendors confine their piles to the formal indoor market, the **Mercado 5 de Octubre** (east side of Av. Lázaro Cárdenas, between Calles 1 and 2 Sur) at the downtown center.

Although most people come to Pochutla for business or to catch a bus, this town offers more than the merely perfunctory. A closer look reveals that Pochutla is really two towns rolled into one—the busy main street and the spacious, completely automobile-free central plaza and mall, just one block downhill to the east.

On the west side of the plaza, the townsfolk have planted a living reminder of Pochutla, whose name comes from the Aztec-language label Pochtlán ("Land of the Pochotes") for the locally plentiful *pochote* tree. You'll see a young specimen with small green leaves, five to a bunch, and spines on the trunk. People say that the *pochote* tree's edible roots sustained many starving families during times of drought and war.

Excitement mounts in Pochutla during the **Fiesta de San Pedro y San Pablo** (June 21–28). Celebrations begin with early morning masses and religious processions, then carnival rides and games, food, and fireworks. Finally, a parade of floats carries a gaggle of mysterious masked characters who climax the festivities with a traditional dance.

Even during non-festival times the nighttime plaza, illuminated with Porfirian-era streetlight globes, is doubly interesting, so much so that you may decide to stay overnight. If so, Pochutla can accommodate you with the traditional **Hotel Pochutla** (Madero 102, tel./fax 958/584-0033, $16 s, $20 d, $24 t), at the plaza's northwest corner. The owners offer 34 rooms arranged around an intimate, plant-decorated inner patio. Although many downstairs rooms are musty, upstairs they are invitingly quaint, with old-world louvered tropical-style doors, some of which open to balconies overlooking the colorful plaza scene. Rooms come with a fan and a private hot-water shower-bath.

For an up-to-date alternative, choose the modern business-class **Hotel San Pedro** (Av. Lázaro Cárdenas, tel. 958/584-1123 or 958/584-1124, www.hotelesdeoaxaca.com/hotelsanpedropochutla.html, $30 d), on the ingress boulevard, about half a mile north of Highway 200. Here you get a choice of 20 clean, comfortable rooms, with cable TV, hot-water shower-bath, air-conditioning, and parking.

Chacalapa

About 14 kilometers (nine mi) uphill from Pochutla along Highway 175, the village of San José Chacalapa nestles in the tropical foothill forest. The village's most inviting roadside attraction is the *palapa* **(Restaurant Los Reyes** (on the west side, 7 A.M.–10 P.M. daily, $3–8). Here you can pick from a long menu of soups, seafood (cocktails, fish fillets, shrimp), *chacales* (local river crayfish), meat, tacos, quesadillas, guacamole, *papa del horno* (baked potato), and sandwiches (hamburger, tuna, chicken, and ham and cheese). After that, relax in the big blue pool or stroll out into the surrounding forest.

For an extended exploration, ask Isidro Reyes Guzmán (restaurantlosreyes@prodigy.net.mx or restaurantlosreyes@hotmail.com), the owner of Restaurant Los Reyes, for a guide to the nearby towering *cascada* (waterfall) and curative sulfur-water lagoon. Also check with Tom Bachmaier of Rancho Alegre (on the road, just before the Balneario, no phone, www.tomzap.com/paraiso.html), who would be a good guide himself.

Along the way, your guide will help you spot, besides the locally abundant *ardillas, gavilanes,* and *aguilas* (squirrels, hawks, and eagles), maybe some *carpinteros, tucanetas, péricos, tigrillos,* and *coatis* (woodpeckers, toucans, parrots, ocelots, and coatimundis). Your guide will probably be able to identify *plantas medicinales* (medicinal plants) in addition to the great forest trees, such as *ceiba, guanacastle, caoba,* and *macuil.*

Moreover, you may want to take a look at some of the attractive local for-sale furniture, crafted from big dried *bejuco* vines by local artisans, such as Agustén Toltepec. Ask at the Restaurant Los Reyes for directions to his house.

You may be so charmed by Chacalapa's natural delights that you'll want to stay overnight. If so, nearby mini-paradise **Balneario El Paraíso** (Rancho El Riego, tel. 958-583-5038$30 d) can accommodate you. Get there from the Chacalapa village center, a few hundred yards north of the restaurant. At the *presidencia,* fork right, off the highway. Within a block, turn right again, at the Alcoholicos Anonimos sign. After exactly 1.6 kilometers (one mi) along a dirt road, turn right into the ranch gate. Here, in addition to a big three-meter (10 ft) deep, spring-fed swimming pool, a kiddie pool, swings, slides, and a shaded *palapa* for picnics, are a pair of tile-floored *cabañas* for rent, with hot-water shower-baths. Although impressive, Balneario El Paraíso's artificially constructed amenities are only part of the attraction. Friendly owner Octavio Ramos and his wife provide meals and are happy to show you around their forested ranch, dotted with mango and orange trees and cinnamon and other spices. Later, explore the surrounding luxuriant stream valley and forest for rewarding views of animals and birds in their natural surroundings. (*Note:* At this writing their pools were filled with water only Friday–Monday.)

San José del Pacífico

This is a little mountaintop town with a tremendous view, so high that the Pacific Ocean is clearly visible far below. The climate is brisk and dry, and pine-clad mountains rise all around, an ideal setting for a few days away from the tropics. What's just as good—the village has a pair of pretty fair restaurants and an invitingly rustic hotel.

Little was spared to create the ◖ **Hotel Puesta del Sol** (from the U.S tel. 011-52-1-951/100-8678, in Mexico long distance tel. 045-951/100-8678, locally tel. 044-951/100-8678, sanjose@sanjosedelpacifico.com, www.sanjosedelpacifico.com, www.tomzap.com/sjose.html, $26–55 s or d), on Highway 175, about a quarter mile north of town. Gardens lead downhill, past the hotel restaurant, to clean and cozy knotty-pine rooms and *cabañas* with fireplaces, all with private hot-water shower-baths.

Food is available either at Hotel Puesta del Sol's **restaurant** (tel. 044-951/100-8678, 8 A.M.–8 P.M. daily, $3–10) with its lovely view, or at the attractively rustic restaurant **Rayito del Sol** (Little Sunbeam), with live karaoke nightly, in the village on the highway nearby.

The main local diversions are natural, such as basking in the sun, hiking mountain trails to panoramic viewpoints, observing wildlife, watching spectacular sunsets, and resting or reading by the fireplace. The Puesta del Sol management arranges guided local walks and tours.

Get to San José del Pacífico by bus or car via Highway 175, either 105 kilometers (65 mi) north of Pochutla or 130 kilometers (81 mi) south of Oaxaca City.

Bahías de Huatulco and Vicinity

The nine azure bays of Huatulco (ooah-TOOL-koh) decorate a couple dozen miles of acacia-plumed rocky coastline east of Puerto Ángel. Between the bays, the ocean joins in battle with jutting, rocky headlands, while in their inner reaches the ocean calms, caressing diminutive crescents of coral sand. Inland, a thick hardwood forest seems to stretch in a continuous carpet to the Sierra.

Ecologists shuddered when they heard that these bays were going to be developed. Fonatur, the government tourism development agency, says it has a plan, however. Relatively few (but all upscale) hotels will occupy the beaches; other development will be confined to a few inland centers. The remaining 70 percent of the land will be kept as pristine ecological zones and study areas.

Although this story sounds sadly familiar, Fonatur, which developed Ixtapa and Cancún, seems to have learned from its experience. Up-to-date sewage treatment was installed *ahead of time;* logging and homesteading were halted; and helicopters patrol the beaches, spotting turtle poachers. If all goes according to the plan, the nine Bahías de Huatulco and their 100,000-acre forest hinterland will be both a tourist and ecological paradise, in addition to employing thousands of local people, when complete in 2020. If this Huatulco dream ends as well as it has started, Mexico should take pride while the rest of the world should take heed.

Getting Oriented

With no road to the outside world, the Bahías de Huatulco remained virtually uninhabited

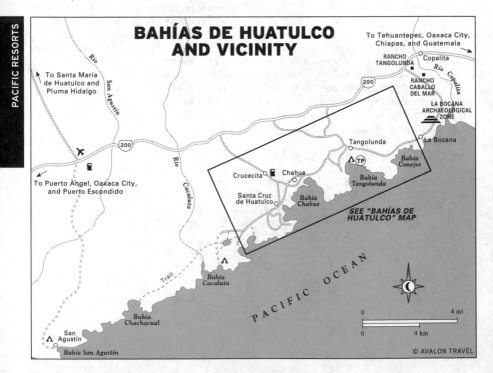

and undeveloped until 1982, about the time that coastal Highway 200 was pushed through. A few years later, the Bahías de Huatulco's planned initial kernel of infrastructure was complete, centering on the brand-new residential service town, Crucecita (pop. 10,000), and nearby Santa Cruz de Huatulco boat harbor and hotel village on Bahía Santa Cruz.

The bays of Huatulco decorate the coastline both east and west of Santa Cruz. To the east, a paved road links Bahías Chahue, Tangolunda, and Conejos. To the west lie Bahías El Organo, El Maguey, and Cacaluta. Of the latter three, only Bahía El Maguey is accessible by paved road. El Organo and Cacaluta are accessible only with the help of a guide; the former on foot or by horseback, the latter by truck or SUV. Isolated farther west are Bahías Chachacual and San Agustín, with no road from Santa Cruz (although a good dirt road runs to San Agustín from Highway 200 near the airport).

Besides Bahía Santa Cruz, the only other bays that have been extensively developed are Chahue, a mile east, and Tangolunda, four miles east. Chahue now has a marina and a sprinkling of small-to-medium-size, medium-priced hotels. Tangolunda has a green and lovely golf course, small restaurant/shopping complex, and six resort hotels (Las Brisas, Quinta Real, Crown Pacific, Barceló Huatulco, Club Gala Resort, and Zaashila) that have all been fully operational since the mid-1990s.

Getting Around

Frequent public **collective taxis** connect Crucecita and Bahías Santa Cruz, Chahue, and Tangolunda. Find the terminal, on Guamuchil, two blocks east of the plaza, at curbside, in front of the Madero shopping center. Private *(especial)* taxis make the same trips for about $3 by day, $4 at night. No public transportation is available to the other bays. Taxi drivers are willing to drive you for a picnic to west-side Bahía El Maguey, or Playa Entrega (a popular beach on Bahía Santa Cruz), for about $5 one-way, from Crucecita or Tangolunda; about the same to Bahía Conejos.

For a half-day trip, taxis will take you to all road-accessible bays for about $15 per hour. On the other hand, you can rent your own car for about $50 per day. Call **Thrifty** (tel. 958/581-9000), **Hertz** (958/581-9092 or 958/581-0588), or **Europcar** (tel. 958/581-9094 or 958/581-0551).

© AMALIA FERREIRA-ESPINOZA/123RF.COM

PACIFIC RESORTS

The bays of Huatulco offer numerous beaches.

Another option is to go by boat. The local boat cooperative (Sociedad Cooperativa Turístico Tangolunda; for reservations call the dock office: tel. 958/587-0081) runs a daily excursion on the 100-passeger catamaran **Fiesta** and, in season, the gigantic 300-passenger **Reventón** (around 10:30 A.M., $20 pp, kids 4–9 half price) to all nine bays, including soft drinks, bilingual guide, and snacks; snorkeling is $5 extra. Alternatively, tour by the similarly big catamaran **Tequila** (from the same dock, tel. 958/587-2303), or contact a travel agent such as **Paraíso Huatulco** (tel. 958/587-0190) or **Prometur** (tel. 958/587-0413).

The cooperative also rents entire boats for all-day tours for up to 10 people for about $100. Drop-off runs to the nearest beach are about $10 per boat round-trip; to the more remote, around $20–30.

Local travel agents offer other tour options: several hours of sunning, swimming, picnicking, and snorkeling at a couple of Bahías de Huatulco beaches cost around $20 per person. Tours to Puerto Ángel, Puerto Escondido, and wildlife-rich lagoons go for $30–50 per person. For reservations, call Paraíso Huatulco or Prometur.

Another option is to get your own guide. An economical option is to hire an English-speaking taxi driver to take you wherever you want to go for several hours, or up to a whole day, for about $15 per hour, depending on the season.

CRUCECITA AND SANTA CRUZ DE HUATULCO

Despite its newness, Crucecita (Little Cross, pop. 10,000) resembles a traditional Mexican town, with life revolving around a central plaza and adjacent market. Crucecita is where the people who work in the Bahías de Huatulco hotels, businesses, and government offices live. Although pleasant enough for a walk around the square and a meal in a restaurant, and perhaps an evening at a bar or disco, it's nothing special—mostly a place whose modest hotels and restaurants accommodate business travelers and weekenders who can't afford the plush hotels near the beach.

PACIFIC RESORTS

THE HOLY CROSS OF HUATULCO

Long before Columbus, the Huatulco area was well known to the Aztecs and their predecessors. The name itself, from Aztec words meaning "Land Where a Tree (or Wood) Is Worshipped," reflects one of Mexico's most intriguingly persistent legends – that of the Holy Cross of Huatulco.

When the Spanish arrived on the Huatulco coast in the 1520s, the local native people showed them a huge wooden cross they worshipped at the edge of the sea. A contemporary chronicler, Ignacio Burgoa, conjectured that the cross had been left by an ancient saint – maybe even the Apostle Thomas – 15 centuries earlier. The cross remained as the Spanish colonized the area and established headquarters and a port, which they named San Agustín, at the westernmost of the Bahías de Huatulco.

Spanish ports and their treasure-laden galleons from the Orient attracted foreign corsairs – Francis Drake in 1579 and Thomas Cavendish in 1587. Cavendish arrived at the bay now called Bahía Santa Cruz, where he saw the cross the natives worshipped. Believing it was the work of the devil, Cavendish and his men tried to chop, saw, and burn it down. Failing at all of these, Cavendish looped his ship's mooring ropes around the cross and with sails unfurled tried using the force of the wind to pull it down. Frustrated, he finally sailed away, leaving the cross of Huatulco still standing beside the shore.

By 1600, pilgrims were chipping pieces from the cross, so much so that in 1612, Bishop Juan de Cervantes had to rescue it. He brought the cross to Oaxaca, where he made four smaller two-foot crosses of it. He sent one specimen each to church authorities in Mexico City, Rome, and Santa María de Huatulco, head town of the Huatulco *municipio*, where it now stands in the shoreline chapel at Santa Cruz de Huatulco. Cervantes kept the fourth copy in the cathedral in Oaxaca, where it has remained, venerated and visible in a side chapel, to the present day.

While in Crucecita, be sure to step into the church on the plaza's west side to admire the heavenly **ceiling mural** of the Virgin of Guadalupe. The mural, the largest of Guadalupe in Mexico, is the work of local artists José Ángel del Signo and Marco Antonio Contreras, whose for-sale art is on display locally. Besides the heavenly Virgin overhead, the muralists decorated the space above the altar with the miraculous story of Don Diego and the Virgin of Guadalupe.

The several deluxe hotels and the mostly travel-oriented businesses of Santa Cruz de Huatulco (on Bahía Santa Cruz, south, about two miles from Crucecita) cluster near the boat harbor. Fishing, tour boats, and ocean liners come and go, vacationers sun themselves on the tranquil yellow-sand Playa Santa Cruz (beyond the restaurants adjacent to the boat harbor), while T-shirt and fruit vendors and boat workers hang around the quay watching for prospective customers. After the sun goes down, not much usually happens in Santa Cruz de Huatulco. Tourists quit the beach for their hotels and workers return to their homes in Crucecita, leaving the harbor and streets empty and dark.

Before you leave Santa Cruz de Huatulco, however, be sure to visit the big **Chapel of the Santa Cruz (Holy Cross) of Huatulco,** on the shoreline side, past the boat harbor. The venerated object on the altar is one of the four smaller crosses, made from the historic original large shoreline cross that had been worshipped for centuries before the Spanish *conquistadores* arrived at the bays of Huatulco in the 1520s. Climb the altar steps and look through the viewing hole of the shoreline, where a replica (albeit smaller) of the original stands, facing the sea.

EXPLORING THE BAHÍAS DE HUATULCO

Isolation has left the Huatulco waters blue and unpolluted, the beaches white and clean. Generally, the bays are all similar: tropical, deciduous (green in the rainy season, July–Jan.), forested rocky headlands enclosing yellow-white coral sand crescents. The water is clear and good for snorkeling, scuba diving, sailing, kayaking, and sailboarding during the often-calm weather. Beaches, however, are typically steep, causing waves to break quickly near the sand, and generally unsuitable for bodysurfing, boogie boarding, or surfing.

Your preparations depend on which bays you plan to explore. For the five developed or partially developed bays—Santa Cruz, Chahue, Tangolunda, Maguey, and San Agustín—you'll need nothing more than transportation, a hat, and sunscreen. Restaurants and stores can supply everything else.

By contrast, the four undeveloped Huatulco bays of El Organo, Cacaluta, Chachacual, and Conejos have neither restaurants, stores, drinking water, nor lots of shade; they're so pristine even coconut palms haven't gotten around to sprouting on them. When exploring, bring food, drinks, hats, sunscreen, and mosquito repellent.

East Side

Bahía Chahue, about a mile from both Crucecita and Santa Cruz, is wide and blue, with a steep yellow dune above the beach, stretching to the marina jetty at the east end. With waves that break quickly near the shore, and recede with strong undertow, Playa Chahue is not good for swimming, boogie boarding, or surfing. Some hotels and restaurants, and a few bars and hangouts are sprinkled along the main Boulevard Benito Juárez, but Chahue beach, three blocks beyond the boulevard, is uncrowded even on weekends and holidays and nearly empty the rest of the time.

About four miles farther east is the breezy and broad **Bahía Tangolunda.** Although hotels front much of the beach, a signed Playa Pública public access road borders the western edge of the golf course (turn right just past the creek bridge). Except for its east end, the Tangolunda beach is steep and the waves break quickly right at the sand. *Palapa* restaurants at the public beach serve food and drinks; or, if you prefer, stroll a quarter mile along the beach for refreshments at the luxurious poolside beach clubs of the Barceló Huatulco and Club Gala Resort.

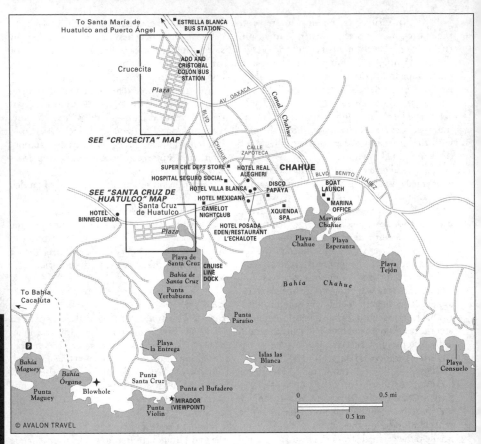

PACIFIC RESORTS

Over the headland about two miles farther east, **Punta Arena** (Sand Point), a forested thumb of land, juts into wide **Bahía Conejos.** Three separate, steep beaches spread along the inner shoreline. The main entrance road arrives at high-duned Playa Punta Arena. Playa Tejoncito (Little Coatamundi) is beyond the rocks far to the right; Playa Conejos (Rabbits) is to the left on the other side of Punta Arena. A few palm-frond *ramadas* for shade and a saltwater flush toilet lavatory occupy the Playa Punta Arena dune. Trees behind the dunes provide a few shady spots for RV or tent campers. (Playa Conejos is a rapidly developing residential zone. By the time you read this, most of the accessible wild dunes and beach may be occupied by houses.)

At **La Bocana,** a signed driveway leads to a parking lot. Walk downhill past that, to a breezy beach and view of the Río Copalita emptying into the sea. Beyond that, a broad beach with oft-powerful surfing rollers (novices beware) stretches for at least a mile east. By the parking lot, restaurants serve drinks and very fresh seafood and a shop rents surfboards for about $14 per day. A spring-fed lagoon above the beach (bring your kayak) appears ripe for wildlife-viewing.

Archaeological Zone

Just past La Bocana, a signed driveway on the right leads to a parking lot and the **Bocana-Río Copalita Archaeological Zone**

PACIFIC RESORTS

(8 A.M.–4:30 P.M. daily, entry $4) where INAH (National Institute of History and Archaeology) investigators have uncovered an early (circa 500 B.C.) town. The zone itself, which occupies about 80 acres, that stretch about half a mile along the Copalita riverbank, may have supported as many as 2,000 people. Scores of dwelling foundations and about 80 burial sites have been excavated, and a number of large structures, including ceremonial plazas, at least one ball court, and an 18-meter-high (60 ft) *templo mayor*. From their research so far, archaeologists reckon that the structures bear architectural resemblance to structures found in southern (Mixe Zoque and Mayan) zones. From radiocarbon dating, archaeologists believe that the site was occupied at least until A.D. 1000, and maybe even until the conquest, when it would have been part of the Aztec village of Copalitlán (Place of Copal). A museum, opened in October 2010, displays a general panorama of the site, and a number of the many intriguing artifacts, recovered during the excavations.

After La Bocana, the road bends inland, paralleling the **Río Copalita wildlife sanctuary**, perfect for adventurous exploring. Several operators guide visitors on river ecotours. Options include bird- and animal-watching walks along riverine forest trails, kayaking river rapids, rafting, and mud baths at a riverside ranch. Furthermore, Rancho Caballo del Mar (entrance on the road, before the Hwy. 200

intersection, tel. 958/584-6545 or 958/587-4886, local cell tel. 044-958/107-8211) offers horseback rides along the river.

West Side

Bahía Santa Cruz has a pair of inviting beaches: **Playa Entrega** and, the most visited, **Playa Santa Cruz,** beyond the shops and restaurants, to the right (facing the ocean) of the boat harbor. Especially during the high winter season and weekends, kids play and vacationers improve their tans at Playa Santa Cruz, and two or three days a week cruise liners dock (and discharge hundreds of tourists ashore) at the adjacent, east side, maritime terminal dock.

Playa Entrega is a small, hidden stretch of sand slipped into the west side of Bahía Santa Cruz. It is the infamous spot where, on January 20, 1831, Vicente Guerrero, president and independence hero, was brought ashore in custody of arch-villain Francisco Picaluga and sent to be executed in Cuilapan, near Oaxaca City, a few months later.

Quarter-mile-long Playa Entrega is the ideal Sunday beach, with calm, clear water and clean yellow sand. Swimming, kayaking, and often snorkeling, sailing, and sailboarding possibilities are excellent. A number of shoreline restaurants serve fresh seafood plates and drinks until around 8 P.M. daily.

Hikers and drivers **get there** via the main east–west street, Boulevard Santa Cruz, which passes the inland edge of the Santa Cruz boat harbor. Continue west, bearing left, at the Y intersection at the Hotel Binneguenda (closed as of this writing) on the right. Mark your odometer. After 1.3 kilometers (0.8 mi) the road bends left and winds uphill, past panoramic viewpoints above Bahía Santa Cruz. Follow the signs and you'll soon be at Playa Entrega.

If, instead of curving left to Playa Entrega, you follow the highway that continues straight ahead at the same spot, you'll be headed for the Bahías El Maguey, El Organo, Cacaluta, and Chachacual (Chah-chah-KOOAHL). At this writing, the planned roads to the latter three of these four bays have not yet been completed. Until authorities get around to finishing them,

land access to the bays of El Organo, Cacaluta, and remote Chachacual will be achievable only by hikers or experienced drivers in off-road vehicles who can navigate the several dirt tracks that wind through the tropical deciduous forest west of Santa Cruz. If in doubt, hire a jeep and a guide (or at least a taxi), or take a boat tour.

Bahía El Organo is closest. About 1.8 kilometers (1.1 mi) along the highway from the Hotel Binneguenda (at this writing, messed up by new construction) look for (or ask a taxi driver to show you) the easy, unofficial 0.8-kilometers (0.5 mi) foot trail to El Organo that takes off downhill through the forest from the road.

The beach is isolated, intimate, and enfolded by rocky shoals on both sides, and sprinkled with driftwood and green verbena vines. Stroll the quarter-mile-long beach, enjoy the antics of the spouting blowhole on the left-side shoal, and, with caution, swim beyond the close-in surf. Surf fishing appears to be fine here. Some trees behind the dune provide shade. Bring food, water, and everything else, including insect repellent.

Back out on the road, continuing straight ahead, the paved highway forks again (about 2.9 km/1.8 mi from the hotel). Either continue straight ahead downhill to El Maguey, or fork right to Cacaluta. The sandy crescent of **Bahía El Maguey** is bordered by tide pools tucked beneath forested headlands. Facing a protected fjordlike channel, the Maguey beach is usually calm, nearly waveless, and fine for swimming, snorkeling, diving, and sailing. It would be a snap to launch a kayak or a rubber boat here for fishing in the bay. Beach access is on foot only, via a downhill staircase. A procession of permanent seafood *palapas* line the beach. Most days, especially weekends and holidays, picnickers arrive and banana towboats and *aguamotos* (mini motor boats) buzz the beach and bay.

Bahías Cacaluta, Chachacual, and San Agustín

The paved road that forks right toward **Bahía Cacaluta** ends at a steel barrier, about 1.1 kilometers (0.7 mi) past the fork, at an unsigned sandy but firm track, negotiable by car, bicycle, or on foot. It continues past the barrier and winds and bumps ahead through the shady tropical forest, past two signed forks that, if you bear left all the way, will lead you to Playa Cacaluta after about 1.9 kilometers (1.2 mi) from the pavement's end.

There, the bay spreads along a mile-long, heart-shaped beach, beckoningly close to a cactus-studded offshore islet. Swimmers beware, for waves break powerfully, surging upward and receding with strong undertow. Many shells—limpets and purple- and brown-daubed clams—speckle the beach. Surf-fishing prospects, either from the beach itself or from rocks on either end, appear excellent.

Bahía Chachacual, past the Río Cacaluta, about four miles farther west from Bahía Cacaluta, is a sand-edged azure nook accessible only with a guide, via forest tracks.

Bahía San Agustín, by contrast, is popular and easily reachable by a Pochutla-bound bus, then by the good dirt road just across the highway (one-way taxi from the highway runs about $8, *colectivo* van $2) from the fork to Santa María Huatulco (at Km 236, a mile west of the airport). After about seven miles along a firm track, accessible by all but the bulkiest RVs, bear right to the road's end to a modest but very crowded village of *palapas* at the bay's sheltered west end. From there, the beach curves eastward along two miles of forest-backed dune.

Besides good swimming, sailing, sailboarding, and fishing prospects, Bahía San Agustín offers some self-contained RV or tent camping options. On your way in, follow the first of two left forks immediately before the road's end. After about a mile, you arrive at **El Playon** (Big Beach). Facilities, besides a long, lovely curving beach, include several beachfront *palapa* restaurants and several sandy lots, ripe for RV and tent camping.

Back on the entrance road, if you follow the second left fork, after a soccer field, you arrive at **El Sacrificio,** a sheltered, family-friendly beach, lapped by gentle waves, lined by *palapa* restaurants, and picturesquely decorated by big, friendly rocks.

Another choice is to turn right about 100 yards before the end of the road and explore the wild, rough, and very fishable, campable, and surfable open-ocean beach.

A few small stores and the road's-end village *palapas* can, at least, supply seafood and drinks and maybe some water and basic groceries.

Adventure Tours

Rancho Tangolunda (on the Bocana-Hwy. 200 road, tel. 958/587-2126, www.rancho tangolunda.com, reservaciones@ranchotangolunda.com) offers a number of options for the adventure-minded visitor. Although most of their clients are in their teens or twenties, there's no elderly age limit. Actvities vary from a half-day to a full three days and nights, and from hiking, rapelling, zip-lining through the forest canopy, rafting (both beginning and advanced), and more.

Alternatively, you might plan a trip with **Aventuras Piraguas** (no phone, www.pira guas.com), a rafting outfitter that guides groups during the June–December high water season. They have no permanent office in Huatulco. They operate out of Veracruz and meet their clientele in Huatulco by appointment.

Guides

Savvy local folks recommend the services of ecologically sensitive guide **Mario Cobos** (tel. 958/587-1833, info@mariocobos.com, www .mariocobos.com). Although Mario's first love is bird-watching, he also offers fishing excursions and backcountry ecotours. His fee begins at $50 per day, for one or two people, with your wheels (with jeep rental—figure a minimum of about $50 extra).

A long list of clients also give veteran guide **Alberto Chavez** (tel. 958/587-0671, spain1965@hotmail.com) rave reviews. He routinely guides small groups on wildlife-viewing excursions, especially in the lush Sierra foothills above the Bahías de Huatulco.

ACCOMMODATIONS

In Huatulco as in other resorts, hotels on the beach are the priciest. Tangolunda's are most expensive, Santa Cruz and Chahue hotels fall in between, and Crucecita's hotels are the cheapest. Virtually all Huatulco lodgings are of modern standard, with private baths with hot water. Many, but not all, have air-conditioning, a plus, especially in the warm spring. More information about most of the hotels listed here is available through the **Huatulco Hotel and Motel Association** (toll-free U.S. and Canada tel. 866/416-0555, local tel. 958/581-0486, fax 958/581-0487, info@hoteleshuatulco.com.mx, www.hoteleshuatulco.com.mx).

Huatulco accommodation rates are highly seasonal. Hotels recommended here are arranged by the customary low-season rates, which rise anywhere between 20 and 100 percent, according to demand, during the high Christmas–New Year's and Easter seasons and some *puente* (bridge) 3–5-day holiday weekends.

Crucecita

Nearly all Crucecita lodgings are within a few blocks of the central plaza. They are generally clean, well-managed posada-style hotels, but most are without restaurants and even fewer (none among the recommendations here) with pools.

UNDER $25

First, the economy **Posada Primavera** (Palo Verde 5, corner of Gardenia, tel./fax 958/587-1167, fax 958/587-1169, $30 s or d in one bed, $35 d or t in two beds), a few blocks north of the plaza, offers six simply furnished but clean, light, high-ceilinged upstairs rooms with bath. Windows look out onto the palmy, bougain-villea-adorned surrounding neighborhood. Rooms come with fans.

$25-50

A couple of blocks south of the plaza, budget-minded visitors should check out the newish (**Posada Leo** (Bugambilias 302, tel. 958/587-0372 or 958/587-2601, posada-leo_hux@hotmail.com, $24 s, $27 d). The six rooms, although a bit cramped for their two double beds, are attractively tiled and furnished

with hand-woven bedspreads, and have shiny modern shower-baths. All rooms come with cable TV and fans; some with air-conditioning for $5 extra. Furthermore, guests enjoy an airy upstairs patio for reading and relaxing.

Nearby, just a block south of the plaza, find **Posada Jois** (Chacah 209, tel. 958/587-0781, joishuatulco@hotmail.com, $30–50 d) between Carrizal and Bugambilias. Past the welcoming female owner's storefront are seven differing rooms on both ground and upper floors. The most attractive are upstairs. One is semi-deluxe, with a king-size bed and bath; another room is for four with two double beds and bath. There is also a pair of rooms with shared baths. All rooms have hot water, TV, and fans. A major plus here is an inviting, shady terrace for guests to use, with tropical plants and soft chairs for relaxing.

On Calle Guamuchil, just half a block east of the plaza, the (**Hotel Los Conejos** (Guamuchil 208, tel./fax 958/587-0054, reservaciones@hotelconejoplaza.com, www.hotelconejoplaza.com, $30 s, $40 d, $55 t or q) offers 10 spic-and-span rooms built around the upstairs balcony of a tranquil, intimate interior patio. The rooms are attractively decorated with ceramic tile floors, white stucco walls, and tasteful, color-coordinated curtains and bedspreads. Rooms come with choice of air-conditioning or fans; all have cable TV, private hot-water shower-baths, but no parking.

About three blocks east from the Crucecita plaza hubbub, the **Hotel Amakal** (Av. Oaxaca 1, tel. 958/587-1500, toll-free Mex. tel. 800/667-5343, fax 958/587-1500, www.hotelamakal.com.mx, hotelamakal_huatulco@yahoo.com.mx, $40 s or d with fan, $50 with a/c) offers semi-deluxe, modern-standard rooms at reasonable prices. A stairway from the small, spartan lobby leads upstairs to 26 clean, light, white-tile-floored, invitingly decorated rooms with modern-standard baths. Parking is only available on the street; credit cards are accepted.

Two blocks south of the plaza, at the corner of Colorin, **Hotel Jaroje** (hah-RO-hay; Bugambilias 304, tel./fax 958/583-4801, Mexico

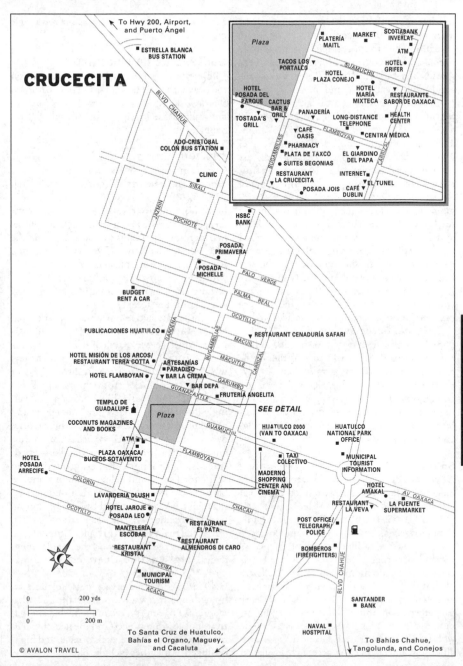

CRUCECITA

To Hwy 200, Airport, and Puerto Ángel

ESTRELLA BLANCA BUS STATION

BLVD CHAHUE

ADO-CRISTÓBAL COLÓN BUS STATION

CLINIC

SIBALI

JAZMIN

POCHOTE

HSBC BANK

POSADA PRIMAVERA

POSADA MICHELLE

PALO VERDE

BUDGET RENT A CAR

PALMA REAL

OCOTILLO

GARDENIA

BUGAMBILIAS

MACUIL

CARRIZAL

PUBLICACIONES HUATULCO

RESTAURANT CENADURÍA SAFARI

MACUITLE

HOTEL MISIÓN DE LOS ARCOS/ RESTAURANT TERRA COTTA

ARTESANÍAS PARADISO

BAR LA CREMA

HOTEL FLAMBOYAN

GARUMBO

BAR DEPA

GUANACAXTLE

FRUTERÍA ANGELITA

TEMPLO DE GUADALUPE

SEE DETAIL

COCONUTS MAGAZINES AND BOOKS

Plaza

GUAMUCHIL

ATM

HUATULCO 2000 (VAN TO OAXACA)

HUATULCO NATIONAL PARK OFFICE

PLAZA OAXACA/ BUCEOS SOTAVENTO

FLAMBOYAN

TAXI COLECTIVO

MUNICIPAL TOURIST INFORMATION

HOTEL POSADA ARRECIFE

COLORIN

MADERNO SHOPPING CENTER AND CINEMA

HOTEL AMAKAL

AV OAXACA

LAVANDERÍA DLUSH

RESTAURANT LA VEVA

LA FUENTE SUPERMARKET

OCOTILLO

HOTEL JAROJE POSADA LEO

CHACAH

MANTELERÍA ESCOBAR

RESTAURANT EL PATA

POST OFFICE/ TELEGRAPH/ POLICE

RESTAURANT KRISTAL

RESTAURANT ALMENDROS DI CARO

BOMBEROS (FIREFIGHTERS)

CEIBA

MUNICIPAL TOURISM

ACACIA

BLVD CHAHUE

SANTANDER BANK

0   200 yds

0   200 m

NAVAL HOSTPITAL

To Santa Cruz de Huatulco, Bahías el Organo, Maguey, and Cacaluta

To Bahías Chahue, Tangolunda, and Conejos

© AVALON TRAVEL

Detail inset:

Plaza

PLATERÍA MAITL

MARKET

SCOTIABANK INVERLAT

ATM

TACOS LOS PORTALCO

GUAMUCHIL

HOTEL PLAZA CONEJO

HOTEL GRIFER

HOTEL POSADA DEL PARQUE

CACTUS BAR & GRILL

PANADERÍA

HOTEL MARÍA MIXTECA

RESTAURANTE SABOR DE OAXACA

TOSTADA'S GRILL

LONG-DISTANCE TELEPHONE

HEALTH CENTER

CAFÉ OASIS

FLAMBOYAN

CENTRA MÉDICA

BUGAMBILIAS

PHARMACY

PLATA DE TAXCO

EL GIARDINO DEL PAPA

CARRIZAL

SUITES BEGONIAS

RESTAURANT LA CRUCECITA

INTERNET

EL TUNEL

POSADA JOIS

CAFÉ DUBLIN

toll-free tel. 800/6234, www.jaroje.mx.tripod
.com, jaroje@yahoo.com.mx, $35 d) offers
15 comfortable rooms, simply but attractively
decorated with color-coordinated drapes, bedspreads, and shiny-tiled baths. Rooms include air-
conditioning, cable TV, and breakfast.

One of Crucecita's loveliest is 【 **Hotel
María Mixteca** (Guamuchil 204, tel. 958/587-
2336 or 958/587-2337, fax 958/587-2338,
andress_3015@hotmail.com, www.travel
bymexico.com/oaxa/mariamixteca, $45 d), just
a block east of the plaza. The 14 rooms are situated around an inviting, tranquil inner patio.
Reflecting the owner's love of the Mixteca region, all rooms are named individually, mostly
for Mixteca towns, such as Juquila, Tlaxiaco,
and Juxtlahuaca. Rooms are high-ceilinged
and attractively decorated in pleasant pastels,
tile, and native art. One room has a queen-size
bed, the rest have two double beds, and many
have airy private balconies. Rates include air-
conditioning, cable TV, wireless Internet access, and parking; credit cards are accepted.

The **Hotel Begonias** (Bugambilias 503, tel.
958/587-0390, reservaciones@hotelbegonias.
com, $30 s or d, $40 two beds), at the southeast plaza corner, offers a semi-deluxe, family-
run alternative. The rooms, although clean and
comfortable, have motel-style walkways passing their windows, decreasing privacy. Rates
for the 13 rooms include fan, air-conditioning,
and cable TV.

$50-100

A very worthy addition to Crucecita's deluxe
lodging options is the new, refined 【 **Hotel
Misión de los Arcos** (Gardenia 902, tel.
958/587-0165, fax 958/587-1903, info@mi-
siondelosarcos.com, www.misiondelosarcos
.com, $55–65 d), a block north of the plaza's
northwest corner. The owners offer 14 spacious, rustic-chic rooms and suites. Walls are
pleasingly white, with accents in beige tile.
Guests in many rooms enjoy views of the leafy
park next door. Some rooms have airy balconies and/or private patios. Rooms all come
with large luxurious baths, cable TV, air-conditioning, and credit cards accepted. There's an

excellent restaurant. Parking is only available
on the street.

Santa Cruz de Huatulco

Although no Santa Cruz hotels are actually on
the beach, they all have inviting pool patios on
their own grounds and are within a five-minute walk of the lovely golden strand of Playa
Santa Cruz.

$50-100

Consider the worthy and inviting 63-
room **Hotel Marina** (Tehuántepec 112, tel.
958/587-0963, -0964, -0965, fax 958/587-
0830 hotelmarinaresort@yahoo.com, www
.hotelmarinaresort.com, reservaciones@hotel
marinaresort.com, $80 d) that perches on the
east side of the Santa Cruz harbor-marina.
Rooms are comfortable and deluxe, and come
with phones, air-conditioning, cable TV, bar,
restaurant, inviting pool patio, and parking;
credit cards are accepted.

Another attractive option is the renovated
Hotel Marlin (Paseo Mitla 107, tel. 958/587-
0055, toll-free Mex. tel. 800/712-7373, fax
958/587-0546, hmarlin@prodigy.net.mex,
www.oaxaca-mio.com/marlin.htm, $75 s or
d), only two blocks from the beach. From
street level, the small lobby leads to an appealingly intimate coral-hued inner pool patio and
adjacent restaurant, enfolded by three stories
of accommodations. Upstairs, the 29 rooms
are thoughtfully decorated with colorful bedspreads, floor-length drapes, attractive and
rustic tile floors, and deluxe modern-standard
bathrooms. Rooms come with air-conditioning, cable TV, phones, and beach club, but no
parking; credit cards are accepted.

On the main Boulevard Santa Cruz, a block
inland from the boat harbor, the popular long-
time **Hotel Castillo Huatulco** (Blv. Santa
Cruz 303, tel. 958/587-0135 or 958/587-0144,
fax 958/587-0131, reservaciones@hotelcastillo
huatulco.com, www.hotelcastillohuatulco
.com, $90 d) offers a recommendable alterna-
tive. Its 106 white stucco and tile neo-colonial-
motif rooms are deluxe, comfortable, and high-
ceilinged. Amenities include, phone, cable TV,

SANTA CRUZ DE HUATULCO

From Crucecita

To Crucecita, Bahía Chahue, Bahía Tangolunda, and Hwy 200 East

HOTEL CASTILLO
HOTEL BINNEGUENDA
TAXI STAND
BANCOMER
BANAMEX
SCOTIA BANK
ARTESANIAS MARKET
CANADIAN RESORT
HOTEL MARINA
BOAT CHARTERS
CAFÉ HUATULCO
BAY EXCURSIONS
Marina
Plaza
HOTEL MARLIN
PARAISO HUATULCO (TOURS)
COCO SOLO GROCERIES
HURRICANE DIVERS
CAPILLA DE LA SANTA CRUZ

To Playa Entrega, Bahías Organo, Maguey, and Cacaluta

BLVD. SANTA CRUZ
CALLE MITLA
OTTLAN DE VALLE
POCHUTLA
COYULA
MONTE ALBAN
CALLE MITLA
ANDADOR
ACATLAN

Playa de Santa Cruz
Bahía de Santa Cruz

0   50 yds
0   50 m

© AVALON TRAVEL

air-conditioning, a palmy pool patio, restaurant, beach club, and parking; credit cards are accepted. Ask for a discount, especially during times of low occupancy.

Chahue

The Bahía Chahue vicinity has, in recent years, acquired a number of new hotels that dot the mostly undeveloped land a few blocks from the beach. At present, however, underdevelopment and isolation make Chahue a less attractive beach neighborhood than either Santa Cruz de Huatulco or Tangolunda. Nevertheless, if you can get a low promotional rate, you might consider staying at one of the hotels recommended here.

$50-100

A block inland from the bayfront boulevard, about four blocks from the beach, find the semi-deluxe **Hotel Real Aligheri** (Calle Zapoteco, tel. 958/587-1242, toll-free Mex. tel. 800/737-0783, hrealigheri@prodigy.net.mx, www.bushhuatulco.com, $55 d). It offers about 20 clean, comfortable rooms with pool, air-conditioning, cable TV, and beach club access.

Nearby, on the same quiet side street, my hurrahs go out to the petite (**Posada Eden Costa** (Calle Zapoteco, tel./fax 958/587-2480, info@edencosta.com, www.edencosta.com, $80 d), behind the larger Hotel Villablanca Huatulco. Here the husband-wife owners—he's French, she's Southeast Asian—set the international theme. The nine rooms and three kitchenette suites, all with a pair of double beds, are simply beautiful, with rustic-chic tile floors and gorgeous *talavera*-accented bathrooms. Rooms come with cable TV, fans, attractive pool patio, and an outstanding on-site restaurant, L'Echalote.

Not so charming, but nevertheless recommendable, is the relaxing **Hotel Villablanca Huatulco** (Blv. Benito Juárez, corner of Zapoteco, tel. 958/587-0606, toll-free Mex. tel. 800/712-7757, toll-free U.S. tel. 888/844-7429, toll-free Canada tel. 877/219-9631, fax 958/587-0660, hotelvillablanca@prodigy.net.mx, www.hotelesvillablanca.com.mx, $80 s or d) next door. Hotel Villablanca guests, mostly upper- and middle-class Mexican weekenders, enjoy simply but comfortably furnished semi-deluxe rooms and junior suites. Amenities include attractively rustic tile floors, blue curtains and bedspreads, modern-standard baths, and private balconies overlooking a palmy pool-patio. Two kids under 12 with parents are free; and the third night is customarily free. All rooms come with air-conditioning, phones, cable TV, restaurant-bar, and beach club access, but parking is only available on the street.

Tangolunda

Several luxury resort hotels spread along the Tangolunda shoreline. The Hotel Las Brisas dominates the sheltered western side-bay, with four stack-like towers that make the place appear, from a distance, like a big ocean liner. As you move east, next comes the elegant Hotel Quinta Real, perching atop its bayview hillside. The Barceló Huatulco hotel and Club Gala Resort stand side by side on the bay's inner recess next to the golf course. The Camino Real Zaashila Huatulco resort spreads gracefully to its east-end cove, while in the middle, away from the beach, the gleaming white Crown Pacific stair-steps up the hillside.

The emphasis of all Tangolunda resorts is on facilities, such as multiple pools, bars, and restaurants, full wheelchair access, live music, discos, shows, and sports, such as tennis, golf, sailing, kayaking, sailboarding, snorkeling, diving, and swimming. Other amenities may include shops, babysitting, children's clubs, and Spanish and arts and crafts instruction.

$100-200

Of the Tangolunda luxury hotels, the **Hotel Crown Pacific** (Blv. Benito Juárez 8, tel. 958/581-0044, toll-free Mex. tel. 800/711-0044, fax 958/581-0221, reservaciones@ crownpacifichuatulco.com, $100 pp) is both the most economical and has some of the most spacious rooms. Despite its lavish facilities, the major drawback of the Crown Pacific is that it's not actually on the beach: Guests must either walk or shuttle a couple of blocks to the beach club. Although standard rates are about $100 per person, bargain packages can run as low as $75 per person for low-season double occupancy, including all meals, drinks, sports, kid's

miniclub, and in-house entertainment, all with air-conditioning.

The (**Dreams Huatulco Resort** (Blv. Benito Juárez 4, tel. 958/583-0400, fax 958/581-0220, toll-free U.S. tel. 866/237-3267, fax 958/581-0220, info.drehu@dreamsresorts.com, www.dreamsresorts.com, $120 pp all inclusive), originally built and operated by the competent Mexican Club Maeva chain, ranks among Mexico's better all-inclusive resorts. The beach setting is gorgeous, the tile floors in the halls and rooms shine, and bright bedspreads, immaculate bathrooms, and private oceanview balconies grace the accommodations. Kids seven years or under stay for free; ages 8–11 go for half-price.

The **Barceló Huatulco** (Blv. Benito Juárez, tel. 958/583-1440, toll-free U.S./Can. tel. 800/227-2356, fax 958/583-0335, huatulco@barcelo.com, www.barcelohuatulco.com, $155 pp all inclusive), originally a Sheraton hotel, is now a worthy member of the worldwide Spanish Barceló chain. Rooms are comfortable, deluxe, and decorated in soothing pastels, with private bay-view balconies, phones, cable TV, and air-conditioning. All lodging, food, drinks, and in-house entertainment are included. Kids ages 2–12 stay for about $55.

Perched at the west end of Bahía Tangolunda, the **Hotel Las Brisas Huatulco** (Lote 1, tel./fax 958/583-0200, fax 958/583-0240, toll-free Mex. tel. 800/227-4727, toll-free U.S./Can. tel. 888/559-4329, lasbrisas.huatulco@brisas.com.mx, www.brisas.com.mx, $200 s or d), formerly Club Med, is now owned and operated by the highly respected Mexican Las Brisas hotel chain. The place is huge, spreading from its grand open-air lobby, from which carts ferry guests to hundreds of spartan-deluxe view rooms, equipped with all modern amenities. Hotel facilities include many sports, three pools, a gym, secluded beaches and coves, kiddie activities, and much more. Two kids under 12 stay for free with parents; breakfast is included.

OVER $200

If the (**Camino Real Zaashila Huatulco**

(Blv. Benito Juárez 5, tel. 958/583-0300, toll-free Mex. tel. 800/910-2300, toll-free U.S./ Can. tel. 800/722-6466, fax 958/581-0468, zaa@caminoreal.com, zaares@prodigy.net.mx, www.caminoreal.com, $250–450 d) hasn't yet gotten an architectural award, it should soon. Builders have succeeded in creating a modern luxury hotel with an intimate feel. This begins right at the reception, a plush round *palapa,* where arriving guests are graciously invited to sit in soft chairs while being attended to by personable clerks, who are also seated, behind rustic, designer desks. Outside, you walk to your room through manicured tropical gardens, replete with gurgling fountains, splashing brooks, and cascading, green lawn terraces. If the Zaashila has a drawback, it's in some of the 148 rooms, which, although luxurious and comfortable, are entirely tile-floored and could use more color and warmth. However, the arrangement of separate units, nested like a giant child's building blocks, resembles a space-age Hopi Native American pueblo, each unit uniquely perched among the whole, affording much privacy and light, especially in upper-floor units. Outside, a few steps downhill, past the big, meandering blue pool, comes the superb beachfront: acres of luscious, billow-washed yellow sand, intimately enclosed between wave-sculpted rocks on one side and a jungly headland on the other. Some units have their own little private pool; all have access to water sports, tennis, golf, and three restaurants.

Playa Conejo

A personable North American couple, Richard and Brooke Gazer, have built **◖ Villa Agua Azul** (overlooking Playa Conejos, tel. 958/581-0265, guarei@hotmail.com, www.huatulco .com.mx/aguaazul, $130–150 s or d year-round), with six elegantly lovely and comfortable guestrooms, into their home. The luxuriously private accommodations stair-step down from the main house to an airy ocean-vista garden pool patio. Rates include a hearty breakfast. For the Christmas–New Year's holiday, add 25 percent. Rooms come with fans and air-conditioning; only nonsmoking adults

18 and over welcome. It's a short downhill walk to a private, intimate beach.

Camping

Authorities permit tent camping and RV parking at some of the Bahías de Huatulco. Self-contained RV parking and tenting is allowed in the spacious, leafy Bahía Tangolunda public beach access park for about $5 per person per day. Although the beach is beautiful and the partly palm-shaded lot is pleasant enough, facilities are limited to toilets and cold-water showers. Get there along the road that goes along the beach to Tangolunda. Turn right at the signed Playa Pública public access road bordering the western edge of the golf course.

Other Huatulco beaches, such as Playa El Maguey, may be available for RV or tent camping. For more information, visit the **Huatulco National Park office** (three blocks east of the Crucecita central plaza, corner of Blv. Chaue, tel. 958/587-0849, 9 A.M.–2 P.M. and 4–6 P.M. Mon.–Fri.), which issues camping permits *(permisos).*

FOOD

Aside from the Tangolunda hotels, most of the good Bahías de Huatulco eateries are either on or near the Crucecita plaza.

Breakfast, Snacks, and Bakery

For inexpensive, homestyle cooking, try the *fondas* (food stalls) at the Crucecita *mercado* (market), between Guamuchil and Guanacastle, half a block off the plaza.

The market stalls are good for fresh fruit during daylight hours, as is the **Frutería Angelita** (just across Guanacastle, 7 A.M.–9 P.M. daily).

Also nearby, the **Panadería San Alejandro** (at the southeast plaza corner of Flamboyan and Bugambilias, tel. 958/587-0317, 6 A.M.–10 P.M. daily) offers mounds of scrumptious baked goodies.

The crowd of satisfied customers will lead you to Crucecita's best-bet snack shop, **◖ Los Portales Taco and Grill** (corner of Guamuchil and Bugambilias, right on the plaza, tel. 958/587-0070, 8 A.M.–midnight daily, $2–6).

Breakfasts, a dozen styles of tacos, Texas chili (or, as in Mexico, *frijoles charros*—cowboy beans), and barbecued ribs are the specialties. Beer is inexpensive, to boot.

For a relaxing drink or a sandwich in Santa Cruz de Huatulco, go to the **Cafe Huatulco** (at the bandstand in the shady Santa Cruz town plaza, a block west of the marina embarcadero, tel. 958/587-1228, cafehuatulco@hotmail.com, 8 A.M.–10 P.M. daily). The mission of the friendly owner, Salvador López de Toledo, and his wife (who operates the kitchen) is to promote the already well-deserved popularity of Huatulco's mountain-grown coffee, which they grind fresh daily for their good cappuccinos and café lattes. Furthermore, Salvador is a good source of information on Huatulco coffee and the mountain *fincas cafeteleras* (coffee farms) where it's grown.

Restaurants

The refined ambience of **Cafe Oasis** (at the southeast plaza corner of Flamboyan and Bugambilias, tel. 958/587-0045, 8 A.M.–midnight daily, $4–12) has made it Crucecita's plaza-front restaurant of choice. Beneath cooling ceiling fans, customers watch the passing scene while enjoying a full bar and a professionally prepared and served menu of breakfast, good espresso, fruit and salads, hamburgers, Mexican and international specialties, and much more.

Lovers of fine Italian cuisine can't miss enjoying a meal at Crucecita's class-act restaurant, **(El Giardino del Papa** (The Pope's Garden; Flamboyan 204, tel. 958/587-1763, 2 P.M.–midnight daily, $17), brainchild of owner Rossana Pandolfini, of Amalfitano, Italy, and chef Mario Saggese of Salerno, who actually was once the pope's bodyguard. He immigrated to Mexico to follow his passion for cooking. Although Mario's suggestions include *calamari criollo, scampi al brandy,* Caesar salad (highly recommended by customers), most everything is tasty. Call for reservations, especially during the winter. Find the restaurant one block west of the plaza's southwest corner.

Diagonally across the plaza, half a block

north of the plaza's northwest corner, step into the cool, airy interior of **(Restaurant Terra Cotta** (at the Hotel Misión de los Arcos, Gardenia 902, tel. 958/587-0165, 8 A.M.–11 P.M. daily, $7–12). Kick back and enjoy the bay-window plaza view while you choose from a list of tasty breakfasts (eggs any style, omelets, waffles), salads (Caesar), baguettes (barbequed pork loin), and Mexican specialties (*mole negro* on chicken, baby back ribs with luscious tamarind sauce).

A worthy restaurant option on the Crucecita plaza-front is **Tostada's Grill** (on the south side, tel. 958/587-1697, 8 A.M.–midnight daily, $11–18). Although it offers plenty of good soups, salads, and pastas, the house specialties come hot off the grill: barbecued ribs, whole lobster, surf and turf brochette, and barbecued snapper, tuna, or *dorado*.

Good, economically priced, local-style food in an open-air, TV-free setting is the specialty of refined but relaxing **(Restaurant La Crucecita** (501 Bugambilias, corner of Chacah, tel. 958/587-0906, 8 A.M.–11 P.M. Thurs.–Tues.), one block south of the plaza. A platoon of loyal local customers arrives daily to enjoy the afternoon five-course *comida corrida*. Pick an entrée (such as *guisado de res, costilla en mole verde,* or chiles rellenos) and you get bottomless fruit *agua* (choice of lemon, orange, jamaica, pineapple), soup, rice, cooked veggies or salad, and dessert, all for $5. The *comida corrida* is served between noon and about 4:30 P.M.

For late lunch or *comida,* local folks crowd into the airy *palapa* of **Restaurant Almendros di Caro** (on Ocotillo, just west of Carrizal, three blocks south, one block east of the plaza's southeast corner, tel. 958/587-0645, 8 A.M.–8:30 P.M. daily), life project of friendly Carina Enriquez Gutiérrez. Here, the big draw is the four-course set lunch, but with plenty of options. Choose your soup, main plate (of pasta, or meat, or seafood, or *antojito*), and you get rice, a drink, and dessert thrown in, all for $5. It's also a good venue for breakfast.

Fine dining in Huatulco has received a big boost at **(Restaurant L'Echalote** (on Calle

Zapateco behind the big Hotel Villablanca in Chahue, tel. 958/587-2480, info@edencosta. com, 2–11 P.M. Tues.–Sun., soups and salads $7–9, fondue for two $22). Although the cooking of owner chefs Thierry Faivre and his Laotion wife, Tina, derives from an entire world of cuisine experience, their creations invariably come with a French touch. Ask Thierry to put on Edith Piaf and it will be better than Paris. Everything they serve is good, from the soup (caldo camarón), salad with goat cheese, and Thai fondue for two. Vive la France! Reservations are highly recommended. **C Restaurant Viena** (Tangolunda, cell tel. 044-958/106-0855, 5–11 P.M. Mon.–Sat., $13–17) of chef Helmut Miklin embellishes the growing Huatulco fine-food tradition. His eclectic and variable menu often includes Grecian- or Tuscan-style salad, gulasch (beef stew), Viennese-style schnitzel with potatoes (veal or pork cutlet), Pork Cordon Bleu, filete de robalo (snook), and apple strudel. Yum! Find Restaurant Viena in Tangolunda, across from the Barceló Huatulco hotel.

ENTERTAINMENT
Nightlife

Bahías de Huatulco entertainment centers on the Crucecita plaza. Although the hubbub cools down on weekdays and during the low season (and hot clubs seem to change as often as the Huatulco breeze), many spots heat up significantly during the winter high season.

A growing platoon of visitors and local expatriates gather for a little bit of Ireland in Huatulco at **Café Dublin** (Calle Carrizal, no phone, noon–after midnight daily low season, 6 A.M.–2 A.M. daily high season), a block east and half a block south of the Crucecita plaza's southeast corner. Good imported beer, Irish coffee, spaghetti and meatballs, hamburgers, satellite TV, and good fellowship keeps the customers happy. In a cozy upstairs room, patrons settle in for the evening, socializing, enjoying recorded music, and watching videos.

Next door to the Café Dublin is the very worthy low- to medium-volume jazz, latin rock, and Karaoke vocal nightspot **El Tunel**

(Calle Carrizal 504, cell tel. 044-958/587-6986, 7–11 P.M. Mon.–Sat.).

One of the longest lasting Crucecita nightclubs is the **La Crema Restaurant-Bar** (at the plaza's northwest corner, tel. 958/587-0702, 6 P.M.–2 A.M. Tues.–Sun.). In high season, it's open nightly, with food and drink, videos, flashing lights, and high-volume salsa music for dancing.

A pair of promising nightspots draw crowds in Chahue. The original was the fancifully decorated disco **El Igloo** (in the basement of the Hotel Real Aligheri, on Zapoteco, about a block north of main Blv. Benito Juárez, tel. 958/589-4489), fixed up to resemble an ice-bound Eskimo house. Programs include mostly salsa, tango, and 1970s and 1980s rock. Hotter still is **Disco Papaya** (on main east–west Blv. Benito Juárez, beach side, approximately two blocks east of the intersection to Crucecita, tel. 958/587-2589, 10 P.M.–3 A.M. Thurs.–Sat.).

Sunset Cruise, Live Music, and Tourist Shows

Lovers of quieter diversions might enjoy going on a wine, snack, and soft-music sunset cruise on the sailboat **Luna Azul** (tel. 958/587-0509). For higher-volume entertainments with your sunset view, go by the catamaran **Tequila** (tel. 958/587-2303) from the Santa Cruz de Huatulco boat harbor.

The **Dreams Huatulco Resort** (Blv. Benito Juárez 4, tel. 958/583-0400, info.drehu@ dreamsresorts.com, www.dreamsresorts.com) in Tangolunda is one of the more reliable sources of hotel nightlife. Live music often plays before dinner (about 6–8 P.M.) in the lobby bar, and "Dreams Night" tourist buffet and shows rev up at least weekly year-round. Contact a travel agent or call the hotel directly for details and reservations (about $55 pp, including everything). Other hotels, such as the **Hotel Crown Pacific** (Blv. Benito Juárez 8, tel. 958/581-0044, toll-free Mex. tel. 800/711-0044, fax 958/581-0221, reservaciones@crown-pacifichuatulco.com) and **Barceló Huatulco** ("Caribe Tropical" and "Broadway" nights; Blv. Benito Juárez, tel. 958/583-1440, huatulco@

barcelo.com, www.barcelohuatulco.com), customarily offer similar buffet and show entertainments in season.

SPORTS AND RECREATION
Swimming, Snorkeling, and Scuba Diving

Swimming is ideal in the calm corners of the Bahías de Huatulco. Especially good swimming beaches are located at **Playa Entrega** in Bahía Santa Cruz and **Bahía El Maguey.**

Generally clear water makes for rewarding snorkeling off the rocky shoals of all of the bays of Huatulco. Local currents and conditions, however, can be hazardous. Novice snorkelers should go on trips accompanied by strong, experienced swimmers or professional guides. Although rentals are generally available, it's best to be prepared with your own equipment.

Huatulco scuba divers enjoy the services of the well-equipped and professional scuba shop **Hurricane Divers** (tel. 958/587-1107, fax 958/587-2576, email@hurricanedivers.com, www.hurricanedivers.com, 9 A.M.–6 P.M. Mon.–Fri., 9 A.M.–4 P.M. Sat.), in the small complex between the Santa Cruz main beach and boat harbor. They start novices out with a pool mini-course, followed by a three-hour ($95) resort dive in a nearby bay. Snorkelers go for about $40, with good equipment furnished. Hurricane Divers' (PADI) open-water certification course takes about four days and runs about $340. With your open-water certificate, you are qualified for the advanced (two-tank $120) dives. After that, you may be ready for more advanced trips, which might include local shipwrecks, night dives, and marine flora, fauna, and ecology tours.

Alternatively, try very experienced (since 1988 in Huatulco) **Buceos Sotavento** (at Plaza Oaxaca complex, upstairs, shop #18, on the Crucecita plaza, southwest corner of Flamboyan and Gardenia, tel./fax 958/587-2166, scubasota@hotmail.com, www.tomzap.com/sotavento.html), which offers similar (PADI) services at very reasonable rates (beginning lesson and dive $75, snorkeling $20, two-tank certified dive $75, three-day open water certification $250).

Fishing and Boat Launching

For a fishing launch *(lancha)* with two or three lines and bait, figure on paying about $25 per hour, for a minimum five-hour excursion. For big-game fishing, best rent a big 30–40 foot boat, with lines and equipment for 4–6, for about $350 for a full day. More reasonable prices might be obtained by asking around among the individual fisherfolk at the Santa Cruz boat harbor or the village at San Agustín.

For example, the local boat cooperative **Sociedad Servicios Turísticos Bahía Tangolunda** (ticket office at the Santa Cruz harbor, tel. 958/587-2303 for catamaran *Tequila*) takes visitors out for fishing excursions from the Santa Cruz boat quay.

Some of the guides already recommended arrange custom fishing outings. Check with **Mario Cobos** (tel. 958/587-1833, info@mariocobos.com, www.mariocobos.com) and **Alberto Chavez** (tel. 958/587-0671, spain1965@hotmail.com). Likewise, both **Hurricane Divers** (tel. 958/587-1107, fax 958/587-2576, email@hurricanedivers.com, www.hurricanedivers.com) and **Buceos Sotavento** (at Plaza Oaxaca complex, upstairs, shop #18, on the Crucecita plaza, southwest corner of Flamboyan and Gardenia, tel./fax 958/587-2166, scubasota@hotmail.com, www.tomzap.com/sotavento.html) also arrange fishing trips.

A number of local boat captains are highly recommended for their experience and skill. For details, contact **Valentin Garcia** (tel. local cell 044-958/589-2015, valentino_fisherman@hotmail.com, www.tomzap.com/valentino.html $60/hr for four) with a 20-foot outboard *lancha*, or Abundio Vasquez Lavarraga and his partner **Efrain Cortez** (tel. 958/109-7170, efrain999@yahoo.com, about $350 for full day) with a 33-foot fishing yacht.

On the other hand, you can leave the negotiations up to a travel agent, who will arrange a fishing trip for you and your friends.

You can also arrange to stop afterward at a beachside *palapa* that will cook up a feast with your catch. For information, inquire at your hotel travel desk, or contact an outside agent, such as **Paraíso Huatulco** (in Plaza Bonita by Bancomer, on Blv. Benito Juárez, in Santa Cruz de Huatulco, tel. 958/587-2878, www.paraisohuatulco.com).

Huatulco's best **boat-launching site** is at easily reachable Bahía Chahue marina, with about 40 slips and an excellent heavy-duty boat ramp. Go to the **marina office** (tel. 958/587-2652, 9 A.M.–3:30 P.M. and 4–7 P.M. Mon.–Fri.) for permission to launch ($15) and slip rental information. Slip rates run about $0.55 per foot per day (between 35 and 80 feet) at the dock. Electricity and water cost extra. Find the marina from the east–west Chahue beachfront boulevard, follow the sign for remolques (trailers) to the big parking lot and ramp.

Tennis, Golf, and Spa

If you're planning on playing lots of tennis, it's best to stay at one of the Tangolunda luxury resorts, such as the Barceló Huatulco or the Las Brisas. Otherwise, the **Tangolunda Golf Course** (tel. 958/581-0037, fax 958/581-0059, tennis courts $10/hour) rents tennis courts. The tennis courts are next to the clubhouse on the knoll at the east side of the golf course.

The breezy green Tangolunda Golf Course (greens fee: $100 for 18 holes, $80 for 9 holes, cart $35, club rental $17, caddy $25), designed by the late architect Mario Chegnan Danto, stretches for 6,851 yards down Tangolunda Valley to the bay. The course starts from a low building complex (watch for bridge entrance) off the Highway 200–Tangolunda highway across from the sanitary plant.

The luxury **Xquenda** (sh-QUEN-dah, "soul" in Zapotec; tel. 958/583-4448 or 958/583-4449, xquenda@huatulcospa.com, www.huatulcospa.com, 9 A.M.–7 P.M. daily) spa and athletic club, in Chahue, west side, on the Santa Cruz–Tangolunda road, offers tennis, paddle tennis, and a lap swimming pool. Spa services include massage, facials, *temazcal* ceremonial hot room, and more.

Horseback Riding

Rancho Caballo del Mar (tel. 958/584-6545 or 958/587-4886, local cell tel. 044-958/107-8211) guides horseback trips along the ocean-view forest trail that stretches from its corral through the eco-preserve zone by the Río Copalita. The four-mile tour, which costs about $40 per person, begins at the ranch site (best go by car or taxi) on the road several miles east past Tangolunda, about a mile before (south of) Highway 200.

SHOPPING
Market and Handicrafts

Crucecita has a small traditional market (officially the Mercado 3 de Mayo) east of the plaza, between Guanacastle and Guamuchil. Although produce, meats, and clothing occupy most of the stalls, a few offer Oaxaca handicrafts. Items include black *barra* pottery, hand-crocheted Mixtec and Amusgo *huipiles*, wool weavings from Teotitlán del Valle, and whimsical duck-motif wooden bowls carved by an elderly but sharp-bargaining local gentleman.

In Santa Cruz de Huatulco, just west of the boat harbor, a warren of dozens of stalls offer nearly everything from T-shirts and Taxco silver to carved wooden fish and lacquer-ware.

Steep rents and lack of business force many local silver, leather, art, and other handicrafts shops to hibernate until tourists arrive in December. The few healthy shops with good selections cluster either around the Crucecita plaza, the Santa Cruz boat harbor, or in the Punta Tangolunda shopping complex adjacent to the Barceló Huatulco hotel (or shops in the hotel itself).

For a fine all-Taxco silver collection, especially rings, go to **Platerea Maitl** (on the Crucecita plaza, west side, between Guancaxtle and Guamuchil, tel. 958/587-1223, 9 A.M.–9 P.M. daily).

One of the few local handicrafts workshops is the charmingly traditional **Mantelería Escobar** (Ocotillo 217, tel. 958/587-0532, 9 A.M.–8 P.M. daily) at the corner of Bugambilias, three blocks south of the Crucecita plaza. This factory uses century-old looms to create lovely all-cotton

PACIFIC RESORTS

Artisans at Mantelería Escobar use antique looms to weave tablecloths.

manteles (tablecloths). Besides their own work, they also sell plenty—blouses, skirts, *huipiles,* and ceramics—from all over Oaxaca.

Another worthwhile Crucecita handicrafts option is **Artesanías Paradiso** (on Gardenia, corner of Guarumbo, tel. 958/587-0268, 9 A.M.–10 P.M. Mon.–Sat., 5–10 P.M. Sun.), just past the plaza's northwest corner. Among the many carefully selected treasures, find masks from Huazaolotitlán, black pottery from San Bartolo Coyotepec, dolls from San Miguel de Allende, *alebrijes* from San Martín Tilcajete, and a whole roomful of fetching one-of-a-kind dresses, blouses, and skirts ranging from traditional to chic.

INFORMATION AND SERVICES
Tourist Information Offices
The Huatulco office of the **Oaxaca Secretary of Tourism** (tel./fax 958/581-0176, 8 A.M.–5 P.M. Mon.–Fri. high season only) is in the Tangolunda hotel zone, inland side, west edge of the hotel-shopping complex.

For year-round information, go to **Huatulco Municipal Tourism** (corner of Guamuchil and Blv. Chahue, tel. 958/587-2880, tel./fax 958/587-2741, turismomunicipal@huatulco.gob.mx, www.huatulco.gob.mx, 9 A.M.–5 P.M. Mon.–Fri., 9 A.M.–2 P.M. Sat.), three blocks east of the plaza.

Health and Emergency
Among the better of the Huatulco private clinics is **Clínica Médico** (403 Sibali, corner of Gardenia, about eight blocks north of the Crucecita plaza, tel. 958/587-0600 or 958/587-0687), with 24-hour emergency service.

For an English-speaking, U.S.-trained doctor, go to IAMAT (International Association for Medical Assistance to Tourists) member and general practitioner **Dr. Andrés González Ayvar** (Blv. Benito Juárez, at the Barceló Huatulco hotel, tel. 958/581-0055 or cell 044-958/587-6065, 11 A.M.–1 P.M. and 8:30–11 P.M. Mon.–Sat.).

Alternatively, go to the 24-hour government clinic, **Centro de Salud** (Calle Carrizal, tel. 958/587-1421), a block east of the Crucecita plaza, or the big modern-standard hospital, **Seguro Social** (tel. 958/587-1182 or 958/587-1183), in Crucecita, on the boulevard to Tangolunda, a quarter mile south of the Pemex gas station.

For routine medications, Crucecita has many pharmacies, such as **Farmacia del Centro** (plaza corner of Flamboyan and Bugambilias, tel. 958/587-0232, 8 A.M.–10 P.M. Mon.–Sat., 9 A.M.–2 P.M. and 5–10 P.M. Sun.), at street level, below the Hotel Begonias.

For police and fire emergencies, call the Crucecita **policía** (tel. 958/587-0210) and the **fire department** (tel. 958/587-0047), both at the Agencia Municipal behind the post office, across the boulevard from the Pemex *gasolinera.*

Newspapers, Books, and Magazines
The small **newsstand** (tel. 958/587-0279, 8 A.M.–10 P.M. daily) at the southwest Crucecita plaza corner may seasonally stock some North

American magazines and newspapers, such as *Newsweek, People, USA Today,* and the daily *News* from Mexico City.

Also, pick up a copy of *Huatulco Magazine* (office: Cerrada de Tlacolula no. 3, tel. 958/587-0342, www.huatulco.magazzine.net), the handy commercial tourist booklet, at your hotel or a store or travel agent, or at the magazine's office in Santa Cruz de Huatulco.

Money Exchange

For cash, you may either use the ATMs available at all of Huatulco's banks, or go inside. In Crucecita, try **HSBC** (corner of Bugambilias and Sibali, tel. 958/587-0324, 8 A.M.–5 P.M. Mon.–Fri.), eight short blocks north of the plaza. Otherwise, go to **Scotiabank Inverlat** (corner of Guamuchil and Carrizal, tel. 958/587-0394, 9 A.M.–4 P.M. Mon.–Fri.) and ATM, with shorter hours, a block west of the plaza. After hours, use either the Banamex ATM, on Carrizal a block west of the plaza a few doors north of the Hotel Grifer, or the Bancomer ATM, on the Crucecita plaza's southwest corner by the newsstand.

You'll find other banks in Santa Cruz de Huatulco: **Banamex** (Blv. Benito Juárez, corner of Pochutla, tel. 958/587-0071, 9 A.M.–4 P.M. Mon.–Fri.) exchanges both U.S. and Canadian travelers checks; **Bancomer** (tel. 958/587-0305, 8:30 A.M.–4 P.M. Mon.–Fri.), on the adjacent corner, across Pochutla, does about the same thing.

Post and Telecommunications

The Huatulco *correo* (post office; tel. 958/587-0551, 8 A.M.–4 P.M. Mon.–Fri.) and *telecomunicaciones* **Telecom** (tel. 958/587-0894, 8 A.M.–7 P.M. Mon.–Fri. and 9 A.M.–12:30 P.M. Sat.) stand side by side, across east-side Blv. Chaue from the Pemex gas station three blocks from the plaza.

For telephone, buy a Ladatel telephone card and use it at public street telephones, or go to one of the *larga distancias* on Carrizal, such as **Caseta Telefónica Gemenis** (Carrizal, tel. 958/587-0735 or 958/587-0736, 9 A.M.–8 P.M. daily) near the Hotel Grifer.

Internet connection is available at **Cuijosnet store** (Carrizal 504, between Flamboyan and Chaca, tel. 958/587-2553, 8 A.M.–10 P.M. daily), next to the Irish pub, Café Dublin.

Immigration and Customs

Both **Migración** (tel. 958/581-9003 or 958/587-0760) and the Aduana (customs) are at the Huatulco airport. If you lose your tourist permit, try to avoid trouble or a fine at departure by presenting Migración with proof of your date of arrival—stamped passport, an airline ticket, or preferably a copy of your lost tourist permit—a day (or at least three hours) before your scheduled departure.

Supermarket and Photography

The supermarket **La Fuente** (on east-side Av. Oaxaca in Crucecita, tel. 958/587-0222, 8 A.M.–10 P.M. daily), a block east of the Pemex station, offers a large stock of groceries, an ice machine, and a little bit of everything else.

For quick digital and film processing and printing, go to **Foto Conejo** (tel. 958/587-0054, 9 A.M.–8 P.M. Mon.–Sat., 9 A.M.–5 P.M. Sun.), just off the Crucecita plaza, across Guamuchil from the market. Besides a photo-portfolio of the Bahías de Huatulco, the friendly owner stocks point-and-shoot cameras and both film and digital supplies and accessories.

Ecology Association

Local ecologists and community leaders monitor Huatulco's development through their informal Green Globe association. They gather weekly at the resort, Camino Real Zaashila Huatulco, in Tangolunda. For more information, please contact one of the local Green Globe activists, Yvonne Kraak (at the Camino Real Zaashila Huatulco, tel. 958/583-0300, Yvonne.kraak@caminoreal.com.mx).

GETTING THERE AND AWAY
By Air

The **Huatulco airport** (officially the Aeropuerto Internacional Bahías de Huatulco, code-designated HUX) is just off Highway 200, 13 kilometers (eight mi) west of Crucecita and 31 kilometers (19 mi) east of Puerto Ángel. The terminal is small, with a pair of snack bars, a few handicrafts and trinket shops, and a modest seasonal book and magazine store, with some English-language paperback novels.

A number of scheduled air carriers connect with Mexican and international destinations: The most direct U.S. flight is via **Continental Airlines** (toll-free Mexico tel. 800/900-5000, airport check-in desk tel. 958/581-9103), which connects daily non-stop with Houston.

Note: **Mexicana Airlines** which ran daily Mexico City–Huatulco flights through its subsidiary Click Airlines for years, went bankrupt and closed operations on August 17, 2010. As of this writing, plans are afoot to restart operations on a much-reduced scale. It's not certain whether Huatulco will be included. We'll have to wait and see. Log on to www.mexicana.com for news and perhaps reservations and tickets.

In the meantime, a number of reliable carriers make Huatulco connections to and from North American gateways, via Mexico City.

Magnicharters (tel. 958/587-1435 or 958/587-1436, www.magnicharters.com.mx) is the most frequent, connecting Huatulco with Mexico City daily.

Interjet (toll-free Mexico tel. 800/001-2345 or 800/911-4538, www.interjet.com.mx), the up-and-coming Mexican airline, also connects Huatulco with Mexico City daily.

Likewise, **Aeromar** (reserve on line, www .aeromar.com.mx) connects Huatulco with Mexico City.

A number of winter–spring seasonal charter flights connect Huatulco with U.S. and Canadian destinations. At this writing, one of the most active is charter airline **Sunwing** (reserve on line, www.sunwing.ca) that connects Huatulco directly with Toronto, returning via Puerto Vallarta.

Also, experienced local light charter airline **Aerotucan** (Mexico toll-free tel. 800/640-4148, Huatulco local tel. 958/587-2427, www.aerotucan.com.mx) regularly connects Huatulco with Oaxaca City.

Huatulco air arrival is simple and straightforward. Nevertheless, since the terminal has no hotel booking agency or money-exchange counter (although customarily there is an ATM), it's best to arrive with a hotel reservation and sufficient pesos to last until you can get to the bank in Santa Cruz de Huatulco or Crucecita. After the typically quick immigrations and customs checks, arrivees have a choice of efficient **ground transportation** to town. Agents sell tickets for collective vans (about $10 pp) to Crucecita, Santa Cruz de Huatulco, and Tangolunda. A private *taxi especial* outside the airport gate only, for three, possibly four passengers, runs about $15 to the same destinations. Prices to the Puerto Ángel vicinity run more than double these, and to Puerto Escondido even more.

Mobile travelers on a budget can roll their suitcase the couple of blocks from the terminal to Highway 200 to catch one of the frequent public buses and *taxis colectivos* ($1–2) headed to Crucecita (east, left) or to the Pochutla (Puerto Ángel) junction (west, right).

A few **car rental** agents are usually on duty for flight arrivals: Thrifty (tel. 958/587-0010, or Mex. toll-free tel. 800/021-2277, www.thrifty.com); or Hertz (at airport, tel. 958/581-9092, in Tangolunda tel. 958/581-0588, Mexico toll-free tel. 800/709-5000, www.hertz.com); or Europecar (at airport tel. 958/581-9094, in Crucecita tel. 958/581-0551, www.europcar.com); or Dollar (tel. 958/581-0532, www.dollar.com).

By Car or RV

Paved highways connect Huatulco east with the Isthmus of Tehuántepec, west with Puerto Ángel and Puerto Escondido, and north with Oaxaca.

Highway 200, the east–west route, runs an easy 161 kilometers (100 mi) to Tehuántepec, where it connects with Highway 190. From there, it continues northwest to Oaxaca or east to Chiapas and the Guatemala border. (A new $2 toll cutoff—fork left about five miles west of, before, Salina Cruz—cuts the time to Tehuántepec and, thence Oaxaca, by at least half an hour.)

In the opposite direction, the Highway 200

route is equally smooth, connecting Huatulco with Pochutla (Puerto Ángel), 40 kilometers (25 mi) west, and Puerto Escondido, 113 kilometers (70 mi), continuing to Acapulco in a long 519 kilometers (322 mi). Allow about three hours to Tehuántepec, 1.5 hours to Puerto Escondido, and to Acapulco, a full nine hours' driving time, in either direction.

Highway 175, the cross-Sierra connection north with the city of Oaxaca, although paved, is narrow, winding, and oft-potholed, with few services in the 129-kilometer (80 mi) high Sierra stretch between its junction with Highway 200 at Pochutla (35.4 kilometers west of Crucecita) and Miahuatlán in the Valley of Oaxaca. The road climbs to 9,000 feet into pine-tufted, winter-chilly Chatino and Zapotec country. Be prepared for emergencies. Allow eight hours northbound, seven hours southbound, for the entire 282-kilometer (175 mi) Huatulco-Oaxaca trip. (You can save an hour by road by taking the new shortcut, from Highway 200, a couple of miles west of the Huatulco airport, via Santa Cruz de Huatulco and Pluma Hidalgo, to Highway 175 and thence to Oaxaca.)

By Bus

Several long-distance bus lines connect Huatulco with destinations east, west, and north. They depart from two separate new terminals in Crucecita.

From the **ADO Terminal** (Rescadillo 108, corner of Blv. Chahue), nine blocks north of the Crucecita plaza, across Bulevar Chahue, luxury-class **Autobuses del Oriente** (ADO GL), first-class **Omnibus Cristóbal Colón** (OCC), second-class **SUR,** and economy-class **Ecobus** connect with points east, west, and north. For all of these buses, tickets are purchased through the same venue (toll-free Mex. tel. 800/702-8000 or www.ticketbus.com.mx).

ADO GL luxury-class buses connect east with Isthmus points of Salina Cruz and Tehuántepec, thence either northwest, with Oaxaca, Puebla, and Mexico City Tapo terminals, or east, with Tehuántepec and Juchitán, thence north with Veracruz.

OCC first-class buses connect west with Pochutla (Puerto Ángel) and Puerto Escondido. OCC buses also connect east with Salina Cruz and Tehuántepec on the Isthmus. From there they connect east, either with Tuxtla Gutierrez and San Cristóbal las Casas or Tapachula in Chiapas; or northwest with Oaxaca City, Puebla, and Mexico City (North, Tapo, and Tasqueña) terminals.

Sur second-class buses connect both west with Pochutla and Puerto Escondido, and east, with Salina Cruz, Tehuántepec and Juchitán.

Finally, economy-class Ecobus departures connect east with Salina Cruz, Tehuántepec, and Juchitán, thence north with Minatitlán, Coatzocoalcos, and Villahermosa.

About one kilometer (0.6 mi) north along Bulevar Chahue (turn off right, one block) at the Crucecita general **Camionera Central** (Central Bus Terminal), a number of lines also offer western, eastern, and northern connections.

Estrella Blanca affiliate, luxury-class **Turistar** (tel. 958/587-1560) connects west, with Pochutla, Puerto Escondido, Pinotepa Nacional, thence north, to Mexico City Sur and Norte terminals.

Also Estrella Blanca affiliate, first class **Elite** (tel. 958/587-1560) connects both east with Salina Cruz, and west, with Pochutla, Puerto Escondido, Pinotepa Nacional, and Acapulco, where connections may be made via Puerto Vallarta and Mazatlán, all the way, to either Nogales or Tijuana, at the U.S. border.

First-class independent **Costeño** buses (tel. 958/587-0680) connect east with Salina Cruz, and west with Pochutla, Puerto Escondido, Pinotepa Nacional, and Acapulco (Ejido terminal), thence north, with Mexico City Tasqueña terminal.

Furthermore, a number of first- and second-class buses of the **Lanesco** cooperative line (combined Estrella del Valle and Autobuses Oaxaca Pacífico, tel. 958/587-2554 and 958/583-4499) connect daily with Oaxaca City by the winding trans-sierra Highway 175 via Pochutla. Under good conditions, the trip runs a minimum of eight hours.

PACIFIC RESORTS

By Van

Although not as comfortable (they're bumpier and often crowded) travel by van is quicker, cheaper, and much more frequent than buses. Competent carrier **Van 2000** (on Guamuchil, two blocks east of the Crucecita plaza, tel. 958/587-2910) offers about eight departures, connecting with Oaxaca City (terminal at Hidalgo 208, tel. 951/516-3154). The trip, about seven hours, takes a shortcut through Pluma Hidalgo in the mountains above Huatulco.

UPLAND EXCURSIONS INTO COFFEE COUNTRY

A century before the Bahías de Huatulco development was even on the drawing board, the cooler, greener Huatulco uplands were home to a community of farmers and fruit and coffee ranchers. Bypassed by the new Highway 200 and the coastal resort development, the foothill region above the Bahías de Huatulco is a treasury of traditional Oaxaca life and natural diversions—wildlife to view, springs and waterfalls to splash in, and jungle coffee ranches to visit.

Ecotouring and Guides

Local tour operators and guides lead tours of archaeological zones, rapelling, fishing trips, river rafting, coffee farms, forest wildlife-viewing, springs, waterfalls, and much more. The following rank among the most experienced and long-lasting of Huatulco tour operators and guides. Although their websites display a number of standard tours, tell them what you want and they can also arrange something special for you. (However, please avoid a quadrimoto tour unless you feel compelled to tear through the forest, scaring away all the animals, on a noisy, polluting four-wheeled motor scooter.)

- **Bahías Plus:** Carrizal 704, Crucecita, tel. 958/587-0216 or 958/587-0932, www.bahiasplus.com; snorkel, bay tour, crocodiles and turtles, Cascadas Mágicas, coffee farms.

- **Paraiso Huatulco:** Plaza Bonita, local 5, Santa Cruz, tel. 958/587-2878 or 958/583-4105, www.paraisohuatulco.com, office also at hotels Barceló Huatulco and Zaashila; horseback ride, sunset cruise, bay tour, rappel, mountain biking, sportfishing, rafting, Cascadas Mágicas, coffee farm.

- **Prometur:** Sabali 304, Crucecita, tel. 958/587-0413, 958/587-1435, www.todohuatulco.com/prometur; bay tour, rafting, rapelling, horseback, Cascadas Mágicas, coffee farm.

You might also hire one of these two excellent guides: **Mario Cobos** (tel. 958/587-1833, info@mariocobos.com, www.mariocobos.com) and **Alberto Chavez** (tel. 958/587-0671, spain1965@hotmail.com).

Pluma Hidalgo

This mini-metropolis of Oaxaca's southern Sierra owes its fame to the excellent coffee, produced by a competent cadre of local *fincas cafeteleras* (coffee farms) sprinkled in the cool vine-hung mountain forests that surround the town. The original impulse for Oaxaca coffee growing dates back to President Benito Juárez's efforts to encourage upcountry coffee growing and shipping via the newly built port of Puerto Ángel around 1870. Although the shipping is now all done by highway, the deep, rich flavor of Pluma Hidalgo coffee is prized by brew fanciers all over Mexico and the world.

SIGHTS

The town of Pluma Hidalgo (pop. 3,000, elev. 1470 meters/4830 feet) nestles on a lush mountainside 26 kilometers (16 mi) by paved road uphill from Santa María de Huatulco. The name "Pluma" originates from the feather-like cloud (thus "plume") that often forms over the verdant ridge above the town.

The main town-center sights are the plaza, the colonial-era church, and the town market, best on Sundays. Just below the market on the north side is one of the most unusually picturesque basketball courts in Mexico. From anywhere on the court (which is fenced in by netting so the ball will not get lost over the adjacent cliff) expansive vistas spread, both up to the Sierra summit and down-valley to the Pacific shore.

The must-do Pluma Hidalgo activity is visiting a coffee farm. On the plaza, on the left as you face the church, is **Abarrotes Ulilsis** (Plaza Principal 2, tel. 958/525-8110, speak in Spanish), the store of coffee grower and dealer Filadelfo Ramirez Ordaz, who sells top-quality organically-grown Pluma coffee for about $5 per half-kilo bag, as well as his locally made coffee liqueur. If he's available, Filadelfo offers to drive visitors out to the coffee plantation area via one of his very old rickety trucks. It's best to make (or ask your hotel desk clerk to make) an appointment with Filadelfo.

If that fails, you can stay at working coffee farm **El Refugio** (off the Santa María de Huatulco–Pluma Hidalgo road, at about mile 5 from Santa María, watch for the sign, tel. 958/583-5021, local cell tel. 044-529/587-7181, robert@hotel.xauki.com, www.ecoturismoen oaxaca.com/hotelrefugio.html).

An on-the-spot alternative would be to visit one of the coffee *fincas* (farms) immediately on foot. Beginning at the plaza, walk past the Posada Isabel hotel and continue downhill along the road to the *panteón* (cemetery). From the cemetery you can enjoy views in three directions across lush mountain-framed river valleys. Past the cemetery, the downhill road leads three kilometers (two mi) past coffee farms, marked by the shiny dark-green-leafed coffee bushes beneath the shady overhead forest canopy. At valley bottom, arrive at a river

PACIFIC RESORTS

THE LITTLE GARDEN THAT GREW OUT OF CONTROL

If you wander downhill a block or two from the Pluma Hidalgo plaza, you'll eventually see a sign that, translated, reads "Welcome to My Garden Biobotanico." Look closer, and you see a small store, surrounded, on all sides with a riot of very recognizable white orchids, yellow angel trumpets, leafy bromeliads, thorny mini-cacti, scarlet ginger, and dozens more species that only a botanist could identify.

"It was a hobby that went *loco*," says grandmotherly Elia Martínez, who follows with a friendly admonition about her plants, to "admire them, but please don't touch."

Her visitors have heeded the warning so well, that now she's the happy owner of a botanist's mini-paradise on a Pluma Hidalgo hillside.

"The plants became my friends; I couldn't stop adding more."

Indeed; now her hobby has become a mini-nursery, that sells more than her little family grocery, that is gradually being crowded out by her out-of-control garden (Calle Matamoros #4, cell tel. 958/106-9859, 9 A.M.–5 P.M. Mon.-Sat.).

© BRUCE WHIPPERMAN

A riot of blossoms welcomes visitors to the garden of Señora Elia Martínez.

and a high, 60-meter (200 ft) gushing cascade on your left.

After a cooling dip in the pond beneath the waterfall and perhaps a picnic lunch, visit the **Tres Cruces** coffee *finca* (9 A.M.–noon Mon.– Fri., free admission) a fraction of a mile back uphill. There you can see where the coffee pickers bring the harvested beans and watch the beans get weighed and recorded in the logbook by the overseer, and then washed and set out to dry. Other *fincas* (farms) that you may visit in the area are La Providencia, San Francisco, and Margaritas. Be sure to wear long pants and carry insect repellent to deter mosquito and no-see-um attacks.

PRACTICALITIES

For a coffee farm overnight, stay at excellent, retreat-like **El Refugio** (off the Santa María de Huatulco-Pluma Hidalgo road, at about mile 5 from Santa María, watch for the sign, tel. 958/583-5021, local cell tel. 044-529/587- 7181, robert@hotel.xauki.com, www.ecoturism oenoaxaca.com/hotelrefugio.html, $25 d) in the luscious foothill tropical forest. They offer 25 clean, comfortable rooms with private bath, home-cooking restaurant, a tour around the farm, a small spring-fed panoramic-view patio and swimming pool, an events salon, and a guide and airport pickup (at additional cost).

If instead you choose to stay in Pluma Hidalgo town, you have the option of the new **Hotel Posada Isabel** (Calle Guerrero, tel. 958/525-8113, joesue24-7@yahoo.com, $20 s, $25 d). The Posada Isabel, located just southwest of the church, offers six clean rooms, some with view balconies, and all with two double beds, private shiny-tile hot-water bathrooms, TV, and parking.

Also, friendly family-owned **Restaurant Luria** (Av. Hidalgo 16, tel. 958/525-8022, $10 s, $15 d) rents three rooms—two with two double beds, the other with one double bed— above the restaurant. Rooms are spartan but clean, with cross ventilation and private tiled bathrooms with fans and hot water.

Furthermore, Restaurant Luria (6 A.M.–9 P.M. daily, $4) offers hearty Mexican country

specialties. Besides Mexican breakfasts, food offerings often include chicken smothered in *mole negro, mole coloradito* (spicy chile usually over pork or chicken), or *estofado* (meat and vegetable stew).

Alternatively, try plaza-front **Restaurant La Flor del Café** (Calle Guerrero 1, 6 A.M.–9 P.M. daily, $3–6), which offers traditional Mexican plates, such as *guisado de res* (beef stew) and *chilaquiles* (spicy baked tortillas and cheese).

Both Internet access and public telephones are available at **Papelería Janice** (Independencia 8, Internet $1/hour) on the plaza. The Pluma Hidalgo doctor is **Victor Vásquez Ramírez** (Hidalgo 21, tel. 958/525- 8016, 2–7 P.M. Mon.–Sat., available 24 hours for emergencies). Besides medical consultations, he also furnishes essential remedies and prescription drugs from his small pharmaceutical supply.

Get to Pluma Hidalgo from the coast via Santa María de Huatulco. Ride with Oaxaca City shuttle **Van 2000** (on Guamuchil, two blocks east of the Crucecita plaza, tel. 958/587- 2910) or *colectivos* that leave frequently from the Santa María de Huatulco turnoff on Highway 200, west of the Huatulco airport entrance (in Santa María you may have to transfer to a Pluma Hidalgo–bound *colectivo*); taxis run uphill from there (about $15 for up to four people). **By car,** turn north off Highway 200 at the Santa María de Huatulco crossing, west of the airport. At the town center, turn left at the (Hwy. 178) Pluma Hidalgo–marked sign. Pass over a scenic mountain-framed river gorge just outside of town. Continue half an hour (26 km/16 mi) uphill to the Pluma Hidalgo right-hand turnoff. Pass the soccer field and continue a fraction of a mile to the town-center church and plaza.

◖ Cascadas Mágicas

The foothill destination of Cascadas Mágicas (or Cascadas Llano Grande for the village where they're located) makes a superb day trip by car or tour. By bus, you might need two days, including an overnight at the La Gloria coffee farm. Along the way, nature lovers will enjoy the leafy foothill country, laced with rivers and springs, gurgling through sylvan, vine-hung woodland, rich with birds, mammals, and fluttering butterflies.

Your first destination, which is a Huatulco must-do, should be the luscious tropical foothill headwaters of the Río Copalita, where you first hike a forest trail and then climb, passing the gorgeous procession of bubbling aqua-blue Cascadas Mágicas waterfalls. You walk past a hanging rope, where folks are swinging above the water, and finally dive in and paddle through the cool, crystal-clear current.

Bring some goodies and enjoy a picnic as you laze in the afternoon sun. Alternatively, on your way back, you could stop at the La Gloria coffee farm for a late lunch and a tour of their vintage, German family house-in-the-jungle; see the coffee process; and visit their *mariposarium* butterfly enclosure.

La Gloria Coffee Farm

About seven kilometers (three mi) back from the Cascadas, you'll pass La Gloria (Apdo. Postal 220, Bahías de Huatulco, Oaxaca 70989, tel. 958/587-0697, lagloria@hispavista.com, www.ecoturismoenoaxaca.com.fincalagloria. html, $20 pp for lunch and tour, $50 pp overnight and three meals), a little German farm in the jungle. The parents of La Gloria's owner-operator Gustav Sherenberg arrived from the wreckage of World War II, seeking a new life in Mexico. The dream that they carved out remains with Gustav (now Gustavo), who, with his son Max, continues to improve on it. (Lately, however, La Gloria has stopped producing coffee, hopefully they will resume when prices rise again.)

The centerpiece, a Saxony-style whitewashed farmhouse and its antique furnishings—polished oak wall telephone, heirloom old-world sideboard, 1940s-vintage shortwave radio—endure for guests to admire and enjoy. The owners invites you to enjoy their farm with them, either for an afternoon, including lunch, or for an overnight, including comfortable and cozy jungle-*cabaña* lodging with lunch, dinner, and breakfast included.

The easiest way to enjoy the Cascadas Mágicas and La Gloria coffee farm is by guide or tour from Huatulco. If you're going independently, you should first head for Xadani, accessible via the signed side road on the north side of Highway 200, 11.4 kilometers (seven mi) west of the Río Copalita bridge and Copalita village (which has a store, *palapa* restaurants, a basic hotel, long-distance telephone; 66 km/41 mi east of Pochutla, 119 km/74 mi west of Salina Cruz).

If by car, set your odometer as you turn off the highway. Continue immediately through a Zimatán village (which has a store with unleaded gasoline) along a good gravel road, paralleling the gorgeous vine-hung, butterfly-decorated Río Zimatán valley. Continue through Xadani to the church (20.4 km/12.7 mi). Proceed, bearing left around the right rear side of the church, then straight ahead another 8.7 kilometers (5.4 mi) to La Gloria coffee farm and about three miles more to the Cascadas Mágicas entrance gate ($5 per car) past El Llano village.

By bus, take a local or long-distance bus from Pochutla or Crucecita, which will take you at least to Copalita, or better, to the Xadani Highway 200 turnoff. From there, you can catch a taxi or a *colectivo* truck ride (offer to pay) to Xadani, thence to La Gloria and Cascadas Mágicas.

EAST TOWARD THE ISTHMUS: CHONTAL COUNTRY

The approximately 145-kilometer (90 mi) Highway 200, stretching east from Huatulco to Salina Cruz, is easy to travel and consequently can pass swiftly without a pause. This, however, would be a pity, for you'd miss a whole swath of interesting and beautiful country—curving sandy beaches, wildlife-rich lagoons, and colorful Chontal villages and markets—along the way. Instead, take a leisurely drive and plan to make some stops.

Santiago Astata

Santiago Astata (pop. 7,000) is near the midpoint (about 76 km/47 mi) between Huatulco and Salina Cruz. This village is the closest thing to a metropolis along this part of the coast. The townsfolk are proud of their indigenous Chontal language (a member of the widespread—from the U.S. Gulf Coast to Central America—Hokan language family) and cultural heritage. To visitors, they like to say *"Nañoje faá loj pijeda"* (Welcome to Santiago Astata).

By far the best time to arrive is during the Tuesday *tianguis* (native town market), when the townspeople are so busy buying and selling that they are less likely to notice a few camera-toting visitors.

Folks will be even less self-conscious (and so distracted that they might not mind having their pictures taken) during the big local **Fiesta del Señor de Piedad** on the second Friday of Lent (second Friday after Ash Wednesday), usually in late February or March.

Even if you don't arrive during any fiesta, you should still take a look inside the church, where you'll find both of the town patrons, Santiago (St. James, on horseback, with sword in hand) and the Señor de Piedad (Lord of Devotion).

Another favorite town diversion is splashing in the **community spring,** known locally as the *aguaje* (ah-GOOAH-hay). Besides all the fun, folks venerate their spring with a small chapel, **La Capilla de la Rosa Mística.** Find it at the roadside a block or two west of the town entrance arch. Afterward, enjoy a snack at one of the several *comedores* (eateries) by the town highway crossing.

For those in need of basic **services,** Astata has a a pharmacy (half a block straight away from the churchfront), a *centro de salud* (clinic; adjacent to the church) with doctor on duty during the daytimes, a public telephone (tel. 995/522-4081), and private doctors Roberto and Rolanda Herrera. You can call the public phone—one of the only phones in town—to contact the doctors. Otherwise, go straight to their home clinic. From the ingress road, turn right, one block from the highway; continue one block, and make a sharp left. Their house compound is immediately on the right.

San Pedro Huamelula

If you missed Astata's Tuesday market, you can get in on Huamelula's market on Thursday by following the signed inland side road from Highway 200, just a fraction of a mile east of Astata. After about five kilometers (three mi), as you enter Huamelula town, you pass a number of schools, including Alma Chontal (Chontal Soul) primary school, a secondary school, and Colegio de Bachilleres del Estado de Oaxaca (Oaxaca State College).

Go through town (you'll see stores, a few *comedores* (eateries), a pharmacy, a doctor) to the old but restored bright birthday-cake yellow-and-blue church, **Templo de San Pedro.** Inside, the same bright yellow and blue continues, right up to the altar, presided over by a very antique Saint Peter. In the right transept chapel, pay your respects to an even older Santa Lucia in the glass case.

Here, the usually serene atmosphere shifts to raucous and jubilant during the **Fiesta de San Pedro** (June 25–26). Processions, fireworks, food, carnival rides, and games climax in traditional dances, including the popular Danza de los Turcos (Dance of the Turks).

East to Salina Cruz

The sights along the eastern stretch past Astata are mostly natural, including mangrove-tufted lagoons, palmy beaches, and breezy viewpoints. What follows is a summary of some ripe possibilities to anticipate along the way. Measure mileage east from Astata or west from the Highway 200 and Trans-Isthmus Highway intersection at the north edge of downtown Salina Cruz.

Moving east from Astata, arrive at the **Laguna Colorada** dirt side road (east from Astata 11 km/7 mi, west from Salina Cruz 66 km/41 mi). The dirt road leads a few miles along the west edge of a glassy, wildlife-rich mangrove lagoon to a beach.

Another several miles along (east 31 km/19 mi, west 47 km/29 mi), another wildlife-rich mangrove lagoon, **Laguna Garrapatera,** is visible from the highway at Kilometer 348. A wave-washed white sandspit borders the lagoon on the ocean side. The lagoon looks fine for kayaking or rubber rafting, and the beach could be great for camping if you can get to it.

At Kilometer 349, Highway 200 rises to a viewpoint overlooking the idyllic green **Río Bamba Valley** (east 32 km/20 mi, west 45 km/28 mi). Several miles farther (east 50 km/31 mi, west 27 km/17 mi) arrive at the dirt road turnoff to surfing and seafood *palapa* restaurant **Playa Cangrejo** (Crab Beach).

Next, pass **Morro Mazatán** town (east 57 km/36 mi, west 21 km/13 mi). Finally, arrive at the signed dirt side road to **Playa Brasil,** which has a great oceanfront breeze-blown sand hill on its west end (east 65 km/41 mi, west 13 km/8 mi).

Puerto Escondido and Vicinity

Decorated by intimate coves and sandy beaches, and washed by jade-tinted surf, Puerto Escondido enjoys its well-deserved popularity. Despite construction of a jet airport in the 1980s, Puerto Escondido remains a place where most everything is within walking distance, no high-rise blocks anyone's sunset view, and moderately priced accommodations and good food remain the rule.

Puerto Escondido (Hidden Port) got its name from the rocky Punta Escondida that shelters its intimate half-moon cove, which perhaps would have remained hidden if local farmers had not discovered that coffee thrives beneath the cool forest canopy of the lush seaward slopes of the Sierra Madre del Sur. They began bringing their precious beans for shipment when the port of Escondido was established in 1928.

When the coast highway was pushed through during the 1970s, Puerto Escondido's then-dwindling coffee trade was replaced by a growing trickle of vacationers, attracted by the splendid isolation, low prices, and high waves. With some of the best surfing breaks in North America, a permanent surfing colony soon was established. This led to more nonsurfing visitors, who, by the 1990s, were arriving in droves to enjoy the comfort and food of a string of small hotels and restaurants lining Puerto Escondido's still-beautiful but no longer hidden cove.

Getting Oriented

Puerto Escondido (pop. 45,000) seems like two towns separated by Highway 200, which runs along the bluff above the beach. The upper town is where most of the local folks live and go about their business, while in the town below the highway most of the restaurants, hotels, and shops spread along a single, touristy, beachfront street mall, **Avenida Pérez Gasga** (known locally as the *adoquín,* ah-doh-KEEN), where motor traffic is allowed only before noon. In the afternoon, chains go up, blocking cars at either end. Beyond the west-end chain, Avenida Pérez Gasga leaves the beach, winding uphill. (Note that beachfront locations are described as being on the *adoquín,* while hillside locations are described as being on Avenida Pérez Gasga.)

Avenida Pérez Gasga winds up to the highway, where it enters the upper town at the *crucero,* Puerto Escondido's only signaled intersection. From there, Avenida Pérez Gasga continues into the upper town as Avenida Oaxaca, also known as National Highway 131.

Getting Around

In town, walk or take a taxi, which should run no more than $4 to anywhere in town. For longer excursions, such as to Lagunas Manialtepec and Río Grande (near National Park Lagunas de Chacahua, westbound), and as far as Pochutla (near Puerto Ángel, eastbound), ride one of the very frequent *urbano* buses that stop at the *crucero,* or rent a car from **Budget** (Blv. Benito Juarez, at the corner of Monte Alban, tel./fax 954/582-0312 or 954/582-0315, budget33@hotmail.com) or **Economica Rent-a-**

PACIFIC RESORTS

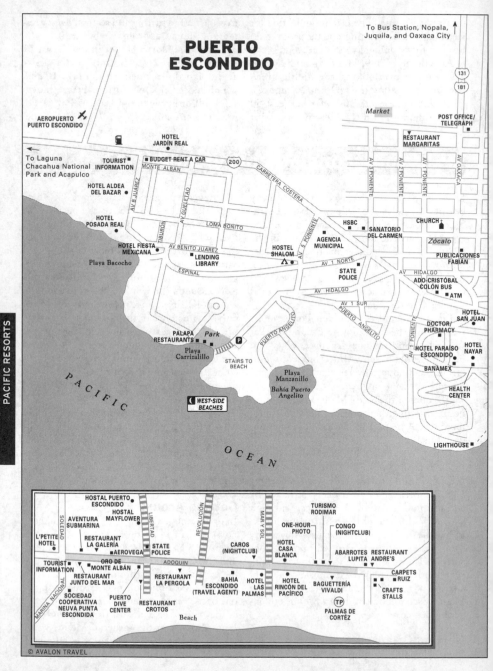

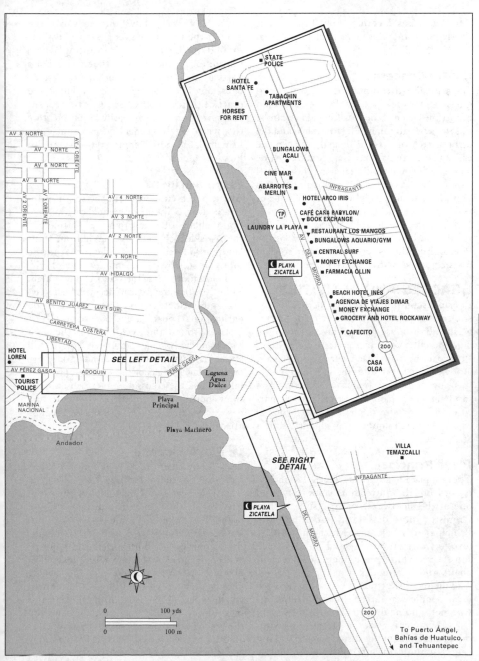

STATE POLICE

HOTEL SANTA FE

TABACHIN APARTMENTS

HORSES FOR RENT

BUNGALOWS ACALI

CINE MAR

ABARROTES MERLIN

INFRAGANTE

HOTEL ARCO IRIS

CAFÉ CASA BABYLON/ BOOK EXCHANGE

TP

LAUNDRY LA PLAYA

RESTAURANT LOS MANGOS

BUNGALOWS AQUARIO/GYM

CENTRAL SURF

PLAYA ZICATELA

MONEY EXCHANGE

FARMACIA OLLIN

BEACH HOTEL INÉS

AGENCIA DE VIAJES DIMAR

MONEY EXCHANGE

GROCERY AND HOTEL ROCKAWAY

CAFECITO

200

CASA OLGA

PACIFIC RESORTS

AV 8 NORTE

AV 7 NORTE

AV 4 ORIENTE

AV 6 NORTE

AV 5 NORTE

AV 4 NORTE

AV 2 ORIENTE

AV 3 ORIENTE

AV 3 NORTE

AV 2 NORTE

AV 1 NORTE

AV HIDALGO

AV BENITO JUÁREZ (AV 1 SUR)

CARRETERA COSTERA

LIBERTAD

HOTEL LOREN

SEE LEFT DETAIL

PÉREZ GASGA

AV PÉREZ GASGA

ADOQUIN

TOURIST POLICE

Laguna Agua Dulce

MARINA NACIONAL

Playa Principal

Playa Marinero

Andador

SEE RIGHT DETAIL

VILLA TEMAZCALLI

INFRAGANTE

PLAYA ZICATELA

AV DEL MORRO

0   100 yds

0   100 m

200

To Puerto Ángel, Bahías de Huatulco, and Tehuantepec

Car (Las Brisas 7, corner of beachfront Calle El Morro, at the south end of Playa Zicatela, tel. 954/582-2557).

Safety Concerns

Occasional knifepoint robberies and muggings mar the once-peaceful Puerto Escondido nighttime beach scene. Walking alone can be unsafe, especially along Playa Bachoco and the unlit stretch of Playa Principal between the east end of Avenida Pérez Gasga and the Hotel Santa Fe. If you have dinner alone at the Hotel Santa Fe, avoid the beach by returning by taxi or walking along the highway to Avenida Pérez Gasga back to your hotel.

Fortunately, such problems seem to be confined to the beach. Visitors are quite safe on the Puerto Escondido streets, often more so than on their own city streets back home.

BEACHES AND ACTIVITIES

Puerto Escondido's bayfront begins at the sheltered rocky cove beneath the wave-washed lighthouse point, Punta Escondida. The shoreline continues easterly along Playa Principal, the main beach, curving southward at Playa Marineros, and finally straightening into long open-ocean Playa Zicatela. The sand and surf change drastically, from narrow sand and calm ripples at Playa Principal to a wide beach pounded by gigantic rollers at Zicatela.

Playa Principal

The best place to appreciate Puerto Escondido is not from the cluttered *adoquín,* but from one of the shady restaurants (such as Los Crotos or Junto del Mar), that front Playa Principal. It's here that Mexican families love to frolic on Sunday and holidays and sun-starved winter vacationers doze in their chairs and hammocks beneath the palms. The sheltered west side is very popular with local people who arrive in the afternoons with nets and haul in small troves of silvery fish. The water is great for wading and swimming, clear enough for casual snorkeling, but generally too calm for anything else in the

cove. However, a few hundred yards east around the bay the waves are generally fine for bodysurfing and boogie boarding, with a minimum of undertow. Although it's not a particularly windy location, sailboarders do occasionally bring their own equipment and practice their art here. Fishing is fine off the rocks or by small boat, easily launched from the beach. Shells, generally scarce on Playa Principal, are more common on less-crowded Playa Zicatela.

Playa Marinero

As the beach curves toward the south, it increasingly faces the open ocean. Playa Marinero begins about 100 yards from the "Marineros," the east-side rocky outcroppings in front of the landmark Hotel Santa Fe. The rocks' jutting forms are supposed to resemble visages of grizzled old sailors. Here the waves can be rough. Swimmers beware: Appearances can be deceiving. Intermediate surfers practice here, as do daring boogie boarders and bodysurfers.

Turn around and gaze inland at the giant Mexican flag, waving in the breeze on the hill above the east-side beach. At dawn on every rainless day, soldiers of the 54th infantry battalion raise the colossal banner, which measures about 18 by 25 meters (82 by 59 ft) and is so heavy that it takes a dozen of them to raise it.

◖ Playa Zicatela

Past the Marinero rocks you enter Mexico's hallowed ground of surfing, Playa Zicatela. The wide beach, of fine golden-white sand, stretches south for miles to a distant cliff and point. The powerful Pacific swells arrive unimpeded, crashing to the sand with awesome, thunderous power. Both surfers and nonsurfers congregate year-round, waiting for the renowned Puerto Escondido "pipeline," where grand waves curl into whirling liquid tunnels, which expert surfers skim through like trains in a subway. At such times, the spectators on the beach outnumber the surfers by as much as 10 or 20 to one. Don't try surfing or swimming at Zicatela unless you're an expert.

© BRUCE WHIPPERMANA

A giant hand sculpture reaches for the sky on Playa Zicatela.

◖ West-Side Beaches: Manzanillo, Carrizalillo, and Bachoco

About a mile west of town, the picture-postcard little blue bays of Bahía Puerto Ángelito and Bahía Carrizalillo nestle beneath the seacliff. Their sheltered gold-and-coral sands are perfect for tranquil picnicking, sunbathing, and swimming. Here, snorkeling and scuba diving are tops, among shoals of bright fish grazing and darting among the nearby coral shelves and submerged rocky outcroppings. Get there by launch from Playa Principal or by taxi. On foot (take a sun hat and water), follow the street that heads west from Avenida Pérez Gasga, uphill across from the Hotel Nayar. Continue to the second street on the left, Avenida 1 Poniente, turn left and go a long block to Avenida 5 Sur. Turn right and continue straight ahead for about a half mile to Bahía Puerto Angelito, which shelters **Playa Manzanillo** at its inner edge. Follow the steps down the cliff. Even more pristine **Bahía Carrizalillo,** a petite strip of golden

sand with a few *palapa* restaurants, is another mile farther west.

Playa Bachoco, yet another mile farther west, down the bluff from the Hotel Posada Real, is a long, scenic strip of breeze-swept sand, with thunderous waves and correspondingly menacing undertow. Swimming is much safer in the inviting pool of the adjacent Hotel Posada Real beach club.

If you're strong, experienced, and can get past the breaking waves, snorkeling is said to be good around the little surf-dashed rocky islet 100 yards offshore.

Although Playa Bachoco's rock-sheltered nooks appear inviting for beach camping, local people don't recommend it because of occasional *rateros* (thugs and drunks) who roam Puerto Escondido beaches at night.

Beach Walking

The *andador* (concrete walkway), which circles the lighthouse point, provides a pleasant, breezy afternoon (or sunset) diversion. From the west chain, follow the street, Marina Nacional, that

Bahía Carrizalillo

© BRUCE WHIPPERMAN

PACIFIC RESORTS

heads toward the beach. Immediately on your left, stairs head down onto the beach cove, where, on the rocks that shelter the cove, at the Capitania del Puerto building, the *andador* heads left along the rocks. It continues, above the spectacularly splashing surf, for about half a mile. Return by the same route, or loop back through side streets to Avenida Pérez Gasga.

For a longer walk, you can stroll as far out of town along Playa Zicatela as you want, in outings ranging from an hour to a whole day. Avoid the heat of midday, and bring along a sun hat, shirt, drinks, and snacks (and perhaps sunglasses) if you plan on walking more than a mile past the last restaurant down the beach. Your rewards will be the acrobatics of surfers challenging the waves, swarms of shorebirds, and occasional finds of driftwood and shells. After about three miles you will reach a cliff and a sea arch, which you can scamper through at low tide to the beach on the other side, **Playa Barra de Colotepec.**

Playa Barra de Colotepec's surf is as thunderous as Zicatela's and the beach even more pristine, being a nesting site for sea turtles. The beach continues for another mile to the jungle-fringed lagoon of the Río Colotepec, where, during the dry winter season, a host of birds and wildlife, both common and rare, paddle and preen in the clear, fresh water.

You could break this eight-mile round-trip into a pair of more leisurely options: Hike A could cover Zicatela only; on Hike B you could explore Playa Barra de Colotepec and the Laguna de Colotepec by driving, taxiing, or busing straight to La Barra, the beach village just west of the Río Colotepec. Access is via the signed side road just before (west of) the Río Colotepec bridge.

Boat Tours

Travel agencies; the local boat cooperative, **Sociedad Cooperativa Turística Nueva Punta Escondida;** and some individuals offer trips for parties of several passengers right from the main town beach. The minimum one-hour trip takes you for a look at a number of sandy little coves west of town, including Carrizalillo (Little Reeds), Puerto Ángelito and its beach, Playa Manzanillo (Little Apple), Coral, and

Puesta del Sol (Sunset). Take drinks, hats, sunscreen, and sunglasses, and don't go unless your boat has a sunroof. Trips can be extended (about $15 per additional hour) to your heart's content of whale-, dolphin-, and turtle-watching, beach picnicking, snoozing, and snorkeling. For more details, visit www.tomzap.com/pe-coop.html.

Alternatively, very competent family-run **Omar's Sportfishing** (local cell tel. 044-954/559-4406, long distance tel. 045-954/559-4406, omarsportfishing-1@hotmail.com or dolfamily@hotmail.com, www.oaxaca-mio.com/omarsportfishing_eng.htm) offers excursions, including dolphin-, whale-, and turtle-watching. You can find Omar on the beach at Puerto Angelito.

ACCOMMODATIONS

The successful hotels in Puerto Escondido are appropriate to the town itself: small, moderately priced, and near the water. They dot the beachfront from Playa Zicatela around the bay and continue up Avenida Pérez Gasga to the highway. Most are either on the beach or within a stone's throw of it, which makes sense, because it seems a shame to come all the way to Puerto Escondido and not stay where you can soak up all the scenery.

Rates for the hotels are listed in ascending order of customary low season room rates. These prices, unless noted, are in effect most of the year, **except for high season** (Christmas–New Year's, Easter, some long weekend holidays, and sometimes July and August), **when they may rise 10-30 percent, depending upon availability.**

Avenida Pérez Gasga-*Adoquín*
UNDER $50
Moving downhill, from the highway, first find the immaculate, best-buy 🄲 **Hotel San Juan** (Felipe Merklin 503, tel. 954/582-0518, tel./fax 954/582-0612, sanjuanhotel@prodigy.net.mx, www.sanjuanhotel.com.mx, $32 per room). For those who like saving money and don't mind (or would enjoy) a 10-minute downhill walk to the beach, this is the place. Rooms,

in four levels, enclose an intimate inner pool patio. They are squeaky clean and invitingly furnished with wall paintings, reading lamps, and color coordinated drapes and bedspreads. Amenities include private hot-water shower-baths, fans, in-house wireless Internet access, morning coffee, a restaurant, and parking. For a splurge, add $13 for air-conditioning with a luxuriously private ocean-view balcony.

Right on the beach amid the tourist-mall hullabaloo is the enduring but somewhat run-down **Hotel Las Palmas** (Av. Pérez Gasga, tel. 954/582-0230, $18 s, $22 d, $27 t). Its main plus is the airy patio, where you can laze beneath the palms every day, feel the breeze, and watch the boats, the birds, and families frolicking in the billows. The big drawback, besides sleepy management and no pool, is lack of privacy. Exterior walkways pass the room windows, which anyone can see through unless you close the curtains, which unfortunately makes the (fan-only) rooms dark and hot. This doesn't seem to bother the legions of return customers, however, since they spend little time in their rooms anyway. There is no parking, nor are credit cards accepted.

The popular **Hotel Loren** (Av. Pérez Gasga 507, tel. 954/582-0057, $38 s or d, $41 t or q), just two blocks uphill from the beach, offers approximately 30 rooms spread through two three-story buildings. Guests in the front-building rooms enjoy private, ocean-view balconies. (However, all rooms, especially the bathrooms, could use a good scrubbing.) The good news is the hotel's inviting blue pool patio and the short five-minute walk to the beach. Reserve a *cuarto con vista* ("a room with a view") in the front building. Reservations are often necessary, especially in the winter. The rooms are basic but comfortable. Add $10 for air-conditioning; parking is available and credit cards are accepted.

The 🄲 **Hotel Rincón del Pacífico** (Av. Pérez Gasga 900, tel. 954/582-0056 or 954/582-0193, fax 954/582-1812, reservaciones@rincondelpacifico.com.mx, www.rincondelpacifico.com.mx, $35 s, $44 d, $50 t with fan only, $58, $68, and $80 with a/c,

$100 larger suites), next door to the Hotel Las Palmas, offers a brighter, renovated prospect. The two tiers of clean, comfortable rooms enfold a shady patio that looks out onto the lively beachfront. As at the Hotel Las Palmas, you must draw drapes for privacy in the hotel's glass-front rooms. This is nevertheless a very popular hotel. Reserve early. Ask for a discount during low-occupancy season (May–June and Sept.–Oct.). Amenities include TV, air-conditioning, and a good restaurant, Danny's; credit cards are accepted (but not American Express), and there is no parking and no pool.

Although it's not right on the beach like its neighbor hotels Las Palmas and Rincón del Pacífico across the *adoquín* walkway, the rooms of the compact, smoke-free **Hotel Casa Blanca** (Av. Pérez Gasga 905, tel. 954/582-0168, fax 954/582-3120, www.ptohcasablanca.com, reservacion@ptohcasablanca.com, $30 s and $38 d) are larger, cooler, and much more private. Some rooms even have private balconies, fine for people-watching on the street below. Guests report that noise is not a problem since cars and trucks are banned on Avenida Pérez Gasga 7 P.M.–7 A.M. Other amenities include a shelf of used paperback books, and, beyond the graceful arches that border the lobby, a petite, inviting pool and patio. The 21 clean, comfortable rooms have fans, private hot-water shower-baths; credit cards are accepted, but there's no parking.

Also perched on the same view hillside as the Hotel Loren, three blocks above the beach, the 1960s-genre **Hotel Nayar** (Av. Pérez Gasga 407, tel. 954/582-0113, fax 954/582-0319, hotel_nayar@hotmail.com, www.oaxaca-mio .com/hotelnayar.htm, $45 s, $50 d, $63 t or q) spreads from its inviting pool patio past the reception to a viewpoint restaurant. Its spacious, simply but comfortably furnished air-conditioned rooms include reading lamps, hot-water shower-baths, fans and air-conditioning, and an in-house wireless Internet connection.

$50-100

Tucked in its own corner, away from the tourist mall bustle, the compact 【 **Le P'tit Hotel** (at the west-end intersection of Soledad and the *adoquín,* tel. 954/582-3178, michelkobryn@ tutopia.com, www.oaxaca-mio.com/leptit .htm, $50 s or d a/c, $10 per extra person) offers an attractive lodging option. Personable French-born owner-builder Michel Kobryn offers 18 rooms and thatched South Seas–style bungalows, all lovingly adorned with colorful tile, original wall art, decorator reading lamps, and sparkling bathrooms. Amenities include cable TV, restaurant, wireless Internet, and an inviting small pool patio; credit cards are accepted.

Back uphill, two blocks below the highway on a short side street off Avenida Pérez Gasga, is the **Hotel Paraíso Escondido** (Calle Union 1, tel. 954/582-0444, fax 954/582-2767, info@hotelpe.com, www.hotelpe.com, $57 s or d, suite $65). A tranquil colonial-chic refuge, the hotel abounds in traditional artistic touches—Mixtec stone glyphs, tiny corner chapels, stained glass, and old-world antiques—blended into the lobby, corridors, and patios. The two levels of rooms nestle around a spacious pool and restaurant patio. The rooms themselves are large, with view balconies, designer tile bathrooms, wrought-iron fixtures, and handcrafted wooden furniture. The hotel is very popular with North American and German winter vacationers; get your reservations in early. The 24 rooms include air-conditioning, pool, kiddie pool, and parking, but credit cards are not accepted.

Playa Zicatela

Beach lovers and surfing enthusiasts enjoy staying on Playa Zicatela, the creamy strand that stretches east and south of the busy *adoquín*. Here, folks relax in street-side cafés and restaurants and stroll and sun on the beach as they watch the surfers conquer (or try to conquer) Zicatela's awesome, oft-thunderous open-ocean waves.

UNDER $50

Three long blocks south along Playa Zicatela stands the very economical and tidy "surfer village" **Rockaway** (Av. del Morro, tel. 954/582-

0668, from outside Mexico tel. 914/906-8000, info@hotelrockaway.com, www.hotelrockaway.com, *cabañas* $22 s or d, $28 t or q, hotel rooms $36 s, $43 d, 56 t), a fenced-in cluster of 15 hotel rooms and 10 clean, concrete-floored bamboo and thatch *cabañas*. Plainly decorated but clean, spacious, and fan-equipped, the *cabañas* sleep up to four and come with private showers and toilets, mosquito nets, and shady, hammock-hung front porches. An inviting, leafy pool patio occupies the center, while a two-story squad of 15 new air-conditioned rooms rises in the rear. Weekly or monthly discounts are negotiable; parking is available. (Note: Prices more than double during the high season, Dec. 20–Easter.)

Back at Playa Zicatela's north-end beginning, find █ **Bungalows Acali** (Av. del Morro, tel. 954/582-0754, casadanycarmen@escondido.com.mx, $32 s, $35 d, $40 t, $55 with a/c). Here, a small colony of rustic *cabañas* clusters around a blue pool in a banana, palm, and mango mini-jungle. The *cabañas* themselves, like a vision out of a South Seas tale,

are built with walls made of sticks (non-see-through) and sturdy plank floors, raised above ground level. Rentals are clean, fan-equipped, with mosquito nets and good bathrooms. Rooms have a fan or air-conditioning, a hot-water shower, and a small refrigerator; parking is available and credit cards are accepted.

Additionally, Bungalows Acali offers three rustic hammock-hung, sunset-view kitchenette bungalows perched on its leafy bamboo- and mango-decorated hillside ($45 for 1–4 guests, fan only; $70 with a/c).

About two long blocks south down the beach, **Beach Hotel Inés** (Av. del Morro, tel. 954/582-0416 or 954/582 0792, info@hotelines.com, $25–120 d) is the life project of German expatriate Peter Voss and his daughter, Inés. Their 45 units occupy the palmy periphery of a lush, pool-café-garden layout, which climaxes with an attractive, stuccoed, two-story complex of rooms at the backside. At the shady poolside tables, longtime repeat guests linger for coffee and conversation after late-morning breakfasts; then, they stroll the

© BRUCE WHIPPERMAN

Most Playa Zicatela hotels, such as the Beach Hotel Inès, welcome guests with a palmy interior patio.

PACIFIC RESORTS

beach in the afternoon, and return for a balmy sunset happy hour. Other days they sunbathe au naturel or relax in the petite but luxurious health club, which provides massages and a hot tub. Most of the rentals are hotel-style rooms, in deluxe and super-deluxe grades, with clean, light interiors, comfortable furnishings, and well-maintained bathrooms. They rent four levels of accommodation, from smallish, but comfortable, hotel-style rooms, to larger cabañas, deluxe apartments, and large super-deluxe suites.

Tucked only a block inland from the beach, at the far south end of the Zicatela development, is (**Casa Olga** (Av. del Morro, no phone, olga_hmex@yahoo.com.mx, $30 s, $35 d, $60 q), which the friendly Mexican owner likes to call "your home away from home." And yes, it could easily be, with five attractively decorated, comfortable rooms on hammock-hung porches, overlooking a lovely green lawn, garden, and blue swimming pool. The upper-story rooms, with two and three beds, are the most invitingly private, with airy ocean views and awning-draped shade. All have private hot-water shower-baths, fans, and use of an outdoor kitchen adjacent to the pool-patio.

It's easy to miss the (**Hotel Flor de María** (at Primera Entrada Playa Marinero, Colonia Marinero, tel. 954/582-0536, fax 954/582-2617, pajope@hotmail.com, www.mexonline.com/flordemaria.htm, $45 d), tucked on a quiet side street above east-side Playa Marinero. That would be a pity, for the Flor de María is an attractive, reasonably priced hotel, half a block from the beach. Rooms rise in two stories around a tranquil, leafy interior patio. At rooftop, a breezy sundeck-bar, with a small but inviting pool and a hammock-hung *palapa,* overlooks a beach-and-bay vista. The approximately dozen immaculate deluxe rooms are simply but thoughtfully decorated, each with two double beds with flowery violet covers and modern-standard hot-water shower-baths and in-house Internet. Additionally, the hotel offers a pair of similarly inviting but more spacious 2nd-floor ocean-view suites and a very good restaurant.

$50-100

Head about three blocks south along Avenida del Morro, which runs along Playa Zicatela, to the three-story **Hotel Arco Iris** (Av. del Morro, Colonia Marinero, tel./fax 954/582-1494 or 954/582-0432, arcoiris@hotel-arcoiris.com.mx, www.hotel-arcoiris.com.mx, $70 s or d). A flowery, shady green garden surrounds the hotel, leading to a gorgeous rear pool and patio. For those who love sunsets, sand, and waves (and don't mind their sometimes insistent pounding), one of the spacious, simply furnished top-floor view rooms might be just the ticket. The Arco Iris's proximity to the famous Puerto Escondido "pipeline" draws both surfers and surf-watchers to the 3rd-floor restaurant La Galera, which seems equally ideal for wave-watching at breakfast and sky-watching at sunset.

OVER $100

Puerto Escondido's class-act hostelry is the (**Hotel Santa Fe** (Av. del Morro, Playa Marinero, tel. 954/582-0170 or 954/582-0266, fax 954/582-0265, from U.S. toll-free tel. 888/649-6407, Mex. toll-free tel. 800/712-7057, info@hotelsantafe.com.mx, www.hotelsantafe.com.mx, $113–260 d). Built in pleasing neocolonial style, with gracefully curving staircases, palm-shaded pool patios, and flower-decorated walkways, the Santa Fe achieves an ambience both intimate and luxuriously private. Its refined but relaxed restaurant, wonderful for morning ocean-view breakfasts, serves a delicious menu, featuring a number of traditional Oaxacan specialties.

The accommodations—spacious, high-ceilinged and comfortable—are thoughtfully appointed with hand-painted tile, rustic wood furniture, and regional handicrafts. Moreover, the recently added room wing has enhanced the hotel's ambience, with a new airy and tranquil elevated view pool-patio that connects gracefully with the original hotel section. The approximately 50 accommodations come in standard, junior, and master-suite grades; there are also 10 kitchenette bungalows that sleep four (kids under 12 are free). All accommodations come with air-conditioning, phones, parking, and credit cards accepted, but no TV.

Apartments and Long-Term Rentals

If you're planning on a stay of two weeks or more, you may be able to save money and yet have all the comforts of home in an apartment rental. First look over the classifieds in the English-Spanish newspaper *El Sol de la Costa* (tel./fax 954/582-2230, elsolinpuerto@ gmail.com, www.elsoldelacosta.com), edited by Warren Sharpe.

Also check with local realtors; the best for rentals is Pat Courtney of **Zicatela Properties** (tel. 954/582-1673, info@zicatelaproperties.com, www.zicatelaproperties.com). Furthermore, associate Vicki Cole also provides help—real-estate matters, immigration papers, residency—for newcomers.

Alternatively, for rentals, you might also contact Nolan Van Way, of **PEP Realty** (tel. 954/582-0085, nvpep@yahoo.com, www.peprealty.com).

Trailer Parks, Camping, and Hostels

Occasional muggings and robberies on the beach have eliminated virtually all camping on Puerto Escondido beaches (with the possible exception of Easter week, when such large crowds flock into town that they spill onto the beaches).

Nevertheless, beachfront camping space is available in the small, palm-shaded trailer park, once closed, now re-opened, **Palmas de Cortés** (east side of Puerto Escondido's Playa Principal, tel. 954/582-3234, cortes@ptoescondido.com.mx, $15–25 for RVs, $5 pp for tents), by the crafts stalls, half a block downhill by the beach. Facilities include security fence, a guard at night, brand-new showers and toilets, hook-ups, and room for about a dozen RVs and maybe some tents.

A good alternative for tenters and hostelers is **Shalom Hostel** (on the east end of Calle Benito Juárez, tel. 954/582-3234, rigeloo@yahoo.com,

www.hostalshalom.com, $7 pp tents, $17 pp *cabañas*, $6 pp dorm), in the Rinconada subdivision, west side of town. Besides tenting in their shady, green, back garden, with heavenly pool-patio, they offer rustic *cabañas* with shared baths and dorm beds. There's a snack restaurant and parking out front.

For a central location, the best hostel-type choice seems to be **Hotel and Youth Hostel Mayflower** (Andador Libertad, tel. 954/582-0367, fax 954/582-0422, minnemay7@hotmail.com, www.tomzap.com/mayflower.html, rooms $35 d, dorm $9 pp). Find it half a block uphill on Andador Libertad, the stair-stepped walkway a block east of the *adoquín*'s west end. Here you can choose from 14 plain but clean hotel rooms with bath or hostel dorm beds. Extras include communal kitchen, in-house Internet, and lots of local information.

Alternatively, nearby, you might consider the smaller, bare-bones but clean **Hostal Puerto Escondido** (Andador Libertad, tel. 954/582-3455, hostalpuertoescondido@hotmail.com, www.mexonline.com/pehostal.htm, $5 pp), also on Andador Libertad, within a block of the *adoquín*. Facilities (communal kitchen and Internet access) are spare, but the price is right.

FOOD
Breakfast and Snacks

In the mornings, you can enjoy breakfast with the baked offerings from the **patisserie** (Playa Zicatela, south end, next to Bungalows Acuario, no phone, 7 A.M.–9 P.M. daily), where you can savor a cappuccino as you watch the surfers conquering the waves.

Baguettería Vivaldi (middle of beachfront Av. Pérez Gasga, across the street from the Hotel Casa Blanca, tel. 954/582-0800, 7:30 A.M.–11 P.M. daily) is the labor of love of friendly Jenny Sinnhuber, who, besides lots of homemade bread, serves a wide selection of delicious breakfasts, and sandwiches for lunch.

You can also get your day started right with breakfast, while watching the beachfront scene, at either airy patio **Restaurant Danny's** (at Hotel Rincón del Pacífico, Av. Pérez Gasga

900, tel. 954/582-0056 or 954/582-0193, www
.rincondelpacifico.com.mx), or **Restaurant
Los Crotos** (on the *adoquín,* west end, tel.
954/582-0025, 8 A.M.–11 P.M. daily, $4–20),
a block from the end of the beach.

Upper Town and *Adoquín*

Many of Puerto Escondido's good restaurants line the *adoquín.* One major exception
is immaculate, strictly home-cooking-style
【 **Margaritas** (Ave. 8 Norte, few doors
east of Calle 2 Poniente, tel. 954/582-0212,
8 A.M.–6 P.M. daily, $6–12, set lunch $3.50),
where all you need is to love good Mexican
food. Find it in the upper town, near the market. Although the long country menu, including eggs in several styles, tacos, tamales,
quesadillas, fish and shrimp any style, and
broiled steaks reveals nothing unusual, everything arrives at your table delicious. The day's
main event is the *comida corrida* (set lunch).
For lunch, you get all of this for $3.50: entrée
(for example, savory beef or pork *guisado* stew,
or *mole* chicken, or chiles rellenos); dessert; and
drink, chosen from a half dozen delicious fruit
aguas (strawberry, lemonade, melon, orange,
and more).

Among three longstanding restaurants on
the *adoquín,* west end block, where the main
beach begins, is **Restaurant La Galería** (on the
inland side, tel. 954/582-2039, 8 A.M.–11 P.M.
daily, $5–14), which usually has customers even
when most other eateries are empty. The reason
is the excellent Italian fare—crusty, hot piz-
zas, rich pastas and lasagna, bountiful salads,
and satisfying soups—which the European-
expatriate owner puts out for her batallion of
loyal customers.

For a refined beachfront option, try the excellent, **Restaurant Junto del Mar** (Beside
the Sea; *adoquín,* west end, tel./fax 954/582-
1803, 7:30 A.M.–11 P.M. daily, $12–15). The
menu offers good breakfasts—rich bottomless
coffee, fresh fruit, omelets, and French toast—
plus many delectable lunch and dinner options.
Specialties include shrimp-stuffed fillets, lobster and shrimp brochettes, and whole garlic-
stuffed fish. Mornings are brightened by the

always-changing beach scene; in the evenings,
the setting turns romantic, with soft candlelight and strumming guitars. Credit cards are
accepted.

Start off the day right: Go for breakfast
at beachfront **Restaurant Los Crotos** (*adoquín,* a block from the end of the beach, tel.
954/582-0025, 8 A.M.–11 P.M. daily, $4–20)
and sit at shaded tables, enjoying the fascinating morning scene. (The restaurant is named
for its lovely garden of reddish Crotos plants,
famously known in Hawaii as *ti.*) Later, at
lunch and dinner, the house specialties—
jumbo shrimp, broiled lobster, and super-fresh
huachinango (snapper) and *robalo* attractively
presented and delicious—seem like an added
bonus.

At the *adoquín* east end, some local Italian
resident entrepreneurs have founded a modest
spaghetti and pizza gourmet ghetto. In some
cases, the results are excellent. For example,
be sure to try the tasty creations of owner-
chef Bendito, at his completely unpretentious
【 **Restaurant Bendito** (*adoquín* east end, no
phone, 8 A.M.–midnight daily, $7–14). Make
up a party and enjoy sampling his delicious
Napoli-style specialties, such as spaghetti put-
tanesca, spinach raviolis, mushroom fettuccine,
and pizza *zavarieta.*

A few doors farther east, restaurant
András (*adoquín* east end, tel. 954/582-1534,
4:30–11 P.M. daily, $8) is another good Italian
option. In a romantic atmosphere of soothing
Italian melodies and gently whirring ceiling
fans, the owner-chef offers a long and varied
menu, featuring plenty of good pizza, but also
salads (such as, *mixta* with ham), pasta (such as,
spinach-stuffed raviolis or fettucini de András);
and desserts (like the lemon pie).

Playa Zicatela

If you have dinner at the restaurant of
the 【 **Hotel Santa Fe** (Av. del Morro,
Zicatela side of the bay, tel. 954/582-0170,
7:30 A.M.–11 P.M. daily, $9–11), you may
never go anywhere else. Savory food, impec-
cably served beneath a luxurious ocean-view
palapa, with evenings accompanied by softly

strumming guitars, brings travelers from all over the world. Although everything on the menu is delicious, the restaurant is proudest of its Mexican favorites, such as rich tortilla soup, bountiful plates of chiles rellenos, and succulent snapper, Veracruz style.

Restaurant Mangos (farther south on Playa Zicatela, next to Hotel Acuario, tel. 954/582-3805, 8 A.M.–midnight daily, $7) packs in a steady stream of youthful customers, with a long menu of innovative breakfasts (crepes, three-egg omelets), salads (plenty of alfalfa sprouts), sandwiches (*cuerno*, large horn croissant), and Mexican specialties (fish-stuffed chiles rellenos).

Farther south a few blocks, past Hotel Rockaway, **Restaurant El Cafecito** (tel. 954/582-0516, 6:30 A.M.–10 P.M. daily, $5–10) is headquarters for a loyal platoon of local surfers and Canadian and American residents who crowd in for bountiful breakfasts, hamburgers, and fresh seafood plates. (Unfortunately, Cafecito's popularity is both a boon and a burden; the customer crowd is sometimes simply too large and noisy for both comfort and good service.)

ENTERTAINMENT AND EVENTS
Nightlife

The amusements along the *adoquín* mall and Playa Zicatela are Puerto Escondido's prime after-dinner entertainment source. You'll find them by following your ears. Right in the middle of the *adoquín* is karaoke bar **Congo** (beach side, open nightly). Those who prefer to gyrate, go to open-air, high volume disco **Tarros** (across from the Hotel Las Palmas).

On Zicatela beach, these days, jazz and latin rock singer **Mayka** performs at Greek Restaurant Oniro (on Zicatela Beach, across from Hotel Arco Iris), while **María Jiménez** entertains with Latin and soft rock melodies (at Hotel Suites Villa del Sol in Bachoco).

For quieter offerings, check out the guitarists who play evenings at the **Hotel Santa Fe restaurant-bar** (Av. del Morro, Zicatela side of the bay, tel. 954/582-0170, 7:30 A.M.–11 P.M.

daily), or go to **Casa Babylon** (Calle El Morro, no phone, 10:30 A.M–2 P.M., 8 P.M.–midnight), right in the middle of Playa Zicatela, for coffee, conversation, and table games. Finally, while the night is still young, take in a movie with popcorn, at the **Cine Mar** (near the Casa Babylon, no phone, 10 A.M.–11 P.M. Thurs.–Tues.).

For more entertainment suggestions, ask friendly and helpful **Gina Machorro** (on the *adoquín*, west end, beach side, tel. 954/582-0276 or 954/582-1186, ginainpuerto@yahoo.com, 9 A.M.–2 P.M. and 4–6 P.M. Mon.–Fri.), who staffs the Avenida Pérez Gasga information booth.

Sunsets and Happy Hours

Many bars have sunset happy hours, but not all of them have good sunset views. Since the Oaxaca coast faces south (and the sun sets in the west), bars and restaurants along west-facing Playa Zicatela, such as **Hotel Santa Fe** (Av. del Morro, tel. 954/582-0170), **Hotel Arco Iris** (Av. del Morro, Colonia Marinero, tel./fax 954/582-1494 or 954/582-0432), and **Restaurant Cafecito** (south end, next to Bungalows Acuario, tel. 954/582-0516,), are the only ones that can offer unobstructed sunset horizons.

If, on the other hand, you prefer solitude, stroll the bayfront *andador* (walkway) that begins on the Playa Principal, west side, on the rocks on the outer western edge of the bay, past the Capitán del Puerto office. The path leads west, past a succession of breezy sunset viewpoints above the waves, about half a mile, to steps that continue uphill to city streets near the lighthouse.

Festivals

Puerto Escondido pumps up with a series of fiestas during the surfing season (also excellent for all around vacationing) with the **Fiestas de Noviembre** (usually Nov. 10–Dec. 10). The main events invariably include surfing and usually sportfishing, cooking, beauty contests, and notably, the dance festival, **Fiesta Costeño**, when a flock of troupes—from Pochutla,

Pinotepa Nacional, Jamiltepec, Tehuántepec, and more—perform regional folk dances.

Visitors who hanker for the old-fashioned color of a traditional patronal fiesta should be sure to arrive in Puerto Escondido by December 8, when seemingly the whole town takes part in the fiesta of the **Virgen de Soledad**. Besides being the patron saint of the state of Oaxaca, the Virgen de Soledad is also protectress of fishermen. To honor her, around 3 P.M. the whole town accompanies the Virgin by boat out to the bay's far reach, and then returns with her to the church plaza for dancing, fireworks, and bullfights.

If you can't be in Puerto Escondido in time to honor the Virgin in December, perhaps you may be able enjoy either Puerto Escondido's **Carnaval** or take a day trip a couple of hours west of Puerto Escondido. There, at **Pinotepa Nacional** (or one of the small towns nearby) you can enjoy the traditionally colorful native Carnaval fiestas with parades, fireworks, and masked traditional dances, on the weekend before Ash Wednesday, the beginning of Lent.

SPORTS AND RECREATION
Surfing, Snorkeling, and Scuba Diving

Although surfing is de rigueur for the skilled in Puerto Escondido, beginners usually learn by starting out with bodysurfing and boogie boarding. Boogie boards and surfboards are for sale and rent ($10/day) at a few shops along the *adoquín* and Zicatela beach. The most experienced shop is **Central Surf** (on Zicatela, by the Bungalows Acuario, tel. 954/582-2285, www.centralsurfshop.com, 9 A.M.–9 P.M. daily).

Beginners practice on the gentler billows of **Playa Principal** and adjacent **Playa Marinero**, while advanced surfers go for the powerful waves of **Playa Zicatela**, which regularly slam foolhardy inexperienced surfers onto the sand with backbreaking force.

Local aficionados organize spontaneous **surfing tournaments** during the summer–fall surfing season, when the surf happens to be up. For information, it's best to contact friendly **Gina Machorro** (on the *adoquín*, west

end, beach side, tel. 954/582-0276 or 954/582-1186, ginainpuerto@yahoo.com), who staffs the Avenida Pérez Gasga information booth.

Clear blue-green waters, coral reefs, and swarms of multicolored fish make for good local snorkeling and diving, especially in little **Puerto Angelito** and **Carrizalillo** bays just west of town. A number of *adoquín* stores sell serviceable resort-grade snorkeling equipment.

A professional dive shop, **Aventura Submarina** (Av. Pérez Gasga 601 A, local cell tel. 954/582-2353, asubmarina@yahoo.com.mx, 9 A.M.–2 P.M.), at the *adoquín* west end, has gained a foothold in Puerto Escondido. It's run by welcoming veteran PADI instructor Jorge Pérez Bravo. The introductory lesson, including two offshore dives, runs about $80, including equipment. For certified open-water divers (bring your certificate), a one-tank night dive costs about $65; a one-tank day dive, about $60.

Alternately, check out equally professional **Puerto Dive Center** (a block farther east on Av. Pérez Gasga, across from the Libertad steps, tel. 954/582-3421, scuba@puertodivecenter.com, www.puertodivecenter.com). They offer a beginner's lesson and dive, $70; certificated one- and two-tank dives, $60 and $80 respectively; open water certification, $320; and snorkeling $25.

Sportfishing

Puerto Escondido's offshore waters abound with fish. Launches go out mornings from Playa Principal and routinely return with an assortment including big tuna, mackerel, snapper, sea bass, and snook. The sheltered west side of the beach is calm enough to easily launch a mobile boat with the help of usually-willing beach hands.

The local **Sociedad Cooperativa Turística Nueva Punta Escondida** (tel. 954/582-1678, www.pescandopuertoescondido@live.com.mx or www.tomzap.com/pe-coop.html), which parks its boats right on Playa Principal, regularly takes fishing parties of three or four out for about $25 an hour, including bait and tackle. Check with boat workers right on the beach, or at their Restaurant Pescador, at the west end of the main town beach (where they will cook up a dinner of the fish you catch).

Individual captains also offer sportfishing excursions. Check out highly recommended **Capitán Carlos Guma** (tel. 954/582-1303, guerra445@hotmail.com, $25/hour with four-hour minimum). He has a 25-foot boat, fine for catching big, fine-eating *dorado* (mahi mahi), tuna, and *pez gallo* (roosterfish).

Alternatively **Omar's Sportfishing** (local cell tel. 044-954/559-4406, omarsportfishing-1@hotmail.com) offers fishing excursions, for about the same prices, with bait and tackle included. You can find Omar on the beach at Puerto Angelito.

Additionally, travel agencies, such as the reliable **Viajes Dimar** (Av. Pérez Gasga 905, tel. 954/582-0734 or 954/582-1551, in Zicatela tel. 954/582-2305, viajesdimar@hotmail.com), arrange fishing trips and much more.

SHOPPING
Market and Handicrafts

As in most Mexican towns, the place to begin your Puerto Escondido shopping is the local **mercado** (Av. 10 Norte), one long block west of the big electric transformer station on upper Avenida Oaxaca. Although produce occupies most of the space, a number of stalls at the south end offer authentic handicrafts. These might include Guerrero painted pottery animals; San Bartolo Coyotepec black pottery; masks from Guerrero and Oaxaca with jaguar, devil, and scary human-animal motifs; the endearing multicolored pottery animals from Iguala and Zitlala in Guerrero; and beautiful crocheted *huipiles* from San Pedro Amusgos.

Back downhill on the *adoquín,* the prices increase along with the selection. Perhaps the most fruitful time and place for handicraft shopping is during the cooler evenings, within the illuminated cluster of crafts stalls just beyond the *adoquín* east-end. Among the finest bargains that, with effort, you will find are the gorgeous handwoven rugs and serapes from Teotitlán del Valle and Santa Ana del Valle near Oaxaca City. The highest-quality examples are

the most tightly woven—typically about 20 strands per centimeter (50 per inch).

Oaxaca's venerable gold jewelry tradition is well represented at the very professional **Oro de Monte Albán** (*adoquín* west end, by Restaurant Junto del Mar, tel. 954/582-0530, 10 A.M.–2 P.M. and 6:30–10:30 P.M. Mon.–Sat.). They have authentic museum-grade replicas of the celebrated Mixtec trove discovered in Monte Albán's Tomb 7.

Next door, the Uribe silversmiting family well represents Taxco tradition at its **Platería Ixtlán** (*adoquín* west end, tel. 954/582-1672, 10 A.M.–10 P.M. Mon.–Sat.). Choose from a host of fetching floral, animal, and abstract designs, in silver and turquoise, garnet, jade, and other semiprecious stones.

INFORMATION AND SERVICES
Tourist Information Offices

Most months of the year, Gina Machorro staffs an **information booth** (on the *adoquín,* west end, beach side, tel. 954/582-1186 or 954/582-0276, ginainpuerto@yahoo.com, 9 A.M.–2 P.M. and 4–6 P.M. Mon.–Fri.). Gina also gives a **walking tour** of Puerto Escondido, including the Puerto Escondido archaeological zone.

Otherwise, you can consult the well-informed staff at the *oficina de turismo* (tel./fax 954/582-0175, 8 A.M.–3 P.M. Mon.–Fri.), who distribute a map of Oaxaca. They are located just off Highway 200, in the little office on the beach side of the highway, a couple of blocks east of the airport Pemex gas station.

Travel Agent and Car Rental

One of the most respected travel agents in town is **Viajes Dimar** (Av. Pérez Gasga 905, tel. 954/582-0734 or 954/582-1551, in Zicatela tel. 954/582-2305, viajesdimar@hotmail.com). They offer a wide range of travel services, especially eco-tours, air and bus tickets, fishing excursions, and more.

Rent a car at **Budget Rent a Car** (Calle Juárez, beach side of Hwy. 200, tel. 954/582-0312, budget33@hotmail.com) in the Bachoco suburb by the airport.

Alternatively, try Gabriel at **Economica**

Rent-a-Car (Las Brisas 7, tel. 954/582-2557) on the downhill street, from Highway 200, at the south end of the Playa Zicatela development. Gabriel also rents out motorbikes.

Health and Emergencies

If you need a doctor, go to the private hospital, **Sanatorio del Carmen** (Calle 3 Poniente, between Calles 2 and 3 Norte, tel. 954/582-1876 or 954/582-0174), three blocks west of the *crucero,* uphill from the highway. There are a number of doctors on call, including general practitioners, and specialists, such as a pediatrician, family medicine doctor, an opthamologist, and an internist, plus a pathology laboratory.

Another medical option is the 24-hour government *centro de salud* (Av. Pérez Gasga, tel. 954/582-2360), below the Hotel Nayar, by Banamex.

Get over-the-counter remedies and prescriptions at one of the good tourist-zone pharmacies, such as the 24-hour **Farmacia La Moderna** (Av. Pérez Gasga, tel. 954/582-0698, 24 hours daily) of Dr. José Luis Esparzar, a block below the *crucero.*

For police emergencies, call the **municipal police** (Hwy. 200, tel. 954/582-0498), ride a taxi to the headquarters in the Agencia Municipal on Highway 200, about four blocks west of the Avenida Pérez Gasga *crucero.* Alternatively contact the **state tourist police** (*adoquín,* west side, tel. 954/582-0721) at the Libertad steps. For fire emergencies, call the *bomberos* (cell tel. 044-954/104-2494) or the police.

Publications, Library, and Movies

One of the few local outlets of English-language newspapers or magazines in Puerto Escondido is **Publicaciones Fabian** (corner of main-street Avenida Oaxaca and Calle 1 Norte, tel. 954/582-1334, 8 A.M.–9 P.M. Mon.–Sat.) in the uphill town. Usually available are the daily Mexico City *News* and magazines such as *Time, Newsweek,* and *Scientific American,* and maybe some new paperback novels.

The local English-Spanish newspaper, *El Sol de la Costa,* provides a load of useful information, including community events listings, informative cultural features, emergency numbers, apartment rental listings, and many service advertisements. Pick up a free copy in one of its many advertiser-businesses along the *adoquín.* If you can't find a copy, contact editor Warren Sharpe (tel. 954/582-2230, elsol@escondido.com.mx, 9:30 A.M.–4 P.M. Mon.–Fri., 9:30 A.M.–2 P.M. Sat.).

English-language books are available at many hotels, plus at least three spots in Puerto Escondido. On Playa Zicatela, browse the used-paperback **Book Exchange** (at Casa Babylon, next to the Bungalows Acuario) as well as the collection at **Cine Mar** (also on Playa Zicatela, no phone, 10 A.M.–11 P.M. Thurs.–Tues.).

Cine Mar's friendly proprietor, Dove Sussman, lives out his bliss by also renting, selling, and screening videos. Three screenings, of hits such as *Inception, True Grit,* and *Social Network,* begin at 7 P.M. daily.

Furthermore, a **lending library** (in the west-side Rinconada district, on east–west Av. Benito Juárez, contact Sheila Clarke tel. 954/582-0276; 10 A.M.–2 P.M. Mon., Wed., and Sat., high season; 10 A.M.–noon Wed. and Sat, low season) is maintained by the International Friends of Puerto Escondido (IFOPE).

Money Exchange

Banamex (Av. Pérez Gasga 314, tel. 954/582-0626, 9 A.M.–4 P.M. Mon.–Fri., 10 A.M.–2 P.M. Sat.), with ATM, uphill from the Hotel Nayar, changes U.S. and Canadian cash and travelers checks. Moreover, **HSBC** (Av. 1 Norte in the upper town, tel. 954/542-1825, 8 A.M.–5 P.M. Mon.–Sat.) also changes money.

After bank hours, a small *casa de cambio* (no phone, 8 A.M.–8 P.M. Mon.–Sat.), on Playa Zicatela, next to Viajes Dimar, changes U.S., Canadian, and Euro currency and travelers checks.

Communications

The *correo* (Av. 7 Norte, tel. 954/582-0959, 8 A.M.–3 P.M. Mon.–Fri., 9 A.M.–1 P.M. Sat.) and *telégrafo* (Av. 7 Norte, tel./fax 954/582-0232, 8 A.M.–7:30 P.M. Mon.–Sat., 9 A.M.–noon

Sun.) stand side by side on Avenida 7 Norte, at the corner of Avenida Oaxaca, seven blocks into upper town from the *crucero*.

For local and long-distance telephone, buy a Ladatel public telephone card at one of several *adoquín* stores and use it in street telephones. First dial 001 for calls to the United States and Canada, and 01 for long-distance calls within Mexico.

On Playa Zicatela, use either the public street phones, or the public long-distance telephone at the desk of the Bungalows Acuario.

Beware of certain prominently situated "Call Home Collect" or "Call Home with Your Credit Card" telephones. Tariffs on these phones can run $10 or more per minute, with a three-minute minimum, costing $30 whether you talk three minutes or not. Ask the operator for the rate; if it's too high, take your business elsewhere.

Internet connection, fax, and long-distance telephone are available at **Coffee Net** (*adoquín*, tel. 954/582-0797, 11 A.M.–10:30 P.M. daily), in the middle of the *adoquín*. Also, on Playa Zicatela, Internet access is available at the store next to the Bungalows Acuario (tel. 954/582-0788, 9 A.M.–11 P.M. daily).

Laundry

Get your laundry done at either **Lavandería Pérez Gasga** (Av. Pérez Gasga, no phone, 8 A.M.–8 P.M. Mon.–Sat., 8 A.M.–5 P.M. Sun.) by Banamex, about two blocks uphill from the west-end chain; or **Lavandería Playa** (on Playa Zicatela, next to Casa Babylon, tel. 954/582-1542, 9 A.M.–10 P.M. Mon.–Sat.).

Groceries

at the east end of the adoquin, on the inland side, **Abarrotes Lupita** (10 A.M.–11 P.M. daily), a fairly well-stocked small grocery, sells meat, milk, ice, and vegetables. Out on Playa Zicatela, a few stores, such as **Abarrotes Merlin** (tel. 954/582-1130, 8 A.M.–11:30 P.M. daily), offer a modest grocery and wine selection.

Photography

On Playa Zicatela, **Centro Photografico**

(tel. 954/582-3307, 9 A.M.–9 P.M. Mon.–Sat., 10 A.M.–7 P.M. Sun.) offers a modest selection of film, cameras, accessories, and color and black-and-white developing and printing services.

Spanish Instruction

The very experienced Puerto Escondido **Language Institute** (tel. 954/582-2055, brian@puertoschool.com, info@puertoschool.com, www.puertoschool.com) offers private or group lessons, homestays, tours, rock climbing, and more, across the highway from Cruz Azul cement store, above Playa Zicatela.

Newcomer **Centro de Idiomas Agua Marí** (Agua Zarca 210, tel. 954/582-0321, doramar26@hotmail.com, www.callilanguageschool.com) offers a very professional and flexible menu of both individual and group Spanish instruction. Find it in the upper town, two blocks west of the market.

Eco-Projects

Locally grown ecological efforts well worth visiting are the two reptile sanctuaries east of Puerto Escondido.

Another local eco-project is the famously successful **turtle sanctuary at Playa Escobillo** (Hwy. 200, Kilometer 181, cell tel. 044-958/587-9882 or 958/589-5908, santuarioescobillo@yahoo.com), about 32 kilometers (20 mi) east of Puerto Escondido. There, a cadre of SEMARNAT (Secretariat of Marine Natural Resources) professionals and volunteers are rescuing, hatching, and returning baby turtles to the ocean. Over the past 20 years, they have helped many hundreds of thousands of baby turtles. They welcome visitors with tours ($10 pp), a restaurant, campground (tent $10 for two), and rustic beachfront-*cabaña* ($20–25 d) lodging.

Meditation and Massage

Healing is the mission of partners Patricia Heuze and Alejandro Villanuevo, who operate **Villa Temazcalli** (Av. Infragante, tel. 954/582-1023, temazcalli@temazcalli.com, ptetemazcalli@yahoo.com.mx, www.temazcalli.com)

PACIFIC RESORTS

meditation and massage center, on the southeast end of town, past the army barracks, two blocks uphill from the highway. Facilities include rustic hot baths, an indigenous-style *temazcal,* and massage room in an invitingly tranquil tropical garden setting. Prices run about $55 each for massage and the hot tub, and about $25 for one, $50 for two, and $60 for three, for the *temazcal.*

GETTING THERE AND AWAY
By Air
The small jetport, officially the **Aeropuerto Puerto Escondido** (code-designated PXM), is just off the highway a mile west of town. The terminal, only a plain waiting room with check-in desks, has no services save a small bar and snack counter. Out in front, *colectivos* ($3 pp) shuttle people to hotels in town. Arrivees with a minimum of luggage, however, can walk a block to the highway and flag down one of the many eastbound local *colectivos,* which all stop at the main town highway crossing. Arrive with a hotel in mind (better yet a hotel reservation in hand), unless you prefer letting your taxi driver choose one, where he will probably collect a commission for depositing you there.

Although car rental agents do not ordinarily meet flights, they will meet you if you have a reservation. Contact **Budget** (tel. 954/582-0312 or 954/582-0315, budget33@hotmail.com).

Be prepared to pay the $12 international departure tax, or its Mexican peso equivalent, if your ticket doesn't already include it. If you lose your tourist card, avoid trouble or a fine by taking your passport and some proof of your arrival date (such as a stamped passport, a copy of your lost tourist card, or an air ticket) to **Migración** (at the airport, tel. 954/582-3369), for help *before* your day of departure.

A few regularly scheduled flights connect Puerto Escondido with other Mexican destinations.

Note: **Mexicana Airlines** (tel. 800/502-2000, www.mexicana.com) which ran daily Mexico City–Puerto Escondido flights through its subsidiary Click Airlines, for years, went bankrupt and closed operations on August 17, 2010. As of this writing, plans are afoot to restart operations on a much-reduced scale. It's not certain whether Puerto Escondido will be included. Telephone the airline for news and perhaps reservations and tickets.

In the meantime, some reliable carriers make Puerto Escondido connections to and from North American gateways via Mexico City.

Up and coming **Aeromar** airlines (tel. 954/582-0977, in Mexico toll-free tel. 800/237-6627. www.aeromar.com.mx) connects daily with Mexico City.

Alternatively, you can try experienced, local, air-taxi service **Aerovega** (tel./fax 954/582-0151, aerovegapto@hotmail.com; in Oaxaca City tel. 951/515-4982, aerovegaoax@hotmail.com, www.oaxaca-mio.com/aerovega.htm), which connects with Oaxaca City.

You can also fly with reliable charter airline **Aerotucan** (tel./fax 954/582-3461; in Oaxaca City tel. 951/502-0532 or 951/502-0840, tel. 951/501-0530 or 951/502-0532, or toll-free Mex. tel. 800/640-4148, info@aerotucan.com.mx, www.aerotucan.com.mx) that routinely runs Oaxaca–Puerto Escondido flights, depending upon passenger demand.

Puerto Escondido is also accessible via the Huatulco airport, one hour east by road.

By Bus
Several long-distance bus lines serve Puerto Escondido from two separate bus stations: the mostly first-class **Autobuses del Oriente** (ADO) terminal on Highway 200, and the (first- and second-class) Puerto Escondido **Camionera Central** (central bus station) on Highway 131, uphill, a mile beyond the north edge of town.

At the latter, **Estrella Blanca** (tel. 951/582-0086) and subsidiary lines (luxury and first-class Futura and Elite and others) travel the Highway 200 Acapulco–Isthmus route. More than two dozen daily *salidas de paso* come through en route both ways between Ixtapa-Zihuatanejo, Acapulco and Pochutla, Huatulco (Crucecita), and Salina Cruz. Additionally, a few departures also connect north to Mexico City, via Acapulco.

Cooperating lines **Autobúses Estrella del Valle** and **Autotransportes Oaxaca Pacífico** (tel. 954/582-0050) provide both first- and second-class connections east to Pochutla, thence north, connecting to Oaxaca City and Mexico City, via Highway 175.

Both **Autobúses Estrella Roja del Sureste** (tel. 954/582-0875) and **Linea Dorada,** formerly La Solteca, second-class bus lines connect north with Oaxaca City (with some departures via pilgrimage town Juquila) along Highway 131 direct from Puerto Escondido.

An additional pair of second-class bus lines, **Transportes Oaxaca-Istmo** and **Fletes y Pasajes,** connect east, via Highway 200, with Pochutla, Huatulco (Crucecita), Salina Cruz, Tehuántepec, and Juchitán.

Operating from the bright new steel-and-glass **ADO bus terminal** (tel. 954/582-1073, on Hwy. 200, half a block west of the *crucero* signal), **Autobuses del Oriente** (ADO) and cooperating bus lines **Cristóbal Colón** (OCC), intermediate-class **Sur** and second-class **Ecobus** provide broad service east, northeast, north, and northwest.

Luxury-class ADO GL express buses connect east with Salina Cruz, thence north via Acayucan on the Gulf Coast, all the way to Veracruz. First-class OCC buses connect with the Isthmus, via Highway 200 with the Oaxaca east coast and Isthmus, connecting all the way east with Tuxtla Gutiérrez and San Cristóbal las Casas in Chiapas and Tapachula, at the Guatemala border, and with the Gulf of Mexico destinations of Coatzacoalcos and Veracruz, northwest, and Villahermosa, northwest. Intermediate OCC destinations include Pochutla, Huatulco (Crucecita), and Salina Cruz. At Huatulco and Salina Cruz, passengers can transfer to Cristobal Colón Oaxaca City–bound buses. At Oaxaca City, at least one of these continues, northwest, via Puebla, to Mexico City (both Tapo and Norte terminals).

Intermediate-class SUR connects east with Pochutla, and Huatulco, thence Isthmus destinations of Salina Cruz, Tehuántepec, and Juchitán.

Second-class Ecobus connects east, via Pochutla and Huatulco, with Tehuántepec and Juchitán, thence north with Minatitlan and Villhermosa on the Gulf of Mexico.

By Car or RV

National Highway 200, although sometimes winding, is generally smooth and uncongested between Puerto Escondido and Pinotepa Nacional (143 km/89 mi, 2.5 hours) to the west. From there, continue another 258 kilometers (160 mi, 4.5 hours) to Acapulco. Fill up at Puerto Escondido before you leave, although gasoline is available at several points along the routes.

Traffic sails between Puerto Escondido and Puerto Ángel, 71 kilometers (44 mi) apart, in an easy hour. (Actually, Pochutla is immediately on Highway 200; Puerto Ángel is an additional six miles to the right, downhill from the Pochutla junction.) Puerto Ángel is alternatively accessible via the very scenic paved (but sometimes potholed) shortcut, via the mini-resorts of Mazunte and Zipolite, from Highway 200, at San Antonio village, Kilometer 198. Huatulco (Crucecita) is an easy 45 kilometers (27 mi) farther east from the Pochutla junction.

To or from Oaxaca City, all paved (but sometimes potholed during the summer rainy season) National Highway 131 connects directly north, along main street Avenida Oaxaca, via its winding but spectacular 254-kilometer (158 mi) route over the pine-clad Sierra Madre del Sur. The route, which rises 7,000 feet through Chatino foothill and mountain country, can be chilly in the winter and has few services along the lonely 161-kilometer (100 mi) middle stretch between San Gabriel Mixtepec and Sola de Vega. Take water and (in the winter) blankets, and be prepared for emergencies. Allow about nine hours at the wheel from Puerto Escondido, eight hours the other way, from Oaxaca City. Fill up with gasoline at the airport Pemex stations on either end before heading out. Unleaded gasoline is consistently available only at the Sola de Vega Pemex *gasolinera* en route. (On the other hand, you could make this drive more leisurely with an overnight at the fascinating pilgrimage town of Juquila en route.)

EXCURSIONS FROM PUERTO ESCONDIDO

Whether you go independently or by escorted tour, outings away from the Puerto Escondido resort can reveal rewarding glimpses of flora and fauna, local cultures, and idyllic beaches seemingly half a world removed from the *adoquín* tourist hubbub.

Farthest afield, to the west of Puerto Escondido, are the colorful festivals, markets, and handicrafts of the indigenous Mixtec towns of **Jamiltepec** and **Pinotepa Nacional** and the crystalline beaches and wildlife-rich mangroves of the **Parque Nacional Lagunas de Chacahua.** To the east lie the hidden beaches of **Mazunte, Zipolite,** and the picture-book **Bahía de Puerto Ángel,** with its turtle museum, au naturel sunbathing on Playa Zipolite, and very accessible off-beach snorkeling at Puerto Ángel. A bit farther beckon the nine breezy Bahías de Huatulco, ripe for swimming, scuba diving, wildlife-viewing, biking, and river rafting.

Closer at hand, especially for wildlife lovers and beachgoers, are the jungly lagoons and pristine strands of the west-side **Laguna Manialtepec,** the nearby hot spring and Chatino sacred site of **Atotonilco,** and a duo of home-grown **reptile conservation sanctuaries.**

◖ Laguna Manialtepec

Sylvan, mangrove-fringed Laguna Manialtepec, about 10 miles west of Puerto Escondido, is a repository for Pacific Mexico wildlife. Unlike Lagunas de Chacahua, Laguna Manialtepec is relatively deep and fresh most of the year, except occasionally during the rainy season when its main source, the Río Manialtepec, breaks through its sandbar and the lagoon becomes a tidal estuary. Consequently lacking a

continuous supply of ocean fry for sustained fishing, Laguna Manialtepec has been left to local people, a few Sunday visitors, and its wildlife.

Laguna Manialtepec abounds with birds. Of the hundreds of species frequenting the lagoon, 40 or 50 are often spotted in a morning outing. Among the more common are the olivaceous cormorant and its relative, the anhinga; and herons, including the tricolored, green-backed, little blue, and the black-crowned night heron. Other common species include ibis, parrots, egrets, and ducks, such as the Muscovy and the black-bellied whistling duck. Among the most spectacular are the huge great blue herons, while the most entertaining are the northern *jacanas,* or lily walkers, who scoot across lily pads as if they were the kitchen floor.

Manialtepec tours are conveniently arranged through travel agencies in Puerto Escondido. Although most of these advertise so-called "ecotours," a pair of genuinely very worthwhile ecotours are led, respectively, by Canadian ornithologist Michael Malone and his equally professional former student, known simply as "Lalo."

If, however, you prefer to organize your own Manialtepec excursion by bus or car, you might find yourself tempted to linger—Manialtepec is ripe for kayaking, boating, and RV and tent camping along its mangrove- and palm-decorated shoreline. A handful of shaded restaurant and lodging compounds along the shore offer the essentials for a week of Sundays in paradise.

Laguna Manialtepec Mini-Resorts

About half a mile past the dormant mini-resort of Las Hamacas at the near (east) end of Laguna Manialtepec is the sleepy little family-run pocket Eden of **La Alejandria** (local cell tel. 044-954/108-3290, tents $10, RVs $15, *cabañas* $25), which nestles along its 100 yards of lakefront, shaded by palms and great spreading trees. It's so idyllic that the *Tarzan* TV series picked La Alejandria for its setting, adding a rustic lake treehouse (now destroyed by hurricanes) to the already gorgeous scene.

LAGUNA MANIALTEPEC

To Río Grande and
Pinotepa Nacional
←
200

Río Manialtepec

Tropical

Deciduous

Forest

El Zacatal

El Corozal

El Carnero

Las
Negras

**LAGUNA
MANIALTEPEC**

Isla El Gallo

La Alejandria

**HOTEL
LA LAGUNA**

200

Las
Hamacas

To Puerto
Escondido
→

Tropical

Deciduous

Forest

Sandy

Beach

La Salina

PACIFIC OCEAN

0   1 mi

0   1 km

© AVALON TRAVEL

PACIFIC RESORTS

Embellishing all this is a homey restaurant/ bar (with a long Mexican-style menu, with familiar breakfasts and lots of seafood, $3–10) screened-in from bugs, decorated with animal trophies, and reminiscent of an old-time East African safari lodge.

La Alejandria rents about six palm-shaded RV spaces with electricity and water (be prepared with your own long extension and hose). Camping spaces are also available. In addition, they rent some rough but serviceable South Seas *cabañas* with private toilet and tepid water; check for mildew and see if everything is working before moving in, however.

Another kilometer west of La Alejandria, find lakefront restaurant and dock ☾ **Isla El Gallo** (local cell tel. 044-954/107-5718), perfect for a day or a week of exploring the lagoon. Consider swimming, kayaking, bird-watching along the mangrove-decorated shoreline, launching your own canoe or boat, or hiring one of El Gallo's boat workers to take you on a lagoon excursion from the dock ($9/hr).

If you decide to linger, next door is resort-style **La Laguna** hotel (tel. 954/582-1997, fax 954/582-0335, U.S. toll-free tel. 800/528-

1234, Mex. toll-free tel. 800/713-0204, www .bestwestern.com, $60 d), which offers 15 modern, invitingly furnished lakefront hotel rooms. The lower rooms' windows, unfortunately, don't open for fresh air. Ask for one of the upper-floor rooms, with doors opening to private balconies and lake views. Tariffs include hot-water shower-baths, in-house Internet, and air-conditioning.

The rooms are nestled around a green tropical patio, with a restaurant and lovely blue pool. A short path leads to a lake-view dock.

Aguas Termales Atotonilco

Also on the west side, a few miles west of Laguna Manialtepec, the Atotonilco hot springs, a Chatino sacred site, provide an interesting focus for a day's outing. The jumping-off point is the village of San José Manialtepec, about half an hour by bus or car west of Puerto Escondido.

At the village, you should hire someone to show you the way up the semi-wild canyon of the Río Manialtepec. The trail winds along cornfields, beneath forest canopies, and past Chatino native villages. Finally, you arrive at the hot springs, where a clear bathtub-sized rock basin bubbles with very hot (bearable for the brave), clear sulfur-smelling water.

Get there by tour, or driving or busing to the Highway 200 turnoff for San José Manialtepec, around Kilometer 116, just east of the Río Manialtepec bridge. Village stables provide horses and guides to the hot springs. It's a very easy three-kilometer (two mi) walk, except in times of high water on the river, which the trail crosses several times.

Excursions East of Puerto Escondido

A pair of grassroots conservation projects on Puerto Escondido's east side are well worth a visit. First, just a few miles east of Puerto Escondido, in Barra de Colotepec, just after (east of) the big Río Colotepec bridge, visit **Producción Ecoturístico Colotepec** (tel. 954/544-1551, 8 A.M.–6 P.M. daily, $3), the turtle, iguana, and crocodile sanctuary of Galo Sánchez. Galo, his wife, family, and neighbors started with a beachfront turtle rescue effort that now includes crocodiles and iguanas. Their aim is to return all of the endangered creatures that they are nursing to the wild. They're happy to receive visitors daily, and ask a nominal donation of about $1 per person; if you can afford more, give it. Get there either by car or *colectivo* from the Puerto Escondido highway crossing. About 6.4 kilometers (four mi) east of town, just after the big Río Colotepec bridge, turn right onto the side road to the village. Continue about 0.6 kilometers (0.4 mi) straight ahead to Galo's house on the left side.

A more elaborate but equally laudable effort has been mounted by Marcelino López Reyes at his **Iguana and Land Turtle Nursery** (no phone, 9 A.M.–6 P.M. Mon.–Sat.) about half an hour by car or bus east of Puerto Escondido. Marcelino, a veterinarian, has been working for about 15 years at the nearby government turtle-hatching station at Escobillo, helping to hatch and return about 1,000,000 *golfina* (olive ridley), *carey* (hawksbill), and *laut* (leatherback) turtles to the wild. For the same number of years, friendly Marcelino has also

devoted himself to his personal mission: to restore local populations of iguanas and land turtles. Although a hurricane nearly demolished his operation, he's back up and running, with dozens of healthy reptilian residents either running free in the branches, in a big outside enclosure, or in cages. Besides the green *iguana verde (Iguana iguana)*, black *iguana prieta (Ctenosaura pectinata)*, and boa constrictors *(Boa constrictor)*, he's also restoring two local species of endangered land turtles, the *tooceanrtuga del monte (Rinoclemys pulcherrima)*, and the *tortuga sabanera (Rinoclemys Ruvida)*. Don't miss visiting him (watch for the *criadero iguana* sign), immediately at the east end, ocean side, of the Río Coazoaltepec bridge about 34 kilometers (21 mi) east of Puerto Escondido, about a mile west of Escobilla, or 37 kilometers (23 mi) west of Puerto Ángel–Pochutla. The best time to find him there is around 5 P.M., after work on weekdays. If he's not there, one of his young assistants will probably be on hand to show you around. He appreciates a donation of about $1, or more if you have it.

The family operates an airy outside restaurant, uphill from the highway, perfect for breakfast, lunch, or simply coffee or a drink.

Tours

Puerto Escondido agencies and guides conduct outings to all of the excursion sites and more. The **Hidden Voyages Ecotours** (www.peleewings.com, $40–65 pp per day) of the Canadian husband-wife team of Michael Malone and Joan Walker (he's an ornithologist; she's an artist-ecologist) lead unusually informative tours seasonally, December–March. Besides their excellent bird-watching and animal-viewing boat tour at Laguna Manialtepec, they also offer a Lagunas de Chacuahua wildlife tour and a sunset tour. Contact them in Puerto Escondido, December 1–April 1, through the competent Viajes Dimar travel agency (Av. Pérez Gasga 906, tel. 954/582-0734 or 954/582-1551 or 954/582-2305, viajesdimar@hotmail.com or michael@peleewings.ca). In the off-season, contact them in Canada (tel. 519/326-5193).

Other Viajes Dimar travel agency tours

include a full-day jaunt east to the turtle museum at Playa Mazunte, continuing to Playa Zipolite, where you can stop for lunch and an afternoon of snorkeling around Puerto Ángel. In the evenings, during the dark of the moon, trips can include night snorkeling ($50 pp) when algae coat everything underwater with an eerie bioluminescent glow. Additionally, they offer an all-day hiking, picnic, and swimming excursion ($50 pp; or $95 for two days, one night, minimum four persons) at a luxuriously cool mountain river and cascade in the sylvan Sierra Madre foothill jungle above Pochutla.

Alternatively, you could also try one of the excellent tours guided by very experienced and well-equipped **Lalo Tours** (tel. 954/582-3050 or 954/582-3060, laloecotours@hotmail.com or laloecotours1@yahoo.com.mx, www.laloecotours.com). Their several tours (full-day tours about $45 pp, half-day $25 pp) include Laguna Manialtepec bird-watching by boat or kayak; bird-watching by footpath in Laguna Manialtepec's barrier sandbar forest; an ocean sunset cruise; and a fascinating night exploration by boat of the ghostly glow of Laguna Manialtepec's phosphorescent waters.

Upland Excursion into Chatino Country

Head north from Puerto Escondido along Highway 131 and you enter the homeland of the Chatino people, who have lived quietly in their remote mountain hamlets longer than anyone can remember. Long neglected and little studied by historians and anthropologists, the Chatinos are now increasingly learning of their distinguished past and appreciating the value of their traditional language and customs.

In the old days, the only reason most outsiders ever came to Chatino country was the miraculous **Virgin of Juquila,** celebrated every December by adoring crowds who overflow Juquila's dozen-odd hotels and bed down in doorways, cars, buses, and the surrounding mountain forest, just to push their way to within 50 feet of the tiny, frail, beloved figurine.

Nopala people tell another story altogether. Theirs is the former domain of the great Chatino kings, whose history is just beginning to be uncovered by scholars. Nopala is also an important center of coffee production, surrounded by several *fincas cafeteleras,* which in February and March harvest and roast a trove of fragrant beans for local, national, and international consumption.

An important consequence of the *fincas cafeteleras* is that they've sparked a renaissance of ecological awareness throughout Oaxaca's entire southern Sierra. Many growers have found markets for their produce among environmentally-aware European and North American buyers, who prefer to buy coffee organically grown, without pesticides and herbicides, just exactly as the local growers have done since coffee was first introduced among Chatino people during the late 19th century.

Encouraged by their contacts with outside eco-activists, certain coffee farm owners and other ecologically aware local entrepreneurs have begun to offer tours, food, and lodging to visitors, who are trickling into Nopala in ever-increasing numbers.

SANTOS REYES NOPALA

Nopala (pop. 6,000, elev. 600 meters/2,000 feet) is tucked into the upper valley of the Río Manialtepec, the heartland of Chatino country. Archaeologists reckon that the Chatino people have been living there for at least 2,000 years. Stelae found at the nearby Cerro La Iglesia archaeological site resemble the famous Olmec-style *danzantes* (dancers) of Monte Albán and are generally believed to date from the same period, around 500 B.C.

Nopala's townspeople nevertheless live very much in the present, enjoying a bit of the profits from their home-grown coffee. The

PACIFIC RESORTS

government, moreover, has provided them with a generous sprinkling of schools: *primarias,* a *secundaria,* and, for the university-bound, a *preparatoria,* unusual for such a small, out-of-the-way town. In the afternoons in town, you can immediately see the positive effect of all this: hundreds of smartly dressed, bright-eyed schoolchildren troop home after their classes are done.

Part and parcel with the increased emphasis on education, Oaxaca's unique new Usos y Costumbres law is having a significant local effect. No political parties, hubbub, or vote payoffs are necessary. A simple town-hall vote of the assembled citizenry is now sufficient to place Nopala's *presidente municipal* in office.

Sights

Nopala, "Land of the Nopales" in the Aztec language (which translates to La B'ya in Chatino), is a pretty little place, perched on a hill surrounded by green mountains. You can best appreciate all this by climbing the stairs (as a formality, ask the police officer on the porch if it's okay) to the top floor of the *palacio municipal,* just uphill from the main-plaza market. On the south (sunny side) rises **Cerro de Atole,** with the cross on top, where everyone climbs on February 24, Día de la Bandera (Day of the Flag), and feasts upon the view, which includes the blue Pacific.

The name of the mountain—*atole,* a nourishing Mexican drink made from corn—comes from the time when every house in town was a *jacal* (thatched hut). In those days, building a new house was a community affair, when all the neighbors would climb the Cerro de Atole to gather the *pasto* (grass) for the new house's roof. When the work was all done, the owner would reward his friends with a party, which would include plenty of *atole.*

On the opposite side, toward the northwest, notice the apparent gash below the mountain summit, which rises perhaps five kilometers (three mi) beyond the town limits. That's the big **Cascada de San Juan Lachao** (about 10 km/6 mi, by road), a waterfall that's a locally popular place for cooling off on a hot

---

TROUBLE IN CHATINO COUNTRY

Juquila's bustle appears so focused by the constant flow of faithful that you might think that the Virgin is all that Juquila is about. Beneath the busy surface, however, lies a complex network of personal relationships held together by political, business, kinship, and *compadrazgo* ties.

In the recent past, this tight social system, fueled by a communal forest property boundary dispute between Juquila and the rival town of Yaitepec, led to a local war that in some years resulted in hundreds of shootings, knifings, and machete slashings. Scores of Juquila and Yaitepec men bear scars of such violent encounters.

Fortunately, however, peace seems to have come to Chatino country, with the shaking of hands over a government-brokered pact in late 1998, fixing the boundary between Juquila and Yaitepec. For a fascinating in-depth look into Chatino social relationships and this dispute, check out James Greenberg's book, *Blood Ties: Life and Violence in Rural Mexico.*

---

day. To the right of that, approximately due north, rises **Cerro La Iglesia** (a steep, one-hour hike), named for the ruined fortified city, an important archaeological site, halfway down its flank. A bit farther to the right (east) of that, also halfway down yet another jungle-clad mountain, you can just make out some of the buildings of **Finca Costoche** (half-hour hike), a locally prominent coffee farm named for the jaguarundi, a wildcat and ferocious chicken-eater common in these parts.

In the northeast foreground, to the right behind the plaza-front buildings, you may be able to make out the mossy, colonial-style facade of the venerable **Templo de Los Reyes Santo Magos** (Church of the Holy Magi Kings), now replaced by the new church on its left. From here, townsfolk hold their yearly patronal festival for three days centering on El

Día de Los Reyes (Jan. 6). Invariably, townsfolk will enjoy a big party, including fireworks, a *calenda* (procession) carrying the images of their patron kings, and the town's favorite dances. These include the Guajalote (offering of the turkey) and Las Chilenas, a courtship dance not unlike the renowned Jarabe Tapatía, the so-called Mexican Hat Dance of Guadalajara.

Also in the foreground, to the east, you can see the redbrick decor of the one-of-a-kind **Hotel Palacio del Chatino,** the town's most prominent hotel and the labor of love of Dr. Elfego Zurita.

As you make your way down from atop the *palacio municipal,* be sure to take a close look at the several stelae embedded into the upper-floor and stairwell walls. Archaeologists, who dug them up at Cerro La Iglesia, believe them to represent Chatino high priests or kings, dating from about 500 B.C. If you look carefully around the bases, you'll see some yet-to-be-deciphered name-dates, presumably of the personages represented. Notice that the upstairs figures have their arms folded over their chests, as in a burial, while the one in the middle of the stairwell is a priest in the act of human sacrifice, holding an obsidian knife in his right hand and a (gulp!) human heart in his left. (*Note:* Plans are afoot in Nopala to open a new museum to display their artifacts; there's a chance that the aforementioned stelae may move to the new museum, on the north side of the plaza.)

Accommodations

Nopala is ready for visitors, with a comfortable hotel and at least three acceptable *comedor* restaurants. The lodging choice is **Hotel Palacio del Chatino** (Hidalgo 55, tel./fax 954/586-0000, $18 s, $28 d), whose bright red-and-white brick decor you probably already saw from atop the *palacio municipal.* The physician-owner polished his little six-room hotel into a first-rate establishment. There are three rooms on top and three on the bottom, all situated around an interior garden. Rooms are clean and comfortably furnished with hot

water, fans, big double beds, and a restaurant on site. The upper ones especially have plenty of air and light and look out on valley and mountain views on two sides. They're hard to beat, especially this far out in the country. Reserve ahead through the owner, Dr. Elfego Zurita.

Food

Nopala can supply you with plenty of local-style food. If you want, start at the big **market,** which operates every day but is even bigger on *tianguis* days, Saturday and Sunday. Hundreds of native Chatino women flood into town in bright *traje* with their loads of *calabazas* (gourds), *cal* (lime or quicklime), *camote* (candied root, like sweet potato), *guajalotes* (turkeys), and much more.

For cooked food, the best market choices are at the clean *fondas* (food stalls) upstairs, in the building opposite the *palacio municipal* on the plaza's east side. *Fonda* **Magali** is especially recommended by guide Frédy Zárate.

For restaurant fare, first choice goes to **Restaurant Quetzal** (at Hotel Palacio del Chatino, Hidalgo 55, tel. 954/586-0000, 8 A.M.–7 P.M. daily, $3–6), set in a cool patio setting. Breakfast choices include the familiar, such as hot cakes and eggs any style, or Mexican choices, such as chiles rellenos, *chilequiles* and *tasajo* (barbequed beef). For afternoon four-course *comida corrida* (set lunch), choose a soup (cream of mushroom or vegetable), rice or mashed potato, and barbequed beef or savory chicken *a la veracruzana,* stewed in spicy tomato and onion sauce.

Or, if you'd rather, go to one of the *comedores,* such as the **Sarita** (on Hidalgo, about two blocks downhill from the market, 8 A.M.–5 P.M. daily, $3–5); or for pizza, go to pizzeria **Kore's** (on Itúrbide, downhill from the plaza, noon–9 P.M. daily, $4–10), next to Frédy Zárate's photo shop.

Information and Services

Nopala's key service establishments are clustered right around the inviting, shady central plaza. Uphill, to the left of and facing the *presidencia municipal,* is the **correo** (post office; 9 A.M.–3 P.M. Mon.–Fri.) and the **telégrafo** (tel. 954/586-0079, 9 A.M.–3 P.M. Mon.–Fri.), across the street adjacent to the basketball court, for fax and money orders.

At the end of the alley adjacent to the post office is Dr. Elfego Zurita's **Farmacia "Willey"** (tel./fax 954/586-0000, 8 A.M.–9 P.M. daily). The *larga distancia* (tel./fax 954/586-0000) telephone office is at the Hotel Palacio del Chatino reception, behind the pharmacy. **Internet access** (8:30 A.M.–3 P.M. and 5–9:30 P.M.daily) is available right next to the Hotel Palacio del Chatino.

While in town, be sure to contact personable, well-informed, local photographer and guide **Frédy Zárate** (house and shop: corner of Zaragoza and Itúrbide, tel. 954/586-0043 or 954/586-0121, fotofredybya@hotmail.com, $25/day). He likes to show people around town and, farther afield, he can take you on excursions to local sights, such as the San Juan Lachao waterfall, the Cerro La Iglesia archaeological site, a coffee farm, and more. He speaks Spanish only, however; if necessary bring someone along to interpret. Contact him ahead of time.

Getting There and Away

By bus: Get to Nopala from Oaxaca City by second-class **Estrella Rojo del Sureste** or **Linea Dorada** from the *camionera central segunda clase* at the Mercado Abastos on Oaxaca City's south side.

From Puerto Escondido, go by the same bus lines, from the central bus station on Highway 131 (tel. 954/582-0875) at the northern edge of town. *Note:* Long-distance buses from either Oaxaca City or Puerto Escondido do not go all the way to Nopala. Get off at San Gabriel Mixtepec and take a taxi or catch a ride from a truck or local *colectivo* the remaining 12 kilometers (seven mi; see driving directions) to Nopala.

From Puerto Escondido, drive 44 curving, sometimes bumpy, uphill kilometers (27 mi) north along Highway 131 to San Gabriel Mixtepec. In the middle of town, when the road makes a sharp turn right, go left at the paved side street. Continue another 12 kilometers (seven mi) along a paved but winding road to Nopala. Allow about 1.5 hours for a safe trip.

By car or RV from Oaxaca: Drive the paved but often potholed Highway 131 south 194 kilometers (120 mi; figure around six hours for safety) to San Gabriel Mixtepec. In the middle of town, where the road cuts sharply left, continue straight onto the paved side street to Nopala. Continue another 12 kilometers (seven mi) along a good but curvy paved road to Nopala.

Excursion to Santa Magdalena Tiltepec

Santa Magdalena Tiltepec (pop. 4,000) is a very modest town perched on a hillside a few miles south of Nopala. A roadside sign a couple of miles before Nopala along the San Gabriel–Nopala road invites visitors to come see the local *artesanías alfarerías* pottery handicrafts. The products, made by both men and women, are rustically-attractive, low-fired, hand-coiled vases, jugs, and *comales* (griddles) in a handsome brown, enhanced by quizzically unique black markings. A number of potters are happy to demonstrate their wares. I stopped in at the house of Señora Ceriales Rojas, on Calle Buena Vista, a few doors uphill from the road's-end town plaza. Señora Ceriales also recommended the work of others, including Jeremia Ríos, Margarita López, and her relative, prize-winning Hipolyta Rojas.

SANTA CATARINA JUQUILA

Much of the life in the Chatino mountain town of Juquila (hoo-KEE-lah, pop. 25,000) revolves around its renowned patron, the Virgin of Juquila, the object of adoration for multitudes who begin converging on the town around the first of December.

The reason for all the hubbub is a small, frail figurine scarcely more than a foot tall, which was donated to Juquila by a priest, Father Jordán de Santa Catalina, of the neighboring town of Amialtepec, in 1713. Father Jordán feared that the image, which was already locally adored, deserved a more secure home than his rude *jacal* (thatched country house).

The love the faithful show for the Virgin of Juquila has grown over the centuries. Somehow, she strikes chords of sympathy in the hearts of Mexicans, perhaps partly because of her frailty and also because she's a simple figurine of a native woman, not unlike a pre-conquest goddess idol.

She was first revered by the Chatino people of Amialtepec during the 16th century when she resided in the town church. But in 1633, the entire town of Amialtepec burned down, and one of the sole remembrances left intact was the Virgin, who from that point forward became a symbol of hope for Chatino people.

◖ Santuario de Nuestra Señora de Juquila

The Juquila town plaza, half a block uphill from the terminus of Avenida Antonio Valdez, the entrance drive into town, is *the* place to appreciate Juquila and the town's beloved patron. Getting there requires some doing, however,

© BRUCE WHIPPERMAN

the sanctuary of Señora de Juquila

especially during festivals. If you're driving, park your car in the lot of the Hotel del Carmen (on the right-hand side of Av. Antonio Valdez, half a block before the plaza) and check in at the desk or order breakfast or lunch, if the restaurant is open. If busing, walk or ride a taxi from the Juquila station about 1.6 kilometers (one mi) ahead along Avenida Antonio Valdez to the plaza.

The neo-baroque shrine-church, the Santuario de Nuestra Señora de Juquila, faces approximately east (unusual for Mexico, where most churches face west). If you face west, toward the church, the *palacio municipal* stands on your left, on the plaza's south side. On your right (north), sloping below the plaza level, stands the town market. Main plaza-front business street Calle Benito Juárez runs south to your immediate left, while on your immediate right, the same thoroughfare continues north as Calle Revolución, where *tianguis* (native town marketplace) spreads out on Friday, Saturday, and Sunday.

Step inside the church, where the tiny Virgin presides above the main altar, surrounded by flowers and encircled by a halo of blue fluorescent light. The faithful continuously arrive and quietly seat themselves in the pews, while others kneel before the altar, gazing at the Virgin. The diminutive figure is decorated with a pearl-garnished silk cape. Her face is of brown complexion, and upon her head rests a regal, native-style crown. In front of the altar stand boxes for donations and personal letters to the Virgin.

At the same time, on the left side of the nave, outside, the faithful line up in an informal procession that leads to the **Capilla de los Veladores,** then the **Capilla de la Manta,** behind the church. Upon entering, the procession passes a succession of images of the virgin, above tables *(veladores)* where worshippers place lighted candles. The procession continues to the adjacent Capilla de la Manta, and mounts a staircase, in order to kiss the Virgin's long cloak *(manta),* which, interestingly, extends through an opening, from the Virgin's image in the nave.

PACIFIC RESORTS

C La Capilla del Pedimento

Despite the supernumerary virgins in the downtown plaza church itself, another nearby hilltop shrine, locally known as La Capilla del Pedimento, also draws multitudes of pilgrims. You'll find it at a signed left turn into a parking lot, about five kilometers (three mi) back, east along the highway out of town.

Past the parking lot are a few trinket stalls and some restaurants where you can purchase nearly everything, from food, drinks, and religious pictures and reproductions of the Virgin to *milagros* (medals for making a wish), candles, and flower gifts for her. Collect your offerings and follow the human flow north of the highway about a quarter mile to the small summit chapel.

There you'll see a large ceramic reproduction of the Virgin in a silken robe (and two or three similar reproductions behind that) hung with *milagro* medals. For an appreciation of the annual mountain of adoration that the Virgin receives, stroll around behind the chapel and marvel at the pile upon pile of offerings, far

© BRUCE WHIPPERMAN

pilgrims at La Capilla del Pedimento

too numerous to count or save, left by untold thousands of pilgrims.

Other commonly visited sights not far away from Juquila include the old Chatino center of **Amialtepec** and the spectacular 50-meter (165 ft) **Cascada Chorro Conejos.** Ask at your hotel desk for a guide to show you the way.

Accommodations

Juquila's probable best-bet hotel is the **Hotel del Carmen** (Av. Antonio Valdez, tel./fax 954/524-0004, $30 s or d, one bed, $40 d or t two beds), at the town center. With an entrance driveway leading steeply downhill to a rear parking lot, this is an especially convenient option for drivers in congested Juquila. The approximately 40 rooms are clean enough for an overnight, with hot-water shower-baths, cable TV, acceptable restaurant, and parking. Some rooms are better than others. Check the mattress before moving in.

Other options, some cheaper, are available around the plaza half a block uphill. The best of these is probably the homey, family-run **Posada los Ángeles** (Calle Benito Juárez 2, Barrio Grande, tel. 954/524-0073, $23 s or d with one or two beds, $30 t), at the plaza's southeast corner. The approximately 20 rooms are clean, simply furnished, and well-maintained, with shaded (as opposed to bare-bulb) lamps. Rooms vary; if possible, get one with a balcony for a plaza-front view.

If Posada los Ángeles is full, try the **Hotel Juquila Plaza** (Av. Revolución 4, tel. 954/524-0066, $28 s or d, $31 t), on the plaza, right in front of the church. Rooms, although clean enough, aren't as thoughtfully furnished or as well-maintained as the Posada del Ángeles. Some, however, have plaza-front views. All rooms have hot-water shower-baths and parking.

If the rush of pilgrims has filled all the above accommodations, you can try others downtown, among them the **Hotel San Nicolas** (Calle Antonio Valdes, tel. 954/524-0120, $28 s or 38 d) and the **Hotel La Conchita** (Calle Hidalgo, tel. 954/524-0015, $30 s or d in one bed, $37 d in two beds), below and behind (southwest of) the church.

Food

Several sources around the plaza offer food. For fruits and vegetables, go to the market on the plaza's north side. A convenient grocery source is **Abarrotes El Centro** (tel. 954/524-0060, 8 A.M.–10 P.M. daily), on the plaza's northeast corner across Avenida Revolución from the market. Hearty country-style food, always wholesome if hot, is available at *fondas* (food stalls) in the market.

A sprinkling of restaurants serve Juquila visitors. Very convenient is the restaurant in the **Hotel del Carmen** (Av. Antonio Valdez, tel. 954/524-0004, about 7:30 A.M.–10 P.M. seasonally, $3–7), on Avenida Antonio Valdez half a block north of the church, with a good standard menu of soups, sandwiches, meats, poultry, and Mexican specialties.

Highly recommended, especially for breakfast, is the eco-conscious **Restaurant Sierra** (no phone, 8 A.M.–1 P.M. daily, $3–5), a block west of the plaza's northeast corner or half a block west of the Hotel del Carmen. Here, for breakfast, you can feast on ham and eggs, toast, coffee, orange juice, and pancakes with maple syrup (miel maple); or, if you prefer Mexican style, chilequiles, enchiladas, or quesadillas. The portions are huge, enough for two.

A number of no-name *comedores* (eateries) along main street Antonio Valdez (such as, at #11A, a block east of the plaza, cell tel. 044-954/103-6689, 8 A.M.–10 P.M. daily, $5) serve wholesome breakfasts and afternoon four-course *comidas corridas* (set lunches). For lunch, choose from entrées such as meat balls *(albondigas)*, or breast of chicken smothered in black *mole* sauce, or beef stew *(guisado de res)*, including fruit drink, rice, soup, and dessert.

Festivals

The big Friday, Saturday, and Sunday *tianguis* (native town market), spreading from the northeast corner of the plaza, is Juquila's main regular event. It swells to a 15-day marathon blowout during the December **Fiesta de la Virgen de Juquila.** The celebration begins quietly in late November with early-morning masses and religious processions; builds with a street carnival, floats, and fireworks; and climaxes around December 8 with traditional and modern dances, tapering off after the December 12 Virgin of Guadalupe festival.

Shopping

Stalls on Avenida Revolución past the plaza's northeast corner offer a variety of local handicrafts and food delicacies. Handicrafts include embroidered *huipiles, cinturones* (belts), *manteles* (tablecloths), and embroidered *servilletas* (napkins). Food includes coffee, coconut candy, and *panela* (brown sugar).

The stands near the church offer a wealth of old-time religious souvenirs. The Hotel del Carmen sells attractive replicas of the Virgin of Juquila.

Services

Juquila, the capital of the big southern Sierra Juquila governmental district, offers some basic services (but unfortunately no bank as of this writing). The *correo* and the *telecomunicaciones* (tel. 954/524-0023, both 9 A.M.–3 P.M. Mon.–Fri.) are in the rebuilt *palacio municipal,* on the south side of the plaza. A public telephone office, **Caseta Mimitel** (tel. 954/524-0277, 7 A.M.–9 P.M.), inside at the rear of the market, offers long-distance and public fax service.

For routine medicines and drugs, try the plaza-front **Farmacia Dolores** (opposite the church). If you get sick, follow the recommendation of your hotel desk or hire a taxi to take you to the local **Hospital Civil** (Carretera Rio Grande, km 1.5, tel. 954/524-0228, 954/524-0225, 954/524-0221, or 954/524-0223). Alternatively, near the plaza, consult with general practitioner Dr. José Luis Zavaleta, on Avenida Revolución, uphill side, at two locations: either at his **Clínica San Juanito** (104 Chapultepec, tel. 954/512-2875) or his **doctor's office** (on the 2nd floor above Abarrotes Zavaleta, tel. 954/524-0237), directly across the plaza from the church.

Getting There and Away

By bus: A pair of long-distance second-class

bus lines serve Juquila from both Oaxaca City and Puerto Escondido. From the Oaxaca City *camionera central segunda clase* near the west-side Abastos market, ride either **Dorado** or **Estrella Roja del Sureste** to Juquila. The same lines connect with Juquila from the Puerto Escondido central bus station (tel. 954/582-0875). *Note:* Not all buses make the 30-kilometer (19 mi) detour to Juquila from the El Vidrio crossing. In such a case, get off the bus at El Vidrio and catch a local *colectivo* taxi for the remaining 30 kilometers.

By car: Juquila is accessible from Puerto Escondido, north via paved but sometimes pot-holed Highway 131, which starts off as the main north–south street through Puerto Escondido. Fill up with gasoline, then follow the winding 88-kilometer (55 mi) route, climbing past the cool, 2,100-meter (7,000 ft) summit to the El Vidrio crossing (where there is a gas station and rough truck-stop *comedores*). There, drivers fork left and continue another 30 kilometers (19 mi) west to Juquila. For safety, allow about 3.5 hours for the entire curvy uphill trip.

The same is approximately true heading south from Oaxaca City. Fill up with gasoline at the airport Pemex station south of town and continue to about three kilometers (two mi) south of Coyotepec, where you fork right on to Highway 131. Continue, winding uphill and down, past Sola de Vega (roadside hotel, restaurant, and unleaded gasoline) to the El Vidrio summit crossing (166 km/103 miles). Turn right at the fork and continue the remaining mostly paved but sometimes bumpy 30 kilometers (19 mi) west to Juquila.

Parque Nacional Lagunas de Chacahua

The Parque Nacional Lagunas de Chacahua spreads for about 20 miles of open-ocean beach shoreline and islet-studded jungly lagoons midway between Pinotepa Nacional and Puerto Escondido. Tens of thousands of birds typical of a host of Mexican species fish the waters and nest in the mangroves of the two main lagoons, Laguna Pastoría on the east side and Laguna Chacahua on the west.

The fish and wildlife of the lagoons, over-fished and overhunted by local people during the 1970s and 1980s, have largely recovered. Commercial fishing is now strictly licensed. Crocodiles were hunted out during the 1970s, but the government is restoring them with a hatchery on Laguna Chacahua.

For most visitors, mainly Mexican families on Sunday outings, access is by boat, except for one unpaved road (passable in the dry season; marginally so in the wet). The boats go from east-side Zapotalito village, where the local fishing cooperative offers full- and half-day excursions to the beaches—Playa Hermosa on the east side and Playa Chacahua on the west.

EXPLORING LAGUNAS DE CHACAHUA

Zapotalito, on the eastern shore of Laguna Pastoría, is the busiest quick access point to the Lagunas de Chacahua. Get there from the Zapotalito turnoff at Kilometer 82, 82 kilometers (51 mi) from Pinotepa and 65 kilometers (41 mi) from Puerto Escondido. (Taxis and local buses run from Río Grande all the way to Zapotalito on the lagoon, while second-class buses from Puerto Escondido and Pinotepa Nacional will drop you on the highway.)

From the Zapotalito landing, the fishing cooperative, Sociedad Cooperativa Turística Escondida, enjoys a near-monopoly for transporting visitors on the lagoons. The boat workers used to make their living by fishing; now they mostly ferry tourists. Having specialized in hauling in fish, most are neither wildlife sensitive nor wildlife knowledgeable. Canopied powerboats, seating about 10, make long, full-day round-trips across the lagoon to lovely Playa Chacahua and village ($110/boat for 10 people, $70/boat for 5). It's best to arrive before 11 A.M. Cheaper (about $30) half-day excursions take

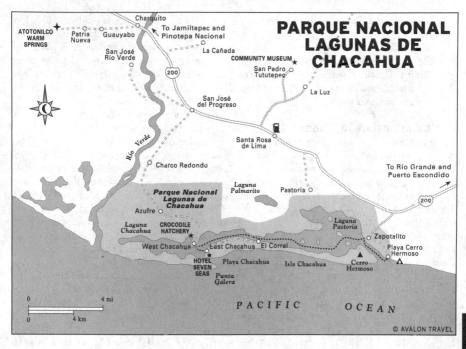

PARQUE NACIONAL LAGUNAS DE CHACAHUA

Charquito
ATOTONILCO WARM SPRINGS
Patria Nueva
Guauyabo
To Jamiltepec and Pinotepa Nacional
San José Río Verde
La Cañada
COMMUNITY MUSEUM
San Pedro Tututepec
200
La Luz
San José del Progreso
Santa Rosa de Lima
Río Verde
Charco Redondo
To Río Grande and Puerto Escondido
Laguna Palmarito
Pastoria
200
Parque Nacional Lagunas de Chacahua
Azufre
Laguna Chacahua
CROCODILE HATCHERY
Laguna Pastoria
Zapotalito
West Chacahua
East Chacahua
El Corral
Playa Cerro Hermoso
HOTEL SEVEN SEAS
Playa Chacahua
Isla Chacahua
Cerro Hermoso
Punta Galera
PACIFIC OCEAN
0   4 mi
0   4 km
© AVALON TRAVEL

visitors to nearby **Playa Cerro Hermosa** at the mouth of Laguna Pastoría for a couple of hours' beach play and snorkeling—if you bring your own snorkeling gear. On the other hand, you can save yourself $30 and drive, taxi, or walk the approximately two miles along the shoreline road from Zapotalito to Playa Cerro Hermoso. Here you'll find a lovely open-ocean beach good for surf-fishing, beach sports, and camping; a wildlife-rich lagoon mangrove wetland; and several *palapa* restaurants.

A much cheaper option for crossing the lagoon to Playa Chacahua is to go like the local people do: Take the *colectivo* boat (about $4) that leaves three or four times a day. It drops you at the Chacahua island dock, from which you can ride a truck (about $2) to Chacahua village.

(*Note:* There are two Chacahua villages, on opposite—east and west—sides of Laguna Chacahua. To distinguish them, I label them east-Chacahua and west-Chacahua, respectively.)

Another cheap route to Playa Chacahua is to drive, taxi, or ride a truck south from San José del Progreso, on Highway 200, about 24 kilometers (15 mi) west of the Zapotalito turnoff. The route, unpaved but passable (with a firm, sandy surface) even in rain, leads south about 23 kilometers (14 mi) to west-Chacahua village. (En route, after eight kilometers, at Charco Redondo village, jog right onto the elevated levee road. Continue another eight kilometers to El Azufre, where you fork left and continue another six kilometers to west-Chacahua village; pop. 1,000). Here you'll find a few stores, *palapa* restaurants, the crocodile hatchery, and a boat landing. Some stores offer secure parking for about $2 per day. The boat crossing to Playa Chacahua and the east-Chacahua village on the opposite side costs $1 per person.

The **Cocodrilario Chacahua** is a crocodile hatchery at west-Chacahua village, on the west shore of Chacahua lagoon. It's also home to a small community of *costeño* families, a run-down hotel, a few stores, and some lagoonside *palapa* restaurants. Past the rickety crocodile caretaker's quarters are a few enclosures housing about 100 crocodiles segregated according to size, from hatchlings to six-foot-long toothy green adults. They're worth seeing while you're at west-Chacahua; ask your boatman to stop there for ten minutes or so.

Boat Excursion to Chacahua

The more expensive, but quick, full-day private excursion to Playa Chacahua, about 23 kilometers (14 mi) away, unfortunately necessitates a fast trip across the lagoon. It's difficult to get the boat operators to slow down. They roar across broad Laguna Pastoría, scattering flocks of birds ahead of them. They wind among the islands, with names such as Escorpión (Scorpion), Venados (Deer), and Pinuelas (Little Pines), sometimes slowing to view multitudes of nesting pelicans, herons, and cormorants. They pick up speed again in the narrow jungle channel between the lagoons, roaring past idyllic, somnolent El Corral village, and break into open water again on Laguna Chacahua.

East-Chacahua Village and Playa Chacahua

The excursion climaxes at the east-lagoon half of Chacahua village across Laguna Chacahua. The main attraction here is **Playa Chacahua,** lovely *because* of its isolation. The unlittered golden-white sand, washed by gently rolling waves, seems perfect for a host of beach diversions. You can snorkel off the rocks nearby, fish in the breakers, and surf the intermediate breaks that angle in on the west side. Once only a few, now several *palapas* crowd the beach, offering food, drinks, and lodging. Don't miss María's enchiladas. Moreover, for beachcombers, wildlife-viewers, and backpackers (who carry their own water), the breezy, jungle-backed beach spreads for 16 kilometers (10 mi) both ways.

The original and still most popular lodging here is the **Restaurant and Hotel Siete Mares** (Seven Seas, tel. 954/560-5690, www.lagunasdechacahua.com, $25 d). The 13

cabañas occupy Chacahua's choicest location. Half of them face the beach, while the other half face the lagoon. For more privacy and tranquility, choose the latter. Rooms come with a fan and private shower and toilet. The Siete Mares's added bonus is friendly owner Doña Meche's restaurant (8 A.M.–9 P.M. daily, $3–8), which keeps satisfied customers returning year after year.

Furthermore, Doña Meche's daughter Juana also rents *cabañas.* You'll find them about 100 yards from the beach, as you walk north along the lagoon-front. Juana is proud of her 17 semi-deluxe **Cabañas Delfines** (tel. 954/120-4453, $23 d with fan, shower-bath, and toilet, $35 d with a/c added, camping $5 pp per night). She also welcomes tenters to her campground, including hammock-hung *palapa* shelters and showers.

If the above accommodations are full, you can also take a look at **El Piojo** *cabañas* (on the beach, tel. 954/559-5073) and those of **Isabel Ortíz** (on the beach, tel. 954/588-6656).

Also, some groceries and fruits and vegetable are available at **Abarrotes Nayeli** (8 A.M.–9 P.M. daily), on the lagoonfront, between Juana's and Reynaldo's *cabañas.*

Furthermore, Internet has arrived at Chacahua, at **La Diva del Manglar Café** (9 A.M.–9 P.M. daily).

RÍO GRANDE

Río Grande (pop. 15,000), on Highway 200, eight kilometers (five mi) east (Puerto Escondido side) of the Lagunas de Chacahua–Zapotalito access road, is a transportation and service point for the region. Right on the highway, find *abarrotes* (groceries), pharmacies and doctors, Ladatel card-operated street telephones, Internet connection, and a 24-hour hospital (off the highway, half a mile east of town).

The downscale **Hotel Río** (Av. Puebla, cell tel. 044-954/103-1217, $15 s or d, $17 s or d with two beds, $20 d with fans, $22 d with fan and a/c) is the two-story building off the highway's north side, at the west end of town. It offers two floors of 22 plain but clean rooms, encircling a spacious parking courtyard. All rooms have private baths, but with tepid (not hot) water.

On the highway corner, directly across Avenida Puebla, the homey, family-run **Restaurant Río Grande** (8 A.M.–9 P.M. daily, *comida corrida* $4) provides hearty meals, especially a daily four-course (soup, rice, entrée, and dessert) *comida corrida.*

On the east edge of town, **Hotel Paraíso Río Grande** (Hwy. 200, tel. 954/582-6195, $15–27) is somewhat-neglected, but nevertheless interesting. Rooms are high-ceilinged with Roman brick overhead and tiled floored below (check for mildew). The hotel lobby's soaring, classically vaulted ceilings and elegant brick arches flow from the expertise of its friendly and articulate architect builder-owner. His life project has been to first build, and now extend, the hotel, using unreinforced brick and concrete only, not unlike ancient Roman buildings, but with the addition of innovative new designs.

Hotel Las Delicias

Green, plumy palm- and *palapa*-shaded **Hotel Las Delicias** (Hwy. 200, Km 108, local cell tel. 044-954/559-2430, food 8:30 A.M.–7 P.M. daily, $7–10; lodging $35 s, $70 d with a/c) provides relaxing food and semi-deluxe lodging not far from Lagunas de Chacahua, only a few miles east of Río Grande. For about $5 entrance fee per person, families can stay the whole day, enjoying a big blue pool, kiddie pool, playground equipment, and plenty of shady room to run around within a fenced garden park. The restaurant serves from a long, very recognizable menu, with lots of breakfast and seafood selections. The several newish hotel rooms, located in a row along the quiet side, away from the highway, are modern, simply decorated, and clean and comfortable, all with private hot-water shower-baths. If you're arriving on a weekend or holiday, it's best to reserve a few days ahead of time.

Roca Blanca

Travelers hankering for an afternoon or a few tranquil days on the beach can have it at Roca Blanca (White Rock), tucked on the shoreline about 10 kilometers (six mi) east of Río Grande or 36 kilometers (22 mi) west of Puerto Escondido. Here, a few rustic *palapa* restaurants front a long curving beach of yellow-white sand, washed by gentle rollers. Islet Roca Blanca perches picturesquely offshore, softening the Pacific swells. On the west side, a lagoon, backed by a scenic jungle of rocky outcroppings, provides shelter for kiddie play and often some impromptu *palapas* that await restoration by new occupants.

If you want to stay, but arrive unequipped for camping, check out the adjacent **cabañas** (cell tel. 044-954/124-6504, $10); call the owner Andres López Solano for information. The *cabañas* are petite, but very rustic, round thatched houses with a bed for two, with showers and toilets in an adjacent building. There's also a lot for parking self-contained RVs and a lagoon-side beach good for setting up a tent, and kayaking or rubber-boating either in the ocean or the lagoon. Be prepared with bug repellent, especially around sunset.

For a more inviting option, check out **Cabañitas Oli** (tel. 954/582-6014, $20 d) on the dune, by the entrance road, about a quarter-mile from Roca Blanca. Here you'll find a cluster of four rustic beach *cabañas,* fine for a few days of beach swimming, strolling, and beachcombing.

Get there by turning off Highway 200 at Cacalote village (Km 102). Continue past the village square a few hundred yards, then turn right at the fork marked by a gigantic tree. Continue another three kilometers (two mi) to Roca Blanca.

SAN PEDRO TUTUTEPEC

Tututepec ("Hill of the Birds" in the Aztec language; pop. 10,000) is a locally important town that perches on the breeze-cooled heights about eight kilometers (five mi) inland from Highway 200. Get there by turning north (right), westbound, or catching a taxi, at the signed side road at Santa Rosa de Lima, 72 kilometers (45 mi) west of Puerto Escondido (or 71 km/44 mi east of Pinotepa Nacional). After about three kilometers (two mi) from the highway, turn left at the fork, which leads a few more kilometers uphill to Tututepec and ends at the town plaza.

Few local residents appear aware of their town's proud tradition as the only Oaxaca kingdom that withstood the 15th-century Aztec invasion and remained independent at the time of the Spanish conquest in 1522. Today's residences are built perfunctorily on the same hilltops where Tututepec's kings raised their pyramids and temples.

Community Museum

A trove of excavated remains give clues to Tututepec's past splendor. Find these in the airy new community museum, **Yucosaa** (in town, a half block from the central plaza, tel. 954/541-0310, 9 A.M.–6 P.M. Tues.–Sun., $3), the local Mixtec-language name for Tututepec.

Inside the museum's luxuriously spacious interior, volunteers preserve Tututepec's treasured artifacts, including a fascinating collection of antique animal-motif pottery *silbatos* (whistles), a host of fetching animal figurines, and a treasury of exquisite polychrome tripod pottery. The museum also displays a number of massive ancient monoliths—of the goddess of fertility, a pair of Quetzalcoatl-like serpents, and a headless jaguar—carved in styles reminiscent of Teotihuacán and Tula (Land of the Toltecs). *Note:* Since the museum is staffed by volunteers, visitation hours may vary from the announced schedule. It's best to telephone the *presidencia municipal* (tel. 954/541-0016 or 954/541-0017, speak in Spanish) ahead of time and verify the schedule and/or make an appointment for a museum visit.

While you're in town, you might climb the concrete stairs leading uphill from the west side of the town plaza to the hilltop mini-park and take a look inside the town church. On the altar is the image of St. Peter, the town patron (who, however, is not the object of the main local festival, which is the Fiesta de Candelaria, around February 2).

Food and Services

While you're in Tututepec, you can avail yourself of reliable eating places and a number of services located in the vicinity of the town plaza. These include *comedor* (eatery) Petra Soriano (no phone, 8 A.M.–6 P.M., Mon.–Sat.) for cooked food, and a couple of *abarroterías* (grocery stores) for groceries, fruit, and vegetables. Nearby services include a **correo, telecomunicaciones** (both 9 A.M.–3 P.M. Mon.–Fri.), and a *centro de salud* (31 de Mayo, Colonia Central, tel. 954-584-0039, open 24 hours daily). Gasoline is available at the Pemex station on Highway 200, not far east of the Tututepec turnoff.

CHARQUITO ATOTONILCO WARM SPRINGS

About 16 kilometers (10 mi) west of the Tututepec side road, Highway 200 passes over the Río Verde, Oaxaca's grand river, which funnels the entire runoff from Oaxaca's central valley into the Pacific a few miles downstream. West of the river, near the Kilometer 48 marker, just over one kilometer (0.6 mi) west of Charquito village, turn left at the Guayabo-labeled side road for Atotonilco hot springs and sacred site.

If driving, set your odometer at the turnoff. Continue through Guayabo (3.4 km/2.1 mi), Patria Nueva (4.5 km/2.8 mi), and a bridge, to the warm spring at 6.8 kilometers (4.2 mi).

This source of warm, sulfury, curative water has been used and revered by untold generations of local people. Folks have built a pair of small chapels on the hill above the pair of springs. If as you approach the site, you bear left at a fork, the first spring will be on your right, below the road, beneath an immense, spreading *guanacastle* tree, and the second is marked by a wide, waist-deep riverbank bathing pool.

A trickle of mostly local people bathe here, especially on Sundays and holidays. If you've got extra time, this might be a pleasant place to set up a tent or park your RV for a day or two (at a respectful distance from the springs themselves; as a courtesy, ask if it's OK to camp). Unless you're under three years old, *do not bathe nude.* Please respect local custom by wearing at least a modest bathing suit while using the springs.

What's remarkable about this place is that the water that bubbles up from beneath this half-acre warm pool remains at the ideal California hot-tub temperature of 40°C (104°F). Simply enter slowly and relax quietly, so as not to stir up mud. The water is most inviting when it remains naturally clear. A toilet, with men and women's halves stands on the hill for public use. A few steps uphill, where a gentle spring drains from the hillside, is a reed-decorated pond, home to a choir of small green frogs.

On the slope above the springs, pay your respects inside the larger of the two chapels, dedicated to the **Virgen de los Remedios.** Here, at the altar, a sign says that people give "thanks to the virgin for the hot waters that have been provided."

West to the Mixtec Coast

In reality, the Costa Chica (Little Coast), which includes the Oaxacan Pacific coast west of Puerto Escondido and the adjoining state of Guerrero coast all the way to Acapulco, isn't very little. Highway 200, heading out of Puerto Escondido, requires approximately 480 kilometers (300 mi) to traverse it.

From Puerto Escondido, you head northwest, first passing settlements, such as San José Manialtepec, on the southern fringe of Chatino-speaking country. Next, you pass the wildlife refuges of Laguna Manialtepec and Parque Nacional Lagunas de Chacahua and continue into the Mixtec coast (Mixteca de la Costa), past its main towns of Tututepec, Jamiltepec, and Pinotepa Nacional.

To many native people of Oaxaca's Costa Chica, Spanish is a foreign language. A large fraction of the *indígenas*—Chatino, Mixtec, and Amusgo—live in remote valleys and foothill villages, subsisting as they always have on corn and beans, without sewers, electricity, or paved roads. Those who live near towns often speak the Spanish they learned by coming to market. In the Costa Chica town markets, you will brush shoulders with them—men, sometimes in pure-white cottons, and women in colorful embroidered *huipiles* over wrapped hand-woven skirts.

Besides the native Mexicans, you will often see African Mexicans—*morenos* (brown ones)—known as *costeños* because their isolated settlements are near the coast. Descendants of African slaves brought over hundreds of years ago, the *costeños* subsist on the produce from their village gardens and the fish they catch.

Costa Chica *costeños* and *indígenas* have a reputation for being unfriendly and suspicious. If true in the past (although it's certainly less so in the present), they have had good reason to be suspicious of outsiders, who in their view have been trying to take away their land, gods, and lives for 300 years.

Communication is nevertheless possible. Your arrival might be the event of the week for the residents of a little foothill or shoreline end-of-road village. People are going to wonder why you came. Smile and say hello. Buy a soda at the store or *palapa*. If kids gather around, don't be shy. Draw a picture in your notebook. If a child offers to do likewise, you've succeeded.

SANTIAGO JAMILTEPEC

About 109 kilometers (68 mi) west of Puerto Escondido and 30 kilometers (18 mi) east of Pinotepa Nacional stands the hilltop town of Jamiltepec (hah-meel-teh-PAYK). Two-thirds of its 20,000 inhabitants are Mixtec and preserve a still-vibrant indigenous culture. A grieving Mixtec king named the town in memory of his infant son, Jamily, who was carried off by an eagle from this very hilltop.

The central plaza, about 1.6 kilometers (one mi) from the highway (follow the signed side road north), stands at the heart of the town. You can't miss it because of the proud town plaza–front clock (and sundials) and the market, always big but even bigger and more

POZAHUANCOS: OAXACA'S SARONGS

To a coastal Mixtec woman, her *pozahuanco* (wraparound skirt) is a lifetime investment symbolizing her maturity and social status, something that she expects to pass on to her daughters. Heirloom *pozahuancos* are of hand-spun thread, dyed in several shades. Women dye them by hand, always including a pair of necessary colors: a light purple *(morada)* from secretions of tidepool-harvested snails, *Purpura patula pansa*; and silk dyed scarlet red with cochineal, a dye extracted from the scale insect *Dactylopius coccus*, cultivated in the Valley of Oaxaca. Increasingly, women are weaving *pozahuancos* with synthetic thread, which has a slippery feel compared to the hand-spun cotton. Consider yourself lucky if you can get a traditionally made *pozahuanco* for as little as $100. If someone offers you a look-alike for $20, you know it's an imitation, made of machine-made polyester thread and synthetic dyes.

© BRUCE WHIPPERMAN

a traditional *pozahuanco*

colorful on Thursday, the day of the traditional *tianguis* (native town market), when a regiment of campesinos crowd in from the Jamiltepec hinterland.

Jamiltepec at midday is a feast of traditional sights and sounds, accessible by simply strolling around the market and side streets. For an interesting side excursion, take a stroll to some of the local *ojos de agua* (community springwater sources). From the plaza's northeast side, head east, downhill, along Calle 20 de Noviembre. After about a block, you'll arrive at a covered *pileta* (basin) built into the hillside rocks on the left, where folks fill bottles and jars with drinking water. Continue downhill another couple of blocks to *ojo de agua* **El Aguacate,** where another covered basin, on the left, supplies drinking water, while a cluster of folks wash clothes and bathe in a natural spring beneath an adjacent shady roof.

If you're interested in a more spectacular water diversion, follow the gravel road by local minibus or car north out of town about 25 kilometers (15 mi) to the **cascada** (waterfall) in the foothill country near San José de las Flores village.

Festivals and Events

Several big festivals are instrumental in preserving local folkways. They start off on New Year's Day and resume during the weeks of Cuaresma (Lent), usually during February and March. Favorite dances, such as Los Tejerones (Weavers), Los Chareos, Los Moros (The Moors), and Las Chilenas, act out age-old events, stories, and fables. Los Tejerones, for example, through a cast of animal-costumed characters, pokes fun at ridiculous Spanish colonial rules and customs.

Soon after, Jamiltepec people celebrate their very popular pre-Easter (week of Ramos) festival, featuring neighborhood candlelight processions accompanied by antique 18th-century music. Hundreds of the faithful bear elaborate wreaths and palm decorations to the foot of their church altars on Domingo de Ramos (Palm Sunday).

Later, merrymaking peaks again, between

July 23 and 26 during the Fiesta de Santiago Apóstol (Festival of St. James the Apostle) and on September 11 with a festival honoring the Virgen de los Remedios. All this celebrating centers in the town church, the **Templo de Santiago Apóstol,** destroyed by a 1928 earthquake but brilliantly restored in 1992–1999, using the same method as the original Dominican padres, who supervised the 16th-century construction of mortar, strengthened with egg yolks. Take a look inside, where the town patron Santiago (St. James, sword in hand) and the Virgen de Los Remedios (Virgin of the Remedies) preside above the altar.

Shopping

Jamiltepec is well worth a stop if only to visit its market (in two locations: around the town center and a half-mile north of town in a big building visible from the highway). Especially worthwhile are the handicrafts shops that sell masks, *huipiles,* carvings, hats, and much more. The market action, busiest on the Thursday *tianguis,* peaks around noon, and shuts down by 6 P.M.

Practicalities

Jamiltepec, capital of the Jamiltepec governmental district, has some recommendable hotels, restaurants, and services (but not yet a bank) near the town plaza. For an overnight, the best is lovely (**Hotel Cádiz** (Calle del Olvido 7, tel. 954/582-8570, $22 s, $26 d), about a quarter mile north of the town center. The dozen-odd rooms are spacious, with designer tile floors, and thoughtfully furnished with color-coordinated drapes and reading lamps. Views from the windows stretch from the surrounding village to far mountain vistas. All rooms come with private hot-water shower-baths, cable TV, fans, and a handy restaurant downstairs. If the Hotel Cádiz is full, take a look at the clean and comfortable **Hotel Maris** (Calle Josefa Ortíz Domínguez, between de la Cruz and Rayón, tel. 954/582-8042, $15–20). Of the 46 rooms, pick one of the light rooms away from the street; rooms come with private bath, cable TV, and fans, but no restaurant.

Additionally, out on the highway, at the west edge of town, consider Jamiltepec's newish, semi-deluxe **Hotel Mirador** (Hwy. 200, cell tel. 044-954/559-2444, $18 s or d in one bed, $25 d with two beds with fan, $20 s or d in one bed, $30 d in two beds with a/c), perched on a hillside with a view, next to Highway 200. Fine for an overnight, the Mirador offers about 15 comfortable (if a bit dark) rooms. All with hot-water shower-baths, parking, and an acceptable restaurant.

For medicines and drugs, go to **Farmacia del Perpetuo Socorro** (Pharmacy of Perpetual Relief; Hidalgo 2, tel. 954/582-9046, 8 A.M.–8 P.M. daily), next to Hotel Díaz, at the plaza's northeast corner, run by a team of friendly sisters. If you need a doctor, they recommend either **Dr. Manuel Mota** (on Hwy. 200, in town barrio Sección 4) or the *seguro social* **hospital** (in town barrio Las Flores, tel. 954/582-8040, 24-hour emergency service).

WEST OF JAMILTEPEC
Huaxpáltepec Pre-Easter Fair

For 32 kilometers (20 mi) west of Jamiltepec, Highway 200 stretches through the coastal Mixtec heartland, intriguing to explore, especially during festival times. The population of San Andres Huaxpáltepec (oo-wash-PAHL-tay-payk), about 10 miles east of Pinotepa, sometimes swells from about 4,000 to 20,000 or more during the three or four days before the day of Jesus the Nazarene, on the fourth Friday of Lent (or in other words, the fourth Friday after Ash Wednesday). The entire town spreads into a warren of shady stalls, offering everything from TVs to stone *metates* (basins for grinding corn). The purchase of a corn-grinding *metate,* which, including *mano* stone roller, sells for about $25, is as important to a Mixtec family as a refrigerator is to an American family. A Mixtec husband and wife usually examine several of the concave stones, deliberating the pros and cons of each before deciding.

The Huaxpáltepec Nazarene fair is typical of the larger Oaxaca country expositions. Even the highway becomes a lineup of stalls;

whole native clans camp under the trees, and mules, cows, and horses wait patiently around the edges of a grassy trading lot as men discuss prices. (The fun begins when a sale is made, and the new owner tries to rope and harness his bargain steed.)

Santa María Huazolotitlán

At nearby Huazolotitlán (ooah-shoh-loh-teet-LAN, pop. 3,000) several resident woodcarvers craft excellent **masks.** Local favorites are jaguars, lions, rabbits, bulls, and human faces. Given a photograph (or a sitting), one of them might even carve your likeness for a reasonable fee (figure perhaps $40–60). Near the town plaza, ask for Che Luna, Lázaro Gómez, or Idineo Gómez, all of whom live in the town barrio Ñií Yucagua.

Textiles are also locally important. Look for the colorfully embroidered animal- and floral-motif *huipiles, manteles,* and *servilletas* (native smocks, tablecloths, and napkins). You might also be able to bargain for a genuine heirloom *pozahuanco* (skirt) for a reasonable price.

Besides all the handicrafts, Huazolotitlán people celebrate the important local **Fiesta de la Virgen de la Asunción** (Aug. 13–16). The celebrations customarily climax with a number of favorite traditional dances, in which you can see why masks are locally important, especially in the dance of the Tiger and the Turtle. The finale comes a day later, celebrated with the ritual dance of the Chareos, dedicated to the Virgin.

Get to Huazolotitlán in about two miles along the paved (but oft-potholed) road that forks south uphill from Highway 200 in Huaxpaltepec. Drive, hitchhike (with caution), ride the local bus, or hire a taxi for about $3.

PINOTEPA NACIONAL AND VICINITY

Pinotepa Nacional (pop. 50,000; 145 km/90 mi west of Puerto Escondido, 253 km/157 mi east of Acapulco) and its neighboring communities comprise the hub of an important coastal indigenous region. Mixtec, Amusgo, Chatino, and other peoples stream into town for markets

and fiestas in their traditional dress, ready to combine business with pleasure. They sell their produce and crafts—pottery, masks, handmade clothes—at the market, then later get tipsy, flirt, and dance.

So many people asked the meaning of their city's name that the town fathers wrote the explanation on a wall next to Highway 200 on the west side of town. Pinotepa comes from the Aztec-language words *pinolli* (crumbling) and *tepetl* (mountain)—thus, "Crumbling Mountain." The second part of the name came about because, during colonial times, the town was called Pinotepa Real (Royal). This wouldn't do after independence, so the name became Pinotepa Nacional, reflecting the national consciousness that emerged during the 1810–1821 struggle for independence.

The Mixtecs, the dominant regional group, disagree with all this, however. To them, Pinotepa has always been Ñií Yo-oko (Little Place). Only within the town limits do the Mexicans (mestizos), who own most of the town businesses, outnumber the Mixtecs. The farther from town you get, the more likely you are to hear people conversing in the Mixtec language, a complex tongue that uses a number of subtle tones to make meanings clear.

Getting Oriented

On Pinotepa's east (Puerto Escondido) side, Highway 200 splits into the town's two major arteries, which rejoin on the west (Acapulco) side. The north, west-bound branch is called Aguirre Palancares; the south, east-bound branch, the more bustling of the two branches, passes between the town-center *zócalo* and church and is called Avenida Porfirio Díaz on the west side and Avenida Benito Juárez on the east. The main north–south street, Avenida Pérez Gasga, runs past both the west-facing church front and the *presidencia municipal,* which faces east, toward the town plaza.

◖ Pinotepa Market

Highway 200 passes a block north of the main town market, by the big, fenced-in secondary school, on the west side, about a mile west of the central plaza. Despite the Pinotepa market's oft-exotic goods—snakes, iguanas, wild mountain fruits, forest herbs, and spices—its people, nearly entirely Mixtec, are its main attraction, especially on the big Monday market day. Men wear pure white loose cottons, topped by woven palm-leaf hats. Women wrap themselves in their lovely striped purple, violet, red, and navy blue *pozahuanco* (saronglike, horizontally striped skirts). Many women carry atop their heads a polished tan *jicara* (gourd bowl for eating), which, although it's not supposed to, looks like a whimsical hat. Older women (and younger ones with babies at their breasts) go bare-breasted with only their white *huipiles* draped over their chests as a concession to mestizo custom. Others wear an easily removable *mandil*, a light cotton apron-halter above their *pozahuancos*. A few women can ordinarily be found offering colorful *pozahuancos,* made with cheaper synthetic thread, for about $50. They told me that traditional all-handmade *pozahuancos* (handspun, hand-sewn, and hand-dyed with naturally gathered pigments) are more commonly available in outlying market towns, notably Pinotepa Don Luis.

Festivals

Although the Pinotepa market days are big, they don't compare to Semana Santa (the week before Easter). People get ready for the finale with processions, carrying the dead Christ through town to the church each of the seven Fridays before Easter. The climax comes on Viernes Santa (Good Friday), when a platoon of young Mixtec men paint their bodies white to portray Jews, and while intoning ancient Mixtec chants shoot arrows at Christ on the cross. On Saturday, the people mournfully take the Savior down from the cross and bury him, and, on Sunday, gleefully celebrate his resurrection with a riot of fireworks, food, and folk dancing.

Although not as spectacular as Semana Santa, there's plenty of merrymaking, food, dancing, and processions around the Pinotepa *zócalo* church on July 25, the day of Pinotepa's patron, Santiago (St. James).

Accommodations

The motel-style **Hotel Carmona** (Av. Porfirio Díaz 127, tel. 954/543-2222, $25 s, $30 d in one or two beds, $35 t with fan, $35 s, $45 d, $50 t with a/c), about three blocks west of the plaza, offers three stories of clean, not fancy but comfortable basic rooms and a big backyard garden with pool and sundeck. For festival dates, make reservations in advance. The 50 rooms come with cable TV and parking.

If the Carmona is full, check out the two high-profile newer hotels, Pepe's and Las Gaviotas, on the north side of the highway, on the west side of town. Of the two, **Pepe's** (Hwy. 200, Km 1, tel. 954/543-4347, fax 954/543-3602, $20 s, $25 d with fan, $28 s, $35 d with a/c) is the much better choice. It offers 35 spacious semi-deluxe rooms, with good TV, hot water, restaurant, and parking. A few doors farther west, the rooms at **Hotel Las Gaviotas** (Hwy. 200, tel./fax 954/543-2838, $22 d with fan, $32 d with a/c) come with TV and parking.

The third choice goes to clean **Hotel Marisa** (Av. Juárez 134, tel. 954/543-2101, $18 s or d in one bed, $20 d or t in two beds with fan, $23 s or d in two beds, $27 t with a/c), downtown on the highway, north side of the street. All rooms come with TV and parking.

Campers enjoy a tranquil spot (best during the dry, calm, clear-water late fall—winter—spring season) on the **Río Arena** about two miles east of Pinotepa. Eastbound, turn left just after the big river bridge. Continue a few hundred yards, past a pump-house on the left, to a track that forks down to the riverbank. Notice the waterfall cascading down the rocky cliff across the river. You will sometimes find neighbors in RVs or tents. Beneath the abandoned Restaurant La Roca (now just a rockwall ruin), poor but friendly sand gatherers sometimes sift through sand on the riverside, planning to sell it to construction sites. The smooth stream is excellent for kayaking (if you have some way of returning back upstream).

Food

For a light lunch or supper, try the very clean

family-run **Burger Bonny** (tel. 954/543-2016, 11 A.M.–10 P.M. daily, $1–4), at the southeast corner of the main plaza. Besides six varieties of good hamburgers, Burger Bonny offers *tortas,* tacos, french fries, hot dogs, microwave popcorn, fruit juices, and *refrescos.*

The second restaurant choice goes to **Tacos Orientales** (Av. Pérez Gasga, 6–11 P.M. daily, three tacos for $2.50), with 15 styles of tacos, from fish to *carnitas.* Find it half a block north of the churchfront.

The hot new Pinotepa restaurant is **El Adobe** (Porfirio Díaz, corner of Progreso, across from Bancomer, no phone, 8 A.M.–10 P.M. daily, $3–6) with an airy 2nd-floor view dining-room. Choose your breakfast (omelet, hot cakes), lunch (hamburger, *torta*), or dinner (chicken salad, spaghetti bolognese, tacos, or quesadilla).

For a quick and convenient on-the-road breakfast, lunch, or dinner, stop by the restaurant of high-profile hotel **Pepe's** (Hwy. 200, Km 1, tel. 954/543-4347, 8 A.M.–10 P.M. daily, $3–6) west of town.

Services

For the freshest fruits and vegetables, visit the town market any day, although it's biggest for the Monday *tianguis* (native town market).

For film and film processing, step in to **Arlette Foto** (tel. 954/543-2766, 8 A.M.–8 P.M. Mon.–Sat., 8 A.M.–3 P.M. Sun.) near the plaza's southwest corner.

Exchange money over the counter or use the ATM at all Pinotepa banks. Try **Bancomer** (corner of Av. Porfirio Díaz and Av. Progreso, tel. 954/543-3022 or 954/543-3190, 8:30 A.M.–4 P.M. Mon.–Fri.), two blocks west of the plaza; **Banamex** (across the street from Bancomer, tel. 954/543-3022, 9 A.M.–4 P.M. Mon.–Fri.); or **HSBC** (Av. Progreso, tel. 954/543-3949 or 954/543-3969, 8 A.M.–5 P.M. Mon.–Fri.), across Avenida Porfirio Díaz and uphill a block from Bancomer.

Find the *correo* (post office; tel. 954/543-2264, 8 A.M.–7 P.M. Mon.–Fri.) about half a mile west of downtown, a block past Pepe's hotel and across the street. Find the

telecomunicaciones office (Av. Pérez Gasga, tel. 954/543-2019, 8 A.M.–7:30 P.M. Mon.–Fri., 9 A.M.–noon Sat.–Sun.) one block north of the plaza church. For telephone, use Ladatel card-operated street telephones, or go to the long-hours *larga distancia* Lada Central telephone and fax office (tel. 954/543-2547), on the plaza, south side. A few doors away, answer your email at **Switch Internet** (on the plaza, 8 A.M.–9 P.M. daily).

For a doctor, go to the 24-hour **Clínica Rodriguez** (Aguirre 503 Palancares, tel. 954/543-2330), one block north, two blocks west of the central plaza churchfront. Get routine medications at one of several town pharmacies, such as the 24-hour **Super Farmacia** (Av. Porfirio Díaz), a block west of the central plaza churchfront.

Getting There and Away

By car or RV, Highway 200 connects west to Acapulco (258 km/160 mi) in an easy 4.5 hours' driving time. The 143-kilometer (89 mi) eastward connection with Puerto Escondido can be done safely in about 2.5 hours. Additionally, the long 385-kilometer (239 mi) Highway 125–Highway 190 route connects Pinotepa Nacional to Oaxaca, via Putla de Guerrero and Tlaxiaco (219 km/136 mi). Although winding most of the way and potholed at times, the road is generally uncongested. It's safely driveable in a passenger car with caution, from Pinotepa to Oaxaca City (nearing Oaxaca City, at Nochixtlán, exit Hwy. 190 and follow the *cuota autopista,* toll expressway) in about eight hours (under dry conditions) at the wheel, and seven hours in the reverse, downhill, direction from Oaxaca City.

By bus, from the new **Camionera Central** (Central Bus Station), about a mile west of downtown, several long-distance bus lines connect Pinotepa Nacional with destinations north, northwest, west, and east. Dominant line **Estrella Blanca** (tel. 954/543-3194), via subsidiaries Turistar, Elite, Futura, Gacela, and Flecha Roja, offers several daily first- and second-class *salidas de paso* (departure buses passing through): west to Acapulco, Zihuatanejo,

Lázaro Cárdenas, and Mexico City; and east to Puerto Escondido, Pochutla (Puerto Ángel), Bahías de Huatulco, and Salina Cruz. Other independent, mostly second-class lines also operate out of the same terminal. **Fletes y Pasajes** connects with inland points, via Putla de Guerrero, Tlaxiaco, and Teposcolula along Highway 125, continuing along Highway 190 via Nochixtlán, to Oaxaca City. **Estrella del Valle** (tel. 954/543-5476) also connects with Oaxaca City, but in the opposite direction, via Highway 200 east to Puerto Escondido and Pochutla (Puerto Ángel), thence north along Highway 175, via San José del Pacifico and Miahuatlán, to Oaxaca City.

On the other hand, second-class **Estrella Roja del Sureste** (tel. 954/543-6017), in addition to connecting with Oaxaca City via Pochutla, thence over the sierra via Highway 175, also connects with Oaxaca City, first following Highway 200 to Puerto Escondido, thence turning inland, north, along Highway 131, over the sierra, via El Vidrio (Juquila) and Sola de Vega, to Oaxaca City.

Also second-class **Boquerón** buses connect north, via Putla de Guerrero, and Juxtlahuaca, with Huajuapan de León in the Mixteca Baja.

EXCURSIONS NORTH OF PINOTEPA

The local patronal festival year begins early, on January 20, at **Pinotepa Don Luis** (pop. 5,000), about 24 kilometers (15 mi), by back roads, northeast of Pinotepa Nacional, with the uniquely Mixtec festival of San Sebastián. Village bands blare, fireworks pop and hiss, and penitents crawl until the finale, when dancers whirl the local favorite dance, Las Chilenas.

Yet another exciting time around Pinotepa Nacional is during **Carnaval,** when nearby communities put on big extravaganzas. Pinotepa Don Luis, sometimes known as Pinotepa Chica (Little Pinotepa), is famous for the wooden masks the people make for their big Carnaval. The celebration usually climaxes on the Sunday before Ash Wednesday,

when everyone seems to be in costume and a corps of performers gyrates in the traditional dances: Paloma (Dove), Tigre (Jaguar), Culebra (Snake), and Tejón (Badger).

Pinotepa Don Luis bubbles over again with excitement during Semana Santa, when the faithful carry fruit- and flower-decorated trees to the church on Good Friday, explode Judas effigies on Saturday, and celebrate by dancing most of Easter Sunday.

San Juan Colorado, a few kilometers north of Pinotepa Don Luis, usually appears as just another dusty little town until Carnaval, when its festival rivals that of its neighbors. Subsequently, on November 29, droves of Mixtec people come into town to honor their patron, San Andres. After the serious part at the church, they celebrate with a cast of favorite dancing characters such as Malinche, Jaguar, Turtle, and Charros (Cowboys).

Amusgo Country

Cacahuatepec (pop. 5,000; on Hwy. 125 about 40 km/25 mi north of Pinotepa Nacional) and its neighboring community San Pedro Amusgos are important centers of the Amusgo people. Approximately 20,000 Amusgos live in a roughly 30- square-mile region straddling the Guerrero–Oaxaca state border. Their homeland includes, besides Cacahuatepec and San Pedro Amusgos, Ometepec, Xochistlahuaca, Zacoalpán, and Tlacoachistlahuaca on the Guerrero side.

The Amusgo language is linguistically related to Mixtec, although it's unintelligible to Mixtec speakers. Before the conquest, the Amusgos were subject to the numerically superior Mixtec kingdoms until the Amusgos were conquered by the Aztecs in A.D. 1457, and later by the Spanish.

Now, most Amusgos live as subsistence farmers, supplementing their diet with occasional fowl or small game. Amusgos are best known to the outside world for their lovely animal-, plant-, and human-motif *huipiles,* which Amusgo women always seem to be hand-embroidering on their doorsteps.

Although Cacahuatepec enjoys a big market

PACIFIC RESORTS

each Sunday, that doesn't diminish the importance of its big Easter weekend festival, as well as the day of Todos Santos (All Saints' Day, Nov. 1), and Día de los Muertos (Day of the Dead, Nov. 2), when, at the cemetery, people welcome their ancestors' return to rejoin the family.

San Pedro Amusgos celebrations are among the most popular regional fiestas. On June 29, the day of San Pedro, people participate in religious processions, and costumed participants dressed as Moors and Christians, bulls, jaguars, and mules dance before crowds of men in traditional whites and women in beautiful heirloom *huipiles*. Later, on the first Sunday of October, folks crowd into town to enjoy the traditional processions, dances, and sweet treats of the fiesta of the Virgen de la Rosario (Virgin of the Rosary).

Even if you miss the festivals, San Pedro Amusgos is worth a visit to buy *huipiles* alone. Three or four shops sell them along the main street through town. Look for the sign of **Trajes Regionales Elia** (tel. 954/582-8697, 9 A.M.–6 P.M. daily), the little store run by sprightly Elia Guzmán, when she's not in Oaxaca City. Besides dozens of beautiful embroidered garments, she stocks a few Amusgo books and offers friendly words of advice and local information.

EXCURSION SOUTH OF PINOTEPA

If you hanker for a little sea breeze and the murmur of the waves, spend a day or a week at **Playa Corralero**, about 28 kilometers (18 mi) south by a paved but potholed, finally sandy but smooth road. Get there by car or the *camionetas* (passenger trucks) that head south on the street one block west from the Hotel Carmona (Av. Porfirio Díaz 127). Along the way, in the beginning, you'll pass rolling tropical forest country, partially tamed to corn and cattle.

About 19 kilometers (12 mi) from Pinotepa, the road forks. The left, paved branch continues to Laguna Corralero village (pop. 2,000), a pleasant small town of fisherfolk on the tidal estuary lagoon. Hikers could probably bargain with a boat worker at the village to ferry them across the lagoon to the open ocean channel and beach (say, "*Ramada Guelaguetza, por el mar*").

Otherwise, hikers should get off the truck at the fork and walk or hitchhike the right-fork road the additional 9.6 kilometers (six mi) to the beach *ramadas* (rustic shelters made of palm fronds). Drivers should likewise turn right at the fork. Along the way, you pass through a thick prickly pear cactus mini-forest along the beach. Finally, you arrive at the beachfront *ramada* restaurants beside a jetty and broad channel, which a dredge keeps open for fishing boats.

The beach itself is of coarse, yellowish sand, rather steep, with the consequent undertow. Waves, which don't appear good for surfing, break strongly and quickly close to shore. The same conditions, however, make the beach perfect for **surf fishing.** If you prefer solitude and don't mind a few cows for company, you can set up camp along the wide, grassy dune and camp most anywhere for 6.4 kilometers (four mi) before the *ramadas*. (*Note:* On the sand, use four-wheel-drive with caution; if not, be very careful to avoid getting stuck, which might happen even with four-wheel-drive.)

On the other hand, if you prefer company, park or tent near the road's-end *ramadas*. The *ramada* **Guelaguetza,** nearest to the beach, run by the friendly López Herrera family, will provide you with plenty of economical fish dinners and *refrescos,* plus shade for your vehicle and tent.

THE MIXTECA

The homeland of the Mixtecs, Oaxaca's "People of the Clouds," spreads over an immense domain encompassing the state's entire northwest, stretching northward from the tropical Pacific coast over the high, cool pine-tufted Sierra to the warm, dry "Land of the Sun" along Oaxaca's northern border. The Mixteca's vastness and diversity have led Oaxacans to visualize it as three distinct sub-regions: Mixteca Alta, Mixteca Baja, and Mixteca de la Costa. These labels reflect the geographical realities of the Mixteca's *alta* (high) and *baja* (low) mountains and the tropical Pacific *costa* (coastal plain and foothills).

The Mixteca Alta comprises the Mixteca's highest, coolest country—all or part of the governmental districts of Nochixtlán, Coixtlahuaca, Teposcolula, and Tlaxiaco.

The Mixteca Baja includes, on the other hand, the warm, dry districts of Huajuapan, Silacayoapan, and parts of Juxtlahuaca along Oaxaca's northern frontier. The Mixteca de la Costa lies south of all this, encompassing the tropical coastal districts of Putla and Jamiltepec on Oaxaca's southwest border.

This chapter traces a counterclockwise circle route through the Mixteca, northwest from Oaxaca City. First, we arrive in Nochixtlán, scarcely an hour from Oaxaca City, and use it as a base for exploring the hidden delights of the southern Mixteca Alta. Next, the route continues north through country renowned for its exquisite and monumental Dominican churches, then on to the warm, sunny Mixteca Baja country around Huajuapan de León. There, our journey curves through the scenic

© BRUCE WHIPPERMAN

HIGHLIGHTS

◖ Tilantongo and Monte Negro Archaeological Zones: The ancient capital of the Mixteca and nearby Monte Negro, with ruins dating back to 500 B.C., make a memorable one-day excursion (page 224).

◖ The Valley of Apoala: This bucolic, spring-fed, mountain-rimmed Oaxacan Shangri-La, replete with scenery and legends, deserves at least an overnight (page 225).

◖ Templo y Ex-Convento de San Pedro y San Pablo: The newly restored gargantuan Capilla Abierta (Open Chapel), big enough for 10,000 acolytes, crowned the Dominican padres architectural efforts in Oaxaca (page 233).

◖ Puente Colosal and Huerta de Juquila: Scramble a mile downhill into a hidden box canyon and explore one of the world's tallest natural bridges, decorated by giant, yet-to-be-deciphered Mixtec petroglyphs (page 243).

◖ Cerro de las Minas Archaeological Zone: A high point of your Mixteca visit will most likely be the chance to climb to the top of the regal pyramids and stroll the broad stately plazas of this archaeological zone (page 247).

◖ Santo Domingo Tonalá: This village is worth a visit, both for the 16th-century Templo de Santo Domingo and the lovely cypress grove behind it (page 256).

◖ Laguna Encantada: This legendary spring-fed lagoon is deep, cold, and crystal-clear emerald green. It's set at the foot of a towering mountain with picture-perfect gnarled *ahuehuete* cypresses inhabiting its banks (page 260).

◖ Tlaxiaco Saturday *Tianguis*: This native market, with its winding, awning-draped stalls of scarlet tomatoes, deep green cucumbers, bright yellow *calabazas* (gourds), lilies, roses, and marigolds, may be Oaxaca's most colorful (page 265).

LOOK FOR ◖ TO FIND RECOMMENDED SIGHTS, ACTIVITIES, DINING, AND LODGING.

back door to the Mixteca Alta—the cool, verdant roof of Oaxaca.

PLANNING YOUR TIME

The Mixteca is a large and fascinating region, rich in history and natural wonders, quickly accessible by tour, bus, or car from Oaxaca City. Your interests, of course, will show you how to use your time. If you have only a day, you can get a quick glimpse of the Mixteca on a day trip, visiting the grand restored 16th-century Dominican churches at Yanhuitlán and Teposcolula and returning to Oaxaca City in the afternoon. If you add a day for a Friday overnight in Tlaxiaco, you could soak in the sights and sounds of the big, colorful **Tlaxiaco Saturday *tianguis*** (native town market) before returning back to Oaxaca City.

Add two days to the above and you'll have time en route to Yanhuitlán for a rewarding two-day side-trip from Nochixtlán for a hotel or camping overnight in the lovely, rustic **Valley of Apoala.** Here you can soak in Apoala's tranquil, bucolic ambience while exploring the limestone Cave of the Serpent, the towering canyon of the Two Colossal Rocks, and the Tail of the Serpent waterfall.

With a week to spend, you could enjoy a grand circle tour of the Mixteca. It would be best to synchronize your trip with the vibrant markets (Fri. in Juxtlahuaca, Sat. in Tlaxiaco) along the way. You can do this by heading north from Oaxaca City on Monday, overnighting in Apoala, then continuing northeast for an overnight or two in Huajuapan, capital of the Land of the Sun, in the Mixteca Baja. Here you'll find a charmingly refined city around a lovely central plaza, dotted with comfortable hotels and good restaurants. The town's sights could begin with the market and continue to the monumental pyramids of the **Cerro de las Minas Archaeological Zone** north of town. A rewarding day trip out of Huajuapan would include the lovely green Valley of the Río Mixteco and a visit to the pilgrimage town of San Pablo and San Pedro Tequixtepec and its community museum that highlights the fascinating, but as yet untranslated, Ñuiñe glyphs.

On Thursday, continue your tour by heading south to **Santo Domingo Tonalá** for a visit to the town's great grove of ancient *sabino* trees and a walk into the nearby Boqueron (Big Mouth) of the spectacular canyon of the Río Mixteco. Continue south for an overnight at Juxtlahuaca; on Friday, stroll the fascinatingly rich native market and marvel at the emerald-green **Laguna Encantada** spring-fed lake. Spend the night in Tlaxiaco, and on Saturday take in the grand market, the cathedral, and the unmissable Botica la Parroquia antique pharmacy.

On Sunday, return back to Oaxaca City, with stops in Teposcolula and Yanhuitlán.

© BRUCE WHIPPERMAN

the Saturday *tianguis* (market) at Tlaxiaco

THE MIXTECA

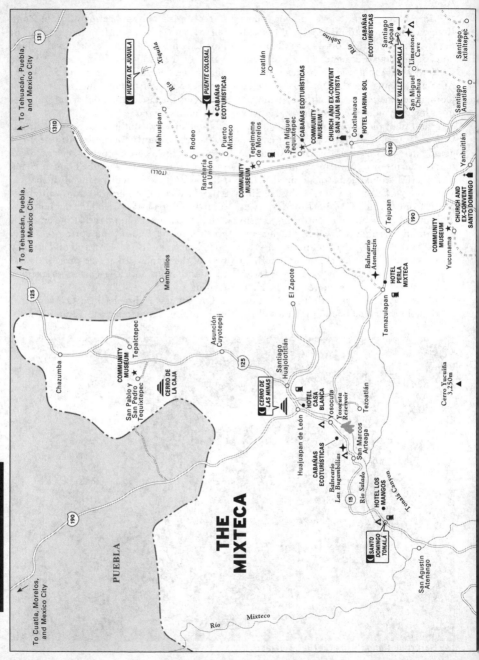

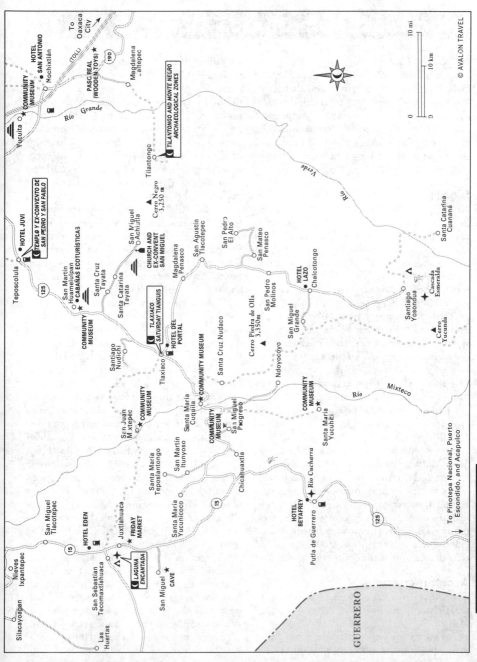

© AVALON TRAVEL

THE MIXTECA

Northwest from Oaxaca City

NOCHIXTLÁN

Nochixtlán (noh-chees-TLAN, pop. 11,000), busy capital of the governmental district of Nochixtlán, is interesting for its colorful market and festivals and especially as a jumping-off point for exploring the wonders of the idyllic mountain valley of Apoala and the remains of the ancient Mixtec kingdoms of Tilantongo and Yucuita.

Sights

Nochixtlán town itself spreads out from its plaza, which is directly accessible from Highway 190, from the Oaxaca side by north–south street Calle Progreso and, from the adjacent, Tamazulapan side, by east–west Calle Porfirio Díaz. The streets intersect at the northwest corner of the central plaza. From there, you can admire the distinguished 19th-century twin-towered **Templo de La Asunción** rising on the plaza's opposite side. Adjacent, to the right of the church, the *presidencia municipal* spreads for a block along Calle Hidalgo. At the plaza's northeast side is the big market, which expands into a much larger *tianguis* on Sunday, when campesinos from all over northwest Oaxaca crowd in to peruse, haggle, and choose from a small mountain of merchandise.

The major patronal **fiesta,** celebrating Santa María de La Asunción, customarily runs August 1–21, climaxing around August 15. Merrymaking includes *calendas* (religious processions), *marmotas* (giant dancing effigies), *mascaritas* (dancing men dressed as women), nearly continuous fireworks, a blaringly loud public dance, and a carnival of food, games, and rides that brightens the entire central plaza.

Accommodations

The town's three recommendable hotels are all on Highway 190, which curves past the edge of town.

For room for parking and a green inner patio, check out the loosely run but family-friendly **Hotel Santillan** (Porfirio Díaz 88, tel./fax 951/522-0351, norbertpcl@hotmail. com, $20 s or d, $27 d in two beds, $29 t), on the highway's west (Tamazulapan) side, convenient for drivers and RVers. The motel-style rooms are arranged in an L-shaped, two-story tier around a spacious inner parking lot, with kiddie pool and patio garden. Additional amenities include a volleyball/basketball court and a pair of shady picnic *palapas.* Upper rooms, probably the best choice, are plainly furnished, but light. All come with hot-water shower-baths, parking, and a family-run restaurant, as well as proximity (half a block west) to the Omnibus Cristóbal Colón–Sur bus station. (Details, however, are not the family's strong point. Inspect your room to see if all is in order and repaired before moving in.)

Right across from the main bus station, check out the brand-new **Hotel San Antonio** (Porfirio Díaz 112, no phone, $20–40 s or d). The 25 semi-deluxe rooms, invitingly furnished in beige-tone bedspreads and drapes, with shiny hot-water bathrooms and spacious modern-standard wash basins and commodes, are stacked in three stories above the bottom-floor parking garage. More expensive rooms come with king-size beds and whirlpool tubs.

On the diagonally opposite, Oaxaca, side of town, find the newish **Hotel Juquila** (Hwy. 190, Km 1, tel. 951/522-0581, $26 s or d in one bed, $32 d or t in two beds) on the highway, about 0.8 kilometers (0.5 mi) from the center of town, a few doors from the ADO bus stop. The hotel's name comes from the owner's devotion to the Virgin of Juquila, for whom he keeps a candle burning in front of a picture of the Virgin on the hotel front desk. Upstairs, the rooms are sparely decorated but very clean. Many are dark, however. Ask for one with *mas luz* (more light). Rooms all come with TV, hot-water showers, and a restaurant downstairs. If you're sensitive to noise, come prepared with ear plugs; the passing trucks and buses may be a problem here.

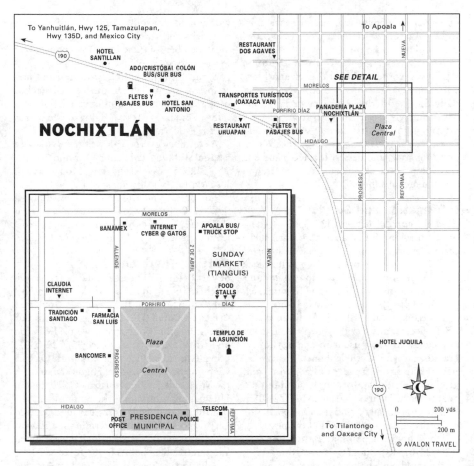

To Yanhuitlán, Hwy 125, Tamazulapan, Hwy 135D, and Mexico City

To Apoala

190

HOTEL SANTILLAN

ADO/CRISTÓBAL COLÓN BUS/SUR BUS

RESTAURANT DOS AGAVES

NUEVA

SEE DETAIL

MORELOS

FLETES Y PASAJES BUS

HOTEL SAN ANTONIO

TRANSPORTES TURÍSTICOS (OAXACA VAN)

PORFIRIO DÍAZ

PANADERÍA PLAZA NOCHIXTLÁN

NOCHIXTLÁN

RESTAURANT URUAPAN

FLETES Y PASAJES BUS

HIDALGO

Plaza Central

PROGRESO

REFORMA

MORELOS

BANAMEX

INTERNET CYBER @ GATOS

APOALA BUS/ TRUCK STOP

ALLENDE

2 DE ABRIL

SUNDAY MARKET (TIANGUIS)

NUEVA

CLAUDIA INTERNET

FOOD STALLS

PORFIRIO

DÍAZ

TRADICIÓN SANTIAGO

FARMACIA SAN LUIS

TEMPLO DE LA ASUNCIÓN

Plaza

BANCOMER

PROGRESO

Central

HOTEL JUQUILA

190

HIDALGO

TELECOM

POST OFFICE

PRESIDENCIA MUNICIPAL

POLICE

REFORMA

To Tilantongo and Oaxaca City

0   200 yds
0   200 m

© AVALON TRAVEL

Food

Nochixtlán offers a sprinkling of budget meal and bakery options. For wholesome (if they're hot) country-style meals, go to the *fondas* (food stalls) in the market, on the north side of the plaza.

In the evenings the action spreads to the market streetfront, across from the church, where a line-up of stalls does big business serving a small mountain of tacos, *tortas*, quesadillas, and especially the Oaxaca specialty, *tlayudas:* giant pizza-sized crisp tortillas loaded with everything from beans and cheese to spicy *chorizo* sausage, cabbage, boiled eggs, and more ($3–6).

Freshly baked offerings are plentiful at **Panadería Plaza** (Porfirio Díaz, no phone, 7 A.M.–9:30 P.M. daily), a block and a half west of the plaza.

Nochixtlán's restaurant of choice is **Dos Agaves** (local cell tel. 044-951/160-4399, 8 A.M.–8 P.M.daily, *comida corrida* $2.50). Although breakfast is fine here, they specialize in hearty four-course *comidas corrida* (set lunch; for example, fresh strawberry punch, rice, cream of carrot soup, and scrumptious meat balls in sauce). Find them on the west side of downtown. From the highway, walk east along Porfirio Díaz a block, turn left and go

THE MIXTECA

one block to Morelos and continue a fraction, to Dos Agaves (which looks like a rustic cowboy bunkhouse) on the left.

Alternatively, try **Restaurant Uruapan** (southwest corner of Porfirio Díaz and Hwy. 190, tel. 951/522-0495, 8 A.M.–9:30 P.M. daily, $3–5). Offerings include especially good Mexican-style breakfasts with fruit; a hearty afternoon four-course *comida* with tasty entrées, such as *guisado de res* (savory beef stew), and soup, rice, and dessert included; and à la carte omelets, tacos, quesadillas, tamales, and much more for supper.

Information and Services

Find the *correo* (tel. 951/522-0309, 8 A.M.–4:30 P.M. Mon.–Fri., 8 A.M.–noon Sat.) at the plaza's southwest corner, west end of the *presidencia municipal.* Skip uphill east, half a block past the *presidencia municipal,* to *telecomunicaciones* (corner of Hidalgo and Reforma, tel. 951/522-0053, 9 A.M.–3 P.M. Mon.–Fri.).

For economical local or long-distance telephone access, buy a widely available Ladatel telephone card and use it in one of the several downtown street telephones. Otherwise, use the long-distance public phone and also connect to the **Internet**, at **Claudia's restaurant** (Porfirio Díaz, tel. 951/522-0190, 9 A.M.–11 P.M. daily). Find it on the north side of Porfirio Díaz, a block west of the plaza.

Stock up with pesos at **Bancomer** (tel. 951/522-0154, 8:30 A.M.–4 P.M. Mon.–Fri.), in the middle of the plaza's west side, with a 24-hour ATM.

A number of attractive all-Oaxaca handicrafts are for sale at the small **Tradición Santiago** (Porfirio Díaz 49, tel. 951/522-0294, 9 A.M.–9 P.M. daily). Offerings include fetching embroidered *huipiles* from remote source villages (such as Yalalag and Tehuacán), genuine homegrown Oaxaca mescal, and the famous green pottery from Atzompa.

Furthermore, beside the toll expressway between Nochixtlán at Km 209, about 16 kilometers (10 mi) past the Huitzo toll gate, watch for the bright toys beside the road. A close look reveals a charming treasury of handmade wooden toys, from windmills and angels to trucks and tractors. They're made by the local members of **Paso Real Toy cooperative** (8 A.M.–8 P.M., toys $2–10).

Simple over-the-counter remedies and prescriptions are available at the big well-stocked drug store, **Farmacia San Luis** (tel. 951/522-0484, 7 A.M.–11:30 P.M. daily) at the plaza's northwest corner.

As for doctors, you can visit the **Centro de Especialidades** (Melchor Ocampo 10, tel. 951/522-0594, 9 A.M.–7 P.M. Mon.–Sat.) of José Manuel Sosa Bolanos, M.D.

For police and fire emergencies, dial tel. 951/522-0430, or go to the *policía municipal,* at their plaza-front station, at the east end (across from the church) of the *presidencia municipal.*

Getting There and Away

Several long-distance bus lines serve Nochixtlán. Luxury and first-class **Autobuses del Oriente** (ADO), first-class **Omnibus Cristóbal Colón** (OCC), and second-class **Sur** (operating jointly out of their west-side station on Porfirio Díaz, Hwy. 190, tel. 951/522-0387) provide broad service southeast with Oaxaca City; northwest both along Highway 190, with the Mixteca Baja (Tamazulapan, Coixtlahuaca, Huajuapan), and along the autopista 135D, continuing to Puebla, Veracruz, and Mexico City Tapo and Tasqueña terminals; and west with Teposcolula, Tlaxiaco, Juxtlahuaca, Putla, and intermediate points in the Mixteca Alta.

Additionally, second-class **Fletes y Pasajes** (Porfirio Díaz, corner of Hwy. 190, tel. 951/522-0585) offers connections northwest with Mexico City via Tehuacán and Puebla and southeast, with Oaxaca.

Enterprising **Transportes Turísticos de Nochixtlán** (Porfirio Díaz 72, tel. 951/522-0503, 6 A.M.–9 P.M. daily, $15), on the west-side highway, offers fast and frequent Suburban van rides to and from Oaxaca City. In Oaxaca City, contact them downtown (Galeana 222, tel. 951/514-0525). They also rent Suburban station wagons for $15 per hour; negotiate for a cheaper daily rate. This would be especially handy for a family or group visit to Apoala.

Drivers can cover the 80 kilometers (50 mi) from Oaxaca City in an easy hour via the *cuota autopista*. If you want to save the approximately $6 car toll (more for big RVs and trailers), figure about two hours via the winding old Highway 190 *libre* (free) route.

YUCUITA, TILANTONGO, AND MONTE NEGRO: FORGOTTEN KINGDOMS
Yucuita

Yucuita (pop. 500) was once far more important than it is today. It started as a village around 1400 B.C., then grew into a town of 3,000 inhabitants around 200 B.C., about the same time that early Monte Albán was flourishing. Later, by A.D. 200, it lost population and became a center secondary to Yucuñudahui, several miles north.

The claim to fame of drowsy, present-day Yucuita, about eight kilometers (five mi) northwest of Nochixtlán, is that it sits atop the old Yucuita, one of the Mixteca's largest and most important (but barely explored) archaeological zones. City officials received donations of so many artifacts that they had to organize a small community museum to hold them. Local volunteers offer, when possible, to open it up for any interested visitor. (Drop by the *presidencia municipal* before noon, preferably on a weekday, early enough to arrange a visit.)

Inside, your guide might point out (in Spanish) interesting aspects of the collection (mostly pottery): 2,000-year-old turkey eggs; human-effigy censers and bowls; 1,000-year-old *manos* and *metates* (stone rollers and grind stones), just like those used today; and a platoon of small, toy-like figurines. The most intriguing piece in the museum is a carved stone relief of a seated figure, appearing Olmec-influenced, holding what looks like a bunch of flowers. Maybe this is related to the meaning of Yucuita, which in Mixtec means Hill of Flowers.

Perhaps your guide will have time to show you around town. In any case, be sure to explore the **Yucuita archaeological zone** by climbing the reconstructed steps (fast

Regal, columned palace-houses speak of Monte Negro's distinguished past as a commercial and ceremonial center.

© BRUCE WHIPPERMAN

THE MIXTECA

becoming part of the ruins themselves) next to the paved through-town highway, about a 1.6 kilometers (one mi) south of the town plaza. If you're agile and adventurous, you can enter the site via a dry **tunnel** that runs about 30 meters (100 ft) from the entrance steps to a big opening and then continues another 30 meters to a final opening, where you can lift yourself out. (*Warning:* Carry a flashlight and a stick to spot and ward off pests, such as scorpions and rattlesnakes, in time to back out. If this scares you, don't try the tunnel.)

Aboveground, what you mostly see is an expansive corn and bean field littered with the stones from the walls and foundations of ancient Yucuita. Pottery shards are common—the colored ones especially stand out. A couple hundred feet to the south of the tunnel opening, inspect the partly reconstructed temple mound with an unfinished stairway and four belowground chambers. Archaeologists say that the entire site, elongated along a north–south axis, is riddled with buried structures, whose remains extend beyond the high hill (the original Hill of Flowers) to the north.

If possible, coordinate your Yucuita visit with the **Fiesta de San Juan Bautista** (June 22–24), when the ordinarily sleepy town is at its exciting best. Many folks return home to Yucuita from all over Mexico and the United States for reunions and to once again enjoy country delicacies, dance the favorite old dances, honor San Juan with grand floral processions, and thrill to rockets bursting and showering stars overhead. (If you can't come in June, then come for the equally popular fiesta to honor the beloved Virgin of Guadalupe around December 18.)

GETTING THERE
Reach Yucuita via minibus from Calle Porfirio Díaz, in front of the Nochixtlán market, or along Highway 190, northwest side of town. Drivers: Head northwest on Highway 190 from Nochixtlán. Continue straight ahead along the old Highway 190, Huajuapan direction (*not* the *cuota* expressway to Puebla and Mexico City). Pass the gas station and continue for about

three kilometers (two mi) until you see a signed right turnoff to Yucuita. Southbound drivers: On old Highway 190, watch for the signed left turnoff to Yucuita before Nochixtlán. If you reach the Pemex *gasolinera,* before the *cuota* expressway, you have gone too far. Turn around and look for the signed Yucuita right turnoff.

◖ Tilantongo and Monte Negro Archaeological Zones

The Tilantongo archaeological zone is the town itself (pop. 4,000), which sits smack on top of storied ancient Tilantongo. In the old days, around A.D. 1050, Tilantongo was the virtual capital of the Mixteca, ruled by the ruthless but renowned Mixtec king 8-Deer of the Tiger Claws. Carved stones built into the Tilantongo town church wall attest to Tilantongo's former glory.

The town government commissioned a mural, now on the outside wall of the *presidencia municipal,* which dramatically portrays the legendary Mixtec Flechador del Sol (Bowman of the Sun) and copies of pages from the Codex Nuttall, a pre-conquest document in blazing color that records glorious events in Mixtec pre-conquest history. See if you can identify 8-Deer (hint: look for the very pictorial 8-Deer hieroglyph) on one of the Codex Nuttall pages reproduced in the mural.

At least as important and more rewarding to explore is the much older Monte Negro archaeological zone atop the towering, oak-studded **Monte Negro** (Black Mountain), visible high above Tilantongo. A graveled road, passable by ordinary cars, easier for high-clearance trucks or jeep-like vehicles, allows access to the top in about an hour. If you have no wheels, you may be able to get a taxi driver to take you up there. If not, perhaps someone with a car might accept the job. Fit hikers should allow about three hours for the eight-kilometer (five mi) uphill climb, two hours for lunch and exploring the site, and two hours for the return. Take plenty of water, wear a hat and strong shoes, and use a strong sunscreen. You must obtain permission from authorities at the *presidencia municipal* (tel. 951/510-4970), who require that a local guide (whom they will furnish, fee about $10, plus lunch) accompany you.

Monte Negro flourished about the same time as early Monte Albán, 500–0 B.C. The 150-acre hilltop zone is replete with ruined columned temples, raised residences of the elite (complete with inner patios), ceremonial plazas, and a ball court, all aligned along a single avenue. Monte Negro's long, north–south orientation is reminiscent of Monte Albán, although its structures are not as grand. For reasons unknown, Monte Negro, like Monte Albán, was abandoned during the Late Urban Stage, around A.D. 800. All that remains are the old city's stone remnants, while its descendants still husband the land you see in all directions from the breezy hilltop. Some of what surrounds you is thick oak forest; other parts are fertile terraced corn and bean fields; while much, in mute testimony to the passage of time, is tragically eroded.

GETTING THERE
Bus passengers can go by the Tilantongo–Nochixtlán bus, which makes the trip about three times a day from Calle Porfirio Díaz, in front of the Nochixtlán market. Drivers: Follow Highway 190 (old *libre* route) to the Jaltepec paved turnoff about 13 kilometers (eight mi) southeast (Oaxaca City direction) from Nochixtlán. Mark your odometer at the turnoff. The road is paved to the Jaltepec plaza (8.2 km/5.1 mi), where you turn right. The road is dirt and gravel, often rough, after that. Follow the Tilantongo (or Teozocoalco) signs. Turn left at a church (17.7 km/10.8 mi) at Morelos villages, and right after a river bridge (23.8 km/14.8 mi). (*Note:* The riverfront at the bridge would make a lovely picnic or overnight camping spot, beneath the shade of the grand old *sabino,* especially during the dry, clear-water fall–spring–summer season.) You'll pull up to the Tilantongo plaza after 29 kilometers (18 mi) and about an hour of steady, bumpy driving.

◖ THE VALLEY OF APOALA
It's hard to describe the valley of Apoala, tucked in the mountains north of Nochixtlán,

with anything less than superlatives. A fertile, terraced, green vale nestles beneath towering cliffs far from the noise, smoke, and clutter of city life. Apoala is no less than a Oaxacan Shangri-La—a farming community replete with charming country sights and sounds, such as log-cabin houses, men plowing the field with oxen, women sitting and chatting as they weave palm-leaf sombreros, dogs barking, and burros braying faintly in the warm dusk. The spring-fed river assures good crops; people, consequently, are relatively well-off and content to remain on the land. They have few cars, almost no TVs, and few, if any, telephones.

What's more, the local folks are ready for visitors. I arrived at a string stretched curiously across the narrow gravel entrance road. I realized that there must be a good reason for this, so I stopped, instead of just barging in. The explanation is that the local folks want to tell you about the wonders of their sylvan valley. The entrance fee is about $5 per group, which includes a guide (an absolute must).

Exploring Apoala
The tour, which takes about two hours, begins at the **Cave of Serpent,** translated from the local Mixtec dialect, which all townsfolk speak. Just before the cave, you pass a crystalline spring welling up from the base of a towering cliff. This spring supplies a large part of the Río Apoala flow, which ripples and meanders down the valley and which folks use to keep their fields green. Another major (and more constant) part of its flow wells up from beneath a huge rock across the creek, below the cave entrance.

Entering the cave, be careful not to bump your head as you descend the tight, downhill entrance hollow. Immediately, you see why your guide is so important: He carries a large battery and light to illuminate the way. In the first of the cave's two galleries, bats flutter overhead as your guide reveals various stalactites and then flashes on the subterranean river gurgling from an underground dark lagoon, unknown in extent. What *is* known, however, is that the water from the lagoon arrives

THE MIXTECA

THE LEGEND OF THE FLECHA DEL SOL (ARROW OF THE SUN)

Once upon a time, the Mixtec warrior chief Yaconooy arrived with his soldiers in present-day Valley of Nochixtlán, looking for land for his people to settle and grow their crops. He found the place deserted, except for a brilliant sun in the sky overhead. Spoiling for a fight, but with no one to battle, Yaconooy shot an arrow at the sun, and wounded it. The Sun's blood colored the horizon, the clouds, and the sky. With this victory over the sun, Yaconooy founded his dynasty, which prospered from his capital, the regal but now-ruined city atop Monte Negro, the Black Mountain, near the modern town of Tilantongo.

© BRUCE WHIPPERMAN

The fresco at Tilantongo City Hall illustrates how the Mixtecs came to settle in the present territory of Oaxaca.

at the springs at Tamazulapan, more than 50 kilometers (30 mi) away. Someone long ago dropped some oranges into the cave lagoon in Apoala, and they bobbed to the surface later in Tamazulapan.

In the other cave gallery (careful, the access is steep and slippery), the light focuses on a towering stalagmite capped by a bishop's visage, complete with clerical miter and long beard. On the other side, you see a stalactite shaped exactly like a human leg.

After the cave, you'll head up-valley between a pair of cliffs that tower vertically at least 150 meters (500 ft). If you speak Spanish or have someone to interpret, be sure to ask the guide to explain the names and uses of the *plantas medicinales* (medicinal plants) along the path. Every plant, even the notorious *mala mujer* (bad woman), which your guide can point out, seems to have some use.

Soon, above and to your left, you'll see the towering 600-meter (2,000 ft) burnt-yellow rampart, **La Peña Donde Murió El Aguila con Dos Cabezas** (The Rock Where the Eagle with Two Heads Died). No kidding. It seems that, once upon a time, a huge eagle

that actually had two heads lived in one of the many caves in the rock face. The problem was, it was killing too many lambs, so one day one of the villagers shot it. The Eagle with Two Heads, however, lives on in the community memory of Apoalans.

Finally, after about 20 minutes of walking and wondering at the natural monuments towering around you, the climax arrives: a narrow, river-cut breach in the canyon, like some antediluvian giant had cut a thin slice through a mountain of butter. The slice remains, between a pair of vertical rock walls called **Las Dos Peñas Colosales** (The Two Colossal Rocks).

The grand finale, down-valley about 1.6 kilometers (one mi), is the waterfall **Cola del Serpiente** (The Serpent's Tail). You walk down a steep forested trail that looks out on a gorgeous mountain and valley panorama. At the bottom, the Río Apoala, having already tumbled hundreds of feet, pauses for spells in several pools, and finally plummets nearly 90 meters (300 ft) in a graceful arc to an emerald green pool surrounded by a misty, natural stone amphitheater.

Local Guides

If you'd like a guide for more local exploring, contact very knowledgeable and personable **Leopoldo Guzman Alvarado,** who, if he can't guide you himself, will find someone who can, such as youthful **Oswaldo López Jiménez.** To contact them in advance, leave a message via the Apoala satellite phone: Dial long distance 01-55/5151-9154.

Accommodations and Food

Camping ($15 per day per group, pay at the *cabaña ecoturística*), by self-contained RV or tent, would be superb here. The community has set aside a choice grassy riverside spot, across the river from the cave at the upper end of town—heavenly for a few days of camping. Clear, pristine spring water, perfect for drinking, wells up at the foot of the cliff at the road's end nearby. Wilderness campers can choose among more isolated spots upstream, ripe for wildlife-viewing. (Swimming, however, is only permitted downstream from the village, preferably at the foot of the waterfall. Always swim with a bathing suit on; skinny-dipping is locally disapproved.)

Non-campers shouldn't miss staying in Apoala's fine *cabaña ecoturística* ($15 pp), where you probably first met your guide. This is a model of Oaxaca's improved second-generation government-built, locally-managed tourist accommodation. Besides three very clean and comfortable modern-standard rooms with either one or two double beds, it features a light, spacious solarium–sitting room–snack café, serving water, beer, and sodas, as well as breakfast, lunch, and early supper.

Guests can also eat their own food there. If you do, bring your own food, since Apoala has only one basic store, the **Conasupo** (9 A.M.–4 P.M. Mon.–Tues. and Thurs.–Fri.), with groceries only, no fruit or veggies. In an emergency, go to the very modest *abarrotes Juana* (grocery), behind the *cabaña ecoturística*, which furnishes basic meals and a few food supplies.

Overnight reservations are strongly recommended. Reserve directly with Apoala through their satellite phone connection (in

Mexico long-distance tel. 01-55/5151-9154; in Mexico City, simply dial as a local call, tel. 5151-9154; from the U.S. tel. 011-52-55/5151-9154). Alternatively, you can get information and lodging reservations in Oaxaca City at the government **tourism office** (703 Av. Juáraz, tel. 951/516-0123, www.aoaxaca.com).

Getting There and Away

Like Shangri-La, Apoala isn't easy to get to. *Colectivo* passengers have it easiest. The Apoala community provides an Apoala-marked **colectivo** ($5), which leaves from Calle 2 de Abril near the corner of Morelos, Nochixtlán (a block north of the plaza's northeast corner). At this writing, it departs at noon Wednesday–Monday, arriving in Apoala around 3 P.M. It departs Apoala for Nochixtlán on the same days at around 6:30 A.M. Check locally for the Apoala *colectivo* schedule with stores or bus or truck drivers parked along Calle 2 de Abril. To check in advance, call the Apoala satellite phone number: Dial long distance 01-55/5151-9154. Otherwise, taxis ($18) and passenger trucks ($4–6) make the same trip hourly until about 5 P.M. from the same spot.

For **drivers,** the 42-kilometer (26 mi) rough dirt and gravel road is a challenge, especially in an ordinary passenger car. The route heads north from downtown Nochixtlán; turn left from Calle Porfirio Díaz (the street that borders the plaza's north side) at the street just past (east) the market. Follow the road signs all the way.

Trucks, vans, and VW Beetles carry nearly all the traffic to Apoala, although a careful, experienced driver in an ordinary car could usually complete the trip with minimal damage. The ideal vehicle (which I've driven three times) would be a high-clearance Jeep-like truck or sport-utility vehicle, with tough tires. Four-wheel-drive, not necessary under dry conditions, is mandatory in rain. Under dry conditions, lighter, maneuverable campers and RVs could make it; large rigs would be marginal at best, because of the narrow, steep, rocky, and winding descent into Apoala Canyon.

THE MIXTECA

Dominican Route South

Of the four missionary orders—Franciscans, Jesuits, Augustinians, and Dominicans—who established an important presence in New Spain, the Dominicans were dominant in Oaxaca. Hernán Cortés had barely begun to resurrect Mexico City from the rubble of old Tenochtitlán when a stream of Dominican padres was heading southeast to Oaxaca. For the next three centuries, until republican reforms forced many of them from Mexico during the late 1800s, the padres earnestly pursued the spiritual thrust of Spain's two-pronged "God and Gold" mission in the New World. The Dominicans converted, educated, protected, and advocated for Oaxaca's native peoples, often in conflict with brutal and greedy Spanish soldiers and colonists.

The Dominicans' legacy remains vibrant to this day. More than 90 percent of Oaxacans consider themselves Catholics, and lovely old Dominican ex-convent/churches decorate the Oaxacan countryside. Some of these outstanding venerable monuments—notably at **Yanhuitlán, Teposcolula, Tlaxiaco,** and **Coixtlahuaca**—grace the Mixteca Alta, not far from the modern town of Tamazulapan, making it a natural base for extended exploration of what has become known as Oaxaca's Dominican route. The Dominican route's more isolated (but very intriguing) northern section—north and west of Tamazulapan—is usually explored via the *autopista* that connects with Coixtlahuaca, from Nochixtlán and Oaxaca City.

TAMAZULAPAN AND VICINITY

Tamazulapan (tah-mah-soo-LAH-pahn, pop. 5,000), partly by virtue of its crossroads position on the National Highway 190, has eclipsed its more venerable, but isolated, neighbor towns and become the major service and business center for the Teposcolula district. You know you're in Tamazulapan immediately as you pass its town plaza, which proudly displays a semicircular columned monument

© BRUCE WHIPPERMAN

Moto-taxis wait for customers in Tamazulapan.

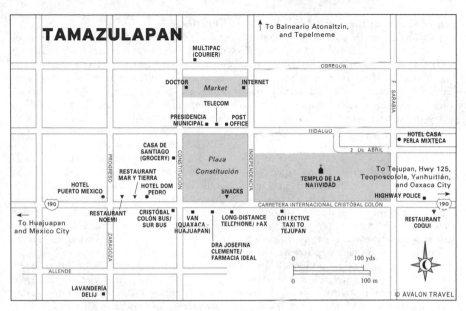

TAMAZULAPAN

right by the highway in honor of Benito Juárez, "Benemérito de las Américas." Upon reflection, nothing seems more appropriate directly on the Pan-American Highway.

Sights

As you stand on the edge of the highway (locally known as Carretera Cristóbal Colón) looking at the Benito Juárez monument, you'll be facing approximately north. The noble, portaled *presidencia municipal* will appear straight ahead behind the square, the **Plaza Constitución.** To your right, beyond the storefronts along plaza-front Calle Independencia, rise the ruddy cupolas of the 18th-century Dominican **Templo de la Natividad.** Bordering the plaza on your left are the stores and services along Calle Constitución.

Walk a block east and step into the cool calm of the venerable Dominican church which, although large and harmoniously decorated, is not architecturally comparable to the masterpieces at Coixtlahuaca, Yanhuitlán, and Teposcolula. What is unique, however, are the two images on the altar, both illuminated. The bottom figure (in the coffin) is an unusually

small image of Jesus on the cross. This figure (known as the Señor Tres de Mayo), is locally paraded and celebrated, along with food, games, dancing, and a basketball tournament, in a festival culminating on May 3, El Día de la Cruz.

Above the figure of Jesus is the larger, but still petite town patron, La Virgen de la Natividad (The Virgin of the Nativity), dressed in blue and white, whom townsfolk celebrate in a fiesta culminating on September 8. As you retrace your steps, exiting through the church garden, you pass the old Dominican convent on the left, now mostly converted to storefronts facing the highway.

Tamazulapan townsfolk love their resort, **Balneario Atonaltzin** (9 A.M.–6 P.M. daily, adults $3, kids $2). You'll see why if you drive, taxi, or walk the 2.5 kilometers (1.5 mi) north along the road to Tepelmeme (east plaza-front Calle Independencia). Soon after a bridge, you'll see the *balneario* (resort) on the right. This spot would be a merely typical Sunday family bathing resort if it were not for its crystalline, naturally disinfected sulfurous springs. The waters gurgle up, cool and clear, from a

THE MIXTECA

pair of sources in the rocky cliff behind the Olympian double-size pool—a lap swimmer's delight (except on Sundays and holidays, when it's filled with frolicking families). Besides the big main pool, there are two kiddie pools, a local-style restaurant, volleyball, dressing areas, a few picnic tables, and campsites. The *balneario* invites overnight tent-camping and self-contained RV parking, for about $10 per car, including the general admission fee.

Two lesser-known but nevertheless interesting spots are the nearby *ojo de agua* swimming hole and the Xatachio archaeological zone. The *ojo de agua* (literally, eye of water), a general term for a natural spring or source of water, is about 90 meters (300 ft) back from the *balneario* (resort) toward town, on the right, below the creek bridge. Step toward the ruined building on the right and you'll see the creek cascading into a big blue pool. Before the Balneario Atonaltzin was built, this was a popular swimming hole. Today, the water appears much less than pure, since it's mostly used by families for washing clothes. Although the steep riverbank near the bridge is nonnegotiable, you can get down to the water via a path to the right around the ruined building, through the brush, up some stone steps, and down again to the creek.

The unexcavated **Xatachio archaeological zone** (shah-TAH-shioh) is accessible via the dirt side road on the left, just past the Balneario Atonaltzin. You'll first spot the zone as a brush-covered hill (actually a former ceremonial pyramid) about 0.8 kilometers (0.5 mi) away on the left. *Note:* Do not try to explore the site on your own. The site lies on communal land, and people are rightly suspicious of possible artifact looters. Go to the *presidencia municipal* on the plaza and ask for permission (preferably through a local spokesperson, such as the owner or manager of your hotel); offer to pay someone (approximately $15) to act as a guide for a couple of hours. Any artifacts you might stumble upon are legally the joint property of the INAH (National Institute of Archaeology and History) and the local community.

Tejupan

If you have time, stop for a few minutes for a look inside the relatively humble, but nevertheless worthy, Dominican church and ex-convent at Tejupan (Tay-HOO-pahn) in the Tamazulapan valley, a 15-minute drive east (Oaxaca City direction) from Tamazulapan. Tejupan is a sleepy farming town, basking in its past glory, visibly represented by its noble, multi-portaled *palacio municipal* and the distinguished 17th-century Dominican **Templo y Ex-Convento de Santiago Apóstol,** across the street. Memorable inside the church is the pretty pink transept chapel, left side, dedicated to the Virgin of Guadalupe. The restored ex-convent section stands to the right of the church front entrance.

Get to Tejupan by bus, taxi, or car via the signed side road off Highway 190 about 11 kilometers (seven mi) southeast of Tamazulapan, or about 13 kilometers (eight mi) northwest of the Highway 190–Highway 125 junction northwest of Yanhuitlán.

Accommodations

Of Tamazulapan's acceptable hotels, most prominent is the four-story **Hotel Dom Pedro** (Cristóbal Colón 24, tel./fax 953/533-0736, $14 s or d in one bed, $16 d in two beds, $18 t), a few doors north of the plaza. The 25 plain but clean upstairs rooms (no elevator) come with toilets and hot-water showers, TV, and parking, but no phone except the long-distance phone at the hotel desk. Credit cards are not accepted.

Although **Hotel Puerto Mexico** (Cristóbal Colón 12, tel. 953/533-0044, $19 s or d, $22 t), a few doors farther west, appears humdrum from the outside, guests enjoy an inviting tropical patio blooming with leafy banana trees. Rooms are clean and carpeted but have the almost universal Mexican small-town bare bulb hanging from the middle of the ceiling. Bring your own clip-on lampshade. Amenities include hot-water showers, parking, TV, and a pretty fair restaurant downstairs, but no phones. Credit cards are accepted.

The star of Tamazulapan hotels is the deluxe, newish ▐ **Hotel Casa Perla Mixteca** (Calle 2 de Abril 3, tel./fax 953/533-0280, toll-free Mex. tel. 800/717-3956, $25 s, $28 d, and $33 t). A major plus here is the hotel's quiet location, removed from the noisy highway truck traffic. Take your pick of 10 designer-decorated rooms, with rustically lovely tile floors, hand-woven bedspreads, reading lamps, and shiny bathrooms with hot-water showers.

Food

For inexpensive prepared food, try the *fondas* (food stalls) inside the market and the night-time taco stands or one of the several sit-down snack bars along the highway by the plaza.

As for restaurants, although the Hotel Puerto Mexico offers breakfast, lunch, and dinner, you might do better by walking a few steps west to **(Restaurant Noemi** (Cristóbal Colón 16, tel. 953/533-0595, 8 A.M.–11 P.M. daily, $2–7) between Hotel Puerto Mexico and Hotel Dom Pedro. The grandmotherly owner puts out Mexican home-style breakfasts, lunches, and suppers, including savory *café de la olla* (pot-brewed coffee, with cinnamon).

Another good choice is **Restaurant Mar y Tierra** (Cristóbal Colón 20, tel. 953/533-0045, 8 A.M.–10 P.M. daily, $4–12), between Hotel Dom Pedro and Restaurant Noemi. In a relaxingly airy patio location, patrons select from a long menu of breakfasts, soups, salads, pastas, seafood, and meat and suppers of Mexican specialties. They also serve a selection of good beers and wines from their bar.

Alternatively, check out the clean, highway-front **Restaurant Coqui** (KOH-kee; Cristóbal Colón 57, tel. 953/533-0109, 7 A.M.–9 P.M. daily), a block and a half east from the plaza. Although she'll cook nearly anything you want, the hard-working owner is best at Oaxacan country delicacies, such as chiles rellenos, enchiladas *tasajos* (beef enchiladas), and Oaxacan tamales, covered with plenty of *mole negro*. (At this writing, however, her asking breakfast prices for scrambled eggs, fruit salad, ordinary coffee, and orange juice have doubled.)

Shopping

Get groceries, fruit, and vegetables at either the town market behind the *presidencia*, or at one of the plaza-front *abarroterías* (grocery stores), such as west plaza-front **Casa de Santiago** (Constitucion 6, tel. 953/533-0015, 8:30 A.M.–3:30 P.M. and 4:30–9:30 P.M. daily).

The market, especially during the big Wednesday *tianguis,* can be a good spot for local indigenous handicrafts shopping. Items might include pottery and palm-leaf woven goods such as *tenates* (tump-line baskets), *petates* (mats), and soft woven Panama hat–like sombreros.

Services

Tamazulapan provides a number of basic services along the blocks near the plaza. At this writing, there is neither bank nor ATM, so make sure to arrive with a supply of pesos (from banks in Nochixtlán, Tlaxiaco, or Huajuapan) or U.S. dollars that you may be able to exchange in local stores or at your hotel.

For public telephone, money orders, and fax, find the *telecomunicaciones* (a block north along Independencia, at corner of Obregón, tel. 953/533-0113, 9 A.M.–3:30 P.M. Mon.–Fri., 9 A.M.–1 P.M. Sat.) behind the *presidencia*. For stamps and sending mail, walk a few doors farther west along Obregón to the *correo* (Obregón, 8 A.M.–4:30 P.M. Mon.–Fri., 9 A.M.–1 P.M. Sat.). Half a block farther along Obregón, you can send a fast, secure mailing via courier service **Multipac** (Obregón 2, 9 A.M.–3 P.M. Mon.–Fri., 9 A.M.–noon Sat.).

For telephone service, go to the *larga distancia* across the highway from the plaza, or one of the three or four Ladatel card-operated public phones sprinkled along the highway and near the plaza. Answer your email at the **Internet store** (across from the plaza, tel. 953/533-0694, 9 A.M.–11 P.M. daily).

At least two **doctors** near the plaza offer consultations and medicines. Choose either **Dra. Josefina Clemente** at her Farmacia Ideal (on the highway directly opposite the plaza, tel. 953/533-0224; pharmacy: 8 A.M.–9 P.M. Mon.–Sat.; consultations: 4–8 P.M. Mon.–Fri.); or **Dr. Fidel A. Cruz Ramírez** (a block and a half north from the highway, on the west Constitución side of the market; no

THE MIXTECA

phone; consultations: 9 A.M.–3 P.M., 5–9 P.M. Mon.–Fri.).

For a police emergency, contact either the **Delegación de Transito highway police** (half a block east of the plaza, on the same side as the highway, tel. 953/533-0472, on duty 24 hours); or the **municipal police** (at the *presidencia municipal,* tel. 953/533-0017).

Get your laundry done at handy **Lavandería Delij** (on Zaragoza, 9 A.M.–8 P.M. Mon.–Sat.), a block and a half south (uphill) from the Hotel Puerto Mexico on the highway.

Getting There and Away

Bus lines **Omnibus Cristóbal Colón** and **Sur** (both across from the plaza, tel. 953/533-0699) operate jointly out of their highway-front station. Their buses connect southeast with Oaxaca City via Nochixtlán; northwest via Huajuapan and Cuautla (Morelos), with Mexico City (Tapo); and south with Teposcolula, Tlaxiaco, and Juxtlahuaca, where you can transfer to a bus headed for Pinotepa Nacional on the Pacific coast.

Good paved roads connect Tamazulapan with all the important Mixteca and Oaxaca destinations: southeast, via Highway 190, 133 kilometers (84 mi), two hours, with Oaxaca City; northwest, 41 kilometers (25 mi), 45 minutes, with Huajuapan; north, by paved (but potholed) secondary road via Tejupan, 35 kilometers (22 mi), 45 minutes, with Coixtlahuaca; and south via Highway 190–Highway 125, 35 kilometers (22 mi), 45 minutes, with Teposcolula.

Frequent (10 per day) **Transportes Atolzín vans** (cell tel. 044/117-8800) connect southeast with Oaxaca City, and northwest with Huajuapan. Check for departures at their small office across the highway from the plaza's southwest corner.

Servicios Turísticos Teposcolula vans connect south with Mixteca destinations of Teposcolula and Tlaxiaco, and west with Huajuapan. They stop for passengers on the highway, by the plaza.

TEPOSCOLULA

Although smaller in population than Tamazulapan, Teposcolula (pop. 2,000)

Teposcolula's central plaza is quiet most of the time.

© BRUCE WHIPPERMAN

continues to outrank it as district capital, a distinction it gained way back in 1740. Its history, however, reaches back much further. When the Spanish arrived in the 1520s, they found well established Mixtec towns on the hillsides above a beautiful lake-filled valley. They drained the lake for farmland and moved the population down to Teposcolula's present location. Abiding by common practice, the Spanish kept the Mixtec name, Teposcolula (Place Surrounded by Springs), tacking on the Catholic patronal title San Pedro y San Pablo. This produced a name so long that practically no one refers to the official San Pedro y San Pablo Teposcolula. People, however, still remember the old pre-conquest settlements on the hillsides. The old palace and temple foundations still stand, as El Fortín (The Fort) on the uphill slope behind the town and Pueblo Viejo (Old Town) on the pine-clad hilltop across the valley.

Orient yourself by standing (or imagining you're standing) on the sidewalk on the through-town highway, facing the tree-shaded town plaza. North will be straight ahead, toward the cartoon-bright, repainted *presidencia municipal* on the far side of the plaza. The main streets are 20 de Noviembre (the highway), Madero (along the plaza's left, west side), and Iturbide (along the plaza's right, east side). Diagonally on your left stands the renowned Templo y Ex-Convento de San Pedro y San Pablo.

◖ Templo y Ex-Convento de San Pedro y San Pablo

Most visitors head right over to the venerable 1538 Dominican church and ex-convent, one of Oaxaca's most important, not only for its historical significance, but also for its monumental architecture, much of which you can view from the exterior by walking around to the church's back (west) side. Here rises the famous, recently-restored **Capilla Abierta** (Open Chapel), with massive, soaring arches and gigantic buttresses. Visitors often wonder why such a huge outdoor chapel was needed right next to an equally massive indoor church. The adjacent grassy expanse provides the reason. It's the **atrium,** the extension of the

© BRUCE WHIPPERMAN

the Capilla Abierta (Open Chapel)

THE MIXTECA

outdoor chapel, the largest in Mexico, where the Dominican builders imagined 10,000 native faithful (so numerous that they were not allowed inside) gathering for mass. Although their vision was fulfilled for a span of perhaps a generation after the conquest, European diseases decimated the Mixtec population by 1600, leaving the huge expanse, equal to three football fields, forever empty.

Step into the main church nave, accessible from outside either the nave's rear door (next to the Capilla Abierta), or from side door on the town plaza. Inside, admire the symphony of glittering *retablos* (altarpieces) that decorate the walls. The tallest and most magnificent towers above the front altar, where the town patron **El Señor de Vidrieras** (Lord of the Glass Box) presides. On the right and left of the patron are the grand apostles, respectively: bald St. Peter and pious St. Paul. And, finally, above all the glitter, high over the altar, presides the omnipresent, all-seeing eye of God.

Local people celebrate their Señor de Vidrieras (named for the glass box they parade him in) during a big eight-day festival culminating on the first Friday of Lent (Cuaresma). Events include traffic-stopping processions, pilgrimages, a flower parade, plenty of fireworks, crowning of a queen, floats, bull roping and riding, and a big community dance.

Find the door to the **ex-convent** (9 A.M.–5 P.M. daily, entrance $2.50) at the rear of the nave. The ex-convent serves largely as a museum of paintings by noted 16th-century artists Andrés de la Concha and Simón Pereyns. As you walk, see if you can recognize the functions—refectory (dining), kitchen, chapel, cloister, monks' cells (upstairs)—of the various rooms that you pass by or through.

During your visit, at the end of the refectory (monks' dining hall) be sure to see the fresh, very recognizable modern or restored painting of Jesus with wounds, at the right hand of a very youthful God the Father, with the Holy Spirit (in the form of a radiant dove) above them. In the middle of the refectory, also notice the interesting painting of St. Michael the Archangel dangling a fish. Also, around the cloister, note the paintings that depict the baptism, school days, mission, and dreams of Santo Domingo.

Archaeological Sites and Casa de la Cacica

If you're interested in historic ruins, you might inquire at the *presidencia municipal* for a guide to lead you to the **El Fortín** and **Pueblo Viejo** archaeological sites. (*Note:* Don't try to go to these sites without permission, since local folks are rightly suspicious of strangers poking around their archaeological zones.)

An interesting, close-by site that you can visit without permission is the Casa de la Cacica (kah-SEE-kah, House of the Chiefess). Walk west about three blocks along the street heading due west from the middle of the church's huge grassy atrium. The street ends at a school, and on the right is the Casa de la Cacica.

The Casa, a complex of buildings, is unique because it's one of the few known stone structures built by the Spanish specifically for indigenous nobles. The Spaniards' motivation was probably to concentrate and thus more easily control the local Mixtec population, who were living in dispersed hillside settlements when the Spanish arrived. They built a noble housing complex and evidently persuaded the local *cacica* (chiefess) to live there, hoping that her people would follow her. Presumably, the House of the Chiefess (under restoration) will eventually become a museum or community cultural center, or both.

Finally, before you leave town, be sure to visit the **carcel** (jail) at the *presidencia municipal* on the plaza. There, the prisoners make and sell handicrafts, such as leather belts, leather-covered mescal flasks, and miniature-shoe key rings.

Accommodations and Food

Teposcolula's first and only hotel (at least in recent times), the **Hotel Juvi** (tel. 953/518-2064, $13 s, $15 d in one bed, $16 d in two beds, $18 t, $20 q) now makes an overnight stay possible. The hotel's layout remains unique—12 rooms around a parking courtyard containing the last remnant, a grain storage crib, of the ancient family homestead. Children of the original ancestors have built a sparsely furnished (but clean) lodging, with bare fluorescent bulbs to go with the shiny bathroom fixtures.

You can buy basic food supplies at a plaza-front *abarrotes* (grocery); a *panadería* (bakery; on Iturbide, tel. 953/537-8683, 8 A.M.–8 P.M. daily), a block behind the *presidencia municipal*; or treat yourself to a hearty afternoon *comida* at the town's good (but pricey) **Restaurant Eunice** (tel. 953/518-2017, 8 A.M.– 8 P.M. Sun.– Fri., $4–12), a block behind the east side of the *presidencia municipal*.

Alternatively, go to the modest but clean restaurant **Temita** (tel. 953/518-2040, 7 A.M.–10 P.M. daily, $3–6), a block east (Oaxaca direction) of the plaza, across from the Cristóbal Colón–Sur bus station.

Information and Services

If you're sick, consult Dr. Brigido Vidal in his **Farmacia Nelly** (on the plaza-front east side, a few doors from the highway, tel. 953/518-2072; consultations: 3–10 P.M.; pharmacy: 9 A.M.–2 P.M. and 5–9 P.M. Mon.–Sat.). Alternatively, go to the **Centro de Salud** (doctor available 8 A.M.–2 P.M. and 4–6 P.M. daily, 24 hours in emergency). Get there via Calle Madero, uphill, passing the *presidencia municipal*'s west side. After two blocks, turn left, and continue three long blocks to the *centro de salud*, on the right.

For police or fire emergencies, contact the police at the *presidencia municipal*, north side of the plaza.

To mail a letter, make a phone call, or use a fax, go either to the *telcomunicaciones* (on Madero, upstairs, half a block north of the plaza's northwest corner, tel. 953/518-2070, 9 A.M.–3 P.M. Mon.–Fri.) or the *correo* (on Madero, downstairs, 11 A.M.–4 P.M. Thurs. only). Otherwise for telephone, fax, or Internet go the **"Mr. Marbo" office** (across the highway from the plaza, tel. 953/518-2103, 7 A.M.–10:30 P.M. daily).

Getting There and Away

Bus transportation to and from Teposcolula is easy and frequent. Bus passengers arrive at and depart from the bus station (Autobuses Sur, Omnibus Cristóbal Colón, and Fletes y Pasajes; on Hwy. 125, tel. 953/518-2000), half a block east from the plaza. Buses connect southeast with Oaxaca City; north with Tamazulapan, Huajuapan, and Mexico City; and south with Tlaxiaco, Juxtlahuaca, and Putla (where connections are available with Pinotepa Nacional on the Pacific coast).

Long-distance vans **Servicios Turísticos Teposcolula** (local cell tel. 044-953/110-9288) connect frequently with Oaxaca and Tlaxiaco, from the small station directly across the highway from the town plaza.

For **drivers,** Highway 125 runs right past Teposcolula's town plaza, about 13 kilometers (eight mi) southwest of its junction with the Oaxaca City–Mexico City Highway 190. To or from Oaxaca City, using the *cuota autopista* (toll expressway), drivers should allow around two hours to safely cover the approximately 125-kilometer (78 mi) Oaxaca City–Teposcolula distance; add at least another hour if going by the old Highway 190 *libre* (free) route via Yanhuitlán. To or from Tamazulapan in the north, allow about 45 minutes for the 35 kilometers (22 mi) via Highway 190–Highway 125 and about an hour for the 47 kilometers (29 mi) along Highway 125 to or from Tlaxiaco in the south.

YUCUNAMA

Teposcolula's petite neighbor, Yucunama (pop. 600), is attractive partly *because* of its small size. Imagine taking a seat on a stone bench one bright, blue summer morning in Yucunama's flower-decorated town plaza. Birds flit in the bushes and perch, singing, in the trees. Now and then, someone crosses the square and returns your *"Buenos días."* You admire the proud, whitewashed bandstand at the plaza center; behind it rises the old church facade, patriotically decorated like a birthday cake in red, white, and green. From the plaza, cobbled streets pass rustic stone houses and continue downhill to verdant fields, which, in the distance, give way to lush oak and pine-tufted woodlands.

Although it sounds too good to be true, it isn't. Yucunama's beauty is probably one reason that Mixtec people have been living there for at least 4,000 years. Its name, which means Hill of Soap, perhaps reflects the town's spic-and-span plaza, clean-swept streets, and newly painted public buildings. It's a pure Mixtec town, for although Yucunama is part of the Teposcolula district, Spanish settlers never lived here. In fact, in 1585 the all-Mixtec townsfolk declared themselves an independent republic. Nothing came of that, but Yucunama's people nevertheless retain their independent spirit.

The remarkable must-see **Bee Nu'u** (House of the People) community museum should be your first stop. The museum now only opens by appointment. Try contacting someone at the dignified, porticoed *presidencia municipal,* across the plaza from the museum. Say (or show them) this: *"¿Puede alguién mostrar el museo para nosotros?"* ("Can someone show us the museum?")

If the *presidencia municipal* is closed, as it sometimes is, you have the pleasant alternative of knocking on the door of welcoming **Señora Cleotilde San Pablo** (local cell tel. 044-951/105-1019, long distance tel. 045-951/105-1019, son Alvaro Emanuel's email kopec_32@hotmail.com, food $5, lodging $10 pp) who runs the town restaurant **Comedor Doña Coti** on the north side of the plaza. She promises to find someone who will open the museum for you. Moreover, Cleotilde will also will fix you a meal and put you up in her large, comfortable house overnight. Contact her in Spanish, of course.

All of these preparations are well worth the chance to look inside the excellent, professionally prepared museum. Its several very interesting exhibits include the original of the Lienzo Yucunama, an *amate* (wild fig bark paper) document from the 1300s that details the 35 tribute payments of a Yucunama Mixtec noblewoman with the name-date 5-Eagle, and her first and second husbands, 12-Flower and 10-Eagle, to her father, who lived in a nearby town. In the cabinet below the *lienzo* stands a copy of the famous **Codex Nuttall** (folded like an accordion), which details, in full color, the exploits of the renowned Mixtec lord 8-Deer. Your guide may be able to provide some details (including odysseys to Coatzacoalcos on the Gulf Coast, and perhaps as far as Panama) of 8-Deer's adventures. If you don't understand Spanish, the museum is well worth bringing a friend to translate for you.

Another fascinating exhibit displays the complete remains of a robust 70-year-old noblewoman (notice her very husky leg bones) and the trove of goods recovered from her grave, one of a score of burials retrieved locally by archaeologists.

Yucunama's richness as an archaeological zone is further evidenced by the two 1996 INAH (National Institute of Archaeology and History) survey maps of the buried remains of a pair of early Classic-period (300 B.C.–A.D. 300) towns nearby. If you're strongly interested, ask at the *presidencia municipal* and you may be able to get permission and a guide. Expect to pay $20 for a full-day guided trip; transportation is extra.

On the other hand, you can step outside the museum and guide yourself on a short stroll to a pair of nearby local sights. Walk down Calle Independencia (from the museum, follow the left side of the plaza, past the *presidencia municipal*) about three long blocks east to the picture-perfect **town fountain,** fed by the old town aqueduct. You may see women doing the day's laundry in the adjacent arched public washhouse basins. A block south and a couple more blocks downhill east, at the end of Calle Libertad, you can marvel at Yucunama's oldest resident, the gigantic 1,000-year-old **Tule,** or *ahuehuete* tree (Mexican bald cypress, *Taxodium mucronatum*), a distant cousin of the California redwood. If you get lost, you can identify El Tule by its tall, bushy green silhouette, or mention El Tule (TOO-lay) to anyone.

Festivals

You'll have even more fun if you arrive during one of Yucunama's festivals. The biggest is the patronal **Fiesta de San Pedro Mártir**

de Verona, which culminates on April 29. Festivities begin on April 26 with a *calenda* (procession) and plenty of mescal, *aguardiente,* and *pulque* for those so inclined to drink liquor. Sometimes town men dress up like women and perform the dance of the *mascaritas* (little masks). The fun continues with more processions, plenty of flowers, food, fireworks, masses, and a dance on April 29.

Other especially festive times in Yucunama include the fiesta of the Virgen del Rosario (first Sun. in Oct.), El Día de los Muertos (Day of the Dead, Nov. 1 and 2), and the Christmas Eve procession, where everyone in town accompanies the infant Jesus to the church, then watches (or does) the traditional dance of the Pastor y Pastorela (Shepherd and Shepherdess).

Getting There and Away

Yucunama is about nine kilometers (six mi) northwest of the Highway 125–Highway 190 intersection. Drivers: Follow the signed, graded gravel road that takes off from the north corner of the intersection. By bus: Ride an **Omnibus Cristóbal Colón, Sur,** or **Fletes y Pasajes** bus to the Highway 125–Highway 190 intersection, then hike the nine kilometers (six mi) or ride a *colectivo* van or truck from there. A number of snack stands and small stores at the intersection provide water and food.

YANHUITLÁN

It sometimes seems a miracle that the Dominican padres, against heavy odds and isolated as they were in the far province of Oaxaca, were able to build such masterpieces as their convent and church in Yanhuitlán. Upon reflection, however, their accomplishments seem less miraculous when you realize the mountain of help the padres received. When Father Domingo de la Cruz began the present church, in 1541, Yanhuitlán retained the prosperity and the large skilled population that it had when it was a reigning Mixtec kingdom prior to the arrival of the Spanish. For a workforce, de la Cruz used the labor of thousands of Mixtec workers and artisans, who

deserve much of the credit for the masterfully refined monuments that they erected.

And monuments, indeed, they still are. Approaching Yanhuitlán from the northwest, the road reaches a hilltop point where the entire Yanhuitlán Valley spreads far below. In the bright afternoon sun, the white-shining, massively buttressed Yanhuitlán church and adjacent atrium (now soccer field), big enough for 15,000 indigenous faithful, dwarfs everything else in sight.

Up close, you see why. The building's exquisitely sculptured Renaissance facade towers overhead, making those standing on the front steps appear like ants. A graceful semicircular arch frames the entrance, while in the niche to the left stands the robed St. Francis of Assisi. In the right niche, Santa Margarita de Alacoque occupies the position customarily reserved in Dominican church facades for Santo Domingo de Guzmán. The Dominican order's revered founder, Santo Domingo de Guzmán, is nevertheless present. Directly above the front portal, a masterful relief of Holy Mother Mary shelters a diminutive Santo Domingo de Guzmán and Santa Catarina de Siena, like small children, beneath her cape.

The church, officially the **Templo y Ex-Convento de Santo Domingo de Guzmán,** is as much a museum of national treasures as it is a place of worship. In fact, it is divided so: The ex-convent, which you enter on the right, has been converted to a **museum** (9 A.M.–4 P.M. daily, $4). Inside, you begin to appreciate the gigantic proportions of the place as you circle the cloister, passing beneath ponderous but delicately designed arches that appear to sprout and spread from stone cloister columns like branches from giant trees. On the stairway leading upstairs at the cloister's corner, don't miss the mural of Jesus dressed like a 16th-century dandy except for his bare feet and the little angel perched on his shoulder.

The nave glows with golden decorations. Overhead, stone rib arches support the ceiling completely, without the need of columns, creating a single soaring heavenly space. Up front, above the altar, Santo Domingo de

THE MIXTECA

Guzmán presides, gazing piously toward heaven, his forehead decorated by a medallion that appears remarkably like a Hindu *tilak*. Before you exit, take a look by the front door for the dramatic painting of Jesus, whip in hand, driving the money changers from the temple.

Get to Yanhuitlán, on Highway 190, by car, van, or Sur, Fletes y Pasajes, or Omnibus Cristóbal Colón bus. By car, from Nochixtlán, head 12 miles (19 km) north along Highway 190 (62 miles from Oaxaca via the toll expressway, allow an hour and a half), or about 23 miles (37 km) south from Tamazulapan (or about the same from Teposcolula via Hwys. 125 and 190.)

Dominican Route North

This corner of the Mixteca hides a treasury of undiscovered gems, just right for adventurers hankering to follow the road less traveled. First, make sure you spend some time at the grand old Dominican church at Coixtlahuaca, the Templo y Ex-Convento de San Juan Bautista. Then continue north to the hamlet of San Miguel Tequixtepec to contemplate the ancient (1590) stone bridge and the community museum's mammoth fossils, then continue on a prehistoric rock painting excursion, and finally enjoy an overnight in San Miguel Tequixtepec's cozy community-built *cabaña* lodging. Carry on north to Tepelmeme de Morelos and culminate your adventure by boulder-hopping down into a tropical canyon to the astonishingly grand Puente Colosal.

COIXTLAHUACA

Coixtlahuaca (koh-eeks-tlah-OOAH-kah, pop. 3,000), although the capital of an entire governmental district encompassing a significant fraction of the Mixteca Baja's *municipios,* is a modest town even by Oaxaca standards. Before the conquest, it was a powerful Chocho-speaking (Chocholteco) chiefdom, so strong that in the 1400s the Coixtlahuaca warriors stopped the invading Aztecs, forcing them to detour through Tlaxiaco. During colonial times and through the 19th century, Coixtlahuaca continued to be an important Chocholteco market center. But depopulation by emigration and increased education and literacy in Spanish have reduced the number of Chocho speakers to a handful of elderly folks in the surrounding countryside.

Most visitors enter Coixtlahuaca by the *cuota autopista* from Oaxaca City. Just inside the edge of town, a big sign on the left marks the road north to San Miguel Tequixtepec. Straight ahead a couple more blocks, most drivers turn right on Independencia, the main town street. Nearly all stores and services are spread along Independencia, which continues several blocks past the town plaza and then the church, both above and to the left of the street. Bus passengers will arrive at the Autobuses Sur station, on Independencia, in the town center.

Sights

Coixtlahuaca's past importance is reflected in its grand church, the **Templo y Ex-Convento de San Juan Bautista,** one of Oaxaca's largest. At this writing, it appeared that its grand open chapel, similar to the one at Teposcolula, is being restored. Inside the church's nave stretches to the proportions of a great European cathedral, its vault soaring overhead, supported by a delicate network of brilliantly painted colored stone arches. Dominican friar Francisco Marín, Coixtlahuaca's first vicar, was the moving force behind all this grandeur, initiating construction in 1546. Although the Reforms forced closure of the convent in 1856, the Dominicans continued to run it as a church until 1906, when locally based "secular" clergy took over.

In addition to its robust proportions, the church has much of interest. As you enter, notice the dark-complexioned image of African padre San Martín de Porres, in a friar's robe, on the right. Farther into the nave, gaze overhead and admire the whirling, rainbow-hued floral designs, lovingly executed by long-dead native artists. All are original, although time and recent replastering have erased much that you don't see. On the right, take a look at the unusually large side altar to the Virgin of Guadalupe and continue to the main altar, where St. John the Baptist, Coixtlahuaca's patron saint, presides at the foot of the towering, gilded *retablo* (altarpiece).

The town is mostly quiet, except for fiestas, which include the patronal festival of San Juan Bautista (around June 24) and the festival of the Señor del Calvario (Lord of Calvary), during the last half of May. The fiestas include processions, carnival games, traditional food, the hazardous *jaripeo* (bull roping and riding), and the Jarabe Chocholteco traditional Coixtlahuaca courtship dance.

Accommodations and Food

The only hotel along the expressway between Nochixtlán and Tehuacán, Puebla, is the local **Hotel Marina Sol** (Calle Independencia, tel. 953/503-5302, $22). Singles, doubles, and triples are available. Although it has been neglected in recent years, renovations are now complete. The owner's motivation is most likely the ongoing restoration of the church across the street and the lavish *parador turístico* (tourist center), recently built nearby (but not yet operating at the time of this writing).

Although the Hotel Marina Sol's rooms are modestly furnished, they're clean and spacious, with private hot-water shower-baths. Summer humidity, however, has, in the past, caused the rooms to accumulate mildew. If so, beds will need fresh linens; don't hesitate to request them before moving in. Guests additionally enjoy a tranquil garden setting, decorated with roses, statuesque Roman cypresses, and a countryside-view deck behind the reception. (You may have to ask around for the manager, who has been present only when guests were expected. If you can't find the manager, or the rooms are unacceptable, it's best to lodge at the *cabañas* in San Miguel Tequixtepec, a few miles north.)

As for food, Coixtlahuaca has two or three local-style *comedores* and taco shops on Independencia, plus the highly recommended **Restaurant Blanquita** (on the entrance road from the expressway, tel. 953/504-5420, 9 A.M.–9 P.M. daily, $2–3), downhill, a block below the road north to San Miguel Tequixtepec. Restaurant Blanquita is open for breakfast, including tasty *huevos a la Mexicana*; lunch, try *guisado de res* (beef stew) or *chilote de pollo* (spicy chicken); and supper, such as quesadillas.

Another Coixtlahuaca pleasant surprise is the fruit store, **Frutería Juquilita** (8 A.M.–8 P.M. daily), on the street above the town plaza and *presidencia municipal*.

Furthermore, some stores also offer a pair of renowned Coixtlahuaca baked specialties: *menudencia* rolls—big, brown, and not too sweet, sprinkled with a bit of sesame—and pancake cubes, made with alcoholic *pulque* instead of water.

Information and Services

Other services along Calle Independencia include a combined *farmacia–larga distancia,* **La Lupita** (Independencia, tel. 953/503-5405, 8 A.M.–8 P.M. daily).

At the town plaza, a few blocks east, before the church, next to the plaza-front library, find the **telecomunicaciones** (9 A.M.–3:30 P.M. Mon.–Fri.) for fax and money orders. Also find a **correo** (8 A.M.–4 P.M. Tues. only) nearby. Additionally, there is a *centro de salud* with **doctor** (8 A.M.–4 P.M. daily), tucked on the side street, between the town plaza and the church grounds.

For handicrafts shoppers, **Artesanías del Sur** (Independencia 20, tel. 953/503-5475), next to the bus station, offers a fetching collection of locally-crafted pottery, woven palm baskets, sombreros, wooden toys and trinkets, and more.

Getting There and Away

The Coixtlahuaca bus terminal is at the middle of main-street Independencia. Second-class **Sur** buses connect southeast with Nochixtlán

THE MIXTECA

(thence Oaxaca City); south with Tlaxiaco via Teposcolula; and northwest, via the toll expressway, with Tehuacán, Puebla, and Mexico.

A local bus connects Coixtlahuaca, with Highway 190 at Tejupan, accessible by collective taxi either northwest to Tamazulapan, or south, to Teposcolula.

To or from Coixtalahuaca, **drivers** can also connect with Oaxaca (or Puebla–Mexico City), via the fast and easy *cuota autopista* (toll expressway); it's approximately 113 kilometers (70 mi), 80 minutes, to Oaxaca (or Puebla, two hours; Mexico City, four hours in the opposite direction).

Furthermore, drivers to and from Coixtlahuaca can take advantage of the short (24 km/15 mi, 45 minutes) connection with Highway 190 (thence Tamazulapan and Teposcolula) via the paved but sometimes potholed road from its Highway 190 junction at Tejupan.

SAN MIGUEL TEQUIXTEPEC

Tequixtepec is the Aztec translation of the town's original Chocho name, Jna Niingui (Hill of the Conch). Local legend says that Tequixtepec was the site of a now-lost temple dedicated to the god of the conch.

The local region comprises the *municipio* of San Miguel Tequixtepec; once rich, fertile, and thickly populated, it has fallen on hard times. Overgrazing, tree cutting, and selling the stones from the old irrigation terraces have degraded the Tequixtepec region into a semi-desert. Many hills are half-eroded, bare stone. Some good land exists at the stream bottoms, but many people are discouraged by such hardscrabble farming. Most residents leave to work for a year in Oaxaca City, Mexico City, or the United States, then come back and live for three or four years on their earnings. The population has dwindled from 3,000 around 1900 to perhaps 400 now.

It turns out, however, that San Miguel Tequixtepec is a village with grit. It shows in the people and their efforts to reverse their fortunes. A major moving force behind the local folks' determination is personable community leader Juan Cruz Reyes, who spearheaded the remodeling of a ruined schoolhouse into a working museum, now a focus for showing off Tequixtepec's valuable touristic assets: a graceful 1909 *presidencia municipal,* a dignified 18th-century church, woven-palm handicrafts, and, in the vicinity, a colonial-era fossil bridge and prehistoric rock paintings.

Sights

If you arrive heading north along the road from Coixtlahuaca, after about eight kilometers (five mi) you cross a creek bridge, where you can gaze upon an adjacent, crumbling, early colonial-era **stone-arched bridge.** It's a remnant of Tequixtepec's glory days, when merchants marketed small fortunes of locally grown silk and red cochineal dye. Tequixtepec tradition says that one such merchant, Don Diego de San Miguel, built the bridge around 1590 to easily transport his valuable silk and cochineal to the formerly big market in Coixtlahuaca. (Although still crossable on foot at this writing, the old bridge is in bad shape. Hopefully, it will be restored, before it falls victim to old age.)

At the town plaza three kilometers (two mi) farther north, make your first stop at the **community museum.** While there are no regular operating hours, a volunteer will often be available to show you the exhibits of local historical lore, fossils (notably, a huge mammoth tusk), local archaeological finds, and handicrafts. If the museum is closed, check at the *presidencia municipal,* across the plaza.

If you've made a prior appointment (tel. 953/503-5407), volunteers will be available to show you around the town, probably starting at the museum, then the town church, the **Parroquia de San Miguel Arcángel,** built of locally quarried rose *cantera* stone and finished in 1766. The vases you see topping the churchyard fence are from Atzompa, near Oaxaca City, and are always ready to be filled with flowers during the town's festivals. Foremost is the big September 27–29 town patronal fiesta in honor of San Miguel. Highlights include traditional dances, such as the Cristianos y Moros (Christians and Moors). Other important fiestas are celebrated on Palm Sunday (Domingo de Ramos) and Sábado de Gloria (the Sat. before Easter Sun.), when people, for the occasion called *mecos*, don masks and do a kind of adult trick or treat. They go from store to store, asking for something to drink and dancing with whomever is present. Yet another important day in Tequixtepec is Sunday, when, between 3 and 4 P.M., teams face off for a game of *pelota mixteca*, the local version of the ancient Mesoamerican ball game.

As you walk around town, be sure to ask your guide to take you to someone who is weaving palm leaves. This won't be difficult, since everyone appears to be doing it during most of their waking hours. Townsfolk gather and sun-dry the leaves of the little local wild palms, which they craft into a number of useful items, notably mats, grain bags, rope, and sombreros. Although their reward (about $0.25 for a sombrero) is pathetically small, at least the raw materials are free and everyone seems to have plenty of time on their hands. This is especially true during the hot (Feb.–June) dry season, when people do their weaving in cool, backyard *cuevas* (caves), most often in the company of others, when work becomes a party.

Something else you shouldn't miss during your around-town walk is a traditional *temazcal* (ritual hot room). Many local traditional curers have built *temazcales* of stone in their backyards for healing, especially for women after childbirth.

Finally, if the season is right, don't miss sampling a *tuna* (cactus apple). Simply pluck one from the leaf-tip of the many neighborhood nopal (prickly pear) cacti. If it's red and ripe, you'll be in for a sweet, delicious treat.

Guides

It is best to have made an appointment before arriving at the Tequixtepec community museum. Call the *presidencia municipal* (tel. 953/503-5407), first. Tell them when you're arriving and that, if possible, you would like someone to show you the museum. Alternatively, you could try contacting the museum president, Alfonso Villegas (tel. 953/538-4415), or Rudolfo Villegas (tel. 953/540-3325), the Presidente Municipal. If your Spanish is rusty, ask a friend or your hotel desk clerk to do it for you. Leave a message (or a fax: ask for *"tono fax, por favor"*) telling them your arrival time. Contact them by mail: the best is fast Mexpost; or send by courier, such as Estafeta, or UPS, with their name and title, then, Domocilio Conocido, San Miguel Tequixtepec, Oaxaca 79360.

Even if you arrive unannounced (but by noon), you still might be able to hire a guide (Spanish-speaking only) to show you around town and even lead you to the rock paintings (probably on a succeeding day) for a modest fee, perhaps $30. The most experienced guide is **Juan Cruz Reyes,** then if he's not available, perhaps **Nazario Zacarias Zacarias, Jacobo Cruz Gúzman,** or **Joventino Cruz Cruz,** who are all capable and competent. All of them can be reached through the *presidencia municipal.*

Hieroglyphic Rock Painting Excursion

Farther afield, but well worth a day's time for travelers interested in antiquities and the great outdoors, are the local *pinturas rupestres* (rock paintings), which adorn the walls of a nearby river canyon. The jumping-off point, for which you certainly will need a guide, is Rancho La Barrete, a few miles from town, where a rocky but easy trail heads down into a shallow canyon, the Arroyo Palo Solo, of the local Río Grande.

As you descend, keep quiet and keep your eyes peeled for armadillo, coyote, deer, fox, skunk, wild turkeys, or any of a host of bird species. Your immediate destination is the **Cueva de la Iglesia**—a sacred site where children used to be baptized on a large flat rock below the cave. In the cave above, you can see an eagle's nest; nearby is a prehistoric painting dubbed the "alligator man."

Farther down the canyon, climb over a low ridge and cross an often-dry tributary, the Río Seca. Soon you will pass Peña Pirul and Peña Amarillo, a pair of painting-decorated cliff

THE MIXTECA

faces pocked with caves, and, above, ancient walls and irrigation terraces. Finally, after passing through a forest of moss-draped trees, comes the climax, the **Peña de los Guerreros** (Rock of the Warriors), adorned with plumed figures carrying shields and feathered lances.

Practicalities

Tequixtepec townsfolk, with government help, have built a pair of comfortable *cabañas* ($10 pp) on the town plaza, adjacent to the *presidencia municipal*. For reservations (ordinarily not necessary) contact Alfonso Villagas, museum president and *cabañas* registrar (tel. 953/538-4415), or simply call the *presidencia municipal* (tel. 953/503-5407).

Each *cabaña* has bunk beds and hot-water showers for overnight visitors. Bring your own towel and soap. Moreover, you can camp by tent or self-contained RV, for which it would be no problem to obtain permission from the generally hospitable townsfolk. Ask Juan Cruz Reyes or one of the other museum volunteers.

Basic fruits, vegetables, and foodstuffs are available at a pair of grocery stores, one of which also runs the long-distance telephone. It's on the corner across the main street, half a block south from the museum. The other, a block north, is run by the friendly sisters Elvia and Cari Córdoba Reyes. Given half a day's notice, the sisters will also cook hearty, wholesome, reasonably priced meals for you.

Getting There

From Oaxaca, get to Tequixtepec by bus via Nochixtlán and Coixtlahuaca. From the Oaxaca City first-class terminal, ride a bus, such as **Sur** or **Omnibus Cristóbal Colón,** to Nochixtlán. Continue via Sur to Coixtlahuaca, where you can catch a *colectivo* north the 11 kilometers (seven mi) to Tequixtepec.

Bus passengers can also get to Coixtlahuaca, thence Tequixtepec, from Tamazulapan, by collective taxi to Tejupan, thence by local bus, from Highway 190 at Tejupan, thence by the paved (but potholed) road to Coixtlahuaca.

For **drivers,** access to Tequixtepec is also best through Coixtlahuaca. From Oaxaca City, simply follow the *cuota autopista* north approximately 113 kilometers (70 mi), 80 minutes, to Coixtlahuaca, and continue another 11 kilometers (seven mi) north via the signed gravel road (that forks left as you enter Coixtlahuaca) to Tequixtepec.

From Tamazulapan, Teposcolula, or Yanhuitlán, access is best via the paved road that intersects Highway 190 at Tejupan, from which Coixtlahuaca is an easy (but potholed) scenic 24-kilometer (15 mi), 30-minute drive.

TEPELMEME DE MORELOS

Before the Spanish conquest, Tepelmeme de Morelos (pop. 1,600), 13 kilometers (eight mi) north of Tequixtepec, was a semi-independent chiefdom, a tributary of Nochixtlán, at times allied with neighboring Mixtec and Ixcatec chiefdoms. The Mixtec connection was so strong that anthropologists sometimes speak of pre-conquest Tepelmeme as a fused Mixtec-Chochotec culture. Tepelmeme's earliest Christian church, founded by the Dominican missionaries not long after the conquest, was built over an earlier Mixtec-style temple at the same spot where the present church stands on the town plaza.

Despite Spanish dominance, Tepelmeme's Chocho-speaking rulers retained influence over their people into the 18th century. At that time, during the 80 years until 1743, their dynasty was united with the Ixcatec kingdom of Ixcatlán, to the northwest. The great majority of Tepelmeme people continued to speak Chocho until around 1900, when improved education and Spanish literacy began to reduce the number of Chocho speakers to the small group of elderly folks who still speak it.

The present town appears to be the rival metropolis of the Coixtlahuaca district, sometimes overshadowing the district capital in hustle and bustle. The source of Tepelmeme's prosperity is its relatively fertile valley soil, not nearly as eroded as many other Mixteca communities. Some farmers, consequently, have money for wells, pumps, and electricity for irrigation. A number are prosperous enough to even own tractors.

Sights

Tepelmeme, laid out along a north–south axis, has two town plazas. The more formal of the two, a *jardín* with grass and a promenade-encircled bandstand, borders the church on its east side and the *presidencia municipal* on the south. Farther south, behind the *presidencia municipal,* is the town's real heart—the scruffy but seasonally busy market plaza.

The community museum, **Niace** (nee-AH-say; located behind the *presidencia municipal*), which in Chocho means Mountain of Honey, has unfortunately been closed in recent years. You might check with the town officials at the *presidencia municipal* (tel. 953/506-6149 or 953/506-6143) to see if the museum has re-opened. Perhaps they will find someone to open it for you. If so, you will have the pleasure of seeing the museum's collection, mainly artifacts, including a huge ceremonial conch shell uncovered from one of the region's several excavated archaeological sites. Most prominent are the copies of the ancient but sophisticated glyphs painted on the cliff face at the awesome Puente Colosal natural bridge.

Townsfolk built the *jardín*-front church, the newly restored **Templo de Santo Domingo de Gúzman,** in 1769 to replace an earlier, conquest-era church. Community adoration culminates here during the major August 2–6 festival in celebration of Santo Domingo. Folks mark his memory with pilgrimages, processions, baptisms, confirmations, fireworks, and a big carnival.

Inside, don't miss the transept chapel (on the left, as you enter), dedicated to the Sacred Heart of Jesus. Here, you'll find several intriguing banners, one for each of the town's *mayordomías,* the community organizations separately responsible for Tepelmeme's 10-odd yearly religious festivals. The pervasive influence of the *mayordomías* is visible during the individual festivals that they each organize.

◖ Puente Colosal and Huerta de Juquila

With a prior appointment, a Tepelmeme guide (call the Tepelmeme *presidencia municipal,* tel. 953/506-6149 or 953/506-6143) will be available to escort you (21 km/13 mi) to the point of departure for the three-kilometer (two mi), two-hour round-trip hike down a forested boulder-strewn creek bottom to Puente Colosal. Here it appears as if a glacier-era lake once filled a deep limestone box canyon. Over eons, the water gradually dissolved the limestone, finally scooping out a yawning, 60-meter-high (200 ft) tunnel through a towering mountain ridge. The result is spectacular Puente Colosal, probably the world's tallest natural stone bridge.

Puente Colosal has most certainly inspired awe in human visitors for thousands of years. Some inscribed their presence, in both primitive rock paintings and refined (probably city-state stage A.D. 1000–1500) Mixtec glyphs, graphically painted on Puente Colosal's stone face. Someday, when archaeologists finally crack the ancient Mixtec code, humanity will know what Puente Colosal inspired them to record for posterity on its stark bedrock walls.

Get there—by permission only, through the Tepelmeme municipal authorities—accompanied by a local guide. A rugged, high-clearance vehicle is necessary for the last few miles of this route: Mark your odometer at the Tepelmeme town plaza. Head north through town to the expressway entrance (two km/1.2 mi). Continue north to the expressway bridge, Puente La Unión (9.6 km/six mi). With caution, just before the bridge, exit left at the unofficial dirt driveway. Cross back over the expressway via the bridge, then, after a fraction of a mile, turn right (10 km/6.3 mi) at the T at Ranchería La Unión. At kilometer 13.4 (mile 8.3), turn left at another T, at Ranchería Puerto Mixteco. Continue down a mountain-rimmed farm valley, past a hillside spring and small dam at Rosario (16.7 km/10.4 mi). Continue down-canyon via the increasingly rough track to road's end (21.7 km/13.5 mi) and the accommodations *cabañas.*

Puente Colosal is at the downstream end of the canyon. Scramble downhill via a steep trail to the shady stream bottom, then boulder-hop the remaining 2.4 kilometers (1.5 mi).

Although the stream bottom is usually dry, **beware of possible flash flooding** from upstream thunderstorms. Take a hat, binoculars, camera, strong shoes, and drinking water.

Experienced and well-equipped wilderness backpackers might enjoy spending an overnight or two beneath Puente Colosal's grand, sheltering rock ceiling. The environs are ripe for wildlife-viewing, expert-grade vertical rock climbing, and exploring past Puente Colosal's downstream portal, where the stream bottom continues into a lush semitropical mountain-walled wild valley.

Even more remote is the locally famous and idyllic Huerta de Juquila grove and waterfall. Access, strictly by museum- or municipal-approved guide only, is also north of Tepelmeme via the expressway to Puente La Unión. In this case, however, you turn left at the T at Ranchería La Unión. The route continues another 29 kilometers (18 mi) into the mountainous backcountry on foot or by horseback. The key intermediate destination is Mahusipan village (jeep-accessible, at 21 km/13 mi), where you continue on foot or by horse approximately another eight kilometers (five mi) to Huerta de Juquila.

Practicalities

For accommodations, Tepelmeme offers rustic *cabañas* (*presidencia municipal*: tel. 953/506-6149 or 953/506-6143, $25 for four) near the road's end, on the way to Puente Colosal. Reserve by contacting the Tepelmeme *presidencia municipal* and specifying how many are in your party and when you'll be arriving.

Tepelmeme has a sprinkling of small basic stores and restaurants. Get groceries at the small mini-super **Lupita** or **Super Centro Mahuizapan** across the street (about three blocks north of the town plaza, past the river bridge, 8 A.M.–9 P.M. daily).

The Lupita's grandmotherly co-owner also displays a collection of handicrafts, from all over the Mixteca. She invites visitors to take a look (while her good-natured husband sighs, explaining that she's "loco" for handicrafts.)

For cooked food, across the street from Lupita, check out country **Comedor Santo Domingo** (local cell tel. 044-953/114-6605, 8 A.M.–10 P.M. daily) with good breakfasts and a hearty *comida corrida* (set lunch).

For stamps and letter-mailing, go to the *correo* (behind the *presidencia municipal*, 5–7 P.M. Mon., Wed., and Fri.). If you're ill, visit the doctor at the **centro de salud** (8 A.M.–2 P.M., 4–6 P.M., Mon.–Fri., 8 A.M.–2 P.M. Sat.) at the *jardín* southeast corner, across the street from the church. You can also make long-distance phone calls at the *larga distancia* at Lupita grocery.

Getting There and Getting Away

Sur maintains a bus station on the north side of town, past the bridge. Get to Tempelmeme easily by Sur bus from the Oaxaca second-class bus station, via the *cuota autopista* and Nochixtl<#\135>n.

You also can get away by Sur bus, northeast, via Puebla to Mexico City, or southeast to Oaxaca via Nochixtlán. Alternatively, you can head south, by Sur to Coixtlahuaca (where you transfer to the local bus to Tejupan and Hwy. 190). There, catch a van or bus at roadside to Tamazulapan or Huajuapan, or south to Teposcolula and Tlaxiaco.

Drivers: From Oaxaca City drive northwest two easy hours, approximately 137 kilometers (85 mi), via the *cuota autopista* to the Tepelmeme exit.

From Highway 190, drivers should go via Tejupan, a few miles southeast of Tamazulapan. Turn east from Highway 190 at the Tejupan crossroad, pass through the town and continue another 25 (paved but potholed) kilometers (15 mi), to the *cuota autopista* near Coixtlahuaca. Head north another 13 kilometers (eight mi) to the Tempelmeme turnoff.

The Mixteca Baja: Land of the Sun

Although its name implies a lowland, the Mixteca Baja is high, seasonally dry, but sunny country. It comprises the 900–1,600-meter (3,000–5,000 ft) mountain valley and plateau land of northwest Oaxaca. Before the conquest, this land was richer and much more densely populated than today. Irrigated stone-terraced fields graced the hillsides and busy market towns supported large populations of Mixtec-speaking people in the fertile valleys. However, after the conquest, the Spanish soldiers and settlers forcibly congregated the indigenous people into more controllable villages and introduced sheep and goats, which quickly ate up much of the natural grassland. Their way of life changed forever; the people abandoned most of their irrigated fields, and their terraces fell into ruin.

Now, however, the people of the Mixteca are making a comeback: They are replanting their fields and rebuilding their terraces. Furthermore, they offer a modicum of hotels and restaurants and a sprinkling of community museums. These smooth the way for visitors to enjoy the wonders of their land, which vary from natural beauty—crystalline springs, stalactite-hung limestone caves, grand cool groves of ancient *sabino* (Mexican cypress) trees, wildlife-rich river canyons—to the exotic color and bustle of indigenous markets, the mystery of ancient ruined cities, and the fascinating puzzle of the yet-to-be deciphered glyphs of the pre-Columbian Ñuiñe language.

HUAJUAPAN DE LEÓN AND VICINITY

Huajuapan de León (pop. 50,000), with good hotels, restaurants, and many services, makes a comfortable base for enjoying the intriguing corners of the Mixteca Baja. Day trips north, via the Tehuacán road, open the fertile, green valley of the Río Mixteco with its colorful hamlets, venerable churches, and ancient archaeological sites. Similarly, excursions south, along the high road to the Mixteca Alta, reveal a wealth of hiking, camping, boating, and fishing opportunities.

What's even better is that the town itself has much to offer. For first-time arrivals, untouristed Huajuapan de León is a pleasant surprise. The town center—plaza, church, and *presidencia municipal*—is removed a few blocks south of the Highway 190 clutter and bustle. Although the present town dates only from colonial times, the surrounding region, which city hall boosters call Tierra del Sol (Land of the Sun), has been inhabited for many millennia. The extensive Cerro de Las Minas (Hill of the Mines) archaeological zone, just 1.6 kilometers (one mi) north of the present town, was a ceremonial, market, and governmental center for thousands of inhabitants during its apex, around A.D. 500. It was excavated and partially restored during the late 1980s.

Huajuapan (a tongue twister, say ooah-WAH-pahn) put itself on the map during Mexico's War of Independence. After two years of seesaw rebellion, national attention focused on Huajuapan, where *insurgente* Valerio Trujano was leading local forces in blocking the advance of a well-disciplined royalist force. Inspired by faith in their patron saint, El Señor de los Corazones (The Lord of the Hearts), the Huajuapan fighters resisted a royalist siege of 111 days, until relieved by Independence hero General José María Morelos on June 23, 1812.

Later, in the early 1820s, Huajuapan's favorite son, Antonio de León (thus, Huajuapan de León) played a crucial role in securing Mexican Independence. He was among the first leaders in conservative Oaxaca to support Agustín de Iturbide's Plan de Iguala, which finally freed Mexico from Spain. Later, León headed the fight against Iturbide when he proclaimed himself emperor and dissolved Congress. León (by then a general at the age of 29) and Nicolas Bravo captured Oaxaca City for republican forces on June 9, 1823.

The Plaza

The town's choice people-watching spot is the tranquil, old-fashioned town plaza, **Plaza**

THE MIXTECA

THE MIXTECA

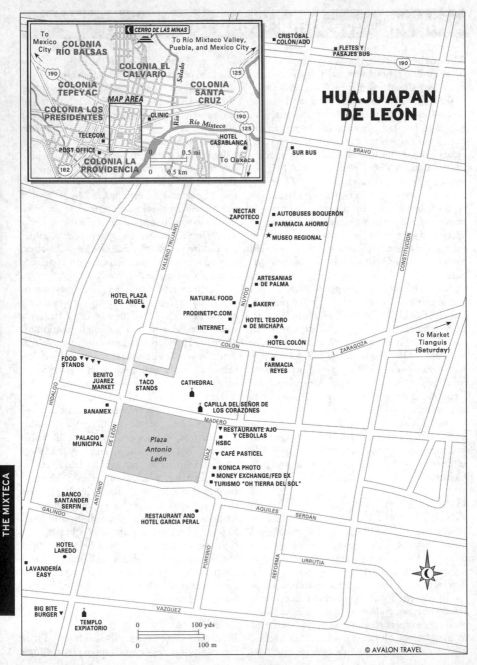

HUAJUAPAN DE LEÓN

Central Antonio de León, bordered by the *presidencia municipal* on its west side. On the plaza's north side stands a distinguished bronze statue of General Antonio de León (1794–1847). Also on the north side, across the street from the plaza, rise the twin spires of the late-19th-century **Catedral de la Virgen de Guadalupe.** A major plaza-front thoroughfare is Antonio de León, on the west side, which becomes Valerio Trujano as it continues north to its highway crossing. On the plaza's east side runs Avenida Porfirio Díaz, which jogs around the backside of the cathedral, becoming Avenida Nuyoo (noo-YOH-oh) as it heads north to the highway.

The plaza's major source of early-evening entertainment is the army of birds, mostly black grackles, who around sunset head from all directions straight for the big, bushy plaza trees. For about an hour, they flutter, cackle, and squabble for perches until they finally settle down for the night.

Stroll over for a look inside the cathedral. For Mexico, this is a new church. Earthquakes repeatedly damaged the previous structures occupying the site since colonial times. The present church, built in the late 1800s, was so severely damaged by earthquakes that it had to be extensively rebuilt and earthquake-proofed in the 1960s. But for the people of Huajuapan, it's not the building, but what it contains, that counts.

Inside, a brilliantly illuminated Virgin of Guadalupe occupies the main front altar, while in the right-side chapel, the **Capilla del Sagrario del Señor de los Corazones,** a painted celebration of baroque glitter climaxes in the beloved, dark-complexioned Señor hanging limply above the altar. On auspicious days, the faithful arrive in a near-continuous stream to pay their respects. As you leave, look on the wall in the small sub-chapel on the left, just outside the door, for the heart festooned with little metal *milagros* (wish offerings), which beseeching pilgrims have left for the Señor.

◖ Cerro de las Minas Archaeological Zone

Be sure to spend at least an hour investigating

the remains of Cerro de las Minas, a major urban-stage (A.D. 300–800) Mixtec town. Artifacts uncovered on this hill just north of town during the 1980s demonstrate characteristics of so-called Ñuiñe glyphs, which archaeologists recognize as one of the five unique writing systems of ancient Mesoamerica.

Similar finds unearthed at contemporaneous Mixteca Baja ruined cities, such as Tequixtepec, Chazumba, Miltepec, Suchitepec, Lunatitlán, and Mixtlahuaca, led archaeologists to name the style by the Mixtec label, Ñuiñe (nyoo-EE-nyay), for the "Hot Country," the Mixteca Baja, where they were discovered.

Before charging up the hill, however, first visit the **Huajuapan Regional Museum** (Museo Regional de Huajuapan; Nuyoo 15, no phone, www.mureh.org.mx, 10 A.M.–2 P.M. and 4–8 P.M. Tues.–Sun.), half a block uphill from the church. Professionally prepared exhibits on the bottom floor give an overview and explanations of the exquisite finds at Cerro de las Minas. Upstairs is a library and beautifully displayed life-size mock-ups—community, costumes, economics, fiestas, religion, and work—of present Mixteca Baja people. Another room exhibits a graphic post-Conquest history and culture of Huajuapan up to modern times, including a description of the interesting tradition of *tequio* (community volunteer work). The museum also sells some books of local history and culture, notably archaeologist Marcus Winter's *Cerro de las Minas* guide to the ruined city uphill.

EXPLORING THE SITE

After the museum, get to the ruins by driving, hiking, or hailing a taxi. Wear sturdy walking shoes, a hat, and take water. From the town center, follow Nuyoo north across the highway and three blocks past the uphill church. Continue straight ahead, up a steep track and turn right to the parking lot, marked by a Zona Arqueología sign. From there, on foot, scramble uphill past the retaining wall to the highest point, **Mound 1,** on the east side.

From the top, the entire Huajuapan Valley spreads in all directions. On the south side, in the distance, rise the downtown cathedral's ruddy twin towers. Far behind them stand the cloud-draped heights of the Mixteca Alta. On the opposite, north side, flat-topped Cerro Yucunitza, the site of another hilltop ruined city, towers over the valley. Below Yucunitza's right shoulder, the Río Mixteco meanders below the high brushy hills of the Mixteca Baja.

Unrestored Mound 1, most certainly a former pyramid, slopes downhill past some reconstructed walls and stairs to a wide ceremonial courtyard. Descend Mound 1 to the courtyard. On its north side are the previously excavated Tombs 4 and 5. On the south side, a staircase descends to a smaller courtyard complex of what appear to be residential walls and patios. Continue west to **Mound 2,** a partly reconstructed ceremonial pyramid. Looking south toward town from its summit, you can view the clear outlines of a partially excavated **ball court** about a hundred yards down the slope.

Continue west, descending the regal, restored ritual staircase down the west side of Mound 2 to a grand 100-yard-square courtyard. Ahead rises **Mound 3,** a brushy hill that most certainly conceals yet another staircase and pyramid summit.

The visible hilltop remains of Cerro de las Minas around you were the ceremonial hub of a small city that, at its apex around A.D. 500, was home to perhaps 4,000 people whose hundreds of homes extended over scores of surrounding hillside acres. Like many of Oaxaca's forgotten cities, the city's original name has been lost over time. What archaeologists do know, however, is that, like Monte Albán and several other of Oaxaca's ancient cities, the inhabitants of Cerro de las Minas mysteriously abandoned it around A.D. 800.

Las Campanas

Las Campanas park, a lovely streamside stroll on Huajuapan's northwest outskirts, is worth at least an hour's visit. At Las Campanas, community efforts have preserved a unique natural desert-like spring and habitat, decorated with rock outcroppings and ferny, shaded nooks. Tables beneath streamside willows make for restful picnicking.

The name Las Campanas (The Bells) derives from the stalactites hanging from the ceilings of shallow, streamside caves. If struck just right, a stalactite will vibrate and ring with a soft, bell-like monotone.

(*Note:* Experienced cavers and hikers might enjoy exploring the cave complex upstream from Las Campanas. A large tree, locally known as Palo Blanco, marks the entrance. The cave extends a mile or two uphill to around Agua Dulce village. *Ordinary travelers should only attempt this led by an experienced guide.* For information and guide recommendations, check with the municipal museum director and/or the tourism office at the *presidencia municipal.*)

Las Campanas, although readily accessible, is not well marked and is easy to miss. Follow the road to Mexico City about 1.6 kilometers (one mi) west of Huajuapan town center. Las Campanas nestles in a shallow arroyo on the left, marked by a left-side (heading in the Mexico City direction) short driveway, leading to a small parking lot. If you pass a government *vivero* (nursery) on the left, you've gone too far; turn around and return one block to Las Campanas.

Shopping

If it's Wednesday or Saturday, the days of Huajuapan's huge *tianguis* (native town market), which is so big that the local government had to move it to the western outskirts of town, it's best to get there by taxi ($3). Stroll beneath the acres of shady *tianguis* (literally, awnings) for your pick of the best, from mounds of luscious bananas, tomatoes, cucumbers, and squashes. During the summer and fall, you'll also see plenty of pears, peaches, guavas, and grapes. Also admire the piles of deep-red chilies and bright-yellow *flor de calabaza* (squash flower) used for flavoring soups and stews. Here and there, you'll glimpse piles of old-fashioned items, such as corn husks (for wrapping tamales), *cal* (lime or quicklime) for soaking corn, red *jamaica* (hah-MAHEE-kah) petals for delicious drinks, nopal (cactus leaves), *tamarindo* and *guaje* pods, yellow *manzanilla* (chamomile) flowers, and hunks of *panela* (brown sugar). Throughout your walk, take note that the women vendors are definitely in charge, although few wear *traje* (traditional indigenous dress).

You'll also find some **handicrafts.** Locally made items include red- and black-streaked pottery, in practical shapes such as *ollas* (pots), bowls, and *comales* (griddles); and stone, carved into *manos* (rollers), *metates* (basins), and *molcajetes* (mortar and pestle) for grinding corn and chilies. Local folks also sell plenty of items woven from palm. These include sombreros, *bolsas* (purses), *petates* (mats), and *cestas* (baskets).

Although few if any local people make textiles, they do import and sell, mostly *huipiles,* from other parts of Oaxaca. You'll probably find some on Wednesday, if you look around the covered section.

Back downtown, on the five non-*tiangius* days (Sun., Mon., Tues., Thurs., and Fri.), you can still enjoy much the same as at the *tianguis,* by meandering the aisles of the downtown **Mercado Benito Juárez** (west side of Trujano), three blocks north of the plaza.

Furthermore, a pair of small stores on Nuyoo, in the town center, offer handicrafts. First, take a look at the woven-palm treasures of the precious little **Artesanías de Palma** (Nuyoo 13, no phone, 9 A.M. 6 P.M. daily), half a block uphill from the cathedral. Stop by and pick a few items from their selection of old-fashioned dress-up costumes, cowboy hats, and *calabazas* for carrying water. Uphill, across Nuyoo from the museum, the mezcal shop **Nectar Zapoteco** (Nuyoo 20, tel. 953/522-0133, 8 A.M.–10 P.M. daily) also stocks some attractive Valley of Oaxaca handicrafts. These include pottery from Atzompa and Coyotepec, leather, and mezcal, in dozens of flavors.

Accommodations
UNDER $25
The budget hotels (none of which accept credit cards) dot the downtown, along Nuyoo and Colón, near the second-class bus stations. **Hotel Colón** (Colón 10, tel./fax 953/532-

0817 or 953/532-1860, $15 s, $22 d one bed, $28 d two beds, $31 t), on the north side of the church, is probably the best super-budget choice. It offers about 20 clean but smallish dark rooms, with cable TV, hot-water shower-baths, all around a parking patio, with *gratis* songs from the owner's bird flock, and a restaurant on site.

Another recommendable budget choice is the **Hotel and Restaurant El Tesoro** (Nuyoo 7, tel. 953/532-4501, $17 s, d one bed, $22 d, t, and q two beds). Choose from around 20 basic rooms with baths, around an inviting plant-decorated restaurant patio, also embellished by birdsong. Clean but small rooms, with TV, in-house Internet, and good restaurant, but no parking, are set back from the busy street and consequently insulated from traffic noise.

For another economical choice, take a look at **Hotel Laredo** (Antonio de León 13, Colonia Centro, just a block south of the plaza, tel. 953/532-0402, $17 s or d one bed, $25 d or t in two beds). The 40 rooms, stacked in three levels around a convenient but morning-noisy parking courtyard, are plain and less than immaculate. If not acceptable, ask them to clean up what's wrong before paying. Amenities include bath, fan, parking, and a passable restaurant.

$25-50
High marks go to suburban resort-style **(Hotel Casa Blanca** (Amatista 1, Colonia Sta. Teresa, tel. 953/532-0779 or 953/532-9364, fax 953/532-0979, $26 s or d in one bed, $50 d in two beds, $60 t), on Highway 190, Oaxaca City side, about 1.6 kilometers (one mi) east of downtown. This is a comfortable option for drivers anxious to avoid downtown traffic and save money. The Casa Blanca's 70 semi-deluxe rooms, in a pair of two-story wings in a spacious garden complex, are carpeted and comfy. Amenities include hot-water shower-baths, cable TV, fans and air-conditioning, relaxing pool-patio, good, airy restaurant, parking, and phones; credit cards are accepted.

If you must stay downtown, but can't find

anything else, you can settle for a night in the **Hotel Plaza del Ángel** (Valerio Trujano 22, tel./fax 953/532-0851, $24 s, $32 d, $40 t). Although not much to look at from the outside, the Ángel has carpeted, and therefore quiet, hallways. Rooms, plain but clean, have private hot-water baths, cable TV, fans, in-house Internet, parking, but no phones nor credit cards accepted.

OVER $50

Visitors who enjoy soaking up Mexico in comfort should choose the immaculate, class-act ◖ **Hotel Garcia Peral** (Porfirio Díaz 1, tel. 953/532-0777 or 953/532-0742, fax 953/532-2000, hotel_garciaperal@hotmail.com, www.garciaperalhotelrestaurant.com, $41 s, $53 d, $70 t), by the southeast corner of the central plaza. The 37 rooms in three floors surround an inviting pool patio blooming with tropical plants and birdsong. Rooms are comfortably furnished, with beige bed covers, reading lamps, attractively rustic tile floors, and modern-standard bathrooms. Amenities include fans, a good restaurant-bar, pool and sauna, and parking; credit cards are accepted.

Food

Huajuapan's best grocery, vegetable, fruit, and economy meals source is the downtown **Mercado Benito Juárez,** (west, on Trujano), two blocks north, from the plaza's northwest corner. For wholesome cooked specialties, visit the airy **andador de fondas** walkway on the Benito Juárez market's north side.

On the other hand, health food fanciers can get plenty of honey, grains, juices, soya, vitamins, supplements, granola, and yogurt at **Natura** (Nuyoo 18, tel. 953/532-2538, 9 A.M.–9 P.M. Mon.–Sat.), a block uphill from the cathedral. Satisfy your hankering for cake, pie, and cookies at the bakery, **Espiga de Oro** (Nuyoo 9, tel. 953/532-3432, 7 A.M.–10 P.M. daily), half a block uphill from the cathedral.

The town center abounds with wholesome cooked food. For inexpensive snacks and meals, try the **taco stands,** on the corner northwest of the church. On the other hand, cross Colón and walk up Nuyoo a few doors and step into the sheltered patio of the hotel and **Restaurant El Tesoro de Michapa** (Nuyoo 7, tel. 953/532-4501, $4–9). Here, you can enjoy a good home-cooked meal accompanied by the melodies of the owner-chef's pet tropical birds.

A cluster of good restaurants serve customers on the east-side plaza-front. In succession, moving south, across from the plaza's northeast corner, first find the Starbucks-like **Italian Coffee Company** (tel. 953/530-5742, 8 A.M.–10 P.M. daily, $1–8). Step into the cool, comfortable interior for a light lunch of either delicious pizza or panini, followed up by a selection of luscious cookies, cakes, and savory café Americano.

Directly upstairs from Italian Coffee Company, on the 2nd floor, you can enjoy both good food and a superbly airy sunset-view and plaza-front perch, at century 21-mod **Zona Zero** (tel. 953/532-0795, 8 A.M.–midnight daily, $8–14), and be entertained with techno tunes and continuously lively TV monitors. As for food, choose from an innovative international menu of breakfasts, soups, salads, pastas, seafood, and meat.

Relaxing courtyard ambience, quiet music, and genteel conversation draw a steady stream of middle- and upper-class patrons to ◖ **Cafetería Pasticel** (two doors south of Zona Zero, next to HSBC, tel. 953/532-2161, 8 A.M.–10 P.M. daily, $3–7). Here, diners start off the day with strong Oaxaca espresso coffee and hearty breakfasts (hotcakes, eggs), and enjoy lunches and suppers of American-style sandwiches (hamburgers, hot dogs, and club) and hearty Oaxacan-style specialties (chicken enchiladas, *chilaquiles,* tacos).

For refined hotel dining, try the airy plaza-view corner restaurant of the **Hotel Garcia Peral** (tel. 953/532-1532, 8 A.M.–10:30 P.M. daily, $7–15). Pick from the long recognizable menu of everything, from cream of asparagus soup and club sandwiches to shrimp salad, filet mignon, or enchilada Oaxacan-style, smothered in black *mole* sauce.

Information and Services

A number of banks around the plaza, all with ATMs, change money. Best for its long hours is **HSBC** (on Porfirio Díaz, tel. 953/532-0169, 9 A.M.–6 P.M. Mon.–Fri., 9 A.M.–3 P.M. Sat.), across from the plaza's northeast corner, south of the church.

If somehow HSBC isn't satisfactory, walk a block to **Banamex** (tel. 953/532-1282, 9 A.M.–4 P.M. Mon.–Fri.), at the plaza's northwest corner.

Get to the *correo* (5 de Febrero 16, on the south side, tel. 953/532-0692, 8 A.M.–4 P.M. Mon.–Fri., 9 A.M.–noon Sat.) from the plaza's southwest corner, by walking south on de León three blocks to 5 de Febrero; turn right and continue another two blocks to the post office on the left side of the street. The *telecomunicaciones* (on Galindo, between Hidalgo and Matamoros, tel. 953/532-0584 or 953/532-3577, 8 A.M.–7:30 P.M. Mon.–Fri.), with money orders, telephone, and fax, is southwest of the plaza. From the plaza's southwest corner, walk a block south, turn right at Hidalgo, and walk a block and a half.

Long-distance telephone and fax are readily available at the **money exchange** (on the plaza, west side, tel. 953/532-2908, 9 A.M.–4 P.M. Mon.–Fri., 9:30 A.M.–2:30 P.M. Sat.–Sun.); it's also a Federal Express and copy shop.

Internet connection is available at **Prodinetpc.com** (Nuyoo 12A, tel. 953/532-2724, 9 A.M.–9 P.M. daily).

If you get sick, one of the best places to go for a doctor is the **Centro de Especialidades de la Mixteca** (Zaragoza 24, tel. 953/532-1355, consultations: 9 A.M.–8 P.M. Mon.–Sat.), three blocks west of the plaza. It has about 15 specialists on call, from gynecologist and pediatrician to internists and a cardiologist.

For routine remedies and prescriptions, go to one of the several pharmacies near the plaza, such as **Farmacia San Jorge** (on Colón, behind the church, tel. 953/532-1399, 8 A.M.–11 P.M. daily), or its second branch (Nuyoo 20, half a block north from the church, tel. 953/532-1123 or 953/532-1584, 8 A.M.–11:30 P.M. daily).

Although Huajuapan has a city *turismo* office on the upper floor of the *presidencia municipal* on the west side of the plaza, you might get more good information by consulting friendly José Flores Cubas, owner of the **Turismo "Oh Tierra del Sol"** (at the plaza's southeast corner, tel./fax 953/532-4555, ohtierradelsol@hotmail.com, 8:30 A.M.–7 P.M. Mon.–Sat).

Get your wash done at **Lavandería Easy** (on Hidalgo, 8 A.M.–8 P.M. Mon.–Sat., 9 A.M.–8:30 P.M. Sun.), one block west, one block south from the plaza's southwest corner.

Getting There and Away

Several first- and second-class bus lines operate out of various terminals, providing direct connections with many Oaxacan and national destinations. The busy, nearly all-first-class **bus terminal** (Hwy. 190 intersection with Nuyoo, tel. 953/532-9309), six blocks north of the plaza, is the hub for **Omnibus Cristóbal Colón, Autobuses del Oriente (ADO), Sur,** and **Autobuses Unidos (AU)** ticket sales, arrivals, and departures. Principal connections, including many intermediate destinations, are southeast with Nochixtlán and Oaxaca City; south via Highway 182 and Tonalá with Juxtlahuaca, where you can transfer on to Tlaxiaco, Putla, and Pinotepa Nacional; and northwest with Puebla and Mexico City.

Second-class **Fletes y Pasajes** (on the highway, across the street, west from the ADO station) offers a broad range of connections in Oaxaca, approximately the same as Sur.

Also, the old (1960s) buses of backcountry bus line **Boqueron** (on Hwy. 182, west edge of town, take a taxi) offer about three connections daily, along the north–south Tonalá–Juxtlahuaca–Putla route all the way to Pinotepa Nacional, on Oaxaca's Pacific coast.

Some independent bus and van stations are scattered along Nuyoo, along the blocks north of the cathedral.

Autobuses Erco (Linea Oro, Nuyoo 19, tel. 953/532-1513) offers first-class express connections with northern destinations of Izucar de Matamoros, Puebla, and Mexico City.

A pair of long-distance van services also provide oft-frequent fast connections. **Servicios Turísticos Huajuapan** (Nuyoo, tel. 953/554-0813) provides broad connections, southeast, with Highway 190, to the destinations of Tamazulapan, Nochixtlán, and Oaxaca; and south, along Highway 182, with Tonalá and Juxtlahuaca.

Furthermore, **Servicios Turísticos Teposcolula** (Nuyoo, local cell tel. 044-953/110-4025) provides connections southeast with Tamazulapan, thence south along Highway 125, with Teposcolula and Tlaxiaco. Find them both, on Nuyoo, about three blocks north of the church, across from the big Farmacia Ahorros.

Drivers have their pick of four major paved highways radiating from Huajuapan. Northwest, Highway 190 connects with Mexico City—316 kilometers (196 mi) via Cuautla, Morelos. Two winding lanes and numerous big trucks along the way usually slow traffic on route. Figure about seven hours under good conditions, in either direction. A quicker alternative is to first head northeast via Highway 125, 118 kilometers (74 mi), two hours, to Tehuacán, Puebla. There, connect with the *cuota autopista,* which will whisk you in another three hours, via Puebla, to Mexico City.

For Oaxaca City, follow Highway 190 for 113 kilometers (70 mi), two hours, southeast to Nochixtlán. Continue via the *cuota autopista* to Oaxaca City, another 80 kilometers (50 mi), about one additional hour.

Drivers can also access points directly south most easily via Tonalá, along the paved (but sometimes potholed), lightly trafficked secondary road, Highway 182, which takes about two hours to Juxtlahuaca (100 km/62 miles). South of Juxtlahuaca 40 kilometers (25 mi; one hour), at the Highway 125 junction, either head left (east) along Highway 125 another 34 kilometers (21 mi), to Tlaxiaco, or go right (south) along Highway 125 via Putla to Pinotepa Nacional on the Pacific coast (a total, from Huajuapan, of 332 km/206 mi). Allow six hours' driving time south to the coast, four hours to Tlaxiaco.

NORTH OF HUAJUAPAN: INTO THE ÑUIÑE REGION

National Highway 125 winds north along the rural, tree-shaded valley of the Río Mixteco, passing a sprinkling of little towns, sleepy except during fiestas, when they liven up with days of processions, barbecues, and carnivals. Along this route, interest climaxes at San Pedro y San Pablo Tequixtepec, where townsfolk welcome visitors to explore their community museum. There, you can view the Ñuiñe-engraved monoliths, whose cryptic inscriptions have convinced archaeologists that they represent a unique written language.

By car, starting early, you could enjoy this 121-kilometer (75 mi) round-trip excursion in a day, allowing time for a picnic in Tequixtepec (35 km/22 mi from Huajuapan) around the midpoint. Bus travelers: Head out by ADO, Sur, or AU bus straight from Huajuapan, on a Tehuacán-bound bus. Ask the driver to let you off at the Tequixtepec entrance road, where you can catch a taxi or the town *colectivo* van and ride the five kilometers (three mi) to town. Afterward, either continue north or return to Huajuapan stopping along the way, if time allows.

Santiago Huajolotitlán

This small town, 6.4 kilometers (four mi) north of Huajuapan, is well known, both for its annual patronal festival and as the place where the Virgin of Guadalupe appeared in 1978. First, stop at the town church, the **Templo de Santiago Apóstol,** built between 1835 and 1840. Inside, to the right as you enter, notice the popular San Isidro Labrador, the patron of farmers, animals, and children, with his customary *yunta* (yoked pair) of oxen and a child. Folks celebrate his memory on May 15, when children bring their animals to church to be blessed.

Also, don't miss the uniquely quaint town patron, **Santiago Caballerito** (Little Saint James), mounted on a small horse, waving a big sword. His festival, celebrated July 26–29, usually includes plenty of fireworks, flowers, music, marches, and *mañanitas* (early morning masses).

Also, on the slope of Cerro del Chilar, northwest of town, is the **Capilla de la Virgen de Guadalupe,** built over the spot where a shepherd saw the Virgin in December 1978. Thousands of believers subsequently flocked to the site, now relatively unfrequented, where the chapel stands.

Río Mixteco Valley and Asunción Cuyotepeji

North of Huajolotitlán, the winding river valley is especially lush during the cooler summer rainy season, when it's abloom with fields of vegetables, tall green corn, and waving wheat. The natural charm climaxes at the riverbank itself, decorated by groves of stately *ahuehuetes* or *sabinos* (bald cypress trees). Here and there, where the highway nears or crosses the river, pause for a stroll along the river and enjoy a spell in the company of the old shady giants.

During mid-August, you also might enjoy getting in on the fun of the **Fiesta de Santa María de la Asunción**, at Cuyotepeji, about 19 kilometers (12 mi) north of Huajuapan. At least take a look inside the church, known for its gilded baroque main *retablo* (altarpiece),

crowned by the Holy Mother ascending to heaven guided by a pair of adoring cherubs.

San Pedro y San Pablo Tequixtepec

You could easily spend your entire day at Tequixtepec (formally, San Pedro y San Pablo Tequixtepec, pop. 1,400), the head town of the *municipio* of the same name. Make your first stop at the community museum, **Memorias de Yucundaayee** (yoo-koon-dah-ah-YAY-ay; adjacent to the town *presidencia municipal*, no phone, 10 A.M.–2 P.M. and 4–7 P.M. Mon.–Thurs.), named with the town's original Mixtec label (Hill of the Standing Conch), which the Aztecs translated to Tequixtepec.

The professionally prepared exhibits display the intriguing glyph-carved monoliths, with Spanish-language explanations of their Ñuiñe writing style. Despite a generation of study and excavations, archaeologists still can say little about the people depicted. For now, their feathered visages remain mute to us; maybe someday

COHETES: BANGS, FLASHES, AND HISSES IN THE NIGHT

Like everyone, Mexicans love celebrations, and every one of them, humble or grand, must be accompanied by *cohetes*. Although *cohetes* literally means "rockets," folks always associate them with the myriad other booming, flaring, whooshing, banging, and whirling incendiary devices that traditionally go along with *cohetes*. And while in most of the United States, bland "Safe and Sane" fireworks are all that ordinary folks set off on the Fourth of July and maybe New Year's, the sky seems to be the only limit during the seemingly innumerable fiestas that Mexicans celebrate everywhere.

One big climax of celebrating peaks during the several weeks before Easter Sunday, when folks start out with a rip-roaring Carnaval (Mardi Gras) and parade the six succeeding Friday afternoons to the cannonades of *cohetes de trueno* (thunder rockets) overhead,

and end up with a grand explosive bash on Easter Sunday.

Whatever the occasion, the *coheteros* (rocketeers) have plenty of tricks up their sleeves, from the familiar, colorfully brilliant *cohetes de luces* (rockets of lights) to a dozen other strictly Mexican varieties. These include *toritos*, a bull-shaped frame, decorated with papier mâché and loaded with flares and firecrackers, that some daredevil wheels or carries on his back through the crowds of merrymakers.

Sometime after that, someone usually scatters some *buscapies* (heel-chasers) that go whizzing, whirling, and shrieking under the feet of the crowd.

Finally, the *cohetero* lights up the *castillo*, a grand framework laced with pinwheels, flares, and smoke bombs, from which a spinning *corona* finally swishes skyward, scattering a trail of stars in the inky firmament overhead.

experts will decipher the Ñuiñe glyphs and understand their messages.

The recently completed **mural** on the museum's front wall depicts the sweep of Tequixtepec history, from pre-Conquest times, through independence, civil war, and reform, clear up to the 20th century, when the tradition of the town's beloved Señor del Perdón began in 1917–1918.

If you have arranged a tour appointment, a museum volunteer will be available to take you on an extensive exploration, including a three-hour round-trip hike to **Cerro de La Caja** (Mountain of the Box), a regal hilltop ruined town. There, among other things, you'll be able to inspect a ponderous box-like monolith, inscribed with a number of graphic Ñuiñe reliefs, one of which includes a personage devouring a captive. Make an appointment by leaving a message, specifically for the *museo comunitario,* with the town long-distance *caseta* (long-distance within Mexico tel. 200/123-7044, 200/123-7045, or 200/123-7046).

Back in town, be sure to visit the church, dedicated to the **Señor del Perdón** (Lord of Forgiveness), who is celebrated in a big regional fiesta and pilgrimage culminating on the second Friday of Lent. At that time, 20,000 people are likely to crowd into little Tequixtepec, sleeping in the plaza, the town pilgrimage shelter, and in scores of buses parked along the road into town. The object of all is to ask forgiveness from the Señor del Perdón, who presides above the church's front altar.

Before you leave, ask your guide for a demonstration of **palm weaving,** which many townsfolk do during their spare moments. Both individual weavers and the museum sell examples of woven sombreros, *petates* (mats), *tenates* (tumpline baskets), and more. Additionally, be sure to step 100 years into the past into the Porfirian-era store of grandfatherly **Faustino "Tino" Moran Castillo** in the center of town opposite the church. Here you might say a good word, make a small purchase, and enjoy a sip of his zingy homemade brandy, which Faustino claims is "very good for your health."

Hint: If you happen to arrive in Tequixtepec

unannounced, Faustino is the one to see first, and can usually find someone to open the museum for you. Furthermore, if you decide to linger in Teqiuxtepec, Faustino and his daughter Abigail are prepared for you. He offers a room in his house for $10 per person, and given a day's notice will arrange for meals for $4 per person. Kindly place a reservation via the town long-distance telephone (tel. 200/123-7044, 200/123-7045, or 200/123-7046).

Santiago Chazumba

The main yearly attractions here at sleepy Chazumba, about 60 kilometers (37 mi) north from Huajuapan, are its two major festivals, in honor of **Santiago** (July 24–26) and the **Señor de Esperanza** (Lord of Hope—the 15 days beginning on Good Friday).

The town's permanent jewel is its church, dedicated to Santiago Apóstol (St. James the Apostle). Although it seems a small miracle that such a monumental building and refined works of art can be found in such an isolated little place, it is the Chazumba townsfolk's intense devotion, rather than divine intervention, that has produced the monumentally resplendent results over centuries of effort. While inside, among all the glitter, don't miss the baptismal chapel to the right of the front door, the Señor de Esperanza in the transept chapel, and Santiago above the front altar.

The Chazumba bus stop supports a few eateries alongside Highway 125. The best seems to be the **Restaurant Los Arcos** (tel. 953/525-0083, 7:30 A.M.–9 P.M. daily), where you can enjoy house specialties, such as *mole de guajalote* (turkey with *mole* sauce), *tamales de frijol* (bean tamales), and *barbacoa* (barbecued beef, pork, or chicken).

Besides food, Restaurant Los Arcos also provides a long-distance telephone and fax (tel. 953/525-0083). Moreover, in town you'll find a *correo* (across the highway, 9 A.M.–1 P.M. and 3–6 P.M. Mon.–Fri.) and a *telégrafo* (9 A.M.–3 P.M. Mon.–Fri.) for money orders and fax.

ADO and **AU** buses, which depart from the Restaurant Los Arcos, connect several times a day north with Tehuacán, Puebla, and Mexico City, and south with Huajuapan, Nochixtlán, Oaxaca City, and intermediate points.

SOUTH OF HUAJUAPAN: ALONG THE HIGH ROAD TO THE MIXTECA ALTA

This lightly traveled, all-paved (but sometimes potholed) route, National Highway 182, branches south from Huajuapan, opening a scenic back door to Oaxaca's cool, green, and culturally rich Mixteca Alta. Along the way, you'll cross rushing mountain rivers, wind through fertile farm valleys, and climb to high ridges where you can gaze back down upon it all.

Pleasant surprises along the way include boating, fishing, camping, and lakeside bungalows at **Yosocuta Reservoir** and riverside hiking and wilderness camping in spectacular **Tonalá Canyon.** A few miles farther, at colonial-era Tonalá town, you can enjoy a cool, shady walk, and a picnic in the town's grand old *sabino* (bald cypress tree) grove. Finally, at the route's end, at Juxtlahuaca, enjoy the color of the grand indigenous Thursday–Friday *tianguis* (native town market), a relaxing stroll, and restful overnight camping in the pine grove beside the crystalline, emerald-green **Laguna Encantada.** With an extra three hours, you can even go for an easy but amazing walking adventure through the stalactite-hung grottoes of the **limestone cave** at nearby San Miguel de la Cueva village.

Yosocuta Reservoir

This big artificial lake, 13 kilometers (eight mi) south of Huajuapan, confined by the government-built Yosocuta dam on the Río Salado, rises and falls with the seasons. From February through June, the reservoir drains, nourishing irrigated crops downstream. Its level consequently falls, leaving an ugly bathtub-like lakeshore ring. However, by October, the lake usually refills to its brim, gently lapping the shoreline at **Parador Yosocuta,** the major lakeside access point.

Here, you have several choices. Lake-view restaurants offer snacks, drinks, and fresh *lobina negro* (black bass) dinners. A concession,

owned by the Yosocuta town fishing cooperative and managed by welcoming Sammy Martínez, offers lake tours by boat ($10–15 per party), fishing excursions ($20/hour), boat rentals, bait, and fishing poles (for sale for about $50); launching fee for your own motorboat runs about $5.

If you decide to stay overnight, Sammy will let you set up your tent on the lakeshore ($2 pp) or park your self-contained RV overnight in the parking lot for free. He also rents out cozy lakeshore four-person duplex cabins (which he calls bungalows, $12 pp per night), with their own hot-water baths and porch-front hammock hooks.

Furthermore, if somehow Lake Yosocuta doesn't suit you, stop instead at the **Balneario las Bugambilias** (10 A.M.–6 P.M. daily, no phone, $6 adults, $3 under 12), a family paradise of pools, water slides, merry-go-round, a restaurant, and a campground. It might be crowded on Sundays and holidays. The *balneario* (resort) is located on the highway, past the town of San Marcos, about eight kilometers (five mi) west of the reservoir.

Also along the road, at San Marcos village, you must stop for a treat at ⬛ **Panadería San Marcos** (7 A.M.–8 P.M. daily), on the highway at the south edge of San Marcos village, a few kilometers past (west of) Yosocuta (but before the *balneario*). Here, you can savor what has to be the Mixteca's, if not all of Oaxaca's, best pastries.

About half a mile before reaching Tonala Canyon, a rustic restaurant, **Comdeor Boquerón,** provides a pleasant place to pause, offering food, drinks, and a panoramic view of the Río Salado valley.

Tonalá Canyon

Past a high, pine-studded ridge and pass, Highway 182 winds down to the fertile, green, Tonalá valley. There, 43 kilometers (27 mi) south of Huajuapan, beneath the foot of **Puente Morelos,** a steel-arch highway bridge, the Río Salado issues through the deep defile of Cañon de Tonalá (known locally as El Boquerón—Big Mouth).

© BRUCE WHIPPERMAN

A sturdy walkway leads through El Boquerón, the grand river gap of the Río Salado.

A trail (and aqueduct) cut into the canyon wall leads to a diversion dam about 1.6 kilometers (one mi) upstream. The trail begins at some stairs not far from the bridge's north footing. It continues spectacularly, above the river along the diversion canal, winding beneath towering 300-meter (1,000 ft) moss-mottled cliffs, green-tufted like a classical Chinese painting. At one point, a great boulder overhangs the trail; at another, a mass of ferns appears to cascade from the vertical rock wall.

At the dam, the trail ends at a small park and commemorative plaque that records that President Gustavo Díaz Ordaz came here during the late 1960s to dedicate the dam, a part of the federal Río Balsas Basin Development Project. A rough informal trail continues past the dam. After 50 downhill yards it leads to a flat spot on the right good for camping, with a bit of shade and safely above the river.

For equipped and prepared wilderness adventurers, the river farther upstream, which runs about 16 kilometers (10 mi) through a wild, deep gorge, might be heaven. Overhead, vultures and eagles soar; coyotes, foxes, and wildcats hunt along the shore; and butterflies flutter among streamside trees and wildflowers. The river, rushing and often muddy during the summer rainy season, slows to a clear, tranquil creek during the dry winter and spring. Although the Yosocuta Dam upstream probably minimizes the hazard, hikers should be aware of possible flash flooding from upstream thunderstorms.

◖ Santo Domingo Tonalá

The sleepy farm community of Santo Domingo Tonalá (pop. 3,000) owns a pair of gems: its 16th-century Dominican-founded church and ex-convent, the **Templo de Santo Domingo,** and the shady, sylvan *sabinera* (cypress grove) behind the church. First, take a look inside the church, behind its front garden, a block north of the town plaza. Just past the entrance hangs an intriguing portrait of Angel Gabriel holding the scales of justice, deciding which of a cluster of beseeching souls will be admitted to Paradise. Farther on stands an image of the beloved African Dominican padre San Martín de Porres. The treasures climax in the right-side chapel, in a glittering, gorgeous small *retablo* (altarpiece), appearing as intricate as filigree and dedicated to the Holy Sacrament. Continue outside to the church's right (east) side and enjoy a turn through the garden within the old convent cloister.

You'll find the *sabinera* two blocks behind the church. Stroll around and soak in the cathedral-like loveliness beneath the ancient trees. Perhaps you will agree that the magnificent, gnarled old veteran *sabinos,* or *ahuehuetes,* are in their own way as magnificent as the stately old-growth groves of their cousins, the California redwoods. They certainly approach the size of redwoods. At the grove's far west end (left as you enter), find the rugged old grandparent of them all, 4.5 meters (15 ft) in diameter and 15 meters (50 ft) around. During your walk, you probably will notice the several small, clear rivulets running through the grove. This is no coincidence; local folks believe *sabinos* to be the most intelligent of trees; they always grow where the water flows.

If you arrive on Sunday, you might be able to see a *pelota mixteca* ball game in the field across the highway at the town entrance road. A direct descendant of the ancient Mesoamerican tradition, the modern game has players batting a big rubber ball back and forth, by hand, not unlike tennis (except without a net or a raquet).

Furthermore, you're in for a treat if you arrive in early May or early August, when Tonalá wakes up for its annual festivals. Between May 1 and May 4, you can get in on the fun (dancing, cockfights, and bull roping and riding) of the **Fiesta de la Santa Cruz.** Three months later, around August 4, join Tonalá folks as they rev up again for more of the same during the **Fiesta de Santo Domingo.**

Ecotourism
What's more, Santo Domingo Tonalá has been increasingly welcoming to visitors. Besides camping, hiking, and wildlife-viewing opportunities in Tonalá Canyon, you can enjoy guided tours of local archaeological sites. These include a cave with *pinturas rupestres* (prehistoric hieroglyphic rock paintings), and walls of ancient crumbling temples (from a time long ago, when the local population is said to have migrated from present Chiapas state).

For information on all this, drop by the local **ecotourism office** (in the Tonalá *presidencia municipal,* tel. 953/531-0023, in Spanish), where Artemio Cruz is in charge. They now have hiking trails for guided tours, navigable either on foot or by mountain bike; and in Tonalá Canyon, a riverside campground and *cabañas* for overnight accommodations.

Accommodations and Food
Consider Tonalá's one hotel, the homey **Los Mangos** (Lázaro Cárdenas 27, tel. 953/531-0023, $15 s, $18 d in one bed, $22 d or t in two beds), marked by a tall mango tree, on the entrance road from the highway. The grandmotherly owner and her daughter offer 10 rooms beside a flowery garden and the loveliest of crimson-blossomed *tabachínes* (flame trees). Check the rooms before moving in; mildew can be a problem here, especially during the rainy summer. Ask for fresh linens if necessary. All rooms have baths, with 24-hour hot water and all the mangos you can eat, in season.

For groceries and fruits and vegetables, go to well-stocked **Comercial Itzoca** (Lázaro Cárdenas, tel. 953/531-0138, 8 A.M.–9 P.M. daily), in the northwest corner of the plaza.

The best place in town for hearty home-cooked meals is the Los Mangos hotel's **restaurant** (Lázaro Cárdenas 27, tel. 953/531-0023, 8 A.M.–8 P.M. daily, $3–8).

Information and Services
Most of Tonalá's essential services are on Lázaro Cárdenas, near the town plaza. For example, if you're sick, go to the *centro de salud* (8 A.M.–2 P.M., 4–6 P.M. Mon.–Sat.), downhill a block past the church. Alternatively, consult with Doctora Aracel Orate at her **Farmacia Diana** (across from the *centro de salud,* pharmacy: 8 A.M.–9 P.M. Mon.–Sat., 8 A.M.–3 P.M. Sun.).

Find both the *correo* (9 A.M.–2 P.M. Mon.–Fri., 9 A.M.–1 P.M. Sat.) and the *telecom* (8 A.M.–3 P.M. Mon.–Fri.) on the plaza, by the *presidencia municipal.* For long-distance telephone and fax go to the *larga distancia* (Lázaro Cárdenas, 9 A.M.–9 P.M. daily), a block downhill from the church, on the right.

For lots of digital photo services, go to **Foto Studio Tonalá** (local cell tel. 044-953/531-0307, 10 A.M.–4 P.M. and 5–9 P.M. Mon.–Sat.), a block south of the plaza.

Getting There and Away
Bus passengers can reach Yosocuta, Tonalá Canyon, and Tonalá town by second-class **Sur** (choose Sur) or **Boquerón** buses, either northbound for Huajuapan or southbound for Juxtlahuaca. By van, **Servicios Turísticos Huajuapan** picks up southbound (Juxtlahuaca), or northbound (Huajuapan) passengers.

From Huajuapan, **drivers** should first take the Mexico City direction along Highway 190 to a signed Highway 182 Juxtlahuaca (or Tonalá) left turn, about 1.6 kilometers (one mi) west of the city center. After another 1.6 kilometers (one mi) turn right at the main street, Avenida Mina, and head out another 13 kilometers (eight mi) to Yosocuta. After a total of 43 kilometers (27 mi), arrive at Tonalá Canyon; continue another five kilometers (three mi) to Tonalá town, continuing to Juxtlahuaca, a total of 100 kilometers (62 mi) to Juxtlahuaca. Heading in the reverse direction, north from Juxtlahuaca, the distances total approximately 51 kilometers (32 mi) to Tonalá, 56 kilometers (35 mi) to Tonalá Canyon, and 87 kilometers (54 mi) to Yosocuta. Figure about two hours at the wheel, either direction.

SANTIAGO JUXTLAHUACA AND VICINITY

Santiago Juxtlahuaca (pop. 30,000) is the largest town and major service and governmental center for the Juxtlahuaca governmental district. It's clear why the town has prospered. It nestles in a deep, fertile valley between a pair of towering oak- and pine-studded mountain ranges. Main roads branch south, west, and north, connecting Juxtlahuaca with the outside world.

A second glance at the surrounding mountains reveals sinuous trails so steep that it's a wonder how anyone could climb them. But people do—the indigenous Mixtec- and Trique-speaking mountain people, for whom Juxtlahuaca's big *tianguis* (native town market) is the focus of their week. They rise long before dawn and bundle up their merchandise—perhaps a basket packed with flowers, potatoes, or carrots; maybe they pile on a few handloomed bright-red-striped *huipiles*. Husband and wife sling the loads on their backs, adjust the tumplines on their foreheads, and begin the steep trek downhill, with hope that this will be a good *tianguis,* and they won't have to haul everything back uphill tomorrow night.

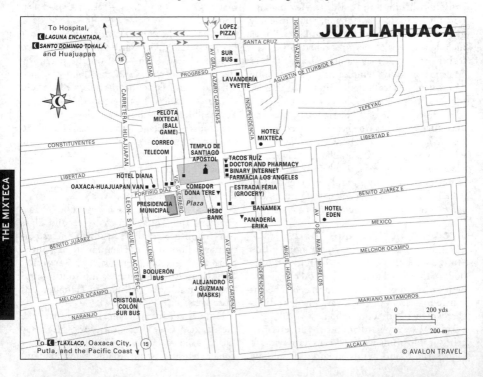

© AVALON TRAVEL

Sights

Orient yourself by the tall, straight-laced bell tower of the town church, the **Templo de Santiago Apóstol**, visible from all over town. The church faces the customary west, downhill. If you stand looking at the church-front, south will be on your right, north on your left. The uphill direction, toward the rear of the church, is east. Main east–west streets are Libertad, which runs along the church's north side; Porfirio Díaz, along the church's south side by the plaza; and Benito Juárez, along the plaza's south side. Important north–south streets are Lázaro Cárdenas, a block behind the church; and Independencia, a block farther east, uphill.

If at all possible, schedule your Juxtlahuaca visit to coincide with its two-day *tianguis* (native town market), big on Thursday, but among Oaxaca's biggest on Friday. Vendors' awnings (known in the Aztec language as *tianguis*) stretch from curb to curb, beginning at the town plaza just downhill from the church, and overflow, filling half of Juxtlahuaca's south-side streets.

The star actors of the *tianguis* are the Trique women, who proudly wear their horizontally striped bright-red wool *huipiles* over their black woolen skirts. (If you wonder why in sunny Mexico they wear wool, it's because afternoons are often cloudy and cool in Juxtlahuaca, especially during the summer and fall rainy season, and doubly so in the Triques' mountaintop villages.)

A number of Trique women congregate in the town plaza, north side, and display their for-sale homespun textiles: *huipiles,* black *enredos* (skirts), and blouses. They don't like having their pictures taken.

From the plaza, plunge into the hubbub of stalls on the south-side street, Benito Juárez. Along your meandering path you'll find loads of lovely fruit, many exotic tropical varieties—*anonas, guanabanas, pitahayas, zapotes*—but also apples, grapes, peaches, pears, and plums in the summer and fall.

You'll also see a fair amount of pottery, especially along Calle Lázaro Cárdenas, the north-south street that runs behind the church.

Varieties include flower-painted, hard-glazed bowls, cups, and plates from Santa Rosa in the Valley of Oaxaca; green ware from Atzompa, also in the Valley of Oaxaca; and red and black jugs, plates, and bowls from Puebla. A few stalls also sell soft woven palm *tenates* and *petates* (tumpline baskets and mats), and sombreros from around Huajuapan de León.

If you're in the market for authentic masks, go to the shop of master craftsman **Alejandro Jesús Vera Guzmán** (Lázaro Cárdenas 301 Sur, corner of Melchor Ocampo, tel. 953/554-0060 or 953/554-1424, alexvera_72@hotmail.com, alexvera_72@yuahoo.com, www.alejandromascaras.com.mx), one block east and one block south of the plaza's southeast corner. His store is adjacent to the southwest corner grocery. He got started creating masks (devils seem to be his specialty) for local fiesta dances; now he sells to the public. His prices aren't cheap; expect to pay $80 and up. From him, however, you're getting the genuine article. If you lend him your photo, he'll even create a mask of you, for around $200.

© BRUCE WHIPPERMAN

THE MIXTECA

Master craftsman Alejandro Jesús Vera Guzmán carves a devilish mask.

While you're strolling around, you might take a look inside the church. Just as you enter the door, look into the small alcove on the right and you'll see the town patron, Santiago (St. James), sword in hand, on his usual white horse, but this time with a cowboy hat atop his head. Up front, above the altar, you'll see Santiago in more traditional dress. Step left, into the left transept chapel, and see the Virgen de Soledad presiding above the altar.

◖ Laguna Encantada

Yet another good reason for coming to Juxtlahuaca is Laguna Encantada (Enchanted Lagoon), a deep crystalline, emerald-green lake beside the Huajuapan highway about three kilometers (two mi) north of town. Laguna Encantada, set like a jewel at the foot of a towering mountain, is a precious asset that, besides furnishing irrigation water, supplies the adjacent communal swimming pool and picnic and camping ground. Even if you don't camp there, you should at least go for a stroll around its shoreline, made picture-perfect by the family of gnarled old *ahuehuete* cypresses inhabiting its banks.

(*Note:* So many men have drowned in Laguna Encantada's cold deep waters that legend says that Laguna Encantada has the spirit of a woman, who takes men that she likes. Notice the crosses on the inner shoreline, adjacent to the hillside, which is especially treacherous because of its steep drop-off to seemingly bottomless depths. Nevertheless, swimming in Laguna Encantada without accident is doable with precautions: You risk drowning by venturing into such cold water that's over your head in depth. Play it safe, and confine your workout to either the shallower, outer shoreline, across the lake from the mountainside, or the safe and sane community bathing pool, where you can reach the shore readily in an emergency.)

Both tent and RV camping prospects at Laguna Encantada could hardly be better. A broad cypress-shaded campground on the lake's north side provides plenty of grassy space to spread out. As a courtesy, ask the caretaker, friendly Natalia Ramos de Morales, or her husband, Francisco, who run the snack stand ($1–4) by the campground and the restaurant on the opposite side, if camping is OK. It will always be both allowed and free; as a courtesy, kindly buy a few tacos and drinks from them at the snack stand, and maybe even a hearty full meal, such as hamburgers, *tortas,* cappuccino, fresh fish, shrimp, and, on Sundays, scrumptious chili-garlic *mole* on roast pork.

Natalia recommends that visitors hike up to the top of the hill, Mogote de la Tialeja, just north of the campground. Natalia (a definite local booster) says that the Mogote, an ancient Mixtec town, is full of artifacts (which must remain in place; Mexican law forbids their removal). Artifacts or not, your reward for the 250-meter (750 ft) summit climb will be an airy, panoramic valley and mountain view.

San Miguel de la Cueva

Townsfolk of San Miguel de la Cueva (pop. 1,000), south of Juxtlahuaca, invite visitors to explore their big limestone cave. An adventurer's delight, the cave has plenty of hanging stalactites, fluttering bats, and a river that flows down from a hidden subterranean lake. Up the road, about 100 yards past the cave, is a petite pretty lake, with picnic shelters, fine for tent or self-contained RV camping. The Río Media Luna (Half Moon), which both enters and exits the tunnel-like cave, provides water (use purification tablets to be safe). A dry path continues about 300 yards through the cave to a separate exit on the north side of a small ridge. With a strong flashlight, good shoes, and a hat, you could hike it yourself, but it's best to get permission and a guide (offer to donate $10) at the *agencia municipal* (which has flashlights) in town. Get there via the signed right-side road from Highway 15, three kilometers (two mi) south of Juxtlahuaca. Continue about 13 kilometers (eight mi) to the hilltop town church, on the right. Go one block straight downhill to the basketball court/town plaza in front of the *agencia municipal.*

To get to the cave, turn right at the bottom of the hill, in front of the *agencia municipal,* and continue exactly 1.6 kilometers (one mi) along the graded dirt road to the cave, visible downhill on the left, beyond a grassy field of big, beautiful summer lilies.

Accommodations and Food

Juxtlahuaca has several hotels, at least three of which are recommendable. Homiest is the family-run **Hotel Mixteco** (Independencia 200, tel. 953/554-0025, $11 s, $14 d, $17 t), near the corner of Libertad, two blocks behind the church. The 13 plainly furnished but clean rooms encircle a picturesque mango and lemon tree–decorated patio. Rooms come with hot-water shower-baths and parking; credit cards are not accepted.

Much fancier is the newish **Hotel Eden** (Calle Mexico 309, tel. 953/554-0706, $20 s, $25 d in one bed, $28 d in two beds, $32 d king-size bed, $33 t), at the corner of Morelos. Choose from three stories of 30 tastefully decorated 1990s-modern rooms, with polished wood highlights, plush maroon carpet, shiny bathrooms, and built-in bed reading lamps, all with hot water, parabolic antenna TV, telephone, and wireless Internet access; credit cards are not accepted. It's best to arrive in the mid-afternoon, whether you have a reservation or not. This place is popular.

If both of the above hotels are full, you'll likely find a room at the **Hotel Diana** (Porfirio Díaz 300, tel. 953/554-1159, $13 s, $18 d in one bed, $22 d in two beds, $25 t), a block downhill from the plaza. The 30 basic but clean rooms come with hot-water shower-baths, TV, and parking; credit cards are not accepted.

As for food, plaza-front taco stands and market *fondas* (food stalls) provide plenty of inexpensive local-style food. Remember: If it's hot, it's wholesome. For dessert, go to the bakery, *panadería* **Erick** (Benito Juárez, no phone, 6 A.M.–9 P.M. daily), half a block uphill from the plaza's northeast corner.

Market vegetable and fruit selection is super, especially during the summer. To be on the safe side, peel, cook, or scrub with soap and water any fruit or vegetable you eat. Stores such as **Estrada Fería** (Lázaro Cárdenas, tel. 953/554-

0026, 9 A.M.–9 P.M. daily), half a block south of Porfirio Díaz and a block uphill from the plaza, opposite HSBC, supply basic groceries.

Juxtlahuaca people are prosperous enough to support a few restaurants. Always busy is the **Comedor Dona Tere** (behind the church on Lázaro Cárdenas, no phone, 7 A.M.–6 P.M. Mon.–Sat., $4 lunch), a block uphill from the plaza, by HSBC. The specialty here is a hearty afternoon four-course *comida,* typically soup, rice, stew, and dessert.

Try **López Pizza** (Lázaro Cárdenas, corner of Santa Cruz, tel. 953/554-1213, 10:30 A.M.–10:30 P.M. daily, $2–7), about four blocks north of the town center, for pizza, spaghetti, calzone, hamburgers, and lettuce and tomato salad.

Alternatively, for tasty Mexican selections, go to spic-and-span **Tacos Ruíz** (Lázaro Cárdenas, corner of Independencia, 8 A.M.–9 P.M. daily), two blocks closer in than López Pizza.

Festivals

Local townsfolk celebrate both **Santiago** and the **Virgen de Soledad** in big festivals. Santiago's festival culminates around July 25, with a number of traditional dances: the Cristianos y Moros (a variation of the Dance of the Conquest; the Moors are the bad guys); the Chilolos (masked men, posing as women, in bells and skirts); and the town favorite, the Diablos (Devils). Much of the same thing goes on during the December 8 Virgen de Soledad festival. In addition, **Carnaval** is big in Juxtlahuaca. On the four days before Ash Wednesday, the beginning of Lent, townsfolk whoop it up with the masked-dance Rubios (Blondes), a parody of the Spanish conquistadores, and the Machos dance.

Juxtlahuaca, moreover, is a center of **pelota mixteca,** the Mixtec version of the ancient Mesoamerican ball game. Although commonly played with a *hule* (natural rubber) ball, the local variation is to use a big leather ball. Players wrap their hands in thick cloth and bat the ball in a court, not unlike tennis. Local teams get ready for the yearly November 20 and February 5 tournaments nearly every

THE MIXTECA

EASTER CALENDAR

Although Christian religious denominations' Easter calendars vary, virtually all Western Christian churches follow the same calendar as the Roman Catholic version, universally used in Mexico. This calendar originated with the Council of Nicaea, which, in A.D. 325, set Easter as the first Sunday after the first full moon of spring (or, more precisely, the first full moon after the vernal equinox, which the church authorities fixed as March 21).

The Easter season customarily kicks off with **Carnaval**, a rip-roaring party that runs the few days preceding **Miercoles de Ceniza** (Ash Wednesday), when all merriment ceases. Ash Wednesday, in turn fixed as the 46th day

before Easter Sunday, occurs most often in February, and marks the beginning of **Lent**, a period of penitence and fasting. The gravity of Lent is literally rubbed in via ashes that the faithful get smeared onto their foreheads during solemn Ash Wednesday Christian church ceremonies worldwide.

In Mexico, religious processions and sober observances continue on each of the subsequent six Fridays. **Domingo de Ramos** (Palm Sunday) immediately follows the fifth Friday, and finally, after the sixth, or **Viernes Santa** (Good Friday), **Domingo Gloria** (Easter Sunday) breaks the fast of Lent as folks celebrate the risen Christ with joy and feasting.

---

afternoon in the long sandy court marked out just below the church.

Information and Services

Change money at the air-conditioned **HSBC** (on Lázaro Cárdenas behind and a block south of the church, tel. 953/554-0427 or 953/554-0428, 9 A.M.–6 P.M. Mon.–Fri., 9 A.M.–3 P.M. Sat.) with ATM. Otherwise, go to Juxtlahuaca's **Banamex** (on Benito Juárez, two blocks uphill from the plaza, tel. 953/554-0417, 9 A.M.–4 P.M. Mon.–Fri.), also with an ATM.

Juxtlahuaca's *correo* (on Porfirio Díaz, no phone, 8 A.M.–4:30 P.M. Mon.–Fri.) is on the northwest plaza corner. The neighboring *telecomunicaciones* (on Porfirio Díaz, half a block downhill from *correo*, fax 953/554-0044, 9 A.M.–3 P.M. Mon.–Fri., 9 A.M.–noon Sat.) provides public fax and money orders. For after-hours long-distance phone and fax, go to either of the two private *larga distancias* on the plaza's south side.

Access the Internet at **Bin@ry Internet** (on Lázaro Cárdenas, south side, corner of Libertad, tel. 953/554-0872, 8 A.M.–10 P.M. daily).

For photographic supplies and services, go to the photo shop **Konica** (9 A.M.–6:30 P.M. Mon.–Sat.).

Get laundry done at **Lavandería Yvet** (on

Lázaro Cárdenas, north end, tel. 953/554-1356, 8 A.M.–8 P.M. daily).

Some doctor-owned pharmacies on Lázaro Cárdenas, such as Doctor Amadeo T. Chaves' **Farmacia Diana Luz** (Lázaro Cárdenas, tel. 953/554-0014, 9 A.M.–10 P.M. daily) are open long hours for consultation, prescriptions, and sales right on the spot. For hospital and emergency medical service, Juxtlahuaca has a **general hospital** (about 1.6 km/1 mi north of town on the Huajuapan highway, tel. 953/554-0307, 953/554-0308, or 953/554-0309).

Getting There and Away

A few long-distance bus lines connect Juxtlahuaca with various Oaxaca and national destinations. Most terminals are downhill near the highway. From their terminal at the foot of Melchor Ocampo, first-class **Omnibus Cristóbal Colón** and second-class **Sur** (tel. 953/554-0181) connect via Highways 182 and 190, north with Huajuapan, continuing to Mexico City (Tapo and Norte terminals), via either Puebla (by the expressway) or Cuautla, Morelos (by Hwy. 190). One weekly (Sunday only) departure connects with Oaxaca.

Additionally, second-class **Sur** offers many connections: north with Huajuapan, continuing to Mexico City; and east with Oaxaca

City, via Tlaxiaco. They all depart out of the Sur **downtown station** (at the north end of Lázaro Cárdenas, corner of Progreso, tel. 953/554-0181).

Aging and worn second-class **Boquerón** buses offer connections south with Putla, continuing to Pinotepa Nacional on the coast; and north with Tonalá and Huajuapan from their stop, also near the foot of Melchor Ocampo.

Furthermore, **Transportes Turísticos Mixteca Baja** passenger vans (on Díaz, corner of Allenda, tel. 953/554-0813), a few doors downhill from the Hotel Diana, provide fast connections north, via Tonalá, with Huajuapan; and northeast, with Oaxaca, via Tlaxiaco.

For **drivers,** paved (but sometimes potholed) mountain roads connect Juxtlahuaca with Oaxaca destinations: north with Huajuapan, 100 kilometers (62 mi), 2.5 hours; south with Putla de Guerrro, via Oaxaca Highway 182 (32 km/20 mi), thence via National Highway 125 (28 km/17 mi), a total of 60 kilometers (37 mi), in about an hour; or east, with Tlaxiaco, via Oaxaca Highway 182 (32 km/20 mi), then via National Highway 125 (48 km/30 mi), a total of 80 kilometers (50 mi), in about two hours.

The Mixteca Alta: Roof of Oaxaca

The Mixteca Alta, Oaxaca's temperate Mixtec highland, is a land poor in gold but rich in scenic and cultural assets: Airy mountain vistas, colorful village markets, pine-scented breezes, beloved old churches, tumbling waterfalls, ancient ruins, and crystalline springs await the traveler who ventures into the Mixteca Alta.

Moreover, travel within the Mixteca Alta is not difficult. Tlaxiaco, with its hotels, restaurants, bus connections, and services, is a good base for exploring the Mixteca Alta. From Tlaxiaco, roads lead out east past cool green mountain vistas to the enigmatic ruins at Huamelulpan and Achiutla, south over the airy Chalcatongo plateau to the Cascada Esmeralda at Yosundua, and west to the friendly little Mixtec-speaking museum towns of Cuquila and San Miguel Progreso.

ASUNCIÓN TLAXIACO

Asunción Tlaxiaco (ah-soon-see-OHN tlah-shee-AH-koh) is far more important than its population of about 20,000 would imply. Tlaxiaco (Place of the Ball Game) is the economic capital of the entire Mixteca Alta, a magnet for many hundreds of vendors from all over central and southern Mexico and thousands more native folks who swarm into town for the **Saturday tianguis** (native town market), second only to the big Saturday market in Oaxaca City.

Tlaxiaco, also capital of its own governmental district, was even more important in times past. During the "Order and Progress" of President Porfirio Díaz (1876–1910), Tlaxiaco's significance perhaps eclipsed even Oaxaca City. Its key position on the trade route between Puebla-Veracruz and the southern Pacific coast, as well as its large hinterland population, made Tlaxiaco a key trading and supply center for much of southwest Mexico. Rich merchants and entrepreneurs, both Mexican and foreign, together with wealthy *hacendados* (landed gentry), constituted a local upper crust who, for a generation, earned Tlaxiaco the unofficial title of "Little Paris."

The Dominican missionary padres certainly understood Tlaxiaco's importance as early as 1550, when Friar Francisco Marín began building the monumental town church, the Templo de la Asunción. Scholars have identified details in the church's decorations that resemble those of the main church in the city of Caceres, Spain. This link has added a piece to one of the puzzles of Oaxaca's great Dominican churches: Where did the Dominican clerics, presumably isolated in the Oaxaca hinterlands, acquire the skill to create the masterpiece churches of

THE MIXTECA

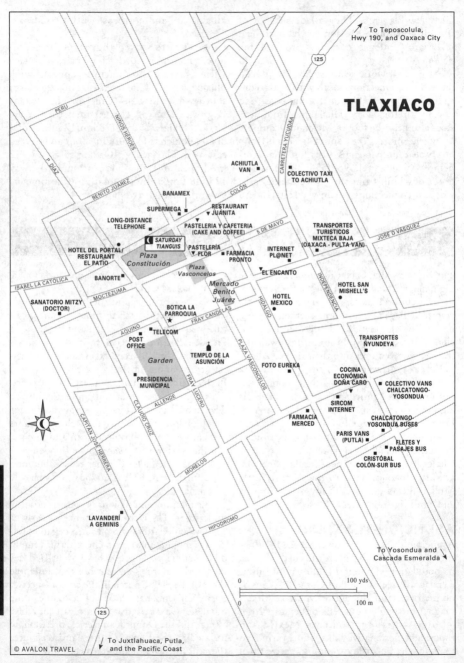

THE MIXTECA

TLAXIACO

To Teposcolula,
Hwy 190, and Oaxaca City

125

PERU

NIÑOS HEROES

P. DIAZ

BENITO JUAREZ

CARRETERA YUCUDAA

COLÓN

ACHIUTLA
VAN

COLECTIVO TAXI
TO ACHIUTLA

BANAMEX

SUPERMEGA

RESTAURANT
JUANITA

LONG-DISTANCE
TELEPHONE

PASTELERIA Y CAFETERIA
(CAKE AND COFFEE)

5 DE MAYO

JOSE D VASQUEZ

TRANSPORTES
TURISTICOS
MIXTECA BAJA
(OAXACA - PULTA VAN)

SATURDAY
TIANGUIS

HOTEL DEL PORTAL/
RESTAURANT
EL PATIO

Plaza
Constitución

PASTELERÍA
FLOR

FARMACIA
PRONTO

INTERNET
PL@NET

BANORTE

Plaza
Vasconcelos

EL ENCANTO

INDEPENDENCIA

HOTEL SAN
MISHELL'S

ISABEL LA CATÓLICA

MOCTEZUMA

Mercado
Benito
Juárez

HOTEL
MEXICO

SANATORIO MITZY
(DOCTOR)

BOTICA LA
PARROQUIA

FRAY CANDELAS

HIDALGO

AQUINO

TELECOM

POST
OFFICE

Garden

TEMPLO DE LA
ASUNCIÓN

PLAZA VASCONCELOS

TRANSPORTES
ÑYUNDEYA

FOTO EUREKA

COCINA
ECONÓMICA
DOÑA CARO

COLECTIVO VANS
CHALCATONGO-
YOSONDUA

PRESIDENCIA
MUNICIPAL

CLAUDIO CRUZ

ALLENDE

FRAY LUCERO

SIRCOM
INTERNET

CHALCATONGO-
YOSONDUA BUSES

FARMACIA
MERCED

PARIS VANS
(PUTLA)

FLETES Y
PASAJES BUS

CRISTÓBAL
COLÓN-SUR BUS

CAPITAN JOSE HERRERA

MORELOS

LAVANDERÍ
A GEMINIS

HIPODROMO

To Yosondua and
Cascada Esmeralda

0   100 yds

0   100 m

125

To Juxtlahuaca, Putla,
and the Pacific Coast

© AVALON TRAVEL

Yanhuitlán, Teposcolula, Coixtlahuaca, and Tlaxiaco? The answer may lie in a previously unknown connection between the Dominican friars and the noted Rodrigo Gil de Montañon, master of Spanish Gothic–Plateresque architecture and builder of the Caceres church.

◖ Tlaxiaco Saturday *Tianguis*

Let **Plaza Constitución,** the hub of the Tlaxiaco market, a few blocks uphill from the cluttered and bumpy through-town highway, be your key to finding your way around town. Main east–west streets Colón and 5 de Mayo run along the north and south sides, respectively, of Plaza Constitución. East of the plaza, they intersect the other main town streets, Independencia and Hidalgo, which both run north, uphill from the highway. The perfect spot to view all of this is the front porch of the Hotel del Portal, which perches on the uphill (north) side of the plaza. From there, you'll see the town clock in the plaza foreground, and in the background, the bell tower of the town church, Templo de la Asunción, a few hundred yards to the southwest. To the right of the church, behind some trees on the west side of a shady *jardín,* stands the town *presidencia municipal.*

the Tlaxiaco Saturday *tianguis*

© BRUCE WHIPPERMAN

Make sure to arrive in Tlaxiaco by noon on Saturday, in time to soak in its spreading, colorful, Saturday *tianguis* (native town market). It's fun to just wander around beneath the rainbow of awnings shading a galaxy of merchandise, both modern and traditional. Especially interesting are the time-tested handmade goods: *calabazas* (gourds) cut and carved into bowls, utensils, and musical instruments; extensive assortments of forest-gathered roots, seeds, bark, dried flowers, and nuts, ready to brew into teas to relieve dozens of illnesses; traditional clothes—hand-embroidered *huipiles* and *blusas* from all over Oaxaca; *canastas, tenates, petates* (reed baskets, sturdy woven palm-leaf baskets, and mats); soft sombreros, not unlike famed "panama hats" also from palm; and leather *cinturones* (belts), *bolsas* (bags), purses, and *billeteras* (billfolds).

The big plus of all the bustle, of course, is the people, especially the native women, who really run the whole show. The men, who help transport the goods, usually stand back (and sometimes, unfortunately, get drunk) and let their spouses do the buying and selling. Perhaps the best two spots for native action are the narrow **Plaza Vasconcelos,** which heads downhill for a block from the southeast corner of Plaza Constitución, and the front steps of the church, a hubbub of native fruit and vegetable sellers.

While you're people-watching in front of the church, the **Templo de la Asunción,** take a break and step into its cool, calm interior. Although begun in 1550, the church, once a Dominican convent, has been continually modified and strengthened since that time. Towering overhead, a network of unreinforced (no steel: all stone and mortar) Gothic arches have, amazingly, supported the entire ceiling for more than 400 years, freeing the nave from the clutter of columns and creating a heavenly, soaring space for worship, rest, and contemplation.

THE MIXTECA

Tlaxiaco's patron, the Virgen de la Asunción, presides from above the altar. High above her, note the all-seeing Eye of God (which looks every bit like its counterparts that decorate many Buddhist and Hindu stupas in India and Nepal).

Townsfolk celebrate their beloved patron in a pair of annual **fiestas.** The first, the official patronal religious festival, Fiesta de la Virgen de la Asunción (accent on the "o" in "Asunción"), kicks off on the third Sunday in August and continues for two more days with processions, food, and fireworks. The second patronal festival begins on the third Sunday of October and includes fireworks, basketball and *pelota mixteca* (traditional ball game) tournaments, and popular dances.

Botica la Parroquia

Just across the street, north, from the church-front, the Botica la Parroquia (Porfirio Diaz, at the corner of Fray Candelas, tel. 953/552-0008, 8 A.M.–9 P.M. daily) is as much a museum as a pharmacy. Its 150 years of continuous

© BRUCE WHIPPERMAN

The author samples the medicinal brandy at the bar of Botica la Parroquia.

operation, begun by the present owner's great-grandfather and handed down through the family, has resulted in a vast and venerable collection of antique bottles, flasks, urns, mortars and pestles, and a regiment of drawers stuffed with locally gathered barks, leaves, mosses, grasses, flowers, mushrooms, seeds, minerals, and animal parts for compounding into remedies to relieve a host of ailments. For example, you can get *siete aguas* (seven waters) for relief of *mal aire* (bad air), a folk name for a common ailment with symptoms of weakness and fever; often, but not always, modern doctors diagnose *mal aire* as malaria. You can also get *catalan* and arnica for aches and pains; and, for whatever else ails you, homemade herbal brandy is dispensed in two-peso portions from a gallon jug on the front counter.

The present owner explains his pharmacy's history and mission: "Grandad was the town doctor. Everyone came to him when they were sick. He hand-prepared all of his prescriptions. My mom still does it."

Accommodations
UNDER $25

A block and a half west of Plaza Constitución stands the downscale old standby, the family-run **Hotel Mexico** (Hidalgo 13, tel. 953/552-0086, $15 s or d, $23 t "old" rooms, $25 s or d, $29 t "new" rooms). Rooms in "new" (private bath) and "old" (shared bath) sections surround a rambling inside patio. All of the 20-odd rooms are clean; the "old" rooms are plainly furnished, while the "new" are thoughtfully decorated with polished wood furnishings, attractive bedspreads, and drapes. Rooms all come with hot water, available only in the morning until 11 A.M.; credit cards are not accepted.

Located a few blocks southeast of the town center, the **Hotel San Mishell's** (Independencia 11, tel. 953/552-0064, $13–21 s, $21–25 d) offers attentive on-site family management. The 20 superior-grade rooms in a two-story wing surround an inviting inner garden patio. Inside, rooms are clean, carpeted, and thoughtfully decorated. Outside the rooms, on a shady garden-view porch, guests enjoy soft chairs for reading and relaxing. Standard-grade (shared bath) rooms occupy a two-story tier beside an adjacent parking patio, and do not have TVs. All guests enjoy hot-water shower-baths, parking, and a breakfast restaurant, but credit cards are not accepted.

$25-50

Of Tlaxiaco's hotels, the semi-deluxe **(Hotel del Portal** (Constitución 2, tel. 953/552-0154, $23–28 s, d one bed; $26–35 d, t two beds), at the north-side plaza-front, affords a superb vantage for soaking in the market action and exploring the colorful town center. Inside, past the reception, you enter an elegantly restored grand patio, softly illuminated by an overhead skylight. The three stories of approximately 50 rooms encircle a back parking courtyard. The rooms come in two grades, standard and semi-deluxe (invitingly decorated, with wall-to-wall carpet), and all are clean, comfortable, and well maintained, with hot-water shower-baths, TV, and parking; Visa and Mastercard are accepted.

Food

Taco stands and upstairs *fondas* (food stalls) at the covered **Mercado Benito Juárez** (one block south of the Plaza Constitución's southeast corner) are your best source of economical meals and snacks. Furthermore, a homey sit-down *comedor,* the **Cocina Economica Doña Caro** (Morelos 13, no phone, 8 A.M.–8 P.M. Mon.–Sat., $4–5), between Independencia and Hidalgo, two blocks east and three blocks south of the plaza's southeast corner, serves from a bountiful menu, for example, *huevos rancheros* and *mexicanos* for breakfast; and choice of either steaming chicken, turkey, or tamales smothered in *mole,* or savory pork and beef *guisados* (stews) for their all-inclusive four-course *comida* lunch or supper.

Basic groceries are available at plaza-front *abarroterías* (grocery stores), notably at **Super Mega** (Constitución, tel. 953/552-0179, 8:30 A.M.–9 P.M. Mon.–Sat., 8:30 A.M.–6:30 P.M. Sun.), on the plaza's northeast side, two doors east of the Hotel del Portal.

Baked goods are also sold at several stalls at the Mercado Benito Juárez and **Pastelería Flor** (Cinco de Mayo, half a block east of the market plaza's southeast corner, tel. 953/552-0555, 9 A.M.–10 P.M. daily), with a host of delights, including chocolate, three-milk, cheese, and lemon cakes, good coffee, and hamburgers, *tortas,* and hot dogs to boot.

A sprinkling of restaurants (some very good) cater to the trickle of visitors and handful of Tlaxiaco residents who can afford to eat out. Tlaxiaco's fanciest is the **Restaurant El Patio** (Constitución 2, tel. 953/552-0154, 8 A.M.–9 P.M. daily, $4–5), in the airy inner courtyard of the Hotel del Portal. Oaxacan cuisine is the main event here; pick from a long list of appetizers, such as roasted onions with leaves of nopal or tortilla soup; for a main dish, you might choose *pierna de puerco* (leg of pork) smothered in rich dark *mole* or Tlaxiaco-style tacos.

For a leisurely *comida corrida* (set lunch) or a bountiful à la carte selection on a warm afternoon, go to refined, airy restaurant **(El Encanto** (Vásquez 6, tel. 953/552-0529, 8 A.M.–9 P.M. Mon.–Sat., $3–7, set lunch $4), a block south and a block and a half east of the main plaza's southeast corner. Find them open also for à la carte breakfast and *cena* (supper).

Information and Services

Change money at Tlaxiaco's plaza-front **Banamex** (Colón 1, tel. 953/552-0166 or 953/552-0133, 9 A.M.–4 P.M. Mon.–Fri., 9 A.M.–1 P.M. Sat.) with ATM.

Alternatively, go to **Banorte** (at the plaza's southwest corner, tel. 953/552-0662, 9 A.M.–5 P.M. Mon.–Fri.) for similar services and ATM.

Find the *correo* (tel. 953/552-2126, 9 A.M.–5:30 P.M. Mon.–Fri., 9 A.M.–1 P.M. Sat.), on the north side of the *jardín* in front of the church. Next door, at *telecomunicaciones* (tel. 953/552-0190, fax 953/552-0465, 8 A.M.–7:30 P.M. Mon.–Fri., 9 A.M.–noon Sat.), you can send or receive a fax or money order.

Telephone long distance or send a fax at the big **SAM** *caseta larga distancia* (Constitución,

MEXICAN NAMES

Nearly every Mexican, from native country folks to pure Spanish bluebloods, goes by his or her Spanish-origin names. Outsiders, confounded by long handles, such as Doña Juana María López de Díaz, wonder how Mexican names got so complicated.

The preceding "Doña Juana" example is especially complicated, because it's a typical woman's name, which is generally more complex than that of a typical man.

So, let's explain a man's name first. Take the national hero, Vicente Ramón Guerrero Saldaña. Vicente is his first given name; Ramón, the second given name, corresponds to the "middle" name in the United States. The third, Guerrero, is customarily the father's first surname; and the last, Saldaña, his mother's first surname. Only on formal occasions are men referred to with all four of their names. Simply, "Vicente Guerrero" would do most of the time.

Now, back to "Doña Juana." I threw a curve at you by introducing "Doña." It's an honorific, used as "Dame," for a distinguished woman. ("Don" is the corresponding honorific for Spanish men.)

So, skipping the honorific, women's names start out like men's: First given name, Juana; second given name, María; and father's first surname, López.

Now, things get more complicated. For unmarried women, the naming is the same as for men. But when a woman gets married, she customarily replaces her second surname with her husband's first surname, preceded by "de," meaning "of." So, in the example, Juana is evidently a married woman, who has substituted "de Díaz" (her husband's first surname being Díaz) for her second surname, all adding up to Juana María López de Díaz.

Thankfully, however, informal names for women also are simplified. Juana, above, would ordinarily shorten her name down to her first given name followed by her husband's first surname: simply Juana Díaz.

All the above notwithstanding, many Mexican women do not go along with this male-dominated system at all and simply use their maiden names as they were known before they were married.

---

on the plaza's north side, next to the Hotel del Portal, tel. 953/552-0313, 953/552-0314, or 953/552-0147, 7 A.M.–11 P.M. daily). Alternatively (and more economically), buy a commonly available Ladatel telephone card and use it to call home in the United States, Canada, or Europe ($2 for four minutes).

Answer your email and access the Internet at **Internet Pl@net** (on Vasconcelos, near corner of Independencia, no phone, 8 A.M.–10 P.M. Mon.–Sat., 10 A.M.–10 P.M. Sun.), two blocks west and a block south of the plaza's southwest corner.

If you need a doctor, ask at your hotel desk for a recommendation or contact one of Tlaxiaco's highly recommended physicians: such as Dr. Javier Noé Alavez Cervantes at **Sanatorio Mitzy** (Moctezuma 4, tel./fax 953/552-0058), a block and a half west from the plaza; or physician-surgeon **Dr. Geraldo Cruz Vela** (Aldama 6, tel. 953/552-0210).

For nonprescription medicines and drugs, try either **Farmacia La Merced** (corner of Morelos and Hidalgo, tel. 953/552-0483, 8 A.M.–9 P.M. Mon.–Sat., 10 A.M.–2 P.M. Sun.), downhill three blocks from the plaza, or **Farmacia Pronto** (Cinco de Mayo, tel. 953/552-0664, 9 A.M.–9 P.M. Mon.–Sat.), half a block east of the plaza's southeast corner.

In police, fire, or medical emergencies call the *policía municipal* (tel. 953/552-1021) or hire a taxi to take you to them.

For film, development, and some digital and film point-and-shoot cameras and supplies, go to Tlaxiaco's Fuji film dealer, **Foto Eureka** (Hidalgo, tel. 953/552-0249, 8 A.M.–9 P.M. Mon.–Sat., 8 A.M.–2 P.M. Sun.), two blocks south, one block east of the plaza.

Tlaxiaco's friendly, family-owned laundry is **Lavandería Geminis** (Capitán José Herrera 20, tel. 953/552-0708, 8 A.M.–9 P.M. Mon.–Sat.). Find it on Herrera: from the plaza's southwest corner, walk a block west, then three blocks south.

Getting There and Away

A welter of taxis, local buses and minivans, and long-distance buses deposit and pick up a small army of passengers daily downhill on Highway 125, locally called Avenida Hipodromo as it runs east–west along the south edge of downtown, and Independencia after it turns north and continues along the east edge of downtown.

Long-distance service includes **Sur** and **Omnibus Cristóbal Colón,** from their station (Hipodromo 24 B, tel. 953/552-0182), half a block west of the Independencia corner. There, buses connect east and southeast with Teposcolula, Yanhuitlán, Nochixtlán, and Oaxaca City; and north with Tamazulapan, Huajuapan, Puebla, Cuautla (Morelos), and Mexico City.

Also, on Hipodromo, a few doors east, second-class **Fletes y Pasajes** (tel. 953/552-0432) long-distance buses connect east and southeast with Teposcolula, Yanhuitlán, Nochixtlán, and Oaxaca City; and north with Mexico City (Tapo terminal) by the expressway, via Coixtlahuaca, Tepelmeme, Tehuacán, and Puebla.

Furthermore, a pair of good van services provide fast and frequent connections. On Independencia, three blocks north of Hipodromo, **Transportes Turística Mixteca Baja** (Independencia, tel. 953/552-0308) connects very frequently with Oaxaca City, via Teposcolula and Nochixtlán, south with Putla (where connections are available for the Pacific coast), and Yosundua (around noon and 6 P.M. daily). Alternatively, reliable **RAMSA** vans (Hipodromo 13), next to Omnibus Cristóbal Colón, connect frequently northeast with Oaxaca City, and south with Putla.

Drivers can connect southerly, to or from Tlaxiaco, with Putla, by Highway 125 (75 km/47 mi), in about two hours; westerly, with Juxtlahuaca via Highways 125 and 182 (80 km/50 mi), also in about two hours; and easterly with Teposcolula (42 km/26 mi), in about an hour, thence another three hours, to or from Oaxaca City.

SOUTH OF TLAXIACO

Although the glorious Cascada Esmeralda (Emerald Waterfall) at the end of the road is reason enough to venture out on this 171-kilometer (106 mi) round-trip excursion, the sights along the way make the journey doubly enjoyable. You'll gaze at a succession of mighty pine- and oak-studded mountains, mile upon mile of green, terraced fields, and, oddly in contrast, one of the most spectacularly eroded landscapes in Oaxaca. Moreover, you'll pass as many log cabins here than on a trip through all of Montana and Wyoming. And if you go on Sunday, you'll get a chance to visit a pair of busy country markets. Finally, self-contained RV or tent campers can enjoy a superbly scenic natural camping site at the dramatic top of Cascada Esmeralda. The all-paved route climbs to the top of the Mixteca Alta—the 2,700-meter (9,000 ft) cool, fertile, Chalcatongo plateau—before descending to Yosundua and the subtropical Esmeralda valley, where on a clear day, folks say, you can glimpse the blue Pacific.

The Road to Chalcatongo

Start out early (8 A.M. by bus, no later than 10 A.M. by car) because in the Mixteca (Land of the Clouds), especially in the summer–fall rainy season, sunny mornings often turn gray, drizzly, and cool by mid-afternoon. By minibus, go from the **Transportistas Ñundeya** minibus terminal (on Independencia, half a block uphill from Hipodromo). Catch one of their morning departures to Chalcotongo and Yosundua.

Drivers, mark your odometer and head south along the southern prolongation of Independencia, from the Highway 125 Independencia-Hipodromo corner. It's best to fill up with gasoline in town before departure (gas on east, Oaxaca City, side only). There is only one gas station en route, at Chalcatongo (although stores along the way do sell unleaded regular). If you want to eat well along the way,

THE MIXTECA

take your own picnic, especially during the winter, when upcountry fresh fruit and veggie supplies are at a low ebb.

At kilometer 16 (mi 10), the road reaches an overlook where you can gaze down upon the **Magdalena Peñasco** (Stony) valley, with erosion so dramatic that, like the scenic Badlands of Dakota, it's a sight in itself. The reason isn't so difficult to figure out. Long ago, the people cut the trees for fuel and houses, then farmed the hills without contour terracing. They let sheep and goats overgraze the meadows, and when downpours began forming gullies, it was too late. Today the entire valley looks like a red, rutted devil's playground.

As you continue downhill, you'll see folks along the road weaving palm leaves, especially on Sunday, as they walk toward the weekly Magdalena Peñasco *tianguis* (native town market). Passing the town square and market, at around kilometer 19 (mi 12), notice one of Magdalena's major public buildings—a turquoise-blue log house—on the right.

Around kilometer 34 (mi 21), continuing through **San Mateo Peñasco,** it's difficult not to be awed by the towering stone-faced mountain on the right. In times past (or maybe even in times present) this awesomely rugged rampart, which local people call simply La Peña (The Rock), must have been a sacred mountain, with its own Señor del Monte (Lord of the Mountain).

Today, a cross stands partway up the slope, where the villagers climb on May 3, the Día de la Santa Cruz (Day of the Holy Cross). Although arduous, the hike to the summit appears doable with effort by fit people wearing hats and sturdy shoes and carrying drinking water. Don't attempt it, however, without permission from the San Mateo Peñasco municipal authorities, who can probably suggest a guide whom you can hire to show the way.

In contrast to the eroded Magdalena valley, the surroundings of **San Pedro Molinos,** at kilometer 45 (mi 28), appear the model of progressive farming practice. Lush valley-bottom fields give way to terraced, mid-slope gardens, which lead to a crown of thick summit

forests. San Pedro Molinos town is marked by its spiffy, portaled *presidencia municipal.*

Farther on, at **Santa Catarina Ticúa** around kilometer 50 (mi 31), note the uniquely picturesque three-story log house, on the right just as you arrive at the town plaza and church. Next, step across the plaza and take a look inside the brilliantly painted 18th-century church, dedicated to martyr Saint Catherine. If you're lucky, you'll arrive on November 24 or 25, when local people are celebrating Santa Catarina with processions, fireworks, sports contests, and dances. If not, at least you can admire the Mixtec pre-Columbian floral designs on the church's walls and ceiling, and maybe afterward, if it's a warm day, you might pause for a dip in the community swimming pool (if it's been maintained; it was algae-stained at my last visit) outside, next to the church.

Chalcatongo

At around kilometer 60 (mi 37), you reach high and cool, sometimes even chilly, Chalcatongo (pop. 2,000). Chalcatongo has two plazas; the first one bordered by the distinguished church, the **Templo de la Natividad,** whose patron, the Virgen de la Natividad, townsfolk celebrate with a fiesta on September 8. Chalcatongo is otherwise quiet except for Thursday, when a regiment of local Mixtec-speaking folks and dozens of vendors from as far as Mexico City crowd in for a big country **tianguis** market.

At the second plaza, one block ahead, one block left, stands the *presidencia municipal.* Although the plazas have a few taco shops, only a few places in town serve complete, country-style meals. The best are the immaculate Restaurant El Paisano and the Restaurant El Fortín, both on the north (Tlaxiaco) side of town where, entering town from Tlaxiaco, the truck route bypass forks right. El Fortín is on the right, just before the fork.

◖ El Paisano (around the corner, just past the Hotel 2000, 7 A.M.–8 P.M. daily, $2–3) serves hearty breakfasts (*huevos a la Mexicana,* pancakes, *chilaquiles* and eggs) until noon, and a filling *comida* (pork in red *mole,* chiles rellenos in tomato sauce) until 5 P.M., and supper choices of tacos, quesadillas, eggs, and *tortas* until closing. **El Fortín,** also highly recommended locally, has similar hours and food, as does a the third restaurant choice, **El Calvario** (corner of Guerrero and Insurgentes, 2nd floor), on the south side, on the highway out of town.

If you decide to stay overnight, Chalcatongo has a good family-run hotel, the **Hotel Lazo** (Cinco de Mayo 67, tel. 953/533 4061, $10 s, $17 d in one bed, $24 d in two beds, $30 t), in the south-side neighborhood. The hotel, built around an inviting interior patio courtyard, offers 24 very clean, comfortable (but smallish) rooms, with 1–3 beds and private hot-water shower-baths.

Yosundua and Cascada Esmeralda

Drivers lucky enough to arrive in Yosundua (at km 82/mi 51) on Sunday will probably find the way to the waterfall blocked by the big, colorful *tianguis* (native town market). Stroll around for a while, then detour downhill, then ahead, via the street that runs in front of the big church, **Templo Santiago Apóstol.** The church is dedicated to Saint James the Apostle, whom townsfolk celebrate July 23–26. Bus passengers should either hire a taxi or hike straight ahead from the Yosundua bus stop about 4 kilometers (2.5 mi) and 300 meters (1,000 ft) downhill to the Cascada Esmeralda.

If you're hungry, stop by the clean, family-run, home-style **Restaurant Manantial** (Restaurant Spring; 8 A.M.–9 P.M. daily, $2–8), named for the town's crystal-clear water source, nearby. It's at the far, southeast edge of town, where the gravel road heads south to the Cascada Esmeralda.

If you miss the last bus back, you can stay at the basic but serviceable **Hotel California** (no phone, $12 s or d one bed, $18 d in two beds), whose personable owner returned from California with a wad of cash and decided to build himself a hotel. He now has 31 mostly empty, spare but clean rooms, with private hot-water shower-baths. You can't miss the place, because, except for the church, it's the biggest building (downhill two blocks on the right as you enter) in town.

Another overnight option, for people who are equipped, is to set up a tent or park their self-contained RV in the informal meadow campground at the top of the Cascada Esmeralda, at kilometer 85 (mi 53). There, the blue-green (brown during the summer rains, however) Río Esmeralda pauses a while in an inviting pool (safe only at low water) before it plunges over the cliff. The road winds another few hundred yards down a steep grade; continue on foot down a steep, short path to the foot of the falls, where you're surrounded by natural beauty. On one side, the waterfall, split into a lacy network of petite cascades, cools you with gentle spray, while on the other, far below, a grand, sun-dappled verdant valley of field and forest nestles beneath a host of sharp, soaring peaks.

EAST OF TLAXIACO

The country east of Tlaxiaco undulates over small fertile vales and green pine-forested hilltops, many crowned with the ruins of ancient buried towns and cities. Two of the largest and most interesting of those ruins are at Achiutla and Huamelulpan, not far from Tlaxiaco.

San Miguel Achiutla

The archaeological site at Achiutla (ah-shee-YOO-tlah, pop. 1,000) stands among Oaxaca's historically most intriguing, partly because it contains both pre- and post-conquest ruins. These include the remains of the earthquake-collapsed original Dominican church and a grand pre-conquest ruined complex, once the site of a renowned 15th-century Mixtec oracle.

GETTING THERE

The gorgeous pine-forested mountains and lush (summer–fall rainy season) valleys you pass along the way are part of the fun of Achiutla. Bus travelers go most conveniently by the minibuses that leave for Achiutla (via Santa Caterina Tayata) from the corner of Calle 5 de Mayo and Highway 125 (Av. Independencia) at the northeast corner of downtown Tlaxiaco. Alternatively, bargain for a taxi to take you to the Achiutla turnoff (signed Santa Catarina Tayata) about

THE MIXTECA

14 kilometers (nine mi) east of town, then catch a truck from there. If so, find out the price—ask, *"¿Cuanto cuesta a Achiutla?"* ("How much to Achiutla?")—before getting on.

For drivers, the road is broad and paved all the way to Achiutla. From Tlaxiaco, along Highway 125, drive east about 14 kilometers (nine mi); or west from Teposcolula about 27 kilometers (17 mi). Set your odometer at the signed Santa Catarina Tayata turnoff. After 1.9 kilometers (1.2 mi), bear left at the fork, and continue through Santa Catarina Tayata (8.4 km/5.2 mi) and follow the left fork (8.7 km/5.4 mi). At 10.3 kilometers (6.4 mi) pass over Río Tayata (Puente Sabino) bridge, above the idyllic grove of ancient *ahuehuete (sabino)* (bald cypress) trees. Some of the gnarled giants, three meters in diameter, must be at least a thousand years old. The adjacent creekside meadows provide good informal camping. (Bring water.) First, however, get permission (which is usually no problem) from the municipal authorities at Santa Catarina Tayata.

At kilometer 17 (mi 10.5) you get the first glimpse of the old San Miguel Achiutla church on the hill straight ahead. Pass over another Puente Sabino bridge at kilometer 18 (mi 11) and continue straight ahead for the old church on the right, ruins on left (20.3 km/12.6 mi). San Miguel Achiutla village is a mile and a half farther, at 22.5 kilometers (14 mi).

EXPLORING THE SITE

The area of historical and archaeological interest lies on an airy, scenic hilltop west of the existing antique church. Christened the Templo de San Miguel Achiutla, the baroque (circa 1700) ex-convent stands on the rise to the south of the road. It supplanted an even older church, now in ruins, on the other side of the road, probably built atop the pre-conquest oracle temple. Beyond that rises a cemetery occupying what appear to be three pre-conquest ceremonial plazas cut, like grand stair steps, into a mountainside that stretches another 1.6 kilometers (one mi) to a high, breezy summit.

First, however, walk south across the broad atrium that leads to the present church. On

the original 1558 Achiutla church, now in ruins

© BRUCE WHIPPERMAN

your way, take a look at the pair of ponderous bronze bells, dated 1848, hanging from the rustic ground-level *campanario* ("bell tower"). The Dominicans built the church probably during the late 1600s, after the original across the road (that was begun in 1558) was destroyed by an earthquake. The new church, dedicated to Archangel St. Michael, grew into a prosperous vicarage, surrounded by a cluster of dependent congregations. Times changed, however. The once-new church is now crumbling and nearly abandoned. Its doors open regularly only for Sunday mass at 10 A.M., after which folks lock up and return downhill for an 11 A.M. mass at the church in town.

A major exception occurs during festivals, celebrating the Sacred Heart of Jesus (June 19), **Carnaval** (Sun., Mon., and Tues. before Ash Wednesday), and especially the **Fiesta de San Miguel** (Sept. 21–29), when masses fill the old church every day.

At this writing, a combined federal-state effort is restoring the old ex-convent section as a museum, similar to what they did at Yanhuitlán. In the future, a museum volunteer might be available to show you around inside the old church.

For the present, the old place is certainly well worth finding the *sacristan* (church-keeper, often nearby) who might open the door for you.

If so, you'll see the inside completely unrestored except for the gilded, baroque main altarpiece, recently refurbished after it collapsed under its own weight. In addition to the native artists' colorful floral designs, the nave walls hold a gallery of precious 16th-century paintings. Don't miss the one showing the angel St. Michael leading a mortal into heaven. Up front, bats flit and flutter out of the baptismal chapel on the left. On the opposite side, note the unusual screened platform high on the south wall, said to have accommodated cloistered nuns who nevertheless wanted to view mass in the nave. The door on the nave's right front leads to an open courtyard, which in turn leads to the ex-convent's former working and living quarters.

Outside, across the road, the crumbling ruin of the original church stands atop the once-famous Achiutla oracle temple. This spot abounds with legends. A Mixtec codex records that one Tilantongo queen was born from a tree in Achiutla. So powerful was Achiutla's magic that people came, believing it to be the home of an all-seeing spirit, an oracle, known then as the Corazón del Pueblo (Heart of the People), who, acting through the local priests, could portend future events. When Cortés threatened his capital, no less than the Emperor Moctezuma sent emissaries to Achiutla. They asked that proper sacrifices be made to the oracle in return for a divination of the result of Cortés's threat. The answer was that Moctezuma's grand empire would be destroyed.

Past the ruined church, climb along paths through the ancient retaining walls, built by long-dead Mixtec masons, to the cemetery's upper levels. Gaze out toward the fertile Achiutla valley far below, encircled by a verdant crown of pine-capped mountains.

Nearby, scattered around you, the cemetery's oldest legible tombstones date from around 1900; many others, unreadably weathered and crumbling, appear much older. Buried beneath those—no one yet knows how deep or old—lie the relics of Achiutla's past.

SERVICES

Drowsy little Achiutla town downhill has a basic grocery store, a *comedor*, a *centro de salud*, police (at the *presidencia municipal*), and gasoline, at a store at the west edge of town.

San Martín Huamelulpan

The community museum at Huamelulpan (oo-wah-may-LOOL-pahn), about two kilometers (1.2 mi) off Highway 125, five kilometers (three mi) east of the Achiutla turnoff, was built partly to display the artifacts uncovered at the town's important archaeological zone. The National Archaeology and History Institute (INAH) installed the museum's archaeological exhibits in 1978. Later, the local community took over and did its own oral history project

DUENDES: SPIRITS OF MEXICO

Once upon a time, most everyone believed that the world was full of spirits that inhabited every object in creation: trees, rocks, animals, mountains, even the wind and the stars. World mythology is replete with examples, from the leprechauns of Ireland and the fairies of Mount Tirich Mir in Pakistan to the spirits who haunt old Hawaiian *heiaus* (temples) and the *duendes* of Mexico.

Such beliefs persist, especially in the Mixteca countryside. Eventually, many a campesino will take his children to his mountainside cornfield to introduce them to the *duendes*, the elfin beings who folks sometimes glimpse in the shadowed thickets where they hide from mortals.

At the upper end of his field, the campesino father addresses the *duendes*: "With your permission we clear your brush and use your water because it is necessary to nourish our corn and beans. Please allow us, for otherwise, we would starve."

Modernized city Mexicans, generations removed from country village life, often scoff at such antique beliefs. That is, until the family doctor fails to cure their weakened spouse or sick child. Then they often run to a *curandero* or *curandera* (folk healer).

"Enduendado," affliction by an angry *duende*, the *curandero* sometimes diagnoses. Often, the cure is simple and savvy: teas and poultices of forest-gathered herbs. Other times, it is mystical, such as "purifying" by passing an egg all over the afflicted one's body to draw out the illness, and then breaking the egg into a bowl. The shape the broken yolk takes, maybe of a snake, might determine the treatment, which may be long and intricate: massage with lotions of herbs and oils, followed by a *temazcal* (sweat bath) rubdown with rough maguey fibers, all consummated by intense prayers to the Virgin of Guadalupe to force the *duende* to cease the affliction.

Many times, the folk cure fails; other times, however, it succeeds, and with enough frequency to convince millions of Mexicans of the power of the village folk healer to purge a *duende*'s poisonous spell.

during the late 1980s, which resulted in the museum's traditional medicine displays.

Note the sign on the post on the right as you reach the town plaza. It reads, roughly: "Please stop and register at the community museum and get a guide to show you the ruins." If you arrive when the museum is closed, ask around for someone to guide you.

Huamelulpan Museum and Archaeological Zone

The museum is officially called the **Museo Comunitario Ihitalulu** (ee-ee-tah-LOO-loo; no phone, 10 A.M.–5 P.M. Tues.–Sun.), meaning "Beautiful Flower." Inside, on the left after you enter, you'll see the archaeological section first, with its especially notable monolith of Dzahui, the Mixtec god of rain, lightning, and thunder (akin to the Zapotec god Cocijo). Also fascinating are burial remains,

including a complete skeleton and bowls for portions of water, food, and *pulque* (alcoholic beverage) for the afterlife. On the museum's opposite side, find the equally intriguing traditional medicine exhibit, detailing methods that *curanderos* (curers), *yerberas* (herbal healers), and *parteras* (midwives) use to treat their clients. Conditions commonly treated include *el parto* (childbirth), *el empacho* (stomach infections), *mal aire* (shivering, and head and body aches; sometimes diagnosed as malaria), and *el espanto* (soul loss, accompanied by severe anxiety). Displays illustrate many remedies, from herbal teas and *temazcal* hot baths to doses of chicken blood and incantations beseeching forgiveness from earth spirits.

EXPLORING THE ZONE

Leave time for a stroll around the archaeological zone. It was first visited in 1933 by Alfonso

Caso of Monte Albán fame, and it has been intensively excavated and partly reconstructed by several others since the 1950s. Finds reveal that Huamelulpan was a small city occupied between 400 B.C. and A.D. 600, approximately the same epoch as Monte Albán.

The zone rambles extensively over many hundreds of acres, running north of town along an approximate east–west line. The most westerly discovered (but unreconstructed) remains lie on the high west-side **Cerro Volado** hilltop. The most intensively reconstructed portion is the so-called Church Group, near the church, a few hundred yards east beyond the town plaza and museum.

Start at the church itself, which has what appears to be a grinning pre-conquest god of death skeleton-monolith built into its right (south) wall. If you continue walking south along the road in front of the church, you will be passing the partly reconstructed **ball court**, reachable by ascending the rise to the left (east) of the road. Notice, at the ball court's south end, the reconstructed half of its I-shaped layout. Continue east, up the second embankment, to a regal **ceremonial courtyard** climaxed on its east side with an elegant staircase and retaining walls. Climb those stairs to another level and yet another courtyard crowned by an equally elegant but smaller **ceremonial platform.**

Huamelulpan community museum volunteers lead visitors on tours of their archaeological zone, including Cerro Volado, for a fee of about $20. Arrive early and you may be able to arrange such a tour on the spot. Guides and **lodging** at Huamelulpan's tourist-house dormitory can also be reserved ahead of time by leaving a message, including time of arrival and number in your party, at the Huamelulpan long-distance telephone *caseta* (tel. 555/510-4949).

Get to Huamelulpan by car or Tlaxiaco-bound second-class Omnibus Cristóbal Colón Sur, Fletes y Pasajes, or van from Oaxaca City, Nochixtlán, Tamazulapan, or Teposcolula. Get off at the Huamelulpan turnoff on Highway 125, about half an hour (21 km/13 mi) past

Teposcolula. In the reverse direction, drive or ride the same bus and van east from Tlaxiaco a similar 21 kilometers (13 mi), half an hour, and get off at the Huamelulpan side-road turnoff. Continue on foot, or by taxi, about two kilometers (1.2 mi) to the museum on the town plaza.

WEST OF TLAXIACO

This is high, cool country of pine-brushed mountains, villages, and cornfields. The people are reserved but quick to return your wave and smile. They see so few outsiders that, although they try to avoid it, they can't help staring as you pass, wondering why you've come. For at least two of these communities, Santa María Cuquila and San Miguel Progreso, visitors have an immediate reason for coming: to see the community museums.

Santa María Cuquila

The Aztecs, to whom the Cuquila (koo-KEE-lah) people were tributaries at the time of the conquest, coined the name Cuquila, which roughly translates to Snakes in the Brush. The Mixtec-speaking local people, however, previously called their village Ñu Kuiñe, which means "Town of the Tiger" in the local tongue.

Now, Cuquila (pop. 2,000) with the help of the government Centro de Desarollo Para los Pueblos Indígenas (www.cedei.gob.mx/cuquila) has organized a museum with a number of historic artifacts, including hieroglyph-inscribed stones found in the big archaeological zone nearby, and documents from the 1580s, such as a map of the town and several yellowed pages recording a plethora of information—town borders, officials' names, events, and perhaps even a little gossip—of early colonial days in Cuquila. The museum also displays examples of locally made present-day pottery and hand-woven *huipiles.*

The town presently runs a handicrafts store, built with the help of the American-based Amigos de las Americas (www.amigoslink .org), on the highway through town. This would be a good spot to stop and maybe see the *artesanos*—potters and weavers—at work, and/or make contacts to visit their home workshops in the village.

The museum committee is currently headed by its president, at this writing, Mario Hilario Baldamero. He and other committee members are qualified to take you on a tour (about three km/two mi, three hours round-trip, offer a donation of about $20) to their "old town" (former population of 3,000) archaeological site on a hill nearby.

Archaeologists reckon that the site was occupied for about 1,300 years, from 400 B.C. to A.D. 900. The ceremonial area, consisting of the remains of a pair of royal residences, a main plaza, two tombs, and a ball court, spreads over about 25 acres. The Cuquila museum is open by appointment, which you can make, or better yet, ask your hotel desk clerk to make by calling the town long-distance telephone (tel. 953/554-0716) or the town *agencia municipal* (tel. 953/596-3398 and 953/596-3399).

Although at this writing they have no guest *cabañas,* they've started a **comedor** (tel. 953/596-3302, 9 A.M.–5 P.M.) at their handicrafts shop.

Get to Cuquila by local van, or Fletes y Pasajes or Sur bus from Juxtlahuaca, Tlaxiaco, or Putla. By car, Cuquila is right on Highway 125, 19 kilometers (12 mi) west of Tlaxiaco, 56 kilometers (35 mi) east of Juxtlahuaca, or 51 kilometers (32 mi) northeast of Putla.

San Miguel Progreso

Three kilometers (two mi) downhill from its signed entry road from Highway 125, San Miguel Progreso (pop. 3,000) welcomes visitors to its museum. The museum committee has arranged the museum displays in four different sections. First are the historic papers, such as a 1780 document defining the town limits and a copy of a 1580 *lienzo* that maps the location of buildings, roads, rivers, and town boundaries. Next comes an excellent exposition of the local wool-weaving craft, then a mock-up of a typical indigenous dwelling.

An archaeological section demonstrates finds, such as stone ax blades, ceramic vases, lance points, and human burial remains, including grave offerings. A final display models the preconquest method of terraced agriculture.

The local area contains a number of interesting sites, enough for a whole day of exploring. These include three unexcavated archaeological zones: Lomatutaya (Where the People Rest), Tuxau (Fifteen Words), and Panteón de los Angelitos (Cemetery of the Little Angels). Also nearby are two sacred caves, where masses are celebrated on May 3, El Día de la Santa Cruz (The Day of the Holy Cross).

Time your arrival on the locally important festival dates, September 29 (Fiesta de San Miguel) or the fifth Friday of Lent (Fiesta de las Tres Caidas de Jesús), when you can get in on the fun of fireworks, food, dancing, processions, music, flowers, and carnival diversions.

To make sure that one of the museum committee members is available to show you the museum and perhaps lead you on a tour, make an appointment (or best ask your hotel desk clerk to make the appointment) through the *agente municipal* (José Cruz Ramírez, tel. 953/556-4635).

Get to San Miguel Progreso by bus or car as described for Cuquila, except that the signed side road (off of Hwy. 125) to San Miguel is about six kilometers (four mi) past Cuquila (from Tlaxiaco) and a corresponding distance closer to Juxtlahuaca and Putla. Continue about three kilometers (two mi) along the downhill side road to San Miguel.

PUTLA DE GUERRERO: LAND OF WATER

After a week traveling in the cool, high Mixteca Alta, the rush of balmy moist tropical air you enjoy when entering the upland valley of Putla de Guerrero (pop. 15,000) feels like another country. Banana trees overhang the road; mangos, in season, sell for a dime apiece; the aroma of roasting coffee scents the air; and people fill their afternoons by splashing in their favorite local swimming holes.

You might want to linger a day or two and bask in the warmth. If so, Putla's colorful market and its modicum of hotels, restaurants, and services can help make your visit interesting and comfortable.

Sights

The town centers on a leafy *jardín,* about four blocks west, downhill from Highway 125. The *jardín,* bordered by the *presidencia municipal* on the south, a line of shops on the north, and the church, at its northwest corner, focuses community activity.

The colorful, bustling market, busiest on Sunday, is a block behind the *presidencia municipal.* Here you'll find stalls offering the handmade textiles—*huipiles, rebozos* (shawls), *blusas,* and *enredos* (wraparound skirts)—for which Putla is well known. Materials vary from wool, homespun and woven by highland Trique women, to cottons, hand-embroidered by coastal Mixtecs.

Accommodations

A relaxing hotel choice in Putla is the **Hotel Beyafrey** (Guerrero 9, tel. 953/553-0294, $15 s, $19 d, $25 t), about three blocks south and two blocks west of the plaza. It has a big blue pool-patio, but is somewhat unkempt. The approximately 30 high-ceilinged rooms come with toilets and hot-water showers, fan, cable TV, and parking. Ask for a room in the quiet rear section upstairs, away from the busy street-front and the trucks that use their parking lot. (Also make sure the room is clean enough and everything works before you move in.)

Another better-managed, but not so laid-back hotel, convenient for bus passengers, is the newish **Hotel Plaza** (Morelos 15, tel. 953/553-0403, $15 s, $18 d in one bed, $22 s, d in two beds, $26 t), on the east side of town half a block below the highway. The hotel's 28 rooms surround an attractively leafy rear patio; uppers open to an inviting balcony walkway that leads to an airy street-view porch up front. (The only drawback is that room windows face

the balcony, and curtains must be drawn for privacy, which renders the rooms dark.) Inside, guests enjoy attractive color-coordinated pink-white decor and shiny hot-water shower-baths, cable TV, and wireless Internet.

Food

You can find plenty of luscious fruits and vegetables and many inexpensive local-variety meals in *fondas* (food stalls) in and around the market. For groceries, try the **Abarrotería Mary Carmen** (at the southwest plaza corner, tel. 953/553-0228, 7 A.M.–8 P.M. daily) across the street from the *presidencia municipal.* For a larger selection, go to the chain grocery **Super Mega** (uphill a block, at the northwest plaza corner, tel. 953/553-0398, 7 A.M.–8 P.M. daily).

For restaurants, start with the choices on the highway. Most inviting is **Restaurant Tito's** (next to the Omnibus Cristóbal Colón terminal, tel. 953/553-1065, 8 A.M.–9 P.M. daily, $4–12), decorated with a gallery of paintings of sentimental old-time Putla scenes, and an airy terrace with a view, especially pleasant for lunch or sunset supper. You also might say a good word to the friendly travel agent–owner Tito Chaves, who's proud of his eclectic menu of salads, pasta, beef brochette, chicken fajita, and seafood (shrimp, fish, octopus).

Also on the highway, next door, downhill from Tito's, you can choose the clean family-run *comedor*-style **Abarrotes-Restaurant Velasco** (tel. 953/553-0047 or 953/553-0099, 8 A.M.–9 P.M. daily, $2–8) for breakfast, lunch, and supper.

Downhill, near the plaza, is what seems to be Putla's most popular local-style eatery, **Sabor de Mi Tierra** (Flavor of My Land; corner of Queretaro and Sonora, local cell tel. 044-953/113-4754, 8 A.M.–8 P.M. daily, $4–7), behind the church. Here, in a no-frills, but immaculate dining room, choose from a long, intriguing, all-local menu: eggs your choice, *entomatado, carne enchilada,* and *tasajo* for breakfast; chiles rellenos, barbequed pork ribs, pork chop or meat balls in spicy sauce, and baked chicken under black *mole* for *comida* or supper.

Entertainment and Events

Ordinarily quiet Putla livens up during its regionally important fiestas. **Carnaval Putleco,** celebrated on the Sunday, Monday, and Tuesday before *miércoles ceniza* (Ash Wednesday), is rich in traditional dances. Local favorites, nearly always performed, are Los Viejos (The Old Ones), El Macho, and Los Copala.

Later in the year, folks crowd the church-front atrium for the **Fiesta de la Natividad,** which kicks off on September 6 with a grand *calenda* and flower-decorated floats, continues with a feast of fireworks on September 7, and culminates on the following day with *peleas de gallo* (cockfights), *jaripeo,* and a big community dance.

Other times, Putla people cool off from the heat by frolicking in the mountain rivers that flow past the town. Join in the fun on a hot afternoon by asking a taxi driver to take you to a *balneario* (bathing spot); one of the best is the Río Cucharra swimming hole, with restaurant and riverview picnic area, about three kilometers (two mi) along Highway 125, uphill from town.

Information and Services

You'll find nearly all of Putla's basic services near the town *jardín*. Change money or use the ATM at **Bancomer** (tel. 953/553-0028, 8:30 A.M.–4 P.M. Mon.–Fri., 10 A.M.–3 P.M. Sat.), a block north from the *jardín's* west side, across from the basketball court. Alternatively, go to **Banamex** (Calle Oaxaca, 9 A.M.–4 P.M. Mon.–Fri.); from the southeast *jardín* corner, walk two blocks east, then south (right) two blocks.

The Putla **correo** (tel. 953/553-1484, 8 A.M.–4:30 P.M. Mon.–Fri., 8 A.M.–noon Sat.) is across from the northwest corner of the basketball court, a block above the *jardín,* right next to **telecomunicaciones** (tel. 953/553-0999, 9 A.M.–3 P.M. Mon.–Fri., 9 A.M.–noon Sat.).

Long-distance phone and fax are available at the **caseta** (tel./fax 953/553-0030, 8 A.M.–8 P.M. daily) on the *jardín's* north side.

Answer your email at **Paquirre Internet** (tel. 953/553-0222, 9 A.M.–10 P.M. daily), at the southwest corner of the basketball court.

For telephones, use the street phones with a Ladatel card, or go to *caseta* **Solivert** (also by the plaza, tel. 953/553-0222, 9 A.M.–9:30 P.M. daily).

For routine nonprescription medicines and drugs, go to the **Farmacia Ahorro** (on the *jardín's* west side, 7 A.M.–10 P.M. daily). If you're ill, however, ask at your hotel desk for a doctor or go to see Doctora Silvia Zarate at her **Farmacia Popular** (at the *jardín's* northeast corner, tel. 953/553-0252, 8 A.M.–2 P.M. and 4–8 P.M. daily). Medical consultations are also available at the **General Hospital** (tel. 953/553-0046), a block north of the *jardín's* east side, across the street from the basketball court.

In police emergencies, call the **policía municipal** (tel. 953/553-0111).

For information and travel services go to **Agencia de Viajes Tito** (tel. 953/553-1065) of friendly Tito Chaves Garcia, on the highway next to Omnibus Cristóbal Colón bus station (which Tito also manages).

Getting There and Away

A few long-distance bus lines and vans operate from stations on or near the highway and connect Putla with many Oaxaca destinations. First-class **Omnibus Cristóbal Colón** (Hwy. 125, tel. 953/553-0163) connects south (one departure per day) with Pinotepa Nacional; north with Mexico City, via Huajuapan; and east, with Oaxaca via Tlaxiaco, Teposcolula, and Nochixtlán. Second-class **Sur** (at Sonora 34A, downtown near the Hotel Beyafrey, tel. 953/553-0350) offers both Mexico City connections via Huajuapan and Puebla and Oaxaca City connections via Tlaxiaco and Nochixtlán. Additionally, second-class **Boquerón** buses from a small terminal downhill from Omnibus

Cristóbal Colón connect south with Pinotepa Nacional and north by the scenic backcountry Juxtlahuaca, Tonalá route to Huajuapan.

Also, from neighboring stations on Highway 125, a pair of van services provide connections with Oaxaca via Tlaxiaco; they are **Transportes Turística Mixteca Baja** (uphill from Omnibus Cristóbal Colón, tel. 953/553-0847), and **RAMSA** vans (cell tel. 953/117-6193).

For drivers, paved Highway 125 connects Putla south with Pinotepa Nacional, on the Pacific coast via 128 kilometers (80 mi) of winding, sometimes potholed, mountain road. Allow three hours for safety. In the opposite direction, Highway 125 and Highway 182 connect Putla north with Juxtlahuaca in about 59 kilometers (37 mi). Winding and sometimes steep grades require slow going. Allow 1.5 hours uphill, 1 hour downhill. About the same is true for the 77-kilometer (48 mi) connection northeast, along Highway 125, with Tlaxiaco, which, for safety, requires about 2 hours uphill, 1.5 hours down.

NORTHERN OAXACA

The vast, extravagantly diverse northern Oaxaca landscape encompasses three of Oaxaca's traditional geo-cultural regions: the pine-tufted northern Sierra, the fertile, tropical Papaloapan basin, and the oases of the desertlike Cañada canyonland. Here, travelers ready to venture north of the Valley of Oaxaca can find their heart's content of high mountains for camping, hiking, and climbing; tropical rivers and grand, glassy lakes for fishing, swimming, and boating; crystalline springs welling from the base of emerald mountains; and country markets where people wear colorful age-old village costumes and speak ancient traditional dialects.

This chapter is organized as a grand circle tour, initially exploring the cool mountain country villages of Benito Juárez and Cuajimoloyas that perch at the first high crest north of Oaxaca City. Continuing north, deeper into the mountains, visitors will find the lushly forested, wildlife-rich country around Ixtlán and Gueletao, the beloved president Benito Juárez's northern Sierra birthplace. The route continues north, down into the luxuriantly fertile Río Papaloapan basin. Using the tropical river town Tuxtepec as a base, we explore the cultural and natural riches of the Chinantec and Mazatec ancestral homelands. The road turns west, into the high Mazateca, to Huautla de Jiménez, a mountain town made internationally famous by the hallucinogenic mushrooms of renowned *curandera* (indigenous medicine woman) María Sabina. Finally, returning west and south toward Oaxaca City, the route traces the tropical orchard oasis country of Teotitlán del Camino and Cuicatlán.

© BRUCE WHIPPERMAN

HIGHLIGHTS

Balnearios Monte Flor and El Zuzul:
Refresh yourself with a swim and a picnic, and even camping overnight, at either or both Monte Flor or El Zuzul crystalline springs (page 297).

A Walk Along the Río Papaloapan:
Enjoy cooling off with a stroll along the river. Take in the views and maybe even a cooling fruit drink and lunch at a river-view *fonda* (food stall) at the Tuxtepec downtown market along the way (page 302).

El Castillo de Moctezuma: Climb the diminutive Aztec-built pyramid (c. 1500) that remains in a relatively good state of preservation in a Tuxtepec neighborhood park (page 303).

San Pedro Ixcatlán and the Islands:
Ride an excursion boat to the charmingly rural, all Mazatec-speaking Isla Soyaltepec and enjoy an overnight in the charming Hotel Villa del Lago (page 309).

María Sabina Mural: In Huautla de Jiménez, be sure to visit the strangely arresting mural on the town hall, which depicts the mission of celebrated hallucinogenic healer María Sabina (page 315).

Las Regaderas: Take an excursion outside Huautla to enjoy the cooling spray of the Las Regaderas waterfalls, which plummet 100 feet into the wild, tumbling river (page 318).

© AVALON TRAVEL

LOOK FOR **(** TO FIND RECOMMENDED SIGHTS, ACTIVITIES, DINING, AND LODGING.

PLANNING YOUR TIME

You can enjoy Northern Oaxaca's charmingly varied sights and grand scenery in an unhurried circle excursion in about a week. You can pick and choose, according to your own interests. Nature enthusiasts would be interested especially in spending a couple of days and a night or two exploring the limestone cave, lush cloud forest, and mountain meadows around Ixtlán de Juárez, perhaps tenting or lodging in local rustic forest *cabañas*. Alternatively, you could enjoy a bit of nearby forest walking and also have time to admire the graceful old colonial-era churches in Ixtlán and nearby

Capulalpan, plus the President Benito Juárez shrine and museum, in his Guelatao birthplace, then spend an overnight in a comfy Ixtlán hotel or forest *cabaña*.

Heading north, over the Sierra summit and down into the lushly tropical Papaloapan basin, be sure to stop at least for a picnic and a swim (and maybe even a tenting or RVing overnight) at the crystalline natural springs **Balnearios Monte Flor** and/or **El Zuzul**. Continue north to Tuxtepec for at least a day and a night, which will give you time for a walk along its airy riverfront, lunch at a riverview restaurant above the market, crossing the

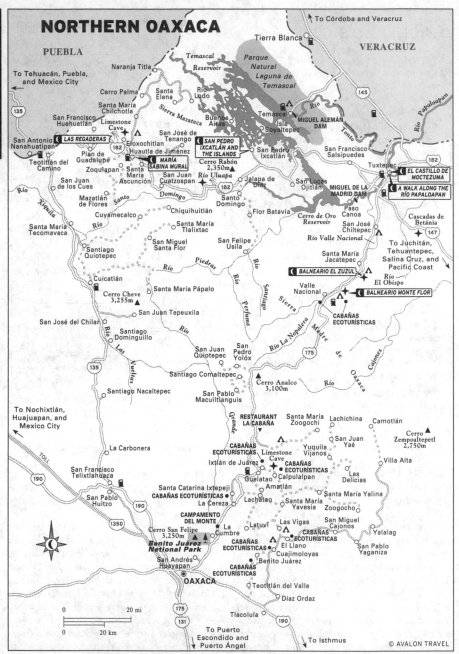

NORTHERN OAXACA

PUEBLA

To Tehuacán, Puebla,
and Mexico City

VERACRUZ

To Córdoba and Veracruz

Tierra Blanca

Naranja Titla
Temascal
Reservoir

Parque
Natural
Laguna de
Temascal

Cerro Palma
Santa
Elena
Río
Lodo

Santa María
Chilchotla
Sierra Mazateca
Buenos
Aires
Temascal
Isla
Soyaltepec

MIGUEL ALEMÁN
DAM

San Francisco
Huehuetlán
Limestone
Cave
San José de
Tenango

San Francisco
Salsipuedes

San Antonio
Nanahuatipan
LAS REGADERAS
Eloxochitlan
Huautla de Jiménez

SAN PEDRO
IXCATLÁN AND
THE ISLANDS

San Pedro
Ixcatlán

Tuxtepec

Teotitlán del
Camino
Plan de
Guadalupe
Zoquiapan
MARÍA
SABINA MURAL

EL CASTILLO DE
MOCTEZUMA

San Juan
de los Cues
Santa
María
Ascunción
San Juan
Cuatzospan
Cerro Rabón
2,350m
Río Uluapa
Jalapa de
Díaz
San Lucas
Ojitlán

MIGUEL DE LA
MADRID DAM

A WALK ALONG THE
RÍO PAPALOAPAN

Mazatlán
de Flores
Santo
Domingo
Santo
Domingo
Flor Batavia
Cerro de Oro
Reservoir
Paso
Canoa
Cascadas de
Betánia

Cuyamecalco
Chiquihuitlán
San José
Chiltepec

Santa María
Tecomavaca
Santa María
Tlalixtac
San Felipe
Usila
Río Valle Nacional

Santiago
Quiotepec
San Miguel
Santa Flor
Santa María
Jacatepec

Cuicatlán
Piedras
BALNEARIO EL ZUZUL

To Juchitán,
Tehuantepec,
Salina Cruz, and
Pacific Coast

Cerro Cheve
3,255m
Santa María Pápalo
Valle
Nacional
Río
El Obispo
BALNEARIO MONTE FLOR

San José del Chilar
San Juan Tepeuxila

CABAÑAS
ECOTURÍSTICAS

Santiago
Dominguillo

San Juan
Quiotepec
San
Pedro
Yolóx

Santiago Comaltepec
Cerro Analco
3,100m

Santiago Nacaltepec
San Pablo
Macuiltianguis

To Nochixtlán,
Huajuapan, and
Mexico City

RESTAURANT
LA CABAÑA
Santa María
Zoogochi
Lachichina
Camotlán

La Carbonera
CABAÑAS
ECOTURÍSTICAS
Limestone
Cave
Yuquila
Vijanos
San Juan
Yaé
Cerro
Zempoaltepetl
2,750m

San Francisco
Telixtlahuaca
Ixtlán de Juárez
CABAÑAS
ECOTURÍSTICAS
Calpulalpan
Villa Alta

San Pablo
Huitzo
Santa Catarina Ixtepeji
CABAÑAS ECOTURÍSTICAS
Guelatao
Amatlán
Las
Delicias

La Cereza
Lachatao
Santa María
Yavesia
Santa María Yalina
Zoogocho

CAMPAMENTO
DEL MONTE
La
Cumbre
Latuvi
Las Vigas
San Miguel
Cajonos
Yalalag

Cerro San Felipe
3,250m
CABAÑAS
ECOTURÍSTICAS
El Llano
Cuajimoloyas
CABAÑAS
ECOTURÍSTICAS
San Pablo
Yaganiza

Benito Juárez
National Park
San Andrés
Huayapan
CABAÑAS
ECOTURÍSTICAS
Benito Juárez

OAXACA
Teotitlán del Valle

Díaz Ordaz

0   20 mi

0   20 km

Tlacolula

To Puerto
Escondido and
Puerto Ángel
To Isthmus

© AVALON TRAVEL

river via the ferry and/or the hanging bridge, and exploring Tuxtepec's in-town 15th-century unrestored Aztec pyramid.

Continue west into the heartland of the indigenous Chinantec and Mazatec peoples. Spend at least a day (or better, stay on overnight at petite Hotel Villa del Lago), at picturesque hilltop lake-view Ixcatlán village. Be sure to take the boat excursion to idyllically isolated Isla Soyaltepec and island village for a bit of strolling and perhaps another overnight in an indigenous Chinantec house. Farther west, pause for at least an hour for some textile shopping at Jalapa de Díaz, where fit hikers would be challenged by a climb to the summit of the Mazatecs' holy mountain, Cerro Rabón.

Next day, farther west, climbing along and above the breathtakingly scenic, green Cañon del Río Santo Domingo, arrive in the capital of the high Mazateca, Huautla de Jiménez, home

of renowned late María Sabina of 1970s Love-Generation magic-mushroom fame. Spend a day strolling the village and vibrant indigenous market and enjoying a hike uphill to the Cerro Adoración panoramic viewpoint. The next day, continuing west, downhill, stop to bask in the cool spray of **Las Regaderas** twin waterfall. Nearby, prepared adventurers might enjoy a day (or an overnight two-day) exploration of the monumental Nindo-Da-Gé (Broad Spring Mountain) cavern at Eloxochitlán village.

With your grand circle tour nearly complete, coast downhill into the cactus-plumed, oasis-dotted Cañada country, for a stop at Cuicatlán, magnet for a host of Cuicatec mountain folks who crowd in daily (and even more on Sunday) for the big town market. Pause for a home-cooked *comida* at the town-favorite Boringen Restaurant before heading south, to arrive back in Oaxaca City by early evening.

Northern Sierra

The vast northern Sierra, the series of rugged mountain ranges that repeatedly rise and fall for a hundred miles, moving north from Oaxaca City, is a repository of a significant fraction of Mexico's increasingly scarce resources: unblemished pine and spruce decorated mountain vistas, colonial-era mountain villages, and vanishing wildlife, including all of Mexico's wild cat species, from the jaguar and the ocelot to the *tigrillo* and jaguarundi. Their survival in the region is due to the sprinkling of northern Sierra communities that carefully husband their communal lands, harvesting their lumber at only a sustainable pace and guarding their holdings against poachers.

These communities welcome visitors. Among the best prepared are Benito Juárez in the south, on the first Sierra ridge above Oaxaca City, and Ixtlán de Juárez near the northern summit. The villagers in Ixtlán de Juárez offer cozy mountain *cabaña* lodgings, campsites, and guides for exploring their lands by bicycle, foot, or car.

UP FROM THE VALLEY: BENITO JUÁREZ AND CUAJIMOLOYAS

This pair of mountain hamlets perch nearly a mile above the Valley of Oaxaca at the first towering crest of the cool, pine-tufted Sierra Juárez. The attraction here is not the towns themselves, but their gorgeous mountain environs and all that that implies: great billowing clouds, summer wildflowers, cool crystalline spring water, and the scent of spruce and pine.

Furthermore, the communities and the Oaxaca government, in their effort to develop the outdoor touristic resources of the northern Sierra, offer a number of food, lodging, and outdoor activity options in Benito Juárez, Cuajimoloyas, Llano Grande, and other villages.

(*Note:* These villages are part of a local network, known cooperatively as **Pueblos Mancomunados,** that welcomes visitors to enjoy and appreciate their wildlife-rich, pine-forested, mountain-top environment. Visitors can make accommodations and guide arrangements either directly through the communities, or more conveniently through their Oaxaca City agent, **Expediciones Sierra Norte.**)

Sights

The modest houses and farms of Benito Juárez village (pop. 1,000) are sprinkled along a single east–west ridge-crest road. The *cabañas ecoturísticas* lodgings and the community center, **Casa del Pueblo,** with the *comedor* and a cozy fireplace, are at the east end, uphill. At that point, signs direct you toward a number of possible diversions: You have your choice of a quarter-mile *tirolesa* (a forest canopy cable ride, $10); horseback riding ($16/hr); a stroll among the springs trickling downhill through the adjacent pine-shaded **Parque Recreativo**; or you can follow the sign marked Mirador, walking along the road (follow each uphill fork) about 2.5 kilometers (1.5 mi) north to the *mirador* (overlook) tower atop a craggy 3,100-meter-high (10,300 ft) perch. Here the view seems limitless. On clear days, early risers can even recognize the sunrise silhouette of Volcán de Orizaba (elev. 5,747 meters/18,856 feet), Mexico's tallest mountain, a hundred miles to the east. On the south side, steeply beneath you, spreads the central valley's verdant checkerboard of meadow, field, and pasture. On the north side, a succession of dark-green mountain ridges stretches northward until the ridges merge and become a deep-purple silhouette on the horizon. On another day, walk or get a ride about 12 kilometers (eight mi) east, past the little settlement of Los Llanos, to another viewpoint, the famous **Peña Larga,** a gigantic 15-meter (50 ft) boulder where you can perch to your heart's content.

Another possibility is to follow the 10-kilometer (six mi) *sendero peaton* walking trail, by mountain bike or on foot. The *cabañas ecoturísticas* manager rents the bikes ($10) and furnishes you with a guide ($12). For more information and cozy *cabaña* reservations, contact the Benito Juárez tourism manager either directly (tel. 951/166-6313), or through

Expediciones Sierra Norte (tel. 951/514-3631, sierranorte@oaxaca.com, sierra_norte@infosel.net.mx, www.sierranorte.org.mx) in Oaxaca City.

Alternatively, you can simply wander around and enjoy yourself. Plenty of folks, Zapotec people (most of whom speak Spanish), are out tending their terraced cornfields, watching their cattle, and doing household chores.

Cuajimoloyas (kooah-hee-moh-LOY-ahs, pop. 1,000), six kilometers (four mi) east along the ridge road from Benito Juárez, is the metropolis of this part of the mountains. Besides lodging and restaurants, it has a pharmacy, health center, small grocery stores, and a long-distance telephone.

You'll be especially lucky to arrive in Cuajimoloyas during either the patronal **Fiesta de San Antonio** (June 11–14) or the **El Día de los Muertos,** which is very big locally, and stretches six days, beginning November 1 and climaxing in a whoopla of favorite traditional dances on November 5 and 6.

Your first stop should be the tourism headquarters on the right side of the road as you enter town, across from the small hotel Yacautzi (Place of the Maguey). The tourism manager can set you up with bicycles ($5/hour), a guide ($15 for three hours), or both. Reserve in advance by leaving a message via the Cuajimoloyas tourism manager (tel. 951/524-5024).

The guided tour takes about three hours by bicycle, or about six on foot. The sights along the way customarily include **El Calvario,** a sacred spring; **Cañon del Coyote,** caves; a climb to the top of **Piedra Colorada,** a gargantuan red monolith; some waterfalls; and the **Llano del Fraile,** a sylvan wildflower-rich camping area, bisected by a trout stream.

A little farther off the beaten track, **Llano Grande** village along the same paved mountain-crest road, 10 kilometers (six mi) farther east, also welcomes lovers of the outdoors. Village offerings include rustic *cabañas,* meals, camping, bicycles, guides, and a menu of activities. These include wildlife-viewing, panoramic vistas, rappelling, and the highest local

Llano Grande's semi-deluxe *cabañas ecoturísticas* are spacious, comfortable, and fireplace-equipped.

viewpoint, sacred **Yaa Tini** peak (elev. 3,200 meters/10,600 feet), where pilgrims still arrive on Easter Sunday to pay their respects to the Lord of the Mountain.

Mountain Guide

A very convenient option is to go with well-equipped Empresa Ecoturística Comunitaria (Community Ecotouristic Enterprise), also known as **Expediciones Sierra Norte** (210 M. Bravo, Oaxaca City, tel. 951/514-3631, sierranorte@oaxaca.com, sierra_norte@infosel.net.mx, www.sierranorte.org.mx). The efficient staff work with a dozen-odd Sierra Norte communities, called **Pueblos Mancomunados,** that include, besides the Benito Juárez–Cuajimoloyas–Llano Grande trio, Yavesia, Latuvi, Amatlán, and Lachatao. Jointly, they have established a 100-kilometer (60 mi) signposted hiking and mountain-biking trail network and offer accommodations in rustic village cabins and campsites.

They make reservations for the cabins and help obtain access and camping permits. They also outfit and guide parties for camping, hiking, and biking outings into the mountains north of Oaxaca City, beginning in the area around Benito Juárez and Cuajimoloyas and extending north toward the other villages. They can furnish camping gear, mountain bikes, transportation, and more.

Accommodations and Food

All three villages offer many lodging choices. The busiest and best organized is Benito Juárez, which offers an assortment of rustic but comfortable lodgings, the most economical of which is the large original tourist accommodation, still called by its original label, **Tourist Yu'u** (dorms $12 pp, guestrooms $10 pp). It accommodates about 20 persons in a dormitory hall, with shared toilet and hot-water showers. The facility also has several four-person bunk-bed private-bath guestrooms that open onto the large common hall. Although well-used, this is still a cozy place if you like lots of company, with a big fireplace, plenty of wool blankets, and a basic kitchen with refrigerator available for guest use. Bring your own soap and towel and, if you plan to cook, most of your own food, especially fresh fruits and vegetables. The local water is crystal pure on this mountaintop.

Additionally, Benito Juárez offers several detached private *cabañas* ($40 d, t, or q), sleeping four, with hot-water baths, fireplace, and kitchenette. For more information and reservations, call the **Benito Juárez manager** (tel. 951/166-6313, 8 A.M.–8 P.M. daily) or **Expediciones Sierra Norte** (tel. 951/514-3631, sierranorte@oaxaca.com, sierra_norte@infosel.net.mx, www.sierranorte.org.mx).

Cuajimoloyas also offers accommodations, including three duplex *cabañas* uphill above the town, and a small, plain hotel, the **Yacautzi** (on the road, left side, as you enter town from Benito Juárez, $15 d hotel rooms, $40 d *cabañas*). Although the hotel offers five clean but unheated basic bare-bulb rooms with double bed, toilet, and hot-water shower, the three *cabañas,* a quarter mile uphill, are much cozier, each with two spacious duplex units sleeping four, with fireplace and a hot-water shower and toilet, shared by respective occupants of the duplex units. Reserve directly through the **Cuajimoloyas tourism office** (tel. 951/524-5024, 8 A.M.–2 P.M. and 4–8 P.M. daily) or through Expediciones Sierra Norte.

The 10 duplex *cabañas* at **Llano Grande** ($45 d, $55 q) consist of 5 larger duplex cabins, with bunk beds for up to four, and 5 smaller, with double beds, for two. Hot-water showers and toilets are shared between the respective occupants of each duplex *cabaña*. Additionally, Llano Grande recently built eight lovely, professionally built and comfortably furnished *cabañas,* with attractive bedspreads and drapes and private modern-standard shower-baths. Four of them accommodate two persons each, while four larger *cabañas* accommodate four persons each.

Furthermore, the Llano Grande community ecotourism office offers packages, including accommodation, meals, and a guide, for about $25 per day per person. Fireplace wood goes for $5 per load. Reserve through the **Llano Grande village telephone** (tel. 951/514-3631), or Expediciones Sierra Norte.

Alternatively, the whole mountaintop area is ripe for tent and some self-contained RV camping. The communities have designated at least four spots. Two walk-in-only campgrounds are close to and administered in Benito Juárez. Closest is in the **Parque Recreativo,** near the village center; and another camping site—with a view—is about 0.3 kilometers (0.2 mi) away on foot.

Farther afield, campers may enjoy a sylvan meadow **Llano de las Tarajeas,** with campsites and good spring water. Find it a total of about 16 kilometers (10 mi) east of Benito Juárez, past Cuajimoloyas. During the summer and fall, this meandering pine-bordered meadow is decorated with a galaxy of wildflowers—lavender buttercups, red lilies, baby blue eyes, white and yellow daisies, and many more. Water comes from a pristine brook, home to some little darting fish. (Foresters have set up a small fish hatchery here, in an attempt to breed more of the little critters, some of whom have become healthy adult rainbow trout.)

To camp at Llano de las Tarajeas, reserve with the **Cuajimoloyas tourism manager** (tel. 951/545-9994, $3 pp per night). **Get there** by car, bus, or on foot. Beginning at Benito Juárez, continue 6.4 kilometers (four mi) east along the ridgeline road, through Cuajimoloyas. Continue another five kilometers (three mi) to the Las Tarajeas sign on the left. Follow more signs another three kilometers (1.8 mi) to the narrow, rough driveway, only marginally passable by big RVs, on the left, to Llano de las Tarajeas.

The latter-day ecotourist influx supports a sprinkling of modest local eateries. In Benito Juárez the best is the **Casa del Pueblo** community *comedor.* In Cuajimoloyas choose between *comedores* **San Antonio** and **La Montaña,** run by friendly Gilda and Sergio Hilser; and in Llano Grande, you have *comedores* **La Curva** (good for both breakfast and groceries), **San Isidro,** and **Katy.** All are open approximately 8 A.M.–8 P.M. daily, and provide breakfasts ($2–5), afternoon *comida* ($3–5), and tacos, tamales, quesadillas, and hamburgers for supper ($3–5).

Campers should arrive with all food provisions in hand, especially fresh fruits and vegetables. Local stores may have only minimal supplies.

Getting There and Away

From Oaxaca City, the best route to Benito Juárez, Cuajimoloyas, and Llano Grande is via the buses of **Sociedad Cooperativa Flecha de Zempoaltépetl** (saym-poh-ahl-TAY-paytl) from the Oaxaca City second-class bus terminal, headed for Cuajimoloyas (and also Llano Grande). They leave approximately six times a day for Cuajimoloyas, via Tlacolula. (They go several places, so say *"¿A Cuajimoloyas?"* before getting on.) For Benito Juárez, get off at the mountain crest, at the junction where the Benito Juárez road splits left (west). Walk or catch a ride the six kilometers (four mi) to the Benito Juárez *cabañas* and Casa del Pueblo. *Note:* Super-fit backpackers could, alternatively, hike or thumb a ride up the car-RV route, described next, via Teotitlán del Valle.

If, however, you're in Tlacolula already, wait for the same Flecha de Zempoaltépetl bus, on the highway, at the corner across from the Tlacolula Pemex gas station and proceed as described.

By car or RV, for experienced and fearless drivers only, it's quickest to drive to Benito Juárez via the spectacularly scenic route via Teotitlán del Valle. Turn left at the signed Teotitlán del Valle Highway 190 turnoff, about 30 kilometers (18 mi) east of Oaxaca City. Continue straight through town, uphill on an initially bumpy road. A mile or two later, past the Teotitlán dam, the graded gravel road gets better. Ordinary cars and most RVs could negotiate it readily under dry conditions, although it might be marginal when wet. Four-wheel-drive vehicles could do it most anytime. At Benito Juárez, at the mountaintop, follow the Martín Ruiz Camino street signs to Cabañas, about 0.8 kilometers (0.5 mi) to the *cabañas ecoturísticas* and the town community center and tourism reception office (turn left half a block uphill past the *cabaña ecoturística*).

Alternatively, drivers can follow the easier but longer paved route that the bus Flecha de Zempoaltépetl takes: Heading east, at the Tlacolula Pemex station, turn left and continue about six kilometers (four mi) to Díaz Ordaz village, where you turn left again. Continue winding uphill about 19 kilometers (12 mi) to the mountaintop and a big road fork, at the Km 19 marker. Turn left sharply for Benito Juárez (six km/four mi); continue straight ahead for Cuajimoloyas (two km/1.2 mi) and Llano Grande (13 km/eight mi).

ALONG THE ROAD TO IXTLÁN

The high road to northern Oaxaca winds far uphill, climbing over lush, pine-clad crests and descending into deep river canyons to the Sierra Juárez, the mountainous birth-land of Benito Juárez, Oaxaca's beloved favorite son. Besides its historical and sentimental significance, the Sierra Juárez's pristine, thickly forested ridges and shadowed stream valleys are a natural garden of springs, meadows, caves, and waterfalls—a de facto wilderness refuge for dozens of endangered species, including all of Mexico's wild cats.

The best hub for exploring the Sierra Juárez is the small town of Ixtlán de Juárez, easily reachable by bus or car, about 60 kilometers (37 mi) north from Oaxaca City via Highway 175.

Although Ixtlán is a worthy destination, journeys are sometimes equally memorable for the bright moments en route. The road to Ixtlán is no exception. You might uncover some pleasant surprises while lingering along the way, such as the invitingly rustic mountain restaurant and refuge Campamento del Monte, or San Andrés Huayapan and Ixtepeji, a pair of little towns with nevertheless big gems of churches.

By bus, ride a Cuenca (koo-AYN-kah) first-class or ADO bus bound for Ixtlán (or Valle Nacional or Tuxtepec) from Oaxaca City's ADO–Cristóbal Colón first-class station, on Highway 190 at the north side of town. Drivers, set your odometer and head out from the junction where Highway 175 splits north from Highway 190, about five kilometers (three mi) east of the Oaxaca City center.

San Andrés Huayapan Church and Reservoir

If you have time, detour into San Andrés Huayapan (left turnoff from Hwy. 175), approximately four kilometers (2.5 mi) uphill from Highway 190. First of all, take a look inside the town's jewel: the distinguished, double-towered 17th-century **Templo de San Andrés.** Past the front door, admire the mural of the Last Supper in the nave and the colorful sculpture of San Andrés in the main altarpiece's central niche.

Afterward, reverse your path by taxi or car to the **Presas de Huayapan** (Dams of Huayapan) on opposite sides of the entrance road, a fraction of a mile uphill from Highway 175. The pair of dams, although built for irrigation, have created a popular, scenic recreation reservoir (prettiest during late-summer high water, when no ugly bathtub-like ring scars the lakeshore), forming petite bays in the folds of the surrounding forested hillsides. Restaurants serve food, and concessionaires rent boats. However, **swimming is not recommended,** due to the lakeshore's steep incline.

Campamento del Monte

About 34 kilometers (22 mi) north, 10 kilometers (six mi) after La Cumbre, you arrive at an attractive chalet-style view restaurant perched on the right (east) side of Highway 175. Although the **《 Restaurant del Monte** (tel. 951/518-6139, $5–7) is certainly worth a stop (especially for fresh trout or baked rabbit) all by itself, the Campamento del Monte (tel. 951/560-3052, local cell tel. 044-951/172-7277, delmontemx@hotmail.com, 9 A.M.–3 P.M. Mon.–Sat., $15 pp, three person minimum per cabin) across the road is the main attraction. A handful of rustic cabins and rooms (at Km 27, Carretera Oaxaca–Guelatao), sprinkled in the pine-oak forest above the highway, offer tranquility and lots of fresh air in a gorgeously secluded pine-shaded setting. The family Pérez Chávez, who first built the restaurant, then the cabins, has named them individually: Toro de Silviero, Laguna Azul, Colmilla Blanco, and Luna de Octubre. Like their names, each cabin is uniquely inviting, built with rustic wood, tile, and brick, with plenty of light, tree-framed mountain and forest vistas, a fireplace with lots of wood, an outdoor grill, hot-water shower-bath, stove, and refrigerator (although you have to furnish your own towels, bedding, and pots, pans, dishes, and utensils). In addition to the cabins, their four rooms (about $50, for up to four) although not individually named, are cozy, with fireplaces and private hot-water shower-baths.

Rentals are popular, so be sure to reserve and mail a 50 percent deposit at least 10 days ahead of time. Although their literature insists on prior reservations, they do rent to drop-ins 3–9 P.M. if they have an available accommodation, which is likely Sunday–Thursday. Bring mosquito repellent, especially necessary early evenings during the summer wet season.

In addition to cabin rentals, the managers also welcome day visitors for about $1 per person. Tenters, RVers, and trailers are also welcome ($7 pp per night), with hot-water showers and toilets provided. Diversions include picnicking, bird- and animal-viewing, and rambling through the sylvan pine- and oak-studded mountainside to local view summits.

Santa Catarina Ixtepeji

This formerly sleepy little canyon community, at the headwaters of the Río Grande, is waking up. Now, folks are welcoming nature lovers to enjoy their great outdoors. They've even established an easily accessible **visitors center** (Hwy. 175 at La Cumbre, tel. 951/560-4037 or 951/560-4039, www.lacumbreextepeji.com, 9 A.M.–6 P.M. daily), 22 kilometers (15 mi) uphill from Highway 190.

At the visitors center, find out about the 4,000-acre (six-square-mile) Ixtepeji (eeks-tay-PAY-hee) **nature preserve** ($2 pp entrance fee), with hiking and biking trails through shadowed spruce, pine, and oak forests, past ferny dells and cold crystal-clear springs, a cascading waterfall, and spectacularly panoramic viewpoints.

Furthermore, the Santa Catarina Ixtepeji community invites you, after a day of such exhilarating exploring, to set up your tent in their *campamento* (campground; $4 pp), stay overnight in one of their **dormitories** ($10 pp) or mountain *cabañas* ($13 pp). A *Cabaña* has three bunk beds; hot-water shower-baths and toilets are shared. A restaurant also serves meals.

In the Santa Catarina Ixtepeji town center, be sure to see the beloved old **Templo de Santa Catarina,** by far the biggest building in Santa Catarina Ixtepeji. The church's main attraction (unless you plan your visit to coincide with the three days of the Fiesta of Santa Catarina, around November 25) is the towering, superb Renaissance facade. Prominent are the eight exquisitely spiraled Solomonic columns, four above and four below. Notice also the facade's empty niches, which once sheltered

St. John the Evangelist, St. Nicolas, and St. Michael, until they were probably toppled by an earthquake. Nevertheless, St. Peter remains on the left, with Bible, flag, and staff, as does St. Catherine, high above, with flowing robe and sword.

GETTING THERE

By bus, ride a Cuenca (koo-AYN-kah) or ADO first-class bus, bound for Ixtlán (or Valle Nacional or Tuxtepec) from Oaxaca City's ADO–Cristóbal Colón first-class terminal, on Highway 190 at the north side of town. Ask the driver to let you off at the La Cumbre–Santa Catarina visitors center (Hwy. 175 at La Cumbre, tel. 951/560-4037 or 951/560-4039, www.lacumbreextepeji.com).

Or hire a taxi to the intersection, five kilometers (three mi) from Oaxaca City, to the corner, where Highway 175 forks north from Highway 190. From there, ride a Santa Catarina *colectivo* ($15 for up to five), which will take you all the way to the Santa Catarina *cabañas*.

Drivers: at La Cumbre, 22 kilometers (15 mi) from the Highway 190 intersection, follow the signed turnoff from Highway 175, to the left, and simply continue for about six kilometers (four mi) down-mountain to the *cabañas*. If, however, you're driving directly to Santa Catarina Ixtepeji town, best continue about five miles farther north, to La Cereza (km 37/mi 23), where a gravel road leads directly downhill to the town center.

AT THE SUMMIT: IXTLÁN DE JUÁREZ AND VICINITY

If a Mexican person told you that he or she lived in Ixtlán, you still wouldn't know where that is, for there are many Ixtláns in Mexico. The prefix *ix-* refers to *ixtle,* the Aztec word for the fibers of the maguey plant. The suffix *-tlan* means "land of" or "place of." The maguey plant is widespread in Mexico, and the Aztecs were so dominant at the time of the conquest that their names for local towns are still used today. So the many Ixtláns are all places that the Aztecs named Land of the Maguey. Oaxaca Ixtlán people gave their town a unique name,

by naming it Ixtlán de Juárez, after their favorite son, revered President Benito Juárez.

People don't grow much maguey around Ixtlán de Juárez anymore, nor do they grow any cochineal, cultivation of which created a number of millionaires in the vicinity. Their money built the ornate old Churrigueresque churches in Ixtlán de Juárez and the neighboring town of Calpulalpan.

What Ixtlán de Juárez people do grow a lot of is wood, in the thick forests coating this part of the northern Sierra. Wisely, they don't cut too much of it, so their forests remain rich habitats for many wild creatures, including all species of Mexican native cats (notably the jaguar and mountain lion), spider monkeys, and tapirs, many of which have disappeared in other parts of southern Mexico. The diversity of species is so rich in Ixtlán de Juárez's woodlands that a panel of international experts convened by the World Wildlife Fund has rated the local forest as one of the world's 17 outstandingly biodiverse ecosystems. What's great for visitors is that the Ixtlán de Juárez community invites them to come see and appreciate their wild treasures through a special community-run ecotourism company.

Sights

Ixtlán de Juárez (pop. 8,000), despite being the capital of its own sprawling governmental district, feels like a village, where the main evening activity is to either watch or join the kids playing basketball on the courts in the central plaza, then get *cena* (supper) before the mom-and-pop *comedores* close around 8:30 P.M. Walk three blocks in any direction and you're in the woods. But don't worry, you won't get lost. Just let the faithful chime of the plaza-tower clock lead you back.

Likewise, the landmark plaza-front *presidencia municipal,* on the plaza's north side, can help get you oriented. Main north–south streets are Sidencio Hernández on the plaza's west side, and 16 de Septiembre on the east side. Crossing those is Revolución, which runs east–west, behind the *presidencia municipal.*

Ixtlán de Juárez's main in-town sight is

its treasured 17th-century **Templo de Santo Tomás Apóstol,** just northwest of the town plaza, behind the faithful, very proper plaza clock. The present *templo,* started by Dominican fathers around 1640, replaced an earlier all-adobe church. Construction was completed about a century later, in 1734. The first thing to notice about old Santo Tomás is that it's made of the same light green *cantera* that you see so much of in Oaxaca City's public buildings. Ixtlán de Juárez's source, however, is local.

Decorating the baroque facade's summit is a bas-relief showing the dramatic confrontation of doubting Thomas with the risen Jesus. Inside, instead of the usual one golden *retablo*

BENITO JUÁREZ: MEXICO'S PRESIDENT FOR ALL SEASONS

Mexico's memory of Benito Juárez, its most revered president, is draped in legend. What's certain is that he was born on March 21, 1806, in the northern Oaxacan *municipio* of San Pablo Guelatao, at the hamlet of Santo Tomás Ixtlán. When his parents of pure Zapotec origin, Marcelino Juárez and Brigida Garcia, died tragically when Benito was three, his uncle took him in. After a quiet childhood, mostly spent shepherding his uncle's flocks in the surrounding hills, Benito left for Oaxaca City in December 1818 to live with his sister, María Josefa.

For Benito, this was a lucky stroke. He became part of the Maza household, where María Josefa lived and worked as a cook. In the genteel, well-to-do Maza family surroundings, young Benito gained exposure to music, books, politics, and people – not possible for a poor boy in the country. Moreover, he met Margarita Maza, who, with the blessing of her parents, later became his wife.

While living with the Mazas, Benito immediately gained the attention of priest and bookbinder Antonio Salanueva, who, recognizing his exceptional qualities, took Benito under his wing and sent him to school in town in January 1819. With Salanueva as his patron, Benito made rapid progress. He entered Oaxaca's new Scientific and Literary Institute in August 1828 to study law. Four years later, he was a practicing attorney. He entered politics, rapidly rose from state to federal legislator, then Supreme Court judge, finally being unanimously elected governor by Oaxaca's legislature on August 12, 1849.

From a successful term as governor, Juárez returned to national prominence. He was elected Mexico's president for two separate terms, both interrupted, first by civil war during the latter 1850s and then by the French Intervention from 1862 to 1867. Victory over the French finally brought peace, and Juárez was elected president for the third time in October 1871. He toiled day and night to realize his dreams for Mexico, but he died from exhaustion on July 18, 1872.

A monument honors Benito Juárez, Mexico's sole pure indigenous president, in Tamazulapan, in the Mixteca.

© BRUCE WHIPPERMAN

© BRUCE WHIPPERMAN

The façade frieze at Ixtlán de Juárez's Templo de Santa Tomás Apóstal depicts the dramatic confrontation of the doubting Thomas with Jesus.

(altarpiece) behind the altar, several more decorate the nave walls, with gilded saints, angels, and masterfully pious 16th- and 17th-century oil paintings. The main *retablo,* behind the altar, shows the kneeling St. Thomas touching the chest of the risen Jesus, the act that, according to the Gospels, removed all doubt of the resurrection's reality. Finally, before you leave, glimpse inside the baptistery, on the right side of the nave, where Benito Juárez was baptized in 1806.

Treat yourself to a *moto* (motorcycle taxi, $4 one-way) ride 600 meters (2,000 ft) uphill to the **El Mirador** mountaintop viewpoint, for a panoramic vista of the entire northern Sierra. While there, feast on fresh trout at the restaurant **Las Truchas** ($7). (You can glimpse El Mirador, on the summit peak, visible far above the town plaza, to the northwest.)

If you're lucky enough to arrive between December 19 and 22, you can join the local folks in the patronal **Fiesta de Santo Tomás**

Apóstol. Festivities include tying up traffic on the highway with *calendas* (religious processions) while bombs blast overhead, *mañanitas* (5 A.M. masses), *jaripeo* (bull riding and roping), and the Betaza traditional courtship dance.

Ecotours

Most of the natural sights around Ixtlán de Juárez are on communal land, so you must make arrangements for a guide from the community-run Ixtlán ecotour agency, **Viajes Ecoturísticos Schiaa Rua Via** (Mountain Where the Clouds Are Born; Calle 16 de Septiembre, tel./fax 951/553-6075, ecoturixtlan@hotmail.com, www.ecoturixtlan.com, 9 A.M.–3 P.M. and 5–8 P.M. daily; tours from $25 pp per day, excluding transportation) to accompany you. Tours range widely over Ixtlán's grand 48,000-acre preserve. They include bird- and animal-watching, cloud forest hikes, mountain biking, rapelling, cave exploring, wilderness camping, and much more.

Especially interesting is their exploration of the eerie moss-draped cloud forest near Los Pozuelos camping shelter. The trail (part of the fabled **Camino Real,** route of long-vanished Aztec, Zapotec, and Mixtec traders who trekked between the Gulf Coast and the Valley of Oaxaca) leads past ice-age remnant wild begonia bushes, giant ferns, dwarf bamboo, and autumn-brilliant liquid amber trees.

All tours leave from the agency's headquarters at the northeast corner of the town plaza. They also rent mountain *cabañas.*

Park and continue on foot downhill. Before the creek, go left at the rough trail, into the woods. After about 90 meters (300 ft), you'll be at Arco de Yagela, a cave that you approach via a yawning, stalactite-walled rock amphitheater (thus *arco,* or arc). Just inside the cave's mouth, a waterfall splashes into springs welling up from beneath the rocks. The cave itself, whose dark cavity beckons a few feet behind the waterfall, can be accessed only with an expert guide and equipment. It has not been completely explored. A small party could camp on the small, level dry space in the arc to the left of the cave mouth, or a larger party could spread out in the big open spot across the creek.

Accommodations and Food

The only recommendable in-town hotel is **Casa de Huéspedes La Soledad** (Calle Francisco Javier Mina, Barrio de la Soledad, tel. 951/553-6171, $10 s, $17 d), with about a dozen clean basic rooms (seven with private baths, the rest with shared bath). Reserve ahead. Get there by walking uphill, past the town plaza, two blocks; turn left at Zapata, turn right at the first street, continue another block north to the hotel on the right.

Viajes Ecoturísticos invites visitors to stay in their forest *cabañas* near the Arco de Yagela cave a few miles out of town. The very substantial facilities include six duplex *cabañas* (tel. 951/553-6075, ecoturixtlan@hotmail.com, $13 pp), each of the accommodation units sleeps four, with double bed, bunk bed, and fireplace with wood included. A hot-water shower-bath and toilet is shared between each

Oaxaca's Sierra Norte is a lushly forested landscape of pastures and deep canyons, sprinkled with small Zapotec-speaking villages.

© BRUCE WHIPPERMAN

pair of duplex units. The entire complex, set in an idyllic, pine-forested stream valley, includes a common dining room serving meals, with touristic services, including mountain bike rentals and guided excursions.

Ixtlán de Juárez offers a sprinkling of food possibilities. Stock up on fruits and vegetables during the Monday **market,** on the town plaza. Otherwise, for some fresh items and a pretty fair grocery selection, go to **Abarrotes Jiménez** (tel. 951/553-6124), just downhill from the plaza's southwest corner.

For an even better produce and grocery selection, visit the new up-and-coming private **Mercado Comunitario** supermarket (8 A.M.–9 P.M. daily), a block north and a block east from the plaza's northeast corner.

Ixtlán de Juárez supports a few restaurants around the plaza. Very recommendable is **Comedor Jemima** (Sidencio Hernández 10, 6:30 A.M.–8 P.M. daily, $4–6), half a block downhill from the plaza's southwest corner.

Another good choice is the popular *comedor* **Farolita** (corner of Zapata and 16 de Septiembre, two blocks uphill from the plaza, tel. 951/553-6441, 9 A.M.–9 P.M. daily) for hearty morning breakfasts and afternoon *comidas.*

Downhill on Highway 175, a block south (Oaxaca direction) from the *gasolinera,* find refined restaurant **Quo Vadis** (tel. 951/553-6322, 7 A.M.–7 P.M. daily, $5), with hearty morning breakfasts and afternoon *comidas.*

Another recommendable local restaurant is the newish **La Cabaña** (near the Hwy. 175 Km 132 marker, 7 A.M.–8 P.M. daily, $4–7), north of town, about 52 kilometers (31 mi) from Ixtlán de Juárez. Inside the spacious, knotty-pine dining room, a small store sells basic groceries and trinkets, and a modest kitchen puts out good breakfasts, spicy *huevos a la Mexicana,* savory *guisado de pollo,* and fresh trout dinner.

Information and Services

Nearly all of Ixtlán de Juárez's services are available near the plaza. Change money at **Banorte** (corner of Revolución and 16 de Septiembre, tel. 951/553-6060 or 951/553-6217, 9 A.M.–4 P.M. Mon.–Fri.) with ATM, a block uphill from the plaza. Also visit the town *biblioteca* (library) next door, south side from the bank.

Find the **correo** (9 A.M.–1 P.M. and 3–6 P.M. Mon.–Fri., 8 A.M.noon Sat.) and, for public fax and money orders, the **telecom** (tel. 951/553-6106, 9 A.M.–3 P.M. Mon.–Fri.) at the plaza's northeast corner. After hours, you can also send a fax, buy a Ladatel card, and use the public long-distance telephone, at the **Jiménez grocery** (Sidencio Hernandez, tel. 951/553-6382 and 951/553-6358), just downhill from the plaza's southwest corner. Answer email at **Internet La Roca** (two blocks north of the plaza, next to Farmacia Soledad, tel. 951/553-6370, 9 A.M.–10 P.M. daily).

If you get sick, go to the **centro de salud** (on Revolución, behind the *presidencia municipal,* open 24 hours). Alternatively, consult one of the town's private doctors. Your choices are **Dr. Vicente Morales** (on the plaza, south side of the basketball court, tel. 951/553-6023, consultations 5–8 P.M. Mon.–Thurs.), or **Doctora Ofelia Maldonado Luis,** at her **Farmacia La Soledad** (16 de Septiembre 17A, tel. 951/553-6003, noon–6 P.M. Mon.–Fri.), two blocks uphill from the plaza.

Both the *gasolinera* and the bus station are on Highway 175, about three blocks west of the plaza. Second-class Cuenca de Papaloapan buses provide several daily connections south with Oaxaca City and north with Valle Nacional, Tuxtepec, and intermediate destinations. Moreover **vans,** provide several daily fast Ixtlán–Oaxaca City connections, from their terminal on Highway 175, near the Cuenca bus stop.

EXCURSIONS AROUND IXTLÁN
Capulalpam, Pueblo Mágico

Little Capulalpam (pop. 3,000) perches on its hillside about 12 kilometers (seven mi) east along the local road from Ixtlán. By virtue of its historic and cultural significance, Capulalpam was recently declared an official

NORTHERN OAXACA

© BRUCE WHIPPERMAN

The celebrated Templo de San Mateo marks the center of picturesque hillside Calpulalpam.

Pueblo Mágico, thus attaining the honored echelon of three-dozen-odd other uniquely typical Mexican villages.

Part of the reason for the town's pride is the **Templo de San Mateo,** completed by the Dominicans in 1718. Ordinarily serene, the church grounds overflow with merrymakers during the **Fiesta de San Mateo,** which climaxes yearly on September 21.

The church's renovated interior soars to a magnificent wooden ceiling. Charmingly naive designs painted by early native artisans decorate the front, below the choir, while a pair of angels, following Jesus's exhortation to become "fishers of men," dangle fish from opposite sides of the front altar. Lining both side walls, several elaborate baroque *retablos* (altarpieces) display a gallery of colorful saints and pious 18th-century oil paintings.

Uphill a few blocks from the church, the town *centro de salud* has a unique twin, the

Centro de Medicinas Tradicionales (Center of Traditional Medicine; tel. 951/539-2060, 9 A.M.–2 P.M. and 4–7 P.M. Mon.–Fri.), across a connecting patio. An herb-drying apparatus out front gives hints of the treatments practiced by the traditional healers inside the conventional-appearing, modern, white stucco building.

Ecotours and *Cabañas*

Riding the wave of its new Pueblo Mágico status, Capulalpam has also made itself into an **ecotourism center** (office in town center, lower floor of library, Felipe Ramírez Domínguez in charge, tel. 951/539-2040, www.capulalpam. com.mx, *cabañas* $14 pp, camping $5 pp). They welcome visitors with a broad menu of outdoor activities (hiking forest trails, river crossing by hanging bridge, cave- and gold-and-silver-mine exploring, biking, trout-farm fishing) by day, and five comfortable duplex *cabañas,* with

NORTHERN OAXACA

fireplaces, toilet and hot-water shower-baths to stay by night, plus a campground to boot.

Guelatao

A government-constructed monumental **Plaza Cívica** has converted this modest mountain town on Highway 175 three kilometers (two mi) south of Ixtlán de Juárez into a shrine for beloved President Benito Juárez, who was born nearby on March 21, 1806.

Juárez's timeless credo, *"El respecto al derechos ajenos es la paz"* ("Respect for the rights of all is peace"), marks the museum on the plaza, two blocks uphill from the town highway crossing. Inside, glass cases preserve a few precious mementos: a photograph, Juárez's death mask, a letter, a diary, a graduation certificate from the seminary in Oaxaca, and a model of the renowned black carriage in which Juárez for years fulfilled his duties of office, one jump ahead of his enemies.

Also on the upper plaza above the lake (by the parking lot) is a bronze sculpture of Juárez's mother, Brigida Garcia, and, at the *presidencia municipal,* a bust of Juárez, together with the historic letter that Juárez wrote to his ambassador in the United States, opposing the meddling of the United States in Mexican affairs.

Just north of the plaza, a shady path borders the petite spring-fed lake from which the town derives its Zapotec name, Guelatao (gooay-lah-TAH-oh), which translates as Enchanted Lagoon. On the lakeshore, see the famous sentimental bronze sculpture of young Benito Juárez, the humble shepherd boy, tending his flock.

The local community joins with the entire country in celebrating the memory of Benito Juárez, "Benemérito de las Américas" ("Hero of the Americas"). Yearly, on March 21, Mexico's president and Oaxaca's governor kick off a six-day fiesta of tournaments, fireworks, and a whirl of traditional dances by performing groups from a host of Zapotec communities.

© BRUCE WHIPPERMAN

This sculpture in Capulalpam honors miners who still work in local silver mines.

© BRUCE WHIPPERMAN

bronze sculpture of Benito Juárez when he was a local shepherd boy in Guelatao

Into the Papaloapan

Humid, tropical air, moving gently westward from the Gulf of Mexico, cools, clouds, and drops a deluge of rain on the northern slope of the Sierra Madre de Oaxaca. The water collects and cascades down the mountains, gathering into great, rushing rivers that finally deepen and wind serenely through a grand tropical lowland plain called the Papaloapan (pah-pah-loh-AH-pahn), after the river system that drains it. The Tonto, the Santo Domingo, and the Valle Nacional join near the town of Tuxtepec to form the Río Papaloapan.

The rivers are the region's prime asset—at high elevations on the Sierra's northern slope, the waters nourish vast, thick forests: pine-oak at the higher elevations and a fantastically lush, tropical hardwood rain forest that spreads downhill into the valleys. There, farmers have replaced the forest with rich fields of corn and tobacco, great thickets of rubber trees, and, in the shady underlay, plantations of shiny-leafed coffee bushes. The government, moreover, has tamed and harnessed the rivers, gathering them into a pair of immense reservoirs—Temascal and Cerro de Oro—for irrigation, recreation, and electric power.

VALLE NACIONAL: LAND OF SPRINGS

As the rainwater makes its way to the valleys, it sometimes wells up as crystalline, mountain-foot springs before gathering into rushing rivers. One of the loveliest of these spring-fed rivers collects at the foot of the Sierra Chinantla, a spur of the Sierra Madre de Oaxaca. It rushes downhill past the town of Valle Nacional, where it's called the Río Valle Nacional.

Valle Nacional (pop. 10,000) is interesting mostly as a springboard to the lush valley and water country that winds north 32 kilometers (20 mi) from its outskirts. The town itself is a commercial service center for the local *ranchos* and *fincas* (farms). Although Valle Nacional is an important coffee-producing center, it would be easier to get an irrigation pump here than a cappuccino. Lunch-table talk centers

mostly around tobacco, coffee, and rubber prices. Although nearly everyone in town has abandoned the original Chinantec tongue for Spanish, things change on Sunday during the big weekly *tianguis* (native town market). Then, you'll most likely rub shoulders with plenty of Chinantec-speaking people, including women in colorful striped local *huipiles*.

Besides Sunday, other good times to arrive in Valle Nacional (officially San Juan Bautista Valle Nacional) are during the local fiestas: one in memory of Saint John the Baptist around June 24, and, even bigger, the **Fiesta de San José,** celebrated for three days beginning March 18. During these times, *calendas* (processions) and floats block the street, fireworks boom overhead, masses fill the church, and merrymakers dance in the plaza.

Centro Ecoturiso San Mateo Yetla

Traveling north along Highway 175 from Oaxaca, a mile before Valle Nacional, just before the long river bridge, stop at the modest, usually tranquil village of San Mateo Yetla. Here, you can enjoy a look around Yetla's jewel of an ecotouristic park, on the shaded bank of the gurgling mountain river, Río Valle Nacional.

The spacious green riverbank park (local cell tel. 283/108-0514, $10 pp general admission) and surrounding forest, besides being a botanist's heaven of native plants, is the launching ground for a swarm of outdoor adventures. These include, kayaking, hiking, swimming, camping, biking, and guided wildlife-viewing (parrots, toucans, monkeys, wild pig-like *jabalí, tigrillos,* jaguarundis, jaguars, and dozens of butterfly and other bird species).

In order to savor at least a small part of all that, guests are invited to stay in one of the park's comfortably rustic river-view *cabañas* (single size $30 d, double size $50 d, t, q) and enjoy meals in their open-air restaurant ($2–6). General admission to the park includes use of picnic ground, campground, swimming pool, and hiking trails.

(Balnearios Monte Flor and El Zuzul

Only a few miles south, past Valle Nacional town, a pair of *balnearios* (developed springs) are perfect for a relaxing afternoon picnic or a pleasant camping or *cabaña* overnight.

Idyllic Balnearios Monte Flor is at Cerro de Marín village, Kilometer 43, about six kilometers (3.5 mi) north of Valle Nacional and 27 kilometers (17 mi) south of Tuxtepec. On the river side of Highway 175 northbound, watch for the small Museo Comunitario sign and rough entrance driveway on the right, at the last village *tope* (speed bump).

Downhill, below the village, under grand, spreading trees, cool, crystalline water wells up beneath a great hillside monolith into a gorgeous natural bathing pool. Kids run around, families splash in the water, chickens scratch in the grass, while downstream, women do their weekly wash. Especially on weekends and holidays, vendors set up tarps and offer soft drinks and barbecued beef, pork, and chicken.

The community welcomes guests to stay at one of their invitingly rustic, lovingly hand-built *cabañas* ($30 for four) and take part in a menu of outdoor activities. These include biking, swimming, and guided wildlife-viewing walks in the surrounding luscious mountainside tropical forest. While you're there, be sure to take a look inside their **community museum** (9 A.M.–5 P.M. daily) to see their collection of locally discovered archaeological artifacts. Tent or self-contained RV parking is available on the community campground ($5 pp, toilets and showers included).

Alternatively, walk downstream from the spring source a couple hundred yards, to the private paradise of friendly Diego Alonzo Francisco and his family. They offer several grassy acres shaded by big old trees, with a few chickens and turkeys pecking around, dogs, and lots of *toronjas* (grapefruit) and mangos in season.

Put up a tent or pull in your self-contained RV for about $5 per person per day, toilets and showers included. Señora Alonzo furnishes all of the drinks and home-cooked food you can eat in the adjacent restaurant. If you prefer, try

© BRUCE WHIPPERMAN

The local community welcomes visitors to enjoy the springwaters of Balneario Monte Flor.

your luck at fishing for *mojarra* or *pepesca* in the spring for your dinner.

The queen of the valley's bathing springs is the local favorite, Balneario El Zuzul, a name everyone from Valle Nacional to Tuxtepec knows fondly. Part of the fun is getting there, because you have to cross the bridge over scenic, swift-flowing Río Valle Nacional. Once across, you see what the fuss is all about: a big, round, stone-edged blue pool of clear, cool spring water, which wells up from the depths for everyone's enjoyment, a perfect antidote for a hot afternoon.

Surrounding the pool is a shady, grassy park, maybe good for tent or RV camping. (Unfortunately, at this writing, its popularity is taking a toll on the El Zuzul park. The green grass, worn by parked cars and thousands of visitors, is disappearing.)

The problem seems to be that no one around is in charge. If you find someone, ask, *";Es bueno campar?"* ("Is it okay to camp?") Expect to pay a fee of about $5 per person.

Get there by driving or taking one of the *colectivo* taxis (less than $1) parked at the signed turnoff road, between Kilometers 36 and 37, about 11 kilometers (seven mi) north of Valle Nacional, or 24 kilometers (15 mi) south of Tuxtepec. Continue 0.5 kilometers (0.3 mi); bear left around the turn, and continue 1.2 kilometers (0.8 mi) over the river bridge to Vega de Sol village on the south bank. Turn right just after the bridge and continue three blocks and turn right into the El Zuzul entry driveway.

Practicalities

Valle Nacional has one main business street, Highway 175, locally called Avenida Benito Juárez, where you'll find most basic services, except for a bank. (Nevertheless, you'll find an ATM at the town plaza, on the right side, northbound, approximately at the center of town.)

Of the town's few hotels, the best by far is **Hotel Valle Real** (Juárez 267, tel. 283/877-4405, lore_vine@yahoo.com.mx, ($27 s, $29 s or d one bed, $32 d, t, or q) in the center of town. The welcoming owner, Texas native Lorena Parra, offers 10 comfortably furnished rooms, with private hot-water baths, cable TV, telephone, air-conditioning, and in-house Internet.

Stores along the main street, notably **La Chinanteca** (tel. 283/877-4405), sell plenty of fresh fruits and veggies, while *abarroterías* (grocery stores), such as **Fruta Mexicana** sell lots of groceries, and a parade of *taquerías, loncherías* and *refresquerías* supply plenty more.

Probably the town's best sit-down restaurant is the very clean, refined (**Desgarenes** (Juárez 29, tel. 283/877-4005, 7 A.M.–6 P.M. daily), beneath the luxurious big *palapa* on the left side of the street, a few blocks north of the plaza. It's open for breakfast, lunch, and early supper.

Find the *correo* (9 A.M.–5 P.M. Mon.–Fri., 9–10:30 A.M. Sat.) and *telecom* (tel. 283/877-4132, 9 A.M.–5 P.M. Mon.–Fri., noon–5 P.M. Sat.) at the *presidencia municipal* on the plaza. Do your telephoning at the Ladatel card-operated street telephones on the town plaza's east side, or at one of the several *casetas larga distancia* on the main street. Internet connection is available at **Cyber del Mar** (Benito Juárez, corner of Veracruz, 9 A.M.–10 P.M. daily).

For a doctor, go to **Doctora Flor de Izis Blas** at her pharmacy, **Corazón de Jesú** (587 Juárez, a block north of the plaza, tel. 283/877-4404 or 283/877-4275, 9 A.M.–2 P.M. and 5–8 P.M. Mon.–Sat., 5–8 P.M. Sun.), or **Doctora Niña de los Angeles** (tel. 283/877-4275).

Gasoline is available at the Pemex station, at the north end of town.

Getting There and Away

The best way to reach Valle Nacional by bus is via a Cuenca bus from the first-class bus station in either Oaxaca City or Tuxtepec. Get away via the small mid-town terminal, where Cuenca and Sur buses connect north with Tuxtepec, and Cuenca buses, south with Oaxaca City, via Ixtlán de Juárez.

From Oaxaca City **drivers** should follow Highway 175 about 177 kilometers (110 mi) north, via Ixtlán de Juárez, to Valle Nacional. The route, although well-maintained much of the way, except for some potholes, is often winding, with three or four steep up-and-down grades en route. For safety, allow about five hours at the wheel for the entire trip to or from Oaxaca City.

SAN JOSÉ CHILTEPEC

Chiltepec (pop. 3,000) is a friendly little Chinantec town with lots of thatched houses surrounded by yards abloom with bananas, red and yellow hibiscus, and crimson torch ginger. Chiltepec is a ripe prospect for an overnight, mainly because of its inviting hotel and riverside *balnearios* (springs).

The hotel **Posada la Chinantla** (Benito Juárez 17, tel. 287/874-7008, $13 s or d), right in the middle of town, would be fine for an overnight. Guests enjoy a shady *palapa,* with comfortable chairs for sitting, set in a flowery garden patio. Six clean, thoughtfully decorated rooms come with hot-water baths and fans.

Visitors also enjoy a sprinkling of *comedores,* especially the charming, rustic *palapa* **⟨** **Restaurant El Río** (Calle Benito Juárez 101, tel. 287-874-7007, 9 A.M.–8 P.M. daily, $5–10). The town's modicum of services includes post office, long-distance telephone, health center, doctor with pharmacy (Doctora Carolina Espinsoa Pérez, upstairs, above Posada La Chinantla, at Benito Juárez 17).

The **Balneario Cocos** is a relaxed local-style place on the winding Río Valle Nacional, with food *palapas* and plenty of shoreline for sunning, frolicking, and splashing. It's best during the warm winter–spring season, when the water is clear and inviting. During the summer rains, the high, sometimes muddy river water sends most bathers to the constantly-clear Balnearios El Zuzul or Monte Flor. Get there, by turning left, just off the highway 1.6 kilometers (one mi) north of town. It provides plenty of grassy space beneath a palm grove, perhaps just right for tenting or parking your RV.

TUXTEPEC: RIVER COUNTRY

Tuxtepec (pop. 140,000), Oaxaca's second-largest city, is the administrative and commercial center of the rich governmental district of the same name. For at least a millennium, the town, at its strategic river-junction location, has been an important trading center.

Archaeologists believe that the Popoluca people, direct inheritors of the ancient Gulf Coast Olmec mother culture, first settled Tuxtepec perhaps 2,000 years ago.

The name Tuxtepec is the Spanish version of the town's Aztec label, Tochtepec, or Hill of the Rabbits, which probably describes the town's original site, atop some low hills about 2.5 kilometers (1.5 mi) west of present downtown Tuxtepec.

At that vital spot, Tuxtepec's early Popoluca people became traders and transporters for the valuable goods—cacao, copper, cotton, feathers, gold—of upstream producers, notably the Mazatecs and Chinantecs. Both still occupy their ancestral homelands: the Mazatecs (People of Mazatlán, Land of the Deer) between the rivers Santo Domingo and Tonto, west of Tuxtepec; and the Chinantecs (People atop the Mountains) in the basin of the Río Valle Nacional, to the southwest.

The ambitious Aztec emperors, expanding their domain in the 1400s, saw strategic Tuxtepec as a key to realizing their dreams of grandeur. Aztec forces under Moctezuma I subdued Tuxtepec in the 1460s. They built a ceremonial pyramid, known locally as the

one of Tuxtepec's current residents

© BRUCE WHIPPERMAN

Castillo de Moctezuma, which still stands in a west-side residential neighborhood.

Aztec governor-generals commanded a Tuxtepec garrison of several thousand warriors for two generations, putting down rebellions and enforcing tribute from Tuxtepec's many subject towns. The codex Mendocino recorded the yearly spoils, including: "eight hundred loads of…red and white blankets…eighty bundles of quetzal feathers…twenty loads of clear amber, set in gold…twenty loads of quartz, enameled and finished with gold…200 loads of cacao…twenty thousand rubber balls…"

Hernán Cortés, almost immediately upon marching into the Aztec capital in 1519, asked Moctezuma II of his empire's source of gold. Moctezuma told him, "In Tochtepec the people wash the soil in bowls with water, and afterward, small grains of gold remain." He went on to say, "Not far from Tochtepec are some mines, said to be worked by Zapotecs and Chinantecs, who are not our subjects. If you desire to send soldiers to investigate, I will furnish emissaries to accompany them."

Cortés immediately dispatched his first gold-searching expedition outside of the Valley of Mexico, to Tuxtepec. They eventually brought back what was estimated, at the time, to be 1,000 pesos' worth—perhaps a modest sackful—of gold dust and small nuggets.

In late 1521, Gonzalo de Sandoval, after passing through the Valley of Oaxaca, took possession of Tuxtepec for Spain. Cortés instructed him to found a new town at Tuxtepec and name it Medellín, after the town in Spain where Cortés was born. Although the name Medellín didn't stick, Cortés persuaded the Spanish king to award him Tuxtepec as part of his Marquesate.

Tuxtepec was only a minor player in Mexican colonial and independence history until it jumped onto the national stage in 1876 when Porfirio Díaz "pronounced" against the reelection of President Lerdo de Tejada. Díaz, a war hero and liberal ally of the revered late President Benito Juárez, threatened civil war. A group of his supporters organized in Tuxtepec, where they formulated the **Plan de Tuxtepec,** which reasserted the principles of the Reform

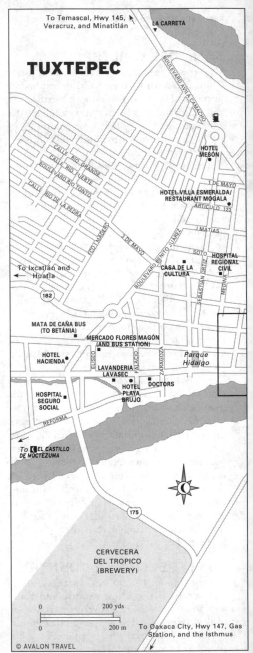

TUXTEPEC

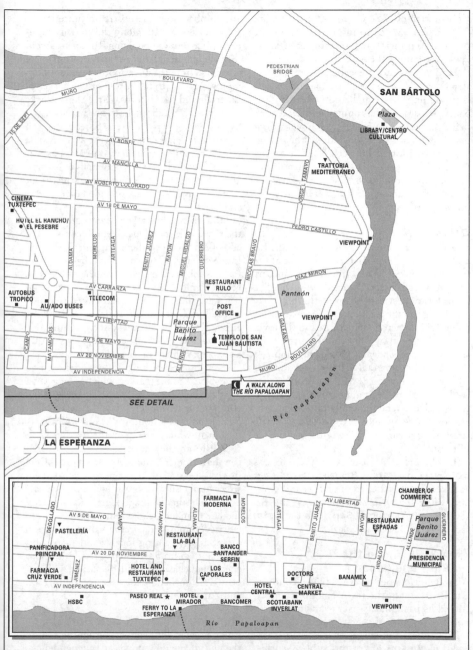

Constitution of 1857 and invented the slogan *"¡No Reelección!"* opposing reelection of the president, a principle that remains as Mexico's law of the land to the present day.

Lerdo de Tejada, nevertheless, refused to step down. So, with the entire state of Oaxaca behind him, Díaz marched on Mexico City. Soon, Tejada fled the country and Díaz took brief de facto control of the government on November 28, 1876. Shortly thereafter, Congress endorsed his action. Díaz served as legal president until 1880, as governor of Oaxaca from 1880 to 1884, then resumed the presidency, ignoring *¡No Reelección!* until revolution forced him into exile in 1911.

Orientation

Tuxtepec is a modern town that spreads for two or three miles along the steep bank of the broad Río Papaloapan, which flows nearly due east past Tuxtepec's busy downtown. The main business streets begin at the Highway 175 bridge at the west end and continue for about 1.5 kilometers (one mi) east to the town plaza. Moving away from the river, the main streets are Independencia, 20 de Noviembre, 5 de Mayo, and Libertad. A fifth street, quieter river-view boulevard El Muro, also runs parallel to the river, beginning at the east end of Independencia and gradually curving northerly, then westerly, until its course is completely reversed as it runs west along the north side of town.

Unlike most Mexican towns, Tuxtepec's main plaza, the **Parque Benito Juárez,** is not at the center of Tuxtepec, but rather at the east end, where the *presidencia municipal* and the town church, **Templo de San Juan Bautista,** face adjacent sides of the plaza.

◖ A Walk Along the Río Papaloapan

Although Tuxtepec owes its existence to the Río Papaloapan, the town has pretty much turned its back on the river ever since trucks and trains replaced the colorful fleet of log rafts, canoes, and barges that used to carry small mountains of cotton, rubber, coffee, and lumber from the upstream hinterlands. Nevertheless, a walk along the river is an entertaining route to enjoying Tuxtepec. Avoid the heat by starting out in the morning or late afternoon from the de facto town center (judging by the hustle and bustle) at the corner of Libertad and Matamoros, three short blocks from the river, about halfway between the highway and the plaza. Here, buses arrive and depart with loads of passengers. While people wait, a host of vendors hawk a varied assortment of goods, from CDs and socks to mangos and machine screws. A number of street-front *comedores* and *loncherías* provide hearty meals and snacks.

From there, head along Matamoros toward the river. After two blocks, you'll come to the end of Matamoros, where you'll turn left onto Independencia. The small riverfront square, **Paso Real,** is immediately on the right. Here you can enjoy the river view, the breeze, and, if it's evening, perhaps a radiant sunset mirrored on the river's glassy surface. Descend the adjacent stairs to the dock, and, for fun, ride the **riverboat** that ferries folks across to **La Esperanza** village on the opposite bank.

Continue east along Independencia two more blocks to the market (which is biggest on Sunday). Find the stairs (inside, on the left) and climb to the second level. Here, take a table at one of the *fondas* (food stalls) and enjoy a refreshment while feasting on the river view.

While at the market, be sure to visit the handicrafts shop **Artesanías Mitla** (9 A.M.–8 P.M. daily), just inside the market's street-front central doorway entrance. Friendly proprietor Irma Santiago Garcia (daughter of the late founder, Señora Anita Morales), who is actually from Mitla, in the Valley of Oaxaca, offers many fetching local woodcrafts, plus black pottery from Coyotepec. You might also check out her stalls 17 and 19, packed with colorful, flowing handmade Mazatec, Chinantec, and Zapotec *huipiles.*

Hanging Bridge to San Bartolo

Enjoy a scenic diversion by continuing east, to the end of the downtown at Independencia.

Either on foot or by taxi, continue straight ahead along airy river-view boulevard El Muro, following (a total of about one km/0.6 mi) along as the river bends northerly to the *puente colgante* (hanging bridge). Cross over to **San Bartolo Tuxtepec,** a sleepy village of yesteryear. Turn right at the first street and stroll up to the town *jardín* and library, where spreading, shady trees frame the view back across the river. One of the few times that San Bartolo wakes up is during its **fiesta** on August 20–24, when, besides the feasts, fireworks, processions, and masses, the town sponsors musical performances, often including marimba and local-style *música cuenqeuña*. If drowsy San Bartolo tempts you to linger, a few taco stands in the park and a sprinkling of restaurants along the main street can supply refreshments.

◖ El Castillo de Moctezuma

This is a 15th-century unreconstructed ceremonial pyramid uncovered around 1916, now the centerpiece of a small neighborhood park in a Tuxtepec west-end suburb. Archaeologists believe that despite its *castillo* label, it was not built as a castle or fortress, but probably served as both a signal post and a ceremonial site for the populous Tuxtepec Aztec colony from around 1460 to 1520.

El Castillo rises gradually from the west side in three steps, to a height of about eight meters (25 ft), and drops precipitously on the east side. Its surface is littered with crumbling masonry walls, which, on the north side, appear to open to a niche or tunnel.

Get there via Calle Reforma, the last street, Tuxtepec side, before the Highway 175 bridge. Turn right and continue three blocks; turn left at the T. Continue four more blocks to a big Refacciones Americano sign at Calle Ruinas. Turn right and continue four more blocks to a big "Procosa" sign on the brick building at Calle Ruinas. Turn right and continue one block to the park and ruins at the corner of Calles Ruinas and Tabasco.

Side Trip to Cascadas de Betania

If you're hankering for a real off-the-beaten track adventure, visit the idyllic blue waterfalls of the Cascadas de Betania (Bethlehem), 19 kilometers (12 mi) east of Tuxtepec.

What you'll find at the end of a quarter-mile forest walk is a gorgeous azure pair of waterfalls, that plunge, in two dramatic 20-foot cascades, into a pool, seemingly right out of an old Tarzan movie (minus the lion and chimpanzee, of course). What you will find, however, is a cool stream for dipping, and plenty of shade for picnicking. The cascades are on private (or communal) land, fenced off from cattle (to keep it pristine and not get muddy.) Please carry away all your refuse.

Get there, via Highway 147, by car or *colectivo* taxi or bus, from the (gas-station) intersection with Highway 175, about six kilometers (four mi) south of Tuxtepec.

Continue east along Highway 147, about 23 kilometers (14 mi) to Betania village at Km 23. Here, you should ask for someone to guide you to the Cascadas Betania. It's a simple route, so a teenager would suffice. Offer to pay (say $10, or 100 pesos), although your offer will probably be refused.

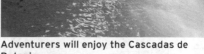

Adventurers will enjoy the Cascadas de Betania.

© BRUCE WHIPPERMAN

The cascades are hidden at the foot of a low forested limestone ridge that borders a cane field, about a quarter mile off the south (right) side of Highway 147, between Km 25 and 26.

Get there by continuing past Betania village. After about two kilometers (1.2 mi), pass a left fork (to Arroyo Limón). Continue about 300 yards to a dirt farm road that forks right (south) from the highway, not far after a big bushy tree. Follow the farm road about 400 yards (a quarter mile) to where the low-forested ridge, on the right, borders a cane (or maybe when you get there, corn) field. From there, a truck track heads faintly right, along the edge of the field. After about 100 yards, the track fades to foot trail, which finally leads, after another 300 yards, into the forest, where you'll soon see the cascades plunging over the ridge. (Most likely, as it usually occurs in Mexican farm fields, a volunteer will appear who will gladly usher you to your destination.)

Accommodations

Tuxtepec serves its many business visitors with a number of good hotels. Most of the fancier establishments lie along west-side Bulevar Benito Juárez (the northern prolongation of Highway 175), or in the quieter neighborhoods away from the downtown. The budget accommodations, most priced under $25, are in the busy downtown, either overlooking or near the river. In all cases, in warm and humid Tuxtepec, air-conditioning is worth the small extra charge.

UNDER $25

Right in the middle of town stands the attractively renovated (**Hotel Mirador** (Independencia 531, tel./fax 287/875-0652, 287/875-0500, or 287/875-0797, $18 s or d one bed, $22 two beds, $25 t, add $4 for a/c) overlooking the river, next to the Paso Real ferry dock. Of the 51 attractively decorated rooms, reserve one of the 2nd-floor ones, numbers 219–223, along the quieter, upper river-view corridor. Rentals all include TV, phone, hot-water bath, and parking. Credit cards are not accepted.

Another good downtown option, also occupying a choice riverfront perch, half a block

east, is the **Hotel Central** (Independencia 565, tel. 287/875-0966 or 287/875-0913, fax 287/875-0801, hotelcentral@yahoo.com, $20 s, $22 d, $24 t). Of the hotel's 24 rooms, reserve one of the three best, numbers 122, 119, and 107, along the airy upper view walkway, overlooking the river. The rooms, clean and simply but invitingly decorated, come with private hot-water baths, TV, phone, air-conditioning, parking, and a good restaurant downstairs. Credit cards are not accepted.

Half a block west is the **Hotel Tuxtepec** (Matamoros 2, tel. 287/875-0934 or 287/875-0944, illatina@hotmail.com, $20 s or d, $25 t with fan; $24 s or d, $29 t with a/c), a few steps off Independencia in the middle of downtown. Lacking a river-view location, the Hotel Tuxtepec management makes up for it by trying harder. Past the reception and appealingly airy street-front restaurant, the small but attractive lobby, set around a bubbling fountain, leads upstairs to 40 immaculate comfortably furnished rooms. Rentals all come with hot-water baths, cable TV, and parking, with credit cards accepted.

$25-50

Moving west one kilometer (0.6 mi), three blocks from the highway and somewhat up the economic scale, try the renovated four-star **Hotel Playa Bruja** (Independencia 1531, tel./fax 287/875-0325, playabruja@hotmail.com, $35 s, $38 d, $42 t). The hotel's 40 clean, comfortably furnished rooms rise in three stories around a small inner pool patio. Rooms all come with air-conditioning, TV, phone, parking, and a restaurant-bar. Credit cards are accepted.

On the highway, a block from the bridge, stands one of Tuxtepec's most relaxing hotels, the spacious four-star (**Hotel Hacienda** (Blv. Benito Juárez 409, tel. 287/875-1500, hhaciendatuxt@hotmail.com, $35 s or d, $40 t). Past the entrance and parking, relegated thoughtfully to the outer periphery, the reception leads to a cool, air-conditioned restaurant (with TV; ask them to turn down the volume), bordering a relaxing pool patio and shady tropical garden. The 60 semi-deluxe rooms in three-story tiers are secluded, clean, and comfortable, though somewhat worn (but undergoing renovation). The most desirable rooms have small balconies overlooking the garden (ask for *"balcón con vista del jardín, por favor"*). Rates are quite reasonable for such amenities, also including air-conditioning, warm-water baths, cable TV, phone, and parking; but credit cards are not accepted. (*Note:* At this writing, the hotel restaurant was closed due to hotel renovations. By the time you read this, however, it should be up and running again, and room prices might have risen by 10 percent.)

Alternatively, consider the refined 1960s motel–style **Hotel El Rancho** (Blv. Avila Camacho 435, tel./fax 287/875-0722, 287/875-0469, or 287/875-0704, elrancho@prodigy.net.mx, www.hotelelranchotuxtepec.com, $35 s, d one bed, $49 d two beds, $57 t). The El Rancho, in a mixed residential-business neighborhood, surrounds an inviting tropical pool and parking patio. Inside, the 49 semi-deluxe rooms are immaculate and thoughtfully and comfortably furnished. Amenities include air-conditioning, bath, cable TV, parking, and a good restaurant-bar. There is limited wheelchair access, and credit cards are accepted. The hotel's only drawback is the room arrangement, on exterior corridors, where guests must unfortunately draw blinds for privacy.

If everything else is full, the hotel that may have a room is the **Hotel Mesón** (Blv. Benito Juárez 1684, tel. 287/875-1200, or 287/875-1292, fax 287/875-1371, hotelmeson@prodigy. net.mx, $42 s or d, $43 t), on Highway 175 about 1.6 kilometers (one mi) from the river bridge. Here, the builder cleverly packed three stories of 65 rooms into a small space. The little pool, unfortunately relegated to a cramped upstairs patio, seems like an afterthought. The rooms inside, however, are clean, private, spacious, tiled, and furnished with comfortable 1980s-standard amenities. Rentals include air-conditioning, bath, cable TV, phone, restaurant-bar, wireless Internet, and parking. Credit cards are accepted.

For not many more pesos, you can stay in Tuxtepec's newest, shiniest lodging, the garden-style **Hotel Villa Esmeralda** (Articulo

123 No. 74, tel./fax 287/875-5111 or 287/875-5112, hotel_villaesmeralda@hotmail.com, www.villaesmeralda.com.mx, $40 s, $49 d, $57 t). The Villa Esmeralda, tucked into a quiet residential neighborhood, offers immaculate semi-deluxe rooms furnished with color-coordinated bedspreads, drapes, tiled floors, and shiny modern-standard baths. Additional pluses are a convenient breakfast restaurant, parking thoughtfully removed to the periphery, and an invitingly tranquil inner patio garden with large lap pool and adjacent kiddie pool. Rooms also come with air-conditioning, phone, cable TV, parking, wireless Internet, and credit cards accepted.

Food

Tuxtepec visitors enjoy plenty of good food. The two town markets, the riverview central market (on Independencia in the town center) and the west-side Mercado Flores Magón (on 20 de Noviembre, two blocks from the Hwy. 175 river bridge), are the best sources of groceries, fruits, and vegetables. At the central market, *fondas* (food stalls) upstairs serve economical, wholesome *comidas* at luxuriously airy river-view tables. Especially recommended among the market *fondas* is 🕻 **Casita María Tere** (Independencia, 7 A.M.–8 P.M. Mon.–Sat., 7 A.M.–4 P.M. Sun., $3–6).

For fresh baked offerings, go early to the **Panificadora Principal** (20 de Noviembre, tel. 287/875-0755, 7 A.M.–9 P.M. Mon.–Sat., 7 A.M.–noon Sun.), on the corner of Degollado, about five blocks east of Highway 175.

A good place to start the day is the relaxing, TV-free 🕻 **Restaurant Bla-Bla** (on 20 de Noviembre, between Morelos and Arteaga, local cell tel. 044-287/104-8570, 7 A.M.–6 P.M. daily, $4–9) in mid-downtown, a block from the river. Choose from a dozen tasty breakfasts, soups, Mexican specialties, poultry, seafood, meats, and much more.

A longtime favorite downtown restaurant, popular for its local-style food and relaxed atmosphere, is town center **Caporales** (Independencia 560, upper floor, tel. 287/875-4405, 8 A.M.–6 P.M. Tues.–Sun., $5–8). Find it across the street, upstairs, from the Hotel Mirador.

Another good choice downtown, half a block west of Caporales, is the immaculate restaurant of the **Hotel Tuxtepec** (Matamoros 2, tel. 287/875-0934, 7 A.M.–11 P.M. daily, $3–10), where you can enjoy a good breakfast, lunch, or supper.

Three stars for refined ambience and attentive service go to the restaurant **El Pesebre** (Blv. Manuel Avila Camacho 435, tel. 287/875-0722 or 287/875-0469, 8 A.M.–10 P.M. daily, $6–12), at the Hotel El Rancho, about 1.6 kilometers (one mi) diagonally northwest of downtown, two blocks from throughway Bulevar Benito Juárez. Here, you can escape from the heat and the hubbub into a cool, air-conditioned, TV-free atmosphere and select from a professionally prepared international-style menu of soups, salads, sandwiches, pasta, eggs, and fish, fowl, and meat entrées.

Its name reveals one attraction of **Casa Blanca de Espadas** (White House of Swords; 5 de Mayo 438, tel. 287/875-6520, 7 A.M.–midnight daily, $10–20). Here, you can join the family crowd for either a sumptuous breakfast buffet (about 20 choices of nearly everything) that gets even larger for *comida* and *cena* (supper). The fun really begins when the waiters begin swishing, cutting, and serving you meat, fish, and fowl with sharp kabob spears.

Another restaurant has ratcheted up culinary standards in Tuxtepec. Authentically prepared Italian-style specialties are the main attraction to the refined dining room of **(Trattoria Mediterraneo** (Blv. Muro 1759, tel. 287/875-8488, 1–11 P.M. Mon.–Sat., 1–10 P.M. Sun., $10), on the river-front boulevard, east side of town. The menu offers many fine choices. For example, start off with roasted artichoke hearts with spinach and mushrooms in olive oil, continue with breast of chicken *a la parmagiana*, and finish off with *tiramusu*. Weekend reservations are recommended.

Entertainment and Events

Tuxtepec's biggest party is the **Feria Tuxtepec,** which customarily runs for about a week during late May or early June, when local people pull all of the rabbits out of their collective hat: election of a queen, grand parade of floats, horse and cowboy parade, cockfights, fireworks, a big commercial exposition, and a folkloric dance festival, including Tuxtepec's own charming **Danza de la Flor de Piña** (Dance of the Pineapple Flower).

If you're in town on July 23 and 24, during the **Fiesta de San Juan Bautista,** be sure to get in on some of the fun around the plaza, including processions, *marmotas* (dancing giants), fireworks, and a community dance.

Tuxtepec folks also make a big celebration of the **Día de los Muertos** (Day of the Dead) on November 1 and 2. At the *panteón* (cemetery), three blocks east of the plaza's northeast corner, whole families arrive in the early evening to clean up and decorate the graves with flowers, candy, candles, and the favorite foods of the deceased, then settle down for an all-night vigil.

Tropical Tuxtepec is warm year-round, and especially so during the warm spring dry season, when folks enjoy the many local *balnearios* (river swimming beaches and natural springs). Some of the best are scattered along Highway 175 south of town.

Information and Services

Tuxtepec has several banks, all with ATMs. The longer hours of **HSBC** (805 Independencia, tel. 287/875-2211, 9 A.M.–6 P.M. Mon.–Fri.) make it a good choice. Find it between Degollado and Jiménez, about three blocks west of the town center. Alternatively, moving east, try **Bancomer** (Independencia 647, tel. 287/875-1959, 8:30 A.M.–4 P.M. Mon.–Fri.), next to the market; or **Banamex** (at Independencia and Rayón, tel. 287/875-1974, 9 A.M.–4 P.M. Mon.–Fri.), farther east.

Find the *correo* (corner of Libertad and Nicolas Bravo, tel. 287/875-0239, 9 A.M.–4:30 P.M. Mon.–Fri., Sat. 9 A.M.–1 P.M.) a block behind the town plaza church. *Telecomunicaciones* (corner of Carranza and Morelos, tel./fax 287/875-0202, 8 A.M.–7:30 P.M. Mon.–Fri., 9 A.M.–12:30 P.M. Sat.–Sun.) provides public fax and money orders.

Find it by walking, from the downtown market, four blocks from the river, inland, along Morelos.

Several **Internet** stores downtown provide email and computer services.

For nonprescription medicines and drugs, go to a *farmacia,* such as **Farmacia Cruz Verde** (Independencia 908, tel. 287/875-0774, 9 A.M.–9 P.M. daily), across from HSBC bank.

Doctors are plentiful in Tuxtepec. Ask at your hotel desk for a recommendation or go to one of the several doctors downtown. Find some of them located in the office complex across Independencia from Scotiabank Inverlat. Here choices include a gynecologist (Eliseo Camacho Delgado, tel. 287/875-3878), ophthalmologist (Julio R. Sáchez), and more.

For more choices, or in an emergency, taxi to either the **Hospital Regional Civil** (Ortiz 310, corner of Calle Sebastian, tel. 287/875-0023) or the **Hospital Seguro Social** (Blv. Benito Juárez/Hwy. 175, tel. 287/875-1366,), on the town side of the river bridge.

For police or fire emergencies, contact the **municipal police** (at the *presidencia municipal,* tel. 287/875-3166).

The local **Cámara Nacional de Comercio** (National Chamber of Commerce; on the plaza's northeast corner of Libertad and Allende, tel. 287/875-0886, 9 A.M.–7 P.M. Mon.–Fri., 9 A.M.–1 P.M. Sat.) try to answer your questions.

Alternatively, travel agents, such as **Viajes Sotelo** (Morelos 118, tel./fax 287/875-2656, 9 A.M.–2 P.M. and 4–8 P.M. Mon.–Fri., 9 A.M.–2 P.M. Sat.), at the center of town, a block from Independencia and a block west of the market, are usually willing to answer travel-related queries.

Get your laundry done at **Lavanderia Lavasec** (Independencia 1683, tel. 287/875-3706 or 287/875-5339, 9 A.M.–2 P.M. and 4–8 P.M. Mon.–Sat., 9 A.M.–2 P.M. Sun.), downtown, on the far west side, two blocks from the Highway 175 river bridge.

Getting There and Away

Long-distance bus lines, from one major terminal and two minor terminals, provide many connections with both Oaxaca and national destinations.

The major **bus station** (near the corner of Matamoros and Libertad, tel. 287/875-0237 for reservations and information) for first-class **Autobuses del Oriente** (ADO) and **Omnibus Cristóbal Colón** (OCC) and mixed first- and second-class lines **Autobuses Unidos** (AU) and **Cuenca de Papaloapan** (Cuenca), is smack in the middle of downtown, three short blocks from the river.

ADO (ah-day-oh) offers broad service, covering much of southeast Mexico. Buses connect south with Oaxaca City via Valle Nacional and Ixtlán de Juárez; northwest with Orizaba, Puebla, Mexico City (Norte terminal), and Veracruz; and northeast with Minatitlán, Coatzacoalcos, Villahermosa, Campeche, Mérida, Cancún, and Chetumal, at the Belize border.

OCC buses connect southeast with Isthmus destinations of Juchitán, Tehuántepec, and Salina Cruz; and Chiapas destinations of Tuxtla Gutiérrez and San Cristóbal las Casas.

AU buses connect north with Puebla and Mexico City; and southeast with Isthmus destinations of Matias Romero, Juchitán, Tehuántepec, and Salina Cruz.

Cuenca buses connect south with Oaxaca City via Valle Nacional and Ixtlán de Juárez; and north and northwest with Loma Bonita, Temascal, Tierra Blanca, Orizaba, Córdoba, and Veracruz.

Additionally, AU and TRV second-class buses operate out of a **second terminal** (at the west-side Flores Magón market on 20 de Noviembre), on the downtown side of the Highway 175 ingress boulevard. Buses connect west several times daily with Mazateca destinations of Ixcatlán and Jalapa de Díaz (but, at this writing, not Huautla de Jiménez) and northwest with Temascal (Miguel Alemán dam and reservoir) and Tierra Blanca.

Small, second-class line **Autobuses Trópico** (Libertad 1215, tel. 287/875-2895), operating from a third terminal (a block and a half west of Matamoros), connects six times daily with Oaxaca City via Valle Nacional and Ixtlán de Juárez.

For **drivers,** mostly good paved roads connect Tuxtepec with both Oaxaca and national destinations. Highway 175 connects south with Oaxaca City via Valle Nacional and Ixtlán de Juárez, over the Sierra Madre, in about 213 kilometers (132 mi). However, steep, winding grades can sometimes slow traffic to a crawl. Allow about five hours for safety in either direction.

Combined Highways 147 and 185 connect Tuxtepec southeast with Tehuántepec, via Matías Romero and Juchitán. The nighttime robberies and hijackings that used to plague the lonely, northern Highway 147 leg of this route have fortunately abated. To be sure, stop at the Highway 175–Highway 147 intersection gas station to check if the highway remains secure. You can ask in Spanish, *"¿Es seguro la carretera a Matias Romero?"* Allow about five hours of road time, either direction, for this 304-kilometer (189 mi) trip.

A paved, but sometimes potholed, route, Highway 182, connects Tuxtepec west with Huautla de Jiménez in the high Mazateca, via Jalapa de Díaz. Allow about 3.5 daylight hours westerly, 3 hours easterly, for this spectacularly scenic 119-kilometer (74 mi) top-of-the-world trip.

TEMASCAL AND MIGUEL ALEMÁN DAM AND RESERVOIR

Temascal (pop. 5,000) is the town where the Mexican government, under the leadership of President Miguel Alemán (1946–1952), began building a huge dam to control and harness the waters of the Río Tonto in 1946. The project, officially the Miguel Alemán Dam, was completed in 1955. A subsequent project, the Cerro de Oro Dam and Reservoir, was completed a generation later. The entire Papaloapan basin benefits from the two reservoirs, now connected, which provide irrigation water, low-cost electric power, and relief from flood devastation.

On the negative side, the dam's social cost was high. Many thousands of Mazatec, Chinantec, and Mixe indigenous campesino families suffered. Thousands had to be moved, some forcibly, from their land and relocated to new, unfamiliar locations.

Today, the Miguel Alemán Dam, towering hundreds of feet, just upstream from the town of Temascal, is the project's most visible reminder. It compares in magnitude with the great hydroelectric projects of the American

© BRUCE WHIPPERMAN

The whale-shaped silhouette of Cerro Rabón, the holy mountain of the Mazatecs, looms above Cerro de Oro reservoir.

West. Its reservoir stretches about 32 kilometers long by 24 kilometers wide (20 by 15 mi) and totals about eight cubic kilometers (two cubic mi) of water, with an average depth of around 12 meters (40 ft). The reservoir's maximum flow can generate about 500 megawatts of electric power, more than enough for the entire state of Oaxaca and nearly enough for a U.S. city the size of San Francisco.

Sights

Follow the road through Temascal town and continue another one kilometer (0.6 mi) uphill to a road fork. Bear right for the Temascal **embarcadero** (wharf), where *palapas* serve fresh fish *comidas* and motorboats on the shoreline wait for passengers. The lake is especially lovely considering that it's artificial. Fortunately, adequate water flows ordinarily keep the level constant and thus avoid the appearance of an ugly bathtub-like ring. From the embarcadero, the lake appears to stretch endlessly, invitingly blue and smooth, among green hills and small islands.

The **shoreline restaurants** specialize in *mojarra* (bass) and *camarón* (shrimp) dinners. Boat workers offer to take you on a two-hour *recorrido* (tour) around the lake for around $25 per boat, for up to about eight persons. Save money by doubling up with others. The prime destination, besides a number of shoreline hamlets, is Soyaltepec, one of the few villages, along with Ixcatlán, that didn't get swallowed up by the reservoir. Ask for young boatman **Alex Vasquez Ramírez,** or kindly **Juan Palma Mina** (who's old enough to tell you how things were here before the dam).

Besides boat rides and swimming, fishing for bass is a major local diversion. Boat workers say that the typical fish amounts to about a quarter pound, and typical catches add up to around 20 fish in a couple of hours. You can launch your own boat for free if you check with the *capitán del puerto,* at the *presidencia municipal* in Temascal; watch for the sign on the main ingress-egress street.

Parking a self-contained RV or setting up a tent is welcomed anywhere around the embarcadero (although level spots appear to be scarce). A small store at the road, just above the embarcadero, could supply water and basic food items. Better-stocked stores in Temascal could supply even more.

Before you leave, reverse your path and instead of turning left for the town, head straight along the upper-level road and take a look at the **Monument to President Miguel Alemán,** on the right before the dam. The main attraction, besides the heroic statue of Alemán, is the big mural in the open building atop the staircase. Here, government artists have tried their best to dramatize the planned benefits of the dam project. A big mural shows two contrasting worlds: before the dam, a forbidding landscape of disease, superstition, poverty, and starvation; and the bright busy modern world—natives reading, surgeons operating, scientists experimenting, engineers building, teachers teaching, farmers harvesting—after the dam.

Temascal town, back below the dam, bustles with plenty of *taquerias* for cooked eats, fruits, vegetables, and groceries, a *centro de salud, correo,* and *telecomunicaciones* near the *presidencia municipal,* and Ladatel card–operated street telephones.

Getting There and Away

Second-class AU and TRV buses connect Temascal east with Tuxtepec (west-side Flores Magón market), and north, with Tierra Blanca and Veracruz.

Drivers, from Tuxtepec follow Bulevar Benito Juárez (the northern prolongation of Hwy. 175). After about 13 kilometers (eight mi), turn left at the Ciudad Alemán sign. Continue approximately another half hour, or 26 kilometers (16 mi), and turn left at the Temascal sign. After another 21 kilometers (13 mi), continue through Temascal town to the dam, a total of 60 kilometers (37 mi) from Tuxtepec.

◧ SAN PEDRO IXCATLÁN AND THE ISLANDS

An alternate gateway to the Miguel Alemán reservoir shoreline is through Ixcatlán, a prime spot for a country stay. The town stands at the eastern boundary of the Mazateca, where many townspeople and virtually everyone in the surrounding countryside speak Mazatec, and women wear the bright blue-and-white horizontally striped local *huipil.* A number of Ixcatlán women embroider blouses and *huipiles.* Be sure to visit the modest **handicrafts shop** (Calle Benito Juárez, no phone, 10 A.M.–4 P.M. daily), maintained by the Campechano family.

You might want to plan your visit to coincide with Ixcatlán's main festival, honoring **San Isidro Labrador** (Saint Isador the Farmer; May 13–15). The fiesta's highlight is the traditional dance La Puta Chichi (Chichi the Prostitute).

Along the Road

The major sight along Highway 182, about half an hour west of Tuxtepec, is the **Puente Pescadito,** which bridges the channel connecting the Temascal and Cerro de Oro reservoirs. *Palapa* restaurants at both ends of the bridge supply refreshments and bass dinners. Below, the riverbanks, accessible on foot or by negotiable dirt roads, are level and invite fishing for *mojarra* (bass) and RV or tent camping.

The grand lake vista spreads for miles south and north. The southern arm, Reservoir Cerro de Oro, began to fill when the **Miguel de la Madrid** dam was built downstream during the 1970s. The reservoir level rose until it finally connected with the Temascal reservoir during the mid-1990s. In joining the two reservoirs, the channel consequently also connects the drainage basins of the Río Tonto, in the north, and the Río Santo Domingo, in the south. Although the Cerro de Oro reservoir is large, with about 260 square kilometers (100 sq. mi) of surface area, this is only a fraction of the size of the Temascal reservoir.

Past the bridge, Highway 182 leads through gently rolling pastoral country—once dense rain forest, now undulating parklike green pasture, sprinkled with palms and leafy trees. Thatched, whitewashed country houses appear atop the hills and around the bends. This is country where an unknown vehicle is an event.

If you're driving, wave as you go by and the people will wave back.

Ixcatlán perches atop a long hill, surrounded by picture-perfect vistas of the verdant countryside; the deeply indented, island-dotted reservoir; and in the background, the precipitous silhouette of Cerro Rabón, the Mazatecs' holy mountain. Besides all this, Ixcatlán has an inviting small hotel, a sprinkling of country *comedores,* services, and excursions to more remote, even uninhabited, islands.

Isla Soyaltepec

If it's no later than 3 P.M., you're early enough for the last trip to Isla Soyaltepec. Once a small isolated town, Soyaltepec (pop. 500) is even more isolated since the reservoir has confined it to an island where most of its friendly, frankly curious inhabitants speak only Mazatec. The only way to go is by boat, for which you can bargain (figure $15–20 for a two-hour round-trip for up to about six people) at the embarcadero on Ixcatlán's west lakeshore (below the Ixcatlán church). Beforehand, ask for highly recommended boatmen Fidel Alto Hermengildo, or Sergio Mota, both of whom live in Soyaltepec. Fidel is the Soyaltepec elementary schoolteacher and can help you find lodging if you decide to stay overnight on his island.

The 9.6 kilometer (six mi) crossing takes about half an hour. Along the way, butterflies flutter, herons stalk their prey, and clouds billow above the mirror-smooth lake surface. On the western horizon rises the gargantuan, loaf-shaped massif of **Cerro Rabón,** often cloaked in a blanket of clouds. You'll pass through a fleet of little islands, some with petite wooded crowns, perfect for an afternoon or overnight soaking in the scenery and solitude. If you do opt for an overnight, be prepared with a tent and mosquito repellent. Have your boatman return to pick you up at an appointed time.

At Soyaltepec, climb (one hour round-trip) to the old village and church on the island hilltop. Half a dozen kids will probably accompany you. Halfway up, you scale a pre-conquest-appearing ponderous stone staircase. At the top, take a look inside the venerable (1744) church, gaze westerly over the many-island-studded lake vista, and get a *refresco* (refreshment) at the hilltop store.

Accommodations and Food

(Hotel Villa del Lago (Calle Benito Juárez, tel. 287/871-3090, $26 s or d) would be a pleasant surprise anywhere, but here in little, out-of-the-way Ixcatlán, it seems a small miracle. The hotel is the labor of love of its friendly owner, Patricia Sarmiento Castillo, who rents six immaculate rooms with air-conditioning and hot-water shower-baths. She has made the hotel even more inviting with an elegantly lovely pool-patio downstairs and a top-level terrace from which guests can enjoy Ixcatlán's dramatic lake-view panorama. Señora Castillo also makes art-to-wear cotton clothing.

The reservoir, whose waters Ixcatlán escaped because of its hilltop perch, has brought fresh fish to Ixcatlán. A scattering of country *comedores* serve good lake bass dinners, notably the homey and clean **El Paraíso** *palapa* (Calle Benito Juárez, 8 A.M.–8 P.M. daily, $4–8) in mid-town, next to the *larga distancia* sign. Best for breakfast is owner Lulu Salina's **el Vaquero** (7 A.M.–9 P.M. daily, $4–10), downhill, overlooking the lake, where, besides the good food, you can feast on the luscious lake view.

Information and Services

Visitors to Ixcatlán can also count on a number of basic services, including a highly respected doctor (known locally only as Doctor Hilario) in addition to Doctor Rene Hipolito Juárez, at the *centro de salud* (Gonzalo Ortega 36, near the town entrance). Other services include pharmacies, grocery stores, a post office, long-distance telephone, and Internet access.

Getting There and Away

Get to Ixcatlán by the **Autobuses Unidos** (AU) or **TRV** bus bound for Jalapa de Díaz, from Tuxtepec's west-side Flores Magón market. Ride to the Ixcatlán side entrance road, then taxi or walk the 6.4 kilometers (four mi) to town.

Drivers: At Tuxtepec, turn left (west) from Highway 175 onto Highway 182 at the Jalapa de

Díaz sign at the traffic circle, about three blocks north of the Río Papaloapan bridge. Continue along Highway 182 west 55 kilometers (34 mi) to the signed Ixcatlán right turnoff. Continue six paved kilometers (four mi) to town.

SAN LUCAS OJITLÁN

While on your way to or from Ixcatlán, you might take the short detour into San Lucas Ojitlán at the signed junction and *gasolinera*, 43 kilometers (27 mi) west of Tuxtepec and 10 kilometers (6 mi) east of the Ixcatlán turnoff.

Ojitlán (pop. 10,000) is the *cabercera* (head town) of a medium-size Chinantec-speaking *municipio.*

Ojitlán's single main street, Independencia, bustles so continuously that few stores take the customary afternoon siesta. A good first stop would be for a cold (Jumex brand) fruit drink from the refrigerator at the friendly general store Centro Comercial del Sureste, known locally as **Tienda de Tinito** (8 A.M.–9 P.M. daily), right in the middle of town. Refreshed, from there, you could cross the street to the Internet

In Ojitlán, stop by Tienda de Tinito for a cold drink.

© BRUCE WHIPPERMAN

store, and/or walk uphill a couple of blocks, to visit both the *correo* and *telecom* (money orders and public fax). Moreover, if you need a doctor, from Tienda de Tinito, walk directly across the street and continue downhill a few blocks to the *centro de salud.*

Ojitlán's hubbub overflows on Wednesday, the regular day of *tianguis* (native town market), when hosts of country folk, including Chinantec- and Mazatec-speaking women in their brilliant *huipiles,* flock into town. Woven and embroidered textiles, mostly huipiles, make up the principal local handicraft. One of the most highly recommended weavers is Juana Muñoz; ask the proprietors of Tienda de Tinito to point you toward her house. If Juana isn't home, someone will most likely direct you to someone else.

Local excitement peaks during the big fiesta in honor of Santa Rosa, on August 28–30. Santa Rosa's popularity is a curiosity, since San Lucas, rather than Santa Rosa, is the official town patron. Community frustration over the local liturgy seems to have led to the preference for Santa Rosa. It turns out that a majority of the faithful prefer the service to be in Spanish, but the local priest and the bishop in Tuxtepec insist on Latin, which no one understands.

Townsfolk do celebrate San Lucas, but with only a token fiesta. You can see evidence of the community preference inside the old church atop the hill, at the end of the main street. Behind the altar, notice the all-female cast of saints, with Santa Rosa in the middle, and San Lucas, conspicuous by his absence.

The Mazateca

JALAPA DE DÍAZ AND VICINITY: THE LOW MAZATECA

By the time you arrive at Jalapa de Díaz, you're well into Mazatec country; walk 0.5 kilometers (0.25 mi) from town in any direction and you'll hear little, if any, Spanish spoken. For women here, wearing the *huipil* is the rule rather than the exception. Local women distinguish three grades of *huipil:* everyday, fancy, and superfancy. The latter are beautifully crocheted all by hand, often displaying a glittering throng of birds and animals, fit for a bride.

You would have little trouble finding Jalapa even if you had no Highway 182 to guide you. Jalapa stands at the foot of the vertical wall of whale-shaped **Cerro Rabón** (elev. 2,350 meters/7,700 feet), arguably Oaxaca's most uniquely prominent landmass.

Sights

The most colorful times to arrive at Jalapa are Thursday and Sunday, for the big country **tianguis,** when sellers' awnings cover half the town, thronging with native folks. Another good time to arrive is during either of the two patronal fiestas,

in honor of San Sebastián (January 19–20) and San Antonio de Padua (June 12–13).

The **Cañon del Río Santo Domingo,** which you can begin to appreciate about eight kilometers (five mi) up the highway from Jalapa, is one of Mexico's little-known wonders. The road climbs, rounding the foot of Cerro Rabón, and enters a vast cirque of verdant, jungle-clad ramparts on one side and the deep, plunging canyon on the other. At about 16 kilometers (10 mi) uphill from Jalapa, you begin to cross rushing creeks: first Arroyo Blanco, then Arroyo Caballo, then finally the blue, boiling **Río Uluapa.** Walk the (sometimes steep and slippery) path, uphill, on the Río Uluapa's right side. After about 300 meters (1000 ft), follow the river's left fork steeply uphill. Continue about 45 minutes over rocks and beneath great, vine-hung trees to a boulder-decorated pool, perfect for paddling (or even tenting for prepared backpackers). Above, see the river flow, from a yawning cave, as a pristine spring, then drop and tumble as a foaming waterfall and cascade.

Climbing Cerro Rabón

At first glance, Cerro Rabón appears tempting to climb. In fact, many local people do it every day. They tend fields on the mountainside and walk down to town afterward. The net rise amounts to about 2,000 meters (6,500 ft) and should be attempted only by fit hikers, with a guide, who start at the crack of dawn with good shoes, hat, food, and a jacket against cold. If the weather turns sour, go back or get shelter in someone's house. Lightning and cloudbursts up there could spell disaster. Clouds (as fog on the mountain) without rain are OK; they cap Cerro Rabón most of the time. This has resulted in the **cloud forest** coating the mountaintop—an eerie ice-age remnant ecosystem of giant tree ferns, hanging moss, bright liquid amber maples, big-leafed orchids, and bromeliads.

Pack something to drink, although springs along the way should suffice for most of the water. You should get formal permission from the authorities at the *presidencia municipal,* who can probably suggest a guide, such as the experienced Antonio Bravo or his son Ángel (they're beekeepers who produce honey at their nearby *rancho*).

Accommodations and Food

Most of Jalapa's business establishments line the main street, Benito Juárez, which leads about half a kilometer (0.25 mi) from the highway to the town plaza, bordered by the *presidencia municipal* on one side and the church, the Templo de San Sebastián, on the other.

Right in the middle of everything is the town's one lodging house, the family-run **Casa de Huéspedes Robertina** (Calle Benito Juárez, tel. 287/877-2009, $15 s or d). The grandmotherly owner and her son rent plain but clean rooms with bath down the hall.

Buy fruits and vegetables at the several curbside market stalls (which multiply into a big native *tianguis* on Thursday and Sunday). Groceries are available at street-front *abarroterías,* such as **Abarrotes Santa Juquila** (Calle Benito Juárez, 8 A.M.–8 P.M. Mon.–Sat., 8 A.M.–5 P.M. Sun.), a block (as you enter) before the plaza. A sprinkling of *comedores* along Juárez supply wholesome, local-style *comidas.*

For good restaurant food, try the locally recommended **Comedor Rosi** (tel. 287/877-2024, 8 A.M.–9 P.M. daily, $2–6) at the *tope* (speed bump) on the Tuxtepec end of Highway 182 through town.

Shopping

Be sure to visit the **Tienda Tres Hermanos** shop (no phone, 9 A.M.–2 P.M. and 4–8 P.M. Mon.–Sat.), on the highway about a block (Tuxtepec direction) before the downtown entrance side road. It's named for owner Fausto's sons: Herme, Paulo, and Roberto of real name Roberto Osorio. Fausto will be happy to show and sell you examples of the lovely *manteles* (tablecloths), *rebozos* (shawls), *camisas* (shirts), and *huipiles* that he, his wife, and his friends craft.

Information and Services

For simple remedies, over-the-counter drugs, and Internet, go to **Farmacia San Felipe** (tel. 287/877-2037, 8 A.M.–2 P.M. and 4–8 P.M. daily), in the town center. If in need of a doctor, visit highly respected **Doctor Ariel Quintana** (tel. 297/877-2062), also in the town center.

Find the town *correo* and *telecomunicaciones* (money orders and public fax) on the ground floor of the downtown *presidencia municipal,* on Benito Juárez, on the downhill side of the town plaza.

Getting There

Bus passengers get to Jalapa just as to Ixcatlán and Ojitlán. Ride second-class **Autobuses Unidos** (AU) or **TRV** buses west from Tuxtepec's market Flores Magón bus terminal.

Drivers: From Tuxtepec, start out exactly as for Ixcatlán (but continue 18.5 km/11.5 mi past the Ixcatlán turnoff) to Jalapa de Díaz, a total of 71 kilometers (44 mi) west of Tuxtepec or 53 kilometers (32 mi) east of Huautla de Jiménez. Heading west, turn left at the town ingress road and continue about half a kilometer (0.25 mi) uphill to the plaza and church.

HUAUTLA DE JIMÉNEZ AND VICINITY: THE HIGH MAZATECA

Huautla de Jiménez (pop. 40,000, elevation 1800 meters/6000 feet), tucked on a lofty

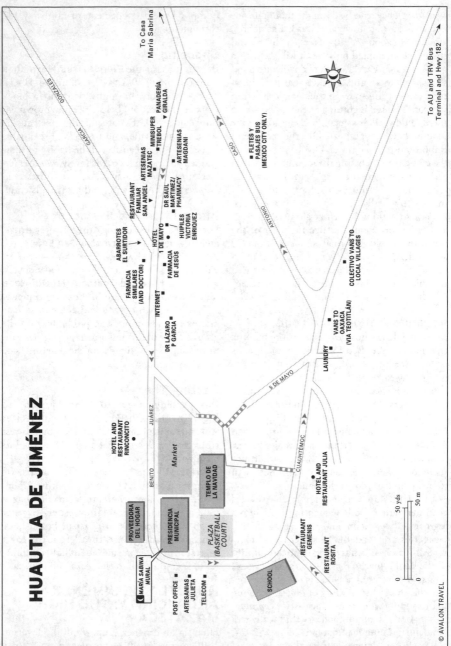

HUAUTLA DE JIMÉNEZ

To Casa
María Sabrina

To AU and TRV Bus
Terminal and Hwy 182

GONZALES

GARCÍA

CASO

ANTONIO

PANADERÍA
GIRALDA

MINISUPER
TREBOL

ARTESENIAS
MAZATEC

ARTESENIAS
MAGDANI

FLETES Y
PASAJES BUS
(MEXICO CITY ONLY)

RESTAURANT
FAMILIAR
SAN ANGEL

DR SAUL
MARTINEZ/
PHARMACY

ABARROTES
EL SURTIDOR

HOTEL
1 DE MAYO

HUIPILES
VICTORIA
ENRIQUEZ

FARMACIA
SIMILARES
(AND DOCTOR)

FARMACIA
DE JESÚS

COLECTIVO VANS TO
LOCAL VILLAGES

INTERNET

DR LÁZARO
P GARCIA

VANS TO
OAXACA
(VIA TEOTITLÁN)

5 DE MAYO

LAUNDRY

JUÁREZ

BENITO

HOTEL AND
RESTAURANT
RINCONCITO

Market

TEMPLO DE
LA NAVIDAD

CUAUHTÉMOC

HOTEL AND
RESTAURANT JULIA

PROVEEDORA
DEL HOGAR

PRESIDENCIA
MUNICIPAL

PLAZA
(BASKETBALL
COURT)

RESTAURANT
GEMENIS

RESTAURANT
ROSITA

MARÍA SABINA
MURAL

POST OFFICE

ARTESANIAS
JULIETA

TELECOM

SCHOOL

50 yds

50 m

0

0

© AVALON TRAVEL

Mazateca mountainside, was put on the world map during the 1960s by María Sabina, a local Mazatec-speaking *curandera* (indigenous medicine woman) who, like many others, used hallucinogenic mushrooms as part of her bag of remedies. The word somehow got out, and a small army of Love Generation devotees of hallucinogens from the United States and Europe, known locally as *gippis* (HEE-pees), quickly descended on Huautla. With them soon came a continuous stream of doctors, journalists, and anthropologists.

María Sabina seemed to enjoy her renown. She was invited far and wide to testify to the efficacy of her remedies at learned international medical conferences. But after a generation of fame, she passed away in 1985 at the age of 90, leaving Huautla to slumber again.

Her legacy, however, remains plainly visible in Huautla today, both in the town mural, and the several institutions that carry her name, such as the María Sabina Cultural Center, the Comedor María Sabina, and the Farmacia María Sabina.

Besides such obvious reminders, a number of new-generation *curanderos* carry on María Sabina's mission. Notable among them is her grandson, Filogonio Garcia, now middle-aged, and his son, Anselmo Garcia. María Sabina's older grandson, Eduardo Vallardares (now deceased), who was María Sabina's constant companion during her heyday, was asked by author Juan Garcia Carrera of his thoughts concerning death. He replied, "By offering you enlightenment, my mushrooms also resign you to the reality of death."

Orientation

Although the town itself spreads over a broad mountainside, the business and service center is concentrated mainly along a few downtown streets. Most important is the east–west Calle Benito Juárez. Addresses start at number one on Juárez and increase to the east. Just downhill from the west end of Juárez are the town market, *presidencia municipal,* and the church, dedicated to the Virgin of the Nativity—all situated around the town plaza–basketball court *(cancha).* A second street, Cuauhtémoc,

downhill from the plaza, runs approximately parallel to Benito Juárez to its intersection with a third street, Antonio Caso, which angles diagonally west, downhill from its east-end intersection, with Benito Juárez. Highway 182 contours along the mountainside three or four blocks downhill from the town plaza.

◖ María Sabina Mural

Make your first Huautla stop at the Huautla town hall outside portico for a look at the vivid mural, painted in 2007 by Mario Enrique Fernández Medina, in honor of María Sabina. The mural, a dramatic panorama of the life of María Sabina, sweeps from left to right. Most striking is the panel of the deep brown face of María Sabina, depicted, with her hallucinogenic mushrooms, leading her followers through a transcendental window to a new, enlightened dimension. There they join with a saint-like visage of María Sabina, who, finally transformed into an eagle, cleanses (symbolized by the egg) the bodies and souls of her clients.

Inside the town hall, a modest museum displays artifacts, documents, photos, and mementos that illustrate Huautla's history from pre-Conquest through the excitement and fame of María Sabina's heyday to the present.

Casa María Sabina

El Fortín, the east-end ridgetop Barrio where María Sabina lived, is well-known and revered by most all Huautlecos. Her old house (Carretera María Sabina 149 A, Barrio El Fortín, Huautla de Jiménez, Oaxaca, local cell tel. 044-236/102-8567, guest rooms $10 pp), a simple iron-roofed stucco dwelling, is being maintained by her grandson Filogonio Garcia and his family as both museum and lodging house for guests interested in the legacy of María Sabina.

Filogonio, a highly respected and sensitive *curandero* (folk healer) carries on his grandmother's tradition, offering professional therapeutic sessions in an adjacent ceremonial room.

As part of their mission, Filogonio and

his family offer a pair of simple, clean guest rooms (with shared hot-water bath), sleeping three and two people, respectively, in the Casa María Sabina.

Find Casa María Sabina in the east-side uphill ridgetop neighborhood. It's best to get there by taxi ($3) from downtown. If, however, you prefer walking (with hat, good shoes, and drinking water), head out east along downtown Calle Benito Juárez, always uphill, asking directions ("¿Casa María Sabina?") and you'll probably arrive at the modest grocery store, at 149A Carretera María Sabina, that the family maintains, after about an hour's walk.

Cerro de Adoración

From Casa María Sabina, continue to sacred site Cerro de Adoración along the dirt road, then path, continuing gradually upward along the right-hand slope of the ridgetop. Your destination is just beyond the highest hill visible ahead along the ridgetop, where, after another half-hour ascent, you'll reach the summit called Cerro de Adoración. Here, you'll find a monument with four crosses where local folks carry offerings, especially around May 3, El Día de la Santa Cruz (The Day of the Holy Cross). Besides meeting folks along the trail carrying wood or herding goats, your reward will most likely be a cool breeze and a breathtaking panoramic vista of billowing clouds and rugged peaks, sprinkled with a dozen seemingly Lilliputian villages on their slopes.

Accommodations

Newish **((** **Hotel Santa Julia** (Calle Cuauhtémoc 12, tel. 236/378-0586, $15 s or d, $17 s or d upstairs, $19 t) is a welcome addition for Huautla visitors. Twenty-one spacious, clean, and comfortably furnished rooms, with hot-water shower-baths, provide the basics, with TV, parking, and restaurant. The most pleasant are the upstairs rooms, some with views, on the sunny south side. Find the hotel on the south, downhill side of the plaza. (If the Santa Julia is full, try its sister hotel, also Hotel Santa Julia (local cell tel. 044-236/105-6986), not so centrally located, however, on

Highway 182, three blocks, downhill, three blocks west, same prices, but with good seafood restaurant.

Third choice goes to **Hotel Rinconcito** (Calle Benito Juárez 8, tel. 236/378-0136, 236/378-0243, or 236/378-0005, fax 236/378-0674, $16 s, $18 d in one bed, $25 d, t in two beds), across Benito Juárez from the market. Husband-wife owners Leonardo Altamirano and Catalina Casamiro rent eight plain but clean rooms with hot-water baths. The best are in front, with sunny views of the market below and the mountains in the distance.

Running a distant fourth choice, two blocks west, is the rough but clean **Hotel 1 de Mayo** (Calle Benito Juárez 30, tel. 236/378-0076, $15 s, $17 d). The three stories of approximately 20 small barebones rooms have hot-water baths.

Food

Go to the town market for the freshest fruits and vegetables. The best grocery selection is at **Minisuper El Trebol** (Calle Benito Juárez 41, tel. 236/378-0027, 9 A.M.–4 P.M. and 6–9 P.M. daily), across from the Hotel 1 de Mayo.

For fresh-baked goods, try the **Panadería Giralda** (Calle Benito Juárez 21, no phone, 7 A.M.–9 P.M. Thurs.–Tues.). Find snacks, such as hamburgers, hot dogs, and *tortas,* at the stand in front of the Hotel Rinconcito, across Benito Juárez from the market.

Huautla's few restaurants are all strictly local country-style. You can expect cleanliness and at least a choice of avocado, beans, *bolillos* (crispy bread rolls), bottled water, cheese, chicken, cucumber, eggs, fruit juice, milk, pork, salsa, spaghetti, steak, tomatoes, and tortillas. A trio of acceptable eateries is on or near Avenida Cuauhtémoc. Find the homey and reliable **((** **Restaurant Rosita** (tel. 236/378-0386, 7 A.M.–10 P.M. daily, $3–6) below the plaza's southwest corner, a few doors down the lane that angles off of Cuauhtémoc. Its airy porch dining room with a view is an extra plus, especially for breakfast and lunch.

Also nearby, you might check out the more basic **Restaurant Gemenis** (Cuauhtémoc 11, 7 A.M.–10 P.M. daily, $3–6), or alternatively, back uphill, on Benito Juárez, the family-run **Restaurant Familiar San Ángel** (7:30 A.M.– 7 P.M. Mon.–Sat., $3–6).

Festivals

The most colorful times to arrive in town are during the patronal celebration **Fiesta de la Virgen de La Natividad** (September 7–8), **El Día de los Muertos** (Day of the Dead, November 1–2), and the **Feria Comercial** (climaxing on the third Friday of Lent, 22 days before Easter Sunday). The Feria Comercial is attended by a host of villagers who crowd in from the surrounding mountains to watch their favorite traditional dances, including the Flor de Naranjo (Orange Tree Flower), Flor de Piña (Pineapple), Flor de Lis (Heaven), and Anillo de Oro (Ring of Gold). If you miss these, at least try to be present on Sunday for the big *tianguis* (native town market), when vendors' awnings fill the entire center of town.

Shopping

Huautla offers some opportunities to shop for its prized, colorful textiles. Around the market, especially, you'll see the reason for the enthusiasm: women in handmade *huipiles* adorned with bright embroidered birds, fruits, flowers, and rainbows of pink-, yellow-, and blue-striped satin.

In addition to the *huipiles,* local women craft and embroider blouses, napkins, shirts, skirts, and tablecloths in floral and animal designs. Buy them at either market stalls, streetfront shops, or at the homes of individual craftspeople; ask Catalina Casamiro, at the Hotel Rinconcito (Calle Benito Juárez 8, tel. 236/378-0136, 236/378-0243, or 236/378-0005) for recommendations.

A number of streetfront shops along Benito Juárez offer quality handicrafts. Three shops stand out. Your first stop should be just east of the Hotel 1 de Mayo, at the shop of **Victoria Enriquez** (on Benito Juárez, tel. 236/378-0449, 8 A.M.–4 P.M. and 6–9 P.M. daily). She's followed her bliss for forty years, crafting lovely *huipiles.*

For a multicolored selection of *huipiles,*

(manteles) embroidered tablecloths, and brightly costumed dolls, continue another few doors east to **Artesanías Magdani** (Benito Juárez 40, no phone, 8 A.M.–8 P.M. Mon.–Sat., 8 A.M.–3 P.M. Sun.).

Next, cross the street to **Artesanías de la Región Mazateca** (Benito Juárez 37, no phone, 9 A.M.–2 P.M. and 4–8 P.M. Mon.–Sat., 9 A.M.–2 P.M. Sun.) for more lovely examples. Finally, return back to the town plaza, where on the west side, lower level, facing the church, **Artesanías Julieta** (9 A.M.–8 P.M. Mon.–Sat.) offers yet more handsomely embroidered *huipiles,* blouses, and dresses.

Information and Services

At this writing, Huautla still has neither a bank nor an ATM. Hopefully one will reopen by the time you read this. If not, it's best to stock up with pesos in Tuxtepec, or at least arrive with some U.S. dollars that you could probably change at the Hotel Santa Julia or Hotel Rinconcito if you're staying there, or the Minisuper Trebol, on Benito Juárez.

A trio of doctors maintain offices on Benito Juárez. Moving east, first find **Dr. Lázaro Pérez Garcia** (Benito Juárez 12, upstairs, 8 A.M.–3 P.M. and 5–8 P.M. Mon.–Sat., also available on call). A block farther east, you'll find **Dr. Saul Martínez,** at his **pharmacy** (Benito Juárez, tel. 236/378-0257, pharmacy: 8 A.M.–10 P.M. daily; consultations: 9 A.M.–1 P.M. and 3–7 P.M. Mon.–Sat.); he's also on call 24 hours a day. Also find **Dr. Flores Ramos** at his **Farmacia Similares** (Benito Juárez 21D, tel. 236/378-0857, 9 A.M.–3 P.M. and 5–9 P.M. Mon.–Sat.).

Nonprescription medicines and drugs are available at additional pharmacies on Benito Juárez, such as **Farmacia de Jesús** (Benito Juárez 16, 8 A.M.–2 P.M. and 4–8 P.M. daily).

The *correo* (8 A.M.–3 P.M. Mon.–Fri.) and *telecom* (tel. 236/378-0397, 8 A.M.–3 P.M. Mon.–Fri., 8 A.M.–1 P.M. Sat.) stand side by side on the plaza's west side, above the shops, across the street (west) from the *presidencia municipal.*

Long-distance telephone is available at the

Hotel Rinconcito desk (Benito Juárez 8, tel. 236/378-0136, 236/378-0243, or 236/378-0005, 8 A.M.–9 P.M.).

Answer email at Internet store **Digital Net** (Benito Juárez 14A, tel. 236/378-0669, 9 A.M.–9 P.M. daily).

Photographic services, such as develop-and-print, cameras, supplies, film, and black-and-white development, have come to Huautla at **Foto Isis** (Benito Juárez 19, tel. 236/378-0062, 9 A.M.–9 P.M. Mon.–Sat., 9 A.M.–3 P.M. Sun.).

Get your laundry reliably done at the small *lavandería* (tel. 236/378-0337, 9 A.M.–3 P.M. and 5–9 P.M. daily), half a block down the alley, adjacent to the Hotel Santa Julia, that runs downhill from Calle Cuauhtémoc.

Getting There and Away

Second-class **Fletes y Pasajes** buses (tel. 236/378-0406) operate out of a terminal on Calle Antonio Caso, which runs diagonally downhill from Calle Benito Juárez. They connect west with Teotitlán del Camino, thence south with Oaxaca City via Cuicatlán; and northwest with Mexico City via Tehuacán and Puebla. Furthermore, on Highway 182, both second-class **TRV** (tel. 236/378-0834) and **Autobuses Unidos** connect with Teotitlan, Puebla, and Mexico City. Additionally, **Autotransportes Turísticos Cañada y Oaxaca** (cell tel. 044-236/102-0530) vans connect, via Teotitlán and Cuicatlán, hourly during the day with Oaxaca City from their terminal at Calle Cuauhtémoc 23. Furthermore, from the street-side, just below the downhill intersection of Cuauhtémoc and Antonio Caso, a lineup of *colectivo* vans connect with a swarm of local villages, such as Eloxochitlán and San Agustín.

Note: as of this writing, no buses nor vans connect Huautla east, down mountain, with Jalapa de Díaz or Tuxtepec. (Although, one of the *colectivos* on Antonio Caso, next to the vans, most likely connects with a downhill town, where you can catch another *colectivo* to Jalapa de Díaz, and thence to Tuxtepec.)

For **drivers,** paved Highway 182 connects Huautla east with Tuxtepec via Jalapa de Díaz, along 122 kilometers (76 mi) of winding but breathtakingly scenic mountain road. For safety, allow 3 hours eastbound, downhill, or 3.5 hours westbound, uphill. In a westerly direction, Highway 182 connects Huautla east with Teotitlán del Camino in 66 kilometers (41 mi) of paved, downhill, winding, scenic mountain road. (From Teotitlán, Hwy. 135 connects south an additional 161 km/100 mi, about 3.5 hours, with Oaxaca City.) Allow 2 hours downhill (westerly) and 2.5 hours uphill (easterly).

Unleaded gasoline is available at the Pemex gas station on the highway a few blocks south, downhill from the town center.

EXCURSIONS AROUND HUAUTLA

The area around Huautla, a verdant, dramatically folded landscape of mountains and deep valleys, hides a number of natural wonders, the best known of which include two spectacular limestone caves and a twin waterfall.

【 Las Regaderas

Easiest to get to and see is Las Regaderas, a pair of waterfalls not far west along Highway 182 from Huautla. Get there by car, AU or TRV bus, or local *colectivo* van to Puente de Fierro, marked by a big Santa María Chicotla sign and arch, about 6.6 kilometers (four mi) west, Teotitlán direction, from Huautla. Just before the bridge, turn right and continue past the arch to a side road. Turn and continue one kilometer (0.6 mi) downhill to the falls.

Las Regaderas (The Showers) plummet 30 meters (100 ft) out of a jungly cliff into a wild, tumbling river. Great trees (apparently identical to California sycamores, *Platanus racemosa*), shade both banks. A steel-cable suspension walkway bridges the river next to a rustic riverside cabin. A short extension bridge accesses the cool spray at the foot of the falls. Some informal riverbank camping sites may be usable during low water, February–May. Security may be a problem, however. Drunkenness seems to be a major local pastime. Ask at the stores past the bridge on the highway: "*¿Es seguro acampar a las regaderas?*"

Shade and cool rushing water are Las Regaderas' prime assets.

© BRUCE WHIPPERMAN

Nindo-Da-Gé

Even more spectacular is Nindo-Da-Gé (Broad Spring Mountain) cave, first explored completely in 1905, near the little town of San Antonio Eloxochitlán (ay-loh-shoh-CHEET-lahn). With a guide, you can explore several of the cave's 19 main galleries, some gigantic, some petite, in half a day. The seemingly endless procession of dripping limestone formations, which have names such as The Infernal Hill, The Fort, The Snail, and Marimba, are even more fun if you dream up your own names.

The town invites visitors to camp locally (town stores can supply food and water) and explore their cave. Recently, authorities completed a road to the cave, which can be reached from town in about two kilometers (1.2 mi) by road, and only another one kilometer (0.6 mi) by foot trail.

The only obstacle to exploring the cave is the reasonable one that for safety reasons you must have a guide recommended by civic authorities. (The guide receives no money; he or she serves as part of their community service obligation. However, do offer a donation, perhaps about $20, in a sealed envelope, to the *ayuntamiento,* city government.)

A town cave committee is in charge. The easiest procedure would be to arrive early enough (say, by 9 or 10 A.M.) to arrange for a guide. A good person to contact would be personable, former cave committee member and friendly schoolteacher, Professor Froilan Rios, whose house stands on the left side of the paved road as you enter town. He recommends Alonzo and Sergio Nieto as the best guides. The minimum excursion requires most of a day. Arrive early and bring at least two strong flashlights (four-celled or more, with extra batteries), good-traction shoes, and enough hard hats (hard plastic construction type) for everyone.

Furthermore, the Eloxochitlán community offers a super extended adventure, an eight-kilometer (five mi), two-day overnight, that, on the second day, continues clear through to the cave's east-end exit, at Cabaña. Your preparations must include all of the equipment above, plus food for all, including your guide, and, at least, sleeping equipment and a super-bright illumination lamp, with extra batteries.

Get to San Antonio Eloxochitlán by bus or car 11 kilometers (seven mi) along the Teotitlán (west) direction on Highway 182, to the San Antonio turnoff gravel road on the right (north). Continue 7.7 kilometers (4.8 mi) to the town church, plaza, and *presidencia municipal.* (You can view some videos of recent explorations of the cave by logging "San Antonio Eloxochitlán You Tube" into Google.)

Sotano de San Agustín

Cave enthusiasts might also enjoy hiking to the Sotano de San Agustín (Pit of San Agustín), near the village of San Agustín, on Highway 182, a few miles northeast of Huautla. The cave was only discovered during the 1990s. With a total depth of about a mile (1,440 meters/4,800 feet) and a number of long single drops (the longest at around 105 meters/350 feet), the San

Agustín cave is considered among the deepest in the world. You can reach the cave entrance accompanied by a local guide (inquire at the San Agustín *presidencia municipal*) via the steep downhill trail from near the town church. As for exploring the cave itself, only super-equipped and experienced speleologists should apply to local authorities for permission to enter.

The Cañada: Canyon Country

Shadowed from rain by mountains on all sides, the dry, tropical Cañada canyonland comprises one of Oaxaca's major geo-cultural regions. It encompasses the Cuicateca—the land of the Cuicatecs—a Mixtec-related people who, for longer than anyone can remember, have hunted and farmed their homeland's cactus-plumed canyon bottoms and temperate upland valleys. Reclusive and traditional, Cuicatec people generally venture out from their home villages only infrequently, mostly to trade at the market towns—sometimes Teotitlán del Camino, more often at Cuicatlán.

TEOTITLÁN DEL CAMINO

Just shy of Oaxaca's border with the state of Puebla stands Teotitlán del Camino (pop. 5,000), the jumping-off point for the Mazateca

highlands to the east and the Cañada to the south. Teotitlán's elevation, 1,100 meters (3,600 ft), places it about 1.6 kilometers (one mi) lower and many degrees warmer than sometimes-chilly Huautla de Jiménez, in the Mazateca highlands. Teotitlán's fortunate combination of warmth, sunshine, and abundant spring water nourishes a local oasis of mangos, bananas, lemons, oranges, and avocados.

Orientation

Despite Teotitlán's significance as the capital of the sprawling governmental district of the same name, it nevertheless feels much like a small town, with a modicum of stores and services within a block or two of the central plaza. Streets run approximately east–west (uphill–downhill) and north–south. The three main

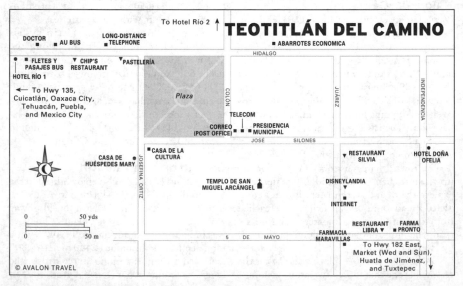

east–west streets are Hidalgo, the Highway 135 ingress street that runs along the plaza's north side; José Silones, between the plaza and the church; and 5 de Mayo, a block south of the plaza along the church's south side. The main north–south streets are Josefina Ortiz de Domínguez, which runs along the west side of the plaza; Juárez, behind and east of the church; and Independencia, the Highway 182 ingress from Huautla, one block farther east (uphill).

Sights

The town's pride is its church, the **Templo de San Miguel Arcángel,** built by Franciscan padres during the 17th century. Outside, an image of angel San Miguel decorates the pinnacle of its Roman Doric–columned facade. Inside, the ceiling is a cheery sky blue, with bright paintings of Saints John (Juan), Matthew (Mateo), Luke (Lucas), and Mark (Marcos) around the central cupola overhead. The broad church atrium out front is usually very quiet, except around September 29, when local folks honor San Miguel with processions, fireworks, and floats ridden by children dressed as angels.

Take a stroll around the adjacent town plaza, where big shady trees provide a welcome refuge from the warm afternoon sun. At night, the plaza becomes the town's central meeting ground, where couples stroll and people relax on benches attractively decorated with bright Puebla tile.

If it's Wednesday or Sunday, another focus of activity is the market on Independencia, about two blocks south of the plaza. The big Teotitlán market structure was obviously built for better times. It's presently empty as a tomb five days a week.

Accommodations

The town has at least two acceptable hotels, a *casa de huéspedes* (guesthouse), and a sprinkling of restaurants, one highly recommended. The best hotel is the new **Hotel Río 1** (José Guadalupe 3, tel. 363/372-0017, $16 s, $18 d in one bed, $22 d two beds, $25 t), three blocks directly north of the plaza. The 24

comfortable, attractively furnished rooms are arranged in a two-story garden-view tier off of a quiet residential street; they come with cable TV, private hot-water shower-baths, parking, and a pool (not operating at this writing) in a back patio.

The other good hotel is the also new brother **Hotel Río 2** (Calle Hidalgo, across from the AU bus station, tel. 363/372-0017, ($17 s, d one bed, $20 d two beds, $23 t) with 13 rooms, comfortably furnished with color-coordinated drapes and bedspreads, and with cable TV, in-house Internet, hot-water shower-baths, and parking.

On the other hand, budget travelers may prefer the plain but homey and clean **Casa de Huéspedes Mary** (tel. 363/372-0242, $7 s, $14 d), diagonally across the street from the plaza's southwest corner.

Food

Go to Teotitlán's best restaurant **Chips** (tel. 363/372-0473, 9 A.M.–10 P.M. daily, $3–10) across Hidalgo from the AU bus station. Kick back and relax in the cool airy, rear *palapa,* away from street noise, and choose from a long selection of nearly everything, from ham and eggs and hot dogs, to tacos and *tlayudas.* Add an extensive seafood selection and you've got it all.

A couple more good food choices are the pub-like **Disneylandia** (Benito Juárez, tel. 236/372-0164, noon–11:30 P.M. daily, *comida* until 7 P.M.), uphill, in the middle of the block; and *comedor* **Libra** (near Benito Juárez–5 de Mayo corner, 8 A.M.–8 P.M. daily, also with *comida* until around 5 P.M.), uphill.

Yet another good choice, convenient to motorists, is the highly recommended **Restaurant Blanca Flor** (Hwy. 135, tel. 363/372-0326, 10 A.M.–10 P.M. daily), on Highway 135, five blocks downhill from the town plaza, just south of the big obelisk monument.

For snacks and refreshments, stop to cool off beneath the shady plaza-front portal of **Paleteria La Michoacana.** Take your pick from a host of flavors of juices, ices, and ice cream.

Get your groceries and yummy Jumex-brand canned juices at the small **Abarrotes Santa Lucia** (8 A.M.–9 P.M. daily), at the southeast plaza corner.

Information and Services

Teotitlán plaza-front establishments can supply most emergency needs. Start with the *correo* (no phone, 8 A.M.–4:30 P.M. Mon.–Fri., 8 A.M.–12:30 P.M. Sat.), in the *presidencia municipal,* southeast plaza corner; and next door, the *telégrafos* (tel. 363/372-0171, 9 A.M.–4 P.M. Mon.–Fri., 9 A.M.–12:30 P.M. Sat.), offers money orders and telegrams, but no fax. For telephone and fax, find the *larga distancia* (Hidalgo, 8 A.M.–9 P.M. daily) by the bus station, half a block downhill from the plaza. Connect to the Internet at **Travel Net** (Benito Juárez 26, at mid-block, uphill, between Silones and 5 de Mayo, tel. 363/372-0480, 9 A.M.–4 P.M. and 5–10:30 P.M. Mon.–Sat., 9 A.M.–4 P.M. Sun.).

For medicines, go to the **Farmacia las Maravillas** (corner of Benito Juárez and 5 de Mayo, tel. 363/372-0374, 7 A.M.–10:30 P.M. daily), of general practitioner Hector Vargas, M.D., behind the church. If las Maravillas doesn't have what you need, continue uphill along 5 de Mayo half a block to **Farmacia Pronto** (8 A.M.–11 P.M. daily).

For medical consultations, visit the town's favorite doctor, **Miguel Ángel Ramírez Tenorio, M.D.** (Hidalgo, 9 A.M.–2 P.M. and 4–8:30 P.M. Mon.–Sat.), a block downhill from the plaza, next to the bus station. Alternatively, go to the 24-hour **Seguro Socialclinic** (Hwy. 182, tel. 363/372-0139), several blocks north of the town center, on Highway 182, uphill from Highway 135–Highway 182 intersection and obelisk monument.

Getting There and Away

Second-class buses operate out of terminals on Hidalgo, downhill from the plaza. First comes **Autobuses Unidos** (AU; tel. 363/383-0972), which connects northwest with Mexico City via Tehuacán and Puebla; and east with

Huautla. Also, **Fletes y Pasajes** buses (tel. 236/372-0282), three blocks farther downhill, connect south with Oaxaca City via Cuicatlán; northwest with Mexico City via Tehuacán and Puebla; and east with Huautla. Additionally, the vans of **Transportes Turísticas Cañada-Oaxaca** (at curbside, on Hidalgo, by Autobuses Unidos) connect south with Oaxaca City via Cuicatlán, and east with Huautla.

For drivers, paved Highway 182 connects Teotitlán east with Huautla in 66 kilometers (41 mi) of scenic but winding uphill mountain road. For safety, allow 2.5 hours (or 2 hours in the opposite, downhill, direction). In a southerly direction, Highway 135 connects with Oaxaca City, via Cuicatlán, in a winding but easy (with caution) 161 kilometers (100 mi). Allow about 3.5 hours of driving time, either direction. In a northerly direction, Highway 135 connects with Tehuacán (63 km/39 mi, one hour). From there, you can continue northwest to Puebla either via the toll expressway in an additional 93-kilometer (70 mi), 1.5-hour trip (or 3 hours via old two-lane Highway 150).

Unleaded gasoline is available at the Pemex *gasolinera* on the highway, about two kilometers (1.2 mi) northwest of the town plaza.

CUICATLÁN

Cuicatlán (pop. 10,000) is the commercial capital of the Cañada, the emporium for the entire high sierra hinterland that rises steeply, east of town. Cuicatlán, like Teotitlán, owes its wealth to abundant sunshine and water. In Cuicatlán, water is synonymous with the Río Grande, the river that passes just west of town. After nourishing a local oasis of fruit, vegetables, and grain, the Río Grande continues its good work downstream. It joins with the swarm of tributaries draining the entire Cañada basin, becoming the Río Santo Domingo, the major electrical power source at the Miguel de la Madrid dam. The river unites with the Río Papaloapan past Tuxtepec, finally feeding thirsty crops and people all the way to the Gulf of Mexico.

Sights

Cuicatlán (Place of Song) is home to a busy market, often packed with Cuicatec-speaking people, especially women, wearing their handmade *huipiles*. Head there via the turnoff road from Highway 135, which, as it becomes Avenida Hidalgo, Cuicatlán's main north–south business street, leads 1.6 kilometers (one mi) north to the plaza at the town center. There stands the church, the **Templo de San Juan Bautista**, on the plaza's east side. Juárez, the main east–west street, runs past the church, half a block east to the *presidencia municipal* and continues uphill. (You can see all this in one grand panorama, if you continue uphill, east on Juárez, and follow the path to El Mirador, at the summit of the rocky hill east of town.)

Back down on Juárez, across the street, south, from the *presidencia municipal* spreads the **market.** Although it's lively enough most days, the market is especially big on Saturdays and Sundays and overflowing around June 24, when merrymakers crowd the streets and celebrate the **Fiesta de San Juan Bautista** with costumes, parades and floats, community feasts, fireworks, and traditional dances.

Step into the cool interior of the church, and pay your respects to Saint John the Baptist reigning high, above Jesus (whom he baptized). Above all, however, see the fluttering Dove of the Holy Spirit and the glorious golden sunrays emanating from the all-seeing eye of God.

Accommodations and Food

Cuicatlán offers three recommendable hotels. The best by far is **Hotel Sochiapan** (Calle Hidalgo 40, tel. 236/374-0001, $22 s, d one bed, $26 d two beds, $30 t) with about 35 immaculate, attractively decorated rooms. The welcoming owner said that she plans to put in a pool. Rooms come with hot-water shower-baths and cable TV.

In the town center, a couple of blocks uphill from the bus station, travelers might find the renovated **Casa Marina** (Calle Hidalgo, no phone, $14 s, $16 d) too convenient to pass up.

It offers about 10 spare but clean rooms around a parking patio, with fans and hot-water showers and toilets; credit cards are not accepted.

Alternatively, you can check out Cuicatlán's most pretentious hostelry, the **Hotel Tijuana** (Juárez 9, tel. 236/374-0116, $16 s, $18 d in one bed, $21 d in two beds, $26 t), one block east, uphill, from the *presidencia municipal*. Past the inviting lobby, a stairway rises to an airy upstairs view patio, encircled by two floors of 14 immaculate, attractively decorated rooms with private hot-water shower-baths and toilets. An unusual feature of the Hotel Tijuana is the downstairs billiards room, next to a crimson-wallpapered sitting room. (The manager said the billiards room closes nightly at 10 P.M.)

As for food, you'll find the freshest fruit and vegetables in the market and the best grocery selection at the **Super El Molino** (tel. 236/374-0008, 7 A.M.–4 P.M. and 5–10 P.M. daily), at the plaza's southeast corner, across the street from the church.

Cuicatlán's best place to eat by far is the clean, seafood-specialty ◖ **Restaurant Boringuen** (Juárez, tel. 236/374-0222, 8:30 A.M.–10 P.M., $3–5), uphill, two blocks east of the plaza, on the same side as the Hotel Tijuana. Here, from her spic-and-span kitchen, the grandmotherly owner puts out a stream of tasty breakfasts (like a cheese omelet), Mexican specialties (leg of pork tacos, *tlayuda*), and shrimp and calamari.

Information and Services

Most of Cuicatlán's service establishments are either on the town plaza or along Calle Hidalgo, the north–south Highway 135 ingress street. Although Cuicatlán still has no bank, you might be able to cash a small travelers check (or at least a $20 bill) at the grocery store **Super El Molino** (tel. 236/374-0008, 7 A.M.–4 P.M. and 5–10 P.M. daily), at the town plaza's southeast corner. A long-distance telephone and Internet access is available at the small *caseta larga distancia* (tel. 236/374-0209, 7:30 A.M.–10:30 P.M. daily), on the plaza at the east corner of Hidalgo.

Buy stamps or mail a letter at the *correo* (Leona Vicario, 9 A.M.–3 P.M. Mon.–Fri., 9 A.M.–2 P.M. Sat.). Also, next door to the *correo,* send a money order or a fax at the *tele-comunicaciones* (Leona Vicario, 9 A.M.–3 P.M. Mon.–Fri., 9 A.M.–12:30 P.M. Sat.). Find them both on Leona Vicario, next to the *presidencia municipal.*

For nonprescription medicines and drugs, cross to the north side of the plaza, to **Farma Pronto** (by the basketball court, tel. 236/374-0326, 7 A.M.–11 P.M. daily).

For a medical consultation, see **Dr. Rudolfo Reyes Escalante** (Calle Centenario 30, tel. 236/374-0033). To get there from the plaza, walk two blocks down Hidalgo to Centenario, then turn right half a block. Alternatively, go to the 24-hour public *centro de salud* (on Hidalgo, tel. 236/374-0299), three blocks downhill from the plaza.

Getting There and Away

Autobuses Unidos (tel. 236/374-0014) second-class long-distance buses operate out of their terminal on Hidalgo, about four blocks downhill from the plaza. Buses connect, either north with Mexico City via Teotitlán, Tehuacán, and Puebla, or south with Oaxaca City.

If, however, you have the inclination to enjoy an adventure into virtually untouristed territory, ride one of the early minibuses that head from the big terminal lot, adjacent, downhill from the bus station, to indigenous Cuicateco mountain villages, such as such Concepción Papalo, San Miguel Santa Flor, and Santa María Tlalixtac.

For **drivers,** Highway 135 connects south with Highway 190 at Telixtlahuaca, thence with Oaxaca City, a total of 101 kilometers (63 mi). The route, paved and in good condition but winding, requires about two hours for safety.

In the northerly direction, Highway 135 connects with Teotitlán del Camino in about 60 kilometers (37 mi), 1.5 hours. From there, continue either east via Highway 182, 66 additional kilometers (41 mi), 2 hours, to Huautla; or north via Highway 135, another 63 kilometers (39 mi) to Tehuacán, 1.5 hours, and thence to Puebla (a total of five hours), and Mexico City (a total of seven hours, or five hours total via the toll expressways 135 D and 150 D).

THE ISTHMUS

A trip to the Isthmus of Tehuántepec from the Oaxaca central highlands sometimes seems like a journey to another country. At the Isthmus, the North American continent narrows to a scarce 160 kilometers (100 mi) in width; the mighty Sierras shrink to mere foothills. The climate is tropical; the land is fertile and well watered. Luxuriant groves hang heavy with almonds, avocados, coconuts, mangos, and oranges. Rivers wind downhill to the sea, springs well up at the foot of mountains, and swarms of fish swim offshore. The Isthmus is a land of abundance, and it shows in the people. Women are renowned for their beauty, independent spirit, and their incomparably lovely flowered skirts and blouses, which young and old seem to wear at any excuse.

And they have excuses aplenty, for the Isthmus is the place of the *velas,* called fiestas in other parts of Mexico. But in the Isthmus, especially in the towns of Tehuántepec and Juchitán, where *istmeño* hearts beat fastest, *velas* are something more special. Most every barrio (neighborhood) must celebrate one in honor of its patron saint. A short list names 20 major yearly *velas* in Juchitán alone. The long list, including all the towns in the Isthmus, numbers more than 100.

If you're lucky to arrive during one of these *velas,* you may even be invited to share in the fun. Local folks dress up, women in their spectacularly flowered *traje* (traditional indigenous dress) and men with their diminutive Tehuántepec sombreros, red kerchiefs, sashes, and machetes. Sometimes entire villages or town barrios celebrate for days, eating, drinking, and dancing to

© BRUCE WHIPPERMAN

THE ISTHMUS

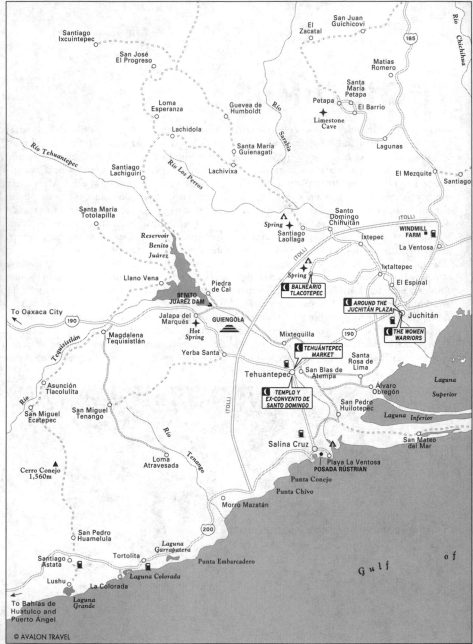

© AVALON TRAVEL

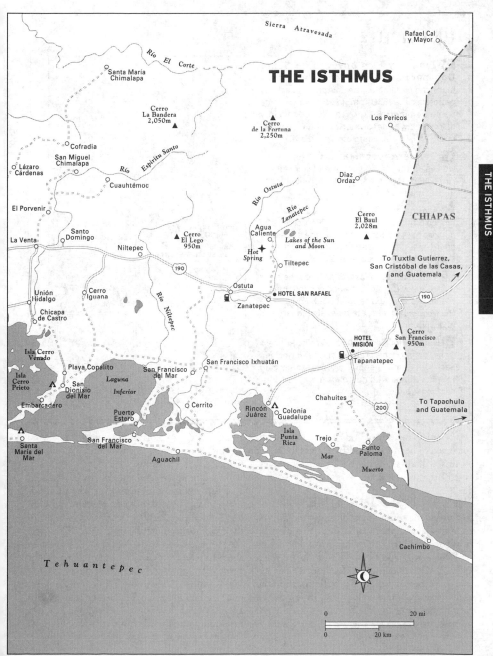

THE ISTHMUS

HIGHLIGHTS

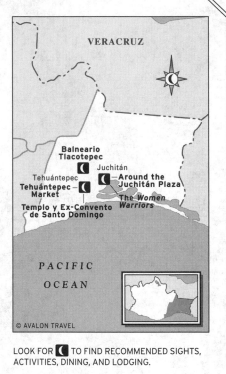

© AVALON TRAVEL

◖ Templo y Ex-Convento de Santo Domingo: Around the Tehuántepec town plaza, the highlight is the church and partially restored, circa 1530 Templo y Ex-Convento de Santo Domingo. Be sure to see the recently discovered wall decorations painted by indigenous artists 450 years ago (page 331).

◖ Tehuántepec Market: The native women, in their extravagant and colorful floral *huipiles*, steal the show at the Tehuántepec market (page 332).

◖ Around the Juchitán Plaza: The flowers, gold filigree, and flowery embroiderered *huipiles* for sale, not to mention the all-female cadre of vendors, are the main attraction on the Juchitán plaza (page 343).

◖ The *Women Warriors:* From the river bridge, enjoy the airy view and cooling breeze, then cross over to the west bank and admire the *Women Warriors*, stainless steel guardians of Juchitán (page 344).

◖ Balneario Tlacotepec: Heroine Princess Donaji donated this precious crystal spring and park for Isthmus people to enjoy, something they have done with gusto for more than four centuries (page 351).

LOOK FOR ◖ TO FIND RECOMMENDED SIGHTS, ACTIVITIES, DINING, AND LODGING.

the beautiful melody of "La Sandunga," which, once you've been captured by its lovely, lilting strains, will always bring back your most cherished Isthmus memories.

PLANNING YOUR TIME

A convenient route to including the Isthmus in your Oaxaca plan would be with a circular side trip, including the vibrant market towns of Tehuántepec and Juchitán en route between Oaxaca City and the Pacific resorts. For example, you could bus, drive, or fly south to the coast, spend some days basking in the South Seas ambience of the Pacific resorts, then begin your return to Oaxaca City east along the coast by either bus, car, or tour, enjoying four days

along the way exploring the colorful markets, cuisine, and sights, both manufactured and natural, of the Isthmus.

For example, be sure to do plenty of strolling, and perhaps some shopping, in the fascinatingly colorful **Tehuántepec Market** hubbub, highlighted especially by the *tehuana* women in their radiantly colorful native dress. Along the way, be sure to do as the local folks do and hop aboard a *motocarro* (small motorcycle truck) for a ride around town. Later, don't miss enjoying at least one deliciously authentic Tehuántepec meal in the showplace Restaurant Scaru. With an additional day, you could enjoy a day trip to Guiengola ruined mountain fortress city, continuing on for a soak in the authentically

hammocks for sale in Juchitán

© BRUCE WHIPPERMAN

rustic *agua caliente* (warm spring) at Jalapa del Marqués village, and/or a lake bass dinner at restful garden Restaurant Del Camino.

The next day, continue east half an hour to Juchitán. Here, soak in the colorful scene with plenty of strolling around the **Juchitán plaza** and market. Along the way, be sure to see the vibrant flower and handicrafts stalls, with riots of roses and lilies and their gold filigree, exquisite flowered *huipiles,* bright hammocks, multicolored pottery, and much more. Take a break with lunch in the airy inner patio of the plaza-front Restaurant Casa Grande. In the later afternoon, don't miss strolling a few blocks west to enjoy the breeze and view from the tranquil Río Los Perros riverbank. And especially don't miss taking a look at the monumental **Women Warriors** stainless steel sculptures overlooking the river.

Finally, enjoy another day by taking a picnic (and your bathing suit) to the historical and uniquely lovely Isthmus excursion park, at the crystalline blue springs that bubble up at **Balneario Tlacotepec,** about an hour by bus north of Juchitán.

Tehuántepec and Vicinity

Although both Juchitán and Salina Cruz are the Isthmus's big, bustling business centers, quieter, more traditional Tehuántepec remains foremost in the minds of most *istmeños* as the former pre-Columbian royal capital, the seat of Cosijopí, the beloved last king of the Zapotecs. Local people are constantly reminded of their rich royal history by virtue of the Templo y Ex-Convento de Santo Domingo, the construction of which was unique in Oaxaca because it was financed by an indigenous monarch, Cosijopí. Moreover, local people can directly see their ancestors' contribution to history by glimpsing the ancient (recently discovered) floral and

THE ISTHMUS

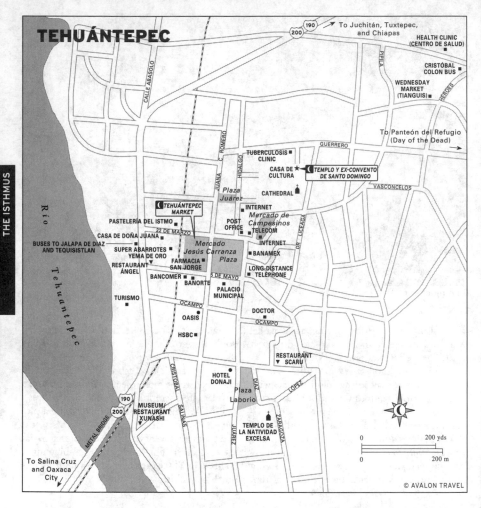

TEHUÁNTEPEC

To Juchitán, Tuxtepec, and Chiapas

HEALTH CLINIC (CENTRO DE SALUD)

CRISTÓBAL COLON BUS

WEDNESDAY MARKET (TIANGUIS)

To Panteón del Refugio (Day of the Dead)

CALLE ABASOLO

ROMERO

JUANA

HIDALGO

PIPILA

HEROES

GUERRERO

TUBERCULOSIS CLINIC

CASA DE CULTURA ★

TEMPLO Y EX-CONVENTO DE SANTO DOMINGO

VASCONCELOS

Plaza Juárez

CATHEDRAL

TEHUÁNTEPEC MARKET

PASTELERÍA DEL ISTMO

CASA DE DOÑA JUANA

BUSES TO JALAPA DE DIAZ AND TEQUISISTLAN

SUPER ABARROTES YEMA DE ORO

RESTAURANT ÁNGEL

22 DE MARZO

FARMACIA SAN JORGE

BANCOMER

BANORTE

INTERNET

Mercado de Campesinos

POST OFFICE

TELECOM

INTERNET

BANAMEX

Mercado Jesús Carranza Plaza

5 DE MAYO

LONG-DISTANCE TELEPHONE

PALACIO MUNICIPAL

DR. LICEAGA

Río

Tehuantepec

TURISMO

OASIS

HSBC

OCAMPO

DOCTOR

OCAMPO

RESTAURANT SCARU

CRISTOBAL

SALINAS

HOTEL DONAJI

Plaza Laborio

DIAZ

LOPEZ

METAL BRIDGE

190
200

MUSEUM/ RESTAURANT XUNASHI

JUAREZ

TEMPLO DE LA NATIVIDAD EXCELSA

ZARAGOZA

To Salina Cruz and Oaxaca City

0   200 yds

0   200 m

© AVALON TRAVEL

animal decorations that their ancestors painted on the walls of the ex-convent nearly half a millennium ago.

The town of Tehuántepec is geographically the center of the Isthmus. Roads, like spokes of a wheel, branch out in all directions, south to Salina Cruz, northeast to Juchitán, and northwest to Oaxaca City. This means that travelers from Oaxaca City most easily reach both Juchitán and Salina Cruz by passing through the fortunate town of Tehuántepec.

HISTORY

Although strictly connected only with a single location, the name Tehuántepec (Hill of the Jaguar) is, in many minds, synonymous with the entire Isthmus region: thus the label the "Isthmus of Tehuántepec." The connection is historical, for Tehuántepec's dominance was born in events of long ago.

The earliest known settlers in the Isthmus left Olmec-style remains, which archaeologists date from as early as 4000 B.C. Much later, around 500 B.C., the Olmecs' inheritors, probably the ancestors of present-day Mixe- and Huave-speaking people, occupied the Isthmus lands. But times changed, and by A.D. 500 the Isthmus had become a strategic funnel: a trade gateway between the great civilizations, such as Teotihuacán and Monte Albán, of the Mexican central highlands, and the rich Mayan cultures of Chiapas, Yucatán, and Guatemala.

Eventually, the more populous Zapotec-speaking people displaced the Mixe and Huave in the Isthmus. By A.D. 1400, the Zapotec kings of Zaachila in Oaxaca's central valley controlled the Isthmus gateway with a mountaintop fort at Guiengola, which guarded their Isthmus capital at the present-day town of Tehuántepec.

The ambitious Aztec emperors also coveted the Isthmus gateway. In the 1440s, they sent armies to Oaxaca to pressure the Mixtec and Zapotec kingdoms, who allied themselves against the Aztecs. But forced by Aztec victories in 1486, many Zapotec people, including their king Cosijoeza, retreated from Zaachila and took refuge in Tehuántepec. There, together with the Mixtecs under King Dzahuindanda, the Zapotecs, attacking from their stronghold at Guiengola, held off the Aztecs, who offered Emperor Moctezuma's daughter in marriage to King Cosijoeza as part of a peace pact.

With tranquility established, Cosijoeza returned to reign once again over Zaachila, leaving his son, Cosijopí, as king of the Isthmus, with his court at Tehuántepec. Later, when the Spanish arrived, King Cosijopí joined with Cortés against the Aztecs. After Aztec power was erased, Cosijopí, along with thousands of his subject-inhabitants of Tehuántepec, converted to Christianity.

ORIENTATION

Although the Río Tehuántepec splits the Santo Domingo Tehuántepec town (pop. 52,000) along a roughly north–south line, the west-side portion, across the river via the Puente Metalico (Metal Bridge), first built for locomotives around 1900, seems like a mere suburb of the town center, east of the river. On the central plaza itself, the *presidencia municipal* occupies the south side, along Calle 5 de Mayo; the main market, **Mercado Jesús Carranza,** lies on the plaza's west, river side, along Calle Juana C. Romero; and to the northeast, past the end of main north–south street Benito Juárez, about a block and a half northeast of the plaza, stands Tehuántepec's most venerable monument, the **Templo y Ex-Convento de Santo Domingo.**

SIGHTS
Around the Plaza

First, take a stroll around the plaza, where you'll find some interesting sculptures, including noble likenesses of Miguel Hidalgo (the Father of Mexican Independence) and a pair of Tehuántepec heroes. On the north side, look for the bronze of a seated **Doña Juana Catalina Romero** (1855–1915), a Tehuántepec legend. She is famous partly for her good works, establishing schools for Tehuántepec children during the days when public education was a rarity in Mexico.

On the plaza's west (market) side, you'll find the bronze bust of **A. Maximino Ramón Ortiz,** the first and only governor of the Isthmus, when it was separated from Oaxaca as the territory of Tehuántepec for a few years during the 1850s. Politics, however, were not Ortiz's first love. He is best remembered as the composer of "La Sandunga," Tehuántepec's beloved theme. His ageless melody seems to perfectly capture the essence of the Isthmus in a gracefully drowsy rhythm that swings slowly, yet deliberately, like the relaxed sway of lovers in a hammock beneath the deep shade of a Tehuántepec grove.

◖ Templo y Ex-Convento de Santo Domingo

From the plaza's northeast corner, walk north along Calle Hidalgo one block to the venerable Santo Domingo church, behind its broad fenced atrium, on the right. The aging landmark (to the left of the new church) is interesting partly because it was one of the few, if not the only, Christian churches in Mexico financed by a native ruler. Cosijopí, the last king of the Zapotecs, was baptized as Juan Cortés de Cosijopí after his friend and ally Hernán Cortés paid for the construction with both cash and the labor of thousands of his subjects. The building was erected under the supervision of Fray Fernando de Albequerque, vicar of Tehuántepec, between 1544 and 1550.

Given the warm relations between King Cosijopí and the Spanish, it is ironic that the Inquisition authorities burned Cosijopí at the stake a generation later for continuing (and for encouraging his people) to worship the old gods.

Enter through an interior side door, off the left-aisle of the very attractive new church. Inside, old Santo Domingo's most remarkable feature is its lovely wooden *tabla* (altarpiece), with an unusual ebony Lord of Creation perched on its crest, with a dog, turtle, and deer in tow. (At last visit, the ebony statue had been removed, but a local priest told me that it would probably be returned after the present church remodeling work is finished.)

The ex-convent section, on the old church's north side, was abandoned not long after the Reforms of the late 1850s forced the Dominicans from Mexico. It had crumbled into a virtual ruin by the mid-20th century, when local people rolled up their sleeves and began restoring it in 1953. In 1982, with the restoration complete, the townsfolk christened their ex-convent as the **Casa de la Cultura** (tel. 971/715-0114, 9 a.m.–2 p.m. and 5–8 p.m. Mon.–Fri., 9 a.m.–2 p.m. Sat.). Now, in the evenings it resounds with the noises of young musicians and dancers at practice.

To take a look inside the restored ex-convent, retrace your steps out across the atrium, turn right at Calle Hidalgo, and walk north. After two short blocks, turn right at Guerrero. Walk one long block. Just after the tuberculosis clinic (formerly *centro de salud*) turn right into an alley, which leads directly south to the Casa de la Cultura and the old convent.

Inside the Casa de la Cultura, look for the faded but still-visible flower and animal motifs that Cosijopí's long-gone artists painted on the walls nearly four centuries ago. Head upstairs

where the ancient wall decorations appear as fresh as if they were painted only a generation ago. In other upstairs rooms you'll see a host of historical mementos, from ancient Olmec-style figurines to a lovely jade necklace, once scattered, but excavated piece by piece and finally reassembled here. (Sometimes the upstairs is closed. If so, it's worth seeking permission from the administrative secretary on the ground floor, in the cloister, to let you go upstairs.)

(Tehuántepec Market

The most colorful downtown action goes on at the **Mercado Jesús Carranza,** just across Romero from the plaza. At midday, the market overflows with life. The center of everything is the corridor street on the market's north side, which connects the plaza with the businesses along the railroad tracks behind the market.

The buzzing *motocarros* (motorcycle minitrucks) that you see depositing and picking up passengers by the railroad track seem to be a unique Isthmus invention. They mostly follow

Women do virtually all the buying and selling at the Tehuántepec Market.

© BRUCE WHIPPERMAN

JUANA CATALINA ROMERO: HEROINE OF TEHUÁNTEPEC

Why Tehuántepec's main downtown streets, which carry such nationally renowned labels as 5 de Mayo, Benito Juárez, and Hidalgo, should include Juana C. Romero among them is a question nearly all adult townsfolk can immediately answer. "Doña Juana," they say, is Tehuántepec's heroine because she "built schools and helped the children of Tehuántepec." Some go on to say that she "got lots of help for Tehuántepec from her friend, Presidente Porfirio Díaz."

When pressed, most Tehuántepec folks acknowledge that she had a close (some even say intimate) relationship with Porfirio Díaz. Juana Catalina was a 21-year-old Zapotec beauty when she was first introduced to Díaz in 1858. At that time, he was an ambitious young captain in the army of President Benito Juárez, struggling to win the bloody see-saw civil War of the Reform that pitted liberal against conservative forces everywhere in Mexico.

Although he must have been charmed by her at their first meeting, most certainly nothing immediate came of it, since, when he proposed to her, she turned him down. People say that she told him, "Yours is a liberal mission, with President Juárez, to save Mexico, while my mission is here in Tehuántepec, helping my people."

Whatever passed between them during later years has been the subject of endless gossip. What is certain, however, is that she never married, and they were certainly close confidantes. Moreover, Don Porfirio had the railroad tracks laid right past her house in downtown Tehuántepec, because, it is speculated, he could hop off the train and visit her any time with no fuss or muss.

Juana Catalina Romero is fondly remembered by Tehuántepec people for her kindness and good works.

© BRUCE WHIPPERMAN

set round-trip routes around town for a fixed price of about $1 (10 pesos). When you get tired of walking, hop on for a breezy whirlwind tour of Tehuántepec's back streets.

Market vendors, especially women in *traje* (traditional indigenous dress), tend to be apprehensive of rubber-necking strangers with cameras in hand. A good strategy is to blend in. Get a *refresco* (refreshment) at one of the food stalls and find a low-profile spot in the shade where you can take in the passing scene.

Get some relief from the heat and bustle inside the roofed market building itself. If you're in the mood for shopping, plenty of handicrafts are available. On the bottom floor, stalls offer the gold filigree jewelry (at this writing, mostly faux-gold filigree, since gold is so expensive) that the Tehuántepec women love to wear. Look farther for lots of woven goods, such as baskets, string bags of *ixtle* fiber, hand fans, and hammocks. One unusual item that you may see during the late spring are large, one-meter-long (three-foot-long) pods of decorative flowers of *coyul.*

Upstairs, via the stairway on the southwest corner by the railroad track, you'll find Tehuántepec's pride—the beautiful embroidered *tehuana* flowered blouses and skirts. Look around, decide what you want, then bargain for it. Asking prices for the prized, embroidered flower–design blouses run as much as $100, a whole outfit about $200, with bargaining.

Behind the market runs the **railway track,** which has the distinct appearance of being abandoned, because dozens of vendors regularly set up where trains should come rolling through.

Pottery, including many big, homely items—bowls, griddles, planters, pots—is for sale at the second downtown market, the lackluster Mercado 5 de Febrero, sometimes known as the **Mercado de Campesinos,** tucked at the plaza's northwest corner. Smaller for-sale items include pots painted with bright flowers as well as woven goods, such as baskets, fans, and handmade brooms and *piñatas.*

Besides the two aforementioned permanent daily markets near the plaza, country people flood into town for *tianguis* (native town market) on Wednesday and Sunday. Visit the Wednesday *tianguis,* set up along north-side Calle Héroes, most easily by riding a *motocarro* from the plaza. Alternatively, from the plaza, walk north along Hidalgo past the church. Two blocks from the plaza, turn right on Guerrero and continue several blocks to the blue-trimmed San Juan Bautista church, where you turn left at Héroes. After a few blocks, you'll see the awnings stretched along side streets.

The Sunday *tianguis* is much bigger, so much so that it's held on the west side across the river, beyond the big Oaxaca highway intersection, in the open space behind the Hotel Gueixhoba.

Casa de Doña Juana Catalina Romero

The railway track so intimately close to the market is due to the speculated intimate relationship between President Porfirio Díaz and local beauty Doña Juana Catalina Romero (1837–1915). Doña Juana Catalina lived in the French-style mansion, now in faded white with fancy blue window awnings in need of serious renovation, which rises by the tracks. Some say that the tracks were built right out front so Díaz could visit her with ease. Until recent years Doña Juana Catalina's elderly granddaughter resided there. Lately, with her retirement, her heirs subsequently sold the house to another family. It is rumored that the state and community are planning to buy it and convert it into a museum.

La Cueva

If you feel like an early-morning or late-afternoon walk, head for La Cueva (The Cave), as local folks call it. It's visible most of the way up the hill called Liesa, across the river about three kilometers (two mi) west of town. La Cueva has been hallowed ground for as long as anyone remembers. Local folks tell stories about the existence of a secret passageway somewhere at the back of the cave that leads all the way to Guiengola, the "old town," now a mysterious ruin on the mountain 16 kilometers (10 mi) to the west.

La Cueva still draws virtually everyone in town for a pilgrimage during both Semana Santa (Good Friday) and Día de la Cruz (May 3). It's best not to try the climb during the heat of the day (allow at least an hour for the whole excursion). In order to get a head start, spend a couple of dollars (20 pesos) on a taxi or *motocarro* (motorcycle mini-truck) to take you to the base of the hill.

Plaza Laborio

A number of smaller plazas dot Tehuántepec's several barrios. If you head south along Juárez two long blocks, you'll arrive at Plaza Laborio and its adjacent blue-trimmed, storybook **Templo de la Natividad Excelsa.** Before you go inside to look around, notice that the right bell tower is tilted at a crazy angle, not unlike the Leaning Tower of Pisa. Laborio (the name of the church's barrio) residents don't seem to worry. "It's been like that for years," they say.

Plaza Laborio is mostly sleepy, except during the August 31–September 11 **Fiesta Laborio,** when residents and visitors celebrate with a long menu of feasts, dancing, fireworks, and *calendas* (processions).

Museum and Restaurant Xunashi

Housed in a colonial-era family mansion-factory, this museum (Callejon El Faro 1A, local cell tel. 971/129-7990, noon–5 P.M. daily, $3) is decorated with a flock of antiques, that range from a giant portrait of the Virgin of Guadalupe and ancient wooden looms, to an entire chapel of devotional memorabilia and a whole kitchen of great pottery jugs.

Welcoming owners Jose Manuel Villalobos and his wife Mari Carmen and their children offer a hearty Mexican *comida* (noon–5 P.M. daily, $6) in their baronial river-view dining room. Get there either by short taxi ride from the plaza, or walking two blocks south from the plaza's southwest corner. Turn right at the Hotel Donaji (corner of Plaza Laborio) and continue another two blocks, to the corner of Cristobal Salinas. Turn left one block, then turn right and continue a short block to the mansion, above, on the right.

Barrio de Santa María

Also worth a visit, across the river, is the Barrio de Santa María. (Get there by bearing left at the street heading diagonally left from the highway, a block or two west of the river bridge; after about two more blocks, go left again.) The main community pride and joy is the (also bright blue and white) **Templo de la Virgen de la Asunción.** The church, by the same architect who built the famous pilgrimage church in Juquila, is the focus of a busy round of barrio events. The bustle climaxes during the August 13–18 **Fiesta Patronal del Barrio de Santa María Reolotoca,** with a *calenda* (procession), parade of flower-decorated bull-drawn carts, and earsplitting popular dances on three successive nights. Bring your earplugs.

ACCOMMODATIONS
Under $50

Tehuántepec offers visitors at least three hotels: one is semi-deluxe, in the west suburb; and a pair downtown is more modest, but very recommendable. A good choice downtown is the **Oasis** (Melchor Ocampo 8, tel. 971/715-0008, fax 971/715-0835, www.hotelesdeoaxaca.com, hoteloasistehuantepec.html, h.oasis@hotmail.com, $18 s, $22 d one bed, $26 d in two beds, $30 t with fans; or $30 s, $35 d with a/c), removed a block south from the plaza hubbub, behind the *presidencia municipal.* Although at first glance the Oasis doesn't appear very exciting, a closer examination reveals the talents of the owner, friendly English-speaking artist Julín (hoo-LEEN) Contreras, whose work decorates the hotel's restaurant wall. (She was also commissioned to do the mural in the council chamber on the 2nd floor of the *presidencia municipal.*)

The hotel building offers four stories of 28 clean and comfortable rooms that enfold in an invitingly leafy and tranquil inner patio. The rooms feature colorful bedspreads and

© BRUCE WHIPPERMAN

Museum and Restaurant Xunashi offers a hearty Mexican lunch in the midst of colonial-era furnishings.

THE ISTHMUS

curtains, walls decorated with the owner's art, and private warm-water shower-baths. In most rooms, windows open to a garden, mountain, or river view. Pottery and plants selected by the owner decorate hotel niches and corridors. In the building's inner patio, a towering *chico zapote* tree stretches skyward. A parking lot provides security for cars. There is a good, relaxed, Restaurant Almendro (Almond Tree). Visa credit cards and dogs and cats are accepted. For lovers of the way Mexico "used to be," this is the place. Besides all of the above, Julín invites guests to visit her on-site art studio and also offers Isthmus culinary tours. A couple of minuses are the hotel's corridor rooms, where curtains must be drawn for privacy, and the hotel's sometimes lackadaisical desk staff.

An arguably better choice downtown is the **Hotel Denali** (Juarez 10, tel. 971/715-0064, fax 971/715-0448, hoteldonaji@hotmail.com, $20 s, $25 d fan only, $30 s, $35 d with a/c), named for Oaxaca's beloved Apothecia heroine and located two blocks south of the plaza on quiet Plaza Laborio. This renovated hotel is very popular locally by virtue of its inviting, plant-decorated inner restaurant patio. The 48 rooms, in a big two-story block, are simply but invitingly decorated, with hot-water shower-baths, cable TV, a small pool-patio, and credit cards accepted.

Over $50

Tehuántepec's fanciest hotel is the four-star **Hotel Guiexhoba** (ghee-ay-SHOW-bah; Carretera Panamericana Km 250.5, Barrio Santa María, tel./fax 971/715-1710 or 971/715-0416, guiexhoba@prodigy.net.mx, $45 s, $58 d, $70 t), which deserves extra points simply for its Zapotec label, the name of a locally abundant white flower with a fragrant scent reminiscent of jasmine. The hotel has a specimen bush, which blooms during the summer rainy season, by the front entrance. Find the hotel on Highway 190, inbound from Oaxaca City on the right before the bridge.

The Guiexhoba's 36 spacious, clean, and comfortable rooms, in two stories, enclose a parking courtyard that fortunately shields rooms on its north side from highway noise. Staff are generally attentive, competent, and courteous. The upstairs rooms away from the highway are quiet and have fewer people walking past the windows, whose drapes, unfortunately, must be drawn for privacy. Amenities include big pool, parking, cable TV, air-conditioning, hot-water shower-baths, credit cards accepted, in-house Internet, and the very good Restaurant Guiexhoba.

FOOD
Groceries and Treats

Tehuántepec's freshest fruit and vegetable sources by far are the luscious mounds of avocados, bananas, carrots, lettuce, mangos, pineapples, radishes, and much more in the plaza market. Likewise, find the best grocery sources, such as the **Super Abarrotes Yema** (tel. 971/715-0489, 8 A.M.–8:30 P.M. daily), by the railroad tracks just west (river side) of the market.

Satisfy your sweet tooth with the baked offerings of the **Super Panadería y Pastelería del Istmo** (tel. 971/715-0808, 8 A.M.–8:30 P.M. daily). Find it on the railroad tracks, just north of the market, on the left. For evening snacks, fill up at the taco stalls lined up behind the *presidencia municipal.*

Restaurants

You'll probably find that it's most convenient to have breakfast at your hotel, such as the **Restaurant Almendro** (Melchor Ocampo 8, tel. 971/715-0008, fax 971/715-0835, www.hotelesdeoaxaca.com) of the Oasis hotel and the restaurant at the Hotel Guiexhoba. Otherwise go to Tehuántepec's best, the refined Restaurant Scaru, three blocks south of the plaza.

Tehuántepec offers a sprinkling of good sit-down restaurants. By far the most colorful is the **Restaurant Scaru** (at south-side cul-de-sac Callejon Leona Vicario 4, tel. 971/715-0646, 8 A.M.–11 P.M. daily, $5–10). Here, in a graceful, airy setting, owners lovingly portray picturesque aspects of traditional Isthmus life. Walls bloom with murals of fruit, festivals, and lovely *tehuanas* in their bright, flowery costumes, while patios are sprinkled with hammocks and sheltered overhead by luxurious handcrafted *palapas.* Saturday and Sunday afternoons 2–6 P.M., a marimba band will play "La Sandunga" to your heart's content. After such a luscious introduction, the food, from a very recognizable menu of salads, soups, eggs, pastas, meats (including some game), fish, and fowl, is no less than you would expect. Get there from the plaza by walking two long blocks south along Juárez to Plaza Laborio. Turn left and walk one block to Callejon Leona Vicario on the left; the restaurant is on the uphill side of the street. Credit cards are not accepted.

Second choice goes to the good but more ordinarily picturesque restaurant at the **Hotel Guiexhoba** (Hwy. 190 Km 250.5, tel. 971/715-1710, 7:30 A.M.–10 P.M. daily, $5–12), across the river. The food, from a typical but tasty menu of breakfast (eggs and pancakes), lunch (hamburgers, soups, and stews), and dinner (meat, fish, fowl, and spaghetti), sometimes comes with a flaming crepe Suzette flourish. Credit cards are accepted.

Back downtown, for a restful *comida,* go to the singularly interesting **Museum and Restaurant Xunashi** (Callejon El Faro 1A, local cell tel. 971/129-7990, noon–5 P.M. daily).

INFORMATION AND SERVICES
Tourist Information

For travel recommendations and help in emergencies, go to the friendly **Turismo office** (on Hwy. 200 south, Salina Cruz direction, no phone, 9 A.M.–7 P.M. daily), overlooking the Río Tehuántepec, two blocks west and two blocks south of the town plaza, before the river bridge.

Health and Emergencies

A number of town pharmacies provide both over-the-counter remedies and prescription drugs. Perhaps the best stocked is the town-center branch of the **Farmacia San Jorge**

(Romero, 8 A.M.–8 P.M. daily), located in a permanent street stall, right on Romero, on the market side of the town plaza.

If you need to consult a doctor, you can always find one at the big 24-hour **Hospital Materno** (Hwy. 190, tel. 971/713-7252) across from the bus station.

Alternatively, you have another highly recommended choice, **Dr. José Manuel Vichido** (Calle Ocampo, tel. 971/715-0862, 9 A.M.–2 P.M. Mon.–Sat.). From the plaza's southeast corner, walk south one block along Juárez; turn left at the first street, Ocampo. The doctor's office is half a block farther on the left.

Police service is available from at least two sources in Tehuántepec. Call either the *policía municipal* (tel. 971/713-7000), or the emergency number (dial 066).

Money

Tehuántepec has some banks, all with ATMs. On the plaza's southeast side, go to up-and-coming **Banorte** (5 de Mayo, 971/715-0140, 9 A.M.–4 P.M. Mon.–Fri.) across from the market. Next door, also find **Bancomer** (5 de Mayo, tel. 971/715-1253, 8:30 A.M.–4 P.M. Mon.–Fri.).

Communications

Both the *correo* (at the plaza's northeast corner, tel. 971/715-0106, 8 A.M.–4:30 P.M. Mon.–Fri., 8 A.M.–noon Sat.), including rapid, secure **Mexpost** service, and *telecomunicaciones* (at the plaza's northeast corner, tel. 971/715-1197, 8 A.M.–5 P.M. Mon.–Fri., 9 A.M.–noon Sat. and Sun.), for money orders and public fax, stand side by side at the plaza's northeast, Calle Hidalgo, corner.

Long-distance telephone, fax, and photocopies are available at **Papelería La Esfera** (at the plaza's southeast corner, tel. 971/715-0042, fax 971/715-2090, 8 A.M.–8 P.M. Mon.–Sat., 9 A.M.–2 P.M. Sun.).

Find Internet access at **Fusion** (Hidalgo, no phone, 9 A.M.–10 P.M. daily), a short block north of the plaza, across from the little Juárez park.

GETTING THERE AND AWAY
By Bus

The vintage Tehuántepec bus station was sup-posed to be replaced years ago by a brand-new terminal, which remains yet unused. Meanwhile, on Highway 190-200, about a mile north of the town plaza, the old **bus terminal** (tel. 971/715-0108 for information and reserva-tions for nearly all departures) still bustles with activity. Get there by taxi or *motocarro* (motor-cycle mini-truck) from the plaza.

Four major bus lines, first-class **Autobuses** **del Oriente** (ADO) and **Omnibus Cristóbal Colón** (OCC), and mixed first- and second-class **Sur** and **Autobuses Unidos** (AU), offer many connections. Departures connect north and east via Juchitán with Tuxtepec, Villahermosa, Palenque, Minatitlán, Coatzacoalcos, Mérida, Cancún and Tulum; northwest with Oaxaca City, Puebla, and Mexico City; southwest with Salina Cruz, Bahías de Huatulco, Pochutla (Puerto Ángel), and Puerto Escondido; and east via Juchitán, Tuxtla Gutiérrez, San Cristóbal las Casas, and Tapachula at the Guatemala border.

SCOOTING AROUND BY *MOTOCARRO*

The city of Tehuántepec's public transpor-tation system was long ago preempted by the town's regiment of *motocarros* – small, motorcycle-driven flat-bed trucks that buzz, putt, squeal, and skid around town continu-ously. The center of the action is the railroad track behind the market, where all Tehuánte-pec *motocarros* faithfully return for passen-gers and cargo.

Motocarros have thus become the end-all answer to how to get around in Tehuántepec's heat. Long ago, everyone (excepting mad dogs and Englishmen) learned that too much mid-day walking can produce a considerable sweat at best and sunstroke at worst. If you get over-heated, do as Tehuántepec people do and take a seat in the shade and cool down with an *agua* or *refresco*. Later, continue your breezy ex-tended tour via *motocarro*. Fares run about $1 for an entire circuit of the town.

Beat the heat by riding around town in a *motocarro*.

© BRUCE WHIPPERMAN

In addition, from an adjacent terminal, a pair of independent second-class cooperating lines, **Oaxaca Istmo** and **Fletes y Pasajes** offer connections northwest with Oaxaca City and west with Bahías de Huatulco, Pochutla (Puerto Ángel), and Puerto Escondido, while Fletes y Pasajes also offers connections northwest with Oaxaca City, southwest with Salina Cruz, and northeast with Juchitán.

By Car

Good paved roads fan out from Tehuántepec in four directions. Highway 190-200 connects northeast with Juchitán (27 km/17 mi), then splits north as Highway 185 at La Ventosa and continues north, via Matías Romero and Minatitlán, all the way to the Gulf of Mexico at Coatzacoalcos, a total of 267 kilometers (166 mi). Allow about 4.5 driving hours, either way, for this relatively easy trip.

For Tuxtepec and northern Oaxaca, from cross-Isthmus Highway 185, turn onto Highway 147 at Matías Romero and continue northwest a total of 304 kilometers (189 mi) from Tehuántepec. Allow about five hours of driving time. *Note:* In the past, some robberies have occurred on the long (two-hour), lonely Highway 147 Matías Romero–Tuxtepec leg. Although security now appears to not be a problem, authorities still advise travelers to restrict their driving to *daytime only* on this stretch.

Highway 190 connects Tehuántepec northwest with Oaxaca City along 250 kilometers (155 mi) of well-maintained but winding highway. Allow about 5 hours in the Oaxaca City direction (uphill), 4.5 hours in the opposite direction.

Highway 200 connects Tehuántepec west with the Oaxaca Pacific coast, via Salina Cruz (15 km/9 mi), Bahías de Huatulco (161 km/100 mi, three hours), Pochutla–Puerto Ángel (200 km/124 mi, four hours), and Puerto Escondido (274 km/170 mi, five hours) on paved, moderately traveled, secure highway.

Combined Highway 190-200 connects Tehuántepec east via Juchitán (27 km/17 mi) and Niltepec to Tapanatepec (126 km/78 mi) near the Chiapas border and beyond to Guatemala. Allow about 3.5 hours of driving time to Tapanatepec.

Drivers should fill up with gasoline at the Pemex *gasolinera* on the west side of the river, about two kilometers (1.2 mi) west of the bridge, where the road splits southwest to Salina Cruz, northwest to Oaxaca City.

EXCURSIONS WEST OF TEHUÁNTEPEC

The interesting destination trio of Guiengola, Jalapa del Marqués, and Tequisistlán can be combined into a full-day auto or taxi excursion (two days by bus) west of Tehuántepec. Along the way, enjoy a vigorous hike through pristine forest to the regal ruined fortress-city at Guiengola, a breezy boat ride on the Jalapa del Marqués reservoir, a soak in the community hot (actually just warm) spring, and a look at what is probably the world's only marble basketball court, topped off by a stop by the marble factory at Tequisistlán.

Guiengola

The mountain fortress Guiengola (ghee-ayn-GOH-lah, Big Rock in Zapotec) may have been abandoned before the Spanish arrived, but it was never forgotten. Local people refer to it as the "old town" and sometimes hear eerie voices up there. If so, they rush down the mountain before dark.

Ghosts notwithstanding, an excursion to Guiengola is a chance to get some fresh air into your lungs as you enjoy the Isthmus tropical forest up close—fluttering butterflies, spiny cactus, flowery trees, and fireflies and hoot owls (if you return at dusk).

At the end of the rough jeep road that winds about six kilometers (four mi) up Guiengola Mountain, you continue on foot via a sometimes steep three-kilometer (two mi), one-hour hike through summer-green (but brown in spring) tropical woodland. If you start early or leave late, you might see *venado* (deer), *javelin* (wild pigs), and, if you're very lucky, a *león* (mountain lion).

You know you're getting close to the ruins when the trail straightens out and you see a

THE ISTHMUS

continuous series of vegetation-covered mounds and walls on both sides. You are following an ancient, regal street, lined with ruined houses of the nobility. Next, break out into the open, where a four-step unreconstructed noble pyramid, called the Pyramid of the Sun, rises at the right. On the opposite side, across a spreading, flat ceremonial plaza, another, even taller, five-step Pyramid of the Moon stands on your left. To the extreme left rises a big ball court, so well preserved that it appears as if a dozen persons could spend a weekend with machetes and a few shovels and put the place in order for a tournament on Monday.

What you see immediately around you is only the ceremonial center. Beneath the surrounding forest are dozens of mounds, remains of temples, ceremonial patios, and regal homes. The state of preservation is exceptional, partly because of the site's isolation. These structures of stone and mud mortar are delicate and mostly unexplored; please refrain from climbing on them.

GUIDES AND GETTING THERE

In Tehuántepec, you can pre-arrange a tour led by highly recommended guide **Victor Velasquez Guzman** (tel. 971/714-4060, local cell tel. 044-971/122-3966, vicveneno@hotmail.com), who lives on Calle Abasolo, four blocks north of the plaza, across Highway 190-200. Victor, who furnishes a translator for his tour, is highly recommended by both Tehuántepec Turismo and Julín Contreras, owner-operator of the Oasis hotel. Alternatively, either Julín (Melchor Ocampo 8, tel. 971/715-0008, fax 971/715-0835, www.hotelesdeoaxaca.com) or Tehuántepec Turismo (on Hwy. 200 south, Salina Cruz direction, no phone, 9 A.M.–7 P.M. daily) may be able to recommend someone else.

If, on the other hand, you lack prior arrangements, arrive early at the Guiengola jumping-off point (from Hwy. 190, about 16 km/10 mi northwest of Tehuántepec) by at least 9:30 A.M., to avoid the midday heat and give you time to possibly contact an on-site guide (not mandatory, but very useful), most likely either José Luis Toral Sánchez or Feliciano Gonzáles Mendez, whom the government has certified as official guardians of Guiengola. You may find one or both of them either at the roadside grocery **Abarrotes Chayote,** or at the uphill parking lot before the trail that leads to the ruins. Abarrotes Chayote and most of the highway-front *palapas* provide lunches (sometimes of armadillo, venison, iguana, coati, and other game), drinks, and bottled water (very necessary, since no water is available along the route). Once you've contacted your guide, you could either continue to Guiengola immediately or with extra time, detour with your guide to Jalapa del Marqués and Tequisistlán and return to explore Guiengola in the late afternoon.

By car, **get there** by driving your own (rugged pickup truck or jeep-like, high clearance) SUV or similar rental vehicle (expensive; contact rental agents in Oaxaca City, Salina Cruz, and Juchitán) to the signed (archaeological symbol) right turnoff that runs from the highway-front Abarrotes Chayote, about 16 kilometers (10 mi) west, Oaxaca City direction, along Highway 190 from Tehuántepec. Otherwise, get to the Highway 190 turnoff by sharing a taxi, or, most cheaply, via the **Autotransportes Galgos de Jalapa** buses, which leave the Tehuántepec parking lot, on Highway 190-200, across from town entry street 5 de Mayo, about every half hour. From the highway turnoff, get to the ruins by continuing by taxi or thumbing a ride (offer to pay) from a truck.

Jalapa del Marqués

During Mexico's big dam boom in the 1950s, planners decided to conserve and control some of the trillions of gallons of water that flow via the Río Tehuántepec into the sea. A good idea, thought most, for flood control and irrigation during the long winter and spring drought.

The result is **Benito Juárez dam and reservoir,** which provides irrigation water, fish, and a tourist attraction for Jalapa del Marqués (pop. 3,000), the biggest town on the reservoir.

The cost for all this was that Jalapa del Marqués, originally on the bank of the Río Tehuántepec, had to be moved eight kilometers (five mi) uphill to its present location next to Highway 190, about 30 kilometers (18 mi) west of Tehuántepec. Now the people have everything new—wide paved streets, a church, and a small museum and Casa del Pueblo cultural center.

Jalapa del Marqués is ready for visitors, with a new hotel and a pair of good restaurants. Just inside the big town entrance gate, find **Hotel Jalapa del Marqués** (Corner Of Highway 190 and Calle Segunda Sur, at the big town entrance gate, tel. 995/721-2467, $18 d w/fan, $24 d a/c), built by the local pharmacist, who offers 10 clean, simply decorated rooms, with cable TV, above the pharmacy.

People in Jalapa del Marqués eat a lot of fish—specifically, *mojarra* (bass). A number of restaurants cook it up and serve it for visitors; for the best, go to **Del Camino** (Hwy. 190 Km 33, 8 A.M.–9 P.M. daily, $3–10, snacks 24 hours), on the Tehuántepec side, about a mile before town. Relax in their tranquil tropical patio setting as you choose from an extensive, professionally prepared and served menu. Or, alternatively, try the more modest **Tecos** (tel. 995/721-2619, 8 A.M.–7 P.M. daily), across the highway, a bit closer to town.

The next thing to do is to go **fishing** and/ or take a **boat ride** on the lake. This is good anytime of year but is best in the dry winter or spring, when the silt from the summer rains has settled and the lake is invitingly clear. Arrive early enough (say by noon) to find one of the boat workers down at the lake before they go home for the day. They charge about $20 for a two-hour ride or fishing trip. Bring your own pole, unless you want to fish by line or net as the locals do.

A popular excursion destination is **Tres Picos,** a Zapotec ruin on the far side of the lake. There, you can explore a trio of conical stone pyramids, about nine meters (30 ft) high, and a submerged ball court. Also, if the water is low and clear enough, perhaps your boatman will take you to see the site of the submerged old Jalapa del Marqués, where you'll be able to see the old church beneath the water or even sit on its bell tower, which at low water protrudes from the lake's surface.

Before or after your boat excursion, take a look inside the **Casa del Pueblo,** on the town plaza about 180 meters (600 ft) downhill from the highway. Besides a number of giant fossil bones, apparently mastodon, it has a sizable collection of locally gathered pre-conquest pottery, including some very phallic-looking figurines. At this writing, the dusty collection was under lock and key. However, if you go to the *presidencia municipal* (on the adjacent side of the plaza), you might find someone who will unlock the door for you.

Get to the plaza and the lakeshore boat landing by the paved main street, marked by a huge concrete Bienvenidos (welcome) portal on the highway. Drivers, mark your odometer. Continue downhill, to the *Presidencia Municipal* (0.2 km/0.1 mi), on the right, uphill plaza corner. Turn right and proceed counterclockwise around the central plaza, first passing the **Casa del Pueblo,** also on the right. On the opposite, downhill side of the plaza, turn right again, and continue around a traffic circle (0.6 km/0.4 mi); after another 2.2 kilometers (1.4 mi) mostly on a dirt road, you arrive at the beach and boat landing. Go swimming (in your bathing suit) and enjoy a lakeside picnic.

Finally, you might join the folks in the community *agua caliente* (warm spring) about one kilometer (0.6 mi) uphill from the highway. People begin arriving around six in the morning, when it's cool. They bring their soap and clothes to be washed and stay for hours, playing in the concrete warm-water tank (hot tub warm, at 39°C/102°F). Wear your bathing suit. If you don't have one, just go in with your clothes on like everyone else. Skinny-dipping, unless you're under three, is liable to land you in jail, besides reinforcing the local people's stereotypical view of the "loose" foreigner. Get there via the dirt street that heads uphill at the highway taxi stop, across from the blue clinical laboratory. After four blocks of walking, bear left at a fork. Soon on the left, in a small valley downhill, you'll see the women washing clothes in big tanks inside a fenced enclosure (to keep animals out). The women are friendly and also careful to keep their waste water from the lower basins, where

© BRUCE WHIPPERMAN

THE ISTHMUS

washing at the community *agua caliente*

you'll be welcome to bathe. (The basins outside the enclosure are for animals only.)

By bus, get to Jalapa del Marqués via either the Tehuántepec central bus terminal or a second-class bus from the parking lot across the highway from the Tehuántepec town entrance street, Calle 5 de Mayo, by the market.

Tequisistlán

This little *municipio,* officially Santa María Magdalena Tequisistlán, was on ground too high to get gobbled up by the reservoir. Consequently, the huge-in-summer (and muddy) **Río Tequisistlán** continues to run

right next to town. During the dry, hot spring this river appears very inviting for a dip into its clear, gurgling water.

Take a look inside the old church in the center of town. Here, folks enjoy the church's completely marble-floored atrium in front, especially handy for dancing during the July 20–24 festival in honor of Santa María Magdalena. On the church's side, you'll find the kicker: probably the world's only **marble basketball court.**

You can see the source of all this by going to the community **marble factory** (Empresa Comunal Industrial de Marmol y Onix, Hwy. 190, local cell tel. 044-995/101-8181, 8 A.M.–2 P.M. Mon.– Fri., 8–11:30 A.M. Sat.), about two kilometers (1.2 mi) west (Oaxaca City direction) of the town highway crossing. If you arrive during working hours, ask someone to "please show" (*"favor de maestrar"*) you around. You'll see dozens of men and machines working beneath a shady open-air roof, cutting, grinding, and polishing dozens of beautiful pieces of marble and onyx.

In the factory office, feast your eyes on the beautifully polished finished products. They will custom-make most anything you want— such as the lovely marble bathroom vanity top you've always wanted, a statuesque marble cat, or some other favorite animal.

Get there by car, via Highway 190 (50 km/30 mi) in the Oaxaca City direction, or an hour by bus from the Tehuántepec bus terminal or parking lot. Get off at the Tequisistlán crossing and walk or taxi to the factory and/or the marble basketball court.

Juchitán and Vicinity

Isthmus people associate the name Juchitán with both the town, Juchitán de Zaragoza, and the governmental district that it heads—a domain larger in extent than either the Distrito Federal or each of the four smallest Mexican states. The district of Juchitán (Place of Flowers) ranges from the Chimalapa, the roadless jungle refuge of dozens of Mexico's

endangered species, south to the warm Pacific and the rich lagoons that border it.

But like any empire, Juchitán is the sum of its small parts—hidden slices of Mexico that few outsiders know, from the crystalline springs of **Tlacotepec and Laollaga** to the seemingly endless groves of the "world mango capital" at **Zanatepec** and the **vibrant market** and near-

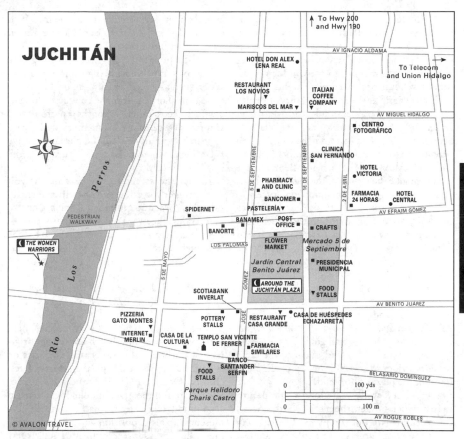

continuous **community festivals**—*velas*—of busy, prosperous Juchitán de Zaragoza.

Orientation

Juchitán (pop. 80,000) bustles with commerce all the daylight and early-evening hours. Main streets 16 de Septiembre and 5 de Septiembre steadily conduct a double stream of traffic to and from the north-side Highway 200 crossing. A few blocks to the west, the Río Los Perros (River of the Dogs, for the otters that hunt fish in the river) courses lazily southward, marking downtown Juchitán's western boundary. Traffic focuses about two kilometers (1.2 mi) south of the highway at the town plaza, the **Jardín Central Benito Juárez,**

the town's commercial and governmental nucleus. On Calle 16 de Septiembre, on the plaza's east side, the long white classical arcade of the *palacio municipal* fills the entire block, from Calle Efrain Gómez bordering the plaza's north edge to Calle Benito Juárez on the south. Governmental offices occupy the upper floor of the *palacio municipal,* while businesses, crafts booths, and food stalls spread across the bottom. Behind the facade, taking up the entire city block east of the plaza, is the town market, Mercado 5 de Septiembre.

SIGHTS
Around the Juchitán Plaza

A fun spot to start off (or end) your day

exploring Juchitán is at a table in the graceful old-Mexico patio of **Restaurant Casa Grande** (Calle Benito Juárez, 7 A.M.–11 P.M. daily) on the plaza's south side. Here, a hearty breakfast or a cool lunch will invigorate you for yet another few hours of relaxed plaza sightseeing.

Stroll out and admire the fine busts of Benito Juárez on the plaza's east side and Margarita Maza, his wife, on the west side, by Calle 5 de Septiembre. On the plaza's north side, find the Monument to the Battle of September 5, 1866, where a Mexican eagle and a heroic Benito Juárez commemorate the victory of the ragtag local battalion over a superior French imperial force.

Step east, across Calle 16 de Septiembre, to the **crafts stalls** beneath the northerly (left) half of the *presidencia municipal* arcade. What you don't find downstairs you'll find in an upstairs market foyer. Stroll the aisles and choose from a host of excellent items customarily including, besides the famous Isthmus embroidered skirts and blouses, handwoven *hamacas* (hammocks); leather huaraches and *bolsas* (purses); woven palm *tenates* and reed *canastas* (baskets), *petates* (mats), and sombreros; and gold-filigree *joyería* (jewelry). You can also find much of the same (besides a riot of flowers) at many of the stalls that line the plaza's north end.

For pottery, walk west along Calle Benito Juárez (which borders the plaza's south side) to the block just west of the plaza. There, along the old town church's rear wall, a lineup of stalls offers an assortment of ceramics, mostly practical traditional housewares, from huge round red *ollas* (jars) and flat *comales* (griddles) to brightly painted piggy banks and flower vases.

Templo de San Vicente Ferrer and Casa de la Cultura

While you're in the vicinity, visit the town's pride, the San Vicente Ferrer church. Reach it by circling the block: Continue west on Calle Benito Juárez, go immediately left at 5 de Mayo, then after one block turn left again at Belisario Domínguez, to the church on the left. Although the church's early history is shrouded in mystery, the present construction

appears by its style to date from the mid-19th century. Its dedication to San Vicente Ferrer, patron of survivors of the sea, appears connected to Juchitán's original founding as a refuge for survivors, perhaps of some ocean disaster, such as a terrible tsunami or hurricane, some time shortly before the conquest. Present-day Juchitecos, inheritors of their patron's zeal and ferocity, celebrate his memory with gusto to match, with no less than eight consecutive *velas*, beginning on the first Saturday of the last 15 days of May.

Across the street from the church, you might linger for a few minutes in the shady side plaza, **Parque Helidoro Charis Castro.** Here stands the bronze bust of Castro, the beloved Juchitecan *maderista* general who led the 13th Juchitecan Battalion in its bloody, but ultimately successful, revolt against dictatorial forces, from 1910 to 1914.

Afterward, look around inside the Casa de la Cultura (tel. 971/711-4589, casacult_ istmo5@hotmail.com, 9 A.M.–2 P.M. and 5–8 P.M. Mon.–Fri., 9 A.M.–2 P.M. Sat.), next door, west of the church. The building, originally a Catholic school, became the Casa de la Cultura in 1972 through the efforts of celebrated Oaxaca painter Francisco Toledo. Rooms around the graceful, old-Mexico patio accommodate a café, a small archaeological museum, an art exposition gallery, and a children's library. The reception staff sells a few Spanish-language books of local history and folklore and folk music CDs.

The *Women Warriors*

As an interesting downtown side-street diversion, cross over the Río Los Perros for a look at the intriguing *Women Warriors* sculptures on the west riverbank. Head west along Calle Benito Juárez. Two blocks west of the plaza, from the middle of the river bridge, notice the two tall sculptures of women (in Juchiteca skirts and blouses, of course), about two stories high, in what appears to be a small neighborhood park.

Few local residents seem to know much about them, except that "they are guarding the people from the river." (Although one person did tell me that they were erected by noted sculptor and lover of Juchitán, Miguel Urban.) Get a better view of the sculptures (which, close-up, you'll see are of stainless sheet steel) by accessing the west riverbank from the pedestrian bridge a block upstream (north) from Benito Juárez.

The riverbank is especially pleasant around sunset, when, standing on the Benito Juárez bridge, you might catch a cooling breeze, enjoy the sky colors, and be entertained by the flocks of black grackles flying overhead and scrapping and cackling in riverbank trees as they settle down for the night.

ACCOMMODATIONS
Under $25
For a good downtown budget option, check out the 27-room **Hotel Victoria** (2 de Abril 29, tel. 971/711-1558, $17 s or d one bed, $19 d two beds with fan; add $5 for a/c) a block east and a block north of the town plaza's northeast corner. What you see is what you get: plain but clean rooms with private, hot-water shower-baths. It's best to arrive by early afternoon or book this hotel, a popular overnight for market vendors, a day in advance.

$25-50
Moving two blocks north from the plaza along 5 de Septiembre, past Miguel Hidalgo, you'll find the welcoming **Hotel Don Alex Lena Real** (16 de Septiembre 48, tel. 971/711-1064 or 971/711-0989, fax 971/711-1064, hotedonalex@hotmail.com, $34 s, $40 d). The 14 very clean rooms with a choice of one king-size or a pair of double beds, come with air-conditioning, phone, cable TV, wireless Internet, and credit cards accepted.

Continuing north, about five blocks from the plaza, find the Hotel Don Alex's sister hotel, the semi-deluxe **Hotel López Lena Palace** (16 de Septiembre 70, tel. 971/711-1388, fax 971/711-1389, hotellopezlena_reservaciones@ hotmail.es, www.hotelesdeoaxaca.com, $40 s, $50 d, $60 t). Builders have included a modicum of extras, such as potted plants, airy staircases, and light, rose-tinted hallways, into the four-story building. The 40 comfortable rooms are tiled, very clean, and attractively decorated. Amenities include cable TV, wireless Internet, phones, air-conditioning, a bar, and a reliable restaurant; credit cards are accepted.

Over $50
Juchitán's most relaxing hotel is the resort-style ⟨ **Gran Hotel Santo Domingo** (Crucero, Hwy. 200, tel./fax 971/711-1050, 971/711-3642, or 971/711-1959, hsto@prodigy.net .mx, www.hotelesdeoaxaca.com, $38 s, $52 d, $65 t), on the highway across from both the bus station and the ingress road to town. The Gran Hotel's choice attraction is an invitingly large and luxurious pool and grassy patio, a welcome refuge for winding down from the heat and bustle. The approximately 60 rooms in a pair of long, double-storied tiers beyond a tropical entrance foyer, are spare but clean, spacious, high-ceilinged, and comfortable, with modern-standard bathrooms, air-conditioning, TV, phones, a good restaurant, parking, and credit cards accepted.

FOOD
Juchitán's downtown plaza food stalls do big business all day and half the night. Especially popular with local people are the market *fondas* (food stalls) at the bottom level, at the south (right) side of the *palacio municipal*. Another, more tranquil *fonda* spot is on the side plaza Helidoro Charis Castro, a block south of the main plaza, in front of the San Vicente Ferrer church.

Try the freshly baked offerings of the **Panadería Internacional** (Efraim Góez, between 8 de Septiembre and 16 de. Septiembre, 9 A.M.–9 P.M. Mon.–Sat., 9 A.M.–3 P.M. Sun.), half a block north of the plaza.

For a snack (sandwich, pizza, salad) and delicious espresso coffee there is soft-seat, 21st-century hip **Italian Coffee Company** (corner of 15 de Septiembre and Hidalgo, tel. 971/711-0773, 9 A.M.–10 P.M. daily, $2–5).

The pizza is hot, the spaghetti is tasty, and the salads are crisp at the **Pizzería Gato Montes** (Wildcat Pizza; Colón 7, tel. 971/711-3945, 5 P.M.–midnight daily, $3–9). Add

VELAS: FIESTAS OF THE ISTHMUS

The Isthmus *velas* amount to a near-continuous regional party. People stay up all night, sometimes for days on end of feasting, drinking, dancing, and parading with family and friends, many of whom return from afar to renew cherished old relationships. What follows is a short list that includes only the most important Isthmus *velas*. (Note: * especially recommended)

DATE	PLACE	FESTIVAL
January 18–21	Jalapa del Marqués	San Sebastián de las Flores
First Friday of Lent	San Pedro Huamelula	Carnaval
February 20–25	Matías Romero	Vela San Matías
First days of April	San Pedro Tapanatepec	Feria de Mango
April 15	Juchitán	Vela Ique Guia
April 25	Juchitán	Vela Ique Guidxi
April 27	Juchitán	Vela Paso Cru
May 3	Juchitán	Vela Guzebenda
May 3–6	Salina Cruz	Santa Cruz
May 5	Juchitán	Vela Quintu
May 8	Juchitán	Vela Guigu Dixta
May 10	Juchitán	Vela San Pedro Cantarito
May 13	Juchitán	Vela San Isidro Guete
May 15	Juchitán	Vela Guela Bene
May 16	Juchitán	Vela Iguu
Last 15 days of May	Juchitán	*Fiesta de San Vicente Ferrer
	Juchitán	Vela Biadxi
	Juchitán	Vela Calvario
	Juchitán	*Vela Angelica Pipi
	Juchitán	*Vela San Isidro Labrador
	Juchitán	*Vela San Vicente Chico
	Juchitán	*Vela San Vicente Grande
	Juchitán	*Vela de Cheguigo
Last week of May	Tehuántepec	Vela Sandunga
June 16	Juchitán	Vela San Antonio

DATE	PLACE	FESTIVAL
June 24	Juchitán	Vela San Juan Bautista
	Juchitán	Vela Taberneros
	Juchitán	Vela Coheteros
June 24–30	San Pedro Huamelula	Fiesta del Apóstol San Pedro
June 27–30	San Pedro Tapanatepec	Fiesta Patronal de San Pedro
July 21–29	Santiago Laollaga	Fiesta de Santiago Apóstol
July	Juchitán	Vela de los Niños
August 13	Juchitán	Vela Asunción
August 15	Juchitán	Vela San Jacinto
August 13–16	Jalapa del Marqués	Fiesta de la Asunción
August 13–18	Tehuántepec	*Fiesta Patronal del Barrio de Santa María Reoloteca
August 31–September 11	Tehuántepec	*Fiesta del Laborio
September 3	Juchitán	Vela de la Familia Pineda
September 4	Juchitán	Vela de la Familia López
September 5	Juchitán	Vela del Triunfo del Batallón Juchiteco de 1866
	Juchitán	Vela Superior
October 1–4	San Francisco Ixhuatan	Vela del Santa Patrón
December 26	Tehuántepec	*Vela Tehuántepec

© BRUCE WHIPPERMAN

Velas (festivals) usually start off with a *calenda* (procession) in which the women dress up in their finest flowered *huipiles*.

movies (starting around 7 P.M.) and your evening will be complete. It's located a block west of the San Vicente Ferrer church, between Belisario Domínguez and Juárez.

The class-act plaza-front restaurant, fine for a midday break, is the refined **((** **Restaurant Casa Grande** (Benito Juárez 12, tel. 971/711-3460, 7 A.M.–11 P.M. daily, $6–12) in the inner patio of an ex-mansion. The mostly business and upper-class patrons choose from an international menu of soups, salads, sandwiches, meats, and pastas, and a number of Oaxacan regional specialties, such as *pechuga de pollo zapoteca* (breast of chicken, Zapotec style), *enchiladas de mole negro* (enchiladas with black *mole* sauce), and *chile relleno de picadillo* (chili pepper stuffed with spiced meat); credit cards are accepted.

On the other hand, local fish lovers frequent seafood restaurant **Mariscos del Mar** (corner of 16 de Septiembre and Hidalgo, no phone, 8:30 A.M.–7 P.M. daily, $3–8), one block north of the plaza, for its long, very correctly Mexican menu of seafood and more. Have it all, including a plethora of clam, oyster, and shrimp cocktails; seafood soups, both clear and creamed; fish, octopus, squid, lobster, and shrimp (cooked 10 ways); and seven styles of *cucarachas* (small prawns).

For good food in a Mexican Bohemian–style atmosphere, check out **Restaurant Los Novios** (The Sweethearts; 5 de Septiembre, tel. 971/712-0555, 7:30 A.M.–5:30 P.M. daily, $4–6), on a block north of the plaza, just past the corner of Hidalgo. Amidst a colorful gallery of the owners' new-Impressionist-mode art, select from an innovative menu of breakfasts (freshly squeezed orange juice and hotcakes with bacon), spaghetti, and fowl (breast of chicken with chipotle sauce).

Alternatively, escape temporarily from Mexico to the coffee shop–style **Restaurant Santa Fe** (Hwy. 200, tel. 971/711-1545, 7 A.M.–midnight daily, $4–10), at the Highway 200 crossing, across from the Gran Hotel Santo Domingo. In the air-conditioned 1970s-mod atmosphere, enjoy fresh coffee and fruit, followed by tasty eggs, waffles, or pancakes for breakfast; several hamburgers and salads for lunch; and, finally, soups, spaghetti, beef, chicken, and fish for dinner. Credit cards are accepted.

FESTIVALS AND ENTERTAINMENT

Juchitán's substantial excess wealth goes largely to finance an impressive round of parties, locally called *velas,* in honor of a patron saint or a historically or commercially important event. The *velas* are organized and financed by entire barrios, and led by *mayordomos,* usually a well-to-do male head of household, but also including his spouse, children, and all relatives and friends, who usually add up to a major fraction of the population of an entire Juchitán barrio. The *mayordomo* family, together with male and female *capitanes* and their closest friends, make up the *mayordomía,* the core committee responsible for carrying off the celebration.

Customary activities include blossom-decorated church masses, parties in the house of the *mayordomo,* community barbecues, a parade of fruit and flower-laden floats, from which the *capitanas,* dressed like brides in their stunningly embroidered Tehuántepec outfits, throw fruit and gifts to the street-side crowds.

(*Note:* Although the *velas* are local affairs, everyone is invited, and can join the fun by paying a nominal entrance fee, customarily $5–10 per adult.)

In all, Juchitecos celebrate 20 in-town *velas,* which fill streets with merrymakers during the last half of April, virtually the entire month of May, and several days each in June, July, August, and September—a total of about 50 days of celebrating for the entire year. This wouldn't be too excessive if it were not for the approximately 20 obligatory national holidays and the other 30 not-to-be-missed *velas* in neighboring Isthmus communities.

Local folks sometimes offer droll commentaries about all this celebrating: "If you go to a *mayordomo* house, I'll tell you what you'll find…no bed, no stove, no shoes, just happy people and lots of friends."

Lacking a local fiesta, you might want to take

in a film at the genteel art **Cinema Casa Grande** (on the plaza, south side, tel. 971-711/0980, mid- to late afternoons Tues.–Sun.). Enter past the patio Restaurant Casa Grande (Benito Juárez 12). Or, alternatively, check out the evening entertainment, beginning around 7 P.M., at the **Pizzería Gato Montes** (Wildcat Pizza; Colón 7, tel. 971/711-3945, 5 P.M.–midnight).

As much a night club as it is a restaurant, the **Restaurant-Bar Las Galias** (Efrain Gómez 15B, dinner entrées $9–12) entertains guests with live Latin music, after 9 P.M. Friday and Saturday nights. Arrive early for fish, chicken, or a good steak, then dance the night away.

INFORMATION AND SERVICES

Tourist Information

The most reliable local government tourism office is in Tehuántepec: **Turismo office** (on Hwy. 200 south, Salina Cruz direction, no phone, 9 A.M.–7 P.M. daily), overlooking the Río Tehuántepec, two blocks west and two blocks south of the town plaza, before the river bridge.

Alternatively, in Juchitán, try travel agent **Zarymar** (5 de Septiembre 100B, tel. 971/711-2867), several blocks north of the plaza, for information, airline tickets, and car rentals.

Health and Emergencies

A ready source of nonprescription medicines and drugs is the 24-hour **Farmacia 24 Horas** (corner of Efrain Gómez and 2 de Abril, tel. 971/711-0316), one block behind the north side of the *presidencia municipal*. Alternatively, go to **Farmacia Similares** (José F. Gomes, at the corner of 5 de Septiembre, tel. 971/711-3126, 9 A.M.–10 P.M. daily), a block south of the plaza's southwest corner.

A number of doctors maintain offices near the plaza. For example, general physician–surgeons Dr. Ruben Calvo López and Dr. Carlos Alonso Ruiz and gynecologist Doctora Anabel López Ruiz hold regular consulting hours at **Clínica San Fernando** (16 de Septiembre, between Efrain Gómez and Hidalgo, tel. 971/711-1569), half a block north of the plaza's northeast corner.

Alternatively, go to the **Clínica Nuestra Señora de Exaltación** (5 de Septiembre, east side, tel. 971/711-0204), with a very professional pharmacy, half a block north of the plaza. Here, general practitioner Doctor Guillermo Gonzales and gynecologist Doctora Catalina Martínez partner with several other medical specialists on call.

In a medical emergency, follow your hotel's recommendation or hire a taxi to the **General Hospital Dr. Macedonio Benítez Fuentes** (Efrain Gómez, tel. 971/711-1441 or 971/711-1985), downtown, near the plaza.

In case of police or fire emergency, dial 066, the public crisis number.

Money

A number of downtown banks, which all have ATMs, help manage Juchitecos' money. They'll also change your money into pesos or U.S. dollars. A good bet is **Banorte** (Efrain Gómez 19, tel. 971/711-1160 or 971/711-3482, 9 A.M.–4 P.M. Mon.–Fri., 10 A.M.–2 P.M. Sat.), half a block west of the plaza's northwest corner. Second choice goes to **Banco Santander Serfin** (corner of Belasario Domínguez and José F. Gomes, tel./fax 971/711-2000, 9 A.M.–4 P.M. Mon.–Fri.), a block south of the plaza.

Communications

The *correo* (tel. 971/711-1272, 8 A.M.–7 P.M. Mon.–Fri., 9 A.M.–noon Sat.) is at the plaza's northeast corner, just west of the *presidencia municipal*. For a public fax or a money order, go to the *telecomunicaciones* (on Aldama, four blocks west of 16 de Septiembre, 8 A.M.–7 P.M. Mon.–Fri., 9 A.M.–noon Sat.).

Internet access is available at **Spider Net** (Efrain Gómez, no phone, 9 A.M.–10 P.M. daily), a few doors east of 5 de Mayo.

Photography and Cameras

A few downtown photo shops offer both digital and film cameras and supplies and services. The best is **Foto Alta Konica** (16 de Septiembre, east side, tel. 971/711-4428, 9 A.M.–9 P.M. Mon.–Sat.), just north of the plaza.

Laundry

One of Juchitán's very few downtown **laundries** (2 de Abril 42, 9 A.M.–2 P.M. and 4–7 P.M. Mon.–Fri., 9 A.M.–6 P.M. Sat.) is three blocks north of the plaza, between Obregón and Aldama.

GETTING THERE AND AWAY
By Bus

A modern long-distance *camionera central* (central bus station), at the Highway 190-200 crossing north of downtown, is the point of departure for all of the first-class and most of the second-class bus connections with both Oaxaca and national destinations. First- and second-class lines service customers from separate waiting rooms (first-class on the left, second-class on the right). The busy but clean station has snack stores and luggage-check service. Long-distance telephone and fax is available at a small office in the second-class waiting room.

Autobuses del Oriente (ADO; tel. 971/711-2565 or 971/711-1022) and affiliated lines offer direct first-class connections north with Gulf of Mexico destinations Minatitlán, Coatzacoalcos, Villahermosa, Palenque, Merida, Cancun, and Tulum; and northwest with Oaxaca City, Mexico City, Veracruz, and Tampico. Additionally, first-class carrier **Omnibus Cristóbal Colón** (OCC; tel. 971/711-2565) and its luxury-class subsidiary, Plus, offer connections northwest with Oaxaca City, Puebla, Mexico City, and Veracruz; southwest with Salina Cruz, Bahías de Huatulco, Pochutla (Puerto Ángel), and Puerto Escondido; and east with Chiapas destinations of Tuxtla Gutiérrez, San Cristóbal las Casas, and Tapachula, at the Guatemala border.

Second-class carriers include **Autobuses del Oriente** (ADO), which offers connections north with Coatzacoalcos; southwest with Tehuántepec and Salina Cruz; and east with Tapanatepec, including all intermediate destinations. Additionally, **Autobuses Unidos** (AU) offers second-class connections northwest with Tuxtepec, Puebla, Mexico City, Orizaba, and Veracruz; and southwest with Tehuántepec and Salina Cruz, including many intermediate destinations. Moreover, **Sur** offers second-class connections north with Coatzacoalcos; northwest with Oaxaca City; southwest with Bahías de Huatulco; and east with Tapanatepec and Tapachula; including intermediate destinations.

Semi-local bus connections with adjacent towns are available via the **Autotransportes Istmeños** buses across the side street, south, less than a block toward town from the *camionera central.*

Mostly second-class **Fletes y Pasajes** buses operate out of a separate terminal, also at the Highway 190-200 crossing but on the west side, adjacent to the Restaurant Santa Fe. Buses connect east with Chiapas destinations of Tuxtla Gutiérrez, Tapachula, and the Guatemala border; northwest, with Oaxaca City, Puebla, and Mexico City; and north with Tuxtepec and Minatitlán.

By Car

Drivers have the same highway choices and destinations as they do for Tehuántepec. Simply subtract 30 minutes driving time (and 27 km/17 mi distance) for northerly and easterly trips; and add the same for northwesterly and southwesterly trips. In Juchitán, fill up with gasoline at the Pemex *gasolinera* at the Highway 190-200 town ingress crossing, next to the bus station.

North of Juchitán

A number of uniquely interesting destinations await travelers willing to venture into the foothill hinterland northwest and north of Juchitán. Foremost among them are the storied former royal Zapotec bathing **springs** that well up, blue and crystalline, at Tlacotepec and Laollaga, an hour's travel northwest of Juchitán.

Equally ripe for exploring is the stalactite-studded **limestone cave** near the town of Santo Domingo Petapa, together with the singularly successful cooperative **company town at Lagunas,** about 1.5 hours north of Juchitán.

Each of these excursions can be enjoyed from Juchitán in a leisurely day by car or a long day by bus.

THE SPRINGS AT TLACOTEPEC AND LAOLLAGA

Both of these bathing resorts were part of the territory of the Zapotec royal family of King Cosijoeza. He often used the springs as a refuge during his protracted war with Aztec emperor Ahuitzotl during the 1490s. A famous traditional story recounts how love resolved the bloody conflict. Tiring of the struggle, Ahuitzotl proposed a peace pact. In exchange for allowing Aztec traders and envoys to pass through the Isthmus lands, Cosijoeza would receive Aztec princess Coyollicatzin in marriage. One day, meditating over the proposition while bathing in the Tlacotepec spring, Cosijoeza was awestruck by a stunning apparition of Coyollicatzin. Despite his apprehension, Coyollicatzin's apparition enchanted him with her beauty. Thus persuaded, Cosijoeza soon took Coyollicatzin in marriage, sealing the pact between the two nations.

Their marriage was a happy one. Children resulted, and Cosijoeza passed the springs at Tlacotepec and Laollaga to their son Cosijopí, the king of the Isthmus lands, and their daughter, Princess Donaji, both of whom continued to exercise authority after the conquest.

☾ Balneario Tlacotepec

Storied Princess Donaji, who after the conquest was baptized as Magdalena Donaji, donated both her Christian name and the springs and royal park at Tlacotepec to the local community, still known as Magdalena Tlacotepec.

Today, the town's springs and surrounding sanctuary are a unique asset for all *istmeño* families to enjoy, which they do en masse on sunny Sundays and holidays. The source, a clear, cool underground river, wells up from a rocky basin and fills a long, meandering, aqua-blue swimming hole. Shoals of little fish that nibble and tickle your feet hide in crannies and flit along the sandy bottom. Shady mango trees overhang the bank and spread over a rustic public strolling ground on one side. On the other, the entrance side, food stalls surround a parking area.

Here you can park your (self-contained) trailer or RV or set up a tent and stay a spell, walking into the surrounding hills in the morning to enjoy wildlife and wildflowers and

Balneario Tlacotepec, once a playground for the Tehuántepec nobility

© BRUCE WHIPPERMAN

THE ISTHMUS

splashing in the cool spring in the afternoons. Custodial personnel, who keep the site clean and secure, collect nominal fees for parking and camping.

Santiago Laollaga

Laollaga (lah-oh-YAH-gah) springs mark the northern boundary of the petite *municipio* of Santiago Laollaga, which you pass through on your way to the springs. A big parking lot overlooks the main series of pools (concrete basins) built into the rocky downhill channel of the Río Laollaga. Shady trees overhang the pools, and a pair of permanent open-air *comedores* on the riverbank serve drinks and food.

Visitors equipped with a self-contained trailer or RV might enjoy a stay, parking in the lot for a day or two. Fees run only a few dollars a day. Unfortunately, the water at the main pools is sometimes a bit tainted by soap from folks washing clothes upstream. You can assure pure water by following the river 0.5 kilometers (0.3 mi) upstream to its source, a natural *ojo de agua* spring welling from the base of the hills. Here, great shady trees spread over a sandy riverbank, ripe for tent camping if you don't mind sharing the spot with a few townsfolk on weekdays, and more on weekends.

Laollaga diversions might include strolls around the town and along dirt roads and trails, into the summer-lush native tropical woodlands. By local bus or car, you could explore farther afield, along the good gravel road (at the northeast corner of town, where you made your last turn left) threading the green-forested Río Los Perros valley and foothill country 25 kilometers (15 mi) northwest to remote Santa María Guienagati.

Arrive during the last 10 days in July and join Laollaga's big **Fiesta de Santiago Apóstol** (July 20–30), which includes four separate *velas,* with fireworks, carnival rides and games, *regada* (fruit-throwing), dances, and *mojigangos* (giant dancing figures).

Small town stores can supply basic groceries. Pharmacies, a private doctor, a *centro de salud,* a post office, and a *caseta larga distancia* can provide essential services.

Getting There

Get to Tlacotepec and Laollaga from Juchitán via Ixtepec, half an hour north of Juchitán. The easiest and cheapest way to go is by one of the Ixtepec-labeled local buses that frequently head north from the Highway 190 crossing in Juchitán, across the street from the main bus station and the gas station. Half an hour later, at Ixtepec, transfer to the blue-and-white Tlacotepec- or Laollaga-labeled local bus.

It's more complicated, but possible, to make your way by car. From the Highway 190-200 crossing at Juchitán, mark your odometer and head north across Highway 190-200, continuing through Ixtaltepec (eight km/five mi) to the railroad tracks at Ixtepec (15.6 km/9.7 mi). Immediately after crossing the tracks, turn left. After one block, turn right at Ixtepec's main street, Calle 16 de Septiembre. Continue five blocks (0.5 km/0.3 mi) and turn left (west) at Galeana (16.1 km/10 mi). Continue west; follow the curve right after about a mile, then after two blocks, at the police post on the right, curve left. Continue about another mile, and at a Y-intersection (19.2 km/11.9 mi) go left and continue, following the Balneario signs to the Tlacotepec springs, a total of about 29 kilometers (18 mi).

Alternatively, for Laollaga, bear right at the abovementioned Y intersection and continue through Chihuitán (turn left at the village corner, at 26.1 km/16.2 mi) to Santiago Laollaga village center (31 km/19.2 mi). Turn right and continue a block, pass over a bridge, and, a block or two farther, at the *presidencia municipal,* turn left. Continue half a mile to the Ojo de Agua sign, turn left and continue to the *balneario* entrance after about three blocks. If you get lost, ask a shopkeeper (or point to this in your guide): *"¿Donde está El Balneario Laollaga?"* (dohn-DAY ays-TAH AYL bal-nee-AH-reeoh lah-oh-YAH-gah?). "Where is the Balneario Laollaga?"

LAGUNAS: COMPANY TOWN

If success can be measured by longevity, the industrial cooperative town of Lagunas, which began producing cement in 1942, has earned its plaudits. Moreover, the unique experiment it represents seems as robust as ever. The idea began back in the 1930s, when investors were eager to exploit a mountain of local limestone that towered conveniently beside the cross-isthmus rail line. The era was, however, that of reformist President Lázaro Cárdenas, when the star of socialism was rising over Mexico from the east. The enterprise must be a cooperative, the government demanded. Investors, realizing the project's unique prospects, agreed, and Cruz Azul, a uniquely Mexican private-public cooperative, was born.

Today, the great mill beside the railroad tracks hums all day and night, producing millions of tons of cement yearly for projects from Chile to Canada. Moreover, besides supporting the livelihoods of thousands of families in the entire local hinterland, the Lagunas mill (judging from the tidy, dust-free town) appears to produce little of the cement dust that has debilitated cement-mill workers, especially in third-world countries, all over the globe.

At the town center, across the tracks from the mill, a monument erected by the workers (the Cooperadores de La Cruz Azul) honors Guillermo Alvarez, Cruz Azul's guiding light, with a pair of eternally flickering electric lamps.

Along Avenida Cooperativismo, facing the plant stand the town Banamex branch, the *correo, telecomunicaciones,* and the plant superintendent's office. Badged workers, all in pressed khakis and hard hats, walk with purpose along the sidewalks. Some turn and continue along the town's main street, Avenida Cruz Azul, and continue past the hamburger shop, *centro comercial* (company store), an immaculate bakery, and the big church, dedicated to the Virgin of Guadalupe. From the commercial center, tree-lined residential streets extend past schools, a hospital, and tidy concrete houses with some of Mexico's rare, American-style unfenced yards with lawns.

SANTO DOMINGO PETAPA: LIMESTONE CAVE

Several miles past Lagunas, Santo Domingo Petapa (pop. 2,000) marks the end of the pavement. Unless you arrive during a national holiday or the August 1–4 town festival in honor of Santo Domingo, Petapa will appear as a typical sleepy Oaxaca country town. Petapa does have, however, at least one claim to fame, and that is the grand limestone cavern on the mountainside three kilometers (two mi) beyond the town.

You will need both local permission and a local guide. The most highly recommended is locally experienced Ismael Juárez.

Lacking prior arrangement, the best procedure would be to arrive early (say by 10 A.M.) on a weekday and inquire for a guide at the *presidencia municipal.* You could smooth all this along by writing a letter, weeks in advance, in Spanish, addressed to the Presidente Municipal, Santo Domingo Petapa, Oaxaca, 70350, telling your date and time of arrival and that you'd be happy to pay for an experienced guide to show you the cave.

Such preparations will give you a good chance of seeing the inside of the cave. Come equipped with sturdy shoes, hard hats (at least plastic), and, if possible, super-bright three- or four-celled flashlights. The cave, 1–2 hours' walk west of town, is large, with a towering, cathedral-like entry portal and a river flowing from its mouth. Your exploration inside will take at least two hours and extend past stalagmites and stalactites approximately one kilometer (0.6 mi) into the mountainside.

THE ISTHMUS

East of Juchitán

From south to north, the grand Isthmus landscape east of Juchitán gradually changes through three distinctive panoramas. In the south, at the Pacific Ocean, the Isthmus begins as three grand, glassy lagoons, the Laguna Superior and Inferior on the west side and the Mar Muerto ("Dead Sea") on the east. This is the home ground of the Huave people, driven to the Isthmus's salty edge an age ago by the Zapotecs, to make their living mostly from the sea. North of that lies the fertile, most prized crescent of pastures, fields, and orchards of the sizable towns of Niltepec, Zanatepec, and Tapanatepec, beside the Pan-American Highway, which connects them all. Farther north rise the trans-isthmus mountains, the Sierra Atravesada, heartland of the Chimalapa, a wild kingdom of sylvan forests, rushing rivers, and deep, shadowed canyons, a final refuge of rare, endangered, and yet-to-be-discovered species of plants and animals.

First access to all this is by the Pan-American Highway 190-200 east of Juchitán, then by side roads north and south from junctions such as La Venta, Zanatepec, and Tapanatepec.

LA VENTA

La Venta (The Windy Place), about 29 kilometers (18 mi) east of Juchitán, lives up to its name. So much so, that the Comisión Federal de Electricidad harnesses the wind's energy with a farm of giant, ultramodern windmills, visible astride Highway 185 for miles, obediently generating many millions of kilowatts for southern Mexico's homes, businesses, and factories.

Get to La Venta by eastbound ADO, Cristóbal Colón, or Sur bus, from either of the central terminals at Tehuántepec or Juchitán. Drivers: Simply head west half an hour along Highway 190-200 to La Venta, at the Highway 185 junction.

The Chimalapa

A rough but mostly paved side road leads north

from La Venta to the backcountry Chimalapa jumping-off point villages of **San Miguel Chimalapa** (23 km/14 mi) and Cuauhtémoc (27 km/17 mi). The immense million-acre Chimalapa de facto wilderness is the communal property of two Zoque-speaking indigenous communities headquartered, respectively, at San Miguel Chimalapa and the more remote **San Martín Chimalapa,** 48 rough kilometers (30 mi) north from the Highway 185 junction at El Mezquite.

The Chimalapa Zoque people are rightly suspicious of strangers, especially now that their lands have become one of Mexico's few remaining storehouses of precious tropical hardwoods, endangered animals, and scarce minerals. Legitimate visitors to the Chimalapa wilderness, if any are allowed at all, are strictly licensed by state and local authorities and must be accompanied by community guides. If you're interested in hiking and camping

The gargantuan windmills of La Venta generate energy for southern Mexico.

© BRUCE WHIPPERMAN

in the Chimalapa, first contact Oaxaca state tourism (703 Av. Juárez, tel./fax 951/516-0123, www.aoaxaca.com, info@aoaxaca.com, 8 A.M.–8 P.M. daily).

PLAYA COPALITO AND SAN DIONISIO DEL MAR

For adventurous travelers, a side trip to the shoreline of the grand lagoons that form the Isthmus's Pacific border will yield experiences and reveal scenes of a Mexico known by scant few Mexicans and even fewer foreign visitors. Get there by bus from Juchitán, first by taxi to the east side via the Unión Hidalgo bus station.

Your destination, Playa Copalito (Little Copal Tree Beach), is a tiny fishing village (but with electricity) of thatched houses and Huave-speaking people. A long, sandy beach built of myriad wave-washed mussel and clam shells winds along the oft mirror-smooth Laguna Superior. Motorboats and *canoas* (canoes) recline lazily on the beach. A few shoreline *copal* trees provide a bit of shade, and grassy (during the summer rainy season) spaces appear fine for RV parking or tent camping.

Here, the main work for locals and diversion for visitors is fishing. *Lanchas* routinely return with a dozen one- or two-pound *lisa* (mullet) and *sierra* (mackerel). Fisherfolk are willing to take visitors on a half-day fishing excursion or exploration for about $20.

Since Playa Copalito is an idyllic but isolated little place, campers should arrive well-equipped with tent, food, and water. Bring insect repellent; mosquitoes may be fierce certain times of the year (although they weren't a problem one wet September). Moreover, security is good here, by virtue of the local naval detachment.

As for food, although a few village stores can supply some essentials, it's best to be prepared with your own fresh fruits and vegetables. The homey *palapa* **Restaurant Playa Copalita** (8 A.M.–7 P.M. daily, $4–10) of the friendly Pinedo Castellanos family, *a su servicio,* will be happy to provide fresh fish dinners.

While you're in the vicinity, the pilgrimage town of **San Dionisio del Mar** would certainly be worth a visit. The miraculous image of San Dionisio at the town church attracts thousands of pilgrims yearly, mostly for the October 6–10 festival. Things get started right away on October 6, when a carnival sets up and food stalls begin serving traditional *atole* (a nonalcoholic corn-juice drink) and tamales for the arriving pilgrims. The next day, the *mayordomía* officials crown the queen, while everyone enjoys a community dance and barbecue at the house of the *mayordomo.* Dances continue for the next two nights, punctuated by processions with fruit and gifts thrown to the celebrants, and nightly fireworks paint the sky red, blue, and green. A basic guesthouse, **Casa de Huéspedes San Dionosio** (at the southeast edge of the village, no phone, $5 pp, $15 pp during festival) is available for separate male and female dormitory accommodations, each with separate, shared tepid-water baths.

Getting There and Away

Get to Playa Copalita and San Dionisio del Mar via Unión de Hidalgo direct from Juchitán or La Venta. Bus travelers: Catch the bus direct to San Dionisio del Mar and Playa Copalita at the east-side Unión Hidalgo bus terminal (take a taxi), in Juchitán.

Drivers head east along Avenida 20 de Noviembre (from about 10 blocks north of the plaza), about a mile, passing over the railroad tracks and continuing about 11 kilometers (seven mi) to Unión de Hidalgo. In Unión de Hidalgo, turn right (south) at the Chicapa de Castro sign. Continue another three kilometers (two mi) to Chicapa de Castro. There, turn left in mid-village and continue southeast another 16 kilometers (10 mi) to Playa Copalita (turn right at the dirt road at the edge of San Dionisio del Mar) or San Dionisio del Mar (continue to the church, at the east end of town), a total of about 39 kilometers (24 mi) from Juchitán.

You can also get to Playa Copalita and San Dionisio del Mar by bus from La Venta. At La Venta, transfer to a local bus or *colectivo* going south half an hour to Unión de Hidalgo, then transfer to the bus bound for San Dionisio–Copalita, via Chicapa de Castro. About 45 bumpy minutes later, get off at the west edge of San Dionisio del Mar at the Playa Copalito right side road (walk about two km/1.2 mi) or continue ahead to San Dionisio del Mar.

From La Venta by car or RV, set your odometer as you head south from Highway 190-200 on the side road to Unión de Hidalgo. At 11.6 kilometers (7.2 mi), make your way through the town, asking townsfolk *"¿El camino a Chicapa?"* ("The way to Chicapa?"). Arrive at Chicapa del Castro (17.5 km/11 mi), where you turn left, heading southeast toward San Dionisio del Mar. After a total of 34.8 kilometers (21.6 mi), turn right at the edge of San Dionisio del Mar, at the dirt road to Playa Copalito (two km/1.2 mi farther), or continue into San Dionisio del Mar, a total of about 35 kilometers (22 mi), to the church at the east end of town.

SANTO DOMINGO ZANATEPEC

The key country town of Santo Domingo Zanatepec (pop. 10,000), on Highway 190-200 about 87 kilometers (54 mi) east of Juchitán, is the point of departure for the wild and spectacularly steep Zanatepec River Canyon. There, accompanied by a guide, you can bask in a warm spring and hike to a pair of wilderness lakes.

Zanatepec, moreover, has a restaurant and hotel. For a break, stop by the mango-shaded **Restaurant Nadxielly** (Hwy 190-200, tel. 994/721-0257, 7 A.M.–midnight daily, $5), where for a few pesos you can eat all the mangos you want in season during April and May. The family-run establishment, set back, but well marked on the highway's north side, offers several breakfasts and good home-style *comidas,* such as pork chops *en chipotle,* or *caldo de pollo* (grandma's chicken-vegetable soup).

Next door stands the beautifully renovated **Hotel San Rafael** (Santa Domingo Zanatepec, tel. 994/721-0257, $18 s, d, t with fan, $30 s, d, or t with a/c). The 20 rooms are comfortably furnished, in graceful old-Mexico style, with colorful tiles and handloomed bedspreads; wireless Internet and parking are included. Be

Zanatepec

© BRUCE WHIPPERMAN

sure to request a room that opens to the tranquil, leafy, rear inner garden patio.

Practicalities

Zanatepec services are located mostly along main street Hidalgo, which heads north, away, from the highway. Find groceries at **Abarrotes Eli** (Hidalgo, 8 A.M.–8 P.M. daily); doctors, such as **Dr. Horacio Hernández** (Hidalgo, 8 A.M.–2 P.M. and 4–6 P.M. Mon.–Sat.) two blocks before the plaza, or Dr. Luis Manuel Sáchez at his *farmacia* (Hidalgo, no phone, pharmacy: 8 A.M.–9 P.M. Mon.–Sat.; consultations: 9 A.M.–2 P.M. and 4–7 P.M. Mon.–Sat.); *telecom* (Hidalgo 200, tel. 994/721-0142, 9 A.M.–3:30 P.M. Mon.–Fri.) and *correo* (Hidalgo 200, no phone), both in the same building, next to the *presidencia municipal;* and *policía* (Hidalgo 198, tel. 994/721-0260) at the *presidencia municipal.*

The Canyon of the Río Zanatepec

The Hotel San Rafael (Santa Domingo Zanatepec, tel. 994/721-0257) also serves as contact point for guide **Hermilo Toledo** ($30 per day, including food), experienced at leading parties on excursions into the Río Zanatepec Canyon during the December–May dry season. (During the rainy season, the river will usually be too high.) Access from the highway is by a gravel road (that can include a stop at the village of Agua Caliente and its warm spring) to the trailhead (14 km/nine mi). Continue on foot (about two hours) up the canyon to a pair of small lakes, the Lago del Sol (Lake of the Sun) and Lago de la Luna (Lake of the Moon). Options include expert-level rock climbing, wildlife-viewing, fishing, and wilderness camping by the river or the lakes. Contact Hermilo Toledo through his brother, Manuel Toledo, who works at the Hotel San Rafael.

SAN PEDRO TAPANATEPEC

"Mango Capital of the World" San Pedro Tapanatepec (pop. 15,000), besides being the main access point for Rincón Juárez on the Mar Muerto, also has a number of hotels, restaurants, and services, both on the highway and in town, about four blocks south of the highway.

Accommodations and Food

A trio of acceptable country hotels offer lodging in Tapanatepec. The fanciest is the **Hotel Casablanca** (Calle Melendez, tel. 994/721-8039, $20 s, $24 d with fan, $26 s, $30 d with a/c) downtown, on the town plaza. The Casablanca offers about 10 comfortably furnished rooms, with private hot-water shower-baths. Find it in the main business district, about four blocks south of the highway.

Back on the highway, the second hotel choice goes to **Hotel Misión** (Hwy. 190-200 Km 924, tel. 994/721-8133 or 994/721-8009, $18 s, $20 d with fan, $25 s, $30 d with a/c). The approximately 35 basic bare-bulb but clean rooms are in a motel-style layout with parking spaces in front of units. All rooms have tepid-water shower-baths and cable TV; credit cards are not accepted. The hotel offers relief from highway truck noise if you get a room in the rear away from the highway.

Also acceptable, partly because of its good, longer-hours restaurant, is the **Posada Flor** (Hwy. 190-200 Km 924, tel. 994/721-8047, $13 s, $18 d with fan; $26 s, $33 d with a/c), across the highway, on the north side, from the Hotel Misión. The approximately 15 basic but clean rooms (by the truck-noisy highway, however, so use ear plugs) have tepid-water shower-baths, cable TV, and parking; credit cards are not accepted.

Any time other than the Fería del Mango (Mango Fair, first week of April) or the Fiesta Patronal de San Pedro (June 27–30), the hotels do not ordinarily require a reservation, provided you arrive before dark.

Groceries are conveniently available at markets on the highway, such as **Abarrotes La Flor** (Hwy. 190-200, tel. 994/721-8282, 8 A.M.–9 P.M. daily).

The first choice for a meal in Tapanatepec goes to the restaurant of the motel-style **Posada Flor** (on the north side of the highway, east end, Hwy. 190-200 Km 924, tel.

994/721-8047, 8 A.M.–10 P.M. daily, $4–10). The second choice goes to the similarly good restaurant at the **Hotel Misión** (Hwy. 190-200 Km 924, tel. 994/721-8133 or 994/721-8009, 8 A.M.–7 P.M. daily, $5–10).

Services

Most of Tapanatepec's service establishments are along the main business street, Calle Martín Melendez, parallel and about four blocks south of the highway. For money, find **Banamex** (Martín Melendez 48, 9 A.M.–4 P.M. Mon.–Fri.) with ATM; for medicine, go to one of the pharmacies on the highway, or **Farmacia Espinoza** (Martín Melendez 78, tel. 994/721-8192, 7 A.M.–9 P.M. daily). A doctor is on duty 24 hours at the **Seguro Social clinic** (16 de Septiembre 47, tel. 994/721-8119).

For a telephone, use one of the card-operated public telephones (Ladatel cards widely purchasable) on the highway and downtown. The *correo* (Av. Juárez, tel. 994/721-8215, 9 A.M.–3 P.M. Mon.–Fri.) and *telecomunicaciones* (Av. Juárez, 9 A.M.–3 P.M. Mon.–Fri.) are both by the *presidencia municipal* (tel. 994/721-8160). Find the **Policía Federal de Caminos** (Federal Highway Patrol; tel. 994/721-8313) on the highway.

RINCÓN JUÁREZ AND THE MAR MUERTO

Adventurers might enjoy exploring what *istmeños* call the Mar Muerto, in contrast with what they call the Mar Vivo (the open ocean). Head out from Tapanatepec south about 23 kilometers (14 mi) by a good paved road to Rincón Juárez village (pop. 1,000). Three or four seafood *palapas* line a sandy beach, lapped by the gentle waves of a spreading, silvery sea. Life follows the drowsy rhythms of daylight and darkness, wind and tides. Early mornings, fisherfolk load their nets and paddle silently out in canoes or buzz out in motorboats to try their luck. Usually, they return with about a 20-pound catch, possibly including jumbo shrimp, clams, or fish for sale to the wholesalers whose trucks arrive in early afternoon.

Visitors also can take pleasure from their own quiet routine, enjoying sunrises and sunsets, watching the flocks of pelicans, cormorants, herons, and lovely flamingo-like roseate spoonbills, and exploring the lagoon either on foot or by boat. Fisherfolk are willing to take parties out for wildlife-viewing or fishing excursions (expect to pay about $40 for half a day). Be prepared with your own binoculars and fishing tackle. Alternatively, launch your own boat or inflated raft right on the beach.

The prettiest spot on the Rincón Juárez shoreline is on the eastern side, at *palapa* **Restaurant Chabelita** (9 A.M.–7 P.M. daily, $5–10) with good *lisa* (mullet) and shrimp lunches and dinners and affording a view of canoes slipping leisurely along the glassy water. If you're planning on staying, it's best to come supplied with fruits and vegetables and drinking water.

Unfortunately, however, despite its calm water, the Rincón Juárez immediate shoreline is useless for most beach diversions because the bottom is coated with muddy, oxygenpoor, black ooze, probably related to the reason that the local body of water is called the Mar Muerto.

Fortunately, there's an alternative, at **Colonia Guadalupe** village, on the shoreline about a mile east (left as you face the water) from Rincón Juárez. There the sandy beach and lagoon floor are clean and welcoming, and you can kick back and enjoy the charms of the beach village, with a sprinkling of fisherfolks' houses and shady *palapas* spread along a sandy spit. Offshore, seagulls and pelicans swoop and dive, and along the inland side lagoon hosts of cormorants, herons, and white ibis stalk, cackle, and preen.

The best spot seems to be **Balneario Playa Sol**, with a sandy, albeit narrow, beachfront, with a clean sandy bottom that extends at least a few hundred feet offshore. Meals are available in the Playa Sol's *palapa* restaurant, there are hammocks in the shade, and a bit of space for tenting and self-contained RV parking. Ask if someone rents horses or can supply a *canoa* or motor *lancha* for a fishing excursion. With your own rubber boat, canoe, motorboat, or kayak you could explore the Mar Muerto to your heart's content.

Other Practicalities

Back in Rincón Juárez, along the road in the middle of the village, on the right side as you enter town, **Los Cocos,** is a store providing both basic groceries and home-cooked *comidas*.

Tenting and RV camping promises to be fine anywhere along the local beach for the foreseeable future. Plenty of shoreline trees provide shade and convenient branches, fine for hammocks.

Get to Rincón Juárez by bus (Tapanatepec-bound first- or second-class) from either the Juchitán or Tehuántepec central terminals. At Tapanatepec, from the highway, continue south via *colectivo* ($6) to Rincón Juárez.

By car, the Rincón Juárez trip requires about two hours, one way, from Juchitán. Set your odometer at the Juchitán Highway 190-200 crossing by the Pemex gas station. Continue east along the highway about two hours to Tapanatepec. After a total of 108 kilometers (67 mi) (or 21 km/13 mi from Hotel San Rafael in Zanatepec), in the middle of Tapanatepec you reach the paved highway turnoff road for Rincón Juárez on the right. Continue through the town and over the only river-crossing bridge. Continue along another 23 kilometers (14 mi) of paved road to Rincón Juárez, a total of about 119 kilometers (74 mi) from Juchitán.

Salina Cruz and Vicinity

Salina Cruz was important long before the conquest. The *salinas* (salt-producing ponds), where untold generations of native folks had been harvesting salt for trade, attracted Hernán Cortés very soon after his arrival in Mexico. He also recognized Salina Cruz's strategic position on the Isthmus, where the long-sought route to China was accessible, not by a torturous trans-Sierra journey but by a short, easy passage over the narrow, low Isthmus. Cortés lost no time in acquiring the *salinas* as part of his personal domain and building ships on nearby Playa La Ventosa with which to explore the Pacific.

His efforts have been amplified by successive generations. Beginning in the 19th century and continuing to the present day, the Isthmus regularly tempts canal builders wanting to carve a sea route between the Atlantic and Pacific. President Juárez's government settled for a rail connection, begun by the American Louisiana railroad company in Salina Cruz around 1870. President Porfirio Díaz presided over the project's climax, with up-to-date Salina Cruz port facilities built by the British company Iglesias, Pearson and Son, Ltd., around 1900.

Since the 1960s, Petróleos Mexicanos (Pemex) and other government authorities have greatly extended those early efforts with a hefty trans-isthmus pipeline funneling Gulf crude oil to a grand petrochemical complex as well as elaborate new shipping docks. From these, great loads of chemicals, crude oil, gasoline, and other fuels, minerals, fruit, and much more move out via truck, train, and ship to Mexico and the Pacific. Salina Cruz has thus become the industrial engine of the southern Mexican Pacific, employing more than 10,000 workers whose wages directly and indirectly support many tens of thousands more.

SIGHTS

Salina Cruz (pop. 80,000), Oaxaca's third-largest city, outstrips both Juchitán and Tehuántepec in hustle and bustle. In Salina Cruz, enterprise reigns and people are working. Crowds with money to spend support a host of town-center markets, stores, offices, hotels, and restaurants. If you need to buy something, Salina Cruz is the place in the Isthmus where you're most likely to get it.

Salina Cruz's big downtown stretches in a two-kilometer (1.2 mi) rectangle north and

THE ISTHMUS

THE ISTHMUS

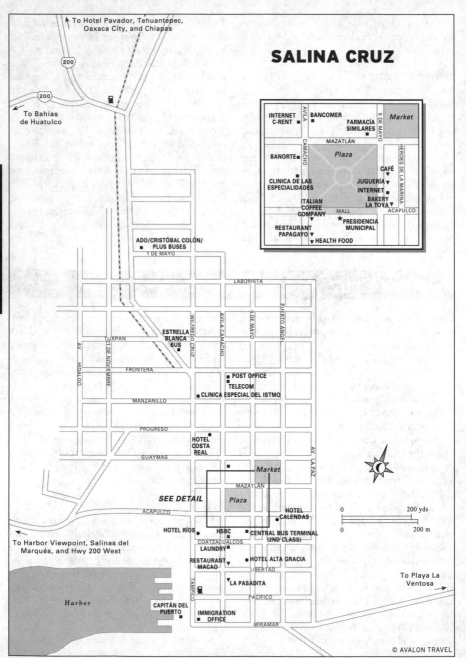

To Hotel Pavador, Tehuantepec, Oaxaca City, and Chiapas

200

200

To Bahías de Huatulco

SALINA CRUZ

INTERNET C-RENT

AVILA

BANCOMER

FARMACÍA SIMILARES

5 DE MAYO

Market

CAMACHO

MAZATLÁN

BANORTE

Plaza

CLINICA DE LAS ESPECIALIDADES

HEROES DE LA MARINA

CAFÉ

JUGUERÍA

INTERNET

BAKERY LA TOYA

ITALIAN COFFEE COMPANY

MALL

ACAPULCO

RESTAURANT PAPAGAYO

★ PRESIDENCIA MUNICIPAL

HEALTH FOOD

ADO/CRISTÓBAL COLÓN/ PLUS BUSES

1 DE MAYO

LABORISTA

WILFREDO CRUZ

AVILA CAMACHO

5 DE MAYO

PUERTO ÁNGEL

ESTRELLA BLANCA BUS

TUXPAN

AV. 21 DE NOVIEMBRE

AV. HIDALGO

FRONTERA

POST OFFICE

TELECOM

CLINICA ESPECIAL DEL ISTMO

MANZANILLO

PROGRESO

HOTEL COSTA REAL

GUAYMAS

Market

SEE DETAIL

MAZATLÁN

Plaza

AV. LA PAZ

ACAPULCO

HOTEL CALENDAS

HOTEL RÍOS

HSBC

CENTRAL BUS TERMINAL (2ND CLASS)

COATZACOALCOS

LAUNDRY

RESTAURANT MACAO

HOTEL ALTA GRACIA

LIBERTAD

To Harbor Viewpoint, Salinas del Marqués, and Hwy 200 West

TAMPICO

LA PASADITA

PACIFICO

To Playa La Ventosa

Harbor

CAPITÁN DEL PUERTO

IMMIGRATION OFFICE

MIRAMAR

0   200 yds

0   200 m

© AVALON TRAVEL

south from the town plaza. Some of the north–south streets change names at the plaza, others don't. On the plaza's east side, 5 de Mayo becomes Héroes south of the plaza, while on the plaza's west side, Avila Camacho retains the same name its entire length. West another block and north of the plaza runs Wilfredo Cruz, which becomes Tampico on the south side, while a block east of 5 de Mayo, Puerto Ángel remains the same both north and south of the plaza. Thankfully, east–west streets do not change names. From a block north of the plaza, moving successively south, are Guaymas, Mazatlán, Acapulco, and, finally, Coatzacoalcos, a block south of the plaza.

Town activity focuses at the very pungent and busy **market,** northeast of the plaza, between Guaymas and Mazatlán. Several blocks south of the plaza are the container docks along the Calle Miramar, which leads to the drowsy beach village of **Playa La Ventosa.**

Once you've gotten your fill of the sights and sounds around the plaza and market, head west to breezy harbor vista point **Faro del Marina.** Drive or ride a Salina-labeled bus or a taxi west along Acapulco, the plaza's south-side street. First you pass *dique* (DEE-kay, dry dock) no. 1 and the naval compound, then cross beneath the great rack of pipelines conducting a small river of oil and chemicals over the road. Continue, winding uphill to the summit parking lot on the right. On the harbor's near side stands the fishing fleet; on the opposite side are the smart gray naval frigates and destroyers. On the right, at the outer pier, great supertankers take on lakes of crude oil, most likely bound for Japan and the United States.

Continue west downhill to Barrio Salinas, named after Hernán Cortés's salt-producing ponds, the **Salinas del Marqués.** Although the ponds, about two kilometers (1.2 mi) west of the foot of the hill, still produce salt, they are as interesting for the wildlife—flocks of waterfowl, both resident and local—that they sustain. People also live from the bounty of the *salinas.* In the afternoons, next to the road that cuts north across the marshes to Highway 200, you can usually see men waist deep in

the pond, throwing nets and hoping to haul in something for dinner.

ACCOMMODATIONS

The continuous flow of Salina Cruz visitors supports several hotels. With the exception of the beachfront hostelries in Playa La Ventosa, they are all (excepting one, Hotel Parador) near the town center.

Under $25

A good low-budget choice is the **Hotel Ríos** (Wilfredo Cruz 405, tel. 971/714-0337, $12 s or d in one bed, $16 d, t, or q in two beds), a block west and half a block south of the plaza. Here, the grandmotherly owner maintains three stories of about 20 plainly furnished but very clean rooms, arranged along corridors around an interior patio. Choose an upper room for more light and privacy. Rooms come with bath (tepid-water shower), fans, and street parking only; credit cards are not accepted.

$25–50

Convenient for travelers with cars or RVs is the **Hotel El Parador** (Carretera Transistmica Km 6, Colonia Aviación, tel./fax 971/716-2951, $35 d). On the highway's east side, about six kilometers (four mi) north of town, El Parador's major attraction is its spacious, palmy, tropical pool patio, perfect for relaxing at the end of a warm, busy day. However, some rooms, although clean, generally lack good ventilation. Consequently, they may smell of *moho* (mildew), especially during the summer–fall rainy season. Inspect various rooms until you find one that is satisfactory. Rooms come with air-conditioning, hot-water shower-baths, and parking; credit cards are not accepted.

Back in the town center, the **Hotel Altagracia** (5 de Mayo 520, tel./fax 971/714-0726 or 971/714-6225, emarin_10949@hotmail.com, $30 s, $34 d, $38 t, $42 jr. suite), just a block and a half south of the plaza, offers another good choice. The 18 rooms, in a compact but invitingly decorated two-story block, are clean, with either one king-size or two double beds. They are tastefully decorated in modern style, with tile floors and some marble baths. Amenities include hot-water shower-baths and air-conditioning, Internet access, but street-only parking; credit cards are not accepted.

Nearer to the plaza, find the **Hotel Calendas** (Puerto Ángel 408, tel. 971/714-4574, calendas_hotel@hotmail.com, $35 s, $40 d, $45 t), one long block east of the plaza, just south of the corner of Acapulco and Puerto Ángel. Savvy managers have created an inviting lodging of about 20 clean, spacious, comfortably furnished rooms in two stories around a quiet interior patio, with hot-water shower-baths, TV, air-conditioning, and parking. Credit cards are accepted.

The fourth choice downtown goes to the pricier **Hotel Costa Real** (Progreso 22, tel./fax 971/714-0293, $44 s, $47 d, $54 t), two blocks north, half a block west of the plaza. A plus here is the good restaurant, which is especially handy for breakfast. Upstairs, although the approximately 30 rooms are clean and comfortable enough, they do not appear particularly well-maintained. Make sure everything works before you pay. Amenities include hot-water shower-baths, air-conditioning, TV, and parking. Credit cards are accepted.

FOOD

Food is plentiful in downtown Salina Cruz. If you're on a tight budget, the *fondas* (food stalls) on the market's south and west sides will satisfy with hearty country-style soups, stews, rice, tamales, and seafood, with all the tortillas you can eat. For dessert, go to one of the close-in *panaderías* (bakeries). For example, try **La Toya** (on Acapulco, 8 A.M.–10 P.M. daily), near the plaza's southeast corner.

Health food fanciers will appreciate the many shelves of grains, food supplements, vitamins, ginseng, herbs, and remedies at the **Centro Naturista Aquarius** (Avila Camacho, tel. 971/714-2180, 8 A.M.–8 P.M. Mon.–Sat.); credit cards are accepted. Find it half a block south of the plaza's southwest corner, just past Restaurant Papagayo.

The first restaurant choice goes to locally popular seafood restaurant ☾ **La**

Pasadita (Avila Camacho, tel. 971/714-0356, 7 A.M.–10 P.M. daily, $6–20), two and a half blocks south of the plaza's southwest corner. Take a seat in their airy, tree-shaded dining room–patio and choose from a long menu that starts out with many breakfast packages, continues with salads and soups (oysters Rockefeller, oyster cream), and finishes with many styles of fish (breaded, with garlic, whole barbecued), and in season, even jumbo prawns (that they call *cucarachas*) and lobster. Credit cards are accepted.

On the other hand, for Chinese food, you have refined **Restaurant Macao Cantonesa** (Avila Camacho, tel. 971/714-3834, 9:30 A.M.–7:30 P.M. daily, $3–7), which carries on Salina Cruz's Asian-food tradition, about two blocks south of the plaza's southwest corner. Diners choose from a long, very recognizable menu, including lots of meat, fish, and chicken dishes, such as almond chicken, pork chow mein, and spareribs. Lighter eaters can skip the meat and ask for rice and vegetables, such as broccoli, cabbage, tomatoes, and mushrooms only and get reduced prices.

Also among the town center's recommendable sit-down eateries is locally popular **Restaurant Papagayo** (Avila Camacho 407, tel. 971/714-2084, 8 A.M.–10 P.M. daily, $2–6), half a block south of the plaza's southwest corner. The Chinese-Mexican owners once offered some Asian food favorites, but now they've switched exclusively to Mexican and international specialties. These include good breakfasts (hotcakes, bacon, eggs), lunches, or dinners (hamburgers, *tortas,* soup, salad, fish, chicken).

For a modicum of tranquility and plain good food, try the dining room of the **Hotel Costa Real** (Progreso 22, tel./fax 971/714-0293, 7:30 A.M.–10:30 P.M. Mon.–Sat., $4–12), two blocks north, half a block west of the plaza's northwest corner.

For dessert, try Starbucks look-alike **Italian Coffee Company** (corner of Acapulco and Avila Camacho, tel. 971/720-2840, 9 A.M.–11 P.M. daily), on the southeast plaza-front corner. Take in the refined, air-conditioned ambience, while relaxing to soothing recorded melodies, sampling the rich espresso coffees, and snacking on sandwiches (*panini,* croissant) or desserts (cakes and brownies).

ENTERTAINMENT AND EVENTS

True to Tehuántepec tradition, Salina Cruz folks sometimes abandon their workaday habits for fiestas. First comes the **Fiesta de la Santa Cruz** (May 3), in a blast that includes coronation of a queen, full-costumed traditional dances, a fruit- and gift-throwing *regada* parade, carnival rides and games, and fireworks.

If you miss that fiesta, you might be lucky and get in on one later, such as the **Fiesta del Pueblo,** an all-purpose town fiesta, for several days beginning May 9; the **Fiesta de Santa Rosa de Lima** (Aug. 26–Sept. 2); the **Fiesta de San Francisco Asis** (Oct. 3–5); and the **Fiesta de San Diego** (Nov. 11–16).

INFORMATION AND SERVICES
Health and Emergencies

A good choice for over-the-counter medications is **Farmacia Similares** (Generics Pharmcacy; Mazatlán, tel. 971/714-1670, open 24 hours daily), a few doors from the plaza's northwest corner.

Probably the most solid in-town medical clinic is the very professional **Clinica Especialidades Medica del Istmo** (Tampico 5, between Manzanillo and Frontera, tel. 971/714-5074). They have several specialists (internist, opthamalogist, pediatrician, gynecologist, pathologist, gastroenterologist, psychiatrist, and dentist) for office consultations and hotel calls.

Alternatively, right on the plaza's west side, the **Clínica de Especialidades Médicas** (Medical Specialties Clinic; Avila Camacho 306, tel. 971/714-4107, 9 A.M.–5 P.M. Mon.–Sat.) offers consultations with either gynecologist, pediatrician, ophthalmologist, or dentist.

In a medical emergency, either follow your hotel's recommendation or have a taxi take you to **Sanatorio del Carmen** (clinic and pharmacy; Calle Francisco Villa 16, tel. 971/714-1180). In a police or fire emergency, contact the **policía municipal** (tel. 971/714-0523).

Money

Several banks, all with ATMs, serve downtown customers. A good first choice is **HSBC** (northeast corner of Avila Camacho and Coatzacoalcos, tel. 971/714-4476, 8 A.M.–6 P.M. Mon.–Fri.), a block south of the plaza. Alternatively, also on Avila Camacho, try **Bancomer** (Avila Camacho, tel. 971/714-0032, 8:30 A.M.–4 P.M. Mon.–Fri., 10:30 A.M.–2:30 P.M. Sat.), on the east side of the street a few steps north of the plaza; or **Banorte** (tel. 971/714-4454 or 971/714-5898, 9 A.M.–4 P.M. Mon.–Fri., 9 A.M.–2 P.M. Sat.), on the west side of the plaza, near the plaza's northwest corner.

Communications

The town **correo** (east side of Avila Camacho, corner of Frontera, tel. 971/714-0040, 8 A.M.–7 P.M. Mon.–Fri., 8 A.M.–4 P.M. Sat.), with Mexpost secure mail service, and the **Telecom** (east side of Avila Camacho, corner of Frontera, tel. 971/714-0891, fax 971/714-0760, 9 A.M.–7:30 P.M. Mon.–Fri.), stand side by side, four blocks north of the plaza. Moreover, a *larga distancia* **telephone office** (7 A.M.–midnight daily) serves customers at the plaza's southeast corner.

A number of small storefronts provide Internet connection. Try **Cybernet** (7 A.M.–7 P.M. daily) near the plaza's southeast corner. Alternatively, go to **C-Rent Internet** (5 de Mayo 705, tel. 971/714-1839, 9 A.M.–2 P.M. and 4–10 P.M. Mon.–Sat.), on the plaza's northwest corner, across Avila Camacho and opposite Bancomer.

Immigration

Being a port of entry, Salina Cruz has a **Migración** (Immigration Office; tel. 971/714-1000 or 971/714-4531, 9 A.M.–1 P.M. Mon.–Fri.), at the foot of Tampico, four blocks south of the plaza. Go there if you lose, or need an extension on, your tourist permit.

If you arrive by private boat and have

inspection documentation from another Mexican port, present it for check-in at the Capitán del Puerto, located just west of Migración, across Tampico. If you arrive without Mexican inspection documentation, first go to Migración for an inspection, then to the Capitán del Puerto.

Car Rental
Rent a VW bug (minimum $40/day) at **Lone Star** (tel./fax 971/716-2650, bubistmo@hotmail.com, 9 A.M.–7:30 P.M. Mon.–Sat.), on the north outskirts, along the Tehuántepec highway, about two kilometers (1.2 mi) from downtown.

Photography and Laundry
The best town source for cameras (Kodak, Konica, and Fuji), developing (both film and digital), and supplies is **Foto Discuento de Oaxaca** (Avila Camacho, tel. 971/714-4300, 9 A.M.–8 P.M. Mon.–Sat.), half a block north of the plaza.

Get your laundry done at **Lavandería Carmel** (southeast corner of Avila Camacho and Coatzacoalcos, tel. 971/714-6105, 9 A.M.–9 P.M. Mon.–Sat., 9 A.M.–noon Sun.), a block south of the plaza's southwest corner.

GETTING THERE AND AWAY
Three terminals serve Salina Cruz bus travelers. The two first-class terminals are on the north side of town. At Calle Laborista 2, corner of Highway 200, about seven blocks north of the plaza, computerized **Omnibus Cristóbal Colón, Plus,** and **Autobuses del Oriente** (ADO) (all bus lines contactable by local tel. 971/714-0703) offer first-class and luxury service (that can also be booked and paid for by credit card via the **Ticket Bus** agency's toll-free Mex. tel. 800/702-8000).

Cristóbal Colón departures connect northwest with Mexico City (Norte and Tapo terminals) via Tehuántepec and Oaxaca City; west with Bahías de Huatulco, Pochutla (Puerto Ángel), and Puerto Escondido; and east with Juchitán, Zanatepec, Tuxtla Gutiérrez, San Cristóbal las Casas, and Tapachula on the Guatemala border. Its subsidiary line, Plus, offers luxury-class connections northwest with Oaxaca City, Mexico City, and Veracruz; and southwest with Bahías de Huatulco.

ADO offers luxury-class connections in three directions: northwest, via Juchitán and Puebla, with Mexico City Tapo terminal; northeast, via Villahermosa, with Mérida and Cancún; and west, via Tehuántepec, with Huatulco, Pochutla (Puerto Angel), and Puerto Escondido.

At the other first-class terminal, also on Highway 200, five blocks north of the plaza, **Estrella Blanca** (tel. 971/714-5548) and its subsidiary lines offer first- and luxury-class connections along the Highway 200 corridor with Huatulco, Pochutla–Puerto Ángel, Puerto Escondido, and Acapulco (where connections may be made northwest, for Zihuatanejo, Puerto Vallarta, and the U.S. border), and Mexico City.

The second-class bus terminal (5 de Mayo, tel. 971/714-0259) is downtown, half a block south of the plaza. Here, **Autobuses Unidos** (AU) offers connections northwest with Oaxaca, Puebla, Mexico City, Orizaba, and Veracruz; and north with Tehuántepec, Juchitán, and Tuxtepec. **Sur** offers connections north, with Tehuántepec, Juchitán, and Coatzacoalcos; east with Zanatepec and Tapanatepec; and southwest with Astata and Bahías de Huatulco.

Drivers have the same highway choices and destinations as Tehuántepec. Simply add 20 minutes to the driving time (and 15 km/nine mi distance) for northerly, northwesterly, and easterly trips; subtract the same for southwesterly trips. Fill up with gasoline at the Pemex *gasolinera* on the highway, Tehuántepec direction, about six kilometers (four mi) north of downtown.

PLAYA LA VENTOSA
Playa La Ventosa is Salina Cruz's sleepy little beach village on the historic Bahía de la Ventosa (Windy Bay), where Hernán Cortés built his

first caravels to explore the Pacific. Get there by car, taxi, or white or orange Ventosa-labeled bus running west along Calle Miramar next to the container docks, four blocks south of the plaza. Drivers, bear left at the fork at the end of Miramar and continue winding over the hill toward the beach. After about three kilometers (two mi), you get a good view of the petrochemical plant on the left, belching a swirling, hellish plume of pollution. Fortunately for Salina Cruz (but not for other towns downwind), prevailing breezes blow the smoke in a northerly direction, away from town.

At about six kilometers (four mi) from downtown, you arrive at Playa La Ventosa. One of the best places to land is **La Palapa de Chava,** the beachfront restaurant at the end of the main street through town. Friendly, knowledgeable owner Salvador Mendoza likes to tell visitors about Playa La Ventosa. He says that wood for Cortés's ships was cut inland and floated downstream via the **Río Tehuántepec,** which empties into the bay's east (left, facing the ocean) side. There, the summer rainy-season flood stains the entire Bahía Ventosa a muddy brown while depositing piles of driftwood on the east-side beach. In the dry winter and spring, the river dries to a clear trickle and the bay becomes clear and blue.

Shift your view west and notice what appears to be a tower atop the headland, a mile or two beyond the foreground bay and beach. This tower has been known for longer than anyone remembers as **El Faro de Cortés** (The Lighthouse of Cortés). The tower's builders cut a window on the seaward side, where historians believe they placed an oil lamp to guide ships to the harbor.

If the story is true, the lighthouse would be nearly five centuries old. How could this be? Without maintenance, mortar crumbles and bricks usually fall after two or three centuries. Restaurant owner Salvador Mendoza answers that experts believe that Cortés built the tower of bricks and mortar, mixed with egg whites and yolks instead of water, which made the mortar durable enough to keep the lighthouse standing straight, without any repairs, through the present day.

Activities

Wander the beach, rocky in the rainy summer and fall, sandy in the dry winter and spring. On the east side, by the river's mouth, collect shells and driftwood, watch the antics of the pelicans, seagulls, and cormorants, and, with your binoculars, look for rarer species. On the west side, explore the tide pools beneath the rocky headland, then head inland and hike the headland's forested arroyos up to the breezy hilltop for a close-up view of El Faro de Cortés.

On another day, go on a fishing excursion and catch a load of silvery *mojarra* (bass), *lisa* (mullet), and *sierra* (mackerel) for a feast for everyone in the neighborhood. Go in your own boat or hire a fisher (figure about $60) to take you out for half a day.

Accommodations

For accommodation, either park your RV, set up a tent, or stay in one of the Playa La Ventosa beachfront lodgings. On the far west side of the beach, beneath the headland, is a secluded, level grassy spot that appears fine for tenting. RV-equipped travelers could simply park at one of a number of likely spots down by the beach.

Otherwise, stay at La Ventosa's rustic best, sleepy **Posada Rústrian** (tel. 971/714-0450, $12 s, $24 d), so relaxing that it's worth reserving well ahead of time if you plan to arrive during high-occupancy times around Christmas, Easter, weekends, and January–April. Posada Rústrian amounts to a downscale mini-resort, perched on a breezy rise with a palm-fringed beach view. Watch for the side road on the left (across from mini-store "Miscelanea de Diaz") as you're entering town. There are no TVs and no phones, simply about 20 basic rooms and a breezy, shaded restaurant with chairs and hammocks for resting, reading, and taking in the view. Rooms (check for maintenance and cleanliness before moving in) have fans and room-temperature private shower-baths.

EAST OF SALINA CRUZ: HUAVE COUNTRY

The country due east of Salina Cruz is one of the low-lying, barrier-sand spits to which many of Oaxaca's Huave-speaking people were marginalized by the more populous Zapotecs long before the Spanish arrived. The Spanish simply continued the segregation that was already in place.

The Huave appear to have grudgingly accepted their lot. They subsist mostly off of the cattle that graze whatever brush, grass, and cactus grow in the sand and the fish and shrimp that they can catch in the ocean and the lagoons.

San Mateo del Mar

San Mateo del Mar (pop. 2,000), seat of the *municipio* of the same name, has a uniquely picturesque church and a native market, making it the major destination of this eastern excursion. Get there by heading one hour east (29 km/18 mi) from the jumping-off spot on Highway 200, near Km 17.

The plaza-center of San Mateo del Mar is a block or two south (turn right) from the entrance road. The main sights are the market, which takes up much of the town plaza; the lagoon, past the plaza, a block south; and the church, just to the east of the plaza, with a unique colorful facade.

The market is where most of the town action takes place. Women are the actors and Huave is the language. Dress appears to be the dividing line: The women who wear *traje*—red blouse, dark skirt, striped cloth headdress trailing a bright ribbon—seem to be the ones who speak Huave only. Besides selling a few vegetables, they mostly offer the local fish and shrimp that their husbands have caught and they've dried in the sun.

Despite their historical shyness (most likely based on a communal memory of hard experience), you might get a smile when you say *"Buenos días"* or *"Buenas tardes."* The Huave reticence shows directly in the way they build their homes. Notice the walls—the older ones

Its market and invitingly picturesque church are prime reasons to visit San Mateo del Mar.

© BRUCE WHIPPERMAN

of sticks or brush, now increasingly of concrete—that surround each family compound. In some country lots, concrete walls appeared to have been built even before any buildings. (This, of course, is not unlike what a significant fraction of town Mexicans do, especially the well-to-do, who have historically surrounded their houses with brawny fences and encased their windows with steel bars.)

GETTING THERE
Go by bus (ask for a "San Mateo del Mar" bus at the Salina Cruz market) or by car. The road (initially paved but potholed, finally good, all-weather gravel; keep your speed down) takes off from near Highway 200 Km 17 about five kilometers (three mi) north of town. If by bus, ride a taxi from town to (ask your taxi driver to drop you at) the San Mateo del Mar bus stop *(parada)*.

By car, on Highway 200, turn right at the highway traffic signal and road that heads east, across the highway from the big electrical sub-station. Drivers, set your odometer. After about five blocks, follow the traffic left; continue straight about three kilometers (two mi), passing through the traffic circle at the Pemex refinery gate. Cross the Río Tehuántepec at kilometer 7.6 (mi 4.7). After the river bridge, follow the right road fork, and continue for about

another 21 kilometers (13 mi) through a couple of hamlets just before San Mateo del Mar, 29 kilometers (18 mi) from Highway 200.

Santa María del Mar

If you have another two hours, continue 16 more kilometers (10 mi) to smaller Santa María del Mar (pop. 500). Here, you'll find a sleepier town plaza and a humbler church. For a bit of beach action, turn north (left) from the plaza to the embarcadero (wharf), on the Laguna Inferior beach, about two kilometers (1.2 mi) from town. A detachment of marines guards the beach, apparently to keep order among the locals. The guards seemed unconcerned with me as I drove past their post.

A battalion of fishing *lanchas* lines a broad, breezy beach. Gentle waves wash the shallow shoreline, and dogs laze in the sun. With the added security of the marines, this appears to be an especially good spot for prepared tenters or RVers (bring water and food). The most exciting time is mid- to late afternoon, when the fisherfolk bring in their catches. They sell whatever they can to buyers who arrive with trucks, and load the rest on wheelbarrows, which they push home for drying. The good shrimp price that the buyers were paying— about $4.50 per pound—reflects both local and world demand.

THE ISTHMUS

BACKGROUND

The Land

On the map of North America, Mexico's state of Oaxaca (wah-HAH-kah) makes up the southern bulge of Mexico, the region where the Mexican coastline thrusts into the Pacific like the belly of a frolicking Pacific dolphin. Oaxaca is a sizable place—with about 95,400 square kilometers (36,800 sq. mi)—and Mexico's fifth-largest state, as big as a midsize U.S. state, such as Indiana, or an entire small European country, such as Portugal.

As in Mexico as a whole, mountains rule Oaxaca's landscape. From the U.S. border, Mexico's grand pair of mother ranges, the Sierra Madre Oriental in the east and Sierra Madre Occidental in the west, sweep southward a thousand miles until they reach Oaxaca, where they bend eastward and practically merge. In Oaxaca, the ranges, respectively called the

Sierra Madre de Oaxaca and the Sierra Madre del Sur, form a broad, rumpled, pine-tufted landscape, dotted with 20 peaks in excess of 3,000 meters (10,000 ft). Only the mostly narrow southern coastal plain, one large valley, and a few scattered lesser vales provide enough level cropland to support large towns. From those few valleys, a handful of streams, blocked and forced by the mountains to twist through deep canyons, make their way to the sea.

A CLOSER LOOK

Imagine navigating a high-altitude airship, borne by the tropical breezes, over Oaxaca's vivid shoreline, mountain, and valley panorama. Start your adventure in the southwest, at Oaxaca's coastal border with its neighboring state of Guerrero. Here, as you drift eastward above the green

© BRUCE WHIPPERMAN

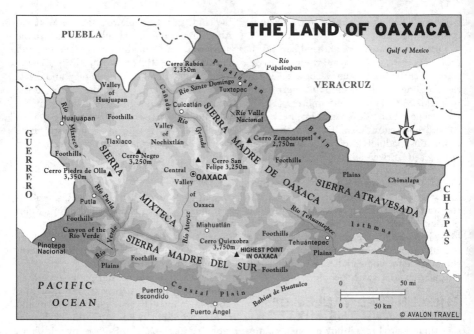

THE LAND OF OAXACA

PUEBLA

Gulf of Mexico

Cerro Rabón 2,350m

Río Papaloapan

Río Santo Domingo   Tuxtepec

VERACRUZ

Valley of Huajuapan

Cuicatlán

Huajuapan   Foothills

Río Valle Nacional

Tlaxiaco

Valley of Nochixtlán

Río Grande

Cerro Zempoatepetl 2,750m

Cerro Negro 3,250m

Cerro San Felipe 3,250m

Foothills

Plains   Chimalapa

Foothills

Cerro Piedra de Olla 3,350m

Central Valley

OAXACA

SIERRA MADRE DE OAXACA

SIERRA ATRAVESADA

GUERRERO

Putla

Río Puxla

of Oaxaca

Río Atoyac

Río Tehuántepec

Isthmus

CHIAPAS

Foothills

Canyon of the Río Verde

MIXTECA

Miahuatlán

Foothills

Tehuántepec

Pinotepa Nacional

Río Verde

SIERRA MADRE DEL SUR

Cerro Quiexobra 3,750m   HIGHEST POINT IN OAXACA

Plains

Plains

Foothills

Foothills   Foothills

PACIFIC OCEAN

Puerto Escondido

Coastal Plain

Bahías de Huatulco

Puerto Ángel

0   50 mi

0   50 km

© AVALON TRAVEL

coastal plain directly below, the broad estuary of the **Río Verde** empties into the sea. The mightiest river system entirely within the state, the Río Verde's tributaries drain a major fraction of western Oaxaca, including the central valley, where it is known as the Río Atoyac.

As you continue easterly, the forest-swathed peaks of the Sierra Madre del Sur stretch ahead, cresting at cloud-capped 3,750-meter (12,300 ft) **Cerro Quiexobra,** Oaxaca's tallest mountain. To your right far below, Pacific waves wash a coastline indented with small bays and lined with wildlife-rich mangrove wetlands and pearly, palm-tufted strands. In succession, you pass over the small resorts of **Puerto Escondido, Puerto Ángel,** and the **Bahías de Huatulco,** where visitors flock year-round to enjoy the delights of South Seas Mexico.

TO THE ISTHMUS AND NORTH

As you continue, the coastal plain gradually broadens as the Sierra shrinks to mere foothills at the **Isthmus of Tehuántepec,** the neck of land where Mexico (and indeed the entire North American continent) shrivels to a scant 200 kilometers (125 mi) in width. East beyond the Isthmus, in the remote region Oaxacans call the **Chimalapa,** you spot a new range of mountains, the **Sierra Atravesada,** rising and stretching east into the neighboring state of Chiapas. The Atravesadas' isolated rugged summits, sylvan forests, and deep gorges shelter one of Mexico's last remaining troves of endangered plants, birds, mammals, and reptiles.

From the Isthmus, other Oaxaca regions beckon. Turning around to the left and heading your airship northwest, you follow the valley of the **Río Tehuántepec,** passing over the bustling, tradition-rich small cities of Juchitán and Tehuántepec and their luxuriant hinterlands of fruit, corn, and cotton. Soon, on your right toward the north, rises the grand **Sierra Madre de Oaxaca.** You see a succession of peaks stretching west a hundred miles, from the rugged homeland of the indigenous **Mixe** (MEE-shay) people in Oaxaca's northeast to the equally mountainous domain of their neighbors, the Sierra **Zapotec** at the northern center of the state.

Drawn by what you might find beyond the mountain crest, you navigate your airship due north, over the Mixe country, above the gigantic spreading massif of **Zempoaltepetl** (saym-poh-ahl-TAY-paytl), 3395 meters (11,138 ft), composed of a dozen separate peaks, the Mixes' holy mountain. Beyond that, the mountains gradually drop to foothills, where you see a great river-laced plain of tropical forest, checkered with pasture, farms, and small towns, stretching north past Oaxaca's northern lowland border with the state of Veracruz all the way to the Gulf of Mexico. The Oaxaca portion, known as the **Papaloapan** (pah-pah-loh-AH-pahn) for the great river system that drains it, encompasses the **Chinantla** and the **Mazateca**, homelands of the indigenous Chinantec and Mazatec peoples.

THE CENTRAL VALLEY OF OAXACA AND THE MIXTECA

Continue your breeze-blown journey, now turning southwest over the Sierra Zapoteca (Zapotec Highland) country to the Valley of Oaxaca, the heartland of the Zapotec people and Oaxacan civilization for more than 3,000 years. Below you spreads Oaxaca's great upland central valley complex: farms, pastures, towns, and villages, radiating in three 50-mile fingers (east, northwest, and south) from the capital city, Oaxaca.

Drawn on by the mystery of the mist-shrouded western mountains, you continue a hundred miles northwest, following the valley of the upper **Río Atoyac,** where the Sierra de Oaxaca rises again. There, you gaze down on a broad mountain and high plateau landscape, much of it tragically eroded. Oaxacans call this the **Mixteca,** the domain of the Mixtec people, proud transmitters of a major share of Oaxaca's ancient tradition. From your high vista, you see a landscape as creased as an old chopping board, dotted with tiny settlements scattered atop rugged mesas and tucked into deep gorges.

A closer look reveals natural divisions in the land. In the center you see the **Mixteca Alta**—high, cool, and cloud-shadowed. To the northwest, bordering the states of Guerrero and Puebla, lies the **Mixteca Baja,** a lower, desert-like plateau-land of cactus, maguey, and dwarf palm. To the south, toward the Pacific, at the place where your imaginary journey began, the mountains drop to the verdant, jungle-draped foothills, lush river canyons, and coastal farms of the **Mixteca de la Costa** (Mixtec coastal region).

CLIMATE

Despite its deep southern latitude, Oaxaca's elevation, cooling sea breezes, and summer rain showers moderate the heat of its plentiful sunshine. Most of the state, excepting the remote mountain summits, basks in the tropics, never feeling the bite of frost.

The seashore and coastal plain, including all of the Isthmus, is truly a land of endless summer. Winter days are typically warm and rainless, peaking at 28–31°C (82–88°F) and dropping to 18–24°C (65–75°F) by midnight.

Summers on the Oaxaca beaches are warmer and wetter. Mornings are usually bright and balmy, warming to around 32°C (90°F). In the early afternoons, clouds often gather and

---

OAXACA FAST FACTS

- **Land area:** 95,470 square kilometers/ 36,860 square miles (fifth largest among 31 Mexican states and the federal district)
- **Tallest mountain:** Cerro Quiexobra, 3,750 meters/12,300 feet
- **Population (2010):** 3,802,000 (10th largest among Mexican states)
- **Indigenous population:** 32 percent of the total
- **Population density:** 40 per square kilometer/103 per square mile

bring short, sometimes heavy, cooling showers. Later, the sun reappears, drying the sidewalks and beaches and warming the breeze just in time to enjoy a dazzling Oaxaca *puesta del sol* (sunset).

Visitors to Oaxaca City experience similar but more temperate seasons. Midwinter days are typically mild to warm, usually peaking between 21 and 24°C (70–75°F). Expect cool but frost-free winter nights between 9 and 16°C (45–60°F). Oaxaca City summers are delightful, with afternoons typically 28–32°C (in the mid- to upper 80s) and pleasant evenings 24–26°C (in the mid-70s), perfect for strolling.

Visitors should take note that Oaxaca's rainfall, like all of Mexico's, is strongly seasonal. Most years, nearly all the rainfall accumulates during the summer and early fall. Rains taper off in October and November and don't usually return until June. May, before the rains, is typically Mexico's warmest month. Relief comes with the cooling summer showers.

Many trees, especially along the coast, respond to the winter–spring drought by losing their leaves by February. This might make a typical late winter–early spring Oaxaca landscape appear barren to the visitor in March, even though the same area will be blooming with greenery by July or August. If you prefer lush, jungle verdure to be part of your Mexico experience, you'll enjoy plenty if you visit during the seven months of July–January.

Flora and Fauna

Luxuriant tropical foliage is one of the reasons that visitors are pleasantly surprised when they visit Oaxaca during the rainy summer–fall season. Then, excursions through Oaxaca's coastal foothill forest can often reward travelers with a bounty of exotic verdure only seen in hothouses back home: Great leafy trees are swathed with mats of vines; giant-leafed **philodendrons** climb toward the canopy, while tropical hangers-on, such as spiny, pineapple-like red **bromeliads** and big, white-flowered **orchids** perch atop available branches.

Tropical forests are not the only places that bloom. Wildflowers sprout everywhere, especially on temperate upland plateaus. There, summer rains bring carpets of roadside blossoms—petite purple daisies, blue and yellow lupine, morning glories, tiny magenta sweet peas, and dozens more.

The dry winter–spring season also brings its surprising rewards. Many trees, especially along the coast, having lost their leaves, flower in February. Hundreds of varieties of the **pea family** bloom in riotous red, pink, yellow, and white. Now and then visitors stop, attracted by something remarkable, such as a host of white flowers blooming from the apparently dead branches of the appropriately named *palo de muerto* (tree of the dead). Other times, strikingly beautiful tree blossoms, such as the yellow, roselike *rosa amarilla,* tempt one's poetic imagination.

In dry country, cactus-like plants rule. Dotted all over the state, fields of **maguey** in ranks and files like obedient botanical battalions wait to be harvested for mescal. In other places, you will often see farmyards fenced with bulging nopal (prickly pear) cacti, their thick leaves studded with red **tunas** (cactus apples). And, on the road some drowsy afternoon, when you least expect it, a big **candelabra cactus** might appear around a bend, bristling with a house-size row of dozens of upright fluted green columns.

VEGETATION ZONES

Plants must adapt to the soil, sun, and rain, and Oaxaca's astonishingly diverse plant population reflects the state's varied landscape. Of Mexico's 14 major vegetation zones, ranging from high desert to tropical rainforest, at least 8 occur in Oaxaca.

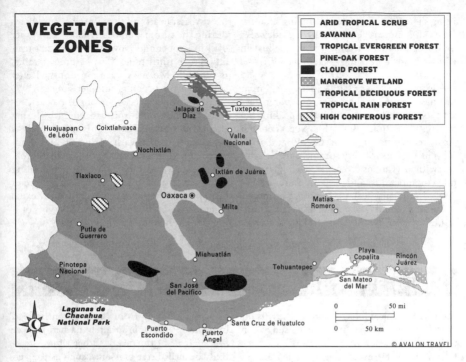

VEGETATION ZONES

- ARID TROPICAL SCRUB
- SAVANNA
- TROPICAL EVERGREEN FOREST
- PINE-OAK FOREST
- CLOUD FOREST
- MANGROVE WETLAND
- TROPICAL DECIDUOUS FOREST
- TROPICAL RAIN FOREST
- HIGH CONIFEROUS FOREST

Huajuapan de León · Coixtlahuaca · Jalapa de Díaz · Tuxtepec · Valle Nacional · Nochixtlán · Tlaxiaco · Ixtlán de Juárez · Oaxaca · Mitla · Matías Romero · Putla de Guerrero · Miahuatlán · Playa Copalita · Rincón Juárez · Pinotepa Nacional · Tehuantepec · San Mateo del Mar · San José del Pacífico · Lagunas de Chacahua National Park · Puerto Escondido · Puerto Ángel · Santa Cruz de Huatulco

0   50 mi
0   50 km

© AVALON TRAVEL

Directly along Oaxaca's paved national highways you can visit six of these zones: Near the seacoast lie extensive swaths of **savanna, deciduous tropical forest,** and **pine-oak forest.** Inland, you can add the **tropical evergreen forest, tropical rainforest,** and **arid tropical scrub** to your botanical itinerary. Oaxaca's remaining major two vegetation zones, the **cloud forest** and **high coniferous forest,** are accessible only on high, often roadless, mountain slopes and summits.

Savanna

In their natural state, Oaxaca's savanna lands appear as flat, palm-dotted grasslands, watery during the summer and dry and brown during the winter and spring. Although much savanna has been converted to pasture or farmland, some pristine stretches lie along the coast, notably along Highway 200 near the Lagunas de Chacahua and along the Isthmus shoreline south of Highway 190, east of Juchitán.

Although grass rules the savanna, palms give it character. One of the most familiar in Oaxaca is the **Mexican fan palm,** or *palma real (Sabal Mexicana),* seasonally festooned with black fruit with leaves spread flat like a señorita's fan. The *palma real,* sometimes called the Oaxaca palm, resembles its cousin, the palmetto of the American southeast. The *palma real,* moreover, doesn't limit itself to the savanna. It appears in many other Oaxaca landscapes, notably in picturesque dwarf form in the cactus forest alongside Highway 190, just north of Huajuapan de León, in arid northwest Oaxaca.

Visitors to Oaxaca's coastal resorts usually enjoy the sight of plenty of **coconut palms** *(Cocos nucifera),* by many measures the world's most useful tree. Local folks, who call it the *cocotero,* use nearly all of its parts: fronds for thatch, mats, and baskets; lumber for construction; and nuts for cooling drinks, fruit, candy, and oil. Nothing seems to symbolize the tropics more than a coconut palm drooping lazily over the beach or its fronds rustling gently in the tropical breeze. The coconut is completely benign with one exception: **Falling coconuts are no joke.** Watch out for them, especially during a breeze.

If you see what look like several grapefruits sprouting from a tree trunk, you are probably looking at a **gourd tree,** or *calabaza (Crescentia alata)*. The mature gourds, brown and hard, were handsomely carved and fitted with gold handles for Aztec emperors to drink chocolate out of. Oaxacans, who still call them by the ancient name *jícaras,* use them as bowls (notably women, on the west Oaxaca coast, who carry them all day at market on their heads, like a hat).

Its petite, pumpkin-shaped gourds both identify and name the **sandbox tree,** or *jabillo,* because they once served as desktop boxes full of sand for drying ink. The Aztecs, however, named it the exploding tree, because its ripe fruit burst seeds forth with a bang like a firecracker. Beware of its poisonous seeds and its irritating sap.

A **mangrove wetland** *(manglar),* a vegetation sub-zone, often borders a savanna's watery seaward edge. Healthy mangrove wetlands are primary nurseries for uncounted forms of aquatic plants and animals. A number of prime spots exist; Laguna Manialtepec, a half-hour drive west of Puerto Escondido, is one of Oaxaca's richest and most accessible mangrove wetlands.

The plant both synonymous with and essential to the mangrove wetland is the **red mangrove,** or *mangle colorado,* a tree that seems to stand in the water on stilts. Its new roots grow downward from above; a time-lapse photo would show it marching, as if on stilts, into the lagoon.

Tropical Deciduous Forest

Great swaths of this "friendly" or "short-tree" forest coat Oaxaca's coastline, especially along coastal Highway 200 around Puerto Ángel and the Bahías de Huatulco. As the label "deciduous" implies, this is the forest where the trees, in response to the dry winter weather, go dormant and lose their leaves. For visitors, the upside to all the winter barrenness is that many trees' leaves show bright fall colors; then, at the height of winter bleakness, they sprout profusions of bright red, yellow, pink, and white winter blossoms from apparently lifeless branches.

One of the most strikingly beautiful of these is the **rosa amarilla,** or yellowsilk shellseed *(Cochlospermum vitifolium).* Although not a rose, it looks every bit like a wild yellow rose when its big flowers sprout from bare branches in the early spring. After the flowers fall, leaves bud and apple-shaped green fruit grows, turning into brown pods, which pop open and release silky fluff.

The **silk cotton tree** *(Ceiba pentandra),* another of the tropical deciduous forest's major actors, yields a form of lightweight, cottony kapok fiber. Local folks, who call it the *cuajilote,* prize it for its spectacular large white (or red in cultivated varieties) blossoms with big, brushy pink stamens. In dense forest the silk cotton tree stays relatively short, but isolated it can grow to a wide-crowned giant with bulging buttresses on the lower trunk.

Lovers of Hawaii will be pleasantly surprised to find that a number of their favorite island plants are Mexican natives. The **frangipani** or **plumeria,** prized by native Mexicans for its heavenly orange blossom–like fragrance, was first classified and named as *Plumeria acutifolia* by French botanist Plumier. Pick some of its white, pink, or yellow whorl-lobed five-petaled flowers and put one behind your ear to get yourself into Mexico's *mañana* mood.

In Oaxaca, as in Hawaii, you always know Christmas is coming because of another famous Mexico native, the **poinsettia,** or *catarina (Euphorbia pulcherrima),* first classified in 1828 by Joel R. Poinsett, an early U.S. ambassador to Mexico. Interestingly, the poinsettia's red blooms, in great abundance at Oaxaca City's Christmas fiestas, are not actually flower petals, but green leaves turned red, known technically as bracts.

Not nearly so benign is the **mala mujer** (bad

The poinsettia (foreground) grows wild in Oaxaca.

woman, *Cnidoscolus urens*), southern Mexico's poison ivy bush. Before venturing out through the Oaxaca coastal forest, ask someone to point out its drooping, oak-like, five-lobed leaves and tiny flowers. Otherwise, you might risk a stinging rash from the nettle-like hairs on the leaf surfaces and the long stalks.

If you go out on your hike but forget your makeup kit, you can improvise with the **lipstick tree,** or *achiote (Bicha orellana)*. It appears as an ordinary shrub, but marked with brownish-green soft burrs above long, heart-shaped leaves. The surprise comes when you crush the burrs and discover their bright red-orange pulp, source of annatto dye, which warriors used to make themselves look fierce and which manufacturers now use to color cheese, silk, and lipstick.

One of the showiest of roadside inhabitants is **mata ratón** (mouse killer, *Gliricidia sepium*). Despite its fragrant spring swirls of pink and white pea-like blossoms, this plant lives up to its name. Oaxacans grind its bark and leaves with cooked corn for a very effective rat and

mouse poison (which, beware, is also poisonous to dogs and cats). It can be further identified by its four- to six-inch-long seedpods.

Pine-Oak Forest

About an hour's drive inland, at elevations of about 1,500 meters (5,000 ft), the tropics give way to the cooling heights of the pine-oak forest, Oaxaca's most extensive vegetation zone.

Although pine-oak forest once covered half of Oaxaca's landscape, people, beginning thousands of years ago with Oaxaca's original farmers, cleared much of it for fields, especially in the central valley and surrounding mountainsides. Nevertheless, extensive upland tracts of pine-oak forest still remain, doing their beneficent work, storing moisture, anchoring soil against erosion, and providing food and shelter for hosts of animals.

As you enter the pine-oak forest from lower elevations, you usually see the oaks first, occurring in two broad families. Mexicans identify them as either the **encino** (evergreen, small-leafed) or the **roble** (deciduous, large-leafed), both resembling oaks that dot the hills and valleys of California and the U.S. Southwest. Clustered in their branches and scattered in the shade are the *bellota* (acorns), which unmistakably mark them as oaks.

At higher elevations the oaks gradually give way to pines, which, in Oaxaca, often grow in pure stands above 1,800–2,100 meters (6,000–7,000 ft). Pines are easy to identify because of their long needle-like leaves, which grow in bundles, in contrast to the shorter needles of other conifers, such as spruce and fir, which commonly grow feather-shaped leaves made of rows of needles individually attached to the leaf stem.

Although pines are easily distinguished from other tree families, individual pine species are often hard to differentiate from each other. Nevertheless, examining the cones (which often conceal edible, tasty nuts) and the needles may yield identifying clues to at least a few members of this populous and very useful Mexican tree family.

Among the varieties you may encounter is the

Mexican white pine *(Pinus ayachuite),* similar to the white pine of the western United States. Local folks, who call it the *pinabete* or *ayacahuite,* know it by its very large (more than 20 centimeters/eight inches) cones and long, 4–6-inch needles, which hang in clusters of five.

Others you might see are the **Montezuma pine,** locally called the *ocote macho* (dark 3–9-inch dark cones, long, drooping needles, five to a bundle), or the **Aztec pine** *(pino real;* shiny, small brown 1–2-inch cones and long, bright green needles in bundles of three—very useful for turpentine, tar, soap, and medicines).

Often associated in the same territory as pines and oaks is Mexico's renowned national tree, the *ahuehuete* (ah-way-WAY-tay), or *sabino.* Nearly every visitor to Oaxaca City sees the country's most famous specimen at the village of Santa María del Tule, half an hour east of the city, where droves of visitors arrive, some on bended knee, to wonder at what is known locally as El Tule. Probably the most massive tree in Latin America, it's as big around at the trunk as it is high: approximately 46 meters (150 ft).

Other more modest but still impressive *ahuehuete* specimens occur in outlying areas, often in majestic groves near water, which accounts for its name, which translates as "old one of the water." When traveling through the inland countryside, especially along stream bottoms in the Mixteca (northwest Oaxaca), you may be able to spot an old *ahuehuete* by its general appearance, unusual for Mexico: a thick, deep green crown and reddish-brown, vertically grooved bark, not unlike a California redwood. Up close you will identify it by its round, reticulated two-inch cones and its feathery green spruce-like leaves (which led botanists to classify it as a type of cypress, namely the Montezuma bald cypress, *Taxodium mucronatum).*

Tropical Evergreen Forest

In rainy foothill and low mountain areas, especially along the north Gulf slope, the lush, dense undergrowth and tall, leaf-crowned trees of the tropical evergreen forest decorate the hillsides. Here, most extensively in the north along Highway 175 around Valle Nacional, and, to a lesser extent, in the southern Sierra foothills along highways north from the Pacific coast, huge trees and vine-strewn thickets often overhang the highway. As the road curls through a dark, isolated, liana-draped canyon, momentarily you might feel as if you're traversing a forgotten corner of some prehistoric lost world, where a last remnant dinosaur might rear up at any moment.

But the bright visions of the tropical evergreen forest invariably dissipate such Jurassic Park images and jolt you back to its vivid jungle realities: A green iguana, looking every bit as primitive as a dinosaur, slithers across the road; a screeching swarm of bright green parrots swoops overhead; or a big, bird-size butterfly flutters in a roadside patch of sunlight. Overhead, huge-leafed climbing plants, such as the **ceriman** *(Monstera deliciosa),* hang by thick ropy vines on the trunks of accommodating trees. Local people, who know the ceriman as the *piñanona,* enjoy its sweet, juicy, corn cob–shaped fruit and find relief from aches and pains by drinking a tea brewed from its leaves.

No Oaxaca jungle trip would be complete without experiencing the **strangler fig,** known by the hideously accurate local label *matapalo* (killer tree). A strangler fig seed, once it sprouts in the crotch of a victim tree, will grow, finally entwining its host in a suffocating embrace. By then, the strangler fig will have planted hairy "air roots" for ground support and will most likely go on living long after its victim has died. In a peculiarly national quirk of character, many Mexicans prize such dead victim-tree trunks. Workers scour the forests, cutting, gathering, and polishing these death embraces, to decorate living room corners or support elaborate outdoor *palapa* roofs, especially in fancy open-air restaurants.

In numerous stretches of Oaxaca's tropical evergreen forest, local folks cultivate **coffee** beneath the shady canopy. Even if coffee *(Coffea Arabica),* known to its Mexican growers as *cafeto,* weren't commercially important, people could still enjoy it as an attractive ornamental, with its shiny, ribbed green leaves and red holly-like berries. Even though coffee shrubs are quite common in Oaxaca's jungly foothills, you have to look carefully for them, because they grow best in the deep shade beneath taller trees. If you don't spot the ripe red berries, look instead for the white flowers, which are as fragrant as those of coffee's cousin, the gardenia.

Another popular import to Oaxaca's tropical forestland is the **African tulip tree** (*Spathodea campanulata*). Often seen right at roadside, a host of spectacular big red blooms caps a lush leafy crown like a host of heavenly scarlet bells.

Nearly as spectacular in its own exotic way is that cousin of the banana, the **heliconia** (*Heliconia latispatha*). Because of the resemblance, Mexicans call it the *platanillo*, or "little banana." In contrast to the fruit of the banana, the heliconia's golden-orange flower-like leaves (bracts), reminiscent of bird-of-paradise blossoms, are the main attraction. To happen upon one for the first time in a garden or in the wild—hanging amongst the greenery in descending golden-orange segments like a ladder for leprechauns—is an experience rarely forgotten.

Tropical Rainforest

This is the "forest primeval" of legend, where heavy rains nourish grand evergreen hardwoods whose great leafy crowns tower up to 60 meters (200 ft) over layers of lesser trees. Here and there, rays of sunlight shine through and nurture luxuriant undergrowth of palms, bamboo, orchids, and bromeliads.

The rainforest gives rise to many unique, sometimes bizarre, adaptations. The big trees fortify themselves against their top-heavy bulk by developing ponderous buttresses, reaching up to a dozen feet from the ground and spreading six or eight feet from the trunk. On the other hand, shorter, lower-canopy trees commonly drop fibrous filaments, which eventually root and grow into strange, stilt-like side-trunks as far as 15 meters (50 ft) from the original trunk.

Oaxaca's rainforests, which once spread in a continuous green swath along its northern border with the state of Veracruz, are steadily being logged and replaced by farms and ranches. Nevertheless, sizable tracts still remain, much in roadless areas on both sides of Highway 175 around Valle Nacional, Isthmus Highway 185, and its offshoot, Highway 147, which runs northwest, through lowland Mixe territory, paralleling the Veracruz border.

The acknowledged king of the Mexican rainforest community is the **mahogany,** which local people, who call it the *caoba,* often point to with pride. The label refers to a number of similar trees of the genus *Swietenia,* which grow throughout the Mexican and Central American rainforests. Although the original mahogany (*Swietenia mahogany*) does not grow in Mexico, some of its cousins, such as *Swietenia macrophylla,* do. Oaxacans prize it for its handsome reddish wood, much valued for furniture. You can identify it by its half-foot-long slender leaves and four-inch woody fruits, curved like a vulture's head, thus the tongue-twisting indigenous label *zopilo zonte-comacuahuitl* (buzzard-head tree).

If, along the roadside, you spot a tall tree with diagonal slashes on its bark (for gathering sap), it's most likely either a rubber tree or the chewing-gum tree, the **chicle,** locally known as the *chicozapote.* Chewing gum, made from the chicle's sap (notice the Chiclets in every store), spread all over the world during the early 20th century and continues to gum up sidewalks and schoolroom desks from San Francisco to Samarkand. Additionally, chicle trees, known to botanists as *Acrasuzapote,* yield hard, very durable wood and, from small pinkish-white flowers, luscious round cream-colored fruits.

Of both commercial and decorative importance is the **rubber tree** (*Castilla elastica*), the source of so-called Panama rubber, once made (before synthetics) for raincoats, tennis balls, and tires. Indigenous Mexicans, who still call it the *hule* (OO-lay), have used it for millennia for making the ball for the ceremonial game of **tlatchtli.** Besides the diagonal grooves (which guide the milky sap into cups) on the trunk, you can identify the rubber tree by its foot-long elliptical leathery dark-green leaves, shiny on the top side and hairy underneath.

Among Oaxaca's most useful rainforest natives is the **chocolate tree** (*Theobromo cacao*), the "food of the gods" of the pre-conquest kings of Mexico. Before the conquest, cacao seeds served as currency. Although these days most people don't like to think of such things, historical records indicate that a healthy slave usually traded for about 100 beans; a small animal for perhaps about 5 beans. Most likely you'll identify the cacao, growing as a smallish tree beneath the forest canopy, by spotting its 25-centimeter (10-inch) pods, which sprout right from the trunk. Workers break open the ripe leathery yellow pods to harvest the trove of beans inside.

Arid Tropical Scrub

Although it looks a lot like a desert, Oaxaca's arid tropical scrub vegetation zone, along its northwest border with the states of Guerrero and Puebla, averages at least as much rainfall as San Francisco, California. In Oaxaca, however, the rain comes within a few summer months, often in cloudburst deluges that quickly drain away, leaving the people, animals, and plants to cope with six months of winter–spring drought.

The arid tropical scrub zone's most successful plants, succulents, such as **cacti** and their cousins the **agaves,** cope by storing moisture in fleshy leaves, trunks, and stems. None is more successful or important than the **prickly pear** *(Opuntia tuna),* which, from its role in Aztec legend and consequent presence on the Mexican flag, is an important national symbol. Moreover, it is especially useful as a fence plant, for cattle food, and, most of all, for its delicious red *tunas,* "cactus apple" fruit, which festoon its fleshy leaves.

The prickly pear is but one member of a broad look-alike family, known in Mexico generally as the **nopal.** Another, especially benign, relative, known by botanists as *Platyopuntia,* is cultivated both for its tasty, spine-free leaves and, in Oaxaca, for red **cochineal** dye. Once commercially very important but now largely supplanted by synthetics, cochineal is still produced in a few Valley of Oaxaca communities. It turns out that a certain scale insect, *Dactylopius coccus,* loves to munch on the *Platyopuntia* cactus leaves. When the insects have eaten their fill, the people gather, dry, and crush their bodies, which yield a brilliant scarlet dye prized by weavers.

Another useful domesticated member of the arid tropical scrub community is the **maguey** (mah-GAY), or century plant, so-called because it's said to bloom once, then die, after 100 years of growth, although its lifetime is usually closer to 50 years. The maguey, moreover, has a number of well-known relatives. These include the very useful mescal, renowned for distilled liquor; lechuguilla, for ixtle fiber; and sisal, also useful for fiber. All of these, of the genus *Agave,* mature as a rose-like cluster of leathery, long pointed gray-green leaves, from which a single flower stalk eventually blooms.

Wondrous gardens of wild cacti proliferate in the arid tropical scrub zone of northwest Oaxaca. Hard to miss is the **bravo** *(Neobuxbaumia mexcalaensis),* which often appears right at roadside, rising as tall (3–6 m/10–20 ft), pencil-shaped fluted columns. Bravos frequently grow in spectacular grand forests stretching to far rocky horizons.

© STEPHAN SCHERHAG/123RF.COM

Cactus-like maguey grows nearly everywhere in the state of Oaxaca.

Often growing in the same habitat is the *candelabro,* or **candelabra cactus** *(Stenoceris weberi),* which, most likely, you will see in a community of stunning many-columned giants, like house-size menorahs, dotting the landscape for miles.

Cloud Forest and High Coniferous Forest

Oaxaca's two rarest plant and wildlife communities lie on the slopes and summits of high, remote mountains. Oaxaca's most accessible cloud forests coat the northern mountains north of Ixtlán de Juárez along Highway 175 and the crest of the Mazatec's holy mountain, Cerro Rabón, near Jalapa de Díaz. The easiest route is to hire a local guide who can take you to these dewy mountaintops where, between 900 and 1,800 meters (3,000–6,000 ft), you will first meet the plant and wildlife community of the cloud forest. Most botanists believe many cloud forest plants to be Ice Age remnants of a time when Mexico's climate was much cooler than today. The proof is in the surprise specimens, many of which appear to have been transported directly across the Gulf of Mexico from the mountain forests of Georgia or North Carolina. In Oaxacan cloud forests, you may see the brilliant reds and oranges of **liquid amber** and the white bark and tan falling leaves of **beech** in the fall, and the lovely white flowers of **dogwood,** in the summer.

Besides those, you might observe some of the cloud forest's even more ancient vestiges, dating from the age of the dinosaurs. They include the giant Mexican **tree ferns** *(Cyathea Mexicana)* with their long feathery fronds, dotted underside with ranks of brown spores. New fronds, which are born curling out of the treetops, account for the tree fern's local name, *rabo de mico* (monkey's tail).

Other such relics are the bromeliads and orchids, which as epiphytes merely enjoy physical support in their hosts' branches (unlike parasites, which feed on their hosts). **Bromeliads,** members of the pineapple family, love the drippy cloud-forest environment, collecting water in their cup-like leaf folds. Of the dozens of Mexican species, one of the best known is the showy *piñuela (Guzmannia lingulata),* whose roseate central leaf cluster matures from green to red, finally appearing as an exotic scarlet flower.

Among the **orchids,** you will most likely first see the very widespread *bayoneta,* or *pata de paloma* (dove's foot), which thrives in every humid Oaxaca environment from mangrove lagoons to cloud forests. You can recognize the *bayoneta* by its clusters of fleshy, drooping green leaves, topped by showy white flowers that age to a mellow golden hue.

Follow your guide even higher and you will reach the zone of **high coniferous forest,** which in Oaxaca exists only as a few scattered roadless, cloud-swathed green alpine islands, with vegetation resembling upper Rocky Mountain slopes in the United States and Canada. In Oaxaca, as you climb above about 3,300 meters (10,000 ft), you will likely pass through a zone of mixed pines, alders, and firs, reigned over by the regal **Montezuma pine** *(Pinus montezumae),* distinguished by its long, pendulous cones and rough, ruddy bark, reminiscent of the sugar pine of the western United States.

Ascending still higher, you may pass through pure stands of **sacred fir** *(Abies religiosa),* which your guide will probably know as *oyamel* or *abeto.* You can identify them by lovely violet-blue cones and typical fir-like needles, which grow in rows along the branches. Even higher, the firs will eventually thin out, giving way to bunchgrass and bushy **Mexican juniper** *(monticola),* with its edible, waxy blue berries.

For more details of Oaxaca's marvelous plants, consult M. Walter Pesman's delightfully readable *Meet Flora Mexicana* (which, unfortunately, has been long out of print, but major libraries often have a copy). Also informative is the more recent popular paperback *Handbook of Mexican Roadside Flora,* by Charles T. Mason Jr. and Patricia B. Mason.

MAMMALS

Although thousands of years of human hunting and habitat encroachment have generally reduced their numbers, many of Oaxaca's native animal species still thrive in the wild. While some animals, sensitive to human presence, such as **jaguars, howler monkeys,** and **tapirs,** are now rarely seen in Oaxaca, others, such as **foxes, coyotes, coatimundis,** and wild pig-like **jabalís,** seem unaffected by, and sometimes even appear to benefit from, human presence.

The excitement of seeing animals in the wild is the reward of visitors who take time to visit them in their own wilderness home grounds. Sylvan stretches, such as the pine-oak woodlands coating mountainsides northeast of Oaxaca City, the thick forests of the Huatulco preserve, or the rich mangrove wetland of Manialtepec near Puerto Escondido, are ripe with wildlife-viewing opportunities for those willing to get off the beaten track and quietly watch and wait.

Armadillos, Coatimundis, Peccaries, and Bats

The benefits of quiet isolation once came to me when, lazing on a tropical beach, I spotted my first **armadillo** (Dasypus novemcinctus). Although it behaved much like the familiar opossum, I was struck by its reptilian-like shell. The armadillo was going about its business, nosing through the forest-edge leaf cover nearby. Not seeming to possess particularly good eyesight, the preoccupied armadillo didn't notice when I crept in for a closer look. He waddled right up and sniffed my shoe, which evidently gave him such a scare that he scuttled back into the woods in a flash.

One of the Mexicans' favorite animals is the raccoon-like **coatimundi** (Nasua narica), known in Mexico as coati, or tejón, the European Spanish name for badger (although the coatimundi is a completely different animal). While many urban Mexicans, charmed by the coatimundi's acrobatic antics and inquisitive nature, keep them as pets, hungry country folks enjoy them for culinary reasons. You can identify one by its long nose and straight, usually vertically held tail. Watch for them at country markets.

The pig-like **collared peccary** (Tayassu

tajacu) is definitely not one of Oaxaca's endangered species. Known in Mexico as the jabalí, the Spanish name for the European wild boar, it is nevertheless an American native, ranging from the southwest United States through Mexico and Central and most of South America. Although it is easily distinguished by its whitish beige, collar-like marking that encircles its neck, the jabalí is sometimes confused with the European wild boar (Sus scrofa), which was introduced into the Americas as a game animal, and now thrives in the wilds of the U.S. Southeast and Pacific Coast.

The jabalí eats most anything and thrives in nearly all environments—often not far from towns and villages. The gray-to-brown short-haired jabalís, although normally shy when encountered alone, sometimes congregate in large groups and become aggressive. People have occasionally reported being chased and, in one case, forced up a tree, by collared peccaries.

Bats (murciélagos, moor-see-AY-lah-gohs) are widespread in Oaxaca, home to more than twice as many bat species as the entire United States. In Oaxaca, bats were once widely worshipped, but today, as everywhere, they are both feared and misunderstood. Even though a tiny minority of Mexican bats are blood-eating vampires, Mexicans nevertheless generally (but mistakenly) call bats vampiros. Shortly before sundown, bats emerge from their cave and forest roosts and silently flit through the air in search of insects. Most people, sitting outside enjoying the early evening, will mistake their darting silhouettes for those of birds, who, except for owls, don't generally fly at night.

Oaxaca's bats carry their vampire cousins' odious reputation with forbearance. They busily go about their good works, pollinating flowers, clearing the air of pesky gnats and mosquitoes, ridding cornfields of mice, and dropping seeds, thereby restoring forests.

Monkeys

Oaxaca's remote mountains and jungles, notably in the **Chimalapa** region in the eastern Isthmus of Tehuántepec, still shelter a number of rare and endangered species. Accompanied by a competent tracker and suitably equipped with a jeep and a week's worth of supplies, you may be lucky enough to catch glimpses of Mexico's two seldom-seen primates, the **spider and howler monkeys.** The black spider monkey, whom your tracker will probably know as the *chango* or *mono de araña,* congregates in groups and uses its spindly arms and legs (thus the "spider" label) and its prehensile tail to reach its favorite wild fruits. Although its entertaining antics and endearingly mischievous ways have earned the *chango* a place as a pet in many Mexican homes, its present rarity is due in large part to its contribution to the diet of many poor indigenous families.

The even rarer howler monkey, called locally *saraguato* or *aullador,* is, by contrast, extremely shy and retiring. Seldom seen even in captivity, howler monkeys *(Alouatta palliata)* withdraw far into the forest as humankind encroaches. Consider yourself lucky if somewhere in Oaxaca's eastern jungle wilderness you can draw close enough to hear a big male howler's far-off booming call. Consider yourself doubly fortunate if, on such an excursion, you also hear the chesty cry of a jaguar, the fabled *tigre.*

El Tigre

The jaguar's cunning, stealth, and strength are the stuff of Mexican legend. In ancient times, the jaguar was the supreme source from whom kings, princes, and warriors drew their power. And when Mexicans recall the old proverb etched in their memories that "Each hill has its own *tigre,*" they remember that untamable presence out there beyond the campfire, the gate, the town limits, lurking somewhere in the darkness.

The legend is well deserved; at 110 kilograms and two meters in length (250 lbs, six ft), the jaguar *(Felis onca)* is America's largest, most powerful cat. With dark reticulated spots over a tan coat, the jaguar resembles a beefy, short-legged leopard. Although hunting and human encroachment have driven jaguars into Oaxaca's deepest forest reaches, a few still live on, mostly in the southern coast and

Sierra and the northeastern Isthmus, where they hunt along thickly forested stream bottoms and foothills. Unlike its more common cousin, the mountain lion, or *león,* the jaguar will eat any game. They have even been known to wait patiently for fish in rivers and stalk beaches for turtle and egg dinners. If they have a favorite food, it is probably the pig-like collared peccary.

Although government rules strictly prohibit jaguar hunting, the temptation for a poor campesino to earn a year's wages by shooting a jaguar and clandestinely selling its pelt is too great for the jaguar to survive for many more years in the wild in Oaxaca.

Despite their fearsome reputation and the demonstrated fact that they will fight back when cornered, little or no evidence indicates that jaguars are deliberate man-eaters.

Ocelots, Margays, and Jaguarundis

Although jaguars are extremely endangered, other Mexican cats are less so. Besides the bobcat and mountain lion, both familiar north of the border, three other wild cat species make their home in Oaxaca. In descending order of size, first comes the **ocelot** *(Felis pardalis).* Its appearance, like a miniature jaguar, with a spotted yellowish-tan coat and stout legs, reflects its Mexican name, *tigrillo.* Full-grown male ocelots measure about 10 kilograms (25 lbs) and one meter in length (three ft). Its soft, fine fur, highly valued as a pelt, has unfortunately led to the ocelot's near-disappearance from Oaxaca's forests.

Approaching large house-cat size is the **jaguarundi,** or *leoncillo,* which, full-grown, weighs in at around six kilograms (13 lbs). Although its species label *(Felis jaguarundi)* clearly puts the brownish jaguarundi in the cat family, its elongated body and long tail (totaling up to 75 cm/30 in) gives it an otterlike overall appearance.

With its spots and diminutive size, a full-grown **margay** appears at first glance to be a baby jaguar. A closer look, however, reveals spots more aligned in rows than the jaguar's.

Moreover, a domesticated margay, in contrast to the untamable jaguar, can be as endearing as your own family cat.

Like their larger cousins, the jaguarundi and margay are gradually disappearing from Oaxaca's forest wildlands. They hunt mostly along stream banks in deep remote valleys and roadless mountainsides. They feast on small game, birds, and fish, and, as a matter of self-preservation, make it their business to see you before you see them.

BIRDS

Oaxaca's coastal wetlands and upland forests straddle the southern zone of the great Pacific Flyway, the major western pathway for hosts of birds migrating south from the United States and Canada. These familiar winter visitors, such as Canada geese and ducks, including the Muscovy, black-bellied whistler, gadwall, baldpate, and shoveler, arrive and join an already-rich resident population of ibis, parrots, jacanas, egrets, herons, and anhingas, swelling the numbers into the millions.

Some of the most commonly seen residents are also the most spectacular and entertaining. The cootlike, blackish **northern jacana** *(Jacana spinosa)* amuses bird-watchers by appearing to walk on water. Actually, its clownishly large feet allow it to scoot across gardens of water-borne lily pads as if they were solid land, earning it the label "lily walker."

Always impressive is the graceful swoop of a **great blue heron** *(Ardea herodius)* gliding to rest in a Oaxacan wetland. Unmistakable because of its regal two-meter (six ft) wingspread and blue-gray coloring, the male great blue heron also sports a proud blue head plume. In the same marshland, you will also probably spot its smaller (about half a meter, or two feet, long), more numerous cousin, the **snowy egret** *(Egretta thula)*, pure white except for its black beak. Although differing sharply in appearance, both species single-mindedly stalk through a pond ever so slowly, freezing rock-still when prey is spotted. After several seconds, pop! Down goes the bill, snaring a hapless crab, fish, or frog.

The great white egret is a familiar hunter in Oaxaca.

© BRUCE WHIPPERMAN

Try not to confuse the snowy egret with the smaller (18-inch) yellow-billed **cattle egret** *(Bubulcus ibis)*, an African native that began appearing in Mexico around 1900. True to their name, cattle egrets usually flock around cow pastures, where they feed on the hordes of bugs that follow livestock. Local Mexican people generally identify all herons and egrets collectively as *garzas*.

Seabirds

Oaxaca's prime beach-bird actors, in addition to the swarms of gulls *(gaviotas)*, terns, sandpipers, and boobies, are **brown pelicans** and big black-and-white **frigate birds.** Their collective feeding rituals, although quite distinct, are equally entertaining. That of the brown *pelicano* (pay-LEE-cah-noh) is the most deliberate. After spotting a school of their preferred prey, the pelicans, singly or in pairs, circle once or twice, then dive headlong into the billows, usually coming up with fish in their gullet. They rest, bobbing over the waves for a spell, seemingly waiting for their comrades to take their turns. Frigate birds *(fragatas)*, by contrast, prefer either being fed or stealing food to hunting for themselves. They often reap bonuses from the efforts of villagers who haul in nets of fish right on the beach. Once the salable part of the catch is gone, kids have great fun throwing the residue overhead to a gaggle of wheeling frigate birds. In contrast to the pelicans' mannerly behavior, it's every frigate bird for itself. Frigates who miss a tossed morsel often try to snatch their fellow's prize.

Parrots

Flocks of small parrots screech, shriek, swoop, chatter, and swarm above Oaxaca's coastal mangrove lagoons and tropical foothills. The best places to spot them are in fields or pastures adjacent to thick forests, far from town. Half a dozen species—mostly green, with a patch of color on their throat or forehead—are common. If you don't get far enough into the country to see them, ask where *péricos* (PAY-ree-kohs) are for sale in big markets, such as Oaxaca City, Tlacolula, Etla, Tehuántepec, Tuxtepec, Pinotepa Nacional, and Valle Nacional.

Although you might be tempted to buy such a market parrot, don't. Like all wild animals, parrots outside of their forest homelands present manifold difficulties. For starters, they quickly chew their way out of bamboo cages. Later, your airline will probably require that you buy a special "parrot ticket" for the flight back home. Moreover, after you arrive, parrots are all but impossible to get through customs. On the other hand, if you must have a pet parrot, best buy a pair (never a single) of certified healthy birds from a pet shop back home.

Among the parrots you're most likely to encounter in Oaxaca is the foot-long **green parakeet** (*Aratinga holochlora*). A long tail and a red throat further mark the species, whose members prefer to flock in the drier woodlands above 1,000 meters (3,000 ft). Another, commonly seen in tropical lowlands, is the **Aztec parakeet** (*Aratinga astec*), at 23 centimeters (nine inches), all green with an olive-brown throat. For superb color drawings and details, see *Bird-Finding Guide to Mexico* by Steve Howell (1999).

REPTILES AND AMPHIBIANS
Snakes

Of Oaxaca's many dozens of snake species, the great majority couldn't harm you even if they tried. Furthermore, most snakes are shy and will clear out if you give them plenty of warning. In Oaxaca, poisonous snakes have been largely driven out of city and tourist areas. In the bush or jungle, however, carry a stick and beat the shrubbery in front of you while watching where you put your feet. When hiking or rock-climbing in the country, don't put your hands in niches you can't see into.

While such precautions minimize potential hazards, outback travelers should be prepared to encounter members of Oaxaca's most notorious snake families, the **rattlesnakes** and the **fer-de-lances.** Each occurs in a number of species, all potently venomous and generally aggressive. Mexican rattlesnakes, or *cascabeles* (kahs-kah-BAY-lays), with the same warning rattle and the diamondback markings as their north-of-the-border U.S. relatives, need little introduction. Their tropical viper-cousins, the fer-de-lances (*Bothrops atrox*), are known locally by various names, such as *nauyaca, cuatro narices, palanca,* and *barba amarilla.* Although about the same full-grown size (two meters/six feet) and general appearance as rattlesnakes, fer-de-lances *lack warning rattles* and are consequently even more dangerous. On treks into the jungle, where the fer-de-lance commonly lives, guard against them by wearing high-topped leather boots, rustling the bushes ahead of you with a stick, and watching carefully where you put your feet.

Snakes in the tropics are not confined to land. Although very unlikely, it is possible that you may encounter a **sea snake** (*culebra marina*) while swimming offshore at an isolated Oaxaca beach. If small, yellow, and black, it will certainly be the *Pelamis platurus*, which, although shy, lives in groups and has been reported to inflict a serious, venomous bite. Some **eels,** which resemble snakes but have gills like fish and inhabit rocky crevices, can inflict nonpoisonous bites and should also be avoided.

The Oaxacan land counterpart of the

poisonous sea snake is the **coral snake** *(coralillo)*, which occurs in several species, all with bright multicolored bands that always include red. Although relatively rare, small, and shy, coral snakes occasionally bite, sometimes fatally.

Gila Monsters, Iguanas, and Geckos

The Gila monster (confined in Mexico to northern Sonora) and its southern tropical relative, the black-with-yellow-spots **escorpión,** are the world's only poisonous lizards. Despite its beaded skin and menacing, fleshy appearance, the *escorpión (Heloderma horridum)* bites only when severely provoked; even then, its venom is rarely, if ever, fatal.

The rest of Oaxaca's many lizard species are much more benign; some are even endearing. Of them, the **iguana,** locally called the *garrobo,* is most popular, mainly because of its tasty flesh. Although usually masked in the bush by its spotted green camouflage, you may glimpse an iguana scurrying, in a flash of green, across the road in front of your car or bus. Despite their fierce dinosaurian aspect, iguanas are peaceful vegetarians, often munching flowers in a favorite treetop.

One of Oaxaca's most endearing reptilian, which was introduced from Europe as a game animal and now lives wild, ranging from South America to central Mexico residents is the **gecko,** known as *guerita* (blondie) in the coastal towns and villages where they are common. Visitors usually encounter them in their hotel rooms. If you hear their homey clicking sound (for which residents affectionately call them *besucona,* the "kissing one"), don't be alarmed. Quite the contrary, for each room cannot be without its resident gecko to properly cleanse it of gnats and mosquitoes. If your room doesn't have one, ask the management to find a *guerita* for you.

Crocodiles

The crocodile *(cocodrilo* or *caiman),* once prized for its meat and hide, came close to vanishing from Oaxaca's coastal lagoons until the government stepped in to ensure its survival. Now officially protected, crocodiles are becoming increasingly common in the wild as government and private hatcheries are breeding more

© BRUCE WHIPPERMAN

Although fierce looking, iguanas are really quite shy.

for the eventual repopulation of lagoons where they once were common. A coastal **crocodile hatchery** open for touring is located in Lagunas de Chacahua, west of Puerto Escondido.

Two crocodile species are native to Oaxaca. The true crocodile *(Crocodilus acutus)* has a narrower snout than its local cousin *(Caiman crocodilus fuscus)*, a type of **alligator** *(lagarto)*. Although past individuals have been recorded up to five meters (15 ft) long, wild native crocodiles are usually young and a few feet or less in length.

Sea Turtles

The story of Mexican sea turtles is similar to that of the crocodiles. They once swarmed ashore on Mexican beaches to lay their eggs. Prized for their meat, eggs, hide, and shell, the turtle populations were severely devastated. Now officially protected, growing numbers (twenty-fold since 1988) of sea turtles are hatching and returning to the sea from Oaxaca's beaches, thanks to the increasing ranks of eco-volunteers who guard against poachers. Very accessible Oaxaca turtle sanctuaries include the entire Bahías de Huatulco, a pair of home-grown sanctuaries near Puerto Escondido, Playa Escobillo, and Playa Mazunte, near Puerto Ángel. There, a government **turtle aquarium and hatchery** occupies the site of a former turtle processing factory.

Of the four locally occurring species, the **olive ridley** *(tortuga golfina)* and the **green turtle** *(tortuga verde)* are the most common. They may often be seen from tour boats, grazing on sea grass offshore from Puerto Escondido, Puerto Ángel, and the Bahías de Huatulco. In contrast, consider yourself very lucky if you glimpse either the uncommon **hawksbill turtle** *(tortuga carey)* or the highly endangered **leatherback** *(tortuga laut)*.

FISH

Shoals of fish abound in Oaxacan waters. Four billfish species are found in deep-sea grounds several miles offshore: **swordfish, sailfish,** and **blue and black marlin.** All are spirited fighters, though the sailfish and marlin are generally the toughest to bring in. The blue marlin is the biggest of the four. Although three-meter, 450-kilogram (10 ft, 1,000 lbs) fish used to be brought in occasionally, one-meter, 90-kilogram (four ft, 200 lbs) marlin and 45-kilogram (100 lbs) sailfish are more typical of late. Recognizing the need for conservation, forward-looking captains now encourage victorious anglers to return these magnificent "tigers of the sea" (especially the sinewy, poor-eating sailfish and blue marlin) to the deep after they've won the battle.

Billfish are not the only prizes of the sea. Serious fish lovers also seek varieties of tunalike **jack,** such as **yellowtail, Pacific amberjack, pompano, jack crevalle,** and the tenacious **roosterfish,** named for the "comb" atop its head. These and the **yellowfin tuna, mackerel,** and **dorado,** which Hawaiians call mahimahi, are among the delicacies sought in Oaxacan waters.

Accessible from small boats offshore and by casting from shoreline rocks are varieties of **snapper** *(huachinango, pargo)* and **sea bass** *(cabrilla)*. Closer to shore, **croaker, mullet,** and **Goliath fish** are often found foraging along sandy bottoms and in rocky crevices.

Sharks and **rays** inhabit nearly all depths, with smaller fry venturing into beach shallows and lagoons. Sometimes, huge **Pacific manta rays** appear to be frolicking, their great wings flapping like birds, not far off Oaxacan shores. Just beyond the waves, local fisherfolk bring in **hammerhead, thresher,** and **leopard sharks.**

Also common is the **stingray,** which can inflict a painful wound with its barbed tail. Experienced swimmers and waders avoid injury by both shuffling (rather than stepping) and watching their feet in shallow, sandy bottoms.

Captains from the wharves at Santa Cruz de Huatulco, Puerto Ángel, and Salina Cruz routinely pilot big boats equipped for four or five anglers to try for the big marlin, sailfish, and swordfish. Launches *(lanchas)* and tackle, suitable for smaller but still exciting catches, can be hired at those same marinas, in addition to Puerto Escondido and many other beach villages along the Oaxacan coast.

History

An age ago—perhaps as long as 20,000 years—small bands of hardy people, ancestors of the adventurers who had crossed the Arctic land bridge from Siberia thousands of years earlier, were hunting and foraging in what is now the Valley of Oaxaca. The forests and meadows abounded with edible plants and game—from squirrels and rabbits to great Ice Age herds of camels, horses, and mammoths. Supplied with abundant food, the people multiplied.

But by around 7000 B.C. the climate had warmed several degrees, and the great game animals were extinct. Perhaps in response, the people began to sow seeds of their favorite edible wild grains, legumes, vegetables, and fruits. As their descendants still do today, those ancient Oaxacans picked out the biggest and healthiest seeds to plant for the succeeding year's crop. After many generations, their fields were blooming with domesticated beans, squash, corn, and avocados nearly as robust as those enjoyed today.

EARLY CIVILIZATION
The Village Era

Millennia later, around 2000 B.C., those early Oaxacans, supplied with the bounty of their fields, no longer had to wander in search of food and were settling into permanent villages. Although initially small—typically only a dozen houses—the villages prospered and grew. Discovered remains reveal that many aspects of Oaxacan village life have remained fundamentally unchanged. Then, as now, planting, harvesting, and preparation of food occupied most of the day. Men used flint ax-heads hafted to wooden handles to clear brush, which they would burn in preparation for seeding. Women ground corn with the familiar *mano* and *metate,* a combination roller-crusher. They patted tortillas and baked them on the flat clay *comal* (griddle) and stewed meats, beans, and chili sauces in round clay pots.

Excavated ceramic figurines reveal the villagers' dress: for women, woven cloth or frond skirts, fiber or leather sandals, and long hair, often attractively braided, plus earrings and necklaces; for men, ordinarily a simple loincloth and sandals.

Village people buried their dead family members, laid out flat, in graves near their houses. A few offerings for the afterlife accompanied the deceased: a bowl with food, drinks, favored personal objects, and jewelry, including a semiprecious stone placed in the mouth.

Gradually, population increased. By 500 B.C. some villages, such as **San José El Mogote** about 16 kilometers (10 mi) northwest of Oaxaca City, had grown into small towns, with as many as 500 residents. At San José El Mogote investigators have uncovered early evidence of social classes—large, regally elevated houses—and specialization, in the form of a factory where workers polished iron-rich magnetite into small mirrors, which were traded hundreds of miles away.

Gradually during the few thousand years when villages were growing into towns, abundant food and burgeoning commercial wealth lifted a small but significant fraction of Oaxacans to a privileged leisure status. They became the artists, architects, warriors, and ruler-priests—with time to think and create. Over time, they devised symbols, writing, and a calendar that tied the constant wheel of the firmament to life on earth, defining the days to plant, to harvest, to feast, to travel, and to trade. Eventually, a grand city arose.

Monte Albán

Around 500 B.C., ancestors of Oaxaca's present-day Zapotec peoples founded what many experts believe to have been the Americas' earliest metropolis. On the central valley summit known today as Monte Albán, they raised monumental platforms, pyramids, palaces, and ceremonial ball courts. These they decorated with inscriptions, in a language yet to be deciphered, recording the exploits of their god-kings. The ordinary family homes of adobe bricks, arranged around central patios, occupied the hillside just below the ceremonial summit.

For centuries, Monte Albán flourished, overflowing halfway down its hillsides. Although starting from a population of perhaps only a few hundred after its founding, Monte Albán flourished to a city of as many as 40,000 at its height a thousand years later. By A.D. 500 Monte Albán encompassed seven square kilometers (three sq. mi), interlaced with vegetable and flower gardens and spreading to several monumental neighborhood sub-centers downhill.

Although Monte Albán ruled, upwards of two dozen subsidiary cities administered local areas throughout Oaxaca. Their ruins litter the present-day state: sites such as Yucuita and Monte Negro near Nochixtlán, in the Mixteca Alta, Cerro de las Minas in the Mixteca Baja, and Dainzu and Lambityeco in the central valley. War appears to have been a scourge of Oaxaca's early cities. Like Monte Albán, and in contrast to most village-era sites, most cities lay atop defensible hilltops.

Monte Albán's days were nevertheless numbered. After dominating Oaxaca and beyond for more than a thousand years, its power was fading fast by around A.D. 750. Although experts argue over what combination of drought, disease, war, or overpopulation ended Monte Albán's glory days, they agree that it was virtually abandoned by A.D. 1000 and eclipsed by a crowd of tussling city-states. A similar mysterious fate befell other southern and central Mexican cities, most notably Teotihuacán, Monte Albán's great rival metropolis in the north.

Teotihuacán

Although founded half a millennium later than Monte Albán, Teotihuacán grew rapidly, attaining population and wealth on a par with the ancient world's great cities by A.D. 300. Its epic pyramids still stand, not far north of Mexico City, along a grand avenue of fearsome, ruby-eyed stone effigies of Quetzalcoatl, the feathered serpent king of gods.

After Teotihuacán was abandoned around A.D. 700, a host of its former vassal cities rose to power, among them Xochicalco, in the highlands in the present state of Morelos, an hour's drive south of Mexico City.

The Living Quetzalcoatl

Xochicalco became renowned as a center of learning, where noble families sent their sons to study the healing arts, astronomy, architecture, and agriculture. A prominent student among them was **Topiltzín** (literally, Our Prince), who left Xochicalco in A.D. 968 to found his own city-state, Tula, north of old Teotihuacán.

After an enlightened 20-year rule, Topiltzín became so revered that his people began to know him as the living incarnation of Quetzalcoatl, the plumed-serpent god of gods. He was not universally loved, however. Jealous priests, who hated Quetzalcoatl-Topiltzín's persuasive opposition to their bloody rites of human sacrifice, drugged him with alcohol. He awoke, bleary-eyed, in bed with his sister. Devastated by shame, Quetzalcoatl-Topiltzín banished himself from Tula with a band of retainers. In A.D. 987, they headed east, toward Yucatán. Although he sent word he would reclaim his kingdom during the 52-year cyclical calendar year of his birth, Ce Acatl, Quetzalcoatl-Topiltzín never returned. Legends say that he sailed east and rose to heaven as the morning star.

The Rise of Oaxacan City-States

By A.D. 1000, the power vacuum left by the demise of Monte Albán had been filled by its dozens of former tributary cities, whose rulers carved out their own little kingdoms, mostly in the central valley and the Mixteca. Each had a dominant town, typically with a population of 5,000–10,000, which ruled a dispersed walking-distance village hinterland of about 250 square kilometers (100 sq. mi) and 10,000 or 20,000 people. Some of these, notably **Zaachila** and **Mitla,** near present-day Oaxaca City, remain thriving towns, still dominating their districts, while others, such as **Yagul,** near Mitla; **Huijazoo,** in the Etla Valley northwest of Oaxaca City; and **Guiengola,** in the Isthmus west of Tehuántepec, are uninhabited ruins.

8-Deer and the Mixtec Invasion

In A.D. 1011, not long after the great Quetzalcoatl-Topiltzín had trekked east, another renowned noble, known to historians as 8-Deer, the calendar name-date of his birth, was born in Oaxaca. Scholars have learned details of his life through pre-conquest hieroglyphic documents, collectively called **codices** (or singularly, codex). Although most were destroyed by Spanish priests all over Mexico early in the conquest, eight Oaxaca codices, folded deerskin hieroglyphic books whitened with lime, survived, all from the Mixtec region of Oaxaca, respectively called Becker I, Becker II, Bodley, Colombino, Nuttall, Sánchez Solis, Selden, and Vienna. Six of these eight Mixtec codices commemorate 8-Deer's adventures. Among the most enlightening, Codex Nuttall records 8-Deer's given name as **Tiger Claw,** portending his ruthless exploits.

As Monte Albán's power faded, the Mixtec city-states, west and northwest of the central valley, thrived. But overpopulation, and perhaps pressure from Xochicalco and the Toltecs (People of Tula), forced ambitious Mixtec nobles to look southward at the fertile lands of the Oaxaca central valley.

The stage for Mixtec expansion was set when 8-Deer Tiger Claw came of age. He moved quickly, forming alliances and setting his rivals against one another. Codex Nuttall depicts one of 8-Deer Tiger Claw's expeditions. It shows him, along with two allies, 4-Tiger and 9-Water, spears and shields in hand, crossing a lake by canoe toward an island, the Hill of Mixtatl. The document records the expedition's three consecutive dates: 10-Serpent, 11-Death, and 12-Deer, of A.D. 1046, when 8-Deer was in his 35-year-old fighting prime.

After bringing the entire Mixteca, from the Tehuacán Valley in the north to the coastal stronghold at Tututepec, under his control, 8-Deer led Mixtec armies southeast from his capital at **Tilantongo** and defeated a number of Zapotec central valley city-states. Although

8-Deer met his end as a sacrifice victim in Cuilapan, not far south of present-day Oaxaca City, in 1061, Mixtec nobles ruled on as an elite minority in Zaachila, Mitla, and other valley city-states. They preserved their dominance by the tactic of political marriage, taking daughters of the Zapotec nobility as near-hostage wives who raised Mixtec-speaking heirs.

Although only a relatively few of the original Mixtec speakers remain living today in Oaxaca's central valley, the old Mixtec influence lives on in the Zapotec-Mixtec stylistic fusion of the architecture, pottery, jewelry, and other remains found at Zaachila, Mitla, Monte Albán, and other sites. Admire the elaborately fine **Greca** mosaic frets decorating the Mitla ruins and you're enjoying the Mixtec influence; likewise, at the Museo de las Culturas de Oaxaca, in the Centro Cultural de Santo Domingo in Oaxaca City, Mixtec artisanship and sophistication gleam from the **golden mask of death** and the trove of gold and turquoise jewelry taken from **Tomb 7** at Monte Albán.

The Aztecs Invade Oaxaca

At the time the Mixtecs were consolidating their rule of the Valley of Oaxaca, the Aztecs (People of Aztlán), a collection of seven aggressive immigrant subtribes, had eclipsed the Toltec civilization that Quetzalcoatl-Topiltzín had founded north of present-day Mexico City. After migrating from a mysterious **western land of Aztlán** (Land of the Herons) into the lake-filled valley that Mexico City now occupies, around 1250, the Aztecs' fiercest tribe, whose members called themselves the **México** (MAY-shee-kah), clawed its way to dominion over the Valley of Mexico. In 1325, the México founded their capital, Tenochtitlán, on an island in the middle of the valley-lake. During the next century, Tenochtitlán grew into a magnificent city, from which Aztec armies, like Roman legions, marched out and subdued kingdoms for hundreds of miles in all directions.

In 1434, the Aztecs, under Emperor Itzcóatl, conquered the northern Mixtec domains in the

Tehuacán Valley; several years later his successor, Moctezuma Ilhuicamina, attacked southward, defeating Atonaltzin, the Mixtec lord of Coixtlahuaca. Besides yielding booty and a small army of captives, the victory opened the path to the entire Mixteca and the Valley of Oaxaca.

By 1488, the Aztecs were firmly fixed in the valley, having established a garrison at **Huaxyacac,** the site of present-day Oaxaca City. From that point, however, the Aztecs found their access to the remainder of the central valley and the coveted southern lands of Tehuántepec blocked by the strong Zapotec city-state of Zaachila. After several years of frustrating bargaining, the Aztecs, then under Emperor Ahuizotl, hammered out a treaty with **Cosijoeza** (koh-see-hoh-EY-zah), the king of Zaachila, for peaceful access toward Tehuántepec in the southeast. Cosijoeza soon regretted the concession. In 1494, the Aztecs broke the agreement and seized and subjugated Mitla, at the eastern end of the Valley of Oaxaca. Enraged, Cosijoeza rushed his forces southeast and fortified their Isthmus hilltop bastion at Guiengola, which blocked the Aztecs' progress to their southern capital at Tehuántepec and Chiapas beyond.

After a seven-month siege of Guiengola, the frustrated Aztecs again resorted to diplomacy. They proposed a new alliance, in the form of a marriage between King Cosijoeza and **Coyollicatzin** (koh-yoh-yee-KAH-tseen), the daughter of the new Aztec Emperor Moctezuma I. The Aztecs' hidden agenda: They expected Coyollicatzin to spy upon Cosijoeza; true love, however, won out as Coyollicatzin refused to play the pawn and remained loyal to her husband Cosijoeza. The Aztecs eventually made peace in return for tribute. Cosijoeza turned his Tehuántepec domain to his son **Cosijopí** and returned home to reign over his Zapotec people at Zaachila in the central valley.

Despite a king's ransom in yearly tribute— mounds of quetzal feathers, dozens of sacks of cochineal, hundreds of pounds of gold, thousands of bolts of cloth—the Aztecs' millions of Oaxacan subjects always seemed to be rebelling someplace until the Spanish conquistadores arrived and toppled the Aztecs from power in 1521.

THE CONQUEST

Although Christopher Columbus and the generation of explorers who followed him had discovered a new world in America, their dreams of riches had eluded them. In Spain's new Caribbean island colonies both gold and native workers, who had mostly died from European diseases, were scarce. A new wave of adventurers, among them **Hernán Cortés,** a minor nobleman from the poor Spanish province of Extremadura, turned their vision toward new fabled empires—perhaps even the elusive Cathay—beyond the setting sun. In Cuba, Cortés patched together a motley force of 550 men, an assortment of small ships, a few horses and cannons and sailed west in early 1519. By the time they landed on Mexico's Gulf Coast on April 22, 1519, Cortés's men, torn by dissension and realizing the impossible odds against them, were near mutiny.

Cortés, however, cut his losses and exploited his opportunities with extraordinary aplomb. He won over the doubters, isolated the dissenters, and ended any thoughts of retreat to Cuba by burning his ships. Next he capitalized on the lucky coincidence that he had landed on the Mexican coastline in the Aztec year of Ce Acatl, exactly the same 52-year cyclical anniversary year in which Quetzalcoatl-Topiltzín had vowed to return from the east to reclaim his kingdom.

As he led his band of adventurers westward over the mountains toward the Aztec capital of Tenochtitlán, Cortés played Quetzalcoatl to the hilt, awing local leaders. Coaxed by **Doña Marina,** his wily native translator-mistress-confidante, local chiefs began to add their armies to Cortés's march against their Aztec oppressors.

Tenochtitlán, Capital of the Empire

A few months later, inside the gates of Tenochtitlán, the Venice-like island metropolis, it was the Spaniards' turn to be awed: by gardens full of animals, gold, and palaces, and a great pyramid-enclosed square where tens of thousands of people bartered goods gathered from all over the empire. Tenochtitlán, with perhaps a quarter of a million people, was the great capital of an empire as large and rich as any in Europe.

Moctezuma II, the lord of that empire, fearing that Cortés was in fact the god Quetzalcoatl incarnate, had followed Cortés's progress toward Tenochtitlán with trepidation. Wishing not to offend, Moctezuma II had sent Cortés sumptuous gifts of gold, coupled with warnings to stay away. Encouraged by the gold, Cortés demanded an early audience with the emperor, who pathetically surrendered himself to Cortés's custody and "donated" his entire empire to the Spanish crown.

Spaniards Enter Oaxaca

With his position temporarily secure, Cortés dispatched emissaries west, east, and south. To Oaxaca he sent Hernando Pizarro and Diego de Ordaz, each with small detachments, to reconnoiter for riches. Pizarro searched for gold in the Papaloapaon basin around Tuxtepec and later the Chinantla, while Ordaz passed through the Mixtec kingdoms of Yanhuitlán and Sosola on his way to the Gulf Coast.

The Aztecs Force a Spanish Retreat

Meanwhile, however, the people of Tenochtitlán were rioting against Spanish brutality. On July 1, 1520, with Moctezuma II mortally wounded by his own countrymen, Cortés and his men, forced by the sheer numbers of rebellious Mexicans, retreated, hacking a bloody path through thousands of screaming Aztec warriors to safety on the lakeshore.

Hearing the news of Cortés's defeat, Mexican garrisons in Oaxaca dealt a similar blow against the local Spanish expeditions, attacking and killing dozens of Spaniards and their indigenous allies.

Although Cortés was down, he wasn't out. In succeeding months, as his forces regathered

strength in the Valley of Mexico, he pushed the conquest of the south. Alonso de Avila arrived in Oaxaca in late 1520 and accepted the ambassadors of Zapotec kings Cosijoeza and Cosijopí, who were more than willing to ally themselves against their Aztec overlords. Concurrently, other Spanish expeditions thrust into Oaxaca: Gonzalo de Sandoval successfully counterattacked against the Aztec garrisons, while Juan Cedeño obtained the submission of the Chinantecs and the northern Zapotecs.

Tenochtitlán Falls and Oaxaca Is Conquered

In late 1521, reinforced by fresh soldiers, horses, a small fleet of armed sailboats, and 100,000 indigenous allies, Cortés retook Tenochtitlán. The stubborn defenders, led by Cuauhtémoc, Moctezuma's nephew, fell by the tens of thousands beneath a smoking hail of Spanish grapeshot. The Aztecs, although weakened by smallpox, refused to surrender. Cortés found, to his dismay, that he had to destroy the city in order to take it.

Soon after Cortés's triumph, the Zapotec kings Cosijoeza and Cosijopí sent ambassadors declaring their submission to him and his king, Charles V. This alarmed the Mixtecs, who, with the backing of the Chinantec king of Tuxtepec, declared war on the Zapotecs. At the request of his new Zapotec allies, Cortés dispatched Francisco de Orozco in December 1521 and Pedro de Alvarado a month later with a few hundred infantry and a handful of cavalry to pacify Oaxaca. After a few skirmishes, Orozco took possession of Huaxyacac, the site of present-day Oaxaca City, which the Aztec garrisons had occupied since 1488. A few hours later, on the same day, December 25, 1521, padre Juan Díaz celebrated the first Catholic mass in Oaxaca territory. A month later at the same spot, Alvarado, with the help of padre Bartolomé de Olmedo, helped negotiate a peace agreement between the Mixtecs and Zapotecs.

With the valley and northern Oaxaca pacified, Cortés sent Alvarado to conquer the Oaxacan Pacific coast. On March 4, 1522,

Alvarado defeated Casandoo, the Mixtec king of Tututepec, and with colonists displaced from the Valley of Oaxaca by Cortés's orders, he founded the Villa Segura de la Frontera (Secure Village of the Frontier). He went on to pacify the whole coast, including Tonameca, Pochutla, Huatulco, and Astata, all the way east to Tehuántepec.

NEW SPAIN

With much of the former Aztec empire firmly in his grip and his lieutenants continuing to lead their forces in triumph in all directions, Cortés anticipated the grand domain that would eventually expand to more than a dozenfold the size of old Spain. He wrote his king, Charles V, "The most suitable name for it would be New Spain of the Ocean Sea, and thus in the name of your Majesty I have christened it."

Even as he was building the new Mexico City atop the ruins of old Tenochtitlán, Cortés dreamed of a kingdom of his own. His first information of the fertile, spring-like Valley of Oaxaca came from his own scouts and from the ambassadors the Oaxacan kings had sent. Cortés moved quickly to carve out his Oaxaca domain, sending orders with Pedro de Alvarado to remove all Spanish settlers from the valley.

When Cortés personally arrived in Oaxaca in 1523 he found to his chagrin that the settlers that he had previously ordered out of the valley had returned and were squatting on the land he wanted for himself. He sent the instigators to Mexico City in chains and dispersed the settlers again. He granted his friends and relatives, including his son Martín and his two illegitimate daughters, *encomiendas* (rights to land and native labor) at strategic points all over Oaxaca, then, in October 1524, marched off on an exhausting two-year expedition to Honduras.

By the time Cortés returned in 1526, the settlers had again returned and reestablished their village at Huaxyacac. Moreover, they had petitioned the king of Spain, Carlos I, for a charter for their settlement, which they had christened **Antequera,** in honor of the ancient Granada town of the same name. To Cortés's great displeasure, the petition was granted, by royal decree, on September 14, 1526.

Undeterred, Cortés took charge and began building his Valley of Oaxaca domain. He staked out the best bottomland, built haciendas, and set his native laborers to planting wheat and sugarcane. Cortés then traveled to Huatulco and Tehuántepec, where he built a port and ships to explore the Pacific. Concurrently, Cortés strengthened his alliance with King Cosijopí, who reciprocated by converting (along with thousands of his Tehuántepec subjects) to Christianity, taking the name Juan Cortés Cosijopí.

Hernán Cortés, Marquis of the Valley of Oaxaca

Cortés realized that his de facto kingdom needed both a queen and royal recognition, so he traveled to Spain in 1528 to get both. A year later he returned with his young noble bride, Juana de Zúñiga, and the grand title of Marqués del Valle de Oaxaca, which included a singularly generous grant of land, subjects, and privileges. For many years thereafter, he and his heirs received upward of 80,000 gold pesos a year from tens of thousands of indigenous subjects on three million acres of domain scattered from the Valley of Mexico through the present states of Morelos, Mexico, Guerrero, and Veracruz to Oaxaca.

Cortés's Valley of Oaxaca holdings, the crown jewel of his domain, encompassed most of the best valley land. In a wide, 350,000-acre swath, it stretched 25 miles, including 34 villages and towns, from Etla in the north to Coyotepec in the south. Excluded, however, was the one-league square (two square miles) of the town of Antequera, which grew into present-day Oaxaca City.

The Missionaries

While the conquistadores scoured the countryside for gold and subjugated the local people, missionaries began arriving to heal, teach, and baptize them. The Dominicans were the first and most numerous in Oaxaca. Padre

Bernardino de Minaya built the first Oaxaca convent, dedicated to Saint Paul, in Antequera around 1530. Other Dominicans settled in Tlaxiaco, Etla, and Tehuántepec, where King Cosijopí financed a church for them in 1538. Other orders—Franciscans, Augustinians, Bethlehemites, and more—eventually joined them. Missionary authorities customarily enjoyed a sympathetic ear from Charles V and his successors, who earnestly pursued Spain's Christian mission, especially when it coincided with their political and economic goals.

Besides saving souls, the missionaries introduced new plants, flowers, and vegetables, and useful European crafts, such as ironwork, glassmaking, wool processing, and pottery glazing. They learned native tongues and wrote catechisms in Zapotec, Mixtec, and other local dialects. Within a few dozen years, the fields, orchards, and vineyards dotted with dozens of churches around the Valley of Oaxaca and beyond testified to the dedication of both the missionaries and their native converts.

Unfortunately, in order to speed the process of conversion, which the missionaries viewed as a sort of divine manifest destiny, native temples, idols, and paintings were destroyed. Historical records were irretrievably lost. The Spaniards also banned native song and dance, fearing that they kept alive old beliefs.

Although the missionaries on the whole provided a kinder, gentler counterbalance to the often brutal and exploitative conquistadores and colonists, they were not entirely blameless. In their zeal to build churches, convents, and monasteries, they also demanded the backbreaking labor of the newly converted. Moreover, those resistant to conversion were dealt with harshly, sometimes beaten, tortured, or killed.

In Oaxaca, however, which was primarily a Dominican stronghold, *indígenas* were spared the worst excesses of the more zealous Franciscans. **Bartolomé de las Casas,** a Dominican friar, devoted his life to fighting for the rights of the native people. This champion of social justice earned the sobriquet "Apostle of the Indians."

The King Takes Control

By 1530, the crown, through the Council of the Indies, had begun to wrest power away from Cortés and his conquistador lieutenants. Cortés had granted many of them rights of **encomienda:** taxes and labor of an indigenous district. In exchange, the **encomendero,** who often enjoyed the status of feudal lord, pledged to look after the welfare and souls of his native charges.

From the king's point of view, though, tribute pesos collected by *encomenderos* translated into losses to the crown. Moreover, many *encomenderos* callously exploited their indigenous wards for quick profit, sometimes selling them as slave labor in mines and on plantations. Such abuses, coupled with European-introduced diseases, began to reduce the native population at an alarming rate.

By 1540, strongly influenced by Dominican padre Bartolomé de las Casas, the outspoken "Apostle of the Indians," the king and his councilors realized that the native Mexicans were in peril, and without their labor New Spain would vanish.

They acted decisively. New laws would shift power toward the crown and limit abuses to the king's native subjects. Decreed in 1542 and enforced by a powerful *visitador* (inspector general), the **New Laws of the Indies** abolished perpetual rights of *encomienda,* outlawed slavery of native Mexicans, and limited their labor and tribute payments.

Although Oaxacan colonists protested vehemently, some native groups benefited. With the support of the new bishop of Antequera, Juan López de Zárate, and the missionary padres, Zapotecs around the Valley of Oaxaca mounted a legal fight against excessive *encomienda* payments.

COLONIAL OAXACA
Congregación

Despite the Valley of Oaxaca marquisate, Spanish garrisons, a score of Spanish-run haciendas, a few mines, and the capital town Antequera, Oaxaca had a sparse population of no more than a thousand Spaniards around 1550. On the other hand, the native population, while reduced, still numbered several hundred thousand, widely dispersed over the entire territory, and largely controlled by the hereditary native nobility. The Spanish authorities, in order to break the hold of the old chiefs on the natives, began moving indigenous populations into *congregaciones:* new townships in potentially productive areas—valleys, mines, and along royal roads. Each township had its *cabercera* (head town) and *sujeto* (subject) villages. Indigenous governing councils, supervised by Spanish agents, were responsible for local order and collection of tribute.

The missionary clergy initially went along with *congregación* because it led to more converts, but after a generation of seeing the cruel reality of people displaced from their land and traditions, opposed it. In 1604, although the policy was officially abandoned and some of the people returned to their original way of life, many did not. Their descendants remain living in the original *caberceras,* which comprise a significant portion of present-day Oaxaca's 570 *municipios* (governmental townships).

The natives, in being shifted toward traditional Spanish occupations, in which they worked mines, harvested sugarcane and wheat, and tended sheep and cattle, were forced to abandon the way of life that had sustained them for millennia. In a few generations, even the memory of their extensive irrigation works—diversion dams and canals that fed terraced fields—was lost.

The severe consequences of this forgotten water-conservation tradition have become acute in modern Oaxaca. An increasing population has led to lack of bottomland, forcing families to poor uplands that, without irrigation, cannot sustain them. Slash-and-burn dry farming, noncontour plowing, overgrazing, and overcutting of forest have turned large tracts of Oaxaca into eroded wasteland.

Population Collapse

In a real sense, European disease, rather than the conquistadores, subdued Mexico. Despite the missionary fathers' most benign efforts and the most beneficial effects of the king's New Laws, typhus, cholera, measles, smallpox, and other European plagues wiped out about 90 percent of the Mexican indigenous population within a few generations after the conquest. Although estimates vary, most experts agree that pre-conquest Mexico's 15–25 million native population had shrunk to a mere 1.3 million by 1650.

Oaxaca's figures reflect a similar tragedy. Of a population that archaeologists estimate at around two million in 1500, only 150,000 remained in 1650. In some cases, such as the mines of Santa Catalina Martir, in 1580, a combination of overwork and disease killed thousands; those remaining simply fled into the hills. In the southern Valley of Oaxaca towns, plagues reduced thriving towns such as Teitipac, Ocotlán, and Miahuatlán from

POPULATION CHANGES IN NEW SPAIN

	EARLY COLONIAL (1570)	LATE COLONIAL (1810)
peninsulares	6,600	15,000
criollos	11,000	1,100,000
mestizos	2,400	704,000
indígenas	3,340,000	3,700,000
negros	22,000	630,000

populations of thousands to a few dozen inhabitants nearly overnight.

Today's Mexicans can look forward to the year 2019, the 500th anniversary of Cortés's landing, when Mexico's native-speaking population will have largely recovered to its pre-conquest level of approximately 25 million.

The Changing Role of the Church

During the colonial era, civil and church authorities increasingly came into conflict with missionary orders, whose independent status derived directly from papal authority, in contrast to locally administered ("secular") clergy who answered to local bishops. Disputes often revolved around treatment of the natives, whose welfare missionaries often outspokenly championed. The kettle, always bubbling, sometimes boiled over. In 1647, Bishop Cerda Benevente of Antequera tried to kick all Dominican fathers out of their churches; in 1749 Bishop Maldonado tried to replace 27 Dominicans with clergy under his control. The issue of power was finally settled in 1767 when the King of Spain expelled all Jesuit missionaries from his New World colonies. This chilled the liberal activist tendencies of clergy everywhere in Mexico and led to an increasingly conservative church establishment.

During Spain's Mexican colonial twilight, the church, increasingly profiting from the status quo, became fat and largely complacent. The biblical tithe—one-tenth of everything, from crops and livestock to rents and mining profits—filled church coffers. By 1800, the church owned half of Mexico. Moreover, all clergy (including the lay church officers) and the military were doubly privileged. They enjoyed right of *fuero* (exemption from civil law) and could be prosecuted by ecclesiastical or military courts only.

The Colonial Economy

In trade and commerce, New Spain existed for the benefit of the mother country. Spaniards enjoyed absolute monopolies by virtue of the complete prohibition of foreign traders and goods. Colonists, as a result, paid dearly for often shoddy Spanish manufactures. The Casa de Contratación, the royal trade regulators, always ensured the colony's yearly balance of payments would result in a deficit, which would be made up by bullion shipments from New Spain mines (from which the crown raked 10 percent off the top).

If New Spain was a tradition-bound feudal domain, Oaxaca was even more so. The crown regulated nearly everything. Any kind of enterprise required a royal license, issued through a bureaucracy that required bribes as part of the cost of doing business. Wealth flowed directly from the labor of the native people. Although Oaxaca people produced lots of corn, wheat, cattle, sheep, wool, and some silk, **cochineal** was by far Oaxaca's most valuable export.

Whatever native people produced, they all had to pay taxes, whether directly to the local collector or as tribute to the *encomendero* owner of the estate where they lived. For many poor native families, the problem of getting enough to eat year-round was doubly acute because of the seasonal nature of their produce. They began to rely upon *alcaldes mayores,* local royal officials, for cash advances on crops, especially cochineal. Through their official posts, *alcaldes mayores* enjoyed a monopoly, which forced local folks to sell to them for a pittance. This hated monopoly payment system, known as *repartmiento,* although officially forbidden, was rampant during the mid-1600s, when a swarm of Oaxaca uprisings led to the killing of Tehuántepec's greedy *alcalde mayor* and a number of his henchmen by an angry crowd of native cochineal producers.

Reform didn't come until the 18th century, when Spanish authorities saw the light and banned the *repartmiento* system, replacing the *alcaldes mayores* with less corruptible salaried agents known as *intendentes.*

The bustling cochineal trade led to boom times in colonial Oaxaca. The region, previously a backwater neglected by Mexico City authorities, benefited from a monopoly on cochineal production after 1745. The population tripled during the 1700s, reaching 20,000 and making the city of Oaxaca (whose name was

COCHINEAL – NATURE'S RICHEST RED DYE

Cochineal (*cochinilla*) is a prized rich scarlet dye, long cultivated in Mexico before the conquest. The Spanish, immediately seeing its export value, expanded production, especially in Oaxaca, where it became a major source of cash for native Oaxacans faced with increasing tribute demands. The rise of the textile industry in England, the Low Countries, France, and Spain further propelled demand for Oaxacan cochineal, renowned as the most brilliant, richest red dye in the world. The word spread, and, by its peak during the 17th and 18th centuries, Spain's cochineal trade extended as far as China. Although largely replaced by cheaper synthetic dyes by 1900, cochineal is still locally cultivated in the Valley of Oaxaca.

The actual source of the dye is the female of a type of scale insect, *Dactylopius coccus*, which feeds off a variety of nopal (prickly pear) cactus. Typically, families or village cooperatives own patches of nopal, from which they brush the female beetles during the fall harvest. The beetles are then dried, ground, mixed with calcium or aluminum salts, and boiled in water. The resulting dye suspension is filtered and evaporated leaving pure crimson cochineal crystals, still preferred by many Valley of Oaxaca weavers.

A demonstration farm, **Rancho la Nopalera** (Km 10.5 Carretera Oaxaca–Puerto Ángel, Calle Matamoros 100, tel. 951/551-0030, fax 951/551-0053, info@aztecacolor.com, www .aztecacolor.com, 9 A.M.-1 P.M. and 2-5 P.M.), dedicated to the revival of cochineal welcomes visitors to see its experimental cactus garden and small museum at Santa María Coyotepec, on the highway about six kilometers (four mi) south of the Oaxaca airport.

© BRUCE WHIPPERMAN

The cochineal beetle thrives on the leaves of nopal cactus, very common in Oaxaca.

officially changed from Antequera in 1786) New Spain's third-largest city by 1800.

The benefits of the new prosperity did not extend equally to all Oaxacans, however. As the administrative center for the entire region, most wealth flowed to Oaxaca City, where a rich elite, of mostly Spanish-born government and church officials and owners of large estates, raked in the lion's share of the profits. Below them, a modicum of treasure and respectability trickled down to the small locally born white and mixed-blood professional and merchant class. Finally, the great majority of mixed and pure native descent who did the hard work—the spinners, weavers, masons, shoemakers, bakers, farmers, and laborers—plugged along as best they could at the city's least desirable margins.

Despite its faults, New Spain lasted three times longer than the Aztec empire. By most contemporary measures, both Oaxaca in particular and New Spain as a whole were prospering in 1800. The native and mixed-blood labor force was completely subjugated and increasing, and the galleon fleets were carrying home increasing tonnages of silver, gold, and cochineal worth many millions of gold pesos. Spanish authorities, however, failed to recognize that Mexico had changed in 300 years.

Criollos: the New Mexicans

Nearly three centuries of colonial rule gave rise to a burgeoning population of more than a million criollos (kree-OH-yohs)—Mexican-born descendants of Spanish colonists, many rich and educated—to whom top status was denied.

High government, church, and military office had always been the preserve of a tiny but powerful minority of *peninsulares*—European-born Spaniards. Criollos could only watch in disgust as unlettered, unskilled *peninsulares* (derisively called *gachupines*—wearers of spurs) were boosted to authority over them.

Although the criollos stood high above the mestizo (mixed native-Spanish), *indígena,* and *negro* (African Mexican) underclasses, that seemed little compensation for the false smiles, the deep bows, and the costly bribes that *gachupines* demanded.

Mestizos, *Indígenas,* and African Mexicans

Upper-class luxury existed by virtue of the sweat of Mexico's mestizo, *indígena,* and black laborers and servants. African slaves were imported in large numbers during the 17th century after typhus, smallpox, and measles epidemics had tragically wiped out as much as 90 percent of the indigenous population. In Oaxaca, a small African-born black population of around 2,000 in 1650 rose gradually to approximately 10,000, both pure and mixed, by 1800. Although the African Mexicans contributed significantly (crafts, healing arts, dance, music, drums, and marimba), they had arrived last and experienced discrimination from everyone.

INDEPENDENCE

The chance for change came during the aftermath of the French invasion of Spain in 1808, when Napoléon Bonaparte replaced Spanish King Ferdinand VII with his brother, Joseph Bonaparte, on the Spanish throne. Most *peninsulares* backed the king; most criollos, however, inspired by the example of the recent American and French revolutions, talked and dreamed of independence. One such group, urged on by a firebrand parish priest, acted.

El Grito de Dolores

"¡Viva México! Death to the Gachupines!" Father **Miguel Hidalgo**'s impassioned *grito,* from the church balcony in the Guanajuato town of Dolores on September 16, 1810, ignited passions. A mostly *indígena,* machete-wielding army of 20,000 coalesced around Hidalgo and his compatriots, **Ignacio Allende** and **Juan Aldama.** Their ragtag mob raged out of control through the Bajío, killing hated *gachupines* and pillaging their homes.

Hidalgo advanced on Mexico City but, unnerved by stiff royalist resistance, retreated and regrouped around Guadalajara. His rebels, whose numbers had swollen to 80,000, were no match for a disciplined, 6,000-strong royalist force. Hidalgo (now "Generalisimo") fled north but was soon apprehended, defrocked, and executed. His head and those of his comrades—Aldama, Allende, and Mariano Jiménez—were hung from the walls of the Guanajuato granary (site of the slaughter of 138 *gachupines* by Hidalgo's army) for 10 years as grim reminders of the consequences of rebellion.

The 10-Year Struggle

Others carried on, however. A former student of Hidalgo, mestizo **José María Morelos,** carried the Independence struggle to Oaxaca in earnest by defeating the Oaxaca capital's royalist defenders on November 25, 1812. He set up a revolutionary government and fanned the flames with his liberationist newspaper *El Correo Americano del Sur* (The American Post of the South) until he was seriously defeated in Michoacán a year later. The victorious royalists retook Oaxaca City on January 29, 1814, sending defending *insurgente* commander Ramón Rayón fleeing north to Tehuacán, Puebla.

Although the royalists seriously damaged the rebel cause by capturing and executing Morelos

José María Morelos

Moreover, in Mexico as a whole, independence had resolved few grievances except to expel the *peninsulares*. With an illiterate populace and no experience in self-government, Mexicans began a tragic 40-year love affair with a fantasy: the general on the white horse, the gold-braided hero who could save them from themselves.

The Rise and Fall of Agustín I

Iturbide—crowned Emperor Agustín I by the bishop of Guadalajara on July 21, 1822—soon lost his charisma. Attempting to assert his authority, Iturbide dissolved the national Congress on October 31, igniting a roar of protests. Among the loudest protesters was Iturbide's military governor of Oaxaca, Colonel Antonio de León. In a pattern that became sadly predictable for succeeding generations of topsy-turvy Mexican politics, ambitious commanders issued *pronunciamientos,* declarations against the government. Supporting *pronunciamientos* followed, and old revolutionary heroes Guerrero, Guadalupe Victoria, and Nicolás Bravo endorsed a "plan"—the Plan of Casa Mata (not unlike Iturbide's previous Plan de Iguala)—to dethrone Iturbide in favor of a republic. Iturbide, his braid tattered and brass tarnished, abdicated in mid-February 1823.

On June 1, 1823, carried away by liberationist zeal, León set up a local provisional government that declared Oaxaca to be a "free and independent" state and wrote a state constitution. Simultaneously, delegates in Mexico City were doing the same, creating the republic of the Estados Unidos Mexicanos (United Mexican States), which Oaxaca soon joined.

The country overflowed with republican zeal. Oaxacans rewrote their state constitution to conform with the federal document, creating a governor, bicameral legislature, local governments, and state departments, including public instruction and the **Institute of Sciences and Arts** (now the Benito Juárez Autonomous University). Graduates of the institute, notably Mexico's famous pair of presidents, Benito Juárez and Porfirio Díaz, both of indigenous descent, gradually began to fill

in December 1815, Morelos's compatriot **Vicente Guerrero** picked up the independence banner and fought on, finally joining forces with opportunistic royalist Brigadier **Agustín de Iturbide** in 1821. Their joint **Plan de Iguala** promised **"Three Guarantees"**—the renowned Trigarantes: Independence, Catholicism, and Equality—which their army (commanded by Iturbide, of course) would enforce. On September 21, 1821, Iturbide rode triumphantly into Mexico City at the head of his army of Trigarantes. Mexico was independent at last.

But the cost of the struggle had been great, especially in Oaxaca. Ten years of war had decimated the cochineal industry and sent Oaxaca's rich Spaniards and their capital fleeing to Mexico City and Europe. The criollo professional and business class now found themselves at the top of the social ladder, but with little money for rebuilding. Everyone tightened their belts as Oaxaca industry reverted to traditional products: soap, *aguardiente* (strong alcohol from cane sugar) distillation, *pulque* (native beer), wool, leather, and pottery.

the leadership vacuum left by the departed Spanish elite.

The Disastrous Era of Santa Anna

Antonio López de Santa Anna, the eager 28-year-old military commander of Veracruz, whose *pronunciamiento* had pushed Iturbide from his white horse, maneuvered to gradually replace him. Throughout the late 1820s the government teetered between liberal and conservative hands six times in three years. Finally, unhappy with the 1828 presidential election result, Santa Anna "pronounced" in favor of the losing candidate, old independence *insurgente* Vicente Guerrero. This put Santa Anna at odds with government commanders all over the country—especially in Oaxaca City, which he attacked—but he soon found himself seriously besieged in the fortress-like convent of Santo Domingo.

But Lady Luck, as usual, intervened in favor of Santa Anna. At the height of the siege, on November 20, 1829, government agents discovered that a Spanish force was being assembled in Cuba to re-invade Mexico. Faced with the external threat, former bitter enemies soon joined hands. On January 5, 1829, Santa Anna rushed from Oaxaca City with a combined force that, a few months later, defeated an abortive Spanish invasion attempt on the Gulf at Tampico. People called Santa Anna "The Victor of Tampico."

In 1831, a rebellious, still-powerful Vicente Guerrero was kidnapped in Acapulco and handed over to agents of conservative President Anastasio Bustamante in Huatulco. He was taken to Oaxaca City and executed at the old convent in Cuilapan on February 14, 1831. Later, upon the initiative of young Oaxaca legislative deputy **Benito Juárez,** Guerrero's remains were placed in an elaborate silver urn and reinterred during six days of solemn ceremonies at Santo Domingo convent in the city.

In late 1832, the national government was bankrupt; mobs demanded the ouster of President Bustamante in retaliation for Guerrero's execution. Santa Anna issued a *pronunciamiento* against Bustamante, which Congress soon obliged, elevating Santa Anna to "Liberator of the Republic" and "Conqueror of the Spaniards" and naming him president in March 1833. More interested in the hunt than the prize, Santa Anna quickly resigned his office to Vice President Gómez Farías.

Santa Anna would pop in and out of the presidency like a jack-in-the-box 10 more times before 1855. First, he foolishly lost Texas to rebellious Anglo-American settlers in 1836. He later lost his leg (which was buried with full military honors) fighting the emperor of France.

Santa Anna's greatest debacle, however, was to declare war on the United States with just 1,839 pesos in the treasury. With his forces poised to defend Mexico City against a relatively small 10,000-man American invasion force, Santa Anna inexplicably withdrew. U.S. Marines surged into the "Halls of Montezuma," Chapultepec Castle, where Mexico's six beloved Niños Héroes cadets fell in the losing cause on September 13, 1847.

In the subsequent Treaty of Guadalupe Hidalgo, Mexico lost two-fifths of its territory—the present states of New Mexico, Arizona, California, Nevada, Utah, and Colorado—to the United States. Mexicans have never forgotten; they have looked upon gringos with a combination of admiration and disgust ever since.

Despite the national debacle, Oaxaca prospered under the 1848–1852 governorship of Benito Juárez. Among his first acts was to deny Santa Anna, who was fleeing from U.S. invaders, transit across Oaxaca territory. Besides keeping the peace, Juárez opened hundreds of elementary schools, a swarm of teacher's academies, and nearly wiped out the state debt. Improved roads and new bridges attracted Italian investment in mines; new coffee production began to replace Oaxaca's lost cochineal output. English entrepreneurs built a textile and hat factory, and artisans in Atzompa, near Oaxaca City, resumed producing their renowned pottery again in earnest. Oaxaca City's population swelled by more than 25 percent, to 24,000, between 1844 and 1854.

But for Santa Anna, however, enough was not enough. Called back as president for the last and 11th time in 1853, Santa Anna, now "His Most Serene Highness," financed his final war against the liberals by selling off a part of southern New Mexico and Arizona, known as the Gadsden Purchase, for $10 million.

REFORM, CIVIL WAR, AND FRENCH INVASION
The Reforms
Mexican leaders finally saw the light and exiled Santa Anna forever. While conservatives fumbled, searching for a king to replace Santa Anna, liberal leaders (whom Santa Anna had exiled or kept in jail) stirred up their own successful revolution. Benito Juárez, having triumphantly returned to the Oaxaca governorship, and others plunged ahead with three controversial reform laws: the Ley Juárez, Ley Lerdo, and Ley Iglesias. These *reformas,* integrated into a new liberal Constitution of 1857, directly attacked the privilege and power of Mexico's corporate landlords, clergy, and generals: Ley Juárez abolished *fueros,* the separate military and church courts; Ley Lerdo forbade excess corporate (read: church) landholdings; and Ley Iglesias reduced or transferred most church power to the state.

Despite their liberal authors' good intentions, some of the reform provisions resulted in negative consequences. Although Ley Lerdo (the "Law of the Divestiture of the Property of the Dead Hand") succeeded in wiping out bloated church landholdings, it also forced thousands of native communities to sell their traditional land. Such sales invariably benefited the few rich individuals who could afford to buy, at the expense of the great mass of native Mexicans who became landless as a result. The consequence was appallingly medieval. It created a new class of super-landowners: *latifundistas,* who soon ruled small kingdoms with impunity all over Mexico.

Oaxaca, fortunately, ran counter to the national trend. Lack of local capital and isolation from Mexico City led to little investment in Oaxaca land, so most communal holdings remained in indigenous hands. Moreover, of the several hundred church parcels sold in Oaxaca, one-third were, surprisingly, bought by native Oaxacans.

Alarmed by the reforms, conservative generals, priests, and businessmen and their mestizo and *indígena* followers revolted. The resulting **War of the Reforms** (not unlike the U.S. Civil War) ravaged the countryside for three long years until the victorious liberal army paraded triumphantly in Mexico City on New Year's Day 1861. In a thumping congratulations from the electors, Juárez outdistanced all rival candidates and became president in March 1861.

Juárez and Maximilian
Benito Juárez, the leading *reformista,* had won the day. His similarity to his contemporary, Abraham Lincoln, is legend: Juárez had risen from humble Zapotec native origins to become a lawyer, a champion of justice, and the president who held his country together during a terrible civil war. Like Lincoln, Juárez's triumph didn't last long.

Imperial France (taking advantage of U.S. preoccupation with its civil war) invaded Mexico in January 1862. Despite a formidable French force, which eventually ballooned to 60,000, Mexican regulars and guerrillas achieved a number of victories, several under the leadership of Oaxacan brigadier general **Porfirio Díaz.** Díaz rocketed to fame as the "Victor of Puebla" whose troops routed the French on May 5 (Cinco de Mayo), 1862. The French nevertheless managed to occupy Mexico City and several state capitals, including Oaxaca City, by summer 1864.

After two costly years pushing Juárez's liberal army into the hills, the French installed the king Mexican conservatives thought the country needed. Austrian Archduke Maximilian and his wife Carlota, the very models of modern Catholic monarchs, were crowned emperor and empress of Mexico in June 1864.

The naive **Emperor Maximilian I** was surprised that some of his subjects resented his presence. Meanwhile, Juárez refused to yield, stubbornly performing his constitutional duties in a somber black carriage one jump ahead of the French occupying army. After Díaz's signal victories at Carbonera and Miahuatlán in Oaxaca in late 1866, the climax came in May 1867, when liberal forces besieged and defeated Maximilian at Querétaro. Juárez, giving no quarter, sternly ordered Maximilian's execution by firing squad on June 19.

Juárez Reelected, Díaz Rebels

Benito Juárez's tumultuous popular approval and reelection to the presidency in October 1867 was not without its costs. His critics, notably Sebastián Lerdo de Tejada and Porfirio Díaz (who retired from active military duty to seek the presidency himself) accused Juárez of heavy-handed constitutional violations. Under Díaz's influence, a number of military commanders stirred up local uprisings. Undeterred, Juárez worked day and night at the double task of reconstruction and reform. Single-mindedly, he pushed to amend the Constitution of 1857, a course that triggered a major armed revolt, the Rebellion of La Noria, by Díaz in 1871 to "restore the purity" of the constitution against Juárez's alleged transgressions. Although his political momentum was weakened, Juárez was reelected president over both Tejada and Díaz in October 1871, but, exhausted, he succumbed to a heart attack on July 18, 1872. In his honor, Oaxaca City fathers renamed their city, officially, **Oaxaca de Juárez.**

The passing of Benito Juárez, the stoic partisan of reform, signaled hope to Mexico's conservatives. They soon got their wish: General Don Porfirio Díaz, the "Coming Man," was elected president in 1876.

ORDER AND PROGRESS
Pax Porfiriana

Don Porfirio is often remembered wistfully, as old Italians remember Mussolini: "He was a bit rough, but, dammit, at least he made the trains run on time."

Although Porfirio Díaz's humble Oaxaca mestizo origins were not unlike Juárez's, Díaz was not a democrat: When he was a general, his officers often took no captives; when he was president, his country police, the *rurales,* shot prisoners in the act of "trying to escape."

Order and progress, in that sequence, ruled Mexico for 34 years. Foreign investment flowed into the country; new railroads brought the products of shiny factories, mines, and farms to respected Gulf and Pacific ports. Mexico balanced its budget, repaid foreign debt, and became a respected member of the family of nations.

Oaxaca also gained material benefits from the Porfiriato, the label Mexican historians attach to Díaz's long rule. The rail link with Mexico City, which arrived in 1892, was the high point of three decades of public works improvement: bridges, roads, ports, electricity, sewage, an elegant theater, an Isthmus rail line, a state museum, and an enlarged Institute of Arts and Sciences. Rich foreign and Mexican investors dug dozens of new mines and built scores of factories, producing shoes, soap, hats, matches, glassware, cigarettes, and beer. In the southern mountains, coffee farms proliferated after the government offered a rebate for planting 2,000 coffee trees or more. Oaxaca City's population doubled, to nearly 40,000, during Díaz's rule.

The human price, nevertheless, was high. The rich, who included hundreds of resident foreigners, soaked up most of the profits while Oaxaca's poor, who lacked the money to benefit directly from the new civic improvements, struggled along as best they could. And although in Oaxaca most natives were able to hold on to their land, nationally Díaz's government did not intervene to prevent more than a hundred million acres—one-fifth of Mexico's land area (including most of the arable land)—being turned over to rich Mexicans and foreigners. Poor Mexicans suffered the most. By 1910, 90 percent of Mexico's *indígenas* had lost their traditional communal land. In the spring of 1910, a smug, now-cultured, and elderly Don Porfirio anticipated with relish the centennial of Hidalgo's Grito de Dolores.

PORFIRIO DÍAZ: HERO OR VILLAIN?

Porfirio Díaz, Mexico's most controversial and longest-serving president, was born in the city of Oaxaca on September 15, 1830. His parents, José de la Cruz Díaz and Petrona Mori, were of poor Mixtec-mestizo origin. Porfirio's father died when he was three, and he spent his childhood working at odd jobs to support his mother while attending public and parochial schools. He entered seminary in Oaxaca in 1843, dropped out after three years, and resumed studies in law at the Institute of Arts and Sciences, where he briefly taught in 1854.

A seminal event occurred for young Porfirio in 1854, when it was publicly announced that the entire faculty of the institute unanimously supported the notorious conservative dictator Antonio López de Santa Anna. Díaz asked that his abstention be recorded, and when publicly accused of siding with the liberal cause, he declared his support for General Juan Álvarez, leader of the liberal rebellion in Guerrero. The die was thus cast: For the next 50 years, Díaz never wavered from the image of a resolute, determined liberal, who possessed the courage of his convictions.

Forced to flee, Porfirio joined a rebel guerrilla band in the northern Sierra and later, in 1856, the Oaxaca National Guard, where he found purpose fighting for Benito Juárez's liberal side during the civil War of the Reforms. His valor and ability elevated him to the rank of brigadier general by the time the liberals triumphed in 1861.

Nearly immediately, during the imperialist French intervention, Díaz's military reputation skyrocketed. His forces defeated the French army at Puebla on May 5, 1862, the still celebrated **Cinco de Mayo** national holiday. After 25 battles and the liberation of Oaxaca, Puebla, and Mexico City from the French, Díaz retired from the military in 1867 at the age of 37.

It turned out that Díaz's insatiable ambition was driving him toward the presidency. He opposed Juárez and Lerdo de Tejada in the 1871 election, which, with no clear winner, was thrown into Congress, where Juárez was re-elected. Díaz revolted unsuccessfully; Juárez died and Lerdo de Tejada became president. Díaz rebelled again, in 1876, promulgating the doctrine of **No Reelección** in his **Plan of Tuxtepec.** Lerdo de Tejada fled, and Porfirio Díaz finally assumed the presidency legally on May 5, 1877.

Mexico, however, remained a hotbed of revolt. Díaz found that he had to put some of his democratic principles aside to remain in office and keep the country together. He reasoned in essence that, after all, if you don't have a government, you can't have democracy. His treatment of captured local rebels – *Matalos*

REVOLUTION AND STABILIZATION
"¡No Reelección!"

Porfirio Díaz himself had first campaigned on the slogan ¡"No Reelección!" It expressed the idea that the president should step down after one term. Although Díaz had stepped down once in 1880, for an interregnum as Oaxaca's governor, in 1884 he got himself elected president again and remained in office for 26 consecutive years. In 1910, **Francisco I. Madero,** a short, squeaky-voiced son of rich landowners, opposed Díaz under the same banner.

Although Díaz had jailed him before the election, Madero refused to quit campaigning.

From a safe platform in the United States, he called for a revolution to begin on November 20. The response in Oaxaca was typical: In the countryside, a few leaders rallied around Madero's banner, but Díaz had them rounded up and then got his nephew, Félix, installed as governor.

After all, *"¡No Reelección!"* is not much of a platform. But millions of poor Mexicans were going to bed hungry, and Díaz hadn't listened to them for years.

Villa and Zapata

In May 1910, those millions of poor Mexicans began to stir. In Oaxaca, a swarm of small

en caliente (Kill them on the spot) – was typically brutal.

Díaz retained enough of his liberal idealism to follow his own *No Reeleccíon* prescription and stepped down from the presidency in 1880 to become governor of Oaxaca, but after that he was re-elected consecutively and held office for 28 more years, until 1911.

The 34-year period (1876-1910) known as the Porfiriato was marked by stability and modernization. A stable Mexico attracted foreign investment. Mostly American and British entrepreneurs and engineers expanded railroads from a mere 400 miles in 1876 to 15,000 miles by 1910. New factories, mills, and mines blossomed along the railroads, which brought raw materials and took away manufactured goods to cities and modernized ports.

In 1908, Díaz hinted in an interview that he would retire in 1910 at the age of 80. This encouraged his growing political opposition, and when Díaz changed his mind and stood for another term in 1910, he was opposed by northern factory owner Francisco I. Madero, who campaigned on Díaz's original *No Reeleccíon* slogan. Díaz had Madero jailed and won election to his eighth presidential term.

But this time, Díaz was too tired to keep the lid on; his long rule collapsed partly because of its own success. Díaz had transformed the country. In many ways it reflected his original liberal vision of a stronger, richer, and better-educated Mexico, with a democratic balance of power and a procedure for orderly succession. But Díaz's failures, driven by cynicism, complacency, and a thirst for dominance, produced a regime that, like a dinosaur, fell under its own weight on May 31, 1911.

Porfirio Díaz, in exile in Paris, complaining of French food and yearning for some home-cooked Oaxacan fare, died on July 2, 1915.

young General Porfirio Díaz, circa 1865

rebellions broke out, then coalesced into a general revolution, which toppled Félix Díaz from the governorship. Simultaneously, up north in Chihuahua, followers of **Francisco (Pancho) Villa,** an erstwhile ranch hand, miner, peddler, and cattle rustler, began attacking the *rurales,* dynamiting railroads, and raiding towns, both in Mexico and the United States. Meanwhile, in Morelos state, just north of Oaxaca, horse trader, farmer, and minor official **Emiliano Zapata** and his *indígena* guerrillas were terrorizing rich *hacendados* and forcibly recovering stolen ancestral village lands. Zapata's movement gained steam and by mid-May had taken the Morelos state capital, Cuernavaca.

Meanwhile, Madero crossed the Río Grande and joined with Villa's forces, who took Ciudad Juárez. Soon the *federales,* government army troops, began deserting in droves, and on May 25, 1911, Díaz submitted his resignation.

As Madero's deputy, General Victoriano Huerta, put Díaz on his ship of exile in Veracruz, Díaz confided: "Madero has unleashed a tiger. Now let's see if he can control it."

Madero's star, nevertheless, was still rising. As he paraded triumphantly into Mexico City, revolutionary state governments were blossoming all over the country. Benito Juárez's son, Benito Juárez Maza, served briefly as Oaxaca's *maderista* governor in 1911–1912 until he was killed in a local skirmish.

The Fighting Continues

Emiliano Zapata turned out to be that very tiger whom Madero had unleashed. Meeting with Madero in Mexico City, Zapata fumed over Madero's go-slow approach to the "agrarian problem," as Madero termed it. By November 1912, Zapata had denounced Madero. *"¡Tierra y Libertad!"* ("Land and Liberty!") the Zapatistas cried, as Madero's support faded. The army in Mexico City rebelled; Huerta forced Madero to resign on February 18, 1913, then ordered him executed four days later.

The rum-swilling Huerta ruled like a Chicago mobster; general rebellion, led by the **"Big Four"**—Villa, Alvaro Obregón, and Venustiano Carranza in the north, and Zapata in the south—soon broke out. Pressed by the rebels and refused U.S. recognition, Huerta fled into exile in July 1914.

Meanwhile in Oaxaca, fighting between liberals and conservatives, much like the wars for Independence and the Reforms, laid waste to the countryside, killing commerce and sending foreign investors fleeing. But unlike the rest of the country, Oaxaca had no majority class of landless campesinos and consequently no great radical cause or leader to champion it.

Disgusted with the barbaric war of attrition ravaging the rest of the country, many Oaxaca leaders publicly repudiated the "Big Four" and declared Oaxaca a "sovereign" republic and tried to deny access to revolutionary outsiders.

Moreover, Oaxacan conservatives made a serious error in betraying and murdering Jésus Carranza, brother of El Primer Jefe (First Chief) Venustiano Carranza. Soon Carranzista battalions invaded Oaxaca and quickly defeated local forces, sending Oaxacan leaders scurrying to Mexico City or to the mountains, where they fought on for years as guerrillas.

The national struggle ground on for three more years as authority see-sawed between revolutionary factions. Finally Carranza, who controlled most of the country by 1917, got a convention together in Querétaro to formulate political and social goals. The resulting Constitution of 1917, while restating most ideas of the Reformistas' 1857 constitution, additionally prescribed a single four-year presidential term, labor reform, and subordinated private ownership to public interest. Every village had a right to communal *ejido* land, and subsoil wealth could never be sold away to the highest bidder.

The Constitution of 1917 was a revolutionary expression of national aspirations and, in retrospect, represented a social and political agenda for the entire 20th century. In modified form, it has lasted to the present day.

Obregón Stabilizes Mexico

On December 1, 1920, General Alvaro Obregón legally assumed the presidency of a Mexico still bleeding from 10 years of civil war. Although a seasoned revolutionary, Obregón was also a pragmatist who recognized that peace was necessary to implement the goals of the revolution. In four years, his government pacified local uprisings, disarmed a swarm of warlords, executed hundreds of *bandidos,* obtained U.S. diplomatic recognition, assuaged the worst fears of the clergy and landowners, and began land reform.

With Obregón as an example, Oaxaca's new governor, **García Vigil,** went to work. Despite the irritant of remnant guerrilla bands in the countryside, Vigil successfully pushed through Oaxaca land reform and wrote a new state constitution, which is essentially in effect today. His tax reform plans, however, ran into trouble with Oaxaca's rich landowners and came to nothing when he was assassinated in 1924.

At the national level, Obregón's success set the stage for Plutarco Elías Calles, Obregón's Secretaría de Gobernación and handpicked successor, who won the 1924 national election. Aided by peace, Mexico returned to a semblance of prosperity. Calles brought the army under civilian control, balanced the budget, and shifted Mexico's revolution into high gear. New clinics vaccinated millions against smallpox, new dams irrigated thousands of previously dry acres, and campesinos received millions of acres of redistributed land.

Simultaneously, Calles threatened foreign oil companies, demanding they exchange their titles for 50-year leases. A moderate Mexican supreme court decision over the oil issue and the skillful arbitration of U.S. Ambassador Dwight Morrow smoothed over both the oil and church troubles by the end of Calles's term.

Calles, who started out brimming with revolutionary fervor and populist zeal, became increasingly conservative and dictatorial. Although he bowed out peaceably in favor of Obregón (the constitution had been amended to allow one six-year nonsuccessive term), Obregón was assassinated two weeks after his election in 1928. Calles continued to rule for six more years through three puppet-presidents: Emilio Portes Gil (1928–1930), Pascual Ortiz Rubio (1930–1932), and Abelardo Rodríguez (1932–1934).

Calles Forms the PRI

In 1929, President Calles united three of Mexico's major constituencies: the country poor (represented by the Confederación Nacional de Campesinos, CNC), the workers (Confederación de Trabajadore Méjicanos, CTM), and the middle classes (Confederación Nacional de Organizaciones Populares, CNOP). Calles christened his new super political party the **Partido Revolucionario Institucional** (Institutional Revolutionary Party), or PRI, or, pronounced simply, the "pree."

The PRI dominated Mexican, and especially Oaxacan, politics during the 60 years after its founding. PRI presidents handpicked their PRI successors, who always got elected. Federal government contracts and salary money flowed from PRI headquarters in Mexico City to state and municipal officials, who were nearly always loyal local members of the PRI.

Oaxaca, isolated from the national economy and with no influential revolutionary ex-general to demand its fair share of national patronage, was consistently underfunded and mostly ignored by the central government. Nevertheless,

despite a severe earthquake in 1931 and general economic depression, Oaxacans managed some modest public works improvements during the 1930s and early 1940s. A paved road to Monte Albán led to important archaeological discoveries; other new highways branched out from the valley to the Mixteca, the Isthmus, and to Puerto Ángel. Oaxaca City residents benefited from a few improvements, such as a new water works and restoration of the opera house. But revolution and hard times had taken their toll: In 1940, Oaxaca City's population, about 40,000, was still the same as in 1910.

Lázaro Cárdenas, President of the People

Although he had received Calles's blessing for the 1934 presidential election, ex-general Lázaro Cárdenas, the 40-year-old former governor of Michoacán, immediately set his own agenda. Cárdenas worked tirelessly to fulfill the social prescriptions of the revolution. As morning-coated diplomats and cabinet ministers fretted in his outer office, Cárdenas ushered in delegations of campesinos and factory workers and sympathetically listened to their problems.

In his six years of rule, Cárdenas moved public education and health forward on a broad front, supported strong labor unions, and redistributed 49 million acres of farmland, more than any president before or since.

Cárdenas's resolute enforcement of the constitution's Artículo 123 brought him the most renown. Under this pro-labor law, the government turned over a host of private companies to employee ownership and, on March 18, 1938, expropriated all foreign oil corporations.

In retrospect the oil corporations, most of which were British, were not blameless. They had sorely neglected the wages, health, and welfare of their workers while ruthlessly taking the law into their own hands with private police forces. Although Standard Oil cried foul, the U.S. government, under President Franklin Roosevelt, did not intervene. Through negotiation and due process, U.S. companies eventually were compensated with $24 million plus

3 percent interest. In the wake of the expropriation, President Cárdenas created Petróleos Mexicanos (Pemex), the national oil corporation that continues to dominate Mexican oil and gas operations to the present day.

Manuel Avila Camacho

Manuel Avila Camacho, elected in 1940, was the last general to be president of Mexico. His administration ushered in a gradual shift of Mexican politics, government, and foreign policy as Mexico allied itself with the United States cause during World War II. Foreign tourism, initially promoted by the Cárdenas administration, ballooned. Good feelings surged as Franklin Roosevelt became the first U.S. president to officially cross the Río Grande, when he met with Camacho in Monterrey in April 1943.

As World War II moved toward its 1945 conclusion, both the United States and Mexico were enjoying the benefits of four years of governmental and military cooperation and mutual trade in the form of a mountain of strategic minerals, which had moved north in exchange for a similar mountain of U.S. manufactures that moved south.

CONTEMPORARY MEXICO AND OAXACA
The Mature Revolution

During the decades after World War II, beginning with moderate President **Miguel Alemán** (1946–1952), Mexican politicians gradually honed their skills of consensus and compromise as their middle-aged revolution bubbled along under liberal presidents and sputtered haltingly under conservatives. Doctrine required of all politicians, regardless of stripe, that they be "revolutionary" enough to be included beneath the banner of the PRI, Mexico's dominant political party.

Mexico's revolution hasn't been very revolutionary about **women's rights,** however. The PRI didn't get around to giving Mexican women, millions of whom fought and died alongside men during the revolution, the right to vote until 1953.

Alemán's government in 1947 began construction of a huge power and irrigation dam in the Río Papaloapan watershed of northern Oaxaca. The resulting **Miguel Alemán Dam,** completed a few years later, created a mammoth 2.3-million-acre reservoir. Although providing a large chunk of the region's growing electricity demand and an assured irrigation supply for a swarm of new pineapple, dairy, cotton, and cattle farms, the project required the painful relocation of many thousands of poor Mazatec, Chinantec, and Mixe *indígena* families.

Political Trouble in Oaxaca

Meanwhile, in Oaxaca City, trouble was breaking out, triggered by the unpopular actions of Governor Edmund Sánchez Cano. Merchants, who objected to his new taxes, and students, who resented the governor's interference in university affairs, got together and occupied the state government palace. Before the dust settled, federal troops were occupying the city and Mexico's second-in-command, the Secretaría de Gobernación, had forced Governor Sánchez's resignation and taken over the state government.

Trouble erupted again in 1951. This time, the dispute had roots among coffee farmers in Oaxaca's southern Sierra. Growers, far removed from Oaxaca City, had been shipping their coffee directly from Pacific ports or by remote roads directly to Mexico City, where they had developed strong commercial and political connections. Although responsible for Oaxaca's major export, coffee growers enjoyed little influence among state officials in Oaxaca City. One of these growers, Mayoral Heredia, had become a close family friend of President Miguel Alemán, who endorsed Heredia's successful PRI candidacy for governor of Oaxaca in 1950.

Upon taking office in December 1950, Heredia replaced the local politicos with his own Mexico City cadre, then proceeded with plans to modernize Oaxaca's agriculture, with subsidies paid by new state taxes. The ensuing dispute revolved fundamentally around the question of power: Who should control

Oaxaca—the city leaders as usual, or Mexico City-oriented appointees?

Soon, most townspeople—notably among them, local businesspeople and university professors and students—lined up angrily against the governor. The governor's sole supporters were the state police, who, in the heat of action, shot two protesting university students. After a one-day national student strike and weeks of daily protests, the merchant-student-professor coalition mounted a **citywide general strike.** Finally, President Alemán had to send in a federal regiment to restore order. Discredited, Governor Heredia was forced to replace his cabinet with city leaders. They reversed his modernization plans: They judged the present dirt roads adequate and found no need for tractors or irrigation. Oaxaca agriculture would sputter along as it had for the past hundred years. Rebuffed, Governor Heredia soon resigned in July 1952.

Political Activism of the 1960s and 1970s

Women, voting for the first time in a national election, kept the PRI in power by electing liberal **Adolfo López Mateos** in 1958. Resembling Lázaro Cárdenas in social policy, López Mateos redistributed 40 million acres of farmland, forced automakers to use 60 percent domestic components, built thousands of new schools, and distributed hundreds of millions of new textbooks. *"La electricidad es nuestra"* ("Electricity is ours"), Mateos declared as he nationalized foreign power companies in 1962.

Despite his left-leaning social agenda, unions were restive under López Mateos. Protesting inflation, workers struck; the government retaliated, arresting Demetrios Vallejo, the railway union head, and renowned muralist David Siqueiros, former Communist party secretary.

Despite the troubles, López Mateos climaxed his presidency gracefully in 1964 as he opened the celebrated National Museum of Anthropology, appropriately located in Chapultepec Park, where the Aztecs had first settled 20 generations earlier.

In 1964, as several times before, the outgoing president's Secretaría de Gobernación succeeded his former chief. Dour, conservative **Gustavo Díaz Ordaz** immediately clashed with liberals, labor, and students. The pot boiled over just before the 1968 Mexico City Olympics. Reacting to a student rebellion, the army occupied the National University; shortly afterward, on October 2, government forces opened fire with machine guns on a peaceful downtown rally crowd, killing hundreds and wounding thousands.

The Mexico City troubles reignited political activism in Oaxaca. Local university students, organized as the **Federación Estudiantil de Oaxaca (FEO),** mounted a successful campaign in support of bus drivers in 1970. In 1972, the students joined with workers and poor farmers, forming the **Coalición de Obreros, Campesinos, y Estudiantes de Oaxaca (COCEO).** They led off with a fight on behalf of sidewalk vendors to prevent the Saturday market being moved to the city's southern outskirts. After that, a disgruntled student splinter faction set off three small bombs: in the PRI-dominated union office, at an English-language library, and in the (empty) folk-dance amphitheater on the hill above the city. Fortunately, no one was injured. Later, in the mid-1970s, the COCEO supported and helped organize rural land invasions by villagers, organized and supported city workers' unions, and backed hillside squatters on the city's northern edge.

The actions in the capital inspired activists in other parts of Oaxaca. In Juchitán, on the Isthmus, students united with workers and poor farmers to form the **Coalición Obero, Campesino, y Estudiantil del Istmo (COCEI).** Unlike its Oaxaca City counterpart, the COCEI had a strong indigenous Zapotec cultural orientation, with women exerting important, although behind-the-scenes, leadership roles. Moreover, their cultural unity produced unusual militancy and political skill. Through a series of actions—strikes, boycotts, marches, and demonstrations—they opposed city-hall cliques and local *caciques* (bosses) at the painful cost of 20 of their number killed or kidnapped by police, soldiers, and hired thugs. Their payment in blood, however, led to significant improvements in working and living conditions for poor people in Juchitán and other Isthmus communities. Moreover, they forced the local establishment politicos to recognize their legitimacy by winning the 1980 local elections and making Juchitán one of the few towns in Mexico without a PRI-dominated city government.

Having had to deal with a generation of Oaxacan political turmoil, the federal government began to direct more resources to Oaxaca. Federal expenditures and employment in Oaxaca City doubled during the 1970s. Improved roads linked villages to the city; electric lines extended into formerly isolated mountain villages; a host of schools and health centers proliferated; and many villages and towns got clean water systems for the first time. With the money and power flowing from Mexico City, Oaxaca's local merchant and professional old guard gradually lost their influence over state government.

New Mexican Industrialization

Despite its serious internal troubles, Mexico's relations with the United States were cordial. President Lyndon Johnson visited and unveiled a statue of Abraham Lincoln in Mexico City. Later, President Díaz Ordaz met with President Richard Nixon in Puerto Vallarta.

Meanwhile, bilateral negotiations produced the **Border Industrialization Program.** Within a 12-mile strip south of the U.S.–Mexico border, foreign companies could assemble duty-free parts into finished goods and export them without any duties on either side. Within a dozen years, a swarm of such plants, called *maquiladoras,* were operating all over the county as hundreds of thousands of Mexican workers assembled and exported billions of dollars worth of shiny consumer goods—electronics, clothes, furniture, pharmaceuticals, and toys—worldwide.

Very few, if any, of Mexico's new *maquiladoras* reached Oaxaca, however. Oaxaca's sparse industry, with few exceptions, remained simple, producing raw materials or goods for local consumption only.

Oil Boom, Economic Bust

Discovery in 1974 of gigantic new oil and gas reserves along Mexico's Gulf Coast added fuel to Mexico's already rapid industrial expansion. During the late 1970s and early 1980s, billions in foreign investment, lured by Mexico's oil earnings, financed other major developments—factories, hotels, power plants, roads, airports—all over the country.

A modest share of Mexico's new oil wealth trickled to Oaxaca, in increased government jobs, infrastructure construction, and the new cross-Isthmus pipelines and Salina Cruz oil refinery, completed in 1977. Soon 3,000 Oaxacan workers were processing 800,000 barrels of Gulf crude a year into gasoline, diesel, jet fuels, and liquified natural gas that was sold and shipped all around the Pacific rim.

The negative side to these expensive projects was the huge dollar debt required to finance them. President **Luis Echeverría Alvarez** (1970–1976), diverted by his interest in international affairs, passed Mexico's burgeoning balance of payments deficit to his successor, **José López Portillo.** As feared by some experts, a world petroleum glut during the early 1980s burst Mexico's ballooning oil bubble and plunged the country into financial crisis. When the 1982 interest came due on its foreign debt, Mexico's largest holding company couldn't pay the $2.3 billion owed. The peso plummeted more than fivefold, to 150 per U.S. dollar. At the same time, prices doubled every year.

In the mid-1980s President **Miguel de la Madrid** (1982–1988) was straining to get Mexico's economic house in order. He sliced government and raised taxes, asking rich and poor alike to tighten their belts. Despite getting foreign bankers to reschedule Mexico's debt, de la Madrid couldn't stop inflation. Prices skyrocketed as the peso deflated to 2,500 per U.S. dollar, becoming one of the world's most devalued currencies by 1988.

Such economic belt-tightening invariably hits the poor hardest, and Oaxacans are among Mexico's poorest. Oaxaca's families average only about $5,000 in income per year—about one-half of the Mexican average, and about a tenth of the U.S. average. With basic food prices not much different from those in the United States, hunger, if not outright starvation, has been an everyday fact for many Oaxacans for as long as they can remember.

Salinas de Gortari, Solidaridad, and NAFTA

Public disgust led to significant opposition during the 1988 presidential election. The conservative National Action Party candidate Michael Clothier and liberal National Democratic Front candidate Cuauhtémoc Cárdenas ran against the PRI's Harvard-educated technocrat Carlos Salinas de Gortari. Although Salinas de Gortari eventually won the election, his showing, barely half of the vote, was the worst ever for an Institutional Revolutionary Party president.

Salinas de Gortari's major international achievement, despite significant national opposition, was the North American Free Trade Agreement (NAFTA), which the Canadian, U.S., and Mexican legislatures ratified in 1993.

The Zapatista Revolt

However, on the very day in January 1994 that NAFTA took effect, rebellion broke out in Oaxaca's neighboring state of Chiapas. A small but well-disciplined campesino force, calling itself **Ejército Zapatista Liberación Nacional** (Zapatista National Liberation Army, EZLN), or "Zapatistas," captured a number of provincial towns and held the former governor of Chiapas hostage.

The Zapatista revolt rattled Oaxaca. In a social trend that had been growing for a generation, indigenous communities all over the state began pushing for their rights under the Mexican constitution.

Prime actors in this movement have been liberationist country Catholic priests and nuns. The Isthmus provides the most successful examples. Under the leadership of clergy, in dozens of communities around Tehuántepec, thousands of indigenous people have organized self-help, cultural, political, and communal work programs. Their moneymaking activities range from raising coffee, sheep, and chickens to milling corn and producing pottery, which they sell in the Tehuántepec, Salina Cruz, and Juchitán markets.

The Zapatista movement has struck the common chord—of autonomy—among virtually all of Oaxaca's indigenous social-political groups. Echoing the Zapatistas in Chiapas, their political goals usually include the right of self-rule by their own traditional means.

A National Tragedy and Recovery

In mid-1994, Mexico's already tense political drama veered toward tragedy. Luis Donaldo Colosio, Salinas's handpicked presidential candidate, was gunned down just months before the August balloting. Fortunately, the nation, instead of disintegrating, united in grief; opposition candidates eulogized their fallen former opponent and later earnestly engaged his replacement, stolid technocrat **Ernesto Zedillo,** in Mexico's first presidential election debate.

In a closely watched, relatively clean election, Zedillo piled up a solid plurality against his opponents. By perpetuating the PRI's 65-year hold on the presidency, Mexican voters had again opted for the PRI's familiar, although imperfect, middle-aged revolution.

A New Economic Crisis

Zedillo, however, had little time to savor his victory. The peso, long propped up by his predecessor's fiscal policies, lost half of its value by January. To stave off a worldwide financial panic, U.S. President Bill Clinton quickly negotiated an unprecedented multibillion-dollar international loan package for Mexico, in February, 1995.

Although economic disaster was temporarily averted, national inflation soared during 1995. More and more families could not afford basic foods and medicines. Malnutrition increased sixfold, and diseases such as cholera and dengue fever resurged in the countryside.

The Political Cauldron Bubbles On

Meanwhile, in June 1995, as negotiations with the rebel Zapatistas sputtered on and off in Chiapas, popular discontent erupted in Oaxaca's western neighbor-state, Guerrero. State police massacred 17 unarmed, protesting, campesinos not far from Acapulco.

On the one-year anniversary of the massacre, a new, well-armed revolutionary group, **Ejército Popular Revolucionario** (People's Revolutionary Army, EPR), made its appearance. Soon, on August 28, EPR guerrillas killed more than two dozen police and soldiers at several southwest Mexico locations, including four sailors at the naval garrison in Huatulco, Oaxaca. Soon, platoons of soldiers and police were scouring rural Guerrero, Oaxaca, Michoacán, and other states, searching homes and arresting suspected dissidents.

At the same time, however, the Zedillo government gained momentum in addressing local grievances both in Chiapas, by building electricity infrastructure and new health clinics, and in Oaxaca, with an unprecedented $1 billion in public works and social expenditures during the upcoming fiscal year.

Nevertheless, the rough federal army and police searches, arrests, and jailings energized a flurry of political action. Oaxacan human rights groups, already protesting against unpunished violence, have upped the pressure for reforms at the state and national level. The official **Comisión Estatal de Derechos Humanos de Oaxaca** (Oaxaca State Human Rights Commission, CEDH) hears complaints and issues "nonbinding and autonomous recommendations" to relevant authorities.

Economic Recovery and Political Reforms

The best news for which the Zedillo government could justly claim credit was the dramatically improving national economy. By mid-1998, annual inflation had dropped below 15 percent, investment dollars were flowing back into Mexico, the peso had stabilized at about eight to the U.S. dollar, and Mexico had paid back every penny of its borrowed U.S. bailout money.

Moreover, a pair of unprecedented events signaled an increasingly open political system. In the 1997 congressional elections, voters elected a host of opposition candidates, depriving the PRI of an absolute congressional majority for the first time since 1929. A year later, in early 1998, Mexicans were participating in their country's first **primary elections**—in which voters, instead of political bosses, chose party candidates.

Although Ernesto Zedillo's presidential ride had been rough, he entered the twilight of his 1994–2000 term able to take credit for an improved economy, some genuine political reforms, and relative peace in the countryside. The election of 2000 revealed, however, that the Mexican people were not satisfied.

End of an Era: Vicente Fox Unseats the PRI

During 1998 and 1999 the focal point of opposition to the PRI's three-generation rule had been shifting to relative newcomer Vicente Fox, former President of Coca-Cola Mexico and clean former PAN governor of Guanajuato.

Fox, who had announced his candidacy for president two years before the election, seemed an unlikely challenger. After all, the minority PAN had always been the party of wealthy businessmen and the conservative Catholic right. But blunt-talking, six-foot-five Fox, who sometimes campaigned in *vaquero* boots and a 10-gallon cowboy hat, preached populist themes of coalition building and "inclusion." He backed up his talk by carrying his campaign to hardscrabble city barrios, dirt-poor country villages, and traditional outsider groups, such as Jews.

In a relatively orderly and fair July 2, 2000, election, Fox decisively defeated his PRI opponent Labastida, 42 percent to 38 percent, leaving PRD candidate Cárdenas with only a feeble 17 percent. Fox's win also swept a PAN plurality (223/209/57) into the 500-seat Chamber of Deputies lower house (although the Senate remained PRI-dominated).

Nevertheless, in pushing the PRI from the all-powerful presidency after 71 consecutive years of domination, Fox had ushered Mexico into a new, more democratic era.

Despite stinging criticism from his own ranks, President Zedillo, whom historians were already praising as the real hero behind Mexico's new democracy, made an unprecedented early appeal for all Mexicans to unite behind Fox.

On the eve of Fox's December 1, 2000, inauguration, Mexicans awaited his speech with hopeful anticipation. He did not disappoint them. Although acknowledging that he couldn't completely reverse 71 years of PRI entrenchment in his one six-year term, he vowed to ride the crest of reform, by revamping the tax system and reducing poverty by 30 percent, by creating a million new jobs a year. He promised, furthermore, to secure justice for all by reforming police, the army, and the federal attorney general's office. On top of all that, Fox called for the formation of an unprecedented congressional "Transparency Commission" to investigate a generation of past grievances, including the 1968 Mexico City University student massacre, and assassinations of, among others, a Roman Catholic cardinal in 1993 and a popular presidential candidate in 1994.

Vicente Fox, President of Mexico

Wasting little time, President Fox headed to Chiapas to confer with indigenous community leaders, shutting down Chiapas military bases and dozens of army roadblocks. Back in Mexico City, he sent the long-delayed **peace plan,** including the **indigenous bill of rights,** to Congress. Zapatista rebels responded by journeying en masse from Chiapas to Mexico City, where, in their black masks, they addressed Congress, arguing for indigenous rights. Although by mid-2001 Congress had passed a modified version of the negotiated settlement, and the majority of states had ratified the required constitutional amendment, indigenous leaders condemned the legislation plan as watered down and unacceptable, while proponents claimed it was the best possible compromise between the Zapatistas' demands and the existing Mexican constitution.

Furthermore, Fox continued to pry open the door to democracy in Mexico. In May 2002, he signed Mexico's first **freedom of information act,** entitling citizens to timely copies of all public documents from federal agencies. Moreover, at the same time, federal attorneys, working with Fox's long-promised **"Transparency Commission"** were questioning a list of 74 former government officials, including ex-President Luis Echeverrí, about their roles in government transgressions.

During 2003, the Mexican economy, having already slowed down in 2002, continued its lackluster performance, increasing public dissatisfaction. In the July 7, 2003, congressional elections, voters took their frustrations out on the PAN and gave its plurality in the Chamber of Deputies to the PRI. When the dust settled, the PRI total had risen to 225 seats, while the PAN had slipped to 153. The biggest winner, however, was the PRD, which gained more than 40 seats, to a total of about 100.

The best news of 2004 was not political, but economic. The Mexican economy, reflecting that of the United States, began to recover, expanding at a moderate (if not robust) rate of about 4 percent, while exports to the United States also increased.

Unfortunately, despite President Fox's successes at the national level, serious political trouble surfaced in Oaxaca in mid-2006. It started mildly enough. In May 2006, Oaxaca's statewide teachers union went on their perennial strike for much-needed higher wages. They accused PRI governor Ulises Ruiz of diverting millions of dollars in education funds to his controversial pet public works projects. Soon, hundreds of teachers were camping out in the *zócalo* and staging daily political rallies. Their rhetoric increasingly focused on the credibility of Governor Ruiz, who consistently refused to negotiate with them.

By mid-June, when teachers began barricading streets around the *zócalo,* Ruiz sent in his police, who brutally manhandled the nonviolent middle-class demonstrators. The protest escalated quickly. The teachers allied themselves with their left-leaning supporters, forming an umbrella protest organization, the APPO (Popular Assembly of the People of Oaxaca), and added the demand that Governor Ruiz must step down.

During the summer months of July, August, and September, the protests turned violent. Highways were blocked, buses were burned, a radio station was occupied, and several people were shot to death. By October, downtown Oaxaca City resembled a ghost town. Tourism had evaporated, and consequently, all businesses, including hotels and restaurants, had shut their doors.

In late October 2006, President Vicente Fox, spurred by the killing of an American news reporter, acted. He sent a brigade of federal troops and police to Oaxaca, who removed the street barricades and dispersed the protestors while inflicting only minimal injuries. The local townspeople, breathing a sigh of relief, turned out, and in two days they swept up the mess, painted over the accumulated graffiti, opened their businesses, and filled the streets, buying flowers to celebrate the November 1–2 Day of the Dead holiday.

Tranquilty seemed to be returning to Oaxaca. Local folks again began strolling around the *zócalo;* restaurants were serving an increasing flow of customers, and hotels were offering lodging discounts on their websites and accepting reservations.

And lastly, what was very important for potential visitors to realize was that, through all of the 2006 political upsets, the people of Oaxaca remained overwhelmingly appreciative of visiting travelers and were again looking forward to sharing their celebrated handicrafts, delicious cuisine, and beloved fiestas with all visitors who come to their lovely city and surrounding valley.

The Election of 2006

Back during the first half of 2006, as Vicente Fox was winding down his presidency, Mexicans were occupied by the campaign to elect his successor. Most headlines went to the PRD candidate, the mercurial leftist-populist Andres Manuel López Obrador, former mayor of Mexico City. Trying hard not to be upstaged was the steady, no-nonsense PAN candidate, Harvard-educated centrist-conservative Felipe Calderón, a leading light of President Fox's cabinet.

On Sunday, July 2, 2006, 42,000,000 Mexicans cast their ballots. In an intensely monitored election marred by very few irregularities, unofficial early returns indicated that voters had awarded Calderón a paper-thin plurality. Four days later, after all returns were certified, the Federal Electoral Institute announced the official vote tally: only about 22 percent for the PRI candidate, Roberto Madrazo, with the remaining lion's share divided nearly evenly, with 38.7 percent going to Obrador and 39.3 percent for Calderón. This result, the Federal Electoral Institute ruled, was too close to declare a winner without a recount.

Besides the close Obrador-Calderón vote, the election results revealed much more. Not only were the 32 electoral entities (31 states and the Federal District) divided equally, with 16 going for Obrador, and 16 for Calderón, the vote reflected a nearly complete north-south political schism, with virtually all of the 16 PAN-majority states forming a solid northern bloc, while the 16 PRD-voting states did the same in the south. Furthermore, the election appeared to signal a collapse of PRI power; with no state (nor the Federal District) giving either a majority or a plurality to Roberto Madrazo.

Election Aftermath

For a month, the questionable ballots were gathered and examined exhaustively by the Supreme Election Tribunal, an impeccable panel of federal judges. They found that the recount shifted the margin by only by a few thousand votes away from Calderón to Obrador. On September 6, 2006, the Federal Electoral Institute declared Calderón the president-elect by a margin of about 240,000 votes, or a bit more than one-half of a percent of the total vote.

Obrador and his supporters screamed foul

and threatened to ignore Calderón and/or block his presidency. In the succeeding weeks, the PRD's obstructionist tactics reached an outrageous climax when a handful of PRD senators and deputies made such a ruckus during a joint session of the federal legislature that they prevented the President of Mexico, for the first time in history, from delivering his annual state of the union address.

Mexican voters, watching the PRD's melodramatic tactics on television, began, in increasing numbers, to say enough was enough. National polls showed that more than two-thirds of Mexicans disapproved of the PRD's protest behavior. By October 2006, many of the PRD's leaders agreed, further isolating Obrador to a mere footnote in Mexican history. Mexico's new democracy, given a gentle shove forward 10 years earlier by President Ernesto Zedillo and nurtured for 6 more years by Vicente Fox, seemed to have again surmounted a difficult crisis and emerged stronger.

Calderón Takes Charge

As he prepared for his December 1, 2006 inauguration, Felipe Calderón not only appeared to be moving ahead with many of his predecessor's original proposals, but he also seemed to be reaching out to the PRI and the PRD with some new ideas. These, although containing many of PAN's pro-business pro-NAFTA ideas, also appeared to borrow considerably from the liberal-populist agenda of Obrador and the PRD. Only much-needed cooperation will allow their country to make progress toward the bright but elusive vision of a just and prosperous motherland for all Mexicans.

Calderón wasted no time getting started. He immediately attacked Mexico's most urgent problem by declaring war on Mexico's drug lords. Right away he replaced most of the federal police chiefs, many suspected of corruption. He then put the Mexican army in charge of his war on drugs, assigning 30,000 Mexican soldiers to seek and destroy criminal drug gangs and networks, especially in the drug-infested border towns of Tijuana, Ciudad Juárez, and Nuevo Laredo.

Peace Reigns in Oaxaca

Concurrently, Felipe Calderón dealt head-on with the violent elements of the Oaxaca political protests. Within a month of his inauguration, Oaxaca police, using a minimum of force, rounded up dozens of the protest ringleaders and sequestered them far away in a Michoacán prison to await trial. To the relief of Oaxaca people, the remainder of the APPO demonstrators were never again allowed to push their protest to the city center.

Calderón Visits the United States

Despite Mexico's immediate security problems, Felipe Calderón found time to tend to the Mexican economy and politics, both national and international. Under his steady hand, during 2007, the Mexican economy continued to bubble along at a moderate annual growth rate of about 2.5 percent, inflation was kept at a low 4 percent, and the peso held its value below 11 pesos to the U.S. dollar.

On the world stage, President Calderón made his first international trip, initially to California for three days, then to the Midwest and New York. On February 13, 2008, he addressed a joint session of the California legislature, emphasizing cooperation. "Collaboration and shared responsibility," he said, were the keys to joint California–Mexico progress. In the same address, he thrust himself into the U.S. immigration debate by declaring that "Mexican and Mexican-American workers are a large reason for the dynamic economy of California," and that Mexican "immigration should be legal, safe, and organized."

Governmental Reforms

With the cooperation of the 31 Mexican states and the Federal District and federal legislators, in September 2008, President Calderón initiated a pair of long-awaited governmental reforms. He announced the **reform of the Mexican Postal Service,** which now will have both new pea green and pink colors and a new name, *Correos de Mexico* (Mail of Mexico). Although detractors scoffed at a mere color and name change, Calderón is backing up the reform with computerized post offices, higher pay for postal workers, and a 25-fold increase (from 7 to 170) in inspectors for Mexico's 1,450 post offices.

Similarly, in September 2008, Calderón announced that Mexico's justice system will be overhauled step-by-step during the next eight years. When complete, the overhaul will replace Mexico's Inquisition-derived European justice system by abolishing both secret trials and coercion (including torture) of the accused. Furthermore, the reform reverses the European legal practice of assuming guilt before innocence. Instead, the accused (as in the United States) will be assumed innocent, until proven guilty by the state.

The War On Drugs

Despite President Calderón's solid early legislation, television news and newspaper headlines often highlighted sensational aspects of what statistics reveal is more of a turf war between drug gangs than against Mexican authorities. By mid-2010, about 24,000 had been killed in drug violence since Calderón took office 3.5 years earlier. Of that number, only about 1 in 20 (1,100 total) were police, soldiers, or government officials. Even fewer were innocent bystanders. Furthermore, more than 90 percent of the violence was confined to four northern border states, with about half of all killings occurring in Ciudad Juárez (which, if you're a drug trafficker, has to be one of the world's most dangerous cities).

What applies to Ciudad Juárez, fortunately, does not apply to anywhere else in Mexico, where, to date, no American or Canadian tourist has been killed as a result of drug violence. (In the winter of 2010–11, one American tourist, in Mazatlán, was hit by a stray bullet. He shrugged it off, saying the same thing could happen in his U.S. hometown.)

Recognizing the difficulty of reducing Mexican drug gang violence, Hillary Clinton, the U.S. Secretary of State, in March 2009, during an official visit in Mexico City with President Calderón and Mexican Foreign Secretary Patricia Espinosa, acknowledged that "We have a co-responsibility," and "We stand with you," in reducing both America's craving for illegal drugs and the thousands of automatic assault weapons smuggled monthly from the United States into Mexico.

On April 3, 2009, following up Hillary Clinton's visit, U.S. Homeland Security Chief Janet Napolitano and Attorney General Eric Holder, met with their counterparts in Mexico City and announced that the U.S. will spend $400 million on more thorough inspection (especially for guns and drugs) in both directions at the U.S.-Mexico border.

Mexican State Elections in 2010

In 9 of the 12 states participating in the state elections on July 4, 2010, the PRI (Institutional Revolutionary Party) surged, gaining new governors, mayors, and municipal council members at the expense of the PAN (National Action Party) and PRD (Democratic Revolutionary Party).

The sole exception was in Oaxaca, where voters ousted the PRI, after 81 years of rule, by a landslide. The coalition party, CUPP (Coalition United for Peace and Progress), a blend of the local PAN, PRD, and PT (Worker's Party) rejected unpopular governor Ulises Ruiz's effort to succeed himself. Gabino Cué (QWAY) Monteagudo claimed victory, thanking López Obrador of PRD and Felipe Calderón of PAN. Louis Ugartehea will be the new mayor of Oaxaca.

Cué Monteagudo, who many believed was cheated at the ballot box in the 2004 election by Ulises Ruiz, planned his strategy to avoid another fraud.

Most Oaxacans, who endured six years of Ulises Ruiz's unresponsive rule, are relieved with his exit. Many blame him for the escalation to violence of the 2006 teacher's strike and its long, troubled aftermath. Folks all over the state now look forward to a sunny, peaceful, and prosperous future for Oaxaca.

Government and Economy

GOVERNMENT AND POLITICS
The Constitution of 1917

Mexico's governmental system is rooted in the Constitution of 1917, which incorporated many of the features of its reformist predecessor of 1857. State constitutions, including Oaxaca's, must conform to the federal Constitution, which, with some amendments, remains identical to the 1917 document. Although drafted at the behest of conservative revolutionary Venustiano Carranza by his handpicked Querétaro "Constitucionalista" congress, the 1917 Constitution was greatly influenced by Alvaro Obregón and generally ignored by Carranza during his subsequent three-year presidential term.

Whereas many articles resemble those of its U.S. model, the Constitution of 1917 contains provisions developed directly from Mexican experience. **Article 27** addresses the question of land. Private property rights are qualified by societal need, subsoil rights are public property, and foreigners and corporations are severely restricted in land ownership. Although the 1917 constitution declared *ejido* (jointly held) land inviolate, recent 1994 amendments allow, under certain circumstances, the sale or use of communal land as loan security.

Article 23 severely restricts church powers. In declaring that "places of worship are the property of the nation," it stripped churches of all title to real estate, without compensation. **Article 5** and **Article 130** banned religious orders, expelled foreign clergy, and denied priests and ministers all political rights, including voting, holding office, and even criticizing the government.

Article 123 establishes the rights of labor: to organize, bargain collectively, strike, work a maximum eight-hour day, and receive a minimum wage. Women are to receive equal pay for equal work and be given a month's paid leave for childbearing. Article 123 also establishes social security plans for sickness, unemployment, pensions, and death.

On paper, Mexico's constitutional government structures appear much like their U.S. prototypes: a federal presidency, a two-house (Senate and Chamber of Deputies) congress, and a supreme court, with their counterparts in each of the 31 states and the Mexico City Distrito Federal. Political parties field candidates, and all citizens vote by secret ballot.

In Oaxaca, local federal elections determine Oaxaca's national legislative delegation: **11 deputies** *(diputados)* of the approximately 500-seat lower house and **four senators** *(senadores)* of the 120-odd upper house seats. **PRI dominance** of Oaxaca elections, although not as complete as in the past, still continues, with a plurality of Oaxaca's deputies and senators usually being PRI members.

Although ideally providing for **separation of powers,** the Constitution of 1917 subordinates both the legislative and judicial branches, with the courts being the weakest of all. The supreme court, for example, can only, through repeated deliberations, decide upon the constitutionality of legislation. Five separate individuals must file successful petitions for writs *amparo* (protection) on a single point of law in order to effect constitutional precedent.

The President, the PRI, and the PAN

Despite Mexico's increasingly active legislative bodies, Mexican presidents still enjoy greater powers than their U.S. counterparts. They can suspend constitutional rights under a state of siege, can officially initiate legislation, veto all or parts of bills, refuse to execute laws, and replace state officers. The federal government, moreover, retains nearly all taxing authority, relegating the states to a role of merely administering federal programs.

Mexican presidents successively built upon their potent constitutional mandate during the last three generations of the 20th century. The **Partido Revolucionario Institucional** (Institutional Revolutionary Party, PRI), whose

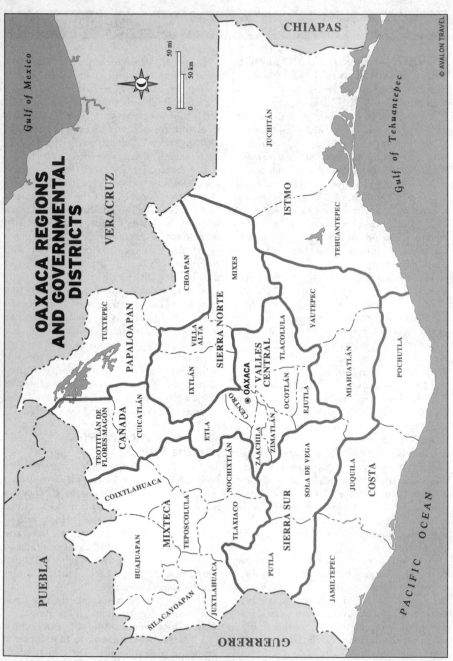

handpicked candidates held the presidency continuously from 1929 to 2000, became an extralegal parallel government, as powerful as or more so than the formal constitutional government. The PRI is organized hierarchically, in three separate labor, farmer, and "popular" (this last is mostly government, business, and professional workers) columns, which send delegates from local committees to state and, ultimately, national conventions.

Past Mexican presidents, as heads of the PRI, traditionally reigned at the top of the party apparatus, sending orders through the national PRI delegates, who in turn looked after their respective state delegations. The delegates reported on the performance of the state and local PRI committees to get out the vote and carry out party mandates. If the local committee's performance was satisfactory, then federal subsidies, public works projects, election funds, and federal jobs flowed from government coffers to the state and local level through PRI organizations. In your hometown, if you were not in the PRI or didn't know someone who was, you might have found it difficult to get a small business loan, crop subsidy, government apartment, teaching job, road-repair contract, or government scholarship.

The successful election of PAN opposition presidential candidate Vicente Fox in 2000, and his PAN successor Felipe Calderón in 2006, although erasing PRI executive dominance, still left the Senate (and later, in 2003 and 2009, also the Chamber of Deputies) under PRI control. Consequently, both Presidents Fox and Calderón found themselves in a similar position as a U.S. president, having to negotiate, with only partial success, with legislators from the opposition party.

State and Local Government

Oaxaca, like all 31 Mexican states, has an elected governor and state legislature. The Oaxaca voters elect 42 representatives to the state legislature, which holds its sessions in the Palacio de Gobierno, adjacent to Oaxaca City's central plaza. With minimal tax powers, the state government is mostly relegated to oversight of federal public works, social welfare, health, and education programs in 30 regional administrative **distritos** (districts).

Distritos vary widely in extent, from the largest, Juchitán, in the Isthmus, to tiny Zaachila, the smallest, in the central valley, not far south of Oaxaca City. Although second smallest in area, Oaxaca's most populous and economically most important district is the Centro district, which contains the capital, Oaxaca City.

Oaxaca's 30 *distritos* are in turn divided, often along ethnic lines, into a host of 570 **municipios** (townships), each with its *cabercera* (head town) and subsidiary *agencias,* usually country villages, each of which oversees a scattering of surrounding *rancherias* (hamlets). Oaxaca's crazy quilt of 570 *municipios,* by far the most of any Mexican state, reflects Oaxaca's ethnic richness. Many of the *municipios* encompass a single ethnic group whose members are united by common kinship, language, and costume.

Its *municipios* are where much of Oaxaca's civic action is. If you get a traffic ticket, you'll probably be told to go to the *municipio's presidencia municipal* (like a city hall) to pay your fine and recover your driver's license. From the *presidencia municipal* reigns the *municipio's* publicly elected *presidente* (like a mayor), *alcaldes* (judges), and *regidores* (administrators) of various ranks, who oversee the *municipio's policía municipal* and organize public works.

Parallel to and interlocking with this formal Spanish-derived hierarchy is the less formal indigenous **consejo de ancianos** (council of elders), members of which attain their status by a cumulative lifetime of civic service. Operating mostly by discussion and consensus, the council of elders (which sometimes includes the *presidente* and other elected officials) gets its way through discussion, persuasion, and final approval or veto of civic proposals.

Oaxaca's former progressive governor and legislature, in 1995, recognized indigenous demands for local election by traditional **Usos y Costumbres** (Use and Custom) procedures. Now, a majority of (but by no means all; notably not Oaxaca City) *municipios* elect their

The *presidencia municipal*, as shown here at Tamazulapan in the Mixteca, is the seat of the local *municipio* (city-county or township) governmental unit.

mayor and city council members in town hall meetings.

Although *municipios* collect minimal monetary taxes, they often require community members to perform *tequio* (public service) in lieu of taxes. For men, such work might be repairing a local bridge or police or fire duty; women, on the other hand, might perform childcare or sweep the city streets or the municipal market.

Since colonial times, authorities have recognized eight traditional Oaxacan ethno-geographic regions: Valles Centrales, Sierra Norte, Papaloapan, Istmo, Costa, Sierra Sur, Mixteca, and the Cañada. Later, during the republican era, these traditional regions were subdivided into governmental-economic districts, now aggregating 30 in number, each presided over by a district capital through which state tax monies are distributed and elections for both state and federal legislative and executive offices are organized. After the capital Oaxaca City, the district capitals, notably Tlacolula, Ocotlán,

and Zaachila in the Valles Centrales; Tuxtepec in the Papaloapan; Juchitán in the Istmo; Juquila in the Sierra Sur; and Juxtlahuaca and Tlaxiaco, in the Mixteca; rank among the state of Oaxaca's most fascinating destinations.

THE ECONOMY
Postrevolutionary National Gains

By many measures, Mexico's 20th-century revolution appears to have succeeded. Since 1910, illiteracy has plunged from 80 percent to about 14 percent; life expectancy has risen from 30 years to about 76; infant mortality has dropped from a whopping 40 percent to about 1.8 percent; and, in terms of caloric intake, most Mexicans are eating about twice as much as their turn-of-the-century forebears.

Decades of near-continuous economic growth account for rising Mexican living standards. The Mexican economy rebounded from its 1982, 1995, and 2002 recessions and has largely recovered from its 2009–2010 recession, because of its plentiful natural resources;

© BRUCE WHIPPERMAN

diversified manufacturing, such as cars, steel, and petrochemicals; increasing tourism; exports of fruits, vegetables, and cattle; and its large, willing, low-wage workforce.

Mexican governments during the 1970s and 1980s skillfully exploited Mexico's economic strengths. The **Border Industrialization Program** has led to millions of jobs in thousands of border *maquiladora* factories, from Tijuana to the mouth of the Río Grande. Foreign trade, a strong source for new Mexican jobs, has burgeoned since the 1980s, due to liberalized tariffs as Mexico joined the General Agreement on Tariffs and Trade (GATT) in 1986 and NAFTA in 1994. As a result, Mexico has become a net exporter of goods and services to the United States, by far its largest trading partner. Although Mexico suffered a peso collapse of about 50 percent (in relation to the U.S. dollar) in 1995, the Zedillo administration acted quickly. Belt-tightening measures brought foreign investment flowing back to Mexico by 1997 and annual inflation, which had initially surged, cooled down to around 4 percent by 2010.

But, during 2004 and 2005, despite high prices for its oil, rock-bottom inflation, large payments of money from Mexicans working in the United States, and a balanced budget, the Mexican economy still didn't produce the million jobs a year it needed to keep up with population increase. Although some of the sluggishness could be blamed on the hurricane that devastated Cancún in the fall of 2005, most experts agree that Mexico's largest economic problem is lack of ability to compete, especially with respect to Asian countries, especially China, which floods Mexico with low-cost

SOCIOECONOMIC STATISTICS: OAXACA VS. MEXICO VS. THE UNITED STATES

	OAXACA	MEXICO	U.S.
Approximate average daily income per active worker	$10	$25	$110
Corn productivity	.5 ton/acre	.5 ton/acre	1.6 ton/acre
Tractor use by farmers	25%	40%	100%
Infant mortality	2%	2%	.7%
Inhabitants per doctor	1,200	670	400
Average grade attained in school	6.0	8.5	13
Illiteracy	20%	9%	3%
Population (year 2000)	3,578,000	101,400,000	298,000,000
Yearly population growth	1.1%	1.2%	1.4%

Sources: Mexican government census, U.S. Census Statistical Abstract, World Bank, and the *U.S. Government Book of Facts*

goods, while Mexico sells very little to China in return. A serious marker of all this appeared in 2004, when China replaced Mexico as the United States' second-largest import source, jumping to about 14 percent of U.S. imports, compared to Mexico, at around 11 percent.

Many economists suggest that Mexico, in order to breathe permanent new life into its economy, needs fundamental structural reforms, such as more flexible labor rules, more effective tax collection (hardly anyone pays any income tax), and the possibility of private investment to modernize the energy and oil industries.

The Oaxacan Economy

Despite huge gains, Mexico's Revolution of 1910 is incomplete. In Oaxaca, it remains especially so. Oaxaca lags behind the rest of Mexico by many measures of economic success. Median income, for example, hovers at about half the national average. Such numbers demonstrate the difficult reality confronting the poorest Oaxacan families.

When asked by 2000 (2010 not yet available) census takers to categorize their incomes, a whopping 28 percent of Oaxacan active wage earners said they received no income. The next two higher categories, totaling about 20 percent (one in five) of the population, reported incomes of $0–2 and $2–4 per day.

A look at more government figures provides clues as to who most of Oaxaca's poor are. According to recent figures, **agriculture**—overwhelmingly corn farming, but also cattle, fruit, and fish—occupies about half of Oaxaca's active workers, but accounts for only one-tenth of the value of Oaxaca's yearly economic output. The remaining nine-tenths is generated by the other half of Oaxaca's workers who are, consequently, responsible for approximately nine times as much production value as the farmers.

At the human level, the typical Oaxacan lives on a farm and is poor, even by Mexican standards. The typically six-member family—dad José, 36; mom María, 31; three kids, 2, 6, and 11; and grandma, 56—earn next to no

cash income and must subsist on what they can produce and gather. This generally is limited to corn, squash, beans, eggs, garden vegetables, an occasional chicken or turkey, and maybe a little wild game. Staples that they don't produce must be bought or bartered for at the village market. So once a week María bundles up some tomatoes, carrots, and potatoes from her garden and maybe one of her half dozen young roosters. With her middle child in tow, she walks the six miles uphill to the village. With luck, María will return by early evening, having sold or traded everything for perhaps a liter of cooking oil, a kilo of sugar, a spool of thread, and a yard or two of bright ribbon.

While María is at the market, José pulls weeds for a few hours in his *milpa* (cornfield). Although his acreage is small, perhaps no more than two or three acres, he usually manages two harvests of corn a year. In a good season, this might amount to two tons, as long as he keeps the mice and rats away from it. Every year he stores about a ton of corn for home consumption and sells the other ton for about $100 to Conasupo, the government commodity agency. If all goes well, he reckons, in three years he'll save enough to replace his family's present stick-and-adobe, dirt-floor house with a new, sturdy two-room concrete house with an interior water tap and a toilet.

Solving the Problems

Like José, many thousands of Oaxacan farmers must struggle to better their lot. The government is generally sympathetic to their efforts and recognizes that Oaxaca, with its plentiful sun and adequate (but sharply seasonal) rainfall, is a potential trove of grain, fruit, fiber, meat, and fish for the rest of the country and maybe even for export. But the problems are manifold. Although Oaxaca has expanses of rich land, especially in the Isthmus, the Papaloapan, and the central valley, about a fifth of Oaxaca's land, especially in the Mixteca, is useless because of severe erosion. Another third is partly so. Before the conquest, much of Oaxaca's farmland was terraced and irrigated, not unlike the millet terraces of

an example of Oaxacan entrepreneurship

Nepal and the rice terraces of Bali. Although Oaxacans largely lost that precious knowledge, it could be relearned, and the old water channels and hillside terraces (which are still visible at many locations) could be restored.

Meanwhile, on the present land, productivity could be greatly increased. To raise corn production from the current half ton per acre to the U.S. level of two tons per acre would require mechanization, fertilizer, an irrigation water supply, and the know-how to make everything come together. At present, however, only about 25 percent of Oaxaca's farmers have access to a tractor (compared to 45 percent nationwide); very few have the money for fertilizer; only about 15 percent have access to irrigation water; and most have completed five years or less of schooling. Nevertheless, a focused, long-term government-to-people partnership, not unlike the Tennessee Valley Authority in the United States, could restore prosperity in the Oaxacan countryside.

One route to a better life for many Oaxacans has been to get out. Census figures indicate that about 40 percent of people born in Oaxaca are living and working in other parts of Mexico, the United States, or Canada. While Oaxacan people don't want to leave home, lack of local jobs forces them to. Unlike northern Mexican states close to U.S. cities filled with people who want to buy Mexican-made shoes, telephones, mops, lamp fixtures, and bicycles, Oaxaca, in the far south, is surrounded by other equally disadvantaged Mexican states. Oaxaca, with few nearby markets, attracts only a dribble of new factories and consequently generates scant new jobs. If Oaxaca had oil or gold, the story would be much different.

Although emigration has slowed Oaxaca's population growth in general, Oaxaca City is an exception. Country people seeking a better life started arriving in Oaxaca City in the 1940s when the population was about 40,000, and they're still coming. Most estimates put Oaxaca City's rising population at around 400,000. All the new neighbors make life more crowded for the average Oaxaca City family—parents with two or three children—who

© BRUCE WHIPPERMAN

typically must manage on about $10 per day. The survival mode for many such city families has been enterprise: Mom takes in laundry or starts a neighborhood store on the front porch; Dad works one or two jobs; and both Mom and Dad sell *taquitos* out front on Saturday and Sunday nights. Oaxacans, like everyone, do what they must to get by.

Tourism

Partly because of their isolation and difficult economic circumstances, Oaxaca folks are in many ways like people of yesteryear. Unlike richer people in some parts of Mexico and much of the United States, Canada, and Europe, most Oaxacans have yet to join the headlong race into the future. And therein lies Oaxaca's charm. The native women's bright traditional costumes, the venerable, monumental buildings, the stick-and-adobe thatched houses, the *vaqueros* on horseback, the oxcarts, all of which symbolize backwardness and poverty in some eyes, are a sentimentally picturesque sight to increasing numbers of visitors, both domestic and foreign.

But as a visitor, *please remember the reality behind Oaxaca's charm.* Please be tolerant, generous in your gratuities, and bargain gently. If you do, Oaxacans will welcome your presence and try even harder to make your visit worthwhile.

State and federal government planners years ago recognized Oaxaca tourism's potential benefits. Their strategy, formulated in the late 1980s, is yielding results. While tourist visitations have burgeoned over the past 20 years, Oaxaca City's proud old monuments have been restored, the central plaza blooms with old Mexico charm, village-run tourist

ECOTOURISM AND SOCIALLY RESPONSIBLE TRAVEL

Latter-day jet travel has brought droves of vacationing tourists to developing countries largely unprepared for the consequences. As the visitors' numbers swell, power grids black out, sewers overflow, and roads crack under the strain of accommodating more and larger hotels, restaurants, cars, buses, and airports.

Worse yet, armies of vacationers drive up local prices and begin to change native customs. While visions of tourists as sources of fast money replace traditions of hospitality, television wipes out folk entertainment, Coke and Pepsi substitute for fruit drinks, and prostitution and drugs flourish.

Some travelers have said enough is enough and are forming organizations to encourage visitors to travel with increased sensitivity to native people and customs. They have developed travelers' codes of ethics and guidelines that encourage visitors to stay at local-style accommodations, use local transportation, and seek alternative vacations and tours, such as language-study and cultural programs and people-to-people work projects.

A number of especially active socially responsible travel groups sponsor tours all over the world, including Oaxaca. These include organizations such as **Global Exchange, Green Tortoise, Green Globe,** and **Third Eye Travel.** They all have websites that can be accessed via Internet search engines, such as Google and Yahoo, or the umbrella website www .sociallyresponsible.com.

The related ecotourism movement promotes socially responsible tourism through the strategy of simultaneous enjoyment and enhancement of the natural environment. Oaxaca has become an ecotourism center partly because of the dedication of Oaxaca-based Ron Mader, founder and moving force behind the superb website www.planeta.com. Log on and you'll find virtually everything you need to know about Oaxaca-based ecotourism, from nature tour companies and village recycling projects to indigenous handicrafts cooperatives and international conferences.

accommodations have sprouted in the countryside, and the coastal Bahías de Huatulco resort continues to grow gradually while retaining its precious tropical forest hinterland.

This is all good news if Oaxaca's increasing tide of visitors doesn't ruin the charm that they came to enjoy in the first place. Instead, let's hope that Oaxaca's culture and natural assets will be enriched *because* of their tourist value. If so, campesinos will preserve, rather than wipe out, the local wildlife because they realize that visitors come *because* of the wildlife. For the same reason, artisans will fashion more enticing handicrafts, people will continue to dress up and dance in their bright costumes, towns will build museums and conserve their old monuments, and archaeologists will restore crumbled cities to their original glory.

People and Culture

Let a broad wooden chopping block represent the high plain, the *altiplano* of Mexico; imagine hacking at one half of it with a sharp cleaver until it is grooved and pocked. That fractured surface resembles Mexico's central highlands, where most Mexicans have lived for millennia. The most severely shattered southern end of the Mexican landscape encompasses Oaxaca, whose rugged topography has isolated its original inhabitants behind high ridges and yawning barrancas for untold generations. In their seclusion, they developed separate tongues and hierarchical societies that viewed outsiders with suspicion and hostility, as odd-speaking, barely human barbarians from across the canyon or behind the mountains. When the Spanish conquerors arrived in Oaxaca, they found a region divided among hundreds of separate subtribes, speaking 16 main languages broken into many dozens of mutually unintelligible dialects. The Oaxacans' own divisions, as much as Spanish horses and steel, led to their quick downfall. The Spanish merely added their own layers atop the existing divisions—of territory, language, caste, class, and wealth—that continue to shape both Mexico and Oaxaca to the present day.

Mesoamerica

Although Oaxacan native peoples are divided by their diverse languages and rugged topography, they nevertheless share many folk customs, not only with each other but with tens of millions of other native peoples in a broad belt, beginning around Mexico's Tropic of Cancer and stretching south and east to Honduras and El Salvador. Anthropologists call the entire region Mesoamerica, a single label reflecting its broad cultural unity. Anthropologists believe that this universal symphony of belief and practice flows from tenaciously held traditions handed down from Mexico's great preconquest civilizations. And nowhere are these folk practices more persistent than in Oaxaca, Mesoamerica's heartland. If you're curious about how most native peoples lived before Columbus and Cortés, you needn't look any farther than the Oaxaca countryside.

POPULATION

The Spanish colonial government and the Roman Catholic religion provided the glue that over 400 years has welded Mexico's fragmented population into a nation. In recent years, increased emigration, mostly to the United States, has slowed the growth of the population of both Mexico at large and Oaxaca. At about 98 million in 2000, and 112 million in 2020, Mexico's population is growing at less than one percent per year, less than half the pace of previous decades. The same is true for Oaxaca's population, which stood at about 3.4 million in the year 2000 and 3.8 million in 2010.

A growing population was not always the case in Mexico. Historians estimate that European diseases, largely measles and smallpox, probably wiped out as many as 20 million—perhaps 95 percent—of Mexico's *indígena* population within a few generations after Cortés stepped

ashore in 1519. Oaxaca's population dropped correspondingly from a pre-conquest level of about two million to a mere 150,000 by 1650. Oaxaca's native peoples, ironically, can look forward to the year 2019, five centuries after Cortés, when their population will have recovered approximately to its pre-conquest level.

By 1600, Mexico's indigenous population had dropped so low that the Spanish began to import sizable numbers of **African slaves,** whose numbers swelled to several tens of thousands by 1650. Although much of the African lineage has been absorbed into Mexico's general population, several thousand African Mexicans still maintain separate small communities in the Costa Chica, the coastal region spreading both east and west from the Oaxaca–Guerrero border.

ETHNIC GROUPS

Although by 1950 Mexico's population had recovered to 25 million, it was completely transformed. The **mestizo,** a Spanish-speaking person of mixed blood, had replaced the pure native Mexican, the *indígena* (een-DEE-hay-nah), as the typical Mexican.

This trend is not as strong in Oaxaca. Although perhaps three of four Mexicans would identify themselves as mestizo, only about half of Oaxacans probably would. Among many native Oaxacans, the label "mestizo" borders on the derogatory, despite the long colonial tradition that, by virtue of their part-European blood, mestizos were elevated to the level of *gente de razón*—people of "reason" or "right."

The typical mestizo family enjoys many of the benefits of the modern world. They typically own a modest concrete house in town. Their furnishings, simple by developed-world standards, will often include an electric refrigerator, washing machine, propane stove, television, and a car or truck. The children go to school every day, and the eldest son sometimes even looks forward to college.

Above the mestizos, a tiny **criollo** (Mexican-born, European blood) minority, a few percent of the total population, inherits the privileges—wealth, education, and political power—of their colonial Spanish ancestors.

In contrast, the typical **indígena** family lives in a small adobe or concrete-block house in a remote valley, subsisting on corn, beans, and vegetables from their small, unirrigated *milpa* (cornfield). They usually raise chickens, a few pigs, and sometimes a cow, and have electricity, but no phone or sewage connection. Their few hundred dollars a year cash income isn't enough to buy even a small tractor or refrigerator, much less a truck. The *indígenas* (or, mistakenly but commonly, Indians), by the usual measurements of income, health, or education, squat at the bottom of the social ladder.

Sizable **African Mexican** communities, or *negros,* descendants of 17th- and 18th-century African slaves, live in the Gulf states and along the Guerrero–Oaxaca coastline. Last to arrive, they experience discrimination at the hands of everyone else and are integrating very slowly into the mestizo mainstream.

SHARED OAXACAN CUSTOMS
Settlement Patterns
Oaxaca's present 570 *municipios* (townships), each with its main town and market, reflect community boundaries often dating back more than a thousand years. Although the Spanish imposed their civic pattern of church, *presidencia municipal* (city hall), and major stores and prominent residences all clustered around a central plaza, the native people still hold to their tradition of concentrating their homes in a number of barrios (neighborhoods) on the outskirts. Native peoples have sometimes stretched the Spanish pattern, reverting to their ancient **"empty town"** custom. Here, only the mestizo and criollo elite permanently live in town, while natives maintain empty in-town houses, which they occupy only during market and ceremonial occasions. Most of their days they spend by their country *milpas* (small, family-owned field).

Birth, Life, and Death
Christian baptism is everyone's first major life event; it's so important that a number of communities believe that a baby is not fully human until baptized. If an unbaptized baby dies, the parents must make haste to bury the body immediately, with little ceremony. If not, the spirit of the unbaptized baby might escape and become a *nagual* (nah-WAHL), a

TAKING PEOPLE PICTURES

Like most folks everywhere, typical Oaxacan people on the street rarely appreciate strangers taking their pictures. The easiest route to overcoming this is a local friend, guide, or even a willing interpreter-bystander who can provide an introduction. Lacking that, you'll need to be at least semi-fluent in Spanish in order to introduce yourself or say something funny to break the ice.

A sometimes useful way to go is to offer to send them a copy of their picture. If they accept, make sure that you follow through. If somehow the picture doesn't come out, at least send them a picture of you and explain what happened.

Although it's becoming less common, some people still believe that they might lose their souls if they let you take their picture. In such a case, humor again might help (or perhaps offering to let them take a picture of you first).

Markets are wonderful picture-taking places but pose challenges. Vendors are often resistant, to the point of hostility, if you try to take their picture behind their sumptuous pile of tomatoes or stack of baskets. The reasons aren't hard to understand. They're grumpy partly because sales are probably disappointing, and, since they have to stay put, they probably feel used. Buying something from them might go a long way toward soothing their feelings.

As for church picture-taking, remember churches are places of worship and not museums. Don't be rude by trying to take pictures of people at the altar. Moreover, churches are usually dark inside, and, unless you have a flash-suppress option or unusually high-speed film, your flash will disturb worshippers.

MESOAMERICAN CALENDAR

The Mixtec and Zapotec ancestors of present-day Oaxacans ordered their lives with the same calendric system as many Mesoamerican linguistic groups, including the Maya, the Aztecs (Nahuatl), the Tarascans (Purépecha), and many others. Their system combined two major calendric cycles. First, they used the agricultural calendar, tied to the seasons and derived from the approximately 365-day (more accurately 365.2422) cycle of the sun through the background of stars and constellations.

The Mesoamerican counting system was basic to the calendar's operation. The Mesoamericans didn't count by decimals, but rather used a vigesimal (20-count) system. They logically divided their agricultural year into 18 "months" of 20 days each, with a five-day short month at the year-end. A given day, for example, might be called, instead of June 11 or June 12, 5-Deer or 6-Deer and so forth.

They tracked ceremonial dates, such as birthdays, with a separate ritual or divinatory calendar of 260 days that combined 20 separate named days with numbers one through 13. Succeeding days were identified as, for example, 2-Water, 3-Monkey, 4-Dog, and so on. A given date was a unique coincidence of both calendars, which you can imagine as a pair of meshed cogwheels, turning in lockstep. As you picture the calendric cogwheels turning, at a given moment a certain cog (marked as 5-Deer, for example) in the solar calendar will always be meshing with some slot (marked as 3-Monkey, for example) in the ritual calendar, producing a unique combination of two numbers and two names (since the solar and the ritual calendars have different – 365 vs. 260 – respective totals of cogs and slots). For example, June 11, 1999, might be represented by the unique coincidence of cog 5-Deer and slot 3-Monkey; June 12, 1999, by 6-Deer and 4-Dog; June 13 by 7-Deer, 5-Water; and so on. (Note that the solar calendar progresses through named "months," such as "Deer" in the example, while the ritual calendar does not.)

In this system dates are unique, but only for a determined time period, because the entire calendric cycle repeats itself after all dual-number–dual-name combinations have occurred. This happens every 52 solar years (or, in days, 52 times 365, 18,980 days). During this time the intermeshed ritual calendar must pass through exactly the same number

malevolent animal that will harm people who cross its path.

Baptism is also the time when the web of *compadrazgo* relationships starts to influence a person's life. This begins when parents designate their *compadres* (best friends) as *padrinos* (godparents) to their newly born. As children mature, with parental consent they designate their own *compadres*. Formal ceremonies often solemnize *padrino* and *compadrazgo* bonds, which might continue through generations of loyal *padrino* and *compadre* relationships.

With babies, nursing often lasts two or three years, or at least until the next child comes along. Preschool children experience little imposed discipline except the responsibility of watching after younger siblings. Loud or disruptive children might get spanked or shunned, however. Formal schooling is usually considered so important that families often sacrifice so that children, especially boys, may attend at least six grades of school. Although children of poorer parents experience few, if any, puberty rites, richer parents often honor their children, especially girls, with a number of Catholic ceremonies, such as first communion, confirmation, blessing of their pet animals, and *quinceana* (coming out) at age 15. Among poorer populations, a girl becomes an adult with marriage, often by age 14 or 15. A boy enters manhood through either marriage or entering *servicio* (community service). He's expected to pay community assessments and perform *tequio* (communal work) service. As a young man matures, he is expected to fulfill the duties of a series of increasingly important

of days. Dividing 18,980 by its number of 260 cogs, you come up with the exactly 73 revolutions that the ritual calendar must undergo in the same 52 solar years.

Besides the Mixtecs and Zapotecs, all other Mesoamerican groups probably feared that cataclysmic events might occur at the end of each 52-year period, measured from some mythical beginning. High priests and presumably the populations at large observed solemn ceremonies, performed sacrifices, and watched the sky for auspicious portents, such as a bright overhead star, a conjunction of planets, or a comet, on the eve of their 52-year cyclical "millennium."

Knowledge of the Zapotec and Mixtec calendars is gradually being accumulated. Scholars believe that they have been used since at least the early urban stage, around 500 B.C., approximately the founding of Monte Albán. Alfonso Caso, the discoverer of Monte Albán's earliest stages, associated a common but undeciphered Monte Albán glyph, of a headdress in profile, with the solar year. For Caso, this indicated that certain personages wearing such headdresses either interpreted, read, or manipulated the calendar. The ritual calendar,

called *piye* in Zapotec, was also certainly used at Monte Albán.

As in other parts of Mesoamerica, persons were named by their birth date, such as 8-Deer, 3-Dog, or 7-Monkey, in the ritual calendar. Such name-dates occur as glyphs associated with personages recorded in stone or on the surviving hieroglyphic paper books, called *codices*, such as the Codex Nuttall.

The Mesoamericans, as the Europeans, had to apply corrections to keep the solar calendar in correspondence with the seasons. This will happen only if the year averages, over the millennia, 365.2422 days. The presently used Gregorian calendar (which was instituted by Pope Gregory VIII in 1582) corrects the solar year approximately to 365.2425 days (compared to the actual 365.2422) by omitting the leap year every three out of four centuries. Therefore, although the years 1700, 1800, and 1900 were not leap years (that is, they were permitted only 365 days, instead of 366), the year 2000 was permitted 366 days. The Mayans, scholars believe, did a little better than this; they corrected the solar calendar to 365.2420 days.

cargos (offices). If successful, at middle age he is rewarded with the rank of *principal* (elder) and admitted to the village council of elders.

Death is usually marked by 24 hours of mourning while the body lies in state at home, usually with candles, incense, and flowers. Wrapped in a *petate* (reed mat) or a coffin, the body is buried, along with the deceased's favored trinkets, and perhaps favorite food. Rituals continue periodically thereafter, especially at nine days as well one year after burial.

Marriage, Family, and Inheritance

Traditional marriage is an alliance between families, initiated by the groom's parents, often through a go-between. Girls marry as early as 14, boys at 16 or 17. The more well-to-do

marry later. Often prospective grooms and brides perform services for the other's family, sometimes even taking up temporary residence (but not sleeping with their intended) while everyone gets acquainted. The contents of the couple's dreams often carry weight in the decision to marry. Polyandry, marriage of a woman to two brothers, although sanctioned in some communities, is not common. On the other hand, well-to-do husbands, while remaining married, sometimes support additional women in separate households.

Although extended families generally encompass two, three, or four generations, couples often establish their own households after the birth of their first child. Even though both the wife's and the husband's relatives enjoy equal kinship status, couples are more likely to live near the husband's relatives. Other practices are male-weighted. Boys usually inherit more land than their sisters, and family names, nearly always Spanish, are inherited from the father. Among some Mixtecs and Mazatecs, the father's first name, interestingly, becomes his children's surname. (This is not unlike the practice among some northern Europeans—"Johnson," "Svensen," and "Mendelsohn," for example.)

Household Life

The basic house has a single room, a cleanly swept hard-dirt floor, stick-and-adobe walls, and a thatched roof. Better houses have more rooms, adobe or concrete walls, a concrete floor, and perhaps a flush toilet. Household goods hang on pegs and nails all around the walls. Overhead, rafters support grain and other heavy storage. Beds are either on floor mats or hammocks. A small altar with saint and candles occupies one corner, with the kitchen in the other. Cooking is either over open fire or on an adobe stove. Tortillas are heated on a flat adobe *comal* (griddle); beans, chilies, and stews are cooked in pottery jars *(ollas)* or metal pots over the open fire. Women grind corn by rolling with their stone *mano* on the *metate* basin. They grind chilies in their *molcajete* (mortar).

Men do the heavier outside work: clearing, burning, farming, building, repairing, plus fishing, hunting, and tending cattle and horses. If fields are far from the homestead, men sometimes take up temporary residence there during planting and harvest. Women cook, sew, wash clothes, gather fruit, flowers, and wild herbs, and tend household animals, such as pigs, goats, chickens, and turkeys. Women do most, if not all, of the marketing. Both men and women carry heavy loads.

Dress

Verbal descriptions pale in comparison to the color and excitement of a Oaxaca town fiesta or big market day. Country people, especially in remote areas, still wear the traditional cottons that blend the Spanish and native styles. Men usually wear the Spanish-origin fiber **sombrero** (literally, shade-maker) on their heads, loose white cotton shirt and pants, and leather **huaraches** on their feet. Women's dress is often more colorful. It can include a *huipil* (long, sleeveless dress), often embroidered in bright floral and animal motifs, or a handwoven **enredo** (wraparound skirt that identifies the wearer with a particular locality). A very common addition is the Spanish-tradition all-purpose woven shawl *(rebozo),* which can carry a baby, a bag of corn, or maybe even a chicken or two, as well as protect from the rain or sun. A **faja** (waist sash) and, in the winter, a **quechquémitl** (shoulder cape) complete the costume.

Making a Living

The great majority of Oaxacan indigenous people cultivate native corn, along with a number of other secondary crops, such as beans, squash, pumpkins, potatoes, chili peppers, and tomatoes. Depending upon soil and climate, they may also harvest potatoes, maguey (for alcoholic drinks), and fruits, such as mangos, papaya, chirimoya, *zapote,* and avocado. Other native crops might be cotton or maguey for *ixtle* fiber, and perhaps cocoa beans, *hule* (rubber), and chicle (chewing gum) for cash. Locally cultivated introduced cash crops include wheat, bananas, coffee, sugarcane, sesame seeds, and peanuts.

Many families or sometimes entire villages specialize in crafts, such as pottery, cloth weaving, or basketry. Although the appearance of cheap, machine-made cloth has weakened the tradition, many Oaxacan women still weave family garments with the ancestral backstrap loom. Treadle looms, introduced by the Spanish and operated by either men or women, are common around Oaxaca City. Potters, both women and men, practice their craft all over Oaxaca. Methods vary; they might confine themselves to the native hand-coiling or the Spanish-introduced potter's wheel, or use a combination of both.

Governmental and Religious Institutions

Although women exercise considerable

behind-the-scenes influence, men customarily occupy the formal community leadership positions. Minor *presidencia municipal* (city hall) positions are usually appointive; senior positions, such as *regidor* (administrator), *alcalde* (judge), and *presidente* (mayor) are often elective. In-town native homes cluster in one or more barrios on the outskirts. A town *regidor* acts as a representative agent for one or more barrios.

Paralleling such formal civil institutions are the religious, which center on the *mayordomía,* the office responsible for the oft-elaborate ceremonial trappings and yearly fiesta of the barrio's patron saint. The barrio's *regidor* or one of its *cofradias* (religious fraternities) designates the *mayordomo* for a one-year *mayordomía* responsibility. If donations for the patronal fiesta are inadequate, the *mayordomo,* often a wealthy individual, is expected to add a generous contribution of his or her own. Although this may spell temporary poverty for the *mayordomo,* the reward is great community prestige. A lifetime of such service will often assure election to the status of elder *(principal* or *anciano)* and exalted (so exalted that elders are rarely prosecuted for wrongdoing) membership in the council of elders, upon whose resources and sage advice the community relies.

RELIGION

Although the vast majority of Oaxacan *indígenas* consider themselves Catholics, their religion blends the catechism of the missionary fathers with ancient native beliefs. Deities in their age-old Mesoamerican pantheon assume thinly disguised identities among the host of Catholic saints. Besides paying obeisance at the village church altar, Oaxacan country folks also appease mountain, water, and underworld spirits with offerings and sacrifices at sacred summits, springs, and caves. Before killing a deer, for example, a hunter often asks permission of the *señor del monte* (lord, or spirit, of the mountain). Sometimes *hechiceros* (wizards) or *ancianos* (elderly) lead entire communities in cornfield ceremonies for a successful harvest, with flower offerings,

candles, food, and sacrificial turkeys and chickens.

Other old beliefs persist. Many folks, especially in remote areas, believe that *animas* (spirits) of the dead, besides the Catholic God and the saints, influence the living. Appeasement of *animas* peaks on November 1 and 2, respectively, the Day of All Saints and the **Day of the Dead,** when many families gather all night at graves of their departed, with candles, flowers, incense, and the deceased's favorite foods. People also appease saints for favors; however, if prayers are not answered, a person may also punish a saint by abusing its figurine. Sometimes evil dwarfs, the devil, or malevolent female spirits lure men to ruin. At birth, people acquire *tonos,* powerful guardian spirits, often in the guise of mountain lions, jaguars, and eagles, who, if treated with respect, might protect them throughout life. Sickness, commonly thought to be afflicted by an evil spell, loss of soul by fright, or "bad air" *(mal aire),* is treated by the incantations of a traditional village healer *(curandero* or *curandera).*

Most Oaxacans consider themselves Catholics.

© BRUCE WHIPPERMAN

THE VIRGIN OF GUADALUPE

Conversion of the *indígenas* was sparked by the vision of Juan Diego, a humble farmer. On the hill of Tepayac north of Mexico City in 1531, Juan Diego saw a brown-skinned version of the Virgin Mary enclosed in a dazzling aura of light. She told him to build a shrine in her memory on that spot, where the Aztecs had long worshipped their "earth mother," Tonantzín. Juan Diego's brown virgin told him to go to the cathedral and relay her instruction to Archbishop Zumárraga.

The archbishop, as expected, turned his nose up at Juan Diego's story. The vision returned, however, and this time Juan Diego's brown virgin realized that a miracle was necessary. She ordered him to pick some roses at the spot where she had first appeared to him (a true miracle, since roses had been previously unknown in the vicinity) and take them to the archbishop. Juan Diego wrapped the roses in his rude fiber cape, returned to the cathedral, and placed the wrapped roses at the archbishop's feet. When he opened the offering, Zumárraga gasped: imprinted on the cape was an image of the brown virgin herself – proof positive of a genuine miracle.

In the centuries since Juan Diego, the brown virgin – La Virgen Morena, or Nuestra Señora La Virgen de Guadalupe – has blended native and Catholic elements into something uniquely Mexican. In doing so, she has become the virtual patroness of Mexico, the beloved symbol of Mexico for *indígenas*, mestizos, *negros*, and criollos alike.

In the summer of 2002, Pope John Paul journeyed to Mexico to perform a historic gesture. Before millions of joyous faithful, on July 31, 2002, the frail aging pontiff elevated Juan Diego to sainthood, thus making him Latin America's first indigenous person to be so honored.

Healers employ other remedies, such as consumption or avoidance of certain foods, sucking (to remove the mysterious object causing the illness), herbs and poultices, and also modern medicine. Especially common is a steam bath in the traditional *temascal,* a permanent wood or stone structure or temporary mat-covered brush hut, which many Oaxacan households maintain individually (rather than communally).

Catholicism, spreading its doctrine of equality of all persons before God and incorporating native gods into the church rituals, eventually brought the native Mexicans into the fold. Within a hundred years of the Conquest, nearly all natives had accepted the new religion, which raised the universal God of all humankind over local tribal deities.

Every Mexican city, town, and village celebrates the cherished memory of their Virgin of Guadalupe on December 12. This celebration, however joyful, is but one of the many fiestas that Mexicans, especially the *indígenas,* rejoice in. Each village holds its local fiesta in honor of its patron saint, who is often a thinly veiled sit-in for some local pre-Cortesian deity. Themes appear Spanish—Christians vs. Moors, devils vs. priests—but the native element is strong, sometimes dominant. During Semana Santa (Holy Week) at Pinotepa Nacional in coastal Oaxaca, for example, Mixtec people, costumed as Jews, shoot arrows skyward, simultaneously reciting traditional Mixtec prayers.

LANGUAGE
Oaxacan Indigenous Languages

Linguists recognize 16 separate languages spoken in Oaxaca today. Experts identify each of them with one of five language families. North American language family names are conventionally derived by combining the names of the northernmost and southernmost languages of the group. Thus, Otomanguean, Oaxaca's most widespread language family, derives its label from Otomi, spoken northwest of Mexico City, and Mangue, spoken in southeast Mexico. All of Oaxaca's native language speakers occupy pretty much the same territories that they did at the time of the conquest. The Otomanguean, by location, moving generally west to east, are: **Amusgo, Chatino, Trique, Mixtec, Chocho, Ixcatec, Popoluca, Cuicatec, Mazatec, Chinantec,** and **Zapotec.** A language pair of eastern Oaxaca, **Mixe** (MEE-shay) and **Zoque** (SOH-kay), probably distantly related to Mayan dialects, are often lumped into a second family, the Mixe-Zoque family. Three other languages are the only representatives of their respective families. **Nahuatl** (the language of the Aztecs) of the Uto-Aztecan family; **Chontal,** of the Hokan-Coahuiltecan family; and **Huave,** of its own family, Huave.

Understanding in Oaxaca is further complicated by a proliferation of **dialects.** Mixtec speakers from Jamiltepec, on the Pacific coast, for example, do not generally comprehend the Mixtec dialect of a town, such as Tlaxiaco, across half a dozen ridges 100 miles away. The

INDIGENOUS LANGUAGES

The 2000 national census figures list populations of those over five years old who speak an indigenous Oaxacan language:

Language	Population	Percentage of Total Oaxacans	Important Centers in Oaxaca
Zapotec	377,000	13.5%	Tlacolula, Juchitán, Pochutla
Mixtec	245,000	8.8%	Tlaxiaco, Huajuapan de León, Jamiltepec
Mazatec	174,000	6.5%	Huatla de Jiménez, Jalapa de Díaz
Chinantec	108,000	3.9%	Valle Nacional, Ojatitlán
Mixe	105,000	3.8%	Ayutla, Zacatepec
Chatino	40,000	1.4%	Nopala, Juquila
Trique	15,200	.55%	Tilapa
Huave	13,700	.49%	San Mateo del Mar, San Dionisio del Mar
Cuicatec	12,000	.43%	Cuicatlán
Nahua	11,000	.39%	Salina Cruz, Tuxtepec
Zoque	5,300	.19%	San Miguel Chimalapa, Santa María Chimalapa
Amusgo	4,800	.17%	San Pedro Amusgos
Chontal	4,600	.16%	Santiago Astata
Chocho	500	.018%	Coixtlahuaca
Popoluca	500	.018%	Santiago Chazumba
Ixcatec	200	.0072%	Ixcatlán
Totals	**1,076,000**	**38.7% of all Oaxacans**	

same is true for Oaxaca's other major languages—Zapotec, Mazatec, Chinantec, and Mixe—and to a lesser degree, for the minor languages.

Few nonindigenous people, whether foreigners or Mexican, have made the intense effort required to speak and understand a Oaxacan native language. All of the Otomanguean languages, like the Chinese dialects, are **tonal.** This means that a given word takes on different meanings depending upon the pitch—low, high, rising, or falling—with which it is enunciated. Consequently, in big market towns, Spanish is often the lingua franca of buying and selling. Nevertheless, at many country markets, aware visitors notice many people, usually older folks, who speak no Spanish at all.

Please take note that the Spanish names for the Zapotec, Mixtec, Mazatec, and Chinantec languages are *Zapoteco, Mixteco, Mazateco,* and *Chinanteco,* while the respective home territories of each group are the Zapoteca, Mixteca, Mazateca, and Chinantla.

INDIGENOUS GROUPS

Although anthropologists and census takers classify them according to language groups (such as Mixtec, Zapotec, or Nahua), *indígenas* typically identify themselves as residents of a particular locality rather than by language or ethnic grouping. And although as a group they are referred to as *indígenas* (native, or aboriginal), individuals are generally made uncomfortable (or may even feel insulted) by being labeled as such.

While the mestizos are the emergent self-conscious majority class, the *indígenas* remain mostly invisible, keeping to their country hamlets, except during town market days and fiestas. Typically, they are politically conservative, socially traditional, and tied to the land. On market day, the typical *indígena* family might make the trip into town. They bag up some tomatoes, squash, or peppers, and tie up a few chickens or a pig. The rickety country bus will often be full, and the mestizo driver may wave them away, giving preference to his friends, leaving the *indígenas* to trudge stoically along the road.

Their lot, nevertheless, has been slowly improving. *Indígena* families now often have access to a local school and a clinic. Improved health has led to a large increase in their population. Official census counts, however, probably run low. *Indígenas* are traditionally suspicious of government people, and census takers, however conscientious, seldom speak the local dialect.

Recent figures nevertheless indicate that about 40 percent of Oaxacans are *indígenas*—that is, they speak one of Oaxaca's 16 native languages. Of these, about a fifth speak no Spanish at all. These fractions, moreover, are changing only gradually. Many *indígenas* prefer the old ways.

Once a year, in mid-July, thousands of indigenous people, from hundreds of ethnically distinct Oaxaca communities, converge on Oaxaca City for the **Guelaguetza** (gay-lah-GHET-sah) folk dance festival. Dazzled by the whirling color and spectacle, visitors begin to grasp the richness and sheer magnitude of Oaxacan folk tradition. Although their diversity is staggering, the simple fact is that the majority—about three of every five—of indigenous Oaxacans speak some dialect of one of two languages, Zapotec or Mixtec. Of these, the most numerous and visible are the Zapotecs, the people whom visitors encounter first in excursions from Oaxaca City.

Zapotecs

The Spanish label "Zapoteco" comes from Aztec, rather than Zapotec, tradition. The Zapotecs call themselves **Ben Zaa,** or "People of the Clouds." The Aztecs heard this as Tsapotécatl, or "Zapote People," a less-than-flattering "fruit eater" label.

Zapotec speakers, who number upward of 400,000, make up about one-third of Oaxaca's native people. The Zapotecs, moreover, are the most visible for more reasons than their numbers. In contrast to the Mixtecs, the Zapotecs, led by their kings Cosijoeza and Cosijopí, allied themselves with the Spanish right from the beginning. Nearly unique among Mexican indigenous groups, Zapotecs have figured prominently in national politics. Mexico's most beloved president, Benito Juárez, was of pure Zapotec origin. Lately, Zapotecs, including many women, have strongly influenced politics and government in the Isthmus through the **Coalición Obero, Campesino, y Estudiantil de Istmo** (Confederation of Workers, Farmers, and Students of the Isthmus, COCEI).

Zapotec influence goes much further. Although frequented by nearly all of Oaxaca's indigenous groups, a number of Oaxaca's largest native markets, such as Oaxaca City, Tlacolula, Tehuántepec, and Juchitán, are run by Zapotecs. Backcountry centers, where Zapotecs own and manage most stalls and stores, are hostile to penetration by mestizo merchants.

Individual Zapotec-speaking persons usually identify themselves more strongly with region or locale than language. (You might expect this, since the several Zapotec regional dialects are virtually separate languages, differing as much as French, Spanish, Italian, and Portuguese.) Living and work patterns, likewise, depend much more on locale—tropical coast, cool mountain, or highland valley—than

ethnicity. Oaxaca's four Zapotec regions (and their important market centers), moving clockwise from Oaxaca's center, are the central valley (Oaxaca City, Tlacolula, Ocotlán), northern Sierra (Ixtlán, Yalalag, Villa Alta), Isthmus (Tehuántepec, Juchitán), and southern Sierra (Miahuatlán, Pochutla).

Zapotec communities, moreover, are generally skillful at resolving disputes. If informal means—neighborly discussion, arbitration, or the council of elders—fail, then the argument will nearly always be resolved in the local court. Blood feuds, common in some Oaxacan indigenous communities, are rare among the Zapotecs.

Although Zapotec speakers are gradually adopting new ways, many still remember the old gods, especially the god of rain, fertility, and lightning, known as Cocijo, in the central valley. On masks you may see him as a lizard. He controls the clouds and may even release *granizo* (hail) onto a wrongdoer's crops. Some southern Zapotecs visualize the world as an island in a vast sea, watched down upon by Cocijo and his retinue-hierarchy of heavenly hosts.

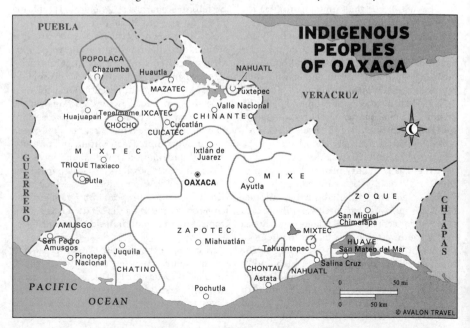

Other old beliefs persist. Influential animals—such as the *correcamino* (roadrunner), who brings good luck; the *tecolote* (small owl), who brings bad; and the *mariposa* (butterfly), who signifies death—are important actors in Zapotec fables. Besides mysterious incantations, Zapotec traditional healers, both men and women, use a wealth of herbal cures: wild garlic for high blood pressure, cloves for toothaches, *rosa de fandango* (a type of mint) for conception, *epazote morada* (a type of basil) for worms.

Although midwives traditionally preside over birthing, fathers are expected to be present to ensure a healthy baby. Pregnant women are often exhorted not to eat honey or mamey fruit. If possible, mothers are treated royally after giving birth. They traditionally remain in bed for three weeks, get plenty of massages, take *temascal* steam baths, and eat lots of chicken, chilies, and salt.

Mixtecs

It's probably not an accident that the Mixtecs' self-label, Nyu-u Sabi "People of the Rain" (or "Clouds"), has the same meaning as the Zapotecs' name for themselves. Linguists estimate that around 3,000 years ago, they were, in fact, the same people. They're not the same today, however. Their languages, although related, are mutually unintelligible, and their homelands are on opposite sides of Oaxaca.

The Mixtecs, who number around 350,000, comprise about a quarter of all Oaxacan native speakers. Nearly all live in three geographic zones in western Oaxaca: the Mixteca Baja, Mixteca Alta, and Mixteca de la Costa. The Mixteca Baja is the dry plateau-land basin of the Río Mixteco, which runs adjacent to the Puebla–Guerrero border, about 160 kilometers (100 mi) west by northwest of Oaxaca City. Major centers are Santiago Juxtlahuaca in the southwest and Huajuapan de León in the north. Bordering the Mixteca Baja to the southwest is the Mixteca Alta, a highland of pine-tufted peaks cut by lush deep canyons. Its major market centers, moving from north to south, are Tamazulapan, Teposcolula, and Tlaxiaco. Bordering the Mixteca Alta on the south is the Mixteca de la Costa, a roughly 160 square kilometers (50 by 50 miles) region of hills and valleys abutting the Guerrero border on the west and spreading southward from the foothills to the mangrove-fringed coastline. Its major centers are Pinotepa Nacional in the center and Santiago Jamiltepec to the east.

A few thousand Mixtec speakers also occupy a pair of intriguingly isolated enclaves: Cuyamecalco (near the market town of San Juan Chiquihuitlán) in the northern Sierra, and around Mixtequilla, the "Little Mixteca" just north of Tehuántepec, in the Isthmus.

Although Mixtec-speaking people have passed down a rich heritage, as a group they are now among Oaxaca's poorest. Of the Mixteca's three regional groupings, the people in the Costa are generally the best off. Santiago Jamiltepec, for example, where Mixtec-speakers compose 70 percent of the population, has many Mixtec shop owners, in contrast to upland Mixtec centers where mestizos often dominate commerce.

Exceptions notwithstanding, most Mixtecs are subsistence farmers. Agriculture is typically based on age-old slash-and-burn methods. Fields lie fallow for five years, then brush is burned, cleared, and the ground planted with corn, usually employing a *coa* (digging stick). Oxen, when they are used for plowing or hauling, are often rented. Irrigation, except near valley-bottom creeks, is not common. On the coast, the warmer climate allows more options for cash crops, such as bananas, mangos, *panela* (brown sugar from cane), cotton, and peanuts, although distribution is limited and local.

Another cash possibility that Mixtecs have not generally developed is coffee, which mestizo, Trique, and European immigrant growers harvest successfully on the Mixteca Alta's semitropical forested mountainsides, using Mixtec day labor.

Moreover, despite their proximity to rich ocean resources, very few coastal Mixtecs fish. Instead, they buy dried fish from the many African Mexicans, descendants of African slaves, whose modest houses and fields dot the coastline.

Nevertheless, the Mixtecs seem to have cornered the palm-frond weaving market. In the dry Mixteca Baja, homeland to wild forests of short palms, people gather and dry the fronds, and whenever two hands are free, everyone—father, mother, children, grandmother, grandfather—weaves them into everything, from mats and hats to toys and baskets.

Lack of good roads hinders market access all over the Mixteca. A large proportion of Mixtec homesteads lie at the end of foot trails, along which produce must be hauled by hand or burro. Even if a farmer could harvest a ton of mangos (potentially worth maybe $500) from his four trees, how could he, his wife, a baby, and two children, and three neighbors haul them five miles by trail, then 20 miles by dirt road, to some market where people have the money to buy his mangos? He tells himself that maybe he and his neighbors will get together, widen the trail and buy a used truck. Yes…someday.

Faced with such odds, instead of saving for that someday truck, many Mixtec farmers opt to accumulate prestige by fulfilling *compadrazgo* (contributing to friends) or *mayordomía* (religious festival) obligations. Although such charitable action often leads to poverty, generosity, in the Mixtec (and Mexican) mind is, after all, much preferable to parsimony.

Coastal Mixtec women enjoy an unusual degree of autonomy. Besides often handling family purse strings and doing all the marketing, they typically keep their own family names and own property independently of their husbands. For some Mixteca Alta and Mixteca Baja men, traveling to the coast is believed to be dangerous, partly for fear that some Costa Mixteca woman, through witchcraft, might steal (or disable) their penis. So, men, watch out for the women, especially around the Pinotepa Nacional market, where they often wear their best finery, which customarily includes an heirloom *pozahuanco* (wraparound skirt) of brilliant natural-dyed red cochineal and deep purple horizontal stripes. From afar, you'll easily recognize them, carrying themselves proudly, with their hat-like *jicara* (gourd bowl) tipped whimsically on their heads. Some women sell handloomed *pozahuancos* in the market. The authentic ones, by which coastal Mixtec women judge each other, sell for $150 or more.

Mazatecs

In contrast to the Zapotecs and Mixtecs, the Mazatec territory, the Mazateca, is relatively concentrated into a roughly 56- by 80-kilometer corner (35 by 50 mi) at Oaxaca's very northern tip. Mazatec villages and farms spread across two very fertile climatic zones: lush semitropical forested uplands and tropical rainforest river bottomland of the Río Papaloapan basin. Major market centers are Jalapa de Díaz and Huautla de Jiménez, both in the western highlands. Important subsidiary centers, many in the highlands around Huautla, are Cosolapa, Santa María Chilchotla, Huehuetlán, Eloxotitlán, San José Tenango, Mazatlán, Chiquihuitlán, and Ayautla. The eastern lowland has no dominant Mazatec center, partly because of the displacement of thousands of

Mazatec-speaking people, after Sunday morning mass

© BRUCE WHIPPERMAN

families during construction of the Miguel Alemán Dam. Although the Mazatecs' homeland spills over into neighboring Puebla and Veracruz states, around 170,000, or about 90 percent, live in Oaxaca.

The Mazatecs' own name for their homeland, Ampaad, which translates as the "Place Where the People Are Born," reflects their own creation myth. Legends say that the great tropical trees of Ampaad gave birth to three types of people: giants; ordinary-size humans, who became the present Mazatecs; and smaller people, who became the monkeys. The label "Mazatec" derives from the Aztec Nahuatl language and translates as "People of the Deer."

Left largely to themselves, the Mazatecs have retained many of their own traditions. Many of these they hold in common with their Chocho-, Popoloca-, and Ixcatec-speaking neighbors, whose tongues linguists sometimes lump into a Mazatec-language subfamily. Their isolation has left Mazatec speakers among the least Hispanicized of Oaxacans; as a group, as many as 40 percent speak little or no Spanish.

In 1944, government planners initiated the **Papaloapan Project,** which called for a huge hydroelectric works in the Mazatec heartland. The project's centerpiece, christened as the Miguel Alemán Dam and Reservoir in 1955, created a mammoth lake in the Mazatec lowland, drowning hundreds of thousands of acres of fertile Papaloapan basin forest and farmland. Although water and electric power were the projected benefits, the human cost turned out to be enormous. Mazatec society was torn by the forced removal of 22,000 poor Mazatec people to unfamiliar, often undesirable territory. Fortunately, the rest of the Mazatec population, largely in the western highlands around Huautla de Jiménez, remained undisrupted. Mexican authorities have since generally avoided such socially disruptive mega-projects.

Although most Mazatec families are subsistence corn, bean, and squash farmers, many cultivate fruits (mango, mamey, zapote, papaya, banana, and avocado) and coffee as cash crops on their fertile acreage. Although some farmer cooperatives have found national and international markets for their fruit and coffee, many individuals seem content to sell their produce for low local prices at Huatla de Jiménez and other Mazateca markets.

Mazatec women are renowned for their costumes and adornments. At markets and festivals especially, watch for them in their famously bright huipiles, horizontally striped in the middle, vertically on the sides. Beneath the huipil they often wear a loom-woven blue and white horizontally striped skirt. Their hair is also part of their decoration. They keep it soft and dark with a preparation called pistle, made from the core of the mamey fruit, and typically braid it with bright ribbons. Many women take pride in their home embroidery and handwoven cotton, silk, and wool, which they sometimes sell at markets.

As in the past, scarcity of priests weakens Catholic influence in the Mazateca. Priestly visits are so rare that many Mazatec campesino couples have two or three children by the time they enjoy a Catholic church wedding ceremony. When a priest does arrive, rustic churches are customarily thronged with husbands and wives bringing children for baptism. For the ceremony, they buy a small lead cross, which they hang with a bright ribbon around their child's neck. In addition to Catholic baptism, Mazatec parents sometimes ask a diviner to read the ancient tonalpohualli 260-day ritual calendar to discover their newborn's tona or tono (guardian spirit).

Mazatec people often gather for non-Catholic religious rites in fields and at sacred springs, caves, or mountains. Mazatec people especially venerate El Rabón peak, which towers over Jalapa de Díaz, and whose one-kilometer-high (0.6 mi) vertical rock wall is said never to have been scaled. There on that lofty summit live the dueñes (earth spirits), who must be appeased with prayers and copal incense for the return of lost souls. In the Mazateca lowland, brujos (witch doctors) carry out similar ceremonies at Cabeza de Tilpan cave near San José Tenango.

Traditional curandero or curandera healers

are very busy in the Mazateca. Among their weapons against illness, many include natural forest-gathered hallucinogens. Common are *hongos alucinantes* (hallucinogenic mushrooms), *semillas de la Virgen* (seeds of the Virgin) or *ololiuhqui,* and *hojas de la pastora* (leaves of the shepherdess). These, used by either the patient or the healer, will induce enlightening visions that may lead to a cure.

Chinantecs

Although Oaxaca's approximately 100,000 Chinantec-speaking people live on some of Mexico's best-watered land, the majority are poor. Inaccessibility, tropical forests that were not easily tillable, and lack of gold or silver relegated the Chinantecs to the margin during colonial times. The Chinantecs' homeland, the Chinantla, is a 112- by 64-kilometer (70 by 40 mi) region around the important market town of Valle Nacional, in northeast Oaxaca. The Chinantla's natural division into eastern lowland (Chinantla Grande) and western upland (Chinantla Pichinche) was apparent to the first Spanish arrivals in the 1520s. For the Spanish conquistadores, the Chinantecs weren't pushovers. After years of seesaw skirmishes, the Spanish mounted their final push at Yetzelalag. Chinantec legend recounts that at the battle's height the Chinantec warriors invoked their gods, who opened the mountain, allowing them to escape. Nevertheless, the Chinantecs submitted to three centuries of labor on Spanish tobacco and sugarcane plantations and cattle ranches.

Although the Spanish colonial policy of *congregación* led to the abandonment of many original town sites, the upland Chinantla retained a number of important market centers. Among the most important and colorful are Sochiapan, Tlacozintepec, Usila, Quiotepec, and San Pedro Yolox in the western uplands; Valle Nacional and San Lucas Ojitlán in the center; and Petlalpa, Lalana, and Jocotepec in the southwest lowlands.

During the 19th century, new colonists introduced coffee, pineapple, and rice agriculture, which, with the Papaloapan Project, continues in modern form today. Although the project forced painful relocations on thousands of lowland Mazatec and Chinantec peoples, it ended their isolation. Government jobs, schools, clinics, electricity, and sanitary and water systems changed life forever in the Chinantec lowlands. At the height of the disorder, swarms of protests erupted. Oaxacan bishops denounced government relocation efforts: "The *indígenas* continue to be the ones always exploited, those who must pay the price of any progress."

For good or bad, the Papaloapan Project lifted the native residents' health, literacy, and general standard of living at the expense of erasing many of their age-old ways of life. In contrast to the Chinantla highlands, few traditional markets function in the lower Chinantla. On the other hand, the government-planned communal and corporate plantations have greatly increased productivity. The Chinantla regularly produces the lion's share of Oaxaca's tobacco, rice, sugarcane, chilies, and pineapples. The workers, however, receive only a minimum of the benefits. Most profits flow to the government agencies, which control everything—seeds, planting, credit, harvesting, and marketing.

Nevertheless, tradition still rules in much of the upper Chinantla. In the minds of many Chinantec-speakers, the old fertility gods "Father and Mother Maize" still command the rain even though their prayers are Catholic. The cosmos is still a battleground between day, ruled by the young and vigorous sun, and night, ruled by the twinkling old stars. Some still believe that Creation's original people, who refused to bow down before the god-sun, were changed to monkeys and banished to the forest forever for their error. In some villages, *rayos,* powerful members of lightning cults, can still hurl lightning bolts against neighboring villages and know how to defend the home village against reverse attacks.

Mixes and Zoques

Their cultural and common Mayan linguistic linkages have led most experts to believe that the original Mixe and Zoque (MEE-shay and SOH-kay) people, together with the Popoloca of present Veracruz state, occupied a single territory. Invasions, first by the Zapotecs and Aztecs and then the Spanish, forced the present territorial divisions. The Mixes (pop. 100,000) occupy the mountainous belt that stretches about 160 kilometers (100 mi) from the central valley's eastern edge to the most easterly Mixe center, San Juan Guichicovi, several miles short of the cross-isthmus highway-rail line. Fifty-five kilometers (35 mi) farther east, Zoque territory (pop. 5,000), divided between two sprawling *ejido* grants, begins. From the Santa María Chimalapa–San Miguel Chimalapa line it spreads east, across the wild Chimalapa mountainous jungle to the Chiapas border. The few remaining Popoloca-speakers are limited to a few isolated villages in eastern Veracruz state.

Despite several costly campaigns, the Spanish force of arms never really conquered the Mixes. If they were conquered at all, it was by 16th-century Dominican missionaries who accomplished with kindness what Spanish guns and steel could not. By the end of the colonial era, they had established nine vicarages, among them Juquila Mixes, San Miguel Quetzaltepec, Asunción Puxmecatan, Ayutla, and San Juan Guichicovi, which all remain important Mixe market towns. Ayutla, closest to the central valley, is dominant.

Anthropologists generally describe Mixe traditions as "less developed" than other Oaxacan groups. They describe a "culture unsuited to the environment," as if the Mixe ways of life first flowered in fairer, more fertile lands and never completely adjusted to the cold, marginal mountainous regions where the Mixes fled in the face of foreign invasions. Such a speculation also explains the Mixes' well-known wariness and avoidance of outside contact. The Zoque, by contrast, adapted relatively easily to Spanish ways and share little of the Mixes' shyness.

Spanish attempts to congregate the Mixes into towns were only minimally successful. Mixe people largely moved back into the countryside, leaving little-used empty houses in town. Today, most live in country hamlets

clinging to mountainsides, with individual houses built on level stilt platforms.

Turbulence has marred the Mixes' recent history. In 1938, President Lázaro Cárdenas wanted to reward the Mixe people for their support of the Republic against the infamous 1865 French Intervention. He persuaded the Oaxaca legislature to award them semi-autonomous status in an all-Mixe district. However, a dispute broke out over the location of the district capital. The towns of Ayutla, Cacalotepec, and Zacatepec had their leading supporters, but Luis Rodríguez of Zacatepec was the most ruthless. While the others protested weakly, he led a four-year reign of terror—kidnapping, cattle rustling, torture, murder, and pillage—with the implicit support of Governor Vicente González. In 1943, Rodríguez cut off the feet and tongue of one prominent opponent and had another assassinated on the steps of the Government Palace in Oaxaca City. Enough was enough for Governor Sánchez Canom, who left Oaxaca City to intervene. But while he was gone, Rodríguez got him replaced. After that, Rodríguez was in complete control, murdering opponents with impunity, collecting tribute from towns and even 10 percent from religious fiestas and holding 500 prisoners in forced labor. Even after his death in 1952, his heirs tried to extend their reign until the 1970s. Despite Luis Rodríguez's notorious legacy, Zacatepec remains the Mixe district capital to the present day.

In 1972, partly in response to the trouble, Mixe people organized themselves into the grassroots social-political Federación Mixe. They soon coalesced with the already-existing local Worker's Federation of Chinantecs, Zapotecs, and Mixes and the national General Union of Workers and Farmers of Mexico (UGOCM).

Mixe and Zoque social traditions closely follow Mesoamerican patterns. Mixe religion has striking parallels to those described in the Maya sacred book, the *Popol Vuh*. Their legends say that the Mixe god Kondoy was hatched from an egg, grew rapidly, and traveled, battling Aztec armies. He returned and arranged the world in the Mixe image, then retired to the Mixe sacred mountain, Zempoaltepetl, where he still lives.

Belief in the *nagual* persists among the Mixes. If an unbaptized baby dies, the parents must make haste to bury the body immediately, with little ceremony. If not, the spirit of the unbaptized baby might escape and become a *nagual,* a malevolent animal that will harm people who cross its path. Sometimes the *nagual* takes human form as a witch that can transform itself into an animal or other scary form and cause general mischief and illness by infusing some type of object into the victim's body. Traditional healers combine a number of remedies, such as *temascal* steam bathing, rubbing with herbs, prayers, sucking, and vision-inducing plants, to remove such infusions.

Chatinos

The southern Sierra country of the nearly 40,000 strong Chatinos is a 3,072-square-kilometer (1,200 sq. mi) enclave surrounded by Mixtecs on the west, Zapotecs on the north and east, and mestizos and African Mexicans on the south coast. Their language, part of the Zapotec subfamily, resembles Sierra Zapotec. Chatino market centers, besides the central and dominant Santa Catarina Juquila, are Panixtlahuaca, San Juan Quiahije, San Pedro Juchatengo, Nopala, and Zacatepec. Besides its commercial and political influence, Santa Catarina Juquila is a major pilgrimage center, especially for the hundreds of thousands of faithful who arrive on December 8 to honor their beloved Virgin of Juquila.

Most Chatino families are subsistence farmers; Zapotec and mestizo traders dominate commerce in the market centers. In addition to the customary corn, beans, and squash, farmers also cultivate coffee, either as day laborers or on their own land, in which case they sell the surplus for cash at the market.

Amusgos

The approximately 48- by 48-kilometer (30 by 30 mi) Amusgo territory straddles the Oaxaca–Guerrero border. Only about 5,000 of 40,000 Amusgo speakers live in Oaxaca, around the small centers of Cacahuatepec and San Pedro Amusgos, while the remainder live on the Guerrero side, near the centers of Ometepec, Xochistlahuaca, and Tlacoachistlahuaca.

Linguists reckon that the Amusgo language, a member of the Mixtec language subfamily, separated from Mixtec between 2000 and 1000 B.C. Around A.D. 1000, the Amusgos came under the domination of the strong coastal Mixtec kingdom of Tututepec. In 1457 they were conquered by the Aztecs and, not long after, by the Spanish in the 1520s. Decimation of the Amusgo population by disease during the 16th century led to the importation of African slave labor, whose descendants, known locally as *negros* or *costeños,* live along the Guerrero–Oaxaca coastline.

Although the Amusgo population eventually recovered, many of the old colonial-era haciendas remained intact until modern times. The Amusgos, isolated from the mainstream of modern Mexican life, retain their age-old corn-bean-squash farming tradition. Moreover, they have received little attention from anthropologists or archaeologists, although several likely archaeological mounds exist near Amusgo villages.

Amusgo women are nevertheless famous for their hand-embroidered *huipiles,* whose colorful floral and animal designs fetch willing customers in Oaxaca tourist centers. Even better, Amusgo women often wear their *huipiles,* appearing as heavenly visions of spring on dusty small-town side streets.

Triques

About 80 kilometers (50 mi) farther north from the Amusgo territory, about 15,000 Trique (TREE-kay) people live in their 32- by 24-kilometer (20 by 15 mi) highland pocket of the Mixteca Alta. You'll see plenty of them in the Juxtlahuaca town market—especially Trique women—selling their brilliant red-striped wool *huipiles* in the middle of the town square. Long ago, the Trique fled into the mountain vastness, from first Mixtec, then Aztec, and finally Spanish, invaders. Some of their main centers are San Isidro Chicahuaxtla, San Juan Copala, and Tilapa, all south of Juxtlahuaca and north of Putla de Guerrero.

The Trique have only grudgingly accepted outside authority. Rebellions broke out often during the colonial era and later. In 1843 Trique forces rebelled against state and federal authorities, who needed five years to jail and execute the responsible leaders. Subsequently, during the later 19th and 20th centuries, coffee became a major Trique product and coffee beans became their money, which traders turned into alcohol and guns. Rebellion, which again required federal forces to suppress, broke out in Copala in 1956. The federal garrison remains in Copala to the present day.

Only at Chicahuaxtla, in the high Mixteca country (just off of Hwy. 125, about 40 km/25 mi west of Tlaxiaco), did Christianity have much effect. This was due to the compassionate persuasion of Father Gonzales Lucero hundreds of years ago. Consequently, much of the Trique's folklore survives to the present day. An oft-told creation myth describes the sun and the moon, gods who once lived in a *calabaza* (calabash), but who broke out and rode a rabbit and a cat into the heavens to light the world. Around March 25, traditional *curanderos* lead services to appease the old gods at a sacred cave near Copala, about 20 kilometers (13 mi) down the highway south of Juxtlahuaca. They sacrifice a lamb and a goat while the gathered crowd offers incense and flowers.

Chochos, Ixcatecs, and Popolocas

Emigration and Spanish literacy are fast reducing the number of speakers of Chocho, Ixcatec, and Popoluca, three related tongues of the dry canyonlands of northwest Oaxaca. Of the three, the Chocho people are dominant in their extensive homeland around Coixtlahuaca and subsidiary centers of Tequixtepec and Tepelmeme. If you're going to hear any of the Chocho language, it will probably be in the market at Tepelmeme de Morelos, just off the

Oaxaca–Puebla expressway about 24 kilometers (15 mi) north of Coixtlahuaca.

Defeated by the Mixtecs in the 1300s and the Aztecs a hundred years later, the Chochos were again subdued by Spanish conquistadores Orozco and Alvarado in 1522 and later converted by Dominican Father Fermín Abrego. Coixtlahuaca was a thriving Chocho and Ixcatec market until around 1900, but loss of topsoil to erosion has forced many families to emigrate.

If you're going to hear any Ixcatec at all, it will be in Ixcatlán, the sole Ixcatec *municipio*, accessible by dirt road about 32 kilometers (20 mi) northeast from Coixtlahuaca. The same is approximately true of Popoloca, whose few remaining speakers in Oaxaca live in the sliver of territory by the Puebla border, around Santiago Chazumba on Highway 125.

Cuicatecs

The Cuicatec language, by contrast, is holding its own, due to the isolation and richness of the homeland of the Cuicatecos ("People of Song"). About 15,000 Cuicatec people inhabit their present territory, mainly the *municipios* of Concepción Pápalo, San Juan Tepeuxila, San Pedro Teutila, and Santiago Nacaltepec in the mountains east of district capital Cuicatlán and south of the Río Santo Domingo canyon.

Archaeological digs around Concepción Pápalo and other sites reveal Toltec influences, hinting that the Cuicatec lands may have been a haven for some of the refugees from the fall of Tula, the Toltec capital in the north, around A.D. 1060.

Historians believe that Cuicatec speakers numbered about 60,000 before the conquest. They were defeated by both the Aztecs, around 1456, and Spanish soldiers, commanded by conquistador Martín Mezquita, in 1526. Nevertheless, during the colonial era, the Cuicatecs resisted both Catholic conversion and forced plantation labor by fleeing into the mountains, where they remain today. Although the Dominicans established a church in Pápalo in 1630 and tried to convert them, Catholic influence remains weak. The old gods, notably *jáiko,* the lord of their sacred mountain, Cerro

Cheve, still live on in the hearts and minds of many Cuicatec people.

Today, you might hear some Cuicatec spoken at the busy market at Cuicatlán, where Cuicatec women come down from the mountains to sell their highland handicrafts: wool serapes and jackets, flower- and animal-motif embroidered *huipiles,* palm-leaf sombreros, *petates* (mats), and *cestas* (baskets).

Cuicatec people also earn cash collectively from the concession in which they allow the paper mill in Tuxtepec to harvest some of their forest trees. The money goes to finance community projects.

Huaves

The Isthmus territory of the Huave people encompasses the shoreline of the big tidal Lagunas Superior, Inferior, and the Mar Muerto. About 15,000 Huave-speaking people live there, notably around the villages of San Mateo del Mar, Santa María del Mar, San Dionisio del Mar, and San Francisco del Mar.

The Huave language, not clearly identified with any other language family, is generally classified in a family of its own. This is supported by studies by colonial historians, indicating that the Huave may have migrated from the Nicaraguan Pacific coast and settled around present-day Jalapa del Marqués on the Isthmus. The more-numerous Zapotecs, invading around 1375, forced them to the edges of the lagoons, where they now live.

Generally ignored and neglected by everyone, the Huaves hold on to many pre-conquest beliefs. In the absence of Catholic priests, native *curanderos* practice thinly veiled pagan rites in some village churches.

Although they subsist mainly on corn, beans, chilies, vegetables, and occasional meat, Huave-speaking people earn cash from their fish catches. Men sell fresh fish to wholesalers who arrive afternoons at the shoreline villages, while women sell the surplus as dried fish at Salina Cruz, Tehuántepec, and Juchitán markets.

Nahuas

Along the coast, in a 32-kilometer (20 mi) strip west of Salina Cruz and with the small town of Morro de Mazatán at its center, lies an enclave of Nahua (Nahuatl- or Aztec-speaking people). Besides this small region, several thousand more Nahuatl speakers live in two other small Oaxaca enclaves in the north, one around Tuxtepec and the other next to the Puebla border, wedged between Mazatec, Ixcatec, Chocho, and Popoluca territories. Such Nahuatl enclaves are probably remnants of early colonies established by the Aztec emperors after their armed expansion into Oaxaca in the 1400s.

Chontals

Finally, 30–40 miles farther west and north lies the Chontal (sometimes known as "Tequistlatec") territory. The Chontals are most visible on the coast, at Santiago Astata and San Pedro Huamelula. Today, about 25,000 speakers of Chontal, a language of the Hokan language family (widespread, from the north Gulf Coast to Central America), live in their approximately 2,560-square-kilometer (1,000 sq. mi) domain.

The Chontals are among the least modernized of Oaxaca indigenous groups. They have always tenaciously resisted invasion (though many in the zone due west of Tequisistlán have adopted the Zapotec language). Although many live near the coast, they do little fishing. They live mostly by corn-based subsistence farming, emigrating to the Isthmus or elsewhere for cash employment.

Relatively unaffected by Catholicism, their traditions remain strong. A popular fable is of their folk-hero King Fane Kansini, whom, legend says, an elderly couple hatched as an infant from an egg that they had found. The old couple soon discovered that the infant had supernatural powers. As he matured, Fane Kansini acquired the burning desire to save his people from the Zapotecs. He invented body armor and a wondrous new kind of arrow, which he used to defeat the Zapotec king in battle and thus save the Chontal people from annihilation. The Chontal-Zapotec mutual enmity continues to the present time.

Festivals and Events

Mexicans love a party. Urban families watch the calendar for midweek national holidays that create a *puente* (bridge) to the weekend and allow them to squeeze in a three- to five-day mini-vacation. Visitors should likewise watch the calendar. Such holidays (especially Christmas and Semana Santa/pre-Easter week) mean packed buses, roads, and hotels, especially around Oaxaca's beach resorts.

Country people, on the other hand, await their local saint's day or holy day. The name of the locality often provides the clue. For example, in Santa Cruz Papalutla, just east of Oaxaca City, expect a celebration on May 3, El Día de la Santa Cruz (Day of the Holy Cross). People dress up in their traditional best, sell their wares and produce in a street fair, join a procession, get tipsy, and dance in the plaza.

It's worth noting that Oaxaca, unique among Mexican states, has no bullfights. Benito Juárez, as governor during the 1850s, was instrumental in outlawing bullfights in Oaxaca. In his honor, they remain banned.

The following calendar lists national and notable Oaxacan holidays and festivals. For many more details, see the destinations cited. Call ahead to confirm dates. If you happen to be where one of these is going on, get out of your car or bus and join in!

January

- January 1: **¡Feliz Año Nuevo!** (New Year's Day; national holiday), especially in Santiago Jamiltepec and Teotitlán del Valle.

- January 6: **Día de los Reyes** (Day of the Kings), especially in Santos Reyes Nopala—traditional gift exchange; townsfolk perform favorite traditional dances.

- January 13–17: **Fiesta del Dulce Nombre de Jesús** (Festival of the Sweet Name of Jesus), in Santa Ana del Valle, Tlacolula, and Zimatlán—troupes perform many traditional dances, including the Dance of the Feathers.

- January 17: **Día de San Antonio Abad**—decorating and blessing animals.

- January 20–21: **Fiesta de San Sebastián,** especially in San Pedro and San Pablo Tequixtepec, Pinotepa Don Luis, and Jalapa de Díaz.

- January 25: **Fiesta del Apóstol de San Pablo** (Festival of Apostle St. Paul), in Mitla—masses, processions, feast, fireworks, *jaripeo* (bull roping and riding), and dancing.

February

- February 2: **Día de Candelaria,** especially in Tututepec—plants, seeds, and candles blessed; procession and bullfights.

- February 5: **Constitution Day** (national holiday)—commemorates the constitutions of 1857 and 1917.

- February 24: **Flag Day** (national holiday).

- February: During the four days before Ash Wednesday (46 days before Easter Sunday), usually in late February, many towns, especially San Juan Colorado, Putla, Pinotepa Don Luis, and Juxtlahuaca, celebrate **Carnaval** with Mardi Gras–style extravaganzas.

- February–March: Celebrations continue during Cuaresma (Lent), especially in Santiago Jamiltepec and Pinotepa Nacional, for several weeks.

March

- Second Friday of Lent (nine days after Ash Wednesday): **Fiesta del Señor del Perdón** (Festival of the Lord of Forgiveness), in San Pedro and San Pablo Tequixtepec—big pilgrimage festival.

- Second Friday of Lent: **Fiesta del Señor de Piedad,** in Santiago Astata.

- Fourth Friday of Lent (23 days after Ash Wednesday): **Fiesta del Señor de Misericordias,** in Santa María Huatulco.

- Fourth Friday before Easter Sunday: **Fiesta of Jesus the Nazarene,** in Huaxpaltepec.

- Week before Palm Sunday: **Week of Ramos,** especially in Jamiltepec.

- Friday before Good Friday (11 days before Easter Sunday): **Feria Comercial** (Commercial Fair), in Huautla de Jiménez—many traditional folk dances.

- March 18–19: **Fiesta de San José,** in Valle Nacional; on the weekend closest to March 10 in San José El Mogote.

- March 21: **Birthday of Benito Juárez,** the "Hero of the Americas" (national holiday), especially in Benito Juárez's birthplace, Guelatao—a whirl of traditional dances.

- March 21–31: **Juegos Florales** (Flower Games), in Oaxaca City.

April

- April: **Semana Santa** (pre-Easter Holy Week, culminating in Domingo Santa—Easter—national holiday), in many locales, especially San Juan Colorado, Pinotepa Don Luis, and Pinotepa Nacional.

- Good Friday, two days before Easter Sunday: **Fiesta de la Santa Cruz de Huatulco** (Festival of the Holy Cross of Huatulco).

- Saturday before Easter Sunday: **Sábado de Gloria** in San Miguel Tequixtepec—people, called *mecos,* don masks and do a kind of adult trick or treat for the occasion.

- First week in April: **Feria del Mango** (Mango Fair), in Tapanatepec.

- April 26–29: **Fiesta de San Pedro Mártir de Verona,** in San Pedro Yucunama.

May

- May 1: **Labor Day** (national holiday).

- May 3: **Fiesta de la Santa Cruz** (Festival of the Holy Cross), in many places, especially Salina Cruz, Tehuántepec, and Unión Hidalgo.

- May 5: **Cinco de Mayo** (national holiday)—celebration of the defeat of the French at Puebla in 1862.

- May 10: **Mothers' Day** (national holiday).

- May 10–12: **Fiesta of the Coronation of the Virgin of the Rosary.**

- May 11–16: **Fiesta de San Isidro Labrador** (Festival of St. Isidor the Farmer), in Ixcatlán.

- May 15–30: **Velas de San Vicente Ferrer,** in Juchitán.

June

- June 2–3: **Fiesta de San Antonio de Padua,** in Jalapa de Díaz.

- June 23–24: **Fiesta de San Juan Bautista** (Festival of St. John the Baptist), especially in Tuxtepec, Valle Nacional, Cuicatlán, and Coixtlahuaca.

- June 25: **Fiesta de San Pedro,** in Santa María Huamelula; June 27–30 in San Pedro Tapanatepec; June 29 in San Pedro Amusgos; June 26–30 in Unión Hidalgo.

- June 29: **Fiesta de San Pablo y San Pedro** (Festival of St. Paul and St. Peter); June 21–28 in San Pedro Pochutla.

July

- July 1–15: **Fiesta of the Precious Blood of Christ,** in Teotitlán del Valle—featuring the Danza de la Pluma (Dance of the Feather).

- Usually on the two Mondays following July 16: **Lunes de Cerro** or **Guelaguetza** in Oaxaca City—all-Oaxaca dance extravaganza.

- July 20–24: **Fiesta de Santa María Magdalena** (Festival of St. Mary Magdalene), in Tequisistlán.

- July 20–30: **Fiesta de Santiago Apóstol** (Festival of St. James the Apostle), in Santiago Laollaga; July 22–27 in Suchilquitongo; July 23–26 in Jamiltepec and in Pinotepa Nacional; and July 25 in Juxtlahuaca.

August

- August 1–5: **Fiesta de Santo Domingo de Guzmán,** in Unión Hidalgo.

- August 13–18: **Fiesta del Barrio de Santa María Relatoca,** in Tehuántepec.

- August 14: **Fiesta de la Virgen de la Asunción** (Festival of the Virgin of the Assumption), in Tlaxiaco; August 15 in Nochixtlán; August 13–16 in Huazolotitlán.

- August 23–24: **Fiesta de San Bartolomé,** in San Bartolo Tuxtepec; August 24–27 in San Bartolo Coyotepec.

- August 26–September 2: **Fiesta de Santa Rosa de Lima,** in Salina Cruz; August 28 in Ojitlán.

- August 31–September 11: **Fiesta Laborio,** in Tehuántepec.

September

- September 7–8: **Fiesta de la Virgen de La Natividad,** in Huautla de Jiménez.

- September 7–9: **Fiesta del Señor de La Natividad** (Festival of the Lord of the Nativity), in Teotitlán del Valle.

- September 11: **Fiesta de la Virgen de los Remedios,** in Jamiltepec.

- September 14: **Charro Day** (Cowboy Day), all over Mexico—rodeos.

- September 15–16: **Independence Day** (national holiday)—mayors everywhere reenact Father Hidalgo's 1810 Grito de Dolores from city hall balconies on the night of September 15.

- September 21: **Fiesta of San Mateo,** in Calpulalpan.

- September 23–30: **Fiesta de la Preciosa Sangre de Cristo** (Festival of the Precious Blood of Christ), in Tlacochahuaya—eight days of processions, dances, fireworks, and food.

- September 27–29: **Fiesta de San Miguel,** in San Miguel Tequixtepec and Teotitlán del

Camino—highlights include traditional dances, such as the Cristianos y Moros (Christians and Moors).

October

- October 1–2: **Fiesta de San Miguel Arcangel,** in Puerto Ángel.

- First Sunday in October: **Fiesta de la Virgen del Rosario** (Festival of the Virgin of the Rosary), in San Pedro Amusgos.

- October 3–5: **Fiesta de San Francisco Asis,** in Salina Cruz.

- October 6–8: **Fiesta de San Dionisio,** in San Dionisio del Mar—pilgrimage.

- Second Sunday in October: **Fiesta del Santo Cristo de Tlacolula** (Festival of the Holy Christ of Tlacolula), in Tlacolula.

- Second Monday in October: **Fiesta de los Lunes del Tule,** in Santa María del Tule—locals in costume celebrate with rites, folk dances, and feats of horsemanship beneath the boughs of their beloved great cypress tree.

- Third Sunday in October: **Fiesta de Octubre,** in Tlaxiaco—includes fireworks, basketball and *pelota mixteca* (traditional ball game) tournaments, and popular dances.

- October 12: **Día de la Raza** (Columbus Day)—national holiday that commemorates the union of the races.

November

- November: **Fiestas de Noviembre,** in Puerto Escondido—features the big folk dance festival **Fiesta Costéño.**

- November 1: **Día de Todos Santos** (All Saints Day)—in honor of the souls of children; the departed descend from heaven to eat sugar skeletons, skulls, and treats on family altars.

- November 2: **Día de los Muertos** (Day of the Dead), especially in Tuxtepec and Cacahuatepec—in honor of ancestors; families visit cemeteries and decorate graves with flowers and favorite foods of the deceased.

Revolution Day, November 20, is an all-Mexico celebration.

- November 11–16: **Fiesta de San Diego,** in Salina Cruz.

- November 13: **Fiesta de San Marcos,** in San Marcos Tlapazola (tourist Yu'u town in the Valley of Oaxaca).

- November 20: **Revolution Day** (national holiday)—anniversary of the revolution of 1910–1917.

- November 22: **Fiesta de Santa Cecilia,** in Unión Hidalgo.

- November 25: **Fiesta de Santa Catarina,** in Santa Catarina Ixtepeji.

- November 29: **Fiesta de San Andrés,** in San Juan Colorado.

December

- December 1: **Inauguration Day**—national government changes hands every six years: 2006, 2012, 2018 . . .

- December 8: **Día de la Purísima Concepción** (Day of the Immaculate Conception).

- December 8: **Fiesta de la Vírgen de la Soledad,** in Oaxaca and Juxtlahuaca.

- Late November–December 8: **Fiesta de la Virgen de Juquila,** in Santa Catarina Juquila—Oaxaca's biggest fiesta.

- December 8–11: **Fiesta de Nuestra Señora de la Concepción,** in Santa María Huatulco.

- December 12: **Día de Nuestra Señora de Guadalupe** (Festival of the Virgin of Guadalupe), nationwide—processions, music, and dancing honoring the patroness of Mexico.

- December 16–18: **Fiesta de la Virgen de la Soledad,** in Oaxaca City.

- December 16–24: **Christmas Week**—week of *posadas* and piñatas, with midnight mass on Christmas Eve.

- December 19–22: **Fiesta de Santo Tomás Apóstol,** in Ixtlán de Juárez.

- December 23: **Fiesta de los Rábanos** (Festival of the Radishes), in Oaxaca City.
- December 24: **Nochebuena** (Christmas Eve), in Oaxaca City and Yucunama.
- December 25: **¡Feliz Navidad!** (Christmas Day; national holiday)—Christmas trees and gift exchange.
- December 26: **Vela Tehuántepec,** in Tehuántepec—everyone in town dances to the lovely melody of the *Sandunga*.
- December 31: **New Year's Eve.**

Arts and Crafts

Oaxaca abounds with attractive, reasonably priced handicrafts. A sizable fraction of Oaxacan families still depend upon homespun items—clothing, utensils, furniture, native herbal remedies, religious offerings, adornments, toys, and musical instruments. Many such traditions reach back thousands of years, to the beginnings of Mesoamerican civilization. The accumulated knowledge of manifold generations of artisans has in many instances resulted in finery so prized that whole villages devote themselves to the manufacture of a certain class of goods.

Shops and markets in Oaxaca City and the Valley of Oaxaca towns of Teotitlán del Valle, Santa Ana del Valle, Tlacolula, Mitla, San Bartolo Coyotepec, San Martín Tilcajete, Santo Tomás Jalieza, Ocotlán, Arrazola, and Atzompa are Oaxaca's most renowned sources of handicrafts. And, although most crafts are not made in the coastal resorts of Huatulco and Puerto Escondido, each has several good private handicrafts stores and a number of crafts markets where local folks maintain stalls stuffed with their homemade goods. Moreover, the rich cornucopia of crafts from other Mexican centers, such as the neighboring state of Guerrero, the Lake Pátzcuaro region of Michoacán, and around Guadalajara, spills over to Oaxaca.

Handicrafts (*artesanías,* ar-tay-sah-NEE-ahs) shoppers who venture away from the Oaxaca City center and the coastal tourist enclaves to the source villages and towns will most likely benefit from lower prices, wider choices, and, most importantly, the privilege of meeting the artisans themselves. There, perhaps in a patio shop on a dusty Teotitlán del Valle side street or an Arrazola family patio, you might encounter the people and perhaps view the painstaking processes by which they fashion humble materials—clay, wool, cotton, wood, metal, straw, leaves, bark, paper, leather—into irresistible works of art.

Bargaining

Bargaining comes with the territory in Mexico and needn't be a hassle. On the contrary, if done with humor and moderation, bargaining can be an enjoyable path to encountering Mexican people and gaining their respect, and even friendship. The local crafts market is where bargaining is most intense. For starters, try offering half the asking price. From there on, it's all psychology: You have to content yourself with not having to have the item. Otherwise, you're sunk; the vendor will probably sense your need and stand fast. After a few minutes of good-humored bantering, ask for *el último precio* (the final price), in which, if it's close, you may have a bargain.

BASKETRY AND WOVEN CRAFTS

Weaving straw, leaves, and reeds is among the oldest of Oaxacan crafts traditions. Mat- and basket-weaving methods and designs go back as far as 5,000 years and are still used today.

The drier regions of Oaxaca are sources of fronds from the dwarf palms that populate the hillsides. In the Mixteca, in places such as Huajuapan de León and Coixtlahuaca and the east side of the Valley of Oaxaca around Tlacolula, you might see people sitting on a doorstep or at a bus stop or even walking down the street while weaving a **petate** (mat) or **tenate** (tumpline basket) of creamy white palm leaf, prized for its soft, pliable texture. All over Oaxaca, nearly everyone uses *petates,* from vacationers, for stretching out on the beach, to local folks, for keeping tortillas warm and shielding babies from the sun. *Tenates* have been raised to nearly a fine art in a number of Oaxaca localities, such as San Luis Amatlán, near Ejutla in the southern Valley of Oaxaca. There, craftspeople interweave dyed fibers with the natural palm, creating attractive, sensitively executed geometric designs.

Carrizo, a bamboo-like reed that grows on stream banks all over Oaxaca state, is the source of stronger, more rigid baskets, usually called *canastas* when they have handles, *tenates* when they don't. Well-known Valley of Oaxaca sources are San Juan Guelavía and Magdalena Teitipac, on the east side, and Santa Ana Zegache near Ocotlán in the south. Familiar variations include the prized *tenate para tortillas,* round at the top and tapering to square at the base, and *cajas para pájaros* (birdcages), sometimes fashioned in two, three, or four levels.

A third important weaving fiber in Oaxaca is **ixtle,** the dried strands from the leaves of maguey and related agave-family plants. Artisans all over Oaxaca craft ixtle into useful items, such as ropes for pulling, string bags for carrying, and hammocks for relaxing.

CLOTHING AND EMBROIDERY

Although *traje* (ancestral tribal dress) has become uncommon in Oaxaca City, significant numbers of Oaxacan native women make and wear *traje,* especially in the Mazateca, Chinantla, and Zapotec Sierra in the north, the Isthmus in the southeast, the coastal Mixteca in the southwest, and the Trique in the Mixteca Alta in the west.

The most common *traje* garment is the **huipil,** a full, square-shouldered, short- to midsleeved dress, often hand-embroidered with animal and floral designs and embellished with ribbons. Probably the most popular Oaxaca

hand-embroidered *huipiles,* from San Pedro Amusgos

© BRUCE WHIPPERMAN

huipiles are the captivating designs from San Pedro de Amusgos (Amusgo tribe; white cotton embroidered with abstract colored animal and floral motifs). Others nearly as prized include the Trique styles from around San Andrés Chicahuaxtla (white cotton, richly embroidered red stripes, interwoven with green, blue, and yellow, and hung with colored ribbons); Mazatec, from Huautla de Jiménez (white cotton with bright flowers embroidered in multiple panels, crossed by horizontal and vertical purple and magenta silk ribbons); and Isthmus Zapotec, from Tehuántepec (brightly colored cotton densely embroidered with either geometric designs or a field of flamboyant, multicolored flowers).

Oaxaca shops and stalls also sell other, less common types of *traje*. These include the **quechquémitl** (shoulder cape), often made of wool and worn as an overgarment in winter, and the **enredo,** a full-length skirt that wraps around the waist and legs like a Hawaiian sarong.

Mixtec women in Oaxaca's warm southwest coastal region around Pinotepa Nacional commonly wear the *enredo,* known locally as the **pozahuanco** (poh-sah-WAHN-koh), below the waist and, when at home, go barebreasted. When wearing their *pozahuancos* in public, they usually tie a **mandil,** a wide apron, around their front side.

Women weave the most prized *pozahuancos* using cotton thread dyed a light purple with secretions of tidepool-harvested snails *(Purpura patula pansa)* and silk dyed deep red with cochineal, an extract from the dried bodies of a locally cultivated scale insect, *Dactylopius coccus.* On a typical day, two or three women will be selling handmade *pozahuancos* at the Pinotepa Nacional market.

Ropa Típica
Colonial-era Spanish styles have blended with native *traje,* producing a wider class of dress, known generally as *ropa típica.* Lovely embroidered *blusas* (blouses), *rebozos* (shawls), and *vestidos* (dresses) fill shop racks and market stalls all over Oaxaca. Among the most popular is the so-called **Oaxaca wedding dress,** made of cotton with a crochet-trimmed riot of diminutive flowers hand-stitched about the neck and yoke. Some of the finest examples are made in San Antonino Castillo Velasco, just north of Ocotlán on the Valley of Oaxaca's south side.

In contrast to women, only a small fraction of Oaxacan men—members of remote groups, such as mountain Mazatec and Chinantecs in the north, the Mixes in the east, and rural Chatinos and Amusgos in the southwest—wear *traje.* Nevertheless, shops offer some fine men's *ropa típica,* such as wool jackets and serapes for the highlands or winter wear, and *guayaberas,* hip-length pleated tropical dress shirts.

Fine *bordado* (embroidery) embellishes much traditional Oaxacan clothing, *manteles* (tablecloths), and *servilletas* (napkins). The women are the ones who define the art of embroidery. Although some work is still handmade at home, cheaper machine-made factory lace and needlework is more commonly available in shops.

Among the most renowned handmade example is the embroidery of Santo Tomás Jalieza, the "town of belts" *(cinturones),* in the Oaxaca central valley south of San Bartolo Coyotepec. Although best known for their attractive embroidered cloth and leather belts, the townsfolk have adapted their colorful designs to clothing, purses, bags, and much more.

LEATHER
Some Oaxaca shops offer selections of locally produced huaraches from around Miahuatlán in the south valley and Yalalag, north in the Sierra Juárez. Shops import most other leather goods from other Mexican centers, such as Guadalajara and León. For unique and custom-designed articles you'll probably have to confine your shopping to the expensive tourist resort shops. For the more usual though still attractive leather items, such as purses, wallets, belts, coats, and boots, veteran shoppers go to Mercado Juárez or Mercado de Artesanías in Oaxaca City.

GLASS AND STONEWORK
Glass manufacture, unknown in pre-Columbian times, was introduced by the Spanish.

Today factories scattered all over Mexico turn out mountains of **burbuja** (boor-BOO-hah), bubbled-glass tumblers, goblets, plates, and pitchers, usually in blue, yellow, green, or red.

Artisans work stone, mostly near sources of supply. Puebla and Tequisistlán (in the Oaxaca Isthmus) are Mexico's main sources of decorative **onyx** (*onix,* OH-neeks). Factory shops turn out the galaxy of mostly roughhewn, cream-colored items, from animal charms and chess pieces to beads and desk sets, which you'll see on some Oaxaca City curio shop shelves.

Cantera, a volcanic tufa stone, occurs in pastel shades from pink to green and is quarried in several locations in the Valley of Oaxaca. The most preferred is the light jade-green *cantera* from Magdalena Etla, northwest of Oaxaca City. It has replaced the original but exhausted green *cantera* source that supplied stone for most of Oaxaca City's original buildings. An open-air *cantera* workshop, with many examples of expertly sculptured *cantera* (by Hwy. 190 in Suchilquitongo, at the Valley of Oaxaca's northeast corner), welcomes visitors.

For a keepsake from a truly ancient Oaxacan tradition, don't forget the hollowed-out stone *metate* (may-TAH-tay, corn-grinding basin) and the three-legged *molcajete* (mohl-kah-HAY-tay), a mortar for grinding chilies. Most examples you'll see in Oaxaca are from Teitipac, in the west valley near Tlacolula (where you'll most likely see for-sale examples during the big Sunday market).

JEWELRY

Gold and silver were once the basis for Mexico's wealth. Her Spanish conquerors plundered a mountain of gold—ritual offerings, necklaces, pendants, rings, plates—masterfully crafted by a legion of indigenous jewelers. Unfortunately, much of that native tradition was lost as the colonial Spanish denied Mexicans access to precious metals and introduced Spanish methods. Nevertheless, a small native gold-working tradition survived the dislocations of the 1810–1821 War of Independence and the 1910–1917 Revolution. Meanwhile, silver crafting, moribund during the 1800s, was revived in Taxco,

Guerrero, during the 1920s, principally through the joint efforts of architect-artist William Spratling and the local community.

Today, spurred by the tourist boom, jewelry-making is thriving in Mexico. Taxco, where guilds, families, and cooperatives produce sparkling silver and gold adornments, is the acknowledged center. Several Oaxaca shops offer Taxco-made jewelry—shimmering ornamental butterflies, birds, jaguars, serpents, turtles, and fish from the pre-conquest tradition. Pieces, mostly in silver, vary from humble but attractive trinkets to glittering necklaces, silver candelabras, and place settings for a dozen, sometimes embellished with precious stones.

Oaxaca also has a healthy local jewelry-making tradition. The acknowledged leader in Oaxaca City is the family firm of **Oro de Monte Albán.** Their several city and coastal resort shops offer replicas of the ancient Mixtec designs, notably of many pieces found at Monte Albán's Tomb 7.

Tehuántepec women *(tehuanas)* have created a demand for elaborate **gold filigree jewelry,** made from fine wires and often decorated with pearls and precious stones. The finest, 10–18 karat (42–75 percent pure) gold, is more often kept in safe deposit boxes and used only on ceremonial occasions. Much more common is *chapa de oro,* gold look-alike filigree that contains no gold at all. Women sell this jewelry in Oaxaca City, at the north-central entrance of the 20 de Noviembre market and in the Isthmus, at the Juchitán and Tehuántepec markets.

Buying Silver and Gold

Silver and gold jewelry, the finest of which is crafted in Taxco, Mexico City, Guanajuato, and Oaxaca, is sold in a number of shops in Oaxaca City, Huatulco, and Puerto Escondido.

One hundred percent pure silver is rarely sold because it's too soft. Silver (most of which is sent from processing mills in the north of Mexico to be worked in Taxco shops) is nearly always alloyed with 7.5 percent copper to increase its durability. Such pieces, identical in composition to sterling silver, should have

".925," together with the initials of the manufacturing jeweler, stamped on their back sides. Other, less common grades, such as "800 fine" (80 percent silver), should also be stamped.

If silver is not stamped with the degree of purity, it probably contains no silver at all and is an alloy of copper, zinc, and nickel, known by the generic label "alpaca," or "German" silver. Once, after haggling over the purity and prices of his offerings, a street vendor handed me a shiny handful and said, "Go to a jeweler and have them tested. If they're not real, keep them." Calling his bluff, I took them to a jeweler, who applied a dab of hydrochloric acid to each piece. Tiny, tell-tale bubbles of hydrogen revealed the cheapness of the merchandise, which I returned the next day to the vendor.

Some shops price sterling silver jewelry simply by weighing, which typically translates to about $1 per gram. If you want to find out if the price is fair, ask the shopkeeper to weigh it for you.

Oaxaca City itself is a gold jewelry center, mainly due to the skill and enterprise of the family-owned Oro de Monte Albán business. They maintain three shops, two in Oaxaca City and one in Puerto Escondido.

People universally prize pure gold, partly because, unlike silver, it does not tarnish. Gold, nevertheless, is rarely sold pure (24 karat); for durability, it is alloyed with copper. Typical purity levels, such as 18 karat (75 percent) or 14 karat (58 percent), should be stamped on the pieces. If not, chances are they contain no gold at all.

WOOD CARVING AND MUSICAL INSTRUMENTS
Masks

Spanish and Native Oaxacan traditions have blended to produce a multitude of masks—some strange, some lovely, some scary, some endearing, but all interesting. The tradition flourishes in Oaxaca and the strongly indigenous neighboring states of Michoacán, Guerrero, and Chiapas. Here campesinos gear up all year for the village festivals—especially Semana Santa (Easter week), early December

Masks, made for traditional dances, also make good souvenirs.

(Virgin of Guadalupe), and that of the local patron, whether it be San José, San Pablo, San Pedro, Santa Barbara, Santa María, or one of a host of others. Every local fair has its favored dances, such as the **Dance of the Conquest, Dance of the Feathers, the Christians and Moors, the Old Men,** or the **Tiger,** in which masked villagers act out age-old allegories of fidelity, sacrifice, faith, struggle, sin, and redemption.

Although artisans craft Oaxaca masks of many materials—from stone and ebony to coconut husks and paper—wood, where available, is the medium of choice. For the entire year, workers carve, sand, and paint to ensure that each participant will be properly disguised for the festival. Although Oaxaca's larger municipalities usually have their cadres of mask makers, towns in the Mixteca region, notably Juxtlahuaca, in the Mixteca Baja, and Santa María Huazolotitlán and Pinotepa Don Luis, in the Mixteca de la Costa, are among Oaxaca's busiest authentic mask sources.

The popularity of masks has resulted in an

entire made-for-tourist mask industry, which has led to mass-produced duplicates, many cleverly antiqued. Examine the goods carefully; if the price is high, don't buy unless you're convinced it's a real antique.

Alebrijes

Tourist demand has made zany wooden animals called *alebrijes* (ah-lay-BREE-hays) a Oaxaca growth industry. Virtually every family in certain Valley of Oaxaca villages—notably Arrazola and San Martín Tilcajete—runs a factory studio. There, piles of copal wood, which men carve and women finish and intricately paint, become whimsical giraffes, dogs, cats, iguanas, gargoyles, and dragons, including most of the possible permutations in between. The farther from the source you get, the higher the *alebrije* price becomes; what costs $5 in Arrazola will probably run about $10 in Oaxaca City and $30 in the United States, Canada, or Europe.

Musical Instruments

Virtually all of Mexico's guitars are made in Paracho, Michoacán (southeast of Lake Chapala), north of Uruapan. There, scores of cottage factories turn out guitars, violins, mandolins, ukuleles, and a dozen more variations every day. Products vary widely in quality, so look carefully before you buy. Make sure that the wood is well cured and dry; damp, unripe wood instruments are more susceptible to warping and cracking.

METALWORK

Several Oaxaca City family factories turn out fine cutlery, forged ironwork, and a swarm of bright tinware mirror frames, masks, and glittering Christmas decorations.

Cutlery tradition—knives, machetes, scissors, swords, and more—arrived in Oaxaca with the Spanish. Today, several family shops offer their wares in town shops and market stalls, notably at the Benito Juárez market in Oaxaca City.

Traditional **ironwork,** admittedly heavy to carry home in your luggage, is made to order, boxed, and shipped at a number of specialty shops in Oaxaca City. Some of the more

© BRUCE WHIPPERMAN

Alebrijes, brightly colored wooden animals, are a hand-carved Oaxacan specialty.

Oaxaca produces superlative and imaginative ironwork.

hope will intercede to cure the ailment or fulfill the wish designated by the *milagro*.

PAPER AND PAPIER-MÂCHÉ

Papier-mâché has risen to nearly a fine art in Tonalá, Jalisco. Many Oaxaca handicrafts stores stock small flocks of Tonalá-made birds, cats, frogs, giraffes, and other animal figurines, meticulously crafted by building up repeated layers of glued paper. The results—sanded, brilliantly varnished, and polished—resemble fine sculptures rather than the humble newspaper from which they were fashioned.

Other paper goods you shouldn't overlook include **piñatas** (durable, inexpensive, and as Mexican as you can get), available in every town market; colorful, decorative **cutout banners** (string overhead at your home fiesta) from San Salvador Huixcolotla, Puebla; and **amate**, wild fig tree bark paintings in animal and flower motifs, from Xalitla and Ameyaltepec, Guerrero.

POTTERY AND CERAMICS

The Valley of Oaxaca is the focus of a vibrant pottery tradition. Many of the most celebrated examples come from the village of Atzompa, a few miles northwest of the city. Traditionally popular for their green-glazed clay pots, dishes, casseroles, and bowls, Atzompa potters have evolved a host of fresh styles, from graceful vases and plates blooming with painted lilies to red clay pots and bowls inscribed with artfully flowing blossoms.

San Bartolo Coyotepec village, south of the city, has acquired equal renown for its **black pottery** *(barro negro),* sold all over the world. Doña Rosa, now deceased, pioneered the crafting of big round pots without using a potter's wheel. Now made in many more shapes by Doña Rosa's descendants, the pottery's celebrated black hue is produced by the reduction (reduced air) method of firing, which removes oxygen from the clay's red (ferric) iron oxide, converting it to black (ferrous) iron oxide. Workers burnish the result to produce an exquisite, pearly sheen.

commonly requested items, such as medieval-style lanterns and garden benches, are available on display.

Tinware (*hojalata,* oh-hah-LAH-tah), especially the colorfully lacquered Christmas decorations—winsome angels, saints, Santas, butterflies, and fruits—constitute Oaxaca City's most sought-after metal craft. Running closely behind are the hosts of old-fashioned lead figures—soldiers, ballerinas, antique automobiles, angels—and fancy silvery mirror frames, metal boxes, birds, flowers, and much more. Many downtown handicrafts shops, in addition to stalls at the 20 de Noviembre market and the Mercado de Artesanías (Handicrafts Market), sell metal work.

Moreover, be sure to ask at the same shops and stalls for **milagros,** one of Mexico's most charming forms of metal work. Usually of brass, they are of homely shapes—a horse, dog, or baby, or an arm, head, heart, or foot. The faithful pin them, along with a prayer, to the garments of their favorite saint, whom they

© BRUCE WHIPPERMAN

Although most latter-day Oaxacan potters are aware of the health dangers of **lead pigments,** some for-sale pottery may still contain lead. The hazard comes from low-fired pottery in which the lead has not been firmly melted into the glaze. Acids in foods such as lemons, vinegar, and tomatoes dissolve the lead pigments, which, when ingested over a period of time, can result in lead poisoning. In general, the hardest, glossiest, high-fired stoneware, that has been twice fired, is the safest for dinnerware.

Although Mexican pottery tradition is as diverse as the country itself, some varieties stand out. Among the most prized is the so-called **Talavera** (or Majolica), the best of which is made by a few family-run workshops in Puebla. The names Talavera and Majolica derive from Talavera, the Spanish town from which the tradition migrated to Mexico in the 1500s. Prior to that, it was extensively crafted on the Spanish Mediterranean island of Majorca (thus the *Majolica* label), from a blending of ancient Arabic, Middle-Eastern, and North African ceramic styles. Shapes include plates, bowls, jugs, and pitchers, hand-painted and hard-fired in intricate bright yellow, orange, blue, and green floral designs. So few shops make true Talavera these days that other, cheaper look-alike grades, made around Guanajuato, are more common, selling for a small fraction of the price of the genuine article. Always ask for proof of the origin (maker and city) of claimed genuine Talavera ware.

WOOLEN WOVEN GOODS

Mexico's finest wool weavings come from Teotitlán del Valle and the neighboring town of Santa Ana del Valle, less than an hour's drive east of Oaxaca City. Although they learned to work wool from the Spanish, the weaving tradition, continued by Zapotec-speaking families, dates back at least a thousand years before the conquest. Many families still carry on the arduous process, making everything from scratch. They gather the dyes from wild plants and the bodies of insects and sea snails. They hand-wash, card, spin, and dye the wool and even travel to remote mountain springs to gather water. The result, they say, is *vale la pena* (worth the pain): intensely colored, tightly woven carpets, rugs, and wall hangings that retain their brilliance for generations.

Although many handicrafts shops and a host of stalls in all the Oaxaca City markets sell the Teotitlán del Valle and Santa Ana del Valle weavings, a trip to Teotitlán del Valle (where Santa Ana del Valle weavers send most of their products for sale) is a must for Valley of Oaxaca first-time visitors.

ESSENTIALS

Getting There

BY AIR
From the United States and Canada

The majority of foreign visitors reach Oaxaca by air, through the Mexico gateways of **Atlanta, Chicago, Dallas, Denver, Houston, Los Angeles, Miami, New York, Orlando, Phoenix, San Antonio, San Francisco, Tijuana,** and **Toronto.** Nearly all flights involve a plane change at the sprawling, super-busy Mexico City Airport, where connections are available, with Oaxaca destinations of either Oaxaca City, or Huatulco and Puerto Escondido, on the Oaxaca Pacific Coast.

For Oaxaca City, go by either **Aeromexico Airlines** (U.S. and Canada toll-free tel. 800/237-6629, www.aeromexico.com) or **Volaris Airlines** (U.S. toll-free tel. 866/988-3527, answers in Spanish, wait to select English option, www.volaris.com.mx). If to Huatulco, go by either **Magnicharters** (www.magnicharters.com) or **Aeromar Airlines** (www.aeromar.com.mx); and, to Puerto Escondido go also via Aeromar.

Fortunately, **two air carriers provide direct Oaxaca connections** that bypass Mexico City completely. They are **Continental Airlines** (www.continental.com), with two

© BRUCE WHIPPERMAN

separate nonstop connections, from Houston, with Oaxaca City and Huatulco; and up-and-coming low-cost **Volaris Airlines,** that connects nonstop with Oaxaca City directly from Tijuana, just across the border from San Diego. The Tijuana connection from San Diego airport is straightforward: Take airport express bus 922 (or taxi) to the San Diego trolley terminal, where you board the blue line trolley to Tijuana, walk across the border, and then taxi to the Tijuana airport.

Although only a few scheduled flights go directly to Mexico City from the northern United States and Canada, **charters** do, especially during the winter. In locales such as Boston, Buffalo, Calgary-Edmonton, Cleveland, Detroit, Minneapolis, Montreal, Ottawa, Seattle, Toronto, Vancouver, and Winnipeg consult a travel agent or website for charter flight options. Be aware that charter reservations, which often require fixed departure and return dates and provide minimal cancellation refunds, decrease your flexibility.

Air travelers can save money by shopping around, through websites such as www. cheaptickets.com and www.priceline.com, and through the airlines, both by telephone and the Internet. Don't be bashful about trying for the best price. Make it clear that you're interested in a bargain. Ask the right questions. Are there special incentive, advance-payment, night, midweek, tour-package, or charter fares? Peruse the ads in your Sunday newspaper travel section for bargain-oriented websites and travel agencies.

From Europe, Latin America, and Australasia

Some airlines fly across the Atlantic directly to Mexico City. These include **Lufthansa,** which connects directly from Frankfurt, and **Aeroméxico,** from Paris and Madrid.

From Latin America, **Aeroméxico** connects directly with Mexico City, from Sao Paulo, Brazil; Santiago, Chile; Lima, Peru; Buenos Aires, Argentina; and San José, Costa Rica. A number of other Latin American flag carriers also fly directly to Mexico City.

A few flights cross the Pacific directly to Mexico, notably **Japan Airlines,** which connects Osaka-Tokyo to Mexico City, via Vancouver. More commonly, travelers from Australasia routinely transfer at Los Angeles, Phoenix, or San Francisco for connections to Mexico City, thence Oaxaca.

Baggage, Insurance, "Bumping," and In-Flight Meals

Tropical and temperate Oaxaca makes it easy to pack light. Veteran tropical travelers often condense their luggage to carry-ons only. Airlines routinely allow a carry-on (not exceeding 45 inches in combined length, width, and girth) and a small bag or purse. Thus relieved of heavy burdens, your trip will become much simpler. You'll avoid possible luggage loss and long baggage check-in lines by being able to check in directly at the boarding gate.

Even if you can't avoid having to check luggage, loss of it needn't ruin your vacation. **Always carry your irreplaceable items in the cabin with you.** These should include all cameras, checks, credit cards, eyeglasses, money, passport, prescription drugs, tickets, and traveler's keys.

At the X-ray security check, insist that your film cameras be hand-inspected. Regardless of what attendants claim, repeated X-ray scanning will fog any film, especially the sensitive ASA 400 and 1,000 high-speed varieties. Digital cameras are not affected by X-ray scanning. (You can assure both protection and hand inspection for your film by packing it in the special lead-lined film bags available in any good camera store.)

Travelers packing lots of expensive baggage, or who (because of illness, for example) may have to cancel a nonrefundable flight or tour, might consider buying **travel insurance.** Travel agents routinely sell packages that include baggage, trip cancellation, and default insurance. Baggage insurance covers you beyond the customary $1,250 domestic, $400 international baggage liability limits, but check with your carrier. **Trip cancellation insurance** pays if you must cancel your

AIRLINES SERVING OAXACA

At this writing, two of the following scheduled airlines (Continental and Volaris) do connect directly (with no plane change) with Oaxaca City (OAX) and Huatulco (HUA). The remainder connect directly with Mexico City (MX), where connecting flights continue on to the Oaxaca destinations of Oaxaca City, Huatulco-Puerto Ángel, and Puerto Escondido. The following airlines are listed alphabetically, with their departure points in geographic order from west to east and south to north.

AIRLINE	ORIGIN	DESTINATIONS
Aeroméxico tel. 800/237-6639 www.aeromexico.com	Los Angeles .... MX Ontario (California) .... MX San Diego .... MX Seattle .... MX Tijuana .... MX Phoenix .... MX Tucson .... MX San Antonio .... MX Houston .... MX New York .... MX Atlanta .... MX Orlando .... MX Miami .... MX	
Air Canada tel. 888/247-2262 www.aircanada.com	Toronto .... MX	
American tel. 800/433-7300 www.aa.com	Dallas .... MX Miami .... MX	

prepaid trip, while default insurance protects you if your carrier or tour agent does not perform as agreed. Travel insurance, however, can be expensive. For example, **Travel Guard Insurance** (toll-free tel. 800/826-4919, www.travelguard.com), one of the most reliable travel insurance companies, offers about $1,000 of travel insurance per person for two weeks for about $50. Carefully weigh both your options and the cost against benefits before putting your money down.

It's wise to reconfirm both departure and return flight reservations, especially during the busy Christmas and Easter seasons. This is a useful strategy—as is prompt arrival at check-in—against getting "bumped" (losing your seat) because of the tendency of airlines to overbook the rush of high-season vacationers. For further protection, if possible get your seat assignment and boarding pass included with your ticket.

Airlines generally try hard to accommodate travelers with dietary or other special needs. When booking your flight, inform your travel agent or carrier of the necessity of a low-sodium, low-cholesterol, vegetarian, or lactose-reduced meal or other requirements. (Furthermore, it's been my experience that special meals ordered ahead of time are better than the on-board standard-fare choices.)

AIRLINE	ORIGIN	DESTINATIONS
Continental tel. 800/231-0856 www.continental.com	Houston .... MX OAX HUA Newark .... MX	
Delta tel. 800/221-1212 www.delta.com	Los Angeles .... MX Dallas .... MX Atlanta.......................... MX New York .... MX	
U.S. Airways tel. 800/428-4322 www.usairways.com	Phoenix .... MX	
Volaris tel. 866/988-3527 www.volaris.com.mx	Tijuana .... MX OAX	

Note: Veteran carrier **Mexicana Airlines** suspended all their dozens of flights in the fall of 2010 due to bankruptcy. As of this writing, plans are afoot to restart operations on a much-reduced scale. Check their website or call center (toll-free tel. 888/882-9994, www.mexicana.com) for more information.

BY BUS

As air travel rules in the United States, bus travel rules in Mexico. Hundreds of sleek luxury- and first-class bus lines with romantic names such as Elite, Estrella de Oro (Star of Gold), and Estrella Blanca (White Star) roar out daily from the border, headed south.

Since U.S. bus lines ordinarily terminate just north of the Mexican border, you must usually disembark, collect your things, and, after having filled out the necessary but very simple paperwork at the immigration office, proceed on foot across the border to Mexico, where you can bargain with a local taxi driver to drive you the few miles ($2–4) to the *camionera central* (central bus station). (*Note:* Mexican border authorities require a valid passport to enter Mexico; United States authorities require a valid passport to return to the United States.)

Finally, after taking a taxi to the bus station, handy words to have in mind are *taquilla* (ticket booth), *guardaequipajes* (baggage checkroom), *llegada* (arrival), *salida* (departure), and *sanitario* or *baño* (toilet or bathroom).

First- and luxury-class bus service in Mexico is generally cheaper and better than in the United States. Tickets for comparable trips in Mexico cost less than half (as little as $100 for a 1,600-km/1,000-mi trip), compared to perhaps $200 in the United States.

In Mexico, as on U.S. buses, you often have to take it as you find it. *Asientos reservados* (reserved seats), *boletos* (tickets), and information must generally be obtained in person at the bus station, and credit cards and travelers checks are sometimes not accepted. Reserved bus tickets are typically nonrefundable; so don't miss the bus. On the other hand, plenty of buses roll south almost continuously. Two basic routes are available, either through Mexico City or down the Pacific coast all the way.

Pacific Coast Route

The route to Oaxaca along the Pacific shore, although the longest, requiring one or two transfers and at least three full 24-hour days, is the most scenic. Try to go luxury or first class all the way; the small additional cost is well worth it. Cross the border at **Tijuana, Mexicali,** or **Nogales,** where you can choose from at least three bus lines (the Estrella Blanca Group buses are best, with luxury class **Futura** and first class **Elite** buses) along the Pacific coast route, via combined National Highways 15 and 200, via Mazatlán, Puerto Vallarta, Zihuatanejo, Acapulco, and, finally, Puerto Escondido, in Oaxaca. At the border, get a bus as far south as you can, most likely **Elite** all the way to Acapulco; or if not, at least to Tepic or Puerto Vallarta, where you change to a bus headed south for, most likely, Lázaro Cárdenas, Zihuatanejo, or Acapulco, at the end of your second day. There, you catch a third bus, which will take you at least to Acapulco, and at most to Puerto Escondido by the end of your third day.

On the other hand, make it easy on yourself and stretch the trip to five days by resting overnight in Puerto Vallarta and Zihuatanejo along the way. In Puerto Vallarta, stay on the beach at either **Hotel Rosita** (tel. 322/223-1033, tel./fax 322/223-2000, U.S. toll-free tel. 877/813-6712, sales@hotelrosita.com, www. hotelrosita.com, $50) or **Casa Corazon** (tel./fax 322/222-6364, U.S.-Canada toll-free tel. 866/648-6893, www.casacorazonvallarta. com, casacorazone1@yahoo.com. $40–50 d). In Zihuatanejo, stay on the beach at **Hotel**

Irma (tel./fax 755/554-8003 or 755/554-8472, www.hotelirma.com.mx, $60–100 d) or budget **Posada Citlali** (tel./fax 755/554-2043, hotelreserv@prodigy.net.mx, $35 d), a block from the beach.

Mexico City Route

This is the quickest bus route to Oaxaca, typically about 36 hours from the south Texas border, a day longer from California or Nogales, Arizona, via Guadalajara. From the western United States, cross the border at Tijuana, Mexicali, or Nogales (ride an Estrella Blanca bus, such as **Elite** or **Futura**). From the United States Midwest, Southeast, and East, cross the border at Laredo to Nuevo Laredo (ride an **Omnibus de Mexico** bus) or McAllen to Reynosa (ride either **Omnibus de Mexico** or **Grupo Senda** bus.) For the most speed and comfort, at only a small extra cost, go by luxury-class bus to Mexico City.

Mexico City has four bus terminals—north, east, south, and west (respectively, Terminal Norte, Terminal Tapo, Terminal Sur, and Terminal Poniente). You will most likely arrive in the Terminal Norte, although a few buses from the west via Guadalajara might arrive at Terminal Poniente. For an overnight rest break, Guadalajara is especially handy, at basic but clean and moderately-priced **Hotel La Serena** (tel.33/3600-0910, fax 33/3600-1974, reservas@aranzazu.com.mx, $38 d), with pool and restaurant, conveniently adjacent to the bus station.

In any case, at Mexico City, if you're heading to Oaxaca City, from Terminal Norte, board an **Autobuses del Oriente (ADO)** or **Cristóbal Colón** bus, via the Puebla expressway (*autopista* or *corta*) to Oaxaca City. If you're heading for the Oaxaca Pacific coast, best board an **Estrella Blanca** affiliate (such as **Turistar** or **Futura**) or an **Estrella de Oro** bus bound for Acapulco, where you can transfer to a Puerto Escondido–bound bus.

If somehow the above connections are not available at Terminal Norte (or Terminal Poniente), share a taxi (don't try it by public transit) to Terminal Sur (or Terminal

Tapo for Oaxaca City via ADO) and catch an Estrella Blanca subsidiary (such as Elite, Turistar, Futura, Flecha Roja, or Transportes Cuauhtémoc) all the way to Puerto Escondido via Acapulco. If you miss the direct Puerto Escondido connection, settle for an express connection to Acapulco, where plenty of local departures head out southeast for Puerto Escondido.

Get across town to your continuing bus terminal via *taxi especial* (private taxi) or *colectivo* (collective taxi). Although such a trip is possible by public transportation, don't try it. If you do, you're either a Mexico City veteran traveling light and know what you're getting into or are willing to bear a load of frustration, pain, and the dirty looks from fellow passengers as you unwittingly poke them with your bulging backpacks and luggage in a crowded subway or local bus.

BY CAR OR RV

If you're adventurous and like going to out-of-the-way places, but still want to have all the comforts of home, you may enjoy driving your car or RV to Oaxaca. On the other hand, considerations of cost, risk, wear on both you and your vehicle, and the congestion hassles in towns may change your mind.

Mexican Car Insurance

Mexico does not recognize foreign insurance. When you drive into Mexico, Mexican auto insurance is at least as important as your passport. At the busier crossings, you can get it at insurance "drive-ins" just north of the border. The many Mexican auto insurance companies are government-regulated; their numbers keep prices and services competitive.

Sanborn's Mexico Insurance (Sanborn's Mexico, P.O. Box 310, McAllen, TX 78502, toll-free 800/222-0158, tel. 956/686-3601, www.sanbornsinsurance.com), one of the best-known agencies, certainly seems to be trying the hardest. It offers a number of books and services, including the *Recreational Guide to Mexico,* a good road map, "smile-by-mile" *Travelog* guide to "every highway in Mexico,"

hotel discounts, and more. Much of this is available to members of Sanborn's Sombrero Club.

Alternatively, look into **Vagabundos del Mar** (tel. 800/474-2252, local tel. 707/374-5511, www.vagabundos.com), an RV-oriented Mexico travel club offering memberships that include a newsletter, caravaning opportunites, discounts, insurance, and much more.

Mexican car insurance runs from a bare-bones rate of about $8 a day for minimal $10,000/$50,000 (property damage/medical payments) coverage to a more typical $14 a day for more complete $20,000/$100,000 coverage. On the same scale, insurance for a $50,000 RV and equipment runs about $30 a day. These daily rates decrease sharply for six-month or one-year policies, which run from about $200 for the minimum to $400–1,600 for complete, high-end (SUV, trailer, boat) coverage.

If you get broken glass, personal effects, and legal expenses coverage with these rates, you're lucky. Mexican policies often don't cover them.

You should get something for your money, however. The deductibles should be no more than $300–500, the public liability per occurrence/medical payments per person/per occurrence should be about double the ($25,000/$25,000/$50,000) legal minimum, and you should be able to get your car fixed in

MEXICO CITY DRIVING RESTRICTIONS

To reduce smog and traffic gridlock, authorities have limited which cars can drive on which days in Mexico City, depending upon the last digit of their license plates. If you violate these rules, you risk getting an expensive ticket. On Monday, no vehicle may be driven with final digits 5 or 6; Tuesday, 7 or 8; Wednesday, 3 or 4; Thursday, 1 or 2; Friday, 9 or 0. Weekends, all vehicles may be driven.

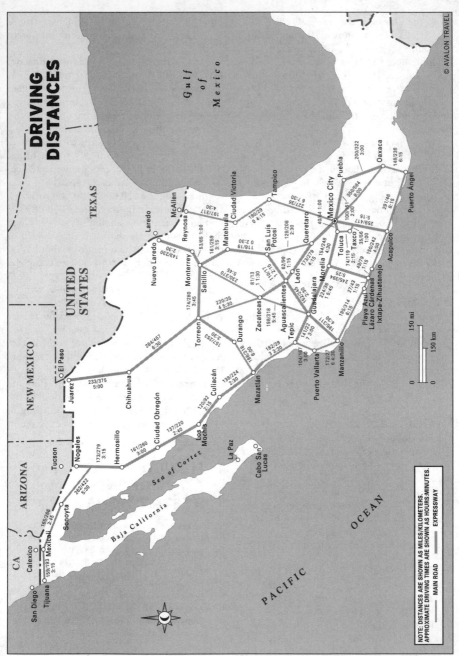

DRIVING DISTANCES

NOTE: DISTANCES ARE SHOWN AS MILES/KILOMETERS.
APPROXIMATE DRIVING TIMES ARE SHOWN AS HOURS:MINUTES.
—— MAIN ROAD   ▬▬ EXPRESSWAY

© AVALON TRAVEL

the United States and receive payment in U.S. dollars for losses. If not, shop around.

A Sinaloa Note of Caution

Although *bandidos* seldom menace Mexican roads (but loose burros, horses, and cattle often do), be cautious in the infamous marijuana-and-opium-growing region of Sinaloa state, north of Mazatlán. It's best not to stray from Highway 15 (or the 15D toll expressway) between Culiacán and Mazatlán or from Highway 40 between Mazatlán and Durango. Curious tourists have been assaulted in the hinterlands adjacent to these roads.

The Green Angels

The Green Angels have answered many motoring tourists' prayers in Mexico. Bilingual teams of two, trained in auto repair and first aid, help distressed tourists along main highways. They patrol fixed stretches of road at least twice daily by truck. To make sure they stop to help, pull completely off the highway and raise your hood. You may want to hail a passing motorist or trucker with a Mexican cell phone to call the **Mexico Tourism-Green Angels hotline** (tel. 800/903-9200, or all-purpose emergency direct tel. 078) for you.

If, for some reason, you have to leave your vehicle on the roadside, don't leave it unattended. Hire a local teenager or adult to watch it for you. Unattended vehicles on Mexican highways are quickly stricken by a mysterious disease, the symptoms of which are rapid loss of vital parts.

Mexican Gasoline

Pemex, short for Petróleos Mexicanos, the government oil monopoly, markets diesel fuel and two grades of unleaded gasoline: 92-octane *premio* (PRAY-mee-oh) and 87-octane Magna (MAHG-nah). Magna is good gas, yielding performance similar to that of U.S.-style regular unleaded gasoline. (My original car, whose manufacturer recommended 91-octane, ran well on Magna.) It runs about $0.65 per liter (or about $2.50 per gallon at this writing). On main highways, Pemex makes sure that major

stations (typically spaced about 30 miles apart in the countryside) stock Magna.

Gas Station Thievery

Although the problem has abated considerably in recent years (by the hiring of young female attendants), boys who hang around gas stations to wash windows are notoriously

ROAD SAFETY

Hundreds of thousands of visitors enjoy safe Mexican auto vacations every year. Their success is due in large part to their frame of mind: Drive defensively, anticipate and adjust to danger before it happens, and watch everything – side roads, shoulders, the car in front, and cars far down the road. The following tips will help ensure a safe and enjoyable trip.

- **Don't drive at night.** Range animals, unmarked sand piles, pedestrians, one-lane bridges, cars without lights, and drunk drivers are doubly hazardous at night.

- Although **speed limits** are rarely enforced, *don't break them.* Mexican roads are often narrow and shoulderless. Poor markings and macho drivers who pass on curves are best faced at a speed of 64 kph (40 mph) rather than 120 kph (75 mph).

- **Drive on sand only sparingly.** Even with four-wheel-drive, you'll eventually get stuck if you drive either often or casually on beaches. When the tide comes in, who'll pull your car out?

- Watch with an eagle eye and **slow down** at the *topes* (speed bumps) at the edges of towns and for *vados* (dips), which can be dangerously bumpy and full of water.

- Extending the **courtesy of the road** goes hand-in-hand with safe driving. Both courtesy and machismo are more infectious in Mexico; on the highway, it's much safer to spread the former than the latter.

light-fingered. When stopping at the *gasolinera,* make sure that your cameras, purses, and other moveable items are out of reach. Also, make sure that your car has a lockable gas cap. If not, insist on pumping the gas yourself, or be super-watchful as you pull up to the gas pump to make certain that the pump reads zero before the attendant pumps the gas.

A Healthy Car

Preventive measures spell good health for both you and your car. Get that tune-up (or that long-delayed overhaul) *before,* rather than after, you leave.

Carry a stock of spare parts, which will be more difficult to get and more expensive in Mexico than at home. Carry an extra tire or two, a few quart bottles of motor oil, oil and gas filters, fan belts, spark plugs, tune-up kit, ignition points, and fuses. Be prepared with basic tools and supplies, such as screwdrivers, pliers including Vice-Grip, lug wrench, jack, adjustable wrenches, tire pump, tire pressure gauge, steel wire, and electrical tape. For breakdowns and emergencies, carry a folding shovel, a husky rope or chain, a gasoline can, and flares or red highway markers.

Car Repairs in Mexico

The American big three—General Motors, Ford, and Chrysler—as well as Nissan and Volkswagen are represented by extensive dealer networks in Mexico. Latecomers Toyota and Honda are also represented, although to a lesser extent. Getting your car or truck serviced at such agencies is straightforward. While parts will probably be higher in price, shop rates run about one-third to one-half U.S. prices, so repairs will generally come out cheaper than back home.

The same may not be true for repairing other makes, however. Mexico has few, if any, other car or truck dealers; consequently, officially certified mechanics for other Japanese, British, and European makes are hard to find outside of Mexico City.

Nevertheless, many ingenious Mexican

DETOUR INTO A CORNFIELD

Driving hazards – poorly marked roads, potholes, pedestrians, roadside horses, cattle, burros, and rattletrap cars and trucks with no lights – make rural nighttime driving in Oaxaca an iffy proposition. Add speed to the mix and you have a recipe for close calls at least and disasters at worst.

I was actually doing about about 50 or 55 kph per hour (30 or 35 miles), and, although the road was paved (something that probably lulled me into complacency), it was dark, wet, gravelly, and completely lacking either a white center line or edge markings.

I blundered into a sharp left curve and in a split second found that I had to either roll my car or leave the road. I chose the latter and hurtled into someone's tall-corn *milpa* (small field). As green stalks slapped the windshield and I bounced up and down like a Ping-Pong ball, I wondered if I was going to go over a cliff (this was hilly country), something that prob-

ably would have postponed publication of this book indefinitely.

This time I was lucky. After a very long second or two, my little truck lurched to a stop, tilted at a crazy sideways angle against a big round boulder. Somehow something managed to seriously crack the front windshield and cave in both passenger-side doors, but the car didn't roll, and miraculously the motor would still run.

What does a writer on a short deadline do on such an occasion? Go get help and get rolling again if possible. The only problem: I was way out in the country, 160 kilometers (100 mi) from the crane (Tow truck? No way!) that seemed necessary to pull my truck from where it was lodged over the boulders and up the long embankment.

It turned out that I couldn't have been in a better place to get help. I climbed out of the cornfield to a nearby village, where, at 9 P.M.

independent mechanics can fix any car that comes their way. Their humble *talleres mecánicos* (tah-YER-ays may-KAH-nee-kohs) dot town and village roadsides everywhere.

Although the great majority of Mexican mechanics are honest, beware of unscrupulous operators who try to collect double or triple their original estimate. If you don't speak Spanish, find someone who can assist you in negotiations. *Always* get a cost estimate, including needed parts and labor, in writing, even if you have to write it yourself. Make sure the mechanic understands, then ask him to sign it before he starts work. Although this may be a hassle, it might save you a much nastier hassle later. Shop labor at small, independent repair shops should run $10–20 per hour. For much more information, and for entertaining anecdotes of car and RV travel in Mexico, consult Carl Franz's *The People's Guide to Mexico.*

Bribes (Mordidas)

The usual meeting ground of the visitor and Mexican police is in the visitor's car on a highway or downtown street. To the tourists, such an encounter may seem mild harassment by the police, accompanied by vague threats of going to the police station or impounding the car for such-and-such a violation. The tourist often goes on to say, "It was all right, though… we paid him $20 and he went away…Mexican cops sure are crooked, aren't they?"

And, I suppose, if people want to go bribing their way through Mexico, that's their business. But calling Mexican cops crooked isn't exactly fair. Police, like most everyone else in Mexico, have to scratch for a living, and they have found that many tourists are willing to slip them a $20 bill for nothing. Rather than crooked, I would call them hungry and opportunistic.

Instead of paying a bribe, do what I've done a dozen times: Remain cool, and if you're really guilty of an infraction, calmly say, "Ticket, please." *("Boleto, por favor").* After a minute or two of stalling, and no cash appearing, the

on Saturday night, everybody was out and about. I asked a man, named German ("Herman"), who, it seems, knew Agustín, who had a tractor. Agustín, German said, was at his girlfriend's house, where we went next.

Agustín came outside for a conference. Given his tractor, it was not a question of if the job could be done, but when.

"Can't we wait until tomorrow?" Agustín asked. "It's dark now. Best to try in the morning."

My deadline pushed me on.

"You may be right, but if possible I'd like to try now. I've got 1,500 pesos ($150) cash. It's yours if you pull my *camioneta* out of the *milpa*."

By this time a small crowd had gathered around. Several of us piled into German's truck and headed to Agustín's place, where Agustín maneuvered a huge green John Deere tractor with two-meter (seven-foot) wheels out of his barn. Agustín's brother went to get a long cable and met us at the site.

With about five guys helping me, we wrapped the cable around the axle. I got behind the steering wheel and, miracle of miracles, Agustín and his tractor, like the strong right hand of God, pulled my *camioneta* straight up the rocky incline and onto the road.

Overjoyed, I immediately wanted to fulfill my promise to Agustín. I started counting out the $10 bills, one by one. When I got to eight or nine, Agustín protested.

"Stop. That's enough."

I distributed the rest of the bills to the other men and was about to leave when someone spied that the crash had flattened the right front tire. Quickly, one of the men replaced it with my spare, and I was ready to go. I thanked everyone all round again and headed out through the Oaxaca night, shaken but unhurt and grateful to my kind rescuers.

officer most likely will not bother with a ticket, but will wave you on with only a warning. If, on the other hand, the officer does write you a ticket, he will probably keep your driver's license, which you will be able to retrieve at the *presidencia municipal* (city hall) the next day in exchange for paying your fine.

Crossing the Border

Squeezing through the border traffic bottlenecks during peak holidays and rush hours can easily take two or three hours. Avoid crossing 7–9 A.M. and 4:30–6:30 P.M. Moreover, with latter-day increased U.S. homeland security precautions, the return, northbound border crossing, under the best of conditions, generally takes at least an hour waiting in your car, along with a hundred or more other frustrated drivers. (*Note:* Mexican officials require a **valid passport** upon entry into Mexico for everyone in your party except babes in arms. A valid passport is likewise required by U.S. officials upon your return to the United States.)

Highway Routes from the United States

If you've decided to drive to Oaxaca, you have your choice of four general routes. At safe highway speeds, from the Mexican border these routes require as many as five days or as few as two days, depending on your route.

The longest but most scenic route is the **Pacific route,** which starts out as Mexican National Highway 15 from the border at Nogales, Sonora, an hour's drive south of Tucson, Arizona. Soon you join Highway 15D *cuota autopista* (toll expressway)—or continue along old *libre* (free) Highway 15—proceeding southward smoothly, over cactus-studded plains mountains that give way to irrigated farms and groves and palmy tropical coastal plain by the time you arrive in Mazatlán. Follow the *periféricos* (peripheral bypasses) that conduct traffic past the congested downtowns of Hermosillo, Guaymas, Culiacán, and Mazatlán. Between these centers, you can speed along via the *cuota* Highway 15D expressway virtually the entire way. If you prefer not to pay

the high tolls (around $60 total for a passenger car, much more for multiple-wheeled RVs) you should stick to the old *libre* Highway 15. Hazards, bumps, and slow going might force you to reconsider, however.

At **Tepic,** the Pacific route leaves Highway 15–15D and continues south via Highway 200, winding past tobacco farms and mango orchards, through lush forest, climbing vine–hung canyons, crossing a score of rivers, past a host of palm-tufted beaches, and passing the renowned vacation lands of **Puerto Vallarta, Manzanillo, Ixtapa-Zihuatanejo,** and **Acapulco.** Finally, several days after you crossed the border, you arrive at the heart of the tropical Oaxaca coast at Puerto Escondido or Puerto Ángel.

A speedier variation on the Pacific route is the **Pacific-Mexico City route,** which starts out as the Pacific route but departs from the Pacific coast, eastward, at Tepic, continuing along Highway 15 or 15D past Guadalajara, via Toluca to Mexico City.

Across town, at the Los Reyes southeast-side suburb, pick up the Puebla–Veracruz expressway Highway 150D, where you continue about an hour past Puebla to a fork. Follow the south fork expressway, via Tehuacán and Nochixtlán, to Oaxaca City. This nearly all-expressway route minimizes the road time from the western U.S. border to three very long, or, to be safe, four days to Oaxaca. *Note:* Be sure to arrive in Mexico City on a day of the week when driving restrictions (determined by the last digit of your license plate) do not apply to your car.

If, however, you're driving to Oaxaca from the central United States, go via the **central route,** crossing the border at El Paso to Ciudad Juárez, Chihuahua. There, National Highway 45, preferably via the *cuota* multilane expressway (or, if not, the old *libre* two-lane highway), leads you southward past high, dry plains and the cities of Chihuahua and Jiménez (use *periféricos* to bypass downtowns). Continue via Highway 49 southwest, through Gómez Palacio and the silver colonial cities of Zacatecas to San Luis Potosí, where you connect with Highway

57 expressway, via Querétaro, to the northern outskirts of Mexico City.

At that point, best use the east-bound *periférico* expressway via Carpio and Tezcoco instead of trying to fight your way through downtown Mexico City. At Los Reyes on the southeast side of town, pick up Highway 150D, the expressway east to Puebla, where you continue southeast via the toll expressway to Oaxaca. To be safe, allow three daytime-only driving days for this route.

Folks heading to Oaxaca from the eastern and southeastern United States probably save the most time by crossing the border from McAllen, Texas, to Reynosa and taking the **eastern route** to Oaxaca. Continue south, via Highway 97 then Highway 101, to Ciudad Victoria, bypassing the downtown by the *periférico*. Then connect with Highway 80 to Tampico. There, again bypass the downtown and pick up Highway 105 south headed for Tempoal de Sánchez. After a long, winding, mountain climb via Huejutla de Reyes, you reach Pachuca and continue southward via expressway Highway 85 to Mexico City. At Carpio in the northern suburb, take the east bypass expressway, via Tepexpan and Tezcoco, continuing to east-bound expressway 150D for Puebla. There, you continue southeast to Oaxaca City. If you start off at dawn each morning, you could probably get to Oaxaca safely in two driving days, under optimal conditions. It's best to do it in three leisurely days, including two overnights.

By Tour

Oaxaca's rich archaeological and cultural heritage provides a focus for some noteworthy tour-study programs.

Road Scholar (11 Lafayette Ave., Boston, MA 02111, 800/454-5768, www.roadscholar.org), formerly known as Elderhostel, offers tours leading participants on Oaxaca explorations emphasizing local traditions, food, and fiestas, plus

HIGHWAY ROUTES FROM THE U.S. BORDER TO OAXACA

ROUTE	VIA	MILES/KM	HOURS AT THE WHEEL	TRAVEL DAYS
Pacific	Nogales-Mazatlán Puerto Vallarta Acapulco-Puerto Ángel	1,911/3,075	46	5
Pacific-Mexico City	Nogales-Mazatlán Guadalajara-Mexico City Puebla-Oaxaca City	1,749/2,814	34	3
Central	Ciudad Juárez-Chihuahua Torreón-Zacatecas Querétaro-Mexico City Puebla-Oaxaca City	1,370/2,204	29	3
Eastern	Reynosa-Ciudad Victoria Tampico-Pachuca-Mexico City Puebla-Oaxaca City	967/1,556	22	2

lots of practice in conversational Spanish. Their Dia de Los Muertos tour focuses on the happy Mexican tradition of celebrating the beloved departed in joyous gravesite, food, flower- and candle-festooned family fiestas. Programs include visits to the archaeological sites of Monte Albán and Mitla and appreciation of indigenous tradition through visits to pottery, weaving, and woodcraft villages and evening excursions to enjoy Oaxacan food and folkloric music and dance. Accommodations can include both hotel rooms and homestays with Mexican families.

Birding tour outfitter **Field Guides** (9433 Bee Cave Road, #1–150, Austin, TX, toll-free 800/728-4953, fax 512/263-0117, www.field-guides.com) leads Oaxaca tours centering on the wildlife-rich foothill forests and lagoons of the tropical coast. Along the way, trips often include archaeological and historical sites and colorful native markets.

Siemer and Hand Travel (767 Bridgeway, Sausalito, CA, 415/331-8400 or toll-free 800/451-4321, fax 415/331-8405, www.siemerhand.com), a broad-based high-end tour agency, specializes in both individual and group educational tours. Their Oaxaca group tours have included "Birding in Oaxaca," in cooperation with the Massachusetts Audubon Society, and "Textiles of Mexico City and the Valley of Oaxaca," in cooperation with the California Academy of Sciences.

Adventuresome travelers hankering for something unusual should check out **Manos de Oaxaca** (Oaxaca tel. 951/571-3695), traditionsmexico@yahoo.com, www.traditionsmexico.com), led by artisan-guide and Oaxaca-lover Eric Mindling. His bliss is leading like-minded folks in explorations of clay and fiber arts by country artisans in the Valley of Oaxaca. The approach is people-to-people, the accommodations sometimes rustic, the prices reasonable, and the rewards potentially great. Other options include a "Flavors of Oaxaca" culinary tour, and a Oaxaca photography workshop.

Getting Around

BY AIR

Travelers on tight time budgets find it useful to save a day by flying, instead of driving or busing, over the Sierra between Oaxaca City and the Pacific resorts of Puerto Ángel, Bahías de Huatulco, and Puerto Escondido.

A pair of light charter airlines (in the general aviation terminal, the building to the right as you face the main terminal) connect Oaxaca City with Huatulco and Puerto Escondido on the Pacific Coast. Contact **Aerotucan** (in Oaxaca City, Calle Emelio Carranza 303, corner of Eucaliptos, tel. 951/502-0840, toll-free outside Oaxaca City tel. 800/640-4148, www.aerotucan.com.mx, infor@aerotucan.com) or **Aerovega** (tel. 951/516-4982), in Oaxaca City.

BY BUS

The bus is the king of the Oaxaca road. A host of lines connect virtually every town and most villages in Oaxaca. Three distinct levels of service—luxury or super-first class, first class, and second class—are generally available. **Luxury-class** (usually called something like Primera Plus or Ejecutivo, depending upon the line): super-deluxe express coaches speed between major towns, seldom stopping en route. In exchange for somewhat higher fares (about $70 Oaxaca City–Puerto Escondido, for example, compared with $50 for first class), luxury-class passengers enjoy rapid passage and airline-style amenities: plush reclining seats, air-conditioning, on-board toilet, video, and aisle attendant.

Although less luxurious, **first-class** service costs less, is frequent, and always includes reserved seating. Additionally, passengers usually enjoy soft reclining seats and air-conditioning (if it's working). Besides making regular stops at or near most towns and villages en route, first-class bus drivers, if requested, will usually stop and let you off anywhere along the road.

Second-class bus seating is unreserved. In outlying parts of Oaxaca, there is a class of buses even beneath second class, but given the condition of many second-class buses, it usually seems as if third-class buses wouldn't run at all. Such buses are the stuff of travelers' legends: the recycled old GMC, Ford, and Dodge school buses that stop everywhere and carry everyone and everything to the smallest villages tucked away in the far mountains. As long as there is any kind of a road to it, such a bus will most likely go there.

Second-class buses are not for travelers with weak knees or stomachs. You will often initially have to stand, cramped in the aisle, among a crowd of campesinos. They are warm-hearted people, but poor, so don't tempt them with open, dangling purses or wallets bulging in back pockets. Stow your money safely away. After a while, you will probably be able to sit down. Such privilege, however, comes with obligation, such as holding an old lady's bulging bag of carrots or a toddler on your lap. But if you accept your burden with humor and

Travel to Juquila from Oaxaca's second-class bus stop.

equanimity, who knows what favors and blessings may flow to you in return.

Tickets, Seating, and Baggage

Online and telephone ticketing has arrived in Oaxaca. The up-and-coming agency **Boletotal** (formerly Ticket Bus, toll-free tel. 800/702-8000, or 800/009-9090, Oaxaca City tel. 951/514-6655, www.boletotal.com. mx), with offices in Oaxaca City, sells tickets for long-distance routes all over the state of Oaxaca, reaching as far west as Acapulco and Mexico City, north to Veracruz, and east to Mérida, Cancún, and the Guatemala border. Participating bus lines are ADO (Autobuses del Oriente) and its affiliates OCC (Omnibus Cristóbal Colón), AU (Autobuses Unidos), Sur, and Cuenca. Otherwise, other first-class (notably Estrella Blanca along the Pacific Coast) and second-class bus lines don't issue tickets online in Oaxaca.

Nevertheless, plenty of buses usually leave daily, so the easiest way to go is to get to the bus station early enough on your traveling day to ensure that you'll get a bus to your destination. You can make this almost foolproof by calling (or asking your desk clerk to call) the bus station ahead for departure information.

At the station, you'll find that although some first-class bus lines accept credit cards and issue computer-printed tickets at their major stations, many reserved bus tickets are sold for cash and handwritten, with a specific *número de asiento* (seat number) on the back. If you miss the bus, you lose your money. Furthermore, airlines-style automated reservations systems have not yet arrived at the smaller Oaxacan bus stations. Consequently, you can generally buy reserved tickets only at the *salida local* (local departure) station. (An agent in Tehuántepec, for example, cannot ordinarily reserve you a ticket on a bus that originates in Oaxaca City, a day's travel down the road.)

Request a reserved seat number, if possible, from numbers 1–25 in the *delante* (front) to *medio* (middle) of the bus. The rear seats are often occupied by smokers, drunks, and general rowdies. At night, you will sleep better on

© BRUCE WHIPPERMAN

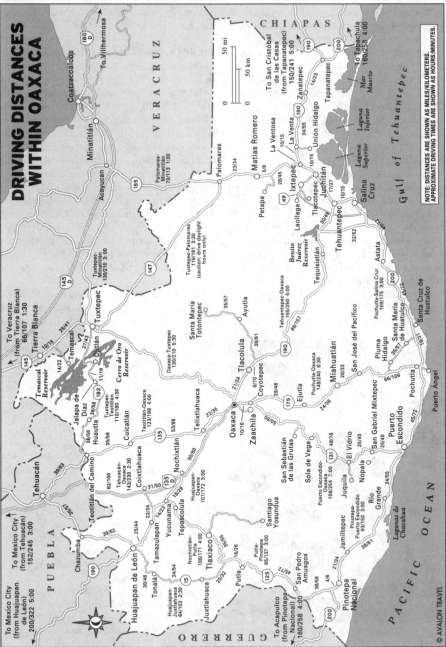

DRIVING DISTANCES WITHIN OAXACA

NOTE: DISTANCES ARE SHOWN AS MILES/KILOMETERS.
APPROXIMATE DRIVING TIMES ARE SHOWN AS HOURS:MINUTES.

© AVALON TRAVEL

the *lado derecho* (right side) away from the glare of oncoming traffic lights.

Baggage is generally secure on Oaxaca buses. Label it, however. Overhead racks are often too cramped to accommodate airline-size carry-ons. Carry a small bag of your crucial items on your person; pack clothes and less essential items in your checked luggage. For peace of mind, watch the handler put your checked baggage on the bus and watch to make sure it is not mistakenly taken off the bus at intermediate stops.

If, somehow, your baggage gets misplaced, remain calm. Bus employees are generally competent and conscientious; if you are patient, recovering your luggage will become a matter of honor for many of them. Baggage handlers are at the bottom of the pay scale; a tip for their mostly thankless job would be very much appreciated.

On long trips, carry food, drinks, and toilet paper. Station food may be dubious and the sanitary facilities ill-maintained.

If you are waiting for a first-class bus at an intermediate *salida de paso* (passing station), you often have to trust to luck that there will be an empty seat. If not, your best option may be to ride a usually much more frequent second-class bus.

BY CAR

Getting around by car in Oaxaca has its pluses and minuses. On the minus side, cars are expensive to rent and roads are often narrow and usually shared with pedestrians, horses, cows, and burros. On the plus side, driving allows you to go where you want on your own schedule.

Rental Car

Car and jeep rentals are an increasingly popular transportation option for Oaxaca travelers. They offer mobility and independence for local sightseeing and beach excursions. (However, street congestion makes for slow and frustrating driving in downtown Oaxaca City. It's

© BRUCE WHIPPERMAN

In Oaxaca, if there's a road to it, a second-class bus probably goes there.

best get around via taxi, $2–3, for anywhere in downtown.) Agents stationed regularly at both the Oaxaca City airport and downtown are Hertz, Alamo, and Europcar; in Puerto Escondido, Budget; and in Huatulco, Thrifty, Hertz, Europcar, and Dollar. Rental car agents also do business in Salina Cruz and Juchitán in the Isthmus, Tuxtepec in Northern Oaxaca, and Huajuapan de León in the Mixteca.

During the winter high season, especially, make reservations in the United States and Canada prior to departure.

Rental agencies generally require drivers to have a valid driver's license, passport, a major credit card, and may require a minimum age of 25.

Oaxaca car rentals are not cheap. With a 15 percent or more "value added" tax tacked on and mandatory Mexican car insurance, they run more than in the United States. The cheapest possible rental car, usually a vintage, well-used, stick-shift VW Beetle, runs $30–50 per day or $200–400 per week, depending on location and season. Prices are steepest during Christmas–New Year's and pre-Easter weeks. Before departure, use the international agencies' (Thrifty, Hertz, Alamo, Budget, and Europcar) toll-free numbers to shop around for availability, prices, and reservations. During non-peak seasons, you may save lots of pesos by waiting till arrival and renting a car through a local agency. Shop around, starting with the agent in your hotel lobby or the local yellow pages (under "Automóviles, renta de").

Car insurance that covers property damage, public liability, and medical payments is an *absolute must* and is required by Mexican law. Although it is customarily included in the price of your rental car, make certain that you're covered before signing the deal. **Collision insurance** may not be included and costs extra. However, major credit cards do furnish coverage that supplements your personal car insurance. Double-check your coverage with both your auto insurance agent and your credit card company before leaving for Mexico.

If you get into an accident in Mexico without insurance, you will be in deep trouble, possibly jail. Safe driving in Oaxaca requires more caution and less speed than back home.

Taxis

The high prices of rental cars make taxis a viable option for local excursions. Cars are luxuries, not necessities, for most Oaxacan families. Travelers might profit from the local money-saving practice of piling everyone in a taxi for Sunday park, beach, and fishing outings. You may find that an all-day taxi and driver (who, besides relieving you of driving, will become your impromptu guide) will cost less than a rental car.

The magic word for saving money by taxi is *colectivo:* a taxi that you share jointly with other travelers. Your first place to practice getting a taxi will be at the airport, where *colectivo* tickets are routinely sold from booths at the terminal door.

If, however, you want your own private taxi, ask for a *taxi especial,* which will probably run about three or four times the individual tariff for a *colectivo.*

Your airport experience will prepare you for in-town taxis, which in Oaxaca do not have meters. **You must establish the taxi price before getting in.** Bargaining comes with the territory in Mexico, so don't shrink from it, even though it may seem a hassle. If you get into a taxi without an agreed-upon price, you are letting yourself in for a more serious, potentially nasty hassle later. If your driver's price is too high, he'll probably come to his senses as soon as you hail another taxi.

After a few days, getting taxis around town will be a cinch. You'll find you don't have to take the high-ticket taxis lined up in your hotel driveway. If the price isn't right, walk toward the street and hail a regular taxi.

In town, if you can't seem to find a taxi, it may be because they are all hanging around waiting for riders at the local stand, called a taxi *sitio.* Ask someone to direct you to it: Say *"Excúseme. ¿Donde está el sitio taxi, por favor?"* ("Excuse me. Where is the taxi stand, please?").

Tours and Guides

For many Oaxaca visitors, locally arranged tours offer a hassle-free alternative to rental car or taxi sightseeing. Hotels and travel agencies, many of whom maintain front-lobby travel and tour desks, offer a bounty of sightseeing, water sports, bay cruise, fishing, and wildlife-viewing tour opportunities.

Hitchhiking

Most everyone agrees hitchhiking is not the safest mode of transport. If you're unsure, don't do it. Hitchhiking doesn't make a healthy steady travel diet, nor should you hitchhike at night.

The recipe for trouble-free hitchhiking requires equal measures of luck, savvy, and technique. The best places to catch rides are where people are already arriving and leaving, such as bus stops, highway intersections, gas stations, RV parks, and on the highway out of town.

Male-female hitchhiking partnerships seem to net the most rides (although it is technically illegal for women to ride in commercial trucks). The more gear you and your partner have, the fewer rides you will get. Pickup and flatbed truck owners often pick up passengers for pay. Before hopping onto the truck bed, ask how much *(¿cuánto cuesta?)* the ride will cost.

Visas and Officialdom

PASSPORTS, TOURIST CARDS, AND VISAS
Your Passport

Your passport is your positive proof of national identity; without it, your status in any foreign country is in doubt. Don't leave home without one. In fact, Mexican border inspection officials require that everyone (except babes in arms) must have a valid passport to enter Mexico; U.S. Immigration rules require that everyone, including **U.S. Citizens, must have a valid passport in order to re-enter the United States.** United States citizens may obtain passports (allow 4–6 weeks) at local post offices. For-fee private passport agencies can speed this process and get you a passport within a week, maybe less.

Entry into Mexico

For U.S. and Canadian citizens, entry by air into Mexico for a few weeks could hardly be easier. At the check-in desk agents immediately inspect your passport. During the flight, airline attendants hand out tourist cards *(tarjetas turísticas)* en route and officers make them official by glancing at passports and stamping the cards at the immigration gate. Business travel permits for 30 days or fewer are handled by the same simple procedures.

Canadian residents must similarly show a valid passport upon entry to Mexico. Nationals of other countries (especially those such as Hong Kong, which issue more than one type of passport) may be subject to different or additional regulations. For advice, consult your regional Mexico Tourism Board Office (U.S./Can. tel. 800/446-3942, www.visitmexico.com) or local Mexican consulate. Very complete and up-to-date Mexico visa and entry information for nationals of virtually all of the world's countries is available at the Toronto, Canada, Consulate website (www.consulmex.com, select "visa and consular services" on the left of the home page).

More Options

For more complicated cases, get your tourist card early enough to allow you to consider the options. Tourist cards can be issued for multiple entries and a maximum validity of 180 days; photos are often required. If you don't request multiple entry or the maximum time, your card will probably be stamped single entry, valid for some shorter period. Request the maximum (180 days is the absolute maximum for a tourist card; long-term foreign residents routinely make semiannual "border runs" for new tourist cards).

Student and Business Visas

A visa is a notation stamped and signed on your passport showing the number of days and entries allowable for your trip. If you need to stay in Mexico more than 180 days, you may apply (sometimes by enduring considerable red tape) at the consulate nearest your home. However, an ordinary 180-day tourist card may be the easiest student or business visa option, if you can manage it.

Entry for Children

Mexican rules for traveling children are very specific: Children under 18 traveling in Mexico must have their own tourist cards and be accompanied either by their parents or by adults carrying an affidavit that gives permission (including relevant dates and locations), notarized by the children's parents. Parents can avoid such difficulties with red tape by getting a passport and a Mexican tourist card for each of their children.

Oaxaca travelers should hurdle all such possible delays far ahead of time in the cool calm of their local Mexican consulate rather than the hot, hurried atmosphere of a border or airport immigration station.

Entry for Pets

A pile of red tape may delay the entry of dogs,

MEXICO TOURISM BOARD OFFICES

More than a dozen Mexico Tourism Board (Consejo de Promoción Turístico de Mexico, CPTM) offices and scores of Mexican government consulates operate in the United States, Canada, Europe, South America, and Asia. Consulates generally handle questions of Mexican nationals abroad, while Mexico Tourism Boards serve travelers heading for Mexico.

For straightforward questions and Mexico regional information brochures, contact the Tourism Board (U.S./Can. tel. 800/446-3942, www.visitmexico.com). If you need more details and read a bit of Spanish, you might find visiting www.cptm.com.mx helpful also. Otherwise, contact one of the North American, European, South American, or Asian Mexico Tourism Boards directly for guidance.

IN NORTH AMERICA

From Alaska, Arizona, California, Colorado, Hawaii, Idaho, Montana, Nevada, Utah, Washington, and Wyoming, contact the **Los Angeles** office (2401 W. Sixth St., 4th Floor, Los Angeles, CA 90057, tel. 213/739-6336, fax 213/739-6340, losangeles@visitmexico.com).

From British Columbia, Alberta, Saskatchewan, and the Yukon and Northwest Territories, contact the **Vancouver** office (999 W. Hastings St., Suite 1110, Vancouver, BC, V6C 2W2, tel. 604/669-2845, fax 604/669-3498, mgarcia@visitmexico.com).

From Arkansas, Colorado, Louisiana, New Mexico, Oklahoma, and Texas, contact the **Houston** office (4507 San Jacinto, Suite 308, Houston TX 77004, tel. 713/772-2581, fax 713/772-6058, houston@visitmexico.com).

From Alabama, Florida, Georgia, Mississippi, Tennessee, North Carolina, Puerto Rico, and South Carolina, contact the **Miami** office (5975 Sunset Dr. #305, Miami, FL 33143, tel. 786/621-2909, fax 786/621-2907, miami@visitmexico.com).

From Illinois, Indiana, Iowa, Kansas, Kentucky, Michigan, Minnesota, Missouri, Nebraska, North Dakota, Ohio, South Dakota, and Wisconsin, contact the **Chicago** office (225 North Michigan Ave., 18th Floor, Suite 1800, Chicago, IL 60601, tel. 312/228-0517, fax 312/228-0515, chicago@visitmexico.com).

From Connecticut, Delaware, Kentucky, Maine, Maryland, Massachusetts, New Hampshire, New Jersey, New York, Pennsylvania, Rhode Island, Vermont, Virginia, Washington D.C., and West Virginia, contact the **New York** office (400 Madison Ave., Suite 11C, New York, NY 10017, tel. 212/308-2110, fax 212/308-9060, mmora@visitmexico.com).

From Ontario, Manitoba, and the Nunavut Territory, contact the **Toronto** office (2 Bloor

cats, and other pets into Mexico. Be prepared with veterinary-stamped health and rabies certificates for each animal. For more information, contact your regional Mexico Tourism Board, or your local Mexican Consulate.

Don't Lose Your Tourist Card

If you do, be prepared with a copy of the original, which you should present to the nearest federal Migración (Immigration) office (on duty at Oaxaca City, Puerto Escondido, and Huatulco airports) and ask for a duplicate tourist permit. Lacking this, you might present some alternate proof of your date of arrival in Mexico, such as a stamped passport or airline ticket. Savvy travelers carry copies of their tourist cards while leaving the original safe in their hotel rooms.

Car Permits

If you drive to Mexico, you will need a permit for your car. Upon entry into Mexico, be ready with originals and copies of your proof-of-ownership or registration papers (state title certificate, registration, or notarized bill of sale), current license plates, and current driver's license. The auto permit fee runs about $30, payable only by non-Mexican bank MasterCard, Visa, or American Express credit cards. (The credit-card-only requirement discourages those

---

St. West, Suite 1502, Toronto, Ontario M4W 3E2, tel. 416/925-0704, fax 416/925-6061, toronto@visitmexico.com).

From New Brunswick, Newfoundland, Nova Scotia, Prince Edward Island, and Quebec, contact the **Montreal** office (1 Place Ville Marie, Suite 1931, Montreal, Quebec H3B2C3, tel. 514/871-1052 or 514/871-1103, fax 514/871-3825, montreal@visitmexico.com).

IN EUROPE

From England, Wales, Scotland, Ireland, Sweden, Estonia, Lithuania, and Latvia, contact the **London** office (Wakefield House, 41 Trinity Sq., London EC3N 4DJ, England, UK, tel. 207/488-9392, fax 207/265-0704, uk@visitmexico.com).

From Hungary, Poland, Slovenia, Slovakia, Germany, Austria, German Switzerland, and the Czech Republic, contact the **Frankfurt** office (Taunusanlage 21, D-60325 Frankfurt-am-Main, Deutschland, tel. 697/103-3383, fax 697/103-3755, germany@visitmexico.com).

From France, Belgium, Luxembourg, Monaco, Russia, and French Switzerland, contact the **Paris** office (4 Rue Notre-Dame des Victoires, 75002 Paris, France, tel. 1/428-69612 or 1/428-69613, fax 1/428-60580, france@visitmexico.com).

From Spain and Portugal contact the **Madrid** office (Carrera San Jeronimo 46, 28014 Madrid, España, tel. 91/561-3520 or 91/561-1827, fax 91/411-0759, spain@visitmexico.com).

From Italy, Turkey, Israel, Cyprus and Malta, contact the **Rome** office (Via Barbarini 3-piso 7, 00187 Roma, Italia, tel. 06/487-4698, fax 06/487-3630 or 06/420-4293, italy@visitmexico.com).

IN SOUTH AMERICA

From Brazil, contact the **Sao Paulo** office (Alameda Administrativo, Rocha Azevedo 882, Conjunto 31, Tercer Andador, Sao Paulo, Brazil, 01410-002, tel. 3088-2129 or 3082-3981, fax 3083-5005, brasil@visitmexico.com).

From Argentina, contact the **Buenos Aires** office (Avenida Reconquista 1056, piso 11, 1003 Barrio Retiro CABA, Buenos Aires, Argentina, tel. 1/4139-6670, fax 1/4139-6771, argentina@visitmexico.com).

IN ASIA

From Japan, Korea, India, Indonesia, Malaysia, Singapore, Thailand, Taiwan, and Vietnam, contact the **Tokyo** office (2-15-1-3F, Nagata-Cho, 2-chome, Chiyoda-ku, Tokyo, Japan 100-0014, tel. 335/030-290, fax 335/030-643, japan@visitmexico.com and pnajar@visitmexico.com).

who sell or abandon U.S.-registered cars in Mexico without paying customs duties.) Credit cards must bear the same name as the vehicle proof-of-ownership papers.

The resulting car permit becomes part of the owner's tourist card and receives the same length of validity. Vehicles registered in the name of an organization or person other than the driver must be accompanied by a notarized affidavit authorizing the driver to use the car in Mexico for a specific time.

Border officials generally allow you to carry or tow additional motorized vehicles (motorcycle, another car, large boat) into Mexico but will probably require separate documentation and fee for each vehicle. If a Mexican official desires to inspect your trailer or motor home, go through it with him.

Accessories, such as a small trailer, boat shorter than six feet, CB radio, or outboard motor, may be noted on the car permit and must leave Mexico with the car.

For more details on motor vehicle entry and what you may bring in your baggage to Mexico, you might also consult the AAA (American Automobile Association) *Mexico TravelBook*. Since Mexico does not recognize foreign automobile insurance, you must buy Mexican automobile insurance.

Crossing the Border and Returning Home

Squeezing through border bottlenecks during peak holidays and rush hours can be time-consuming. Avoid crossing 7–9 A.M. and 4:30–6:30 P.M.

Just before returning across the border with your car, park and have a customs *(aduana)* official **remove and cancel the holographic identity sticker that you received on entry.** If possible, get a receipt *(recibo)* or some kind of verification that it's been canceled *(cancelado)*. Tourists have been fined hundreds of dollars for inadvertently carrying uncanceled car entry stickers on their windshields.

At the same time, return all other Mexican permits, such as tourist cards and hunting and fishing licenses. Also, be prepared for

Mexico exit inspection, especially for cultural artifacts and works of art, which may require exit permits. Certain religious and pre-Columbian artifacts, legally the property of the Mexican government, cannot be taken from the country.

If you entered Mexico with your car, you cannot legally leave without it except by permission from local customs authorities, usually the Aduana (Customs House) or the Oficina Federal de Hacienda (Federal Treasury Office).

All returnees are subject to U.S. immigration and customs inspection. These inspections have become generally more time-consuming since September 11, 2001. The worst bottlenecks are at busy border crossings, especially Tijuana and, to a lesser extent, Mexicali, Nogales, Juárez, Nuevo Laredo, and Matamoros, all of which should be avoided during peak hours.

United States law allows a fixed value ($800 at present) of duty-free goods per returnee. This may include no more than one liter of alcoholic spirits, 200 cigarettes, and 100 cigars. Up to 10 percent duty will be applied to the first $1,000 (fair retail value, save your receipts) in excess of your $800 exemption. You may, however, mail packages (up to $100 value each) of gifts duty-free to friends and relatives in the United States. Make sure to clearly write "unsolicited gift" and a list of the value and contents on the outside of the package. Perfumes (over $5), alcoholic beverages, and tobacco may not be included in such packages.

Improve the security of such mailed packages by sending them by Mexpost class, similar to U.S. Express Mail service. Even better (but much more expensive), send them by Federal Express or DHL international couriers, which maintain offices in Oaxaca City, Puerto Escondido, Huatulco, Tuxtepec, Salina Cruz, Juchitán, and other larger Oaxaca towns.

U.S. Government Customs and Wildlife Information

For more information on U.S. customs regulations important to travelers abroad, read or download the useful pamphlet *Know Before You Go* by visiting the U.S. Customs and

Border Patrol website (www.cpb.gov). Click on "Travel" at the top of the home page, then scroll down to *Know Before You Go.*

For more information on the importation of endangered wildlife products, contact the Fish and Wildlife Service (1849 C. St. NW, Washington, DC 20240, toll-free tel. 800/344-9453, www.fws.gov).

Recreation

ON THE BEACH

It's easy to understand why many Oaxaca vacationers stay right at the beach. And not just at the popular crystalline stretches around the Bahías de Huatulco, Puerto Ángel, and Puerto Escondido. Some adventurers flee the resorts to find even more pristine strands hidden in far corners along the entire Oaxaca coast. There they discover solitude and wildlife-rich shorelines varying from mangrove-edged lagoons and algae-decorated tide pools to shoals of pebbles and sand of a dozen colors and consistencies.

Sand makes the beach, and Oaxaca has plenty, from warm black mica dust to cool, velvety white coral. Some beaches drop steeply to turbulent, close-in surf fine for fishing. Others are level, with gentle, rolling breakers made for surfing and swimming.

Oaxaca's beaches yield fascinating troves of shells and treasures of flotsam and jetsam. **Beachcombing** is more rewarding during the summer storm season when big waves deposit acres of fresh shells—among them clams, combs of Venus, conch, cowries, limpets, olives, sand dollars, scallops, starfish, and whelks.

During the summer–fall rainy season, beaches near river mouths are often fantastic outdoor galleries of wind- and water-sculpted snags and giant logs deposited by the downstream flood.

© BRUCE WHIPPERMAN

Playa Principal, Puerto Escondido

SPRINGS, CAVES, AND WATERFALLS

A trove of crystalline springs (aguas termales), limestone caves (grutas), and gushing waterfalls (cascadas) fills the state of Oaxaca. (The * means especially recommended.)

- **The Valley of Oaxaca:** *Hierve El Agua, *San Sebastián de las Grutas

- **Pacific Resorts and Southern Sierra:** Chacalapa, Balneario El Paraíso, Aguas Termales Atotonilco, Charquito Atotonilco Warm Springs, Huatulco (*Cascadas Magicas)

- **The Mixteca:** *Apoala, *Tamazulapan, Juxtlahuaca (*Laguna Encantada, *San Miguel de la Cueva), Yosundua (Cascada Esmeralda)

- **Northern Oaxaca:** Ixtlán de Juárez (Arco de Yagela), Valle Nacional (*Balnearios Monte Flor and El Zuzul), San José Chiltepec, Tuxtepec (*Cascadas de Betania), Jalapa de Díaz (*Río Uluapa), Huautla de Jiménez (Las Regaderas, *Nindo-Da-Gé, and Sotano de San Agustín)

- **The Isthmus:** Jalapa del Marqués, *Magdalena Tlacotepec, *Santiago Laollaga

Cascada Esmeralda

© BRUCE WHIPPERMAN

SNORKELING AND SCUBA DIVING

Many exciting clear-water sites, such as the **Bahías de Huatulco** and **Playa Estacahuite** near Puerto Ángel and **Playa Angelito** near Puerto Escondido, await both beginner and expert snorkelers and divers. Veteran divers usually arrive during the dry winter and early spring when river outflows are mere trickles, leaving offshore waters clear. In Huatulco and Puerto Escondido, professional dive shops rent equipment, provide lessons and guides, and transport divers to choice sites.

While convenient, rented equipment is often less than satisfactory. To be sure, serious divers bring their own gear. This might include wetsuits in the winter, when some swimmers begin to feel cold after an unprotected half hour in the water.

SURFING, SAILING, AND KAYAKING

Oaxaca has the Mexican Pacific's acknowledged best (but most challenging) surfing beach, the renowned **Playa Zicatela** "pipeline" at Puerto Escondido. The surf everywhere is highest and most exciting during the July–November hurricane season, when big swells from storms far out at sea attract platoons of surfers to favored beaches.

Other lesser but still popular intermediate-level surfing spots are **Playa Zipolite** near Puerto Ángel, **La Boca** at Huatulco, and Playa Chacahua, an hour's drive west of Puerto Escondido.

Sailboarders and sailboaters can often find the moderately breezy conditions that they love during the Oaxaca winter or spring. Then they gather to enjoy the near-ideal conditions at many coves and inlets near the resorts.

Kayakers who, by contrast, are happiest in tranquil waters, also do well in the winter and spring in sheltered coastal bays and coves, notably the **Bahías de Huatulco.** Mangrove lagoons, furthermore, especially **Laguna Manialtepec** near Puerto Escondido, and Laguna Chacahua farther west, or Laguna Corrallero, near Pinotepa Nacional, near

Oaxaca's western border, offer abundant kayaking opportunities.

While beginners can have fun with the equipment available from rental shops, serious surfers, sailboarders, sailboaters, and kayakers should pack their own gear.

POWER SPORTS

Power sports, such as waterskiing, parasailing, and personal watercraft riding, are not widespread on Oaxaca beaches. In parasailing, a motorboat pulls while a parachute lifts you, like a soaring gull, high over the ocean. After 10 minutes, they deposit you (usually gently) back on the sand. Personal watercraft are like snowmobiles except they operate on water, where, with a little practice, even beginners can quickly learn to whiz over the waves.

Although the luxury hotels at the Bahías de Huatulco provide experienced crews and equipment for such activities, practice while sober and with caution. Moreover, you, as the paying patron, have a right to expect that your providers and crew are themselves both cautious and sober besides being well equipped.

BEACH BUGGIES AND ATVS

Some visitors enjoy racing along the beach and rolling over dunes with beach buggies and ATVs (all-terrain vehicles—*motos* in Mexico); balloon-tired, three- or four-wheeled motor scooters; and mini-jeeps. While certain resort rental agencies cater to the growing use of such vehicles, limits are in order. Of all the proliferating high-horsepower beach pastimes, these are the most intrusive. Noise, exhaust and gasoline pollution, injuries to operators and bystanders, and scattering of wildlife and destruction of their habitats have led (and I hope will continue to lead) to the restriction of beach buggies and ATVs on beaches and in forest habitats.

FISHING

Experts agree that the Oaxaca coast is a world-class deep-sea and surf fishing ground. Sportfishing enthusiasts routinely bring in dozens of species from among the several hundred that have been identified in Oaxaca waters.

Surf Fishing

Most good fishing beaches away from the immediate resort areas will typically have only a few locals (mostly with nets) and fewer visitors. Oaxacans do little sportfishing. Most either make their living from fishing or do none at all. Some local folks catch fish for supper with nets. Consequently, few Oaxaca shops sell fishing equipment. Plan to bring your own, including hooks, lures, line, and weights.

In any case, the cleaner the water, the more interesting your catch. On a good day, your reward might be *sierras, cabrillas,* porgies, or pompanos pulled from the Oaxaca surf.

You can't have everything, however. Foreigners cannot legally take Mexican abalone, clams, coral, lobster, rock bass, sea fans, seashells, shrimp, or turtles. Nor are they supposed to buy them directly from fisherfolk.

Deep-Sea Fishing

Santa Cruz de Huatulco, Salina Cruz and, to a lesser extent, Puerto Escondido and Puerto Ángel are well-known jumping-off-spots for the big prize marlin and sailfish.

A deep-sea boat charter generally includes the boat and crew for a full or half day, plus equipment and bait for 2–6 persons, not including food or drinks. The full-day price depends upon the season. Around Christmas and New Year's and before Easter (when reservations will be mandatory), a boat can run $400 at the Bahías de Huatulco, less during low season and at the other spots.

Renting an entire big boat is not the only choice. *Pangas* (outboard launches seating up to six passengers) are available for as little as $50, depending on the season. Once, six of my friends hired a *panga,* had a great time, and came back with a boatload of big tuna, jack, and mackerel. A restaurant cooked them up as a banquet for a dozen of us in exchange for the extra fish, and I discovered for the first time how heavenly fresh *sierra veracruzana* can taste.

Bringing Your Own Boat

If you're going to be doing lots of fishing, your own boat may be your most flexible and economical option. One big advantage is you can go to the many excellent fishing grounds the charter boats do not frequent. Keep your equipment simple, scout around, and keep your eyes peeled and ears open for local regulations and customs, plus tide, wind, and fish-edibility information.

Fishing Licenses and Boat Permits

Anyone, regardless of age, who is either fishing or riding in a fishing boat in Mexico is required to have a fishing license. Although Mexican fishing licenses are obtainable from certain bait and tackle stores and car insurance agents or at government fishing offices everywhere along the coast, save yourself time and trouble by getting both your fishing licenses and boat permits by mail

---

FISH

A bounty of fish dart, swarm, jump, and wriggle in Oaxaca's surf, reefs, lagoons, and offshore depths. While many make delicious dinners (albacore, dorado, pez gallo), others are tough (sailfish), bony (bonefish), and even poisonous (puffers). Some grow to half-ton giants (marlin, Goliath fish, sunfish), while others are diminutive reef-grazers (parrot fish, damselfish, angelfish) whose bright colors delight snorkelers and divers. Here's a sampling of what you might find underwater or on your dinner plate.

The **best-eating** of the bunch are albacore, dolphinfish (*dorado*), red snapper, roosterfish, snook (*robalo*), triggerfish (*pez Puerco*), wahoo, yellowfin tuna, and yellowtail (*jurel*).

- **albacore** (*albacora, atún*): 2–4 feet in size; blue; found in deep waters; excellent taste
- **angelfish** (*angel*): one foot; yellow, orange, blue; reef fish
- **barracuda** (*barracuda, picuda*): two feet; brown; deep waters; good taste
- **black marlin** (*marlin negro*): six feet; blue-black; deep waters; good taste
- **blue marlin** (*marlin azul*): eight feet; blue; deep waters; poor taste
- **bobo** (*barbudo*): one foot; blue, yellow; found in surf; fair taste
- **bonefish** (*macabi*): one foot; blue or silver; found inshore; poor taste

fresh mahimahi (*dorado*), ready to eat

© BRUCE WHIPPERMAN

ahead of time from the Mexican Department of Fisheries. Call at least a month before departure and ask for (preferably faxed) applications and the fees (which are reasonably priced, but depend upon the period of validity and the fluctuating exchange rate). On the application, fill in the names (exactly as they appear on passports) of the people requesting licenses. Include a cashier's check or a money order for the exact amount, along with a stamped, self-addressed envelope. Address the application to the **Mexican Department of Fisheries** (Oficina de Pesca, 2550 5th Ave., Suite 15, San Diego, CA 92103-6622, U.S. tel. 619/233-4324, fax 619/233-0344).

Freshwater Fishing

Oaxaca has four large reservoirs: Yosocuta, in the Mixteca near Huajuapan de León; Cerro de Oro and Miguel Alemán, in the north near Tuxtepec; and Benito Juárez Reservoir, in

- **bonito** *(bonito):* two feet; black; deep waters; good taste
- **butterfly fish** *(muñeca):* six inches; black, yellow; reef fish
- **chub** *(chopa):* one foot; gray; reef fish; good taste
- **croaker** *(corvina):* two feet; brownish; found along inshore bottoms; rare and protected
- **damselfish** *(castañeta):* four inches; brown, blue, orange; reef fish
- **dolphinfish, mahimahi** *(dorado):* three feet; green, gold; deep waters; excellent taste
- **grouper** *(garropa):* three feet; brown, rust; found offshore and in reefs; good taste
- **grunt** *(burro):* eight inches; black, gray; found in rocks, reefs
- **jack** *(toro):* 1-2 feet; bluish-gray; offshore; good taste
- **mackerel** *(sierra):* two feet; gray with gold spots; offshore; good taste
- **mullet** *(lisa):* two feet; gray; found in sandy bays; good taste
- **needlefish** *(agujón):* three feet; blue-black; deep waters; good taste
- **Pacific porgy** *(pez de pluma):* 1-2 feet; tan; found along sandy shores; good taste
- **parrot fish** *(perico, pez loro):* one foot; green, pink, blue, orange; reef fish
- **puffer** *(botete):* eight inches; brown; inshore; poisonous
- **red snapper** *(huachinango, pargo):* 1-2 feet; reddish pink; deep waters; excellent taste
- **roosterfish** *(pez gallo):* three feet; black, blue; deep waters; excellent taste
- **sailfish** *(pez vela):* five feet; blue-black; deep waters; tough, poor taste
- **sardine** *(sardina):* eight inches; blue-black; offshore; good taste
- **sea bass** *(cabrilla):* 1-2 feet; brown, ruddy; reef and rock crevices; good taste
- **shark** *(tiburón):* 2-10 feet; black to blue; in- and offshore; good taste
- **snook** *(robalo):* 2-3 feet; black-brown; found in brackish lagoons; excellent taste
- **spadefish** *(chambo):* one foot; black-silver; found along sandy bottoms; reef fish
- **swordfish** *(pez espada):* five feet; black to blue; deep waters; good taste
- **triggerfish** *(pez puerco):* 1-2 feet; blue, rust, brown, black; reef fish; excellent taste
- **wahoo** *(peto, guahu):* 2-5 feet; green to blue; deep waters; excellent taste
- **yellowfin tuna** *(atún amarilla):* 2-5 feet; blue, yellow; deep waters; excellent taste
- **yellowtail** *(jurel):* 2-4 feet; blue, yellow; offshore; excellent taste

the Isthmus not far from Tehuántepec. Their shorelines are scenic and easily accessible, and their waters are home to several varieties of fish, mostly *mojarra* (bass), plentiful enough for local folks to a make living cooking fish dinners.

TENNIS AND GOLF

Most Oaxacans are working too hard to be playing much tennis and golf. Consequently, tennis and golf courses are nearly completely restricted to Oaxaca City and the Bahías de Huatulco. If you are planning on a lot of golf and tennis, check into one of the several Oaxaca City or Bahías de Huatulco hotels with easy access to these facilities. Use of hotel tennis courts is sometimes included in your hotel tariff. If not, fees will run about $10 per hour. Golf greens fees, which begin at about $50 for 18 holes, are usually extra.

Accommodations

Oaxaca has lodgings to suit every style and pocketbook: world-class resorts, small beachside hotels, bed-and-breakfasts, homey *casas de huéspedes* (guesthouses), friendly trailer parks, community-maintained tourist lodgings, and many miles of breezy beaches, ripe for camping.

In Oaxaca City, the busy **high seasons,** when hotel reservations are generally necessary, are July, Day of the Dead (late Oct.–early Nov.), and mid-December–Janurary 6, the Day of the Kings. On the coast, high seasons are also mid-December–January 6, plus mid-February–Easter, and the months of July and August. Excellent, quiet **low-season** times to visit anywhere in Oaxaca are November after the Day of the Dead and the month of January after January 6, when prices are low and the weather is consistently temperate and dry.

The dozens of accommodations described in this book are positive recommendations— checked out in detail. They are good choices from which you can pick according to your taste and purse.

Hotel Rates

The rates listed in this book are U.S. dollar equivalents of peso prices, taxes included, as quoted by the hotel management at the time of writing. They are intended as a general guide only, and probably will only approximate the asking rate when you arrive. Some readers unfortunately try to bargain by telling desk clerks that, for example, the rate should be $30 because they read it in this book. This is unwise, because it makes hotel managers and clerks reluctant to quote rates for fear readers might hold their hotel responsible for such quotes. As private businesses, hotels are free to raise their rates; conversely, if the price is too high, customers are entitled to take their business elsewhere.

In Oaxaca, hotel rates depend strongly upon inflation and season. To cancel the effect of the fluctuating Mexican peso, rates are reported in U.S. dollars. However, when settling your hotel bill, you should always insist on paying in pesos cash or by credit card, which by law must be marked in pesos.

Saving Money

The hotel prices quoted here are **rack rates:** the maximum tariff, exclusive of packages and promotions, that you would pay if you walked in off the street and rented an unreserved room for one day. Savvy travelers seldom pay the maximum. Since most hotel clerks will tell you that their hotel doesn't give **discounts** *(discuentos),* it's best not to use that forbidden word. Instead, always inquire if there are any **promotions or packages** (*promociones o paquetes,* proh-moh-see-OH-nays oh pah-KAY-tays). At any time other than the high seasons, you can generally bargain for a lowered price. Don't be shy; if the hotel asking price is $60, offer $40. At best, you'll get what you want; at worst, you can always take your business elsewhere. Often discounts (Shh!) come as one or two free days for a one-week stay. Promotional packages available during slack seasons sometimes include free extras, such as breakfast, a car rental, a boat tour, or a sports rental. A travel agent and/or Internet travel site can be of great help in shopping around for such bargains.

You will virtually always save money if you deal in pesos only. Insist on booking your lodging for an agreed price in pesos and paying the resulting hotel bill in pesos, rather than dollars. The reason is that dollar rates quoted by hotels are often based on the hotel desk exchange rate, which is sometimes as much as 10 percent less favorable than the bank exchange rate. For example, if the desk clerk tells you your hotel bill is $1,000, instead of handing over the dollars, ask him or her how much it is in pesos. Using the desk conversion rate, the clerk might say something like 10,000 pesos (considerably less than the 11,000 pesos that the bank might give for your $1,000). Pay the 10,000 pesos or have the clerk mark 10,000 pesos on your credit card slip, and save yourself $90.

GUESTHOUSES, BED-AND-BREAKFASTS, AND HOMESTAYS

A significant fraction of Oaxaca City lodgings fall into these categories. On city residential side streets, often several blocks removed from the tourist zone, are many of the *casas de huéspedes* (guesthouses), bed-and-breakfasts, and homes where increasing numbers of families are renting rooms to visitors.

Such lodgings vary from scruffy to spic-and-span, humble to luxurious. At minimum, you can expect a plain room, a shared toilet and hot-water shower, and plenty of atmosphere for your money. Rates are highest in Oaxaca City and the Bahías de Huatulco, ranging between $20 and about $100 for two. Discounts are often available for long-term stays.

Note: Oaxaca bed-and-breakfasts are generally rather expensive, since they are a lodging style sought out by mostly North American travelers accustomed to paying high prices. If you want to save money, check out the Mexican version of the same thing, the homier *casa de huéspedes.*

In addition to the guesthouse, bed-and-breakfast, and homestay-style lodgings listed in the destination chapters of this book, you should also consult the many classified advertisements of the local tourist newspapers, especially in Oaxaca City and Puerto Escondido. Moreover, Spanish Language School, common in Oaxaca City, usually recommends a list of homestays (family accommodations) to their participants.

APARTMENTS AND HOUSE RENTALS

For longer stays in Oaxaca City, many visitors prefer the convenience and economy of an apartment or house rental. Choices vary, from spartan studios to deluxe homes big enough for entire extended families. Prices depend strongly upon season and amenities, from $350 per month for the cheapest to around $1,000 for the most luxurious.

At the low end, you can expect a clean, furnished apartment with kitchen and bathroom and once- or twice-a-week housecleaning service. Higher up the scale, houses vary from moderately luxurious homes to sky's-the-limit mansions, blooming with built-in designer luxuries, such as a swimming pool or tennis court, and including at least a gardener, cook, and maid.

Shopping Around

You can find many guesthouses, bed-and-breakfasts, and apartment rentals through on-the-spot local contacts, such as the tourist newspapers' want ad sections, websites, neighborhood For Rent *(Renta)* signs, and local listing agents. If you prefer making rental arrangements prior to arrival, you can usually email, fax, or telephone managers—many of whom speak English—directly.

COMMUNITY *CABAÑAS ECOTURÍSTICAS*

More than a dozen rural communities, mostly on the east side of the central Valley of Oaxaca, the Northern Sierra, and the Mixteca, encourage visitors to come and stay in their tourist lodges, called *cabañas ecoturísticas* (ecotouristic cabins). These are government-built, rustic but comfortable, modern-standard cabins, managed and maintained by a community-appointed *gerente* (manager). *Cabañas* typically have two separate one-room units that sleep up to six people each and share a single flush toilet and shower-bath between them. Units rent for about $10–20 per night per person, or $30–50 per group, with towels, blankets, flush toilets, and hot-water showers.

LOCAL HOTELS

Locally owned and operated hotels make up most of the recommendations in this book. Many veteran travelers find it hard to understand why people come to Oaxaca and spend $200 a day for a super-luxury hotel room when simpler but comfortable alternatives can run as little as $30.

In Oaxaca City, many such hotels are within easy walking distance of the town center, with its lovely plaza, restored old monuments, restaurants, and shops. In the Puerto Escondido and Puerto Ángel resorts, most of them are either right on the beach or very near it. Local hotels, which depend as much on Mexican tourists as foreigners, generally have clean, large rooms, often with private view balconies, ceiling fans, and toilet and hot-water bath or shower. What they often lack are the plush extras—air-conditioning, cable TV, phones, tennis courts, exercise gyms, spas, and saunas—of the luxury resorts.

Booking local hotels is straightforward. Many of them can be emailed and all of them can be dialed or faxed directly (from the United States, dial 011-52, followed by the telephone or fax number) for information and reservations. If your Spanish is rusty, ask for someone who speaks English (ask, in Spanish: *"¿Por favor, hay alguien que habla Inglés?"*—por fah-VOR, AY ahhl-ghee-AYN KAY AB-lah een-GLAYS?). Always ask about money-saving packages (pah-KAY-tays) and promotions (proh-moh-see-OH-nays) when reserving.

INTERNATIONAL-CLASS RESORTS

Oaxaca visitors enjoy several beautiful, well-managed, international-class resort hotels in Oaxaca City and the Bahías de Huatulco. Their super-deluxe amenities, moreover, need not be overly expensive. While high-season room tariffs ordinarily run $100–300, low-season packages and promotions sometimes cut these prices by half. Shop around for savings through travel agents, and by calling the hotels directly through their toll-free 800 numbers.

CAMPING, *PALAPAS,* AND TRAILER PARKS

Although Oaxaca has only a sprinkling of formally maintained places for camping, many inviting beach and inland country spots are customarily used informally.

Beach Camping

Camping at beaches is popular among middle-class Mexican families, especially during the Christmas–New Year's week and during Semana Santa, the week before Easter. During other times of the year, tent and RV campers usually find prospective camping spots not crowded. The best beach spots typically have a shady palm grove for informal camping and a *palapa* (palm-thatched) restaurant that serves drinks and fresh seafood. (Heads up for falling coconuts, no joke, especially in the wind.) Cost for parking and tenting is often minimal, typically only the price of food at the restaurant.

Beach days are often perfect for swimming, strolling, and fishing; nights are usually balmy—too warm for a sleeping bag, but fine for a hammock (which allows more air circulation than a tent). Good tents, however, keep out mosquitoes and other pests, which may be further discouraged with good bug repellent. Tents are generally warm inside, requiring only a sheet or light blanket for cover.

As for **camping on isolated beaches,** opinions vary, from dire warnings of *bandidos* to bland assurances that all is peaceful along the coast. The truth is probably somewhere in between. Trouble is most likely to occur in the vicinity of resort towns, notoriously, on the out-skirt beaches of Puerto Escondido, where a few local thugs have harassed isolated campers.

When scouting out a place to camp, a good general rule is to arrive early enough in the day to get a feel for the place. Buy a soda at the *palapa* or nearby store and take a stroll around. Say *"Buenos días"* to the people along the way; ask if the fishing is good: *"¿Pesca buena?"* Use your common sense. If the people seem friendly, ask if it's *seguro* (safe). If so, ask permission: *"¿Es bueno acampar acá?"* ("Is it OK to camp around here?"). You'll rarely be refused.

Beach *Palapas*

Visitors can still rent beachfront *palapas* (thatched houses) in Puerto Escondido; west of Puerto Escondido, at Playas Zipolite, Mazunte, and Ventanilla (near Puerto Ángel); and east of Puerto Escondido, at Roca Blanca and Playa Chacahua. Amenities typically include beds or hammocks, a shady thatched porch, cold running water, a kerosene stove, and shared toilets and showers, for about $10 per day per person.

The bad news is that security has been a problem in some *palapas,* notably at Puerto Escondido. The good news is that the Puerto Ángel area has some of the better *palapas,* such as Lo Cósmico and Shambhala. The best news of all is that *palapas* are usually right on the beach, so you can walk right out your front door onto the sand, where surf, shells, and sea-birds will be there to entertain you.

Mountain and Backcountry Camping

Oaxaca's mountain and rural backcountry offer many additional camping opportunities. Private owners and communities maintain pic-nic areas and informal campgrounds at choice sites, such as springs, waterfalls, caves, *sabineras* (giant cypress groves), and on rivers and reservoir shorelines.

Invariably, camping sites are on private (*particular*—par-tee-koo-LAHR) or com-munal land. As a courtesy, you should obtain permission to set up camp either from the site manager, the closest neighboring restaurant or house, or at the nearest *presidencia municipal* or *agencia.* Such permission, sometimes for a small fee, is usually granted almost automati-cally. Please reciprocate by keeping your camp-fire, if permitted, modest and under control, respecting local etiquette (don't swim or sun-bathe in the nude), cleaning up thoroughly, and carrying away all your trash.

For an informative and entertaining dis-cussion of camping in Mexico, check out *The People's Guide to Mexico* by Carl Franz.

RV Trailer Parks

Campers who prefer company to isolation usu-ally stay in trailer parks. Oaxaca has five mod-est but recommendable RV trailer parks: two in Oaxaca City, two in Zipolite by the beach, near Puerto Ángel, and one in Puerto Escondido, on the beach.

Food and Drink

Some travel to Mexico for the food. True Mexican food is old-fashioned, homestyle fare requiring many hours of loving preparation. Such food is short on meat and long on corn, beans, rice, to-matoes, chilies, spices, onions, eggs, and cheese.

Mexican food is the unique end-product of thousands of years of native tradition. It is based on corn—*teocentli,* the Aztec "food of the gods"—called *maíz* (mah-EES) by present-day Mexicans. In the past, the typical Mexican woman spent much of her time grinding and preparing corn: soaking the grain in limewa-ter (which swells the kernels and removes the tough seed-coat) and grinding the bloated seeds into meal on a stone *metate.* Finally, she would pat the meal into tortillas and cook them on a hot, baked mud griddle.

Sages (men, no doubt) have wistfully imag-ined the gentle pat-pat-pat of women all over Mexico to be the heartbeat of Mexico, which

© BRUCE WHIPPERMAN

Lining up for a kilogram of tortillas is a daily ritual.

they feared would someday cease. Fewer women these days make tortillas by hand. The gentle pat-pat-pat has been replaced by the whir and rattle of automatic tortilla-making machines in myriad *tortillerías,* where women and girls line up for their family's daily kilo-stack of tortillas.

Tortillas are to the Mexicans as rice is to the Chinese and bread is to the French. A Mexican family meal, more often than not, is some mixture of sauce, meat, beans, cheese, and vegetables wrapped in a tortilla, which becomes the culinary be-all: the food, the dish, and the utensil all wrapped into one.

This most Mexican style of meal usually includes one or two of a number of specialties known by Mexicans as **antojitos** and known to everyone else as "Mexican food." These are the familiar burritos, chiles rellenos, enchiladas, guacamole, nachos, quesadillas, refried beans, tacos, tamales, and other combinations of beans, cheese, corn, eggs, meat, sauces, and spices that make up the menus of Mexican restaurants in the United States and Canada.

HOT OR NOT?

Much food served in Mexico is not "Mexican." Eating habits, as most other Mexican customs, depend upon social class. Upwardly mobile Mexicans typically shun the corn-based native food in favor of the European-style food of the Spanish colonial elite: chops, cutlets, fish, clams, octopus, omelets, pasta, potatoes, rice, soups, salads, and steaks.

Such fare is often as bland as Des Moines on a summer Sunday afternoon. *"No picante"*—not spicy—is how the Mexicans describe bland food. *"Caliente"* or *"Calor,"* the Spanish words that describe "hot" water or weather, do not, in contrast to English usage, also imply spicy *(picante).*

VEGETARIAN AND ORGANIC FOOD

Strictly vegetarian cooking is the exception in Mexico, although a few macrobiotic-vegetarian restaurants and health-food stores have opened in Oaxaca City, Puerto Escondido, Puerto Ángel, and the Bahías de Huatulco. Meat is such a delicacy for most Oaxacans that they can't understand why people would give it up voluntarily. If vegetable-lovers can manage with beans, cheese, corn, eggs, fruit, and *legumbres* (vegetables) and not be bothered by a bit of *manteca de cerdo* (pork fat), Mexican (and Oaxacan) cooking will suit them fine.

Although much Oaxacan produce would probably qualify north of the border as de-facto organic, a system for classifying food as organic is just beginning in Oaxaca City and the coastal tourist resorts of Puerto Escondido and the Bahías de Huatulco.

If all you require is strictly vegetable fare, Oaxaca is a snap. Most restaurants, all the way down to a humble Mexican *comedor* or *fonda* (food stall) will almost always be able to fill up some hot corn tortillas with fresh diced tomatoes, avocados, beans, and onions, add some piquant fresh *salsa,* and serve it all up as several tasty and nutritious hot tacos.

SEAFOOD

Early chroniclers wrote that Aztec Emperor Moctezuma employed a platoon of runners to bring fresh fish 480 kilometers (300 mi) from the sea to his court every day. On the Oaxaca Pacific coast, fresh seafood is fortunately much more available from scores of shoreline establishments, ranging from thatched beach *palapas* to five-star hotel restaurants.

Oaxaca seafood is literally there for the taking. When strolling on the beach, I have seen well-fed, middle-class local vacationers breaking and eating oysters and mussels right off the rocks. Villagers up and down the coast use small nets (or bare hands) to retrieve a few fish for supper, while communal teams haul in big nets full of silvery, wriggling fish for sale right on the beach.

Despite the plenty, Oaxaca seafood prices reflect high worldwide demand, even at the humblest seaside *palapa.* The freshness and variety, however, make even the typical dishes seem like bargains at any price.

FRUITS AND JUICES

Squeezed vegetable and fruit juices (*jugos,* HOO-gohs) are among the widely available delights of Oaxaca. Among the many establishments—restaurants, cafés, and *loncherías*—willing to supply you with your favorite *jugo,* the **jugerías** (juice bars) are often the most fun. Colorful fruit piles usually mark *jugerías.* If you don't immediately spot your favorite fruit, ask anyway; it might be hidden in the refrigerator.

Besides your choice of pure juice, a *jugería* will often serve **licuados.** Into the juice, they whip powdered milk, your favorite fruit, ice, and sugar to taste for a creamy afternoon

CATCH OF THE DAY

- *Ceviche* (say-VEE-chay): a chopped raw fish appetizer as popular on Oaxaca beaches as sushi is on Tokyo side streets. Although it can contain anything from conch to octopus, the best ceviche consists of diced young *tiburón* (shark) or *sierra* (mackerel) fillet and plenty of fresh tomatoes, onions, garlic, and chilies, all doused with lime juice.

- *Filete de pescado:* fish fillet breaded (*empanizada*), sautéed *al mojo* (ahl-MOH-hoh) with butter and garlic, or smothered in *mole.*

- *Pescado frito* (pays-KAH-doh FREE-toh): fish, pan-fried whole; if you don't specify that it be cooked *a medio* (lightly), the fish may arrive well done, like a big, crunchy french fry.

- *Pescado veracruzana:* a favorite everywhere. Best with *huachinango* (red snapper) smothered in a savory tomato, onion, chili, and garlic sauce. *Pargo* (snapper), *mero* (grouper), and *cabrilla* (sea bass) are also popularly used in this and other specialties.

- **Shellfish:** *ostiones* (oysters) and *almejas* (clams) by the dozen, *langosta* (lobster) and *langostina* (crayfish) *asado* (broiled), *al vapor* (steamed), or *frito* (fried). Pots of fresh-boiled *camarones* (shrimp) are sometimes sold on the street in markets by the kilo; restaurants will make them into *cóctel* (cocktail) or prepare them *en gabardinas* (breaded) at your request.

delicious *aguas*, served at *jugerías* (juice bars)

© BRUCE WHIPPERMAN

pick-me-up or evening dessert. One big favorite is a cool banana-chocolate *licuado,* which comes out tasting like a milk shake, minus the calories.

ALCOHOLIC DRINKS

The Aztec chiefs often sacrificed anyone caught drinking alcohol without permission. The later, more lenient, Spanish attitude toward getting *borracho* (soused) has led to a thriving Mexican renaissance of alcoholic beverages: aguardiente, Kahlua, mescal, pulque, and tequila.

Mescal, distilled from the fermented juice of the maguey (century) plant, was introduced by the Spanish colonists in Oaxaca, where the best *mescales* are still made. Mescal and **tequila,** the best of which is made near Guadalajara from the blue agave subspecies of maguey, both come 76 proof (38 percent alcohol) and up. A small white worm, endemic to the maguey plant, is often added to each bottle of factory mescal for authenticity.

Pulque, Mexico's ancestral alcoholic beverage, although also made from the sap of the maguey, is locally brewed (but not distilled), to a small alcohol content, between beer and wine. The brewing houses are sacrosanct preserves, circumscribed by traditions that exclude both women and outsiders. The brew, said to be full of nutrients, is sold to local *pulquerías* and drunk immediately. If you are ever invited into a *pulquería,* it will be an honor you cannot refuse.

Aguardiente, by contrast, is the notorious fiery Mexican "white lightning," of locally fermented and distilled can juice, and is a dirt-cheap ticket to oblivion for poor Mexican men.

While pulque comes from an age-old indigenous tradition, **cerveza** (beer) is the beverage of modern mestizo Mexico. Full-bodied and often tastier than "light" U.S. counterparts, Mexican beer enjoys an enviable reputation.

Those visitors who indulge usually know their favorite among the many brands, from light to dark: Superior, Corona, Pacífico, Tecate (served with lime), Carta Blanca, Modelo, Dos Equis, Bohemia, Victoria, Indio, Tres Equis, and Negra Modelo. Nochebuena, a flavorful dark brew, becomes available only around Christmas.

Mexicans have yet to develop much of a taste for *vino* (wine), although some domestic wines, such as the Baja California labels Monte Xanic, Domecq, and Cetto, are always quite drinkable and sometimes excellent.

A TROVE OF FRUITS AND NUTS

Besides carrying the usual temperate fruits, *jugerías* (juice bars) and traditional markets are seasonal sources of many delectable, exotic (followed by an *) varieties.

- **avocado** *(aguacate* – ah-wah-KAH-tay): Aztec aphrodisiac

- **banana** *(platano):* many kinds – big and small, red, purple, and yellow

- ***chirimoya**:** green scales, white pulp, sometimes called an *anona*

- ***ciruela**:** looks like (but tastes better than) a small yellow-to-red plum

- **coconut** *(coco):* coconut "milk," called *agua coco*, is a delicious-nutritious thirst quencher

- **grapes** *(uvas):* August–November season

- ***guanabana**:** looks, but doesn't taste, like a green mango

- **guava** *(guava):* delicious juice, widely available canned

- **lemon** *(lima real* – LEE-mah ray-AHL): uncommon and expensive; use lime instead

- **lime** *(limón* – lee-MOHN): abundant and cheap; douse salads with it

- ***mamey**** (mah-MAY): yellow, juicy fruit, excellent for jellies and preserves

- **mango:** king of fruit, April–August. Grown in profusion in Tapanatepec, Oaxaca, the mango "world capital."

- **orange** *(naranja* – nah-RAHN-ha): often greenish-yellow skin, but much sweeter than most California oranges

- **papaya:** said to aid digestion and healing

- **peach** *(durazno* – doo-RAHS-noh): delicious and widely available as canned juice and fruit

- **peanut** *(cacahuate* – kah-kah-WAH-tay): home roasted and cheap

- **pear** *(pera):* fall season

- **pecan** *(nuez):* for a treat, try freshly ground pecan butter

- ***piña anona**:** looks like a thin ear of corn without the husk; tastes like pineapple

- **pineapple** *(piña):* huge, luscious, and cheap

- **strawberry** *(fresa* – FRAY-sah): local favorite

- **tangerine** *(mandarina):* sweet, juicy, and common around Christmas

- **watermelon** *(sandía* – sahn-DEE-ah): perfect on a hot day

- **yaca*** (YAH-kah): relative of the Asian jackfruit, with pebbly green skin, round, and as large as a football; yummy mild taste

- ***zapote**** (sah-POH-tay): yellow, fleshy fruit, said to induce sleep

- ***zapote colorado**:** brown skin, red, puckery fruit, like persimmon; commonly, but incorrectly, called *mamey*

© BRUCE WHIPPERMAN

Pecans *(nuez)* are commonly sold in native markets.

BREAD AND PASTRIES

Excellent locally baked bread is a delightful surprise to many first-time visitors to Oaxaca. Small bakeries everywhere put out trays of hot, crispy-crusted **bolillos** (rolls) and sweet **panes dulces** (pastries). They range from simple cakes, muffins, cookies, and doughnuts to fancy fruit-filled turnovers and puffs. Half the fun occurs before the eating: Grab a tray and tongs, peruse the goodies, and pick out the most scrumptious. With your favorite dozen finally selected, you take your tray to the cashier, who deftly bags everything up and collects a few pesos (two or three dollars) for your entire mouthwatering selection.

Tips for Travelers

ACCESS FOR TRAVELERS WITH DISABILITIES

Mexican airlines and hotels (especially the large ones) have become sensitive to the needs of travelers with disabilities. Open, street-level lobbies and large, wheelchair-accessible elevators and rooms are available in nearly all Pacific Mexico resort (and some smaller, especially boutique) hotels. Furthermore, nearly all street-corner curbs accommodate wheelchairs.

Both Mexico and United States law forbids travel discrimination against otherwise qualified people with disabilities. As long as your disability is stable and not liable to deteriorate during passage, you can expect to be treated like any passenger with special needs.

Make reservations far ahead of departure and ask your agent to inform your airline of your needs, such as a boarding wheelchair or in-flight oxygen. Be early at the gate to take advantage of the pre-boarding call.

For many helpful details to smooth your trip, get a copy of *Survival Strategies for Going Abroad* by Laura Hershey, published in 2005 by **Mobility International USA** (132 E. Broadway, Suite 343, Eugene, OR 97401, tel. 541/343-1284 voice/TTY, fax 541/343-6812, www.miusa.org). Mobility International is a valuable resource for many disabled lovers of Mexico, for it encourages disabled travelers with a goldmine of information and literature and can provide them with valuable Mexico connections. They publish a regular newsletter and provide information and referrals for international exchanges and homestays.

Similarly, **Partners of the Americas** (1424 K St. NW, Suite 700, Washington, D.C. 20005, tel. 202/628-3300 or 800/322-7844, fax 202/628-3306, info@partners.net, www.partners.net), with chapters in 45 U.S. states, works to improve understanding of disabilities and facilities in Mexico and Latin America. It maintains communications with local organizations and individuals whom disabled travelers may contact at their destinations.

TRAVELING WITH CHILDREN

Children are treasured like gifts from heaven in Mexico. Traveling with kids will ensure your welcome most everywhere. On the beach, take extra precautions to make sure they are protected from the sun.

A sick child is no fun for anyone. Fortunately, clinics and good doctors are available even in most small towns. When in need, ask a storekeeper or a pharmacist, *"¿Dónde hay un doctor, por favor?"* (*"¿DOHN-day eye oon doc-TOHR por fah-VOHR?"*). In most cases, within five minutes you will be in the waiting room of the local physician or hospital.

Children who do not favor typical Mexican fare can easily be fed with always available eggs, cheese, *hamburguesas,* milk, oatmeal, corn flakes, tomatoes, avocados, bananas, cakes, and cookies.

Your children will generally have more fun if they have a little previous knowledge of Mexico and a stake in the trip. For example, help them select some library picture books and magazines so they'll know where they're going and what to expect, or give them responsibility for packing and carrying their own small travel bag.

Be sure to mention your children's ages when making air reservations; child discounts of 50 percent or more are sometimes available. Also, if you can arrange to go on an uncrowded flight, you can stretch out and rest on the empty seats.

For more details on traveling with children, check out *Adventuring with Children* by Nan Jeffries.

SENIOR TRAVELERS

Age, according to Mark Twain, is a question of mind over matter: If you don't mind, it doesn't matter. Mexico is a country where whole extended families, from babies to great-grandparents, live together. Elderly travelers will benefit from the respect and understanding Mexicans accord to older people. Besides these encouragements, consider the number of retirees already in havens in Puerto Vallarta, Guadalajara, Manzanillo, Oaxaca, and other regional centers.

Certain organizations support and sponsor senior travel. Leading the field is **Road Scholar** (formerly Elderhostel, 11 Ave. de Lafayette, Boston, MA 02111-1746, toll-free tel. 800/454-5768, www.roadscholar.org). Check out their list of Mexico programs, which has regularly included a 10-day Oaxaca-based Spanish-language and culture program.

Some books also feature senior travel opportunities. One of the pithiest is *Unbelievably Good Deals and Great Adventures You Can't Have Unless You're Over 50,* by Joan Rattner Heilman, published by McGraw Hill (2008). Its 200 pages are packed with details of how to get bargains on cruises, tours, car rentals, lodgings, and much, much more.

The **Internet** is a gold mine of senior-oriented travel information. Near the top of the list is the **Transitions Abroad** site (www.transitionsabroad.com), which offers a gold mine of useful resources for seniors inerested in traveling and living abroad.

GAY AND LESBIAN TRAVELERS

The great majority of visitors find Oaxaca people both gracious and tolerant. This extends from racial color-blindness to being broadminded about sexual preference. As long as gay and lesbian visitors don't flaunt their own preference, they will find acceptance most anywhere in the state of Oaxaca.

As a result, both Oaxaca City and, to an equal smaller extent, the coastal resorts have acquired a growing company of gay- and lesbian-friendly hotels, bars, and entertainments. For example, for Oaxaca City hotel, restaurant, and nightlife details, visit the gay-oriented travel website www.go-oaxaca.com; for a list of gay-friendly bars, nightclubs, and businesses, log on to www.go-oaxaca.com/lifestyles.html.

Some gay- and lesbian-oriented Internet and print publishers also offer excellent travel guidebooks. One of the most experienced is **Damron Company** (tel. 415/255-0404 or 800/462-6654, www.damron.com), which publishes, both in print and by Internet subscription, the *Damron Women's Travel Guide* and *Damron Men's Travel Guide* guidebooks, containing a wealth of gay and lesbian travel information, including more than a dozen listings in Oaxaca City.

If you're interested in more gay and lesbian travel information, advice, and services, check out the San Francisco **Purple Roofs** Internet agency (wheretostay@purpleroofs.com, www.purpleroofs.com). They offer lesbian and gay-friendly Oaxaca hotel and travel agent listings, plus a multitude of services, from tours and air tickets, to travel insurance and hotel reservations.

Health and Safety

STAYING HEALTHY

In Oaxaca as everywhere, prevention is the best remedy for illness. For those visitors who confine their travel to the beaten path, a few basic common-sense precautions will ensure vacation enjoyment.

Resist the temptation to dive headlong into Mexico. It's no wonder that people get sick—broiling in the sun, gobbling peppery food, guzzling beer and margaritas, then discoing half the night—all in their first 24 hours. An alternative is to give your body time to adjust. Travelers often arrive tired and dehydrated from travel and heat. During the first few days, drink plenty of bottled water and juice, and take siestas.

Immunizations and Precautions

A good physician can recommend the proper preventatives for your Oaxaca trip. If you are going to stay pretty much in town, your doctor will probably suggest little more than updating your basic typhoid, diphtheria-tetanus, hepatitis, and polio shots.

For camping or trekking in remote tropical areas—below 1,200 meters (4,000 ft)—doctors often recommend a gamma-globulin shot against hepatitis A and a schedule of chloroquine pills against malaria. While in backcountry areas, use other measures to discourage mosquitoes—and fleas, flies, ticks, no-see-ums, "kissing bugs," and other tropical pesties—from biting you. Common precautions include sleeping under mosquito netting, burning *espirales mosquito* (mosquito coils), and rubbing on plenty of pure DEET (n,n dimethyl-meta-toluamide) "jungle juice," mixed in equal parts with rubbing (70 percent isopropyl) alcohol. Although super-effective, 100 percent DEET dries and irritates the skin.

Sunburn

For sunburn protection, use a good sunscreen with a sun protection factor (SPF) rated 15 or more, which will reduce burning rays to one-fifteenth or less of direct sunlight. Better still, take a shady siesta-break from the sun during the most hazardous midday hours. If you do get burned, applying your sunburn lotion (or one of the "caine" creams) after the fact usually decreases the pain and speeds healing.

Safe Water and Food

Although municipalities have made great strides in sanitation, food and water are still potential sources of germs in some parts of Oaxaca. Although water is nearly always safe everywhere, except in a few upcountry localities, it's still probably best to drink bottled water only. Hotels, whose success depends vitally on their customers' health, generally provide *agua purificada* (purified bottled water). If, for any reason, the available water is of doubtful quality, add a water purifier, such as Potable Aqua brand (get it at a camping goods stores before departure) or a few drops per quart of water of *blanqueador* (household chlorine bleach) or *yodo* (tincture of iodine) from the pharmacy.

Pure bottled water, soft drinks, beer, and fresh fruit juices are so widely available it is easy to avoid tap water, especially in restaurants. Ice and *paletas* (iced juice-on-a-stick) may be risky, especially in small towns.

Washing hands before eating in a restaurant is a time-honored Mexican ritual that visitors should religiously follow. The humblest Mexican eatery will generally provide a basin to *lavar las manos* (wash the hands). If it doesn't, don't eat there.

Hot, cooked food is generally safe, as are peeled fruits and vegetables. These days milk and cheese in Mexico are generally processed under sanitary conditions and sold pasteurized (ask, "*¿Pasteurizado?*") and are typically safe. Mexican ice cream used to be both bad-tasting and of dubious safety, but national brands available in supermarkets are so much improved that it's no longer necessary to resist ice cream while in town.

In recent years, much cleaner public water and increased hygiene awareness have made salads—once shunned by Mexico travelers—generally safe to eat in tourist-frequented Oaxaca cafés and restaurants. Nevertheless, lettuce and cabbage, particularly in country villages, are more likely to be contaminated than tomatoes, carrots, cucumbers, onions, and green peppers. In any case, you can try dousing your salad in *vinagre* (vinegar) or plenty of sliced *limón* (lime) juice, the acidity of which kills most bacteria.

First-Aid Kit

In the tropics, ordinary cuts and insect bites are more prone to infection and should receive immediate first aid. A first-aid kit with aspirin, rubbing alcohol, hydrogen peroxide, water-purifying tablets, household chlorine bleach or iodine for water purifying, swabs, bandages, gauze, adhesive tape, Ace bandage, chamomile *(manzanilla)* tea bags for upset stomachs, Pepto-Bismol, acidophilus tablets, antibiotic ointment, hydrocortisone cream, mosquito repellent, knife, and good tweezers is a good precaution for any traveler and mandatory for campers.

HEALTH PROBLEMS
Traveler's Diarrhea

Traveler's diarrhea (known in Southeast Asia as "Bali Belly" and in Mexico as *turista* or "Montezuma's Revenge") sometimes persists, even among prudent vacationers. You can suffer *turista* for a week after simply traveling from California to Philadelphia or New York. Doctors say the familiar symptoms of runny bowels, nausea, and sour stomach result from normal local bacterial strains to which newcomers' systems need time to adjust. Unfortunately, the dehydration and fatigue from heat and travel reduce your body's natural defenses and sometimes lead to a persistent cycle of sickness at a time when you least want it.

Time-tested protective measures can help your body either prevent or break this cycle. Many doctors and veteran travelers swear by Pepto-Bismol for soothing sore stomachs and stopping diarrhea. Acidophilus, the bacteria found in yogurt, is widely available in the United States in tablets and aids digestion. Warm *manzanilla* (chamomile) tea, used widely in Mexico (and by Peter Rabbit's mother), provides liquid and calms upset stomachs. Temporarily avoid coffee and alcohol, drink plenty of *manzanilla* tea, and eat bananas and rice for a few meals until your tummy can take regular food.

Although powerful antibiotics and antidiarrhea medications such as Lomotil and Imodium are readily available over *farmacia* counters, they may involve serious side effects and should not be taken in the absence of medical advice. If in doubt, consult a doctor.

Chagas' Disease and Dengue Fever

Chagas' disease, spread by the "kissing" (or, more appropriately, "assassin") bug, is a potential hazard in the Mexican tropics. Known locally as a *vinchuca,* the triangular-headed, two-centimeter (0.75-inch) brown insect, identifiable by its yellow-striped abdomen, often drops upon its sleeping victims from the thatched ceiling of a rural house at night. Its bite is followed by swelling, fever, and weakness and can lead to heart failure if left untreated. Application of drugs at an early stage can, however, clear the patient of the trypanosome parasites that infect victims' bloodstreams and vital organs. See a doctor immediately if you believe you're infected.

Most of the precautions against malaria-bearing mosquitoes also apply to dengue fever, which does occur (although uncommonly) in outlying tropical areas of Mexico. The culprit here is a virus carried by the mosquito species *Aedes aegypti.* Symptoms are acute fever, with chills, sweating, and muscle aches. A red, diffuse rash frequently results, which may later peel. Symptoms abate after about five days, but fatigue may persist. A particularly serious, but fortunately rare, form, called dengue hemorrhagic fever, afflicts children and can be fatal. See a doctor immediately. Although no vaccines or preventatives are available, other than generally deterring insects, you should nevertheless see a doctor immediately.

Scorpions and Snakes

While camping or staying in a *palapa* or other rustic accommodation, watch for scorpions, especially in your shoes, which you should shake out every morning. Scorpion stings and most snake bites are rarely fatal to an adult but are potentially very serious for a child. Get the victim to a doctor calmly but quickly.

Tattoos

All health hazards don't come from the wild. A number of Mexico travelers have complained of complications from black henna tattoos. When enhanced by the chemical dye PPD, an itchy rash results that can lead to scarring. It's best to play it safe: If you must have a vacation tattoo, get it at an established, professional shop.

MEDICAL CARE

For medical advice and treatment, let your hotel (or if you're camping, the closest *farmacia*) refer you to a good doctor, clinic, or hospital. Mexican doctors, especially in medium-size and small towns, practice like private doctors in the United States and Canada once did before health insurance, liability, and group practice. They will come to you if you request it; they often keep their doors open even after regular hours and charge reasonable fees.

You will receive generally good treatment at the many local hospitals in Oaxaca's tourist centers and larger towns. If you must have an English-speaking, American-trained doctor, the **International Association for Medical Assistance to Travelers (IAMAT)** (1623 Military Rd., #279, Niagara Falls, NY 14304, tel. 716/754-4883; or 2163 Gordon St., Guelph, Ontario N1K 1B5, tel. 519/836-0102, or 1287 St. Clair Ave. W, Toronto, Ontario M6E 1B8, tel. 416/652-0137, info@iamat.org, www.iamat.org) publishes an updated booklet of qualified member physicians, some of whom practice in Oaxaca City, Puerto Escondido, and Huatulco. IAMAT also distributes a very detailed *How to Protect Yourself Against Malaria* guide, together with

© BRUCE WHIPPERMAN

Oaxaca doctors often meet their patients in streetfront clinics.

MEDICAL TAGS AND AIR EVACUATION

Travelers with special medical problems should consider wearing a medical identification tag. For a reasonable fee, **Medic Alert** (2323 Colorado Ave., Turlock, CA 95382, California 95382, tel. 209/668-3333, toll-free tel. 888/633-4298, www.medicalert.org) provides such tags, as well as an information hotline that will inform doctors of your vital medical background.

In life-threatening emergencies, highly recommended **Aeromedevac** (Gillespie Field Airport, 681 Kenney St., El Cajon, CA 92020, toll-free tel. 800/462-0911, from Mexico 24-hr toll-free tel. 800/832-5087, www.aeromedevac.com) provides high-tech jet ambulance service from any Mexican locale to a U.S. hospital for roughly $20,000.

Alternatively, you might consider the similar services of **Med-Jet Assist** (Birmingham, Alabama, Intl. Airport, 4900 69th St., Birmingham AL, 35206, toll-free U.S. tel. 800/527-7478, www.medjetassist.com; in emergencies, world-wide, call U.S. tel. 205/595-6626 collect).

worldwide malaria risk and communicable disease charts.

For more useful information on health and safety in Mexico, consult Drs. Robert H. Paige and Curtis P. Page's *Mexico: Health and Safety Travel Guide* (Tempe, AZ: Med to Go Books, 2004) and Dirk Schroeder's *Staying Healthy in Asia, Africa, and Latin America* (Berkeley, CA: Avalon Travel Publishing, 2000).

WATER SAFETY

As viewed from Oaxaca beaches, the Pacific Ocean usually lives up to its name. Many protected inlets, safe for child's play, dot the coastline. Unsheltered shorelines, on the other hand, can be deceiving. Smooth water in the calm forenoon often changes to choppy in the afternoon; calm ripples lapping the shore in March can grow to hurricane-driven walls of water in November. Such storms can wash away sand, changing a wide gently sloping beach into a steep rocky one plagued by turbulent waves and treacherous currents.

Undertow, whirlpools, crosscurrents, and occasional oversized waves can make ocean swimming a fast-lane adventure. Getting unexpectedly swept out to sea or hammered onto the beach bottom by a surprise breaker are potential hazards.

Never attempt serious swimming when tipsy or full of food; *never* swim alone where someone can't see you. *Always* swim beyond the breakers (which come in sets of several, climaxed by a big one, which breaks highest and farthest from the beach). If you happen to get caught in the path of such a breaker, avoid it by diving straight under it and letting it roll harmlessly over you. If you do get caught by a serious breaker, try to roll and tumble with it (as football players tumble) to avoid injury.

Poisonous sea snakes, although rare and shy, do inhabit Oaxaca waters. Much more common, especially around submerged rocks, is the toothy **moray eel** that sometimes inflicts a painful bite. Don't stick your fingers or toes anywhere you can't see.

Now and then, swimmers get a nettle-like **jellyfish sting.** Furthermore, take care around **coral reefs** and beds of **sea urchins; corals** can sting (like jellyfish), and you can get infections from coral cuts and sea-urchin spines. Shuffle along sandy bottoms to scare away stingrays before stepping on one. If you're unlucky, its venomous tail-spines may inflict a painful wound.

If you suffer a coral scratch or jellyfish sting, experts advise you to wash the afflicted area with ocean water and pour alcohol (rubbing alcohol or tequila) over the wound, then apply hydrocortisone cream available from the *farmacia.*

Injuries from sea-urchin spines and stingray barbs are painful and can be serious. Physicians recommend similar first aid for both: remove the spines or barbs by hand or with tweezers, then soak the injury in as-hot-as-possible fresh water to weaken the toxins and provide relief. Another method is to rinse the area with an antibacterial solution—rubbing alcohol, vinegar, wine, or ammonia diluted with water. If none are available, the same effect may be achieved with urine, either your own or someone else's in your party. Get medical help immediately.

CRIME AND PERSONAL SAFETY

Occasional knifepoint robberies and muggings have marred the once-peaceful Puerto Escondido nighttime beach scene. Walk alone and you invite trouble, especially along Playa Bachoco and the unlit stretch of Playa Principal between the east end of the *adoquín* and the Hotel Santa Fe. If you have dinner alone at the Hotel Santa Fe, avoid the beach and return by taxi or walk along the highway to Avenida Pérez Gasga back to your hotel.

Fortunately, such problems seem to be confined to the beach. Visitors are quite safe on the Puerto Escondido streets themselves, often more so than on their own city streets back home.

Safe Conduct

Mexico is an old-fashioned country where people value traditional ideals of honesty, fidelity, and piety. Crime rates are low; visitors are often safer in Mexico than in their home cities.

This applies even more strongly in Oaxaca. Don't be scared away by headlines about kidnappings and drug-related murders in border cities such as Tijuana and Ciudad Juárez, or car hijackings in bad Mexico City neighborhoods. Violent crime is nearly unknown in Oaxaca City. Around the *zócalo,* women are often seen walking home alone at night. Nevertheless, some Oaxaca neighborhoods are friendlier than others. If you find yourself walking in a locality at night that doesn't feel too welcoming, do not hesitate to hail a taxi.

Although Oaxaca is very safe with respect to violent crime, you should still take normal precautions against petty theft. Stow your valuables in your hotel safe, don't wear showy jewelry or display wads of money, and especially at a crowded market, keep your camera and valuables protected in a waist belt, secure purse, or zipped pockets. If you're parking your car for the night, do it in a secure garage or a guarded hotel parking lot.

Even though four generations have elapsed since Pancho Villa raided the U.S. border, the image of a Mexico bristling with *bandidos* persists. And similarly for Mexicans: despite the century and a half since the *yanquis* invaded Mexico City and took half their country, the communal Mexican psyche still views gringos (and, by association, all white foreigners) with revulsion, jealousy, and wonder.

Fortunately, the Mexican love-hate affair with foreigners does not usually apply to individual visitors. Your friendly *"buenos dias"* ("good morning") or *"por favor"* ("please"), when appropriate, is always appreciated, whether in the market, the gas station, or the hotel. The shy smile you will most likely receive in return will be your small, but not insignificant, reward.

Women

Your own behavior, despite low crime statistics, largely determines your safety in Mexico. For women traveling solo, it is important to realize that the double standard is alive and well in Mexico. Dress and behave modestly and you will most likely avoid embarrassment. Whenever possible, stay in the company of friends or acquaintances; find companions for beach, sightseeing, and shopping excursions. Ignore strange men's solicitations and overtures. A Mexican man on the prowl will invent the sappiest romantic overtures to snare a gringa. He will often interpret anything but a firm "no" as a "maybe," and a "maybe" as a "yes."

Men

For male visitors, alcohol often leads to trouble. Avoid bars and cantinas; and if, given Mexico's excellent beers, you can't abstain completely, at least maintain soft-spoken self-control in the face of challenges from macho drunks.

The Law and Police

While Mexican authorities are tolerant of alcohol, they are decidedly intolerant of other substances such as marijuana, psychedelics, cocaine,

MACHISMO

I once met an Acapulco man who wore five gold wristwatches and became angry when I quietly refused his repeated invitations to get drunk with him. Another time, on the beach near San Blas, two drunken campesinos nearly attacked me because I was helping my girlfriend cook a picnic dinner. Outside Taxco I once spent an endless hour in the seat behind a bus driver who insisted on speeding down the middle of the two-lane highway, honking aside oncoming automobiles.

Despite their wide differences (the first was a rich criollo, the campesinos were *indígenas*, and the bus driver mestizo), the common affliction shared by all four men was machismo, a disease that seems to possess many Mexican men.

Machismo is a sometimes reckless obsession to prove one's masculinity, to show how *macho* one is. Men of many nationalities share the instinct to prove themselves. Japan's *bushido* samurai code is one example. Mexican men, however, often seem to try the hardest.

When confronted by a Mexican braggart, male visitors should remain careful and controlled. If your opponent is yelling, stay cool, speak softly, and withdraw as soon as possible. On the highway, be courteous and unprovocative; don't use your car to spar with a macho driver.

Drinking often leads to problems. It's best to stay out of bars or cantinas unless you're prepared to deal with the macho consequences. Polite refusal of a drink may be taken as a challenge. If you visit a bar with Mexican friends or acquaintances, you may be heading for a no-win choice of a drunken all-night *borrachera* (binge) or an insult to the honor of your friends by refusing.

For women, machismo also requires cautious behavior. In Mexico, women's liberation is long in coming. Few women hold positions of power in business or politics. Machismo requires that female visitors obey the rules or suffer the consequences. Keep a low profile; wear bathing suits and brief shorts only at the beach. Follow the example of your Mexican sisters: Make a habit of going out in the company of friends or acquaintances, especially at night. Many Mexican men believe an unaccompanied woman wants to be picked up. Ignore such offers; any response, even refusal, might be taken as a "maybe." If, on the other hand, there is a Mexican man whom you'd genuinely like to meet, the traditional way is an introduction arranged through family or friends.

Mexican families, as a source of protection and friendship, should not be overlooked – especially on the beach or in the park, where, among the gaggle of kids, grandparents, aunts, and cousins, there's room for one more.

and heroin. Getting caught with such drugs in Mexico usually leads to swift and severe results.

Equally swift is the punishment for nude sunbathing, which is both illegal in public and offensive to Mexicans. Confine your nudist colony to very private locations.

Although with decreasing frequency lately, traffic police in Oaxaca sometimes seem to watch foreign cars with eagle eyes. Officers seem to inhabit busy intersections and one-way streets, waiting for confused tourists to make a wrong move. If they whistle you over, stop immediately or you will really get into hot water. If guilty, say *"Lo siento"* ("I'm sorry") and be cooperative. Although the officer probably won't mention it, he or she is usually hoping that you'll cough up a $20 *mordida* (bribe) for the privilege of driving away. Don't do it. Although the officer may hint at confiscating your car, calmly ask for an official *boleto* (written traffic ticket), if you're guilty, in exchange for your driver's license (have a copy), which the officer will probably keep if he or she writes a ticket. If after a few minutes no money appears, the officer will most likely give you back your driver's license rather than go to the trouble of writing the ticket. If not, the worst that usually will happen is you will have to go to the *presidencia municipal* (city hall) the next morning and pay the $20 to a clerk in exchange for your driver's license.

The customarily tranquil state of Oaxaca has occasionally experienced episodes of public unrest. Recent conflicts have been the result of the longstanding backlog of unsettled grievances that run from local land disputes and protest strikes by underpaid teachers, such as the teacher strike that paralyzed Oaxaca City for several months during 2006, all the way up to unsolved political kidnappings and assassinations.

Since 2006, aggrieved, often local community delegations have petitioned local authorities for redress and set up camp in plain view for visitors to see in the Oaxaca *zócalo*. There is no reason for visitors to be alarmed about such lawful demonstrations as long as they remain as peaceful as they have been for the past five years.

Pedestrian and Driving Hazards

Although Oaxaca's potholed pavements and "holey" sidewalks won't land you in jail, one of them might send you to the hospital if you don't watch your step, especially at night. "Pedestrian beware" is especially good advice on Mexican streets, where it is rumored that some drivers speed up rather than slow down when they spot a tourist stepping off the curb. Falling coconuts, especially frequent on windy days, constitute an additional hazard to unwary campers and beachgoers.

Driving along Mexican country roads, where slow trucks and carts block lanes, campesinos stroll the shoulders, and horses, burros, and cattle wander at will, is hazardous—doubly so at night.

Information and Services

MONEY
The Peso: Down and Up

Overnight in early 1993, the Mexican government shifted its monetary decimal point three places and created the "new" peso (now known simply as the "peso"), which, at this writing, trades at about 12 per U.S. dollar. Since the peso value sometimes changes rapidly, U.S. dollars are a more stable indicator of value than pesos, and are therefore used in this book to report prices. You should, nevertheless, always use pesos to pay for everything in Mexico.

Since the introduction of the new peso, the centavo (one-hundredth of a new peso) has reappeared, in coins of 5, 10, 20, and 50 centavos. Incidentally, the dollar sign, "$," also marks Mexican pesos. Peso coins *(monedas)* in denominations of 1, 2, 5, 10, and 20 pesos, and bills, in denominations of 10, 20, 50, 100, 200, 500, and 1,000 pesos, are common. Since banks like to exchange your travelers checks for a few crisp large bills rather than the often-tattered smaller denominations, ask for some of your change in 50- and 100-peso notes. A 500-peso note, while common at the bank, may look awfully big to a small shopkeeper, who might be hard-pressed to change it.

Banks, ATMs, and Money-Exchange Offices

Mexican banks, like their North American counterparts, have lengthened their business hours. Hong Kong Shanghai Banking Corporation (HSBC) maintains the longest hours: some branches as long as 8 A.M.–6 P.M. Monday–Saturday. Banamex (Banco Nacional de Mexico), generally the most popular with local people, usually posts the best in-town dollar exchange rate in its lobbies, for example, *Tipo de cambio: venta 11.799, compra 11.933,* which means it will sell pesos to you at the rate of 11.799 per dollar and buy them back for 11.933 per dollar.

ATMs (automated teller machines), or *cajeros automáticos* (kah-HAY-rohs ahoo-toh-MAH-tee-kohs), have become the money sources of choice in Mexico. Virtually every bank has a 24-hour ATM, accessible by a swarm of U.S. and Canadian credit and ATM cards, with proper "PIN" ("NIP," pronounced "NEEP" in Spanish) identification codes. *Note:* Some

BaNorte is one of Mexico's largest banks.

Mexican bank ATMs will "eat" your ATM card if you don't retrieve it within about 15 seconds of completing your transaction. Retrieve your card *immediately* after completing your transaction.

Since one-time Mexican bank charges (typically $2–3 per transaction) do not depend on the amount you withdraw, you might as well save on fees by withdrawing the maximum ($300–500).

Even without an ATM card, you don't have to go to the trouble of waiting in long bank service lines. Opt for a less-crowded bank, such as Bancomer, Banco Serfín, BaNorte, or a private money-exchange office *(casa de cambio)*. Often most convenient, such offices often offer long hours and faster service than the banks, for a fee (as little as $1 or as much as $4 per $100).

Keeping Your Money Safe

Travelers checks, the once-popular traditional prescription for safe money abroad, are now not widely accepted by Oaxaca hotels and restaurants, although they are by banks. So, even if you plan to use your ATM card, you might buy some U.S. dollar travelers checks (a well-known brand such as American Express or Visa) as an emergency reserve. Canadian travelers checks and currency are not as widely accepted as U.S. travelers checks, and European and Asian travelers checks are even less so. Unless you like signing your name or paying lots of per-check commissions, buy denominations of $100 or more.

In Oaxaca as everywhere, from Paris to Perth, **thieves** circulate among the tourists. Keep valuables in your hotel *caja de seguridad* (security box). If you don't particularly trust the desk clerk, carry what you cannot afford to lose in a money belt. Pickpockets love crowded markets, buses, and airport terminals where they can slip a wallet out of a back pocket or dangling purse or a camera from its belt case in a blink. Guard against this by carrying your wallet in your front pocket, your camera in your purse or daypack, and your purse, waist pouch, and daypack (which clever crooks can sometimes slit open) on your front side.

© BRUCE WHIPPERMAN

Don't attract thieves by displaying wads of money or flashy jewelry. Don't get sloppy drunk; if so, you may become a pushover for a determined thief.

Don't leave valuables unattended on the beach; share security duties with trustworthy-looking neighbors, or leave a bag with a shopkeeper nearby.

Tipping

Without their droves of visitors, Mexican people would be even poorer. Deflation of the peso, while it makes prices low for outsiders, makes it rough for Mexican families to get by. The help at your hotel typically get paid only a few dollars a day. They depend on tips to make the difference between dire and bearable poverty. Give the *camarista* (chambermaid) and floor attendant 20 pesos every day or two. And whenever uncertain of what to tip, it will probably mean a lot to someone—maybe a whole family—if you err on the generous side.

In restaurants and bars, Mexican tipping customs are similar to those in the United States: tip waiters and bartenders about 15 percent for satisfactory service.

Credit Cards

Credit cards, such as Visa, MasterCard, and, to a lesser extent, American Express and Discover, are widely honored in the hotels, restaurants, crafts shops, and boutiques that cater to foreign tourists. You will generally get better bargains, however, in shops that depend on local trade and do not so readily accept credit cards. Such shops sometimes offer discounts for cash sales.

Whatever the circumstance, your travel money will usually go much further in Oaxaca than back home. Despite the national 15 percent ("value added" IVA) sales tax, local lodging, food, and transportation prices will often seem like bargains compared to the developed world. In both Oaxaca City and the Oaxaca Pacific resort towns, hearty restaurant dinners run $4–10, while basic, but comfortable and clean hotel rooms go for as little as $30.

COMMUNICATIONS
Using Mexican Telephones

Although Mexican phone service has improved in the last decade, it's still sometimes hit-or-miss. If a number doesn't get through, you may have to redial it more than once. When someone answers (usually *"Bueno"*) be especially courteous. If your Spanish is rusty, say, *"¿Por favor, habla inglés?"* (¿POR fah-VOR, AH-blah een-GLAYS?—"Please, do you speak English?"). If you want to speak to a particular person (such as María), ask, *"¿María se encuentra?"* (¿mah-REE-ah SAY ayn-koo-AYN-trah?).

Since November 2001, when telephone numbers were standardized, Mexican phones operate pretty much the same as in the United States and Canada. In Oaxaca City, for example, a complete telephone number is generally written like this: 951/514-4709. As in the United States, the "951" denotes the telephone area code, or *lada* (LAH-dah), and the 514-4709 is the number (except in the case of a cell phone) that you dial locally. If you want to dial this number **long distance** *(larga distancia),* first dial "01" (like "1" in the United States and Canada), then 951/514-4709. All Mexican telephone numbers, with only three exceptions, begin with a three-digit *lada,* followed by a seven-digit local number. (The exceptions are Monterrey, Guadalajara, and Mexico City, which have two-digit *ladas* and eight-digit local numbers. The Mexico City *lada* is 55; Guadalajara's is 33; Monterrey's is 81. For example, a complete Guadalajara phone number would read something like 33/6897-2253.)

Although **Mexican cellular telephones** are as universally used as those in the United States and Canada, at this writing they operate a bit differently. In order to call a local cellular number, for example, the Oaxaca local number 951/514-4709, you must prefix it with "044." Thus, in Oaxaca City and Valley, dial 044-951/514-4709. However, outside of Oaxaca City and the Valley of Oaxaca, for example, in Puerto Escondido, you call a cellular number in Oaxaca City by first dialing "045." Thus, from Puerto Escondido calling Oaxaca, simply dial 045-951/514-4709.

In Oaxaca towns and cities, direct long-distance dialing is the rule—from hotels, public phone booths, and efficient private computerized telephone offices. The cheapest, often most convenient, way to call is by buying and using a public telephone **Ladatel telephone card** *(tarjeta telefónica)*. Buy them in 30-, 50-, and 100-peso denominations at the many outlets—minimarkets, pharmacies, liquor stores—that display the blue and yellow Ladatel sign.

Another equally economical option is to do your phoning in a *caseta larga distancia* (local phone office). Typically staffed by a young woman and often connected to a store or café, the *larga distancia* becomes an informal community social center as people pass the time waiting for their phone connections.

The most convenient, but **costliest telephoning option** is to use your hotel room telephone, which can run as much as $0.50 per minute to call locally, and $5 per minute to call the United States, Canada, or Europe.

Getting your own cell phone adapted for Mexico at home before you leave and using it on your trip probably won't help much, since it will probably run about $80 per month stateside cost, plus about $100 or more in Mexico, for, say, 400 monthly minutes.

Buying and using a Mexican cell phone in Mexico is nearly as expensive. Although they are reasonably priced ($25–50), they must be used with phone cards, which cost $0.25–0.50 per minute.

Calling Mexico and Calling Home

To call Mexico direct from the United States, first dial 011 (for international access), then 52 (Mexico country code), followed by the Mexican area code and local number. For example, from the United States, call a Oaxaca local number such as 951/514-4709 by dialing 01152-951/514-4709. Again, you must **dial cellular phone numbers a bit differently,** by entering a "1" before the area code. Thus, if Oaxaca City local number 514-4709 were a

cellular number, from the United States you must dial 01152-1-951/514-4709.

For station-to-station **calls to the United States and Canada from Mexico,** dial 001 plus the area code and the local number. For example, to call San Diego (area code 619) local number 388-5390, from Mexico, simply dial 001-619/388-5390. For calls to other countries, ask your hotel desk clerk or see the easy-to-follow directions in the local Mexican telephone directory.

Beware of certain private "To Call Long Distance to the U.S.A. Collect" (or "by Credit Card") telephones installed prominently in airports, tourist hotels, and shops. Tariffs on these phones often run as high as $10 per minute (with a three-minute minimum), for a total of $30, whether you talk three minutes or not. Always ask the operator for the rate, and if it's too high, buy a 30-peso ($3) Ladatel phone card for a (six-minute) call home.

Post, Telegraph, and Internet Access

Mexican *correos* (post offices) operate similarly, but more slowly and much less securely, than most of their counterparts all over the world. (Hopefully this may improve, due to the recent Mexican post-office reform measures.)

Mail services usually include *lista de correo* (general delivery, address letters *"a/c lista de correo"), servicios filatelicas* (philatelic services), *por avión* (airmail), *giros* (postal money orders), and Mexpost secure and fast delivery service, sometimes from separate Mexpost offices.

Mexican ordinary (non-Mexpost) mail has been sadly unreliable and pathetically slow. If, for mailings within Mexico, you must have security, use the efficient, reformed government Mexpost (like U.S. Express Mail) service. For fast and absolutely secure private mailings inside Mexico, use the excellent, widely available **Estafeta** courier service. For international mailings, check the local Yellow Pages for widely available (but very expensive, $30 for a letter to the United States) DHL, Federal Express, or UPS courier service.

PACKING CHECKLIST

Use this list as a last-minute check to make sure that you've packed all of the items essential to your Mexico trip:

NECESSARY ITEMS

___ camera, film (expensive in Mexico)
___ comb
___ guidebook, reading books
___ inexpensive watch, clock
___ keys, tickets
___ lightweight clothes, hat for sun,
___ money, ATM card, maybe traveler's checks
___ mosquito repellent
___ prescription eyeglasses
___ prescription medicines and drugs
___ purse, waist-belt carrying pouch
___ sunglasses, sunscreen
___ swimsuit
___ toothbrush, toothpaste
___ passport
___ windbreaker

USEFUL ITEMS

___ address book
___ birth control
___ checkbook, credit cards
___ contact lenses
___ dental floss
___ earplugs
___ first-aid kit
___ flashlight, batteries
___ immersion heater
___ lightweight binoculars
___ portable radio/cassette player
___ razor
___ travel booklight
___ vaccination certificate

NECESSARY ITEMS FOR CAMPERS

___ collapsible gallon plastic bottle
___ dish soap
___ first-aid kit
___ hammock (buy in Mexico)
___ insect repellent
___ lightweight hiking shoes
___ lightweight tent
___ matches in waterproof case
___ nylon cord
___ plastic bottle, quart
___ pot scrubber/sponge
___ sheet or light blanket
___ Sierra Club–style metal cup, fork, and spoon
___ single-burner stove with fuel
___ Swiss army knife
___ tarp
___ toilet paper
___ towel, soap
___ two nesting cooking pots
___ water-purifying tablets or iodine

USEFUL ITEMS FOR CAMPERS

___ compass
___ dishcloths
___ hot pad
___ instant coffee, tea, sugar, powdered milk
___ moleskin (Dr. Scholl's)
___ plastic plate
___ poncho
___ short (votive) candles
___ whistle

Government Telecom offices are all over Oaxaca.

Telégrafos (telegraph offices), usually near the post office, send and receive *telegramas* (telegrams) and *giros* (money orders). *Telecomunicaciones* (Telecom), the new high-tech telegraph offices, add computerized telephone and public fax to the available services.

Internet and computer services, including personal email access, has arrived in Oaxaca cities and towns, large and small. Internet "cafés" are becoming increasingly common, especially in the Oaxaca City, Huatulco, Puerto Escondido, and Puerto Ángel resort centers. Online rates run $1–2 per hour.

Electricity and Time

Mexican electric power is supplied at U.S.-standard 110 volts, 60 cycles. Plugs and sockets are generally two-pronged, nonpolar (like the pre-1970s U.S. ones). Bring adapters if you're going to use appliances with polar two-pronged or three-pronged plugs. A two-pronged polar plug has different-sized prongs, one of which is too large to plug into an old-fashioned nonpolar socket.

The entire state of Oaxaca and all surrounding states operate on U.S. Central Time, the same as Mexico City and central U.S. states such as Nebraska, Illinois, Tennessee, and Louisiana.

RESOURCES

Glossary

Many of the following words have a socio-historical meaning; others you will not find in the usual English–Spanish dictionary.

abarrotes groceries, grocery store

aguardiente Mexican "white lightning": cheap distilled liquor made from sugarcane

aguas watch out!

alcalde mayor or municipal judge

alebrije fanciful wooden animal, mostly made in Arrazola and Tilcajete villages

alfarería pottery

andador walkway, or strolling path

antojitos native Mexican snacks, such as tamales, chiles rellenos, tacos, and enchiladas

artesanías handicrafts

artesano, artesana craftsman, craftswoman

asunción the assumption of the Virgin Mary into heaven (as distinguished from the *ascención* of Jesus into heaven)

atole a popular nonalcoholic drink made from corn juice

audiencia one of the royal executive-judicial panels sent to rule Mexico during the 16th century

autopista expressway

ayuntamiento either the town council or the building where it meets

balneario hot springs; can refer to a natural feature, a recreational spa, or a resort

barrio a town or village district or neighborhood, usually centered around its own local plaza and church

bienes raices literally "good roots," but popularly, real estate

bola small crowd of people

boleto ticket, boarding pass

brujo, bruja male or female witch doctor or shaman

caballero literally "horseman," but popularly, gentleman

cabaña ecoturísticas bungalow lodging for tourists

cabercera head town of a municipal district, or headquarters in general

cabrón literally, a cuckold, but more commonly, bastard, rat, or S.O.B.; sometimes used affectionately

cacique local chief or boss

calenda procession, usually religious, as during a festival

camionera bus station

campesino country person; farm worker

canasta basket, traditionally made of woven reeds, with handle

cantera local volcanic stone, widely used for colonial-era Oaxaca monuments

Carnaval celebration preceding Ash Wednesday, the beginning of the fasting period called Lent. Carnaval is called Mardi Gras in the United States.

casa de huéspedes guesthouse, often operated in a family home

cascada waterfall

caudillo dictator or political chief

centro de salud health center/clinic

charro gentleman cowboy

chingar literally, to "rape," but also the universal Spanish "f" word, the equivalent of "screw" in English

Churrigueresque Spanish baroque architectural style incorporated into many Mexican colonial churches, named after José Churriguera (1665-1725)

científicos literally, scientists, but applied to President Porfirio Díaz's technocratic advisers

coa (estaca) digging stick, used for planting corn

Cocijo Zapotec god of rain, lightning, and thunder

cofradia Catholic fraternal service association, either male or female, mainly in charge of financing and organizing religious festivals

colectivo a shared public taxi or minibus that picks up and deposits passengers along a designated route

colegio preparatory school or junior college

colonia suburban subdivision/satellite of a larger city

comal a flat pottery griddle, for cooking/heating tortillas

comedor restaurant

comida casera home-cooked food

comida corrida economical afternoon set meal, usually with four courses – soup, rice, entrée, and dessert

compadrazgo the semi-formal web of village and barrio compadre and padrino relationships that determine a person's lifetime obligations and loyalties

compadre a semi-formalized "best friend" relationship that usually lasts for life

comunal refers to the traditional indigenous system of joint decision-making and land ownership and use

Conasupo government store that sells basic foods at subsidized prices

correo mail, post, or post office

criollo person of all-European, usually Spanish, descent born in the New World

Cuaresma Lent (the 46 days of pre-Easter fasting, beginning on Ash Wednesday, and ending on the Saturday before Easter Sunday)

cuota toll, as in cuota autopista, toll expressway

curandero, curandera indigenous medicine man or woman

damas ladies, as in "ladies room"

Domingo de Ramos Palm Sunday

ejido a constitutional, government-sponsored form of community, with shared land ownership and cooperative decision-making

encomienda colonial award of tribute from a designated indigenous district

farmacia pharmacy or drugstore

finca farm

finca cafetelera coffee farm

fonda food stall or small restaurant, often in a traditional market complex

fraccionamiento city sector or subdivision, abbreviated "Fracc."

fuero the former right of Mexican clergy and military to be tried in separate ecclesiastical and military courts

gachupín "one who wears spurs"; a derogatory term for a Spanish-born colonial

gasolinera gasoline station

gente de razón "people of reason"; whites and mestizos in colonial Mexico

gringo once-derogatory but now commonly used term for North American whites

grito impassioned cry, as in Hidalgo's Grito de Dolores

hacienda large landed estate; also the government treasury

hamaca hammock

hechicero a "wizard" who often leads native propitiatory ceremonies

hidalgo nobleman or noblewoman; called honorifically by "Don" or "Doña"

hojalata tinware, a popular craft of Oaxaca

huarache popular dish consisting of a fried masa base with a variety of toppings

huipil traditional emroidered dress

indígena indigenous or aboriginal inhabitant of all-native descent who speaks his or her native tongue; commonly, but incorrectly, an **indio** (Indian)

jacal native label for thatched, straw, and/or stick country house

jaripeo bull roping and riding

jejenes "no-see-um" biting gnats, most common around coastal wetlands

judiciales the federal "judicial," or investigative police, best known to motorists for their highway checkpoint inspections

jugería stall or small restaurant providing a large array of squeezed vegetable and fruit *jugos* (juices)

juzgado the "hoosegow," or jail

lancha launch (a small motorboat)

larga distancia long-distance telephone service, or the *caseta* (booth or office) where it's provided

licencado academic degree (abbrev. Lic.) approximately equivalent to a bachelor's degree in the United States

lonchería small lunch counter, usually serving juices, sandwiches, and *antojitos*

machismo; macho exaggerated sense of maleness; person who holds such a sense of himself

manañita early-morning mass

mano a hand, or the stone roller used to grind corn on the flat stone *metate*

mayordomo community leader responsible for staging a local Catholic religious festival

mescal alcoholic beverage distilled from the fermented hearts of maguey (century plant)

mestizo person of mixed native and European descent

metate a slightly concave, horizontal stone basin for grinding corn for tortillas

milagro literally a miracle, but also a small religious wish medal, often pinned to an altar saint by someone requesting divine intervention

milpa a small, family-owned field, traditionally planted in corn, beans, and squash

mirador viewpoint, overlook

molcajete a stone mortar and pestle, used for hand-grinding, especially chilies and seeds

mordida slang for bribe; "little bite"

olla a pottery jug or pot, used for stewing vegetables, meats, beans, coffee

padrino, padrina godfather or godmother, often the respective *compadres* of the given child's parents

palapa an open, thatched-roof structure, usually shading a restaurant

panela rough brown cane sugar, sold in lumps in the market

panga outboard motor-launch *(lancha)*

papier-mâché the craft of glued, multilayered paper sculpture, centered in Tonalá, Jalisco, where creations can resemble fine pottery or lacquerware

Pemex acronym for Petróleos Mexicanos, the national oil corporation

peninsulares the Spanish-born ruling colonial elite

peón a poor wage-earner, usually a country native

periférico peripheral boulevard

petate all-purpose woven mat, from palm fronds

piciete native tobacco, widely cultivated in Northern Oaxaca state

piñata papier-mâché decoration, usually in animal or human form, filled with treats and broken open during a fiesta

plan political manifesto, usually by a leader or group consolidating or seeking power

Porfiriato the 34-year (1876–1910) ruling period of president-dictator Porfirio Díaz

Las Posadas Christmas, especially on Christmas Eve, procession, in which participants, led by costumed Holy Mary and Joseph, knock on neighborhood doors and implore, unsuccessfully, for a room for the night

pozahuanco horizontally striped hand-woven wraparound skirt, commonly worn in the Oaxaca's coastal Mixtec district

pozole stew of hominy in broth, usually topped by shredded meat, cabbage, and diced onion

presidencia municipal the headquarters, like a U.S. city or county hall, of a Mexican *municipio*, county-like local governmental unit

preventiva local, state, or federal police, especially charged with directly foiling crooks

principal, anciano a respected elder, often a member of a council of elders, whom the community consults for advice and support

pronunciamiento declaration of rebellion by an insurgent leader

pueblo town or people

puente literally a "bridge," but commonly a long holiday weekend, when resort hotel reservations are highly recommended

pulque the fermented juice of the maguey plant, approximately equivalent in alcoholic content to wine or strong beer

puta whore, bitch, or slut

quinta a villa or upscale country house

quinto the colonial royal "fifth" tax on treasure and precious metals

ramada a shade roof, usually made of palm fronds; in coastal Mexico, *ramadas* often shelter homes or restaurants

regidor a community official, often a town council member, responsible for specific government functions, such as public works

retablo altarpiece, often of ornately carved and gilded wood

retorno cul-de-sac

ropa típica traditional dress, derived from the Spanish colonial tradition (in contrast to *traje*, traditional indigenous dress)

rurales former federal country police force created to fight *bandidos* (bandits) and suppress political dissent

Sabi Mixtec god of rain

sabino "Mexican" or "Montezuma" bald cypress tree, *Taxodium mucronatum*

Semana Santa Holy Week, the week preceding Easter Sunday

servicios the indigenous ladder of increasingly responsible public tasks that, if successfully performed, leads to community approval, prestige, and leadership for a given individual by middle age

tapete wool rug, made in certain east-side Valley of Oaxaca villages

taxi especial private taxi, as distinguished from *taxi colectivo*, or collective taxi

telégrafo telegraph office, lately converting to high-tech **telecomunicaciones** *(telecom)*, that also offers computerized telephone and public fax services

temazcal traditional indigenous sweat room, rock-enclosed and heated by a wood fire, usually used for healing, especially by women after childbirth

tenate basket of woven palm leaf, with tumpline instead of a rigid handle

tepache a wine, fermented from *panela* (sugarcane juice)

tequio an obligatory communal task, such as local road work, street sweeping, or child care, expected of all adult villagers from time to time

tianguis literally "awning," but now has come to mean the awning-decorated native town market

tlacoyos fired or toasted cakes made of masa; similar to corn tortillas but fatter

tono a usually benign animal guardian spirit

topil lowest municipal job, of messenger, filled by youngest teenage boys

traje traditional indigenous dress

vaquero cowboy

vecinidad neighborhood

yanqui Yankee

zócalo the popular label originally for the Mexico City central plaza; now the name for central plazas all over Mexico, including Oaxaca

Spanish Phrasebook

Your Mexico adventure will be more fun if you use a little Spanish. Mexican folks, although they may smile at your funny accent, will appreciate your halting efforts to break the ice and transform yourself from a foreigner to a potential friend.

Spanish commonly uses 30 letters – the familiar English 26, plus four straightforward additions: ch, ll, ñ, and rr, which are explained in "Consonants," below.

PRONUNCIATION

Once you learn them, Spanish pronunciation rules – in contrast to English – don't change. Spanish vowels generally sound softer than in English. (Note: The capitalized syllables below receive stronger accents.)

Vowels

a like ah, as in "hah": *agua* AH-gooah (water), *pan* PAHN (bread), and *casa* CAH-sah (house)

e like ay, as in "may:" *mesa* MAY-sah (table), *tela* TAY-lah (cloth), and *de* DAY (of, from)

i like ee, as in "need": *diez* dee-AYZ (ten), *comida* ko-MEE-dah (meal), and *fin* FEEN (end)

o like oh, as in "go": *peso* PAY-soh (weight), *ocho* OH-choh (eight), and *poco* POH-koh (a bit)

u like oo, as in "cool": *uno* OO-noh (one), *cuarto* KOOAHR-toh (room), and *usted* oos-TAYD (you); when it follows a "q" the **u** is silent; when it follows an "h" or has an umlaut, it's pronounced like "w"

Consonants

b, d, f, k, l, m, n, p, q, s, t, v, w, x, y, z, and ch
pronounced almost as in English; **h** occurs, but is silent – not pronounced at all.

c like k as in "keep": *cuarto* KOOAR-toh (room), Tepic tay-PEEK (capital of Nayarit state); when it precedes "e" or "i," pronounce **c** like s, as in "sit": *cerveza* sayr-VAY-sah (beer), *encima* ayn-SEE-mah (atop).

g like g as in "gift" when it precedes "a," "o," "u," or a consonant: *gato* GAH-toh (cat), *hago* AH-goh (I do, make); otherwise, pronounce **g** like h as in "hat": *giro* HEE-roh (money order), *gente* HAYN-tay (people)

j like h, as in "has": *Jueves* HOOAY-vays (Thursday), *mejor* may-HOR (better)

ll like y, as in "yes": *toalla* toh-AH-yah (towel), *ellos* AY-yohs (they, them)

ñ like ny, as in "canyon": *año* AH-nyo (year), *señor* SAY-nyor (Mr., sir)

r is lightly trilled, with tongue at the roof of your mouth like a very light English d, as in "ready": *pero* PAY-doh (but), *tres* TDAYS (three), *cuatro* KOOAH-tdoh (four).

rr like a Spanish r, but with much more emphasis and trill. Let your tongue flap. Practice with *burro* (donkey), *carretera* (highway), and Carrillo (proper name), then really let go with *ferrocarril* (railroad).

Note: The single small but common exception to all of the above is the pronunciation of Spanish **y** when it's being used as the Spanish word for "and," as in "Ron y Kathy." In such case, pronounce it like the English ee, as in "keep": Ron "ee" Kathy (Ron and Kathy).

Accent

The rule for accent, the relative stress given to syllables within a given word, is straightforward. If a word ends in a vowel, an n, or an s, accent the next-to-last syllable; if not, accent the last syllable.

Pronounce *gracias* GRAH-seeahs (thank you), *orden* OHR-dayn (order), and *carretera* kah-ray-TAY-rah (highway) with stress on the next-to-last syllable.

Otherwise, accent the last syllable: *venir* vay-NEER (to come), *ferrocarril* fay-roh-cah-REEL (railroad), and *edad* ay-DAHD (age).

Exceptions to the accent rule are always marked with an accent sign: (á, é, í, ó, or ú), such as *teléfono* tay-LAY-foh-noh (telephone), *jabón* hah-BON (soap), and *rápido* RAH-pee-doh (rapid).

BASIC AND COURTEOUS EXPRESSIONS

Most Spanish-speaking people consider formalities important. Whenever approaching anyone for information or some other reason, do not forget the appropriate salutation – good morning, good evening, etc. Standing alone, the greeting *hola* (hello) can sound brusque.

Hello. *Hola.*
Good morning. *Buenos días.*
Good afternoon. *Buenas tardes.*
Good evening. *Buenas noches.*
How are you? *¿Cómo está usted?*
Very well, thank you. *Muy bien, gracias.*
Okay; good. *Bien.*
Not okay; bad. *Mal or feo.*
So-so. *Más o menos.*
And you? *¿Y usted?*
Thank you. *Gracias.*
Thank you very much. *Muchas gracias.*
You're very kind. *Muy amable.*
You're welcome. *De nada.*
Goodbye. *Adios.*
See you later. *Hasta luego.*
please *por favor*
yes *sí*
no *no*
I don't know. *No sé.*
Just a moment, please. *Momentito, por favor.*
Excuse me, please (when you're trying to get attention). *Disculpe or Con permiso.*
Excuse me (when you've made a boo-boo). *Lo siento.*
Pleased to meet you. *Mucho gusto.*
How do you say...in Spanish? *¿Cómo se dice...en español?*
What is your name? *¿Cómo se llama usted?*
Do you speak English? *¿Habla usted inglés?*
Is English spoken here? (Does anyone here speak English?) *¿Se habla inglés?*
I don't speak Spanish well. *No hablo bien el español.*
I don't understand. *No entiendo.*
How do you say...in Spanish? *¿Cómo se dice...en español?*
My name is ... *Me llamo ...*

Would you like . . . ? *¿Quisiera usted...*
Let's go to . . . *Vamos a ...*

TERMS OF ADDRESS

When in doubt, use the formal *usted* (you) as a form of address.

I *yo*
you (formal) *usted*
you (familiar) *tu*
he/him *él*
she/her *ella*
we/us *nosotros*
you (plural) *ustedes*
they/them *ellos* (all males or mixed gender); *ellas* (all females)
Mr., sir *señor*
Mrs., madam *señora*
miss, young lady *señorita*
wife *esposa*
husband *esposo*
friend *amigo* (male); *amiga* (female)
sweetheart *novio* (male); *novia* (female)
son; daughter *hijo; hija*
brother; sister *hermano; hermana*
father; mother *padre; madre*
grandfather; grandmother *abuelo; abuela*

TRANSPORTATION

Where is . . . ? *¿Dónde está... ?*
How far is it to . . . ? *¿A cuánto está... ?*
from...to . . . *de...a ...*
How many blocks? *¿Cuántas cuadras?*
Where (Which) is the way to . . . ? *¿Dónde está el camino a ... ?*
the bus station *la terminal de autobuses*
the bus stop *la parada de autobuses*
Where is this bus going? *¿Adónde va este autobús?*
the taxi stand *la parada de taxis*
the train station *la estación de ferrocarril*
the boat *el barco*
the launch *lancha; tiburonera*
the dock *el muelle*
the airport *el aeropuerto*
I'd like a ticket to . . . *Quisiera un boleto a ...*
first (second) class *primera (segunda) clase*
roundtrip *ida y vuelta*

reservation *reservación*
baggage *equipaje*
Stop here, please. *Pare aquí, por favor.*
the entrance *la entrada*
the exit *la salida*
the ticket office *la oficina de boletos*
(very) near; far *(muy) cerca; lejos*
to; toward *a*
by; through *por*
from *de*
the right *la derecha*
the left *la izquierda*
straight ahead *derecho; directo*
in front *en frente*
beside *al lado*
behind *atrás*
the corner *la esquina*
the stoplight *la semáforo*
a turn *una vuelta*
right here *aquí*
somewhere around here *por acá*
right there *allí*
somewhere around there *por allá*
road *el camino*
street; boulevard *calle; bulevar*
block *la cuadra*
highway *carretera*
kilometer *kilómetro*
bridge; toll *puente; cuota*
address *dirección*
north; south *norte; sur*
east; west *oriente (este); poniente (oeste)*

ACCOMMODATIONS
hotel *hotel*
Is there a room? *¿Hay cuarto?*
May I (may we) see it? *¿Puedo (podemos) verlo?*
What is the rate? *¿Cuál es el precio?*
Is that your best rate? *¿Es su mejor precio?*
Is there something cheaper? *¿Hay algo más económico?*
a single room *un cuarto sencillo*
a double room *un cuarto doble*
double bed *cama matrimonial*
twin beds *camas gemelas*
with private bath *con baño*

hot water *agua caliente*
shower *ducha*
towels *toallas*
soap *jabón*
toilet paper *papel higiénico*
blanket *frazada; manta*
sheets *sábanas*
air-conditioned *aire acondicionado*
fan *abanico; ventilador*
key *llave*
manager *gerente*

FOOD
I'm hungry *Tengo hambre.*
I'm thirsty. *Tengo sed.*
menu *carta; menú*
order *orden*
glass *vaso*
fork *tenedor*
knife *cuchillo*
spoon *cuchara*
napkin *servilleta*
soft drink *refresco*
coffee *café*
tea *té*
drinking water *agua pura; agua potable*
bottled carbonated water *agua mineral*
bottled uncarbonated water *agua sin gas*
beer *cerveza*
wine *vino*
milk *leche*
juice *jugo*
cream *crema*
sugar *azúcar*
cheese *queso*
snack *antojo; botana*
breakfast *desayuno*
lunch *almuerzo*
daily lunch special *comida corrida (or el menú del día depending on region)*
dinner *comida (often eaten in late afternoon); cena (a late-night snack)*
the check *la cuenta*
eggs *huevos*
bread *pan*
salad *ensalada*
fruit *fruta*

mango *mango*
watermelon *sandía*
papaya *papaya*
banana *plátano*
apple *manzana*
orange *naranja*
lime *limón*
fish *pescado*
shellfish *mariscos*
shrimp *camarones*
meat (without) *(sin) carne*
chicken *pollo*
pork *puerco*
beef; steak *res; bistec*
bacon; ham *tocino; jamón*
fried *frito*
roasted *asada*
barbecue; barbecued *barbacoa; al carbón*

SHOPPING
money *dinero*
money-exchange bureau *casa de cambio*
I would like to exchange traveler's checks. *Quisiera cambiar cheques de viajero.*
What is the exchange rate? *¿Cuál es el tipo de cambio?*
How much is the commission? *¿Cuánto cuesta la comisión?*
Do you accept credit cards? *¿Aceptan tarjetas de crédito?*
money order *giro*
How much does it cost? *¿Cuánto cuesta?*
What is your final price? *¿Cuál es su último precio?*
expensive *caro*
cheap *barato; económico*
more *más*
less *menos*
a little *un poco*
too much *demasiado*

HEALTH
Help me please. *Ayúdeme por favor.*
I am ill. *Estoy enfermo.*
Call a doctor. *Llame un doctor.*
Take me to ... *Lléveme a ...*
hospital *hospital; sanatorio*

drugstore *farmacia*
pain *dolor*
fever *fiebre*
headache *dolor de cabeza*
stomachache *dolor de estómago*
burn *quemadura*
cramp *calambre*
nausea *náusea*
vomiting *vomitar*
medicine *medicina*
antibiotic *antibiótico*
pill; tablet *pastilla*
aspirin *aspirina*
ointment; cream *pomada; crema*
bandage *venda*
cotton *algodón*
sanitary napkins use brand name, e.g., Kotex
birth control pills *pastillas anticonceptivas*
contraceptive foam *espuma anticonceptiva*
condoms *preservativos; condones*
toothbrush *cepilla dental*
dental floss *hilo dental*
toothpaste *crema dental*
dentist *dentista*
toothache *dolor de muelas*

POST OFFICE AND COMMUNICATIONS
long-distance telephone *teléfono larga distancia*
I would like to call ... *Quisiera llamar a ...*
collect *por cobrar*
station to station *a quien contesta*
person to person *persona a persona*
credit card *tarjeta de crédito*
post office *correo*
general delivery *lista de correo*
letter *carta*
stamp *estampilla, timbre*
postcard *tarjeta*
aerogram *aerograma*
air mail *correo aereo*
registered *registrado*
money order *giro*
package; box *paquete; caja*
string; tape *cuerda; cinta*

AT THE BORDER
border *frontera*
customs *aduana*
immigration *migración*
tourist card *tarjeta de turista*
inspection *inspección; revisión*
passport *pasaporte*
profession *profesión*
marital status *estado civil*
single *soltero*
married; divorced *casado; divorciado*
widowed *viudado*
insurance *seguros*
title *título*
driver's license *licencia de manejar*

AT THE GAS STATION
gas station *gasolinera*
gasoline *gasolina*
unleaded *sin plomo*
full, please *lleno, por favor*
tire *llanta*
tire repair shop *vulcanizadora*
air *aire*
water *agua*
oil (change) *aceite (cambio)*
grease *grasa*
My...doesn't work. *Mi...no sirve.*
battery *batería*
radiator *radiador*
alternator *alternador*
generator *generador*
tow truck *grúa*
repair shop *taller mecánico*
tune-up *afinación*
auto parts store *refaccionería*

VERBS
Verbs are the key to getting along in Spanish. They employ mostly predictable forms and come in three classes, which end in *ar*, *er*, and *ir*, respectively:

to buy *comprar*
I buy, you (he, she, it) buys *compro, compra*
we buy, you (they) buy *compramos, compran*

to eat *comer*
I eat, you (he, she, it) eats *como, come*
we eat, you (they) eat *comemos, comen*

to climb *subir*
I climb, you (he, she, it) climbs *subo, sube*
we climb, you (they) climb *subimos, suben*

Here are more (with irregularities indicated):

to do or make *hacer* (regular except for *hago*, I do or make)
to go *ir* (very irregular: *voy, va, vamos, van*)
to go (walk) *andar*
to love *amar*
to work *trabajar*
to want *desear, querer*
to need *necesitar*
to read *leer*
to write *escribir*
to repair *reparar*
to stop *parar*
to get off (the bus) *bajar*
to arrive *llegar*
to stay (remain) *quedar*
to stay (lodge) *hospedar*
to leave *salir* (regular except for *salgo*, I leave)
to look at *mirar*
to look for *buscar*
to give *dar* (regular except for *doy*, I give)
to carry *llevar*
to have *tener* (irregular but important: *tengo, tiene, tenemos, tienen*)
to come *venir* (similarly irregular: *vengo, viene, venimos, vienen*)

Spanish has two forms of "to be":

to be *estar* (regular except for *estoy*, I am)
to be *ser* (very irregular: *soy, es, somos, son*)

Use *estar* when speaking of location or a temporary state of being: "I am at home." "*Estoy en casa.*" "I'm sick." "*Estoy enfermo.*" Use *ser* for a permanent state of being: "I am a doctor." "*Soy doctora.*"

NUMBERS

zero *cero*
one *uno*
two *dos*
three *tres*
four *cuatro*
five *cinco*
six *seis*
seven *siete*
eight *ocho*
nine *nueve*
10 *diez*
11 *once*
12 *doce*
13 *trece*
14 *catorce*
15 *quince*
16 *dieciseis*
17 *diecisiete*
18 *dieciocho*
19 *diecinueve*
20 *veinte*
21 *veinte y uno or veintiuno*
30 *treinta*
40 *cuarenta*
50 *cincuenta*
60 *sesenta*
70 *setenta*
80 *ochenta*
90 *noventa*
100 *ciento*
101 *ciento y uno or cientiuno*
200 *doscientos*
500 *quinientos*
1,000 *mil*
10,000 *diez mil*
100,000 *cien mil*
1,000,000 *millón*
one half *medio*
one third *un tercio*
one fourth *un cuarto*

TIME

What time is it? *¿Qué hora es?*
It's one o'clock. *Es la una.*
It's three in the afternoon. *Son las tres de la tarde.*
It's 4 A.M. *Son las cuatro de la mañana.*
six-thirty *seis y media*
a quarter till eleven *un cuarto para las once*
a quarter past five *las cinco y cuarto*
an hour *una hora*

DAYS AND MONTHS

Monday *lunes*
Tuesday *martes*
Wednesday *miércoles*
Thursday *jueves*
Friday *viernes*
Saturday *sábado*
Sunday *domingo*
today *hoy*
tomorrow *mañana*
yesterday *ayer*
January *enero*
February *febrero*
March *marzo*
April *abril*
May *mayo*
June *junio*
July *julio*
August *agosto*
September *septiembre*
October *octubre*
November *noviembre*
December *diciembre*
a week *una semana*
a month *un mes*
after *después*
before *antes*

Suggested Reading

Some of these books are informative, others are entertaining, and all of them will increase your understanding of both Mexico and Oaxaca.

HISTORY

Blanton, E. Richard, Gary M. Feinman, Stephen A. Kowaleski, and Linda M. Nicholas. *Ancient Oaxaca*. Cambridge, New York, and Melbourne: Cambridge University Press, 1999. A scholarly account of pre-Columbian Oaxaca history, for the serious reader.

Brunk, Samuel. *Emiliano Zapata: Revolution and Betrayal in Mexico*. Albuquerque, NM: University of New Mexico Press, 1995. A detailed narrative of the renowned revolutionary's turbulent life, from his humble birth in Anenecuilco village in Morelos through his de facto control of Mexico City in 1914–1915 to his final betrayal and assassination in 1919. The author authoritatively demonstrates that Zapata, neither complete hero nor complete villain, was simply an incredibly determined native leader who paid the ultimate price in his selfless struggle for land and liberty for the campesinos of southern Mexico.

Calderón de la Barca, Frances. *Life in Mexico, with New Material from the Author's Journals*. Charleston, SC: Bibliobazaar, 2006. A new copyright and printing of the humorous original 1843 book, by the brilliant, celebrated Scottish wife of the Spanish ambassador to Mexico.

Casasola, Gustavo. *Seis Siglos de Historia Gráfica de Mexico (Six Centuries of Mexican Graphic History)*. Mexico City: Editorial Gustavo Casasola, 1978. Six fascinating encyclopedic volumes, in Spanish, of Mexican history in pictures, from 1325 to the present. Now out of print, but large city and university libraries may have copies.

Chance, John K. *Conquest of the Sierra*. Norman, OK: University of Oklahoma Press, 1989. Professor Chance uses archival sources to trace the evolution of colonial society, principally the northern Sierra Zapotec communities and how they adapted their religion, customs, and settlement patterns in response to the pressures of Spanish rule.

Collis, Maurice. *Cortés and Montezuma*. New York, NY: New Directions Publishing Corp., 1999. A reprint of a 1954 classic piece of well-researched storytelling, Collis traces Cortés's conquest of Mexico through the defeat of his chief opponent, Aztec Emperor Montezuma. He uses contemporary eyewitnesses—notably Bernal Díaz del Castillo—to revivify one of history's greatest dramas.

Cortés, Hernán. *Letters from Mexico*. Translated by Anthony Pagden. New Haven, CT: Yale University Press, 1986. Cortés's five long letters to his king, in which he describes contemporary Mexico in fascinating detail, including, notably, the remarkably sophisticated life of the Aztecs at the time of the conquest.

De las Casas, Bartolome. *A Short Account of the Destruction of the Indies*. New York, NY: Penguin Books, 1992. The gritty but beloved Dominican Bishop, renowned as Mexico's "Apostle of the Indians" writes passionately of his own failed attempt to moderate and humanize the Spanish conquest of Mexico.

Díaz del Castillo, Bernal. *The Discovery and Conquest of Mexico*. New York, NY: Da Capo Press, 2003. A fascinating, still-fresh soldier's tale of the conquest from the Spanish viewpoint.

Garfias, Luis. *The Mexican Revolution*. Mexico City: Panorama Editorial, 1985. A concise Mexican version of the 1910–1917 Mexican revolution, the crucible of present-day Mexico.

Gugliotta, Bobette. *Women of Mexico, the Consecrated and the Common*. Encino, CA: originally published by Floricanto Press, 1989. Lively legends, tales, and biographies of remarkable Mexican women, including several from Oaxaca. Libraries, Amazon.com, and others have used copies.

León-Portilla, Miguel. *The Broken Spears: The Aztec Account of the Conquest of Mexico*. New York, NY: Beacon Press, 1992. Provides an intriguing contrast to Díaz del Castillo's account.

Meyer, Michael, and William Sherman. *The Course of Mexican History*. New York, NY: Oxford University Press, 2003. An insightful, interestingly written 700-plus-page college textbook in paperback. A bargain, especially if you can get it used.

Novas, Himilce. *Everything You Need to Know About Latino History*. New York, NY: Penguin Group, 2007. Chicanos, Latin rhythm, La Raza, the Treaty of Guadalupe Hidalgo, and much more, interpreted from an authoritative Latino point of view.

Ridley, Jasper. *Maximilian and Juárez*. London: Orion Pub. Group, 2001. This authoritative historical biography breathes new life into one of Mexico's great ironic tragedies, a drama that pitted the native Zapotec "Lincoln of Mexico" against the dreamy, idealistic Archduke Maximilian of Austria-Hungary. Despite their common liberal ideals, they were drawn into a bloody no-quarter struggle that set the Old World against the New, ending in Maximilian's execution, the insanity of his wife, and the emergence of the United States as a power to be reckoned with in world affairs.

Ruíz, Ramon Eduardo. *Triumphs and Tragedy: A History of the Mexican People*. New York, NY: W. W. Norton, Inc., 1992. A pithy, anecdote-filled history of Mexico from an authoritative Mexican American perspective.

Shorris, Earl. *Life and Times of Mexico*. New York, NY: W. W. Norton, 2006. A grand 750-page narrative of the divided soul of Mexico, driven by 3,000 years of history, as told by Mexicans, from the ancient Olmecs, Benito Juárez, and Emiliano Zapata, to *maquiladora laborers,* prostitutes, and a movie director.

Simpson, Lesley Bird. *Many Mexicos*. Berkeley, CA: University of California Press, 1962. A much-reprinted, fascinating broad-brush portrait of Mexican history.

ARCHAEOLOGY

Flannery, Kent, and Joyce Marcus. *The Cloud People*. New York, NY: Academic Press, 2003. Eminently authoritative authors trace the divergent evolution of the Zapotec and Mixtec peoples as revealed by the archaeological record.

Marcus, Joyce, and Kent Flannery, contributor. *Zapotec Civilization*. London and New York, NY: Thames and Hudson, 1996. The distinguished authors elegantly illustrate and trace the evolution of Valley of Oaxaca civilization, from 10,000 b.c. to the conquest, using the results from recent finds and hundreds of maps, drawings, and photos.

Winter, Marcus. *Oaxaca, the Archaeological Record*. Mexico, D.F.: Minutiae Mexicana, 1992. A distinguished Oaxaca resident archaeologist skillfully traces a concise history of Oaxaca's pre-conquest inhabitants, based on finds at Monte Albán, Mitla, and many other sites. Dozens of maps and site descriptions make this 100-page pamphlet an especially useful guide.

UNIQUE GUIDE AND TIP BOOKS

American Automobile Association. *Mexico TravelBook*. Heathrow, FL: American Automobile Association, 2003. The American Automobile Association (1000 AAA Drive, Heathrow, FL 32746-5063, www.aaa.com, 800/922-8228) offers short but sweet summaries of major Mexican tourist destinations and sights. Also includes information on fiestas, accommodations, restaurants, and a wealth of information relevant to car travel in Mexico. Available in bookstores, or free to AAA members at affiliate offices.

Church, Mike and Terry. *Traveler's Guide to Mexican Camping*. Kirkland, WA: Rolling Homes Press (order by tel. 800/922-8228, or through www.rollinghomes.com). This is an unusually thorough guide to trailer parks all over Mexico, with much coverage of the Pacific Coast in general and Oaxaca region in particular. Detailed maps guide you accurately to each trailer park cited and clear descriptions tell you what to expect.

Forgey, Dr. William. *Traveler's Medical Alert Series: Mexico, A Guide to Health and Safety*. Merrillville, IN: ICS Books, 1991. Useful information on health and safety in Mexico. Out of print, but available through Amazon. com.

Franz, Carl. *The People's Guide to Mexico*. Emeryville, CA: Avalon Travel Publishing, 13th edition, 2006. An entertaining and insightful A-to-Z general guide to the joys and pitfalls of independent economy travel in Mexico.

Gilford, Judith. *The Packing Book*. New York, NY: Ten Speed Press, 2006. The secrets of the carry-on traveler, or how to make everything you carry do double and triple duty. All for the sake of convenience, mobility, economy, and comfort.

Graham, Scott. *Handle With Care: Guide to Socially Responsible Travel in Developing Countries*. Chicago, IL: The Noble Press, 1991. Should you accept a meal from a family who lives in a grass house? This insightful guide answers this and hundreds of other tough questions for people who want to travel responsibly in the third world. It's out of print, but available through Amazon.com.

Jeffrey, Nan. *Adventuring with Children*. Ashland, MA: Avalon House Publishing, 1996. This unusually detailed book starts where most travel-with-children books end. It contains, besides a wealth of information and practical strategies for general travel with children, specific chapters on how you can adventure—trek, kayak, river-raft, camp, bicycle, and much more—successfully with the kids in tow.

Werner, David. *Where There Is No Doctor*. Berkeley, CA: Hesperian Foundation (1919 Addison St., Suite 204, Berkeley, CA 94704, tel. 888/729-1796, www.hesperian. org), 1992. How to keep well in the tropical backcountry.

Whipperman, Bruce. *Moon Acapulco, Ixtapa & Zihuatanejo*. Berkeley, CA: Avalon Travel, fourth edition, 2008. The most comprehensive guidebook, with an abundance of detail of not only the famous resorts, but the little-known untouristed treasures, from the mountains to the sea, of Oaxaca's neighboring state of Guerrero.

FICTION

Bowen, David, ed. *Pyramids of Glass*. San Antonio, TX: Corona Publishing Co., 1994. Two dozen-odd stories that lead the reader along a month-long journey through the bedrooms, the barracks, the cafés, and streets of present-day Mexico.

Boyle, T. C. *The Tortilla Curtain*. New York, NY: Penguin-Putnam, 1996; paperback edition, Raincoast Books, 1996. A chance intersection of the lives of two couples, one affluent and liberal Southern Californians, the other poor homeless illegal immigrants, forces all to come to grips with the real price of the American Dream.

Cisneros, Sandra. *Caramelo.* New York, NY: Alfred A. Knopf, 2002. A celebrated author weaves a passionate, yet funny, multigenerational tale of a Mexican-American family and of their migrations, which, beginning in Mexico City, propelled them north, all the way to Chicago and back.

De la Cruz, Sor Juana Inez. *Poems, Protest, and a Dream.* New York, NY: Penguin, 1997. Masterful translation of a collection of love and religious poems by the celebrated pioneer (1651–1695) Mexican feminist-nun.

De Zapata, Celia Correas, ed. *Short Stories by Latin American Women: The Magic and the Real.* New York, NY: Random House Modern Library, 2003. An eclectic mix of more than 30 stories by noted Latin American women. The stories, which a number of critics classify as "magical realism," were researched by editor Celia de Zapata, who got them freshly translated into English by a cadre of renowned translators.

Doerr, Harriet. *Consider This, Señora.* New York, NY: Harcourt Brace, 1993. Four expatriates tough it out in a Mexican small town, adapting to the excesses—blazing sun, driving rain, vast untrammeled landscapes—meanwhile interacting with the local folks while the local folks observe them, with a mixture of fascination and tolerance.

Finn, María, ed. *Mexico in Mind.* New York, NY: Vintage Books, 2006. The wisdom and impressions of two centuries of renowned writers, from D. H. Lawrence and John Steinbeck to John Reed and Richard Rodríguez, who were drawn to the timelessness and romance of Mexico.

Fuentes, Carlos. *Where the Air Is Clear.* New York, NY: Farrar, Straus, and Giroux, 1971. The seminal work of Mexico's celebrated novelist.

Fuentes, Carlos. *The Years with Laura Díaz.* Translated by Alfred MacAdam. New York, NY: Farrar, Straus, and Giroux, 2000. A panorama of Mexico from Independence to the 21st century through the eyes of one woman, Laura Díaz, and her great-grandson, the author. One reviewer said that she, "as a Mexican woman, would like to celebrate Carlos Fuentes; it is worthy of applause that a man who has seen, observed, analyzed and criticized the great occurrences of the century now has a woman, Laura Díaz, speak for him."

Jennings, Gary. *Aztec.* New York, NY: Atheneum, 1980; reprinted by Forge Books, 2006. Beautifully researched and written monumental tale of lust, compassion, love, and death in pre-conquest Mexico.

Nickles, Sara, ed. *Escape to Mexico.* San Francisco, CA: Chronicle Books, 2002. A carefully selected anthology of 20-odd stories of Mexico by renowned authors, from Steven Crane and W. Somerset Maugham to Anaïs Nin and David Lida, who all found inspiration, refuge, adventure, and much more in Mexico.

Perez-Riverte, Arturo. *Queen of the South.* New York, NY: Plume Books, 2005. In a gripping good read, the author tackles the dangerous world of Mexican drug trafficking. The story immediately races along with protagonist Teresa Mendoza, fleeing for her life from Mexico, to Morocco. There, learning from her every step, threading her way through a snake nest of dangerous men, she finally triumphs as the ringleader of a big drug trafficking ring.

Peters, Daniel. *The Luck of Huemac.* New York, NY: Random House, 1981. An Aztec noble family's tale of war, famine, sorcery, heroism, treachery, love, and, finally, disaster and death in the Valley of Mexico.

Traven, B. *The Treasure of the Sierra Madre.* New York, NY: Hill and Wang, 1967. Campesinos, *federales,* gringos, and *indígenas* all figure in this modern morality tale set in Mexico's rugged outback. The most famous of the mysterious author's many novels of oppression and justice in Mexico's jungles.

Villaseñor, Victor. *Rain of Gold.* New York, NY: Delta Books (Bantam, Doubleday, and Dell), 1991. The moving, best-selling epic of the gritty travails of the author's family. From humble rural beginnings in the Copper Canyon, they flee revolution and certain death, struggling through parched northern deserts to sprawling border refugee camps. From there they migrate to relative safety and an eventual modicum of happiness in Southern California.

ARTS, CRAFTS, AND ARCHITECTURE

Baird, Joseph. *The Churches of Mexico, 1530–1810.* Berkeley, CA: University of California Press, 1962. Mexican colonial architecture and art, illustrated and interpreted, with many monumental examples from Oaxaca.

Chibnik, Michael. *Crafting Tradition: The Making and Marketing of Oaxaca Wood Carvings.* Austin, TX: University of Texas Press, 2003. Authoritative study of the phenomenally popular growth of *alebrijes,* Oaxaca's fanciful wooden animals. This carefully researched work covers all you need to know about the history, crafting, artistry, and the social and economic ramifications of Oaxacan woodcrafts in particular and handicrafts in general.

Fishgrund, Andrea Stanton. *Zapotec Weavers of Teotitlán.* Santa Fe, NM: University of New Mexico Press, 1999. Authoritative, richly color-illustrated description of the history, economics, and techniques, both traditional and contemporary, of the textile weavers of Teotitlán del Valle, in the Valley of Oaxaca.

Martínez Penaloza, Porfirio. *Popular Arts of Mexico.* Mexico City: Editorial Panorama, 1981. An excellent pocket-sized exposition of Mexican art and handicrafts.

Morrill, Penny C., and Carol A. Berk. *Mexican Silver.* Atglen, PA: Shiffer Publishing Co. (4880 Lower Valley Road, Atglen, PA 19310), 2001. Lovingly written and photographed exposition of the Mexican silvercraft of Taxco, Guerrero, that was revitalized through the initiative of Frederick Davis and William Spratling in the 1920s and 1930s. Color photos of many beautiful museum-quality pieces supplement the text, which describes the history and work of a score of silversmithing families who developed the Taxco craft under Spratling's leadership. Greatly adds to the traveler's appreciation of the beautiful Taxco silvercrafts.

Mullen, Robert J. *The Architecture and Sculpture of Oaxaca, 1530s to 1980s.* Tempe, AZ: Arizona State University, 1995. An informative stone-by-stone guide to Oaxaca's monumental buildings, mostly churches. The author's solid commentary vivifies visits to every church of note in Oaxaca and transforms what might be humdrum sightseeing for the reader-traveler into recognition, understanding, and appreciation.

Sayer, Chloë. *Arts and Crafts of Mexico.* San Francisco, CA: Chronicle Books, 1990. All you ever wanted to know about your favorite Mexican crafts, from papier-mâché to pottery, toys, and Taxco silver. Beautifully illustrated by traditional etchings and David Lavender's crisp black-and-white and color photographs.

PEOPLE AND CULTURE

Castillo, Ana, ed. *Goddess of the Americas.* New York, NY: Riverhead Books, 1997. Here a noted author has selected from the works of seven interpreters of Mesoamerican female deities to provide readers with visions of the Virgin of Guadalupe that range as far and wide as Sex Goddess, the Broken-Hearted, the Subversive, and the Warrior Queen.

Casumano, Camille. *Mexico, a Love Story: Women Write About the Mexican Experience.* Berkeley, CA: Seal Press, 2006. A dozen-odd writers share stories, some poignant, some entertaining, and all endearing, that express their love for Mexico and its people.

Chinas, Beverly Newbold. *Isthmus Zapotecs: A Matrifocal Culture of Mexico.* Forth Worth, TX: College Publishing, 1997. In a detailed academic study, the author explains how an indigenous, female-dominant culture functions in Oaxaca.

Cohen, Jeffrey. *Cooperation and Community: Economy and Society in Oaxaca.* Austin, TX: University of Texas Press, 2000. A pithy, authoritative account of the history, economy, politics, and folkways of the Santañeros—the people of the weaving village of Santa Ana del Valle, in the Valley of Oaxaca. Here, time-honored customs—*compadrazgo, guelaguetza, promesas*—fuse with latter-day realities to produce a culture simultaneously modern and traditional.

Cordrey, Donald, and Dorothy Cordrey. *Mexican Indian Costumes.* Austin, TX: University of Texas Press, 1968. A lovingly photographed, written, and illustrated classic on Mexican native peoples, including many Oaxacan groups.

Edinger, Steven T. *The Road from Mixtepec.* Fresno, CA: Asociación Cívica Benito Juárez (P.O. Box 12320, Fresno, CA 93706), 1996. A compassionately researched and photographed account of the people of San Juan Mixtepec, in the Mixteca Alta region of Oaxaca. The author, through his solid anecdotal narrative, relates the story of how a people whose means of existence have been gradually degraded for the past 400 years maintain their lives, spirit, and traditions only by repeated emigration to work as marginal farm laborers in northern Mexico and the United States.

Finerty, Cathcrine Palmer. *In a Village Far From Home.* Tucson, AZ: University of Arizona Press, 2000. After a successful Madison Avenue career, the author packed up and eventually found herself the volunteer nurse in an isolated western Mexico village. From her eight-year diary, she shares the joys and sorrows of a cast of village characters, from a valiant Catholic padre and his frowning bishop, to Chuy, her indigenous housekeeper, and Chila, her landlord.

Greenberg, James B. *Blood Ties: Life and Violence in Rural Mexico.* Tucson, AZ: University of Arizona Press, 1993. The author reveals, with a wealth of personal anecdotes, the cultural underpinnings beneath decades of deadly feuding between two leading Chatino towns in Oaxaca's southern Sierra.

Haden, Judith Cooper, and Matthew Jaffe. *Oaxaca, the Spirit of Mexico.* New York, NY: Artisan, division of Workman Publishing, Inc., 2002. Simply the loveliest, most sensitively photographed and crafted coffee-table book of Mexico photography yet produced. Photos by Haden, text by Jaffe.

Leslie, Charles M. *Now We Are Civilized.* Detroit, MI: Wayne State University Press, 1960. A now-classic anecdotal study of the worldview and ways of the Zapotec people of Mitla, Oaxaca.

Martinez, Zarela. *The Food and Life of Oaxaca.* New York, NY: Macmillan, 1997. Martinez, a New York restaurateur, leads her readers on an intriguing tour of Oaxacan folkways by way of the palate. Features chapters on Oaxaca's seven *moles,* 150 recipes, and two dozen photos of finished gastronomical creations.

Nader, Laura. *Harmony, Ideology, Justice, and Control in a Zapotec Mountain Village.* Palo Alto, CA: Stanford University Press, 1990. How some northern Sierra Zapotecs solve disputes, using religion-based ideas of harmony to achieve justice and social control.

Palmer, Colin A. *Slaves of the White God: Blacks in Mexico.* Cambridge, MA: Harvard University Press, 1976. A scholarly study of why and how Spanish authorities imported African slaves into the Americas and how they were used afterward. Replete with poignant details taken from Spanish and Mexican archives describing how the Africans struggled from bondage to eventual freedom.

Romney, Kimball, and Romaine Romney. *The Mixtecans of Juxtlahuaca.* Huntington, NY: Robert E. Krieger Publishing Co., 1973. The authors study the contemporary Mixtec culture of the western Mixteca. Pithy examples, especially of the organization of fiestas, still ring true despite the two generations that elapsed since the research was done.

Stephen, Lynn. *Zapotec Women.* Durham, NC: Duke University Press, 2005. Study of how women run much of the local economy and a significant fraction of the politics in the Oaxaca Isthmus districts of Tehuántepec and Juchitán.

Toor, Frances. *A Treasury of Mexican Folkways.* New York, NY: Bonanza Books, 1947; reprinted 1985. A lovingly illustrated encyclopedia of vanishing Mexicana—costumes, religion, fiestas, burial practices, customs, legends—compiled during the celebrated author's 35 years' residence in Mexico in the early 20th century.

Sabina, María. *María Sabina Selections.* Berkeley, CA: University of California Press, 2003.

María Sabina (1894–1985) was the celebrated traditional healer and tutor to an entire new age generation, from mellow hippies, to straight-laced psychiatrists, seeking cures through María's magic mushrooms. Although she was not a poet, she has nevertheless left behind a poetic legacy of essays and chants, compiled by her family and followers in her Northern Oaxaca mountain-top hometown of Huautla de Jiménez.

Trilling, Susana. *Seasons of My Heart.* New York, NY: Ballantine Publishing Group, 1999. The celebrated Oaxaca author, chef, and cooking teacher leads her readers on a culinary journey of the seven regions of Oaxaca. Along the way, they stop by market towns, mountain hamlets, shoreline villages, and lush highland valleys, visiting the friends with whom she refined the dozens of recipes that introduce the best of Oaxacan cooking. *Seasons of My Heart* is the companion volume to Trilling's National Public Television series on Oaxacan cooking.

Wauchope, Robert, ed. *Handbook of Middle American Indians.* Volumes 7 and 8. Austin, TX: University of Texas Press, 1969. Authoritative, fascinating, but aging studies of important native-speaking groups in northern, central (vol. 8), and southern (vol. 7) Mexico.

GOVERNMENT, POLITICS, AND ECONOMY

Campbell, Howard. *Zapotec Renaissance: Ethnic Politics and Cultural Revival in Southern Mexico.* Albuquerque, NM: University of New Mexico Press, 1994. A history of how the Zapotecs around Juchitán, Oaxaca, fought city hall and won.

Dillon, Samuel, and Preston, Julia. *Opening Mexico: The Making of a Democracy.* New York, NY: Farrar, Strauss and Geroux, 2005. Former Mexico City *New York Times* bureau chiefs use their rich personal insights and investigative journalistic skill to tell the story of the latter-day evolution of Mexico's uniquely imperfect democracy. Their story begins during the 1980s, tracing the decay of the 71-year-rule of the PRI, to its collapse, with the election of opposition candidate Vicente Fox in 2000.

Murphy, Arthur D., and Alex Stepick. *Social Inequality in Oaxaca.* Philadelphia, PA: Temple University Press, 1993. A sociopolitical history of grassroots underclass activism in Oaxaca City during the 1960s, 1970s, and 1980s.

Poleman, Thomas T. *Agricultural Development in the Mexican Tropics.* Palo Alto, CA: Stanford University Press, 1964. The successes, failures, and consequences of Mexico's great dam project in Oaxaca's Papaloapan basin.

Rubin, Jeffry W. *Decentering the Regime.* Winston-Salem, NC: Duke University Press, 1997. Ethnicity, radicalism, and democracy in Juchitán, Oaxaca.

FLORA AND FAUNA

Goodson, Gar. *Fishes of the Pacific Coast.* Stanford, CA: Stanford University Press, 1988. More than 500 beautifully detailed color drawings highlight this pocket version of all you ever wanted to know about the ocean's fishes (including common Spanish names) from Alaska to Peru.

Howell, Steve N. G., and Sophie Webb. *A Guide to the Birds of Mexico and Northern America.* Oxford: Oxford University Press, 1995. All the serious bird-watcher needs to know about Mexico's rich species treasury. Includes authoritative habitat maps and 70 excellent color plates that detail the males and females of around 1,500 species. (For a more portable version, check out Steve Howell's *Bird-Finding Guide to Mexico,* 1999.)

Mason Jr., Charles T., and Patricia B. Mason. *Handbook of Mexican Roadside Flora.* Tucson, AZ: University of Arizona Press, 1987. Authoritative identification guide, with black and white illustrations, of all the plants you're likely to see in the Oaxaca region.

Morris, Percy A. *A Field Guide to Pacific Coast Shells.* Boston, MA: Houghton Mifflin, 1974. The complete beachcomber's Pacific shell guide.

Pesman, M. Walter. *Meet Flora Mexicana.* Globe, AZ: D. S. King, 1962. Delightful anecdotes and illustrations of hundreds of common Mexican plants. Out of print.

Wright, N. Pelham. *A Guide to Mexican Mammals and Reptiles.* Mexico City: Minutiae Mexicana, 1989. Pocket-edition. Lore, history, descriptions, and pictures of commonly seen Mexican animals.

Internet Resources

A number of websites may be helpful in preparing for your Oaxaca trip.

GENERAL TRAVEL
Internet Travel Sites
www.travelocity.com,
www.expedia.com
These are major sites for airline and hotel bookings.

Travel Insurance
www.travelinsure.com,
www.worldtravelcenter.com
Both sites are good for general travel insurance and other services.

Mexico Car Insurance
Sanborn's Insurance
www.sanbornsinsurance.com
Sanborn's Insurance is the long-time, very reliable Mexico auto insurance agency, with the only north-of-the-border adjustment procedure. Get your quote online, order their many useful publications, and find out about other insurance you many have forgotten.

SPECIALTY TRAVEL
Go Oaxaca
www.go-oaxaca.com/overview/
gay.html
A small page that lists a number of gay-friendly bars, restaurants, nightclubs, and a few gay-friendly hotels in Oaxaca City.

Mobility International
www.miusa.org
Site of Mobility International is expertly organized and complete, with a flock of services for travelers with disabilities, including many people-to-people connections in Mexico.

Purple Roofs
www.purpleroofs.com
One of the best general gay travel websites is maintained by San Francisco–based travel agency Purple Roofs. It offers, for example, details about several gay-friendly Oaxaca hotels, in addition to a wealth of gay-friendly travel-oriented links worldwide.

Road Scholar
www.roadscholar.org
Site of Boston-based Road Scholar, Inc. (formerly Elderhostel, Inc.), with a very popular program of ongoing study tours, includes a Oaxaca program of Spanish Language and Oaxacan culture.

U.S. GOVERNMENT
U.S. State Department
www.state.gov/travelandbusiness
The U.S. State Department's very good travel information site, includes lots of headings and links to a swarm of topics, including Mexican consular offices in the United States, U.S. consular offices in Mexico, travel advisories, and links to other government information, such as importation of food, plants, and animals, U.S. customs, health abroad, airlines, and exchange rates.

MEXICO IN GENERAL
MexConnect
www.mexconnect.com
This is an extensive Mexico site, with dozens upon dozens of subheadings and links, especially helpful for folks thinking of traveling, working, living, or retiring in Mexico, including Oaxaca.

Mexico Desconocido
www.mexicodesconocido.com.mx
This is the site of the excellent magazine *Mexico Desconocido* (Undiscovered Mexico) that often features unusual, untouristed destinations, many in the state of Oaxaca. It links to a large library of past articles, which are not unlike a Mexican version of National Geographic Traveler, featuring solid, hard-to-

find information, in good English translation, if you can get it. (The site is so voluminous that the automatic translator tends to bog down at the effort.)

On the initial home page, find the small magnifying glass and dialog box, labeled "buscar" ("find") at the upper right. I typed in "Oaxaca" and got 206 informative hits about places and things in Oaxaca, each linked to an article in the magazine.

Mexico Online
www.mexonline.com
Very extensive, well-organized commercial site with many subheadings and links to Mexico's large and medium destinations, and even some in small destinations. For the state of Oaxaca, they cover Oaxaca City, Huatulco, and Puerto Escondido. For example, for Oaxaca, their linked page www.mexonline.com/cityguide-oaxaca.htm is typical, with manifold links about many dozens of accommodations, from luxury hotels to modest bed-and-breakfasts. It's excellent.

Mexico Tourism Board
www.visitmexico.com
The public-private Mexico Tourism Board (Consejo de Promoción Turítica de Mexico) maintains a moderately helpful general site for destination travel information. It has lots of summarily informative sub-headings, not unlike an abbreviated guidebook. If you can't find what you want here, call the toll-free information number (tel. 800/446-3942) or email contact@visitmexico.com.

If you can read some Spanish, its Spanish-language version, www.cptm.org.mx, is much more specific and detailed.

On the Road in Mexico
www.ontheroadin.com
This helpful site, with regularly updated information and photos of Mexico trailer parks and campgrounds, includes accurate and very usable maps to lots of out-of-the-way locations, many along the Pacific coast, including Puerto Escondido, Puerto Ángel, and Huatulco.

OAXACA CITY AND OAXACA IN GENERAL
Ecoturism in Oaxaca
www.ecoturismoenoaxaca.com
A good up-and-coming site with broad partial coverage of outdoor recreation sites, ripe for hiking, climbing, rapelling, bicycle riding, rafting, and more. Includes hotels, cabins, camping sites, and restaurants.

Oaxaca Bed-and-Breakfasts
www.oaxacabedandbreakfast.org
Modest but helpful site of the Oaxaca Bed-and-Breakfast Association. The dozen-odd accommodations, of English-savvy owner-operators, run $65–100 per night. A number of them are recommended in this book.

Oaxaca Mio
www.oaxaca-mio.com
Excellent commercial site, with lots on history, culture, sights, hotels, and services in Oaxaca City and Valley. Oaxaca coast coverage, including Puerto Escondido and Huatulco, is still informative, but not so extensive.

Oaxaca Secretary of Tourism
www.oaxaca.travel
Very detailed website of the Oaxaca Secretary of Tourism. Good Tourist Guide section with archaeological sites, recipes, churches, museums, festivals, myths and legends, murals, handicrafts, and more. The site goes the extra step farther and provides extensive detailed information. (Accessible by clicking on the homepage interactive Oaxaca map symbol, bottom of the homepage, left side. This gets you to an interactive Oaxaca City map. On the right of that, select the Valles Centrales map, for selections for off-the-tourist-track outlying villages.)

Oaxaca Times
www.oaxacatimes.com
The website of the *Oaxaca Times* newspaper has links to restaurants, galleries, handicrafts shops, services, plus a handy classified section usually including a long list of Oaxaca City

apartment, house, homestay, and bed-and-breakfast rentals.

Planeta.com
www.planeta.com

Superb life project of Latin America's dean of ecotourism, Oaxaca resident Ron Mader, who furnishes a comprehensive English-language clearinghouse of everything ecologically correct, from rescuing turtle eggs on the Oaxaca Coast to preserving the cloud forests in the Oaxaca's northern Sierra Juarez. Contains dozens of pages competently linked for maximum speed. Check out www.planeta.com/oaxaca.html for a block-long list of information-packed links to everything you need to know about Oaxaca.

Vacation Rentals
www.vrbo.com, www.choice1.com

A pair of very useful sites for picking a vacation rental house, condo, or villa, with information and reservations links to individual owners. Prices vary from moderate to luxurious. Coverage extends over much of the Mexican Pacific, and, especially in www.vrbo.com (Vacation Rentals by Owner), many listings are in Oaxaca City, Puerto Escondido, and Huatulco.

OAXACA COAST
El Sol de la Costa
www.elsoldelacosta.com

Extensive and authoritative commercial site of the excellent Puerto Escondido bilingual tourist newspaper *El Sol de la Costa* (Warren Sharpe, editor and publisher). It's especially useful for restaurants, sights, and services and also includes much cultural background, especially on local indigenous culture and traditions. A handy classified section usually lists a number of vacation rentals by owner.

Huatulco Hotel Association
www.hoteleshuatulco.com.mx

Useful site of the Huatulco Hotel Association, with links to about four dozen hotels, ranging from modest to plush (but mostly plush), including prices for some of the hotels. The remaining information (restaurants, events, tour operators, water sports, and land sports) would be more useful if it were in English.

Huatulco Magazzine
www.huatulco.magazzine.net

Site of the reliable local free tourist magazine, with a plethora of links to its advertisers, from real estate and rental cars to handicrafts shops and three-, four-, and five-star hotels.

Puerto Real Estate
www.puertorealestate.com

Very good website of Puerto Escondido Real Estate; besides home sales, it lists and photo-illustrates many vacation rental villas, condos, and apartments ($300–3,000/week) and offers trip-planning services.

Tomzap
www.tomzap.com/oaxaca.html

This project of Mexico lover Tom Penick is a very informative site, especially for down-scale corners of Oaxaca. It's unusually detailed about Puerto Escondido, Puerto Ángel, Zipolite, Mazunte, and the Bays of Huatulco. Information includes hotels, travel, history, surfing, scuba and snorkeling, and much more, with much helpful advice on what to enjoy and what to avoid. It's very Good. (*Note:* Be aware, however, that some information is out of date.)

Zicatela Properties
www.zicatelaproperties.com

Excellent site of Puerto Escondido's Zicatela Properties real estate company. It's especially good for moderately priced apartment, condo, and vacation home rentals (as low as $250/week). It also lists a number of services to help newcomers settle into Puerto Escondido.

Index

List of Maps

www.moon.com

DESTINATIONS | ACTIVITIES | BLOGS | MAPS | BOOKS

MOON.COM is ready to help plan your next trip! Filled with fresh trip ideas and strategies, author interviews, informative travel blogs, a detailed map library, and descriptions of all the Moon guidebooks, Moon.com is all you need to get out and explore the world—or even places in your own backyard. While at Moon.com, sign up for our monthly e-newsletter for updates on new releases, travel tips, and expert advice from our on-the-go Moon authors. As always, when you travel with Moon, expect an experience that is uncommon and truly unique.

KEEP UP WITH MOON ON FACEBOOK AND TWITTER
JOIN THE MOON PHOTO GROUP ON FLICKR

MAP SYMBOLS

Expressway	▐ Highlight	✕ Airfield	⚑ Golf Course
Primary Road	○ City/Town	✈ Airport	ⓟ Parking Area
Secondary Road	◉ State Capital	▲ Mountain	▲ Archaeological Site
Unpaved Road	⊛ National Capital	✚ Unique Natural Feature	⚱ Church
Trail	★ Point of Interest		⛽ Gas Station
Ferry	• Accommodation	⌇ Waterfall	⬭ Glacier
Railroad	▼ Restaurant/Bar	⚑ Park	⬖ Mangrove
Pedestrian Walkway	■ Other Location	⯃ Trailhead	▨ Reef
Stairs	⋀ Campground	⛷ Skiing Area	⬚ Swamp

CONVERSION TABLES

°C = (°F - 32) / 1.8
°F = (°C x 1.8) + 32
1 inch = 2.54 centimeters (cm)
1 foot = 0.304 meters (m)
1 yard = 0.914 meters
1 mile = 1.6093 kilometers (km)
1 km = 0.6214 miles
1 fathom = 1.8288 m
1 chain = 20.1168 m
1 furlong = 201.168 m
1 acre = 0.4047 hectares
1 sq km = 100 hectares
1 sq mile = 2.59 square km
1 ounce = 28.35 grams
1 pound = 0.4536 kilograms
1 short ton = 0.90718 metric ton
1 short ton = 2,000 pounds
1 long ton = 1.016 metric tons
1 long ton = 2,240 pounds
1 metric ton = 1,000 kilograms
1 quart = 0.94635 liters
1 US gallon = 3.7854 liters
1 Imperial gallon = 4.5459 liters
1 nautical mile = 1.852 km

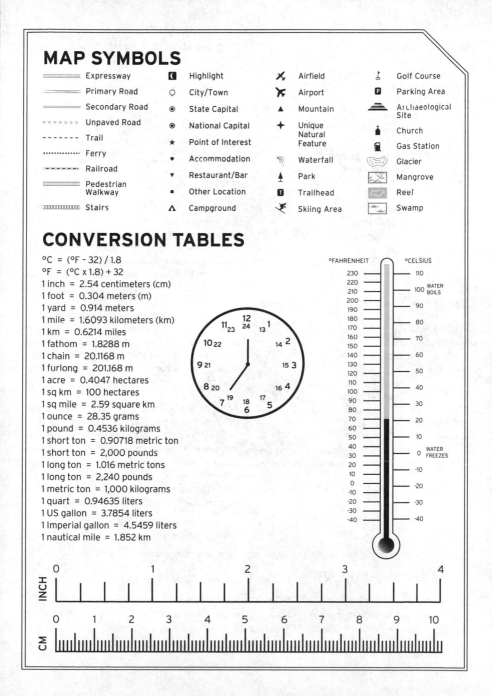

MOON OAXACA

Avalon Travel
a member of the Perseus Books Group
1700 Fourth Street
Berkeley, CA 94710, USA
www.moon.com

Editor: Kevin McLain
Series Manager: Kathryn Ettinger
Copy Editor: Naomi Adler Dancis
Graphics and Production Coordinator:
    Elizabeth Jang
Cover Designer: Elizabeth Jang
Map Editor: Mike Morgenfeld
Cartographers: Chris Henrick, Kaitlin Jaffe
Proofreader: Natalie Mortensen
Indexer: Rachel Kuhn

ISBN-13: 978-1-59880-924-4
ISSN: 1533-3949

Printing History
1st Edition – 2000
6th Edition – October, 2011
5 4 3 2 1

Text © 2011 by Bruce Whipperman.
Maps © 2011 by Avalon Travel.
All rights reserved.

Some photos and illustrations are used by permission
and are the property of the original copyright owners.

Front cover photo: *Danzante* relief, Monte Albán
© imagebroker.net/SuperStock

Title Page photo: contented cat in Puerto Ángel
© Bruce Whipperman

Interior color photos: All © Bruce Whipperman,
except p. 18 © abalcazar/istock.com, and p. 19 ©
Tomas Hajek/123rf.com

Printed in Canada by Friesens

Moon Handbooks and the Moon logo are the property
of Avalon Travel. All other marks and logos depicted
are the property of the original owners. All rights
reserved. No part of this book may be translated or
reproduced in any form, except brief extracts by a
reviewer for the purpose of a review, without written
permission of the copyright owner.

All recommendations, including those for sights,
activities, hotels, restaurants, and shops, are based
on each author's individual judgment. We do not
accept payment for inclusion in our travel guides,
and our authors don't accept free goods or services
in exchange for positive coverage.

Although every effort was made to ensure that
the information was correct at the time of going
to press, the author and publisher do not assume
and hereby disclaim any liability to any party for any
loss or damage caused by errors, omissions, or any
potential travel disruption due to labor or financial
difficulty, whether such errors or omissions result
from negligence, accident, or any other cause.

KEEPING CURRENT

If you have a favorite gem you'd like to see included in the next edition, or see anything
that needs updating, clarification, or correction, please drop us a line. Send your
comments via email to feedback@moon.com, or use the address above.